Globe Law
and Business

International
Advertising Law

A Practical Global Guide
Second Edition

Consulting Editors **Paul Jordan** and **Andrew Butcher**

Consulting editors
Paul Jordan and Andrew Butcher

Managing director
Sian O'Neill

International Advertising Law: A Practical Global Guide, Second Edition
is published by

Globe Law and Business Ltd
3 Mylor Close
Horsell
Woking
Surrey GU21 4DD
United Kingdom
Tel: +44 20 3745 4770
www.globelawandbusiness.com

Printed and bound by CPI Group (UK) Ltd, Croydon CR0 4YY, United Kingdom

International Advertising Law: A Practical Global Guide, Second Edition

ISBN 9781787423909
EPUB ISBN 9781787423916
Adobe PDF ISBN 9781787423923
Mobi ISBN 9781787423930

Table of contents

Introduction

Paul Jordan
Bristows LLP

1.   Introduction

Advertising law and regulation are found in a wide variety of sources, such as legislation, common law (ie, law developed through decisions of the courts) and self-regulatory codes; and they overlap with a diverse range of other areas of law. This makes the selection of a finite number of topics to cover in a text of this nature a difficult task. In making our decision, we considered the questions that in-house advertising and marketing lawyers are likely to encounter most frequently in their day-to-day work, but the needs of private practice lawyers have also been kept in mind. Furthermore, the book adopts a straightforward and practical approach to the explanation of the key concepts and regulations within each area, meaning that non-lawyers in advertising and marketing roles should also find *International Advertising Law: A Practical Global Guide* an extremely useful source of information and guidance.

In Europe in particular, the areas of law with which advertising lawyers must be familiar – such as data protection, intellectual property and consumer protection – are largely harmonised across the EU member states. For this reason, in addition to the importance of internet-based marketing activities and the international nature of many campaigns, advertising lawyers are increasingly expected to have an international overview of the regulatory regimes to which their campaigns are subject. However, within Europe, this can often be a challenge where there are in fact differences in the local implementation of EU directives. This text therefore covers not only the key European markets (including a post-Brexit United Kingdom), but also selected other important markets, including the United States, Canada, Australia and Russia.

As a consequence of the large number of countries covered, it is not possible for every chapter to provide an in-depth discussion of each of the issues touched upon. This is not the intention of this publication. The goal is rather to provide guidance that allows a comparison to be made of the applicable regimes between countries and the key risk areas in particular jurisdictions to be identified.

Each chapter is written by a leading expert in the relevant country and begins with an overview of the legal and regulatory regime for advertising in that country, before providing more detail on the following topics: comparative advertising; online behavioural advertising; sales promotions; ambush marketing; direct marketing; product placement; native advertising and social media influencers; and certain industry-specific regulation (which includes consideration of the regulation of ads for gambling, alcohol, pharmaceuticals, financial products and services, food, tobacco and the rapidly expanding e-cigarette product category).

To avoid repetition, the individual chapters do not provide an introduction to each of the above topics; instead, we do so in this introduction. Furthermore, as a result of differences in market practice and the approach of local regulators, the reader may find that greater emphasis is placed on certain topics rather than others within a particular chapter, and that the distribution of emphasis varies between chapters. Indeed, even across the European chapters, emphasis may vary. This is because, as mentioned above, despite a significant degree of harmonisation across the European Union in areas such as consumer protection and data protection, EU directives may be implemented differently in different member states, national regulators may interpret the law differently and market practice may differ.

2. Comparative advertising

In its broadest sense, 'comparative advertising' is any type of advertising that, either explicitly or even by implication, identifies a competitor or a competitor's products. Comparative advertising is a powerful tool and one that is commonly used in highly competitive sectors such as telecommunications and supermarkets. Because of the power of comparative advertising, and the potential harm that can be caused to a referenced competitor by an unfair or untruthful comparison, in many jurisdictions comparative advertising must adhere to strict criteria in order to remain on the correct side of the law. As the reader will discover, in most countries there is significant overlap between the regulation of comparative advertising and trademark law.

3. Online behavioural advertising

Online behavioural advertising comes in various forms. However, broadly speaking, 'online behavioural advertising' refers to the technique of collecting and analysing information based on users' web browsing activity in order to display online advertising that is intended to be more relevant to the user. It usually involves the creation of 'interest segments' based on the information collected, with different advertising then being served to different users based on the interest segment that the user is judged to fall into. For example, a user who frequently browses the sports section of an online news service may be placed within a segment identified as being interested in sports. As a result, that user might then be served ads for sports products and services when he or she visits a different and unrelated site.

Online behavioural advertising is often enabled via the use of 'cookies' (and other similar technologies), Cookies are small text files placed on a user's computer (or other connected device) by the advertising provider; they can then be used to identify the same user (or more specifically, the same browser) when he or she returns to the site or another site that has access to the cookie.

Public awareness of cookie usage online and online behavioural advertising has increased over the past decade. In Europe, this has been partly due to changes in the European Union's e-Privacy Directive, which raised the level of consent required in relation to the use of cookies. Various self-regulatory industry initiatives (eg, the Your Online Choices initiative) have also played a part in raising consumer awareness and understanding of online behavioural advertising. However, in other parts of the world – such as certain Asian and South American countries – online behavioural advertising is entirely unregulated.

4. Sales promotions

Sales promotions encompass straightforward temporary discounting, buy-one-get-one-free offers and two-for-one offers, in addition to prize promotions such as prize draws, skill-based competitions and 'instant win' promotions.

In this area of advertising law in particular, the level of regulation varies quite dramatically between jurisdictions. A particular risk to bear in mind here is the legislative controls around gambling and the potential for a prize draw to be deemed an unlicensed lottery. Readers will see some crossover between this section and the sub-section on gambling in the industry-specific section at the end of each chapter.

5. Ambush marketing

The most common example of ambush marketing is where a non-official sponsor creates an association with a significant event, such as the Olympic Games or the football World Cup. This can occur to the detriment of official sponsors, which might have paid significant sums for the sponsorship rights to create such an association.

Ambush marketing is difficult to combat and in many countries some forms of ambush marketing are, in fact, lawful. However, host countries of major sporting events such as the Olympic Games are increasingly being required by the event organisers to enact legislation to assist in the protection of official sponsors' expensively acquired rights.

6. Direct marketing

Broadly speaking, direct marketing can be defined as marketing communications addressed to and/or targeted at particular individuals – for example, by mail, email or telephone. The legal and regulatory concerns with direct marketing largely stem from data protection and privacy law. In particular, electronic direct marketing (eg, email and text messaging) is generally subject to more stringent requirements.

7. Product placement

Product placement is the inclusion, for marketing purposes, of a product or brand in audio-visual content (eg, a television programme, film or radio programme) where the producer of the programme or the broadcaster is paid for the inclusion.

The practice of product placement has been commonplace in feature films and US television shows for a number of years, but has historically been relatively rare in Europe due to strict regulations. However, the practice is now increasing in Europe as a result of the 2007 Audiovisual Media Services Directive, which relaxed the applicable rules to some extent.

Many jurisdictions permit product placement only in a very limited number of programme genres and may also require that the presence of product placement be flagged to the viewer prior to the start of the programme.

8. Native advertising and social media influencers

Advertisers continue to work incredibly hard to deliver engaging 'organic' content to their customer base. Big brands have been expanding their marketing budgets significantly over the last few years in the area of native advertising. But is it always clear to consumers that targeted content or influencer endorsements are ultimately controlled and paid for by advertisers? Following increasingly strict regulation in the United States, the rest of the world is now wrestling with how best to increase transparency and identify commercially incentivised content as 'advertisements'. This latest edition highlights this growth area and provides guidance as to how countries around the world are now dealing with this topic.

9. Industry-specific regulation

To conclude, each chapter provides a brief discussion of the key issues in the regulation of ads for gambling, alcohol, pharmaceuticals, financial products and services, food, tobacco and e-cigarettes in the relevant jurisdiction. The aim of this section is to identify prohibited activities, the main areas of risk when advertising in these important sectors, and the key pieces of legislation and regulation to consider.

10. And finally...

I would like to recognise the sizeable contributions of Bristows colleagues Andrew Butcher, Jamie Drucker, Sara Sefton and Jake Palmer. Their intellect, hard work and enthusiasm throughout this project have been greatly appreciated.

Argentina

Juan Carlos Ojám
Ojam Bullrich Flanzbaum

1. Overview of the legal and regulatory regime for advertising

Argentina does not have a uniform legal system regarding advertising; instead, multiple regulations (acts, decrees, resolutions) and self-regulatory codes, of varying degrees of effective application, must be considered when advertising in Argentina.

Before examining the specifics of Argentine advertising law, an understanding of the specific hierarchy of laws is helpful. At the top is the Constitution, which governs the government and its powers, and sets out the principles on which governance is based. It is a single law and is superior to all other regulations, which must respect its provisions; otherwise, they may be declared unconstitutional. Also standing at the top of the hierarchy alongside the Constitution and its principles are the international treaties ratified by Congress.

Below them are the different acts passed by Congress; which are followed in hierarchical order by decrees (issued by the executive power) and resolutions (issued by governmental offices). Finally, there are self-regulatory documents and other unofficial regulations, which are binding only on those parties that agree to them. This hierarchical structure allows for the correct application of the legal system in Argentina, ensuring that every act, decree, resolution and self-regulatory regulation complies with the constitutional principles.

The bodies that apply these regulations also vary in their structure and level of specialisation. The government offices that apply the advertising regulations include:

- the Secretariat of Domestic Trade (SCI);
- the National Administration of Drugs, Food and Medical Technology (ANMAT);[1]
- the National Entity of Communications (ENACOM);[2] and
- the Undersecretariat of Consumer Defence.

---

1   Established by Decree 1490/1992, ANMAT is a decentralised body that operates within the scope of the National Public Administration, which cooperates in the protection of human health by ensuring the quality of the products that it regulates: drugs, foodstuffs, medicinal products, diagnosis reagents, cosmetic products, dietary supplements and household cleaning products.

The private entities involved in the self-regulation of advertising include:

- the Advertising Self-Regulatory Council (CONARP);
- the Argentine Marketing Association;
- the Direct and Interactive Marketing Association (AMDIA);
- the Cable and Internet Advertising Bureau;
- the Argentine Chamber of Commerce; and
- the Argentine Advertising Council.

CONARP is the main self-regulatory body; it was created jointly by the Argentine Association of Advertising and the Argentine Chamber of Advertisers (CAA), which represent the main stakeholders in the advertising industry – both advertising agencies and advertisers.

Argentina's Federal Congress has also passed regulations on advertising in:

- the Consumer Defence Act (Act 24240);
- the Fair Trade Practices Decree (274/2019);[3]
- the Alimentary Code (Act 18284 – applicable only to foodstuffs); and
- the Audio-visual Communication Services Act (Act 26522).

These provisions allow for the imposition of fines, the seizure of products and even the suspension of trading rights in case of non-compliance.

The Civil and Commercial Code (Act 26994), in force since August 2015, has established a legal framework for information and advertising in Argentina. Sections 1100 to 1103 set out the following relevant rules:

- The advertiser must provide information to consumers on all essential characteristics of the products and services advertised, the conditions of sale and all other relevant circumstances.
- The following types of advertising are prohibited:
  - advertising that contains false or confusing indications regarding essential elements of the product or service that could mislead consumers;
  - advertising that makes comparisons of products or services that have the potential to mislead consumers;
  - advertising that is abusive or discriminatory; and

---

2   Established by Decree 267/2015, ENACOM is an autonomous and decentralised entity that operates within the scope of the Head of the Cabinet of Ministers of the Nation. Its role as communications regulator is to:
- ensure that all users have quality services;
- promote technological convergence; and
- create a stable market conditions to guarantee access to internet, fixed and mobile telephone, radio, postal and television services.

This entity is the successor to the Federal Authority of Audio-visual Communication Services.

3   On 22 April 2019, Decree of Necessity and Urgency 274/2019 was published in the *Official Gazette*, replacing the previous Fair Trade Practices Act (Act 22,802).

- advertising that induces consumers to behave in a way that is detrimental or dangerous to their health or safety.
- Affected users or consumers may seek from the courts:
  - the cessation of illegal advertising;
  - the publication of rectification notices; and
  - where appropriate, convictions.
- The details included in advertising are considered to be incorporated in the contract with the consumer and are legally binding on the advertiser.

Some of these acts of Congress are complemented in detail by various decrees, resolutions and dispositions. In particular, ANMAT Resolution 4980/2005 regulates the advertisement of:
- special non-prescription medical products;
- foodstuffs;
- cosmetics;
- personal hygiene products;
- perfumes;
- dental products;
- household supplies;
- *in vitro* diagnostic products;
- dietary supplements; and
- medical technology devices.

CONARP has also established its own Code of Ethics and Advertising Self-Regulation, which applies to all advertising; although CONARP has no authority to impose pecuniary sanctions in case of non-compliance. More recently, CONARP released a document entitled *Commercial Communication on the Internet*, which addresses issues such as online behavioural advertising, social media influencers and other related matters. However, this document is not binding on CONARP's members, as it only sets out guidelines and principles.

Despite this array of applicable regulations (which in some cases may lead to the application of the same principle twice by different authorities), there are common guiding principles: ads must be truthful, lawful, ethical and decent; and must not disparage competitors.

The principle of truthfulness is unarguably the fundamental principle of advertising in Argentina, and is inferred from the National Civil and Commercial Code, the Fair Trade Practices Decree, the Consumer Defence Act and the CONARP code. Section 11 of the Fair Trade Practices Decree forbids any kind of presentation, advertising or marketing that, due to inaccuracies or concealments, could confuse, deceive or mislead consumers with regard to the characteristics, properties, nature, origin, quality, purity, mixture, quantity, use, price, commercialisation conditions or production techniques of products, services or real estate. Section 7 of the Consumer Defence Act, on the other hand, provides that the statements made in ads are legally binding on the seller and will be deemed to be included in the contract with the consumer. The CONARP code also provides for this principle in its Sections 11, 12, 13 and 16.

Generally, controversial forms of marketing, such as subliminal and viral marketing, are also prohibited, although only expressly through the CONARP code (Sections 15 and 39.4).

In most cases, modification of an infringing ad will be required in order to ensure that it complies with the applicable regulations; although in some cases, its complete withdrawal may be required. Government offices such as the SCI and ANMAT can apply pecuniary sanctions. The sanctions applied by the SCI include fines ranging from ARS 26.40 to ARS 264 million, which can be doubled in case of repeat infringement. The fines imposed by ANMAT range from ARS 1,000 to ARS 1 million, depending on the gravity and scope of the infringement.

Advertisers should also consider the risk of infringing the IP rights of third parties. Although comparative advertising is not prohibited as long as it is not misleading, the use of third parties' trademarks may constitute trademark infringement under the Trademarks Act (22362). Intentionally false claims about competitors may also lead to actions before the courts on the basis of infringement of the fair trade practice regulations, with the corresponding liability for damages.

## 2.	Comparative advertising

Although it is relatively uncommon in Argentina, direct comparative advertising is not forbidden, as long as it:

- complies with the necessary legal parameters;
- is truthful and objective; and
- is not misleading or denigrating.

Comparative advertising is regulated by the Civil and Commercial Code and specifically by the Fair Trade Practices Decree, which defines it as advertising that explicitly or implicitly alludes to a competitor, its brand or its products or services. Section 15 of the decree provides that comparative advertising is permitted provided that:

- it does not mislead, deceive or confuse consumers between the advertiser and a competitor, or between the products or services of the advertiser and those of a competitor;
- it compares products or services that satisfy the same needs or have the same purpose;
- it involves an objective comparison between one or more essential, relevant, representative and verifiable characteristics of the products or services, which may include the price;

- its purpose is to highlight the advantages of the advertised products or services;
- it does not discredit or denigrate the IP rights or circumstances of a competitor;
- it does not obtain undue advantage from a competitor's brand reputation or designation of origin;
- it does not present a product or service as an imitation or replica of a trademarked product or service; and
- in the case of products covered by a denomination of origin, geographical indication or specific denomination, it compares other products of the same denomination.

Section 10 of the Fair Trade Practices Decree also indicates that comparative advertising will be considered an act of unfair competition if the above terms are breached.

Comparative advertising is also regulated in several annexes of ANMAT Resolution 4980/2005, applicable only to ANMAT's specific industries, and in the CONARP code.

The ANMAT resolution provides that comparative advertising must not:
- create confusion through the comparison;
- ridicule or disparage the other product;
- distort the image of the other product;
- attack the reputation or prestige of third parties;
- seek to encourage the rejection of third parties' products or customers;
- mention active principles, components, ingredients or substances that are not contained in the advertised product; or
- mention possible adverse or side effects of active principles, components, ingredients or substances that are not contained in the advertised product.

The CONARP code provides that comparative advertising must:
- be respectful of IP rights;
- aim to inform consumers of the verifiable advantages of the advertised product;
- refer to equivalent products and qualities;
- be precise and reflect the truth, under the same conditions; and
- be presented in an objective manner in order for the comparison to be verifiable.

Therefore, according to the code, comparative advertising must not:
- create confusion by means of the comparison;
- ridicule or disparage the other product;

- distort the image of the other product;
- attack the reputation or prestige of third parties; or
- seek to encourage the rejection of third parties' products or customers.

Where the benefits of a product or service are highlighted in comparison with the product or service of a competitor, the code provides that the comparison must:
- accord with local and international applicable regulations; or
- be performed using a technical or scientific procedure that can validate the authenticity of the comparison and the statistical or technical relevance of its conclusions.

Moreover, where the demonstration is publicly performed, it must be replicable under the same conditions and using the same products and other elements. Comparative demonstrations at sales points or in public places must scientifically replicate laboratory tests, and must be performed by specialised technical personnel under a protocol that guarantees the rigour, reliability and reproducibility of the demonstration and its results, such that consumers are not misled or otherwise induced to error with regard to the qualities or performance of any of the products.

Although, in comparative advertising cases, the affected competitor must usually request the intervention of government authorities or self-regulatory bodies, ANMAT and the CONARP can also intervene *ex officio* upon detecting a possible violation of the applicable regulations. However, any resolution issued by CONARP will be binding only if both parties are members.

ANMAT has established a surveillance programme – called the Programme for the Monitoring and Supervision of Advertisements and Promotion of Products Subject to Sanitary Surveillance – under which the cessation of a supposedly infringing ad can be requested; and it can liaise with ENACOM to enforce its decisions. Procedures undertaken by ENACOM and ANMAT can overlap and lead to the imposition of separate sanctions for the same ad.

The SCI is responsible for enforcing the Fair Trade Practices Decree and will intervene at the request of affected competitors. This decree represents a significant change from the previous regime in this regard. The complainant, as affected competitor, participates in the proceedings and may now present evidence to the SCI, which will process the respective appeal and impose sanctions accordingly.

On another note, the general parameters on the use of third-party trademarks set out in the Trademarks Act apply to comparative advertising between competitors and may constitute grounds for judicial intervention. This act provides for the imposition of sanctions and fines on those that use the trademarks of third parties without authorisation when advertising their own products. This was confirmed in the leading case on the matter, *Coca-Cola v Pepsi*.[4] Several other court rulings have confirmed that comparative advertising is to be suppressed only where the competitor's trademark is denigrated or discredited; such advertising will be legitimate as long as it does not denigrate or discredit the trademarks of third parties, and does not confuse the consumer.

3.   Online behavioural advertising

In Argentina, there are no specific laws relating to online behavioural advertising. However, general rules are set out in the applicable self-regulatory regimes and in the underlying principles on the regulation of direct marketing.

The CAA has signed up to the Self-Regulatory Principles for Online Behavioural Advertising developed by the World Federation of Advertisers, which apply consumer-friendly standards to online behavioural advertising. These are based on the following principles:

- Education principle: Entities should make an effort to educate consumers and businesses about online behavioural advertising, how it works and the ways in which consumers can avoid it.
- Transparency principle: Mechanisms should be adopted to inform consumers about data collection and data use associated with online behavioural advertising.
- Consumer control principle: Users of websites should be informed of the mechanisms that allow them to choose whether they want their data to be collected and used for online behavioural advertising.
- Data security principle: Entities should ensure the reasonable security of data which is collected and used for online behavioural advertising purposes.
- Material changes principle: Entities should obtain consumers' consent before modifying the way in which data is used and obtained.
- Sensitive data principle: Sensitive data should benefit from enhanced protection.
- Accountability principle: Entities should develop and implement policies and programmes for further adherence to these principles.

Interpreted broadly, the Personal Data Protection Act (Act 25326) could also apply to this matter. Section 27 states that:

> the compilation of domiciles, distribution of documents, advertising or direct sales and other similar activities, it is allowed to manage data suitable for establishing certain profiles with promotional, commercial or advertising purposes, or for determining consumption habits, as long as such data appears in documents that

---

4   Fed R Civ Com P; *The Coca Cola Company y otros, Cámara Nacional de Apelaciones en lo Civil y Comercial Federal*, sala III, 1 November 1993.

are accessible to the public, or has been provided by the owners, or has been obtained with their consent

This act does not specifically address online behavioural advertising, as it does not deal with the creation of consumer profiles and the identification of their habits (based in particular on their browsing history). However, to the extent that consumption habits can be interpreted from the use of cookies and other web surfing activity, with users' consent, this regulation could be stated to cover the creation of profiles based on consumers' online behaviour.

Accordingly, in order for online behavioural advertising to be lawful, the data subject should have given his or her express consent for the treatment of his or her personal data, either in writing or through equivalent means (eg, an online tick box), in an explicit manner. The data subject should also have been previously notified of:

- the purpose for which the data will be gathered and used;
- the existence of the relevant data file(s), and the register or database in which the data will be stored;
- the identity and address of the person responsible for the database; and
- the right to access, modify or delete his or her data.

A draft Act on Personal Data Protection, known as *Mensaje* 147/2018, was sent by the executive power to the Congress in 2016. It has not yet been enacted, but the most relevant changes or additions it proposes include:

- an obligation to notify the data subject of any security incidents involving personal databases; and
- an obligation to conduct an impact assessment regarding the protection of personal data where it is probable that there is a high risk of affecting the rights of data subjects.

In case of violation of the Personal Data Protection Act, the National Directorate for the Protection of Personal Data (DNPDP) is responsible for applying sanctions. If data is unlawfully obtained, in addition to civil liability for damages arising from breach of the Personal Data Protection Act, the DNPDP may apply sanctions including:

- a warning;
- suspension of use of the data files;
- a fine ranging from ARS 1,000 to ARS 100,000; and
- in the most serious cases, closure or cancellation of the file, register or database.

4. Sales promotions

The regulatory regime on sales promotions is spread across a number of congressional acts, decrees and administrative resolutions. Of these, the core regulation is the Consumer Defence Act.

Section 4 of the Consumer Defence Act obliges sellers to provide consumers with clear and detailed information on the essential features of the products or services that they offer, and of their marketing conditions. Section 8 states that the contents of ads are legally binding and are considered part of the offer to customers; thus, the advertiser is contractually liable for any breach of the terms of its own promotions. The SCI, together with the local authorities of each province and of the Autonomous City of Buenos Aires, is responsible for ensuring compliance with this act.

With reference to 'special offers', the AMDIA Code of Ethics states that characterising a product as 'free' will always mean free of all costs and charges. The code also states that in special promotions involving price reductions, the quality and quantity of the product cannot be modified.

Companies often give out prizes to consumers as a marketing strategy. This is regulated by the Fair Trade Practices Decree. Pursuant to Section 14 of the decree, companies may offer prizes as long as:

- these are not awarded randomly; and
- the grant of the prize is not conditioned in whole or in part on the acquisition of a product or the contracting of a service.

The prohibition on the random award of prizes or gifts aims to avoid distorting consumers' behaviour as a result of the prizes. However, this practice is nonetheless considered acceptable as long as the following conditions are met:

- Each ad includes the phrase (in Spanish) "Promotion without purchase requirement", in a way that ensures it can be easily read or heard by consumers, together with the start and end date of the offer and its territorial scope;
- Each ad includes the full requirements for participating in the draw or directions on how to obtain such information;
- Where any additional elements are required to participate in the promotion (eg, submission of a purchase receipt or product packaging), such elements are distributed for free in at least one store in the capital city of each province, and in one store in each city with more than 50,000 inhabitants, for the duration of the promotion; and
- The stores in which the advertised product or service is sold exhibit the following information:
  - a complete list of the stores in which the elements required to participate in the promotion are distributed for free;

- a complete list of prizes;
- the full requirements for participating in the promotion; and
- the mechanism for distributing the prizes, including the time and place for their distribution.

Up until 2018, pursuant to Decree 588/98, the National Lottery Organisation had to authorise any contest or promotion carried out through mass media channels for the purpose of advertising products, services or shows in which the winner was selected at random. In turn, in 2000, the Federal Administration of Public Revenue held that the prizes obtained in contests or promotions carried out within the framework of sales promotions of products or services were subject to tax under the 1973 Tax Act emergency levy on prizes won in draws. However, in February 2018, Decree 95/2018 was issued, which dissolved the National Lottery Organisation. As a result, national authorisation to carry out contests or draws is no longer required. Whether provincial authorisation will be required, and whether tax will be imposed under the 1973 emergency levy, will depend on the laws of each province.

Article 7 of the Anti-Alcohol Act (24788) prohibits any contest that consists of the intake of alcoholic beverages for purposes other than tasting them or testing their quality. On conviction, the organiser of such a contest will be subject to a fine of between ARS 2,000 and ARS 20,000 and a penalty of between six months' and two years' imprisonment.

5.   Ambush marketing

The only express regulation on ambush marketing is set out in Section 32 of the CONARP code, which states that advertisers should not suggest that a company is sponsoring an event or its media coverage when it is not in fact an official sponsor.

Apart from that, there are no congressional acts or regulations that expressly cover ambush marketing. Thus, ambush marketing claims should be based on:

- the unfair competition legislation;
- the general civil and commercial regulations; or
- the Trademarks Act.

When ambush marketers use competitors' trademarks, they may be liable for trademark infringement, pursuant to the Trademarks Act. However, ambush marketers do not usually employ the trademarks of third parties, but rather creatively allude to a high-profile event and use their own trademarks to suggest a connection or affiliation with it. Without actual trademark infringement, victims of ambush marketing are commonly left with a claim for unfair competition as their best means of challenging this practice.

The Fair Trade Practices Decree sets out the following prohibitions that could apply to ambush marketing:

- Section 10 describes as unfair practices:
  - acts of deception that may mislead consumers as to the existence or nature, mode of manufacture or distribution, main characteristics, purity, mixture, fitness for use, quality, quantity, price, conditions of sale or purchase, availability, results of use, attributes, benefits or conditions of products or services; and
  - acts of confusion that may mislead consumers as to the business origin or establishment of the products or services themselves, so that they are deemed to have a different origin.
- Section 11 also prohibits misleading or deceptive advertising, as it prohibits any kind of presentation, advertising or marketing that, through inaccuracies or concealments, may mislead, deceive or confuse as to the characteristics or properties, nature, origin, quality, purity, mixture, quantity, use, price, conditions of marketing or techniques of production of products or services.

Many authors disagree on the limits between association in advertising and the right of free expression; and on whether the rights of third parties are in fact infringed by ambush marketing (some would argue that they are not).

Actions against ambush marketing campaigns usually start by issuing a cease and desist letter to the infringing party on the grounds of the Trademarks Act or unfair competition. However, given the short duration of these kinds of events, this course of action may not be effective in safeguarding the affected party's interests. Another approach is to seek a preliminary injunction from the courts. In Argentina, preliminary injunctions are granted without informing the defendant, but require that the following conditions be met:

- The plaintiff must present evidence that proves, with a sufficient degree of certainty, that it is the rights holder and that its rights are being infringed. Any type of material evidence is acceptable (eg, commercial and/or legal documents, products and ads, photographs and videos, references to websites, letters exchanged with the defendant). With respect to certain evidence, notarial certification regarding its authenticity might also be required. If trademark infringement is invoked, the certificate of trademark registration should be attached.
- It must be proved that delay is likely to cause irreparable harm to the rights holder.
- The court may require the provision of security or equivalent assurance sufficient to protect the defendant and prevent abuse. The amount of this security will be decided by the judge and will depend on the type, extent and importance of the measure to be executed. The security may be supplied by means of a cash deposit to the judicial bank or a bond.

Once the security (if any) has been provided, the injunction will become effective immediately after the defendant has been notified. If the security is provided quickly, the injunction may take effect within three to seven days of filing of the complaint.

To obtain compensation for damages, the plaintiff must prove the damage caused due to the infringement; to this end, in case of trademark infringement, it may be useful to prove reputation and confusion among consumers. Ultimately, given the difficulties of proving and quantifying damages, this must be ascertained in a discovery proceeding instituted after the injunction has been granted.

As Argentina has no specific legislation on ambush marketing, the Trademarks Act and the Fair Trade Practices Decree may be insufficient to prevent such activity, as there is also little case law on this issue.

6. Direct marketing

Section 27 of the Personal Data Protection Act allows for the creation of consumer profiles for advertising purposes based on individual consumption habits if such data is publicly available – whether provided by the data subjects themselves or obtained with their consent. However, the data subject may at any time request the withdrawal or blocking of his or her name from any such databases. This provision therefore permits targeted postal and electronic marketing, as long as certain requirements are met.

For direct marketing to be lawful, one of the following conditions must be met:

- The data is publicly available;
- The data has been provided by the data subjects themselves; or
- The data subjects have given their express consent to the gathering and use of their personal data, in writing or through other similar means, in a prominent and explicit manner.

The data subjects should also be notified in advance of:

- the purpose for which the data will be used;
- the existence of the relevant data file, register or database;
- the identity and domicile of the person responsible for the data file, register or database;
- the consequences of providing the data; and
- the right to access, modify or delete the data.

However, according to Section 5 of the Personal Data Protection Act, consent is not considered to be necessary where the data:

- is limited to the data subject's name, national identity card number, tax or social security identification, occupation, date of birth, address or telephone number; or

- arises from a contractual relationship – either professional or scientific – with the data subject and is necessary for the development or fulfilment of that contractual relationship.

Decree 1558/2000, which regulates the Personal Data Protection Act, states that any ads disseminated by post, telephone, email, Internet or any other long-distance method of communication must clearly include an option for the recipient to request the withdrawal or blocking, either totally or partially, of his or her data from the relevant database. The data subject can also request the name of the person responsible for the relevant database.

The DNPDP is responsible for applying sanctions in case of violation of the Personal Data Protection Act. In addition to civil liability for damages arising from breach of the act, the DNPDP may:

- warn the infringer;
- apply sanctions such as the suspension, closure or cancellation of the file, register or database; or
- impose fines of between ARS 1,000 and ARS 100,000.

Disposition 4/2009 of the DNPDP replicates the terms of Decree 1558/2000 on direct advertising, and also requires the database owner to include in any communication details of the mechanism provided for withdrawing or blocking personal data from the database.

Section 33 of the Consumer Defence Act similarly safeguards the rights of consumers by prohibiting any sort of direct marketing that could incur an automatic monetary charge if this has not been requested by the recipient. This provision applies even if the direct marketing scheme includes delivery of the advertised product, which the consumer is not obliged to return to the advertiser. Section 47 provides for the imposition of fines ranging from Ps100 to Ps5 million in case of infringement.

Likewise, the AMDIA Code of Ethics, approved by DNPDP Disposition 4/2004, sets out principles to ensure that:

- the collection, use and treatment of data are conducted safely and with consent; and
- data subjects have the right to rectify or remove their data from the relevant databases.

In particular, it provides that direct marketing offers must be clear and complete, and must include the nature, price, forms of payment and obligations assumed when ordering a product. Offers cannot include vulgar or obscene content; and any image of a product that is used in an ad must be a faithful representation of that product. The name of the seller and the purpose of the offer must be included, and offers must not be disguised as market research.

Section 32(5) of the CONARP code states that "compliance with any obligation arising from direct marketing activities must be immediate and efficient". It also states that "all obligations assumed at the moment of the offer by the seller, the intermediaries and the consumer must be clear to the consumer"; and that "sellers must avoid using any harassment techniques". This same provision covers the door-to-door delivery of advertised products.

Sections 39(1) and 39(2) of the CONARP code address the subject of communication through new media. With regard to email marketing, the code provides that the subject and context of such emails must make clear that they constitute advertising. Consequently, electronic communications for advertising purposes must not provide ambiguous information that might influence consumer choice; and sellers must therefore inform consumers of the full process for acquiring the advertised product. Section 39 states further that electronic advertising messages that were not requested by the consumer can be sent only if:

- there is evidence that the consumer may be interested in the offer; and
- the message includes a simple mechanism for the consumer to indicate that he or she no longer wishes to receive such communications in the future.

Finally, in 2015, the Telephone Services Act (Act 26951) was published. This Act established the national Do Not Call Register, under the scope of the DNPDP. The act aims to protect users of telephone services from unsolicited advertising, offers, sales and gifts of products or services by telephone.

7. Product placement

In Argentina, product placement has increased significantly in recent years. The general principles on advertising also apply to product placement. Some commentators argue that product placement violates the basic principle whereby advertising should be clearly identifiable as such. However, the decisions that have been issued on product placement range from its absolute prohibition to its unrestricted acceptance.

While there are certain congressional acts in which product placement is mentioned, these do not assess it in depth. For instance, Section 4 of the Audio-visual Communication Services Act lists, among its definitions, 'non-traditional advertising', which is defined as "any form of audio-visual commercial consisting of displaying or referring to a product, service or trademark, as part of a programme, in exchange for a fee or similar consideration".

In addition, the Advertising, Promotion and Consumption of Tobacco Products Act (Act 26687) ('Tobacco Advertising Act') bans product placement involving tobacco products. In Section 2(d), it defines the 'advertising and promotion' of tobacco products as all types of communications, recommendations or commercial actions aimed at the direct or indirect promotion of tobacco products. Section 5 prohibits the product placement of tobacco products by stating that it is prohibited to advertise or promote tobacco products, either directly or indirectly, in any communication medium.

8.   Native advertising and social media influencers

In Argentina, there are no specific regulations on native advertising, and thus the general regulations on online advertising and the underlying principles on direct marketing apply.

Promotions or sponsored posts on social media (eg, Facebook, LinkedIn and Twitter) are becoming an increasingly popular method of online advertising. Again, Argentina has no specific regulations on social media influencers, as this phenomenon has emerged only recently, due to ongoing technological advances, the growing popularity of new social media and the reduced effectiveness of more traditional forms of online advertising.

Decree 274/2019 on Fair Trade Practices requires access to essential information about products and services that are advertised through physical or digital channels. Therefore, native advertising and advertising through social media influencers should respect the general principles set out in the decree.

Pursuant to the decree and the Consumer Defence Act, social media influencers should ensure that they post truthful and accurate information, as their posts are subject to the general principles on advertising directly linked to consumer protection.

The terms of CONARP in relation to advertising through emails, websites, mobile and other channels will also apply, as follows:

- Where the purpose of an electronic communication is to advertise, it should not conceal this purpose or provide ambiguous information that may affect consumers' purchasing decisions; and
- Electronic communications must include a simple and transparent mechanism that allows the consumer to express his or her wish not to receive future commercial communications, which should be easy to locate, understand and use.

It further provides that, when advertising through social media:

- the terms and conditions are subject to contracts law which applies to all users of the platform. Advertising in social media will be considered appropriate only where users have expressed their prior consent to receive messages with such characteristics; and
- communications that are inconvenient for minors must be clearly identified as such in the subject of the message.

CONARP's guidance entitled *Commercial Communication on the Internet* sets out some further points and suggestions that should be borne in mind in relation to native advertising and social media influencers:

- Native advertising must always be identifiable as advertising and make clear the identity of the issuer as well as its commercial purpose.
- The code recognises that initially, a social media post is targeted only at the influencer's specific followers; but as it is possible to expand this specific scope, due to reposting and the potential for content to go viral, extreme care when advertising through this medium is advised. Communications on social media should always take into account the type of recipient; and should be legal, truthful, honest, loyal and trustworthy.
- Influencers also generate content beyond that associated with the advertiser. Thus, where there is a contractual relationship between the advertiser and the influencer, this should be clearly identifiable to the user. The content of a blog can take various forms, depending on:
  - the relationship between the advertiser and the influencer;
  - the extent of control over the content exercised by the adviser or the influencer; and
  - the type of dissemination.
- In the case of gifts given to advertise, if the social media influencer expresses a positive opinion about the product or service and the advertiser uses that testimony for commercial purposes, the principles of responsible advertising should be observed.
- In the absence of a commercial relationship between the social media influencer and the advertiser, advertising on social media is not to be understood as a commercial communication, since there is no active intervention of the advertiser in the creation or dissemination of the content. However, a post will be considered to be a commercial message if the advertiser adopts and incorporates that content as its own within its communications and intentionally promotes it.

9. Industry-specific regulation

9.1 Gambling

The advertisement of gambling on radio or television requires the prior authorisation of the competent authority, pursuant to Section 81 of the Audio-visual Communication Services Act. The enforcement authority for this act is ENACOM, a decentralised public entity that operates under the national executive power.

In the City of Buenos Aires, as well as in some provinces, local regulations oblige advertisers to include the warning (in Spanish) "Compulsive gambling is injurious to health" in all ads in magazines and newspapers, and on billboards.

In general, however, the regulation of gambling advertising will vary, depending on the state in which it is being disseminated.

9.2 Alcohol

Section 6 of the Anti-alcohol Act sets out the following conditions that apply to the advertisement of alcoholic beverages:

- Ads must not be targeted at people under the legal drinking age (18 years);
- Ads must not depict underage individuals drinking alcoholic beverages;
- Ads must not suggest that alcohol consumption improves physical, intellectual or sexual performance, or encourages any form of violent behaviour; and
- Ads must include the wording (in Spanish) "Drink moderately" and "Sale forbidden to people under 18 years of age".

The Argentine Chamber of Distillers, the Chamber of the Argentine Brewing Industry and the Chamber of Wineries have together established a strict self-regulatory regime regarding alcohol advertising. The most relevant conditions of this regime are as follows:

- Ads must state that excessive consumption may lead to addiction;
- Ads must not suggest that the consumption of alcoholic beverages has beneficial effects on health, strength or longevity;
- Ads must not be targeted at teenagers or appear in programmes, films, events or publications that are mostly watched or read by underage individuals;
- Ads must not falsely state that the advertised products have features that are in fact absent;
- The actors or models used in ads must be at least 23 years old; and
- Ads must not suggest that alcohol helps to reduce anxiety or depression.

Should any member of these bodies violate these regulations, another member may file a complaint before an arbitration court, to which CONARP will appoint three arbitrators. The decision of the first-instance arbitration court may be appealed in writing before a second-instance arbitration court. The second-instance arbitration court will be comprised of three members appointed by the Coordinator of the Food Products Industries.

9.3 Pharmaceuticals

Section 19(c) of the Medicines Act (Act 16463) imposes an absolute prohibition on any inducement to self-medicate through non-prescription medicines, while Section 19(d) states that prescription-only medicines must not be advertised to the general public and, accordingly, forbids all types of advertising concerning prescription medicines.

The Medicines Act also establishes penalties in cases of infringement, which include:

- warnings;
- fines;
- seizure of the advertised medicines;
- suspension of the advertiser's activities;
- removal of its authorisation to sell or produce medicines; and
- in serious cases, even the complete closure of an establishment.

The advertisement of pharmaceutical products is also governed by Resolution 20/2005 of the Ministry of Health on the advertisement of non-prescription medicines. The resolution provides that all ads for non-prescription medicines and dietary supplements must comply with the ethical criteria set out by ANMAT in Disposition 4980/2005 and others. ANMAT has the authority to issue fines ranging from ARS 1,000 to ARS 1 million, in accordance with Disposition 1710/2008.

The most important general regulations provide that ads must, among other things:

- be aimed at the proper use of the product;
- respect public health interests;
- be clear, truthful and not deceptive;
- not cause anguish or fear;
- not advertise properties of the product that have not been approved by the appropriate health authority;
- not advertise products that have not been authorised by ANMAT;
- not suggest that a medical product is a different type of product or that a non-medical product is a medical product; and
- identify the different ingredients of the product.

The most important specific regulations concerning the advertisement of non-prescription medicines state that ads must:

- clearly express the conditions that the product aims to combat;
- specify expected indications authorised by ANMAT;
- specify the commercial name of the product, which must state the medicines' active ingredients; and
- include the legend "Read the package insert thoroughly, and in case of doubt ask your doctor or pharmacist".

The most important specific regulations regarding the advertisement of dietary supplements provide that:

- ads must match the dietary supplement definition included in the Alimentary Code;

- ads must include the legend "Supplements insufficient diets. Ask your doctor or pharmacist"; and
- the provision of free samples to underage individuals is prohibited.

ANMAT Disposition 3634/2005, governing dietary supplements, provides that ads must not:
- associate the consumption of alcohol with these supplements, either directly or indirectly;
- link them with health or success; or
- depict people under the age of 18.

Resolution 627/2007 of the Ministry of Health has established Good Practices for the Advertising of Prescription Medicines, which are governed by the following principles:
- The promotion of medicines that have not yet obtained the corresponding commercialisation authorisation is prohibited;
- All contents of the ad must accord with the characteristics of the product as set out in the certificate of registration authorised by ANMAT; and
- The advertisement and promotion of medicines must encourage their rational use and present them objectively.

ANMAT's Programme for the Monitoring and Supervision of Advertisements and Promotion of Products Subject to Sanitary Surveillance allows for the assessment of ads for prescription and non-prescription drugs, dietary supplements and other products mentioned in Resolution 20/2005 of the Ministry of Health. It allows ANMAT to directly notify infringers and request the cessation of infringing advertising, and aims to promote interaction between governmental and non-governmental organisations to assist in the monitoring of advertisements. Finally, ANMAT Disposition 6516/2015 requires all companies that produce products which are subject to sanitary surveillance to notify it of all advertising (traditional and non-traditional) addressed to the general public, and to present the corresponding ads in the format that they will be disseminated.

9.4   Financial products and services

The advertisement of financial products and services is governed by Communication A5482 of the Central Bank of the Argentine Republic, together with the modifications and special regulations introduced by Communications A5795, A11278, A5928, A5823 and A5828.

These regulations relate to savings accounts, salary accounts, free universal accounts and special accounts. They state that commercial banks, financial companies and saving societies must exhibit information boards in branches relating to each account they operate, which must be of a specified size and present the basic characteristics of the account.

The rates offered to the public should also be presented on similar boards, including a clear explanation of the scope of any warranty (eg, the type of operation, percentage offered and amount of warranty). In the case of ads relating to deposits, a limited warranty should be provided for their return or non-existence. Advertised rates should express the annual nominal interest rate and the annual effective interest rate for operations in Argentine pesos, foreign currencies or securities.

Printed ads (in newspapers and magazines, and on billboards) that promote different alternatives for investment should clearly include the annual nominal interest rate and the annual effective interest rate.

Moreover, Communication A5482 establishes that financial entities that work electronically – for instance, through electronic cashiers or online (ie, online banking) – should exhibit boards that present the costs charged for transfers through those channels.

Communication A5482 contains rules aimed at the protection of users of financial services. It states that financial entities and non-financial companies that control the issue of credit cards must provide consumers and small and medium-sized companies with easy and direct access to the following information:

- In branch: Detailed documents explaining the products and services offered, including precise costs and commissions associated with them; and a full copy of all agreements and their annexes in case a service contract is signed; and
- Online: All costs, commissions, interest rates, total financial cost, promotions and retributions offered.

Communication A5482 further obliges financial services companies to hire a person "responsible for attention to users of financial services", who will be responsible for verifying that all advertising complies with the applicable regulations. This person should be mentioned in the boards exhibited in branch, including his or her full name, position and contact information, among other things.

In addition, Communication A5482 provides that advertising through all means (on site, online, via graphical media such as newspapers and magazines, and in any other medium) must include and clearly state the following information:

- the annual nominal interest rate;
- the annual effective interest rate;
- the total financial cost;
- the lowest applicable interest rate;

- the highest applicable interest rate; and
- the average of the interest rates.

Ads regarding payment in instalments are also covered by this communication, which requires that such ads state the full instalment payable per month, including all costs, except for taxes other than value added tax.

9.5   **Food**

Chapter 5 of the Alimentary Code establishes a general framework for food advertising. Section 221 provides that the content of all food ads must match the definition, composition and denomination of the advertised product as set out in Chapters 6 to 19 of the aforementioned code. Moreover, Section 235 prohibits ads that:

- state that a product has medicinal or therapeutic properties; or
- recommend its consumption for reasons of stimulus, wellbeing or health.

On the other hand, Annex III of ANMAT Resolution 4980/2005 sets out detailed regulations on food advertising. It requires that all ads for foodstuffs:

- include the sales denomination and the commercial name of the product;
- describe it objectively in a clear and precise manner; and
- include any consumption instructions or warnings, if applicable.

It further provides that food ads must not:

- advertise any product that has not previously been approved by ANMAT;
- claim that a product is new if it has been sold for two years or more;
- include any statement such as 'recommended by experts' or 'proved by clinical tests' unless the advertiser has actually carried out such scientific tests in a well-known institute, in Argentina or abroad (the results of those tests must be provided to ANMAT upon request);
- claim that the consumption of a product guarantees good health; or
- include any message which:
  - suggests that the product is a medicinal product or has therapeutic effects;
  - states that health might be endangered if the product is not consumed;
  - is targeted at children under 12 without adult counsel;
  - states that a specific product can be used as the only food in a diet;
  - falsely claims that the advertised product is 'natural'; or
  - uses any word, sign, name, symbol or illustration that could mislead consumers with regard to the nature, composition, origin, quality,

quantity or performance of the product, or the way in which the product must be consumed.

The regulations set out in Resolution 4980/2005 are applicable to all ads, including those placed on the Internet.

9.6 Tobacco

Sections 5 and 8 of the Tobacco Advertising Act impose a general prohibition on the advertisement, promotion and sponsorship of tobacco-based products in public places, online, at certain events and through other means of communication. However, three exceptions to the general principle are set forth in Section 6. Accordingly, these products can be advertised:

- inside the stores in which they are sold;
- in publications targeted exclusively at people or institutions involved in the tobacco business; and
- through direct communications to individuals over 18 years of age.

In such cases, the ad must include a white rectangle, covering at least 20% of its total size, which includes one of the following warnings in black lettering:

- "Smoking causes cancer";
- "Smoking causes emphysema";
- "Smoking causes addiction";
- "Smoking causes impotence";
- "Smoking causes heart and respiratory diseases";
- "Tobacco smoke causes disease and death";
- "Smoking during pregnancy causes irreversible harm to the unborn child";
- "Smoking causes breathing difficulties";
- "Smoking reduces your life expectancy"; or
- "Smoking may cause leg amputation".

Each of these legends includes an image as determined by Resolution 497/2012 of the Ministry of Health.

Infringers of the Tobacco Advertising Act will be fined sums equivalent to the cost of 10,000 to 100,000 packs of 20 cigarettes of the most expensive type. In case of repeat infringement, this fine can be increased to the equivalent of 1 million packs. The Ministry of Health, which is responsible for enforcing the act, can also close down an infringing store or institution, and confiscate or destroy materials or products that do not comply with the law.

9.7 E-cigarettes

The import, distribution, commercialisation and advertisement of e-cigarettes are forbidden pursuant to ANMAT Resolution 3226/11, which also applies to e-cigarette accessories. This resolution was ratified by ANMAT on 2016, after detailed analysis of scientific studies confirmed that the existing evidence is insufficient to confirm that these devices help smokers to quit. They further established that the short-term side effects of e-cigarettes are frequent and moderate, but can sometimes be serious – including acute poisoning and potentially severe damage from the explosion of some components.

Australia

Stephanie Scott
Stephen von Muenster
von Muenster Legal

1. Overview of the legal and regulatory regime for advertising

In Australia, the advertising and marketing communications industry is regulated by government, by the courts and by the industry itself through a regime of proactive self-regulation. There exists a broad coalition of laws, regulations, determinations, standards and industry codes that impacts directly on the nature and type of content that can be published, and that restricts the claims and messages of all commercial communications.

This coalition – which may apply on a case-by-case basis to influence and restrict advertising and marketing communications in Australia – can be summarised as follows.

1.1 Consumer protection

The Australian Consumer Law prohibits all those engaged in trade or commerce – including advertisers – from communicating misleading or deceptive material to consumers. The law is usually enforced by the Australian Competition and Consumer Commission (ACCC) or invoked by competitors; and penalties for breach include corrective advertising orders, injunctions, fines and damages.

(a) Digital Platform Inquiry

In December 2017 the ACCC was directed to consider the impact of "online search engines, social media and digital content aggregators on competition in the media, advertising services markets" and the collection of users' personal data. The final report of the Digital Platform Inquiry was released on 19 June 2019. The report made 23 recommendations to ensure that Australian consumers are treated fairly and that their privacy is respected, including multiple ways in which the Privacy Act could be amended to enhance protection for consumers.

First, the report suggests that the definition of 'personal information' in the act be amended to include technical data, including all identifiers that could be used to distinguish individuals. This would bring breaches of data privacy within the remit of the act and mean that consumers could benefit from Privacy Act protections.

Second, the report recommends that the Privacy Act require a better disclosure notice upfront for platforms that collect data, explaining how a user's data will be collected, used and disclosed, including 'layered' notifications; and using short terms and conditions in plain language.

The report also recommends that consumer consent be obtained for the collection, use and disclosure of personal data. This would mean that the collection and use of data would be subject to an opt-in system. This would undoubtedly impact on the amount of data that can be collected, used and disclosed as consumers become more aware of their rights to data privacy.

General recommendations include:

- the potential creation of a special branch of the ACCC to handle all matters relating to data privacy and digital platform content. Digital platforms would be monitored by dedicated, trained officers tasked with proactively calling out breaches, essentially creating a police-like force to safeguard data privacy;
- broader review of Australia's privacy framework, with greater emphasis on individual rights; and
- a requirement that digital platforms disclose additional information about their use of personal data in ways that they have not been required to do previously.

(b) Digital Advertising Services Inquiry

In February 2020, the government responded to the findings of the Digital Platforms Inquiry in support of the ACCC's focus on digital platforms, technology and advertising, directing the ACCC to set up a new Digital Platforms Branch to undertake two new inquiries:

- The Digital Advertising Services Inquiry will focus on the practices of ad tech and advertising agencies, investigating and reviewing the supply of ad tech services and advertising agencies; and
- The Digital Platforms Services Inquiry will review digital platform and advertising services by digital platforms, as well as anti-competitive behaviour and data practices by digital platforms and data brokers, to investigate and enforce issues in digital markets.

The direction is a response to recent concerns relating to self-referencing and the lack of transparency in respect of digital platforms such as Google and Facebook. It also reflects the recent increased use of compulsory notices by the ACCC and the grant of A$25 million to the Office of the Australian Information Commissioner (OAIC) to realise its increased enforcement and control powers.

(c) Publishers

An example of the law's struggle to keep pace with the digital age and the increasing regulation of online platforms is the recent case of *Voller v Nationwide News Pty Ltd* [2019] NSWSC 766. Dylan Voller, an Aboriginal Australian from Darwin, was incarcerated at Alice Springs Correctional Centre when the centre was featured on the ABC TV programme *Four Corners* episode "Australia's Shame" in July 2016. Footage showed Voller shackled to a restraining chair in the prison. Voller gave evidence at the Royal Commission into the Protection and Detention of Children in the Northern Territory in December 2016. At the time, various news outlets reported on the content, with articles shared via social media and news platforms.

In February 2019, Voller sued *The Sydney Morning Herald*, *The Australian*, *The Centralian Advocate*, *Sky News Australia* and *The Bolt Report* over a series of "false and defamatory" imputations made about him in the comments section of Facebook. Separate from the question of defamation, the critical question was whether the media companies could be held to be responsible for "publishing" comments which they did not write or moderate.

In June 2019, the Supreme Court of New South Wales (NSW) held that media companies could be held liable for defamatory comments made by third parties on their public platforms. Justice Rothman said the media organisations' public Facebook pages were not merely "a conduit of the comment" and operated for commercial purposes, which encouraged the publication of comments. The content was likely to promote comments and the sorts of comments likely to flow from the posting of the content were likely to include defamatory material.

Following the decision, media outlets not sued by Voller – including Bauer, Seven West Media and the *Daily Mail* – intervened, lodging an appeal to have the decision overturned. In June 2020, the NSW Court of Appeal upheld the decision, stating that media platforms were liable as publishers of third-party Facebook posts, because they "encouraged and facilitated" comments when they set up public Facebook pages.

The implication for the advertising sector is that organisations with public social media pages must moderate the comments to ensure they are not personally liable for defamatory publication.

1.2   Copyright

The Copyright Act 1968 (Cth) prevents advertisers from using in advertising any unauthorised reproduction or adaptation of original creations such as books, computer programs, scripts, lyrics, paintings, sculptures, drawings, photographs, musical scores, films, videos, broadcasts, sound recordings or the choreography of a performance. Copyright proceedings are brought by an aggrieved party and orders sought usually include injunctions, damages and an account of profits.

1.3   Moral rights

Moral rights exist independently under the Copyright Act from the copyright that may exist in original material, and may continue to be exercised by an author or performer even though the copyright ownership has transferred to another person. Moral rights prevent:

- advertisers from using works without attribution of the work;
- false attribution; and
- derogatory treatment of a person's work in advertising.

An artist or creator who asserts that a moral right has been infringed without consent can seek remedies including damages and the publication of corrections.

1.4   Trademarks

The Trademarks Act 1995 (Cth) prevents advertisers from using, as a brand or "badge of origin", any letter, word, name, signature, numeral, device, brand, heading, label, ticket, aspect of packaging, shape, colour, sound or scent that has been registered as a trademark by another person. Trademark proceedings are brought by the owner of a registered trademark and orders sought usually include injunctions, damages and an account of profits.

1.5   Defamation

The national uniform defamation laws (2006) governing defamation in the various states and territories of Australia protect personal reputation and prevent advertisers from defaming individuals in their commercial communications. A defamed party will usually seek damages for loss of and damage to reputation.

1.6   Injurious falsehood

'Injurious falsehood' is a common-law action that protects business interests. An injurious falsehood case may be brought against an advertiser where it is alleged that its advertising and marketing communications contain false statements concerning the property, products or services of another person or entity. The usual remedy is an injunction and damages.

1.7   Privacy laws

The Privacy Act 1988 (Cth) (as amended) protects personal information (information about an identified person or from which a person is reasonably identifiable) and regulates the ways in which a consumer's personal information can be collected, stored and used, including for direct marketing purposes. The OAIC has the power to direct a cessation of Privacy Act breaches and to seek the imposition of penalties during court proceedings.

1.8 Discrimination, indecency, hate speech and causing offence

Various Australian federal and state/territory criminal laws apply that prohibit discrimination, racial vilification and causing offence. These laws are enforced by the responsible state, territory or federal government department, and fines for infringement may be imposed.

1.9 Spam laws

The Spam Act 2003 (Cth) regulates the ability of an advertiser to send electronic commercial messages to consumers. This act is enforced by the Australian Communications and Media Authority, which has the power to seek the payment of fines or to approach a court to seek penalties and corrective orders.

1.10 Trade promotion lottery laws

Various state and territory lottery laws regulate the conduct of prize draws and competitions conducted by advertisers for the promotion of products and services. The laws are enforced by the gaming offices of each Australian state and territory, which have the power to charge offenders criminally for breaches of their regulations, with the courts imposing fines. Advertisers can also be prevented from conducting future competitions.

1.11 Mandatory industry codes of practice

Many mandatory codes of practice exist in Australia that must be complied with by force of law. Such codes are industry and product specific, and must be determined and complied with by advertisers, depending upon the products and services offered to consumers. Breaches will often result in sanctions, directions to cease selling products or services, and fines.

1.12 Voluntary industry codes of practice

The Australian Association of National Advertisers (AANA) is the main advertising industry body representing the rights and responsibilities of Australia's major advertisers and their industry partners. The AANA promotes consumer confidence in and respect for general standards of advertising through the Advertising Standards Bureau (ASB). The ASB's responsibility is to ensure that all advertising, wherever it appears, meets the high standards laid down in the industry codes, particularly the codes administered by the ASB.

The Australian Influencer Marketing Council (AIMCo), a division of the not-for-profit Audited Media Association of Australia (AMAA), provides leadership and best practice guidance to the advertising sector with regard to influencer marketing. The AIMCo Code of Practice establishes the baseline of accepted practices when engaging an influencer. Although breaches of the voluntary codes do not attract fines and penalties, components of the codes restate legislation, the breach of which may attract civil or criminal penalties, and advertisers can be directed to withdraw or modify advertising that does not comply.

2. Comparative advertising

Comparative advertising is legal in Australia, but should be used with caution. This section summarises the applicable laws and regulations for this type of advertising.

2.1 Trademark and copyright law

The use of competitors' trademarks in comparative advertising is permissible under the Trademarks Act. Section 122(1)(d) of that act provides that "a person does not infringe a registered trademark when ... the person uses the trademark for the purposes of comparative advertising". As demonstrated by *Easyway Australia Pty Ltd v Infinite Plus Pty Ltd* [2011] FCA 351, where a competitor's trademark is not displayed in the ad, the court will look to the market and the context of the ad to determine whether the impugned vendor is identifiable.

There is no exception in the Copyright Act 1968 (Cth) that allows the reproduction of a copyright work (eg, a brand's logo) in comparative advertising. However, there is a provision that allows the inclusion of artwork 'incidentally' in a film or broadcast. Whether the inclusion of a third party's brand in an ad is 'incidental' will be determined on a case-by-case basis and there are currently no decided cases in Australia on this point.

2.2 Misleading and deceptive conduct

Section 18 of the Australian Consumer Law (found as Schedule 2 to the Australian Competition and Consumer Act 2010 (Cth)) prohibits a person from engaging in conduct in trade or commerce that is misleading or deceptive, or is likely to mislead or deceive. The main risk that advertisers face when using comparative advertising is that comparisons which are misleading or deceptive may breach Section 18 of the Australian Consumer Law.

The laws prohibiting misleading and deceptive conduct apply to all forms of advertising. However, comparative advertising is more likely to be subject to scrutiny, both by the competitor and by a regulator such as the ACCC.

(a) Comparing like with like

To avoid breaching the Australian Consumer Law, accuracy is essential. For this reason, advertisers need not necessarily compare 'like with like'. An ad may compare a 'superior' product with an 'inferior' product, as long as the comparison is truthful and accurate. This applies even if the competitor also produces a more comparable superior product.

For example, in *Gillette Australia Pty Ltd v Energizer Australia Pty Ltd* (2002) 56 IPR 1 a television commercial compared a Duracell alkaline battery against an Eveready carbon zinc battery, which had a shorter battery life, but was less expensive. In *Telstra Corporation Ltd v SingTel Optus Pty Ltd* [2007] FCA 824, Optus ads compared Optus's A$49 Cap Plan against Telstra's A$40 Phone Plan. In both cases, the ads were clear, accurate and truthful, and the court held them to be lawful even though the competitor also sold other products more comparable to the 'superior' product.

Each case will be assessed on its merits. Where the products being compared are clearly identified and the statements made about the products are truthful, there will be no breach of the Australian Consumer Law.

(b) Comparing prices

Any price comparisons made in advertising must accurately state the price difference and this accuracy must be maintained for the life of any such advertising campaign. Should a competitor change its prices in response to an ad, the comparative advertising may be rendered misleading. Thus, many advertisers elect to include disclaimers stating that a price or calculation was accurate as at a certain date, to avoid this issue. However, while such disclaimers mitigate risk, they do not eliminate it altogether. Whether the comparison will be seen as unlawful will depend on the overall impression created by the ad.

Additionally, as the focus of the Australian Consumer Law is consumer protection, price differences must not be overstated or understated. In *Luxottica Retail Australia Pty Ltd v Specsavers Pty Ltd* [2010] NSWSC 37, a Specsavers ad attempted to compare its prices favourably against the prices charged by OPSM. It stated the average price paid by OPSM customers, along with the average saving if Specsavers' products were purchased instead. The saving at Specsavers was in fact much larger than the saving claimed in the ad. Even though Specsavers painted OPSM more favourably than it should have, Specsavers was still found to have engaged in misleading or deceptive conduct because the price comparison was inaccurate.

(c) Remedies

The remedies often sought in pursuing claims for misleading or deceptive conduct regarding comparative advertising include injunctions, damages and corrective advertising – for example, retracting or amending any misleading claims made.

3. Online behavioural advertising

Online behavioural advertising uses cookies to deliver ads to individuals through an internet-enabled device based on:

- their web browsing activity;
- interests demonstrated on that device; or
- the 'behaviour' of that device.

3.1 Australian Guide for Online Behavioural Advertising

On 8 April 2011, the Australian Senate Environment and Communications References Committee released a report entitled *The Adequacy of Protections for the Privacy of Australians Online*. As a result of the recommendations in this report, the Australian Guide for Online Behavioural Advertising was developed by the Australian Digital Advertising Alliance (ADAA) and was released in March 2011. This was the first self-regulatory guide for online behavioural advertising in Australia. The guide was designed to complement existing Australian privacy laws and to provide an additional layer of protection for consumers.

The aims of the guide were fourfold:

- to promote transparency and choice by giving consumers clear notice as to which data is collected, how it is collected and what it is used for, and by giving them the ability to exercise choice over online ads;
- to promote internal good practices in relation to privacy, data security and the handling of sensitive data;
- to promote consumer awareness, with the launch of www.youronline choices.com.au; and
- to promote accountability, with the introduction of an easily accessible complaints procedure and ongoing monitoring and review of the guide.

3.2 Australian Best Practice Guidelines for Interest Based Advertising

In September 2014, the Interactive Advertising Bureau released the Australian Best Practice Guidelines for Interest Based Advertising for and on behalf of the ADAA.

The guidelines build on the Guide for Online Behavioural Advertising, comprising seven self-regulatory principles for best practice. These principles do not seek to regulate the content of online ads and apply only to online behavioural advertising by third-party companies such as online advertising networks, as opposed to the website publisher itself. The seven principles can be summarised as follows:

- Personal information and third-party online behavioural advertising: Third parties that want to combine online behavioural advertising data with personal information must treat the online behavioural advertising data as if it were personal information and in accordance with Australia's Privacy Act.
- Provision of clear information to users: Clear notice must be given to consumers about what data is collected, how it is collected and what it is used for.
- User choice over online behavioural advertising: Consumers must be able to make a choice as to whether they consent to the collection of data for online behavioural advertising; and they must be given clear, user-friendly options to manage their advertising choices.

- Secure data: Companies must ensure that data is stored securely and is kept only for as long as it fulfils a legitimate business need or as required by law.
- Careful handling of sensitive segmentation: Online behavioural advertising categories uniquely designed to target children under 13 cannot be created. Companies seeking to use online behavioural advertising in relation to sensitive market segments must obtain explicit consent.
- User education: Companies should provide easily accessible, user-friendly information about online behavioural advertising. A consumer education website providing consumer-friendly, non-technical information on online behavioural advertising has been developed by the industry.
- Accountability: All businesses are accountable for:
    - upholding the principles in the guidelines;
    - developing easily accessible mechanisms for consumers to lodge complaints directly to companies; and
    - committing themselves to an ongoing review of the guidelines and their implementation.

At the time of writing, the ADAA associations and other signatories to the Australian Best Practice Guidelines for Interest Based Advertising were:
- the Interactive Advertising Bureau of Australia;
- the Association for Data-Driven Marketing & Advertising;
- the Australian Association of National Advertisers;
- the Communications Council;
- the Australian Interactive Media Industry Association;
- the Media Federation of Australia;
- Adconian Media Group;
- Fairfax Digital;
- Google;
- Microsoft;
- NineMSN;
- realestate.com.au;
- Sensis Digital Media;
- Network Ten; and
- Yahoo!.

4.   Sales promotions

Trade or 'sales' promotions describe a marketing technique aimed at increasing consumer demand for certain products or services as well as brand recognition for the promoter. A variety of mechanisms are employed to engage the consumer, but the most common is the giving away of prizes. Numerous federal, state and territory laws and regulations govern the conduct of trade and consumer promotions in Australia. State and territory lottery laws will apply if there is any element of chance in a promotion, and permits may be required to conduct the promotion.

Additionally, all promotions (not just prize draws or competitions) in Australia are subject to consumer protection requirements under the Australian Consumer Law as found in Schedule 2 to the Competition and Consumer Act 2010 (Cth). Relevantly, under the Australian Consumer Law, a person must not, in trade or commerce:

- engage in conduct that is misleading or deceptive (Section 18);
- make a false or misleading representation about products or services (Section 29); or
- offer any rebate, gift, prize or other free item with the intention of not providing it at all or as offered (Section 32).

4.1 Game of skill or chance, or both?

A game of chance is a game in which there is a degree of chance, regardless of any degree of skill. Conversely, 'skill' refers to any element that controls or influences the outcome of a game or activity that is within the control of a player or players. If a promotion involves any random element, it is deemed to be a game of chance. Each entry in a game of chance must have a fair and equal chance of winning. Some examples of games of chance include promotions with the following mechanisms:

- barrel or electronic draw – for example, "Purchase a [specially marked product], complete the entry form and place it in the entry box to go into the draw to win a prize";
- instant win – for example, "Purchase a [specially marked product] to receive a scratch card, and scratch to reveal whether you are an instant winner";
- first past the post – for example, "The first 100 entrants to purchase a [specially marked product] will each win a prize"; and
- chance for a chance – for example, "The first entrant drawn wins the opportunity to choose 1 of 10 envelopes, only 1 of which will contain a prize".

Permits may be required to conduct a game of chance, subject to:

- the entry mechanism of the promotion;
- the Australian states and territories in which the promotion is conducted; and
- the total maximum prize pool value awarded in these states and territories.

Games of chance can be distinguished from other forms of promotional activity, such as cashbacks, loyalty programmes, gift-with-purchase promotions, guaranteed offers and games of skill. Although these latter promotional activities are not regulated by lottery laws and do not generally require permits, they must still comply with the Australian Consumer Law. Permits may be required if the promotional activities involve any element of chance (eg, "The first eligible entry drawn will win a prize"). Specifically, games of skill do not require permits and are defined as requiring that every entry be individually judged against objective criteria and that there be no possibility of a tie.

4.2 Permits

If a promotion contains any element of chance, the promotion must comply with the lottery laws in each state and territory in which the promotion is conducted (in addition to the Australian Consumer Law). Lottery laws vary between each state and territory, and therefore national promotions must comply with the individual lottery laws in all states and territories. Promotions extending to New Zealand must also comply with New Zealand's lottery laws.

Some states and territories require the application and issuance of permits before the advertising for the promotion and the promotion itself commence (depending on the entry mechanism and prize value of the promotion); while other states and territories, and New Zealand, have 'standing' permits that allow the promotion to proceed provided that it complies with certain standing requirements. Table 1 on the next page summarises the permit requirements in Australia and New Zealand.

Upon lodgement of a permit application, a permit fee must be paid to the lottery department in each state or territory in which a permit must be obtained (with the exception of the Northern Territory, where there is no fee). The permit fee is calculated based on the total maximum recommended retail value, including goods and services tax (GST), of all prizes to be awarded in the applicable state or territory.

Any electronic drawing systems used to randomly draw winners in a promotion require prior approval from the South Australian lottery department if the promotion is conducted in that state. Once a random electronic drawing system is approved, it can be used for all future promotions that use a random system to draw winners. The NSW lottery department also requires that the promoter obtain certain electronic draw procedure reports if the promotion is conducted in that state, which may be called upon at any time by the authorities.

4.3 Free entry

The lottery laws in Australia and New Zealand require that entry into a sales promotion be free. However, the promoter may require that entrants purchase

Table 1. Permit requirements for sales promotions containing an element of chance

Category	Area	Conditions
Permit areas	Australian Capital Territory	Permit required when prize value is greater than A$3,000. Standing permit rules apply to promotions with a prize value of less than A$3,000.
	New South Wales	Authority required when prize value is greater than A$10,000. Standing permit rules apply to promotions with a prize value of less than A$10,000.
	Northern Territory	Permit not required regardless of prize value if a permit has been granted in any other Australian state or territory. Otherwise, permit required when prize value less than A$5,000. Standing permit rules also apply.
	South Australia	Permit required when prize value is greater than A$5,000 – but a permit is required regardless of prize value if an 'instant win' element exists in the promotion. Standing permit rules apply to promotions with a prize value of less than A$5,000.
Non-permit areas	Queensland	Standing permit rules apply.
	Tasmania	Standing permit rules apply.
	Victoria	Standing permit rules apply.
	Western Australia	Standing permit rules apply.
	New Zealand	Standing permit rules apply.

certain product(s) at the recommended retail price in order to enter the promotion. The most common method of entry is via a website or social media platform; however, the promoter may also require that entrants enter the promotion via a communication mechanism (eg, mail, telephone or SMS) at a cost not exceeding A$0.55, including GST (except in Victoria, where the maximum entry cost is A$1.00, including GST). Costs are current at the time of writing, but are subject to change.

4.4 Specified terms and conditions

The Australian Consumer Law and lottery laws also require that all relevant information on a promotion, including the rights of the promoter and limitations on entry and prizes, be disclosed to entrants at the time of entering the promotion via a set of 'terms and conditions' or 'conditions of entry'. The terms and conditions for a promotion must be readily accessible by entrants before they enter the promotion in order to be enforceable pursuant to contract law and the Australian Consumer Law. Entrants must not be charged to access the terms and conditions.

For promotions involving an element of chance, the terms and conditions must be approved by the lottery departments in each state and territory in which a permit is required to conduct the promotion. Additionally, if the promotion involves any electronic element and is conducted in Western Australia, the final terms and conditions must be provided to the Western Australia lottery department prior to the start of the promotion.

4.5 Advertising the promotion

If artwork for a promotion does not contain the full terms and conditions, the artwork must include a reference to where the full terms and conditions may be accessed, and the terms and conditions must be accessible at that location. The promotional artwork must also contain certain minimum disclosures, or 'abbreviated terms and conditions', required to adequately communicate the promotion to consumers for compliance with the various state and territory lottery laws and the Australian Consumer Law. Advertising for a game of chance must include the permit numbers from each state or territory gaming authority on all marketing collateral.

4.6 Amendments to a promotion

If any amendments must be made to the terms and conditions of a promotion after the permit application has been submitted to the NSW, Australian Capital Territory, South Australia, Northern Territory and/or Western Australia lottery department(s) (as applicable), the lottery department(s) must be notified of the proposed amendments. If the permit application has already been processed and permit approval granted by the NSW, Australian Capital Territory, Victoria and/or South Australia lottery department(s) (as applicable), an amendment application must be lodged and various amendment fees will be payable to each department (as applicable).

Once a promotion has commenced or its advertising is in the market, lottery departments will not generally allow any amendments to the promotion, and the promotion must therefore be run in accordance with the representations and disclosures made to consumers via the promotional advertising for compliance with the Australian Consumer Law and the terms and conditions originally approved by the lottery departments.

5. Ambush marketing

The classic contemporary example of ambush marketing in Australia is a 2000 Qantas television ad featuring choirs on the Sydney Opera House steps, which caused many people to believe that Qantas, and not Ansett, was the official airline sponsor of the 2000 Sydney Olympics. Ambush marketing has become a recurring issue in Australia. Following the 2016 Summer Olympics in Rio de Janeiro, the Australian Olympic Committee took Telstra (a past Olympic team sponsor) to court over its 'I Go To Rio' campaign, which stated that Telstra was the "official technology partner of Seven's Olympic Games coverage" and appeared on the network which had secured television rights for the Olympic broadcast.

Numerous laws in Australia directly and indirectly regulate ambush marketing, including consumer protection laws, IP laws and event-specific legislation. These laws seek to prevent ambush marketing from weakening the commercial investment of an event's official sponsors or suppliers by diluting or depriving them of public recognition and association with the event.

5.1 Consumer protection laws

Pursuant to the Australian Consumer Law in Schedule 2 to the Competition and Consumer Act 2010 (Cth), any marketing activity that falsely or deceptively suggests or implies an association, sponsorship or affiliation between a brand and an event may constitute misleading or deceptive conduct (Section 18 of the act) and/or contain false or misleading representations (Section 29).

A distinction must, however, be made between:

- marketing activity that indirectly implies an affiliation with an event, which may only lead to confusion and may not give rise to a cause of action under the Australian Consumer Law; and
- marketing activity that makes direct and misleading claims of association with an event, which may result in deception or a misrepresentation under the Australian Consumer Law.

Additionally, ambush marketing may be actionable under the common law action of passing off if it causes:

- damage to the reputation or goodwill of an official sponsor or supplier to an event; or
- wrongful appropriation in the sense of causing potential customers to associate the product or business of an official sponsor or supplier with that of the marketed brand, where no such connection exists.

5.2 Event-specific legislation

In addition to the above laws that generally regulate ambush marketing, various Australian federal and state laws restrict certain marketing practices for specific events, including the following:

- The Olympic Insignia Protection Act 1987 (Cth) protects Olympic insignia and prohibits the commercial use of certain Olympic expressions without licence from the Australian Olympic Committee;
- The Major Sporting Events (Indicia and Images) Protection Act 2014 (Cth) regulates the use of protected indicia and images to sell, advertise or otherwise promote products or services in connection with a defined major sporting event (eg, the International Cricket Council T20 World Cup 2020);
- The Melbourne 2006 Commonwealth Games (Indicia and Images) Protection Act 2005 (Cth) protects against the use of fraudulent or obvious imitations of designs or symbols associated with the Commonwealth Games;
- The Australian Grands Prix Act 1994 (Vic) prevents ambush marketing in connection with the Australian Grand Prix in Melbourne;
- The Major Sporting Events Act 2009 (Vic) restricts ambush marketing relating to major sporting events and to venues for events in Victoria, including aerial advertising;
- The Major Sports Facilities Act 2001 (Qld) regulates the advertisement and promotion of national and international events staged in Queensland, including advertising in air space or on a building or other structure visible from these events; and
- The Commonwealth Games Arrangements (Brand Protection) Amendment Act 2013 (Qld) bans the unauthorised use of certain references and images where the use is for commercial or promotional purposes or would suggest a sponsorship-like arrangement with the 2018 Gold Coast Commonwealth Games, as well as conduct suggesting a sponsorship or affiliation with the games that does not exist.

5.3 How to protect official sponsorship rights in Australia

The exclusivity of official sponsorship rights to an event in Australia can be protected in a variety of ways, including:

- securing first-tier advertising rights (eg, in broadcasts) for official sponsors of the event;

- registering any trademarks in respect of the event (including any titles, logos or images that only official sponsors can use to distinguish themselves from other parties), as well as in respect of the advertisement of the event by official sponsors. If a trademark is unregistered, the trademark owner can seek to enforce its rights only on the basis of consumer protection laws, which often requires evidence of reputation in the trademark, unlike an action for the infringement of a registered trademark under the Trademarks Act 1995 (Cth);
- entering into an official sponsorship agreement with the governing body of the event which contemplates ambush marketing and the circumstances in which the governing body will intervene to assist the sponsor – for example, the confiscation of competing marketing material from the venue;
- issuing formal public thanks to official sponsors for their support of the event;
- imposing conditions on tickets to the event and controlling what patrons are permitted to bring into the event (eg, any promotional material of competitors);
- managing the numerous layers of sponsorship opportunities between events, venues, promotions, teams and athletes; and
- preparing template letters of demand, which can be quickly served on competitors to enforce the rights of official sponsors in respect of the event in reliance upon the above laws.

6.   Direct marketing

6.1   Privacy

The Privacy Amendment (Enhancing Privacy Protection) Act 2012 (Cth), which took effect on 12 March 2014, amended the Privacy Act 1988 (Cth) significantly, including introducing a new set of Australian Privacy Principles (APPs).

APP 7 deals with direct marketing. However, it does not apply to the extent that the Spam Act 2003 (Cth) or the Do Not Call Register Act 2006 (Cth) applies. APP 7 restricts the use and disclosure of personal information by organisations for the purpose of direct marketing. Organisations will be permitted to use or disclose personal information for direct marketing only if:

- they collected the information from the individual;
- the individual would reasonably expect the organisation to use or disclose the information for the purpose of direct marketing;
- the organisation provides a simple means for the individual to easily request not to receive direct marketing communication from the business; and
- the individual has not already made a request to opt out.

Where the direct marketing involves the use or disclosure of sensitive information (eg, medical information), consent will be required. An exception is provided for contracted service providers to federal government agencies.

In all cases, individuals will have the right to:

- request the source of their personal information;
- opt out of receiving direct marketing communications from the organisation; and
- opt out of disclosure of their personal information for third-party marketing.

6.2 Privacy Amendment Act

The Privacy Amendment (Enhancing Privacy Protection) Act 2012 ('Privacy Amendment Act') was introduced to the Australian Parliament on 23 May 2012 and was passed with amendments on 29 November 2012. The Privacy Amendment Act introduced many significant changes to the Privacy Act 1988 (Cth), which came into force on 12 March 2014.

Most importantly, the Privacy Amendment Act introduced the APPs, which replaced the National Privacy Principles and the Information Privacy Principles contained in the 1988 act. The APPs apply to all organisations that collect 'personal information' and that have a minimum annual turnover of A$3 million.

This raises an important question for organisations using online behavioural advertising: when does the collection and pooling of information to create a user profile of an individual for marketing purposes amount to the collection of 'personal information' as defined in the 1988 act, thereby requiring full compliance with all of the APPs?

Under the old act, 'personal information' was defined as: "information or an opinion (including information or an opinion forming part of a database), whether true or not, and whether recorded in a material form or not, about an individual whose identity is apparent, or can reasonably be ascertained, from the information or opinion." When the Privacy Amendment Act took effect, the old definition of 'personal information' was replaced with the following definition:

information or an opinion about an identified individual, or an individual who is reasonably identifiable:

(a) whether the information or opinion is true or not; and

(b) whether the information or opinion is recorded in a material form or not.

Significantly, this new definition contemplates information about an individual that, when linked to other information (which may be held by the same entity or another entity), identifies an individual or renders the individual reasonably identifiable. The central issue is to determine whether, when data is compiled from various sources to create user profiles, the threshold of 'reasonably identifiable' has been reached.

The Privacy Amendment Act applies to information about an individual who is 'identified' or 'reasonably identifiable'. The Explanatory Memorandum in that act provides some guidance regarding when information about an individual may be seen as reasonably identifiable:

Whether an individual can be identified or is reasonably identifiable depends on context and circumstances. While it may be technically possible for an agency or organisation to identify individuals from information it holds, for example by linking the information with other information held by it or another entity, it may be that it is not practically possible. For example, logistics or legislation may prevent such linkage. In these circumstances, individuals are not 'reasonably identifiable'.

The Explanatory Memorandum goes on to note that whether an individual is reasonably identifiable from certain information requires a consideration of a number of factors, including the cost, difficulty, practicality and likelihood that the information will be linked in such a way as to identify an individual. This approach is consistent with the recommendations contained in *For Your Information: Australian Privacy Law and Practice* (Australian Law Reform Commission Report 108), which suggest that an individual is reasonably identifiable when he or she can be identified from information in the possession of an agency or organisation, or from that information and other information which the agency or organisation may access, without unreasonable cost or difficulty.

Guidance issued by the OAIC in its 2017 publication *What is Personal Information?* plays an important role in helping organisations, agencies and individuals to understand the meaning of 'identified' and 'reasonably identifiable' in the definition of 'personal information' and their obligations in this regard. The objective test, which has practical regard to the context in which the 'identifiability' of information arises, should be applied when determining whether a user profile falls within the definition of 'personal information'.

The decision will always be contextual and must be considered on a case-by-case basis.

Common examples of personal information include an individual's name, signature, address, telephone number, date of birth, medical records, bank account details, employment details and commentary or opinion about a person. In most cases, the background data collected as part of online behavioural advertising will be classified as personal information under the Privacy Act. As such, online behavioural advertisers should:

- treat all user profiles as personal information, unless the underlying data set contains only anonymous, de-identified information that cannot be linked or combined with any other data to become personally identifiable information; and
- comply with the provisions of the Privacy Amendment Act in collecting and handling personal information, including the APPs.

6.3   Notifiable Data Breach Scheme

The requirements of the Notifiable Data Breach (NDB) Scheme are contained in Part IIIC of the Privacy Act and apply to breaches that occur on or after 22 February 2018.

The NDB Scheme mandates that where a data breach occurs which "is likely to result in serious harm to an individual whose personal information is involved", it must be reported to the OAIC and any individual at risk of serious harm must be notified promptly. The NDB Scheme applies to any regulated organisation or agency to which the Privacy Act applies.

Notification must include:

- the name and contact details of the organisation or agency;
- a description of the data breach;
- a description of the personal information concerned;
- an explanation of how the organisation or agency intends to respond to the breach; and
- directions for the individual as to the steps that should be taken.

The OAIC provides advice and guidance in respect of the NDB Scheme, handles complaints, conducts investigations and takes regulatory action in respect of non-compliance by regulated organisations and agencies.

6.4   Spam

All commercial electronic messages sent in Australia must comply with the Spam Act 2003 (Cth). This act is supplemented by the Australian e-Marketing Code of Practice that was registered with the Australian Media and Communications Authority in March 2005. The code has the force of law and establishes industry-wide rules and guidelines for the sending of commercial electronic messages in accordance with the Spam Act. The code's rules and guidelines provide practical and specific guidance in relation to the sending of messages in the context of current electronic marketing practices. The code automatically applies to all entities (both individuals and organisations) that are undertaking e-marketing activity.

Under the Spam Act, 'commercial electronic messages' include messages sent by way of email, instant messaging and mobile wireless technology (including SMS, MMS, Wireless Access Protocol and 3G, along with technologies thereafter devised), by entities to individuals for the purposes of selling, advertising or promoting certain products and services. 'Commercial electronic messages' in this context do not include fax or voice-to-voice telemarketing, even where a voice call is a pre-recorded human voice (although the Do Not Call Register – see section 6.5 – will apply).

The Spam Act prohibits the sending of commercial electronic messages to an individual unless that individual has consented to receive such communications. Both the Spam Act and the code clearly establish that consent can take the form of express consent or inferred consent. 'Express consent' arises where an individual takes an active step to indicate that he or she consents to receive future marketing material, after first being made clearly aware that he or she is consenting to receive commercial messages in the future. This means that the consumer must be advised that he or she may receive promotional or advertising material from the relevant advertiser in the future by way of email, instant messaging or mobile wireless technology.

Establishing 'inferred consent' is more difficult. The Spam Act and the code state that this can come about in two ways:

- where the advertiser sending the commercial electronic messages and the relevant individual have an existing business or other relationship, and there is a reasonable expectation of receiving commercial electronic messages from that advertiser; and
- where a person conspicuously publishes a work-related email address and a company wants to send that person a commercial electronic message that relates to his or her line of work (although this option does not apply if a person indicates that he or she does not want to receive commercial electronic messages at that address).

In addition to the consent of the recipient, the Spam Act requires all commercial electronic messages (as defined) to contain clear and accurate sender identification and a functional 'unsubscribe' facility in order to opt out of receiving such messages.

6.5   Do Not Call Register

The Do Not Call Register was established under two pieces of Commonwealth legislation:

- the Do Not Call Register Act 2006 (Cth); and
- the Do Not Call Register (Consequential Amendments) Act 2006 (Cth).

The Do Not Call Register commenced in 2007, with a general prohibition beginning on 31 May 2007 on making (or causing to be made) telemarketing calls to numbers on the register. Under the Do Not Call Register Act, it is illegal to make telemarketing calls to numbers on the Do Not Call Register – although there are exceptions for charities, educational and religious organisations, and political parties.

Advertisers that make telemarketing calls can avoid possible penalties by checking, or 'washing', their lists against the Do Not Call Register.

It is legal for advertisers to call customers with whom they have a relationship and who have consented to receive the call, even if the customer's number is listed on the Do Not Call Register. It is important for advertisers to be able to establish that express consent has been given – for example, if the customer willingly opted in via the Internet or a mobile telephone in response to a particular campaign.

The Australian Media and Communications Authority (ACMA) has also implemented the Telecommunications (Do Not Call Register) (Telemarketing and Research Calls) Industry Standard 2007, which commenced on 31 May 2007. The standard establishes a minimum set of requirements for making telemarketing and research calls and aims to provide greater certainty for consumers on the minimum level of conduct that they can expect from those making unsolicited telemarketing and research calls.

The standard applies to:

- all telemarketing calls made to an Australian number to offer, advertise or promote products, services, interests in land, business opportunities or investments, or to solicit donations;
- all research calls to conduct opinion polling and to carry out standard questionnaire-based research; and
- calls made for the foregoing purposes by public interest entities (eg, charities, registered political parties and religious organisations) that are exempt from the general prohibition on calling numbers listed on the Do Not Call Register when making specific types of telemarketing calls.

ACMA has released the *Do Not Call Register Act 2006 Compliance Guide* to provide telemarketers with advice about measures they can take to comply with the Do Not Call Register legislation.

6.6 ADMA Direct Marketing Code of Practice

The Association for Data-driven Marketing and Advertising (ADMA) operates a Direct Marketing Code of Practice which is a self-regulatory code. Compliance with the code is a prerequisite of ADMA membership.

7. Product placement

Although there are laws prohibiting the display of specific products (eg, tobacco), product placement remains largely unregulated in Australia. Nonetheless, there are certain constraints imposed upon product placement activities and these – as well as the lack of constraints – are discussed in the remainder of this section.

7.1 Industry codes

A number of industries in Australia have their own voluntary advertising codes of practice (as discussed further below), but it is arguable that these codes do not extend to coverage of product placement. Instead, they are primarily concerned with more traditional forms of advertising.

However, product placement is considered by the Commercial Television Industry Code of Practice. Under Section 1.20 of that code, which applies to factual television programmes (documentaries, current affairs and infotainment programmes), if a licensee enters into a commercial arrangement and the third party's products or services are endorsed or featured in the programme, the licensee must disclose the existence of that commercial arrangement. This disclosure must be made during the programme itself or in the credits for the programme. It should adequately bring the existence of any such commercial arrangement to the attention of viewers in a way that is readily understandable to a reasonable person. These rules also apply where the presenter of a factual programme is paid to endorse a third party's product.

The same code notes that where a licensee receives payment for material that is presented in a programme or a segment of a programme, that material must be distinguishable from other programme material – either because it is clearly promoting a product or service, or because of labelling or some other form of differentiation.

The code of practice is silent with regard to commercial arrangements for non-factual programmes. This lack of regulation means that a television network may accept payment from an advertiser for promoting a brand in a non-factual television programme without disclosure either during the programme or in the credits.

7.2   Consumer protection laws

All advertisers must comply with the Australian consumer protection laws, including when engaging in product placement.

Most relevantly, product placement must not be seen as misleading or deceptive; otherwise, it may infringe the Australian Consumer Law (see Schedule 2 to the Competition and Consumer Act 2010 (Cth)). Section 18 of the Australian Consumer Law provides that a person in trade or commerce must not engage in conduct that is misleading or deceptive or that is likely to mislead or deceive. Section 29 prohibits a person from falsely representing that products or services promoted have have sponsorship or approval from, or an affiliation with, a third party or a third party's products or services. The legal test is whether a reasonable, casual and attentive yet not over-analytical viewer or reader of the advertising material would be likely to be misled or deceived.

The risk of breaching these laws when engaging in product placement is relatively low, as by its nature product placement does not generally make representations as to the standard, quality, value, grade, composition, style or model of a particular product. Furthermore, given that products are often placed in fictional settings, it is doubtful that the 'reasonable viewer' would be likely to be misled or deceived by any representations made.

8. Native advertising and social media influencers

8.1 Native advertising

Influence takes many different forms. Native advertising is typically associated with 'advertorials', where a respected publisher or journalist from a masthead, relying on readers' trust, receives payment to promote products or services and the paid content appears in an editorial environment without disclosure. The core issue is that the content appears and is perceived by consumers as organic editorial content, when it is in fact native advertising.

The legal issues are similar to those surrounding social media influencers. Any influencer must disclose rewards and commercial connections with brands and products if it would be misleading or deceptive not to do so in the circumstances. This is important because consumers trust what is written by reputable sources and a breach of that trust may result in a breach of the Australian Consumer Law.

The Australian Consumer Law prohibits misleading or deceptive conduct and specific product misrepresentations, including testimonials (Sections 18 and 29). Conduct is assessed on a case-by-case basis, having regard to:
- the nature of the communication;
- the context;
- the likely audience of the post; and
- the consumer impression – that is, how a consumer may perceive the claim from the dominant impression created by the advertising as a whole (the 'take-out').

8.2 Social media influencers

Brand engagement – usually through a collaboration between a brand and social influencer or socially active brand ambassador – has become a mainstream marketing channel in Australia, with influencers playing a direct role in shaping the purchasing decisions and buying patterns of their followers and communities.

The increase in influencer-led marketing in recent years has heightened awareness of inadequate disclosures, fake followers and influencer hijacking by brands and ghosting influencers.

AIMCo was established by the AMAA in September 2019 to set best practice standards around influencer marketing. On 1 July 2020, the AIMCo Guiding Council (comprised of founding member companies representing all sides of the influencer marketplace) released the industry's inaugural Code of Practice to support brands, agencies and creators and drive trust, accountability and transparency in this growing sector.

The code articulates areas of responsibility and makes recommendations for all involved in the influencer marketing ecosystem, spanning vetting, advertising disclosure and contractual considerations, including content rights usage and reporting metrics.

The long-awaited framework for transparent industry conduct is a key focus of the code which raises awareness of existing disclosure requirements, including:

- Section 2.7 of the AANA Code of Ethics, as part of the advertising and marketing sector's self-regulation, which requires that "Advertising or Marketing Communication shall be clearly distinguishable as such to the relevant audience"; and
- disclosure requirements under the Australian Consumer Law, specifically in respect of misleading and deceptive conduct through the publication of advertising content which fails to disclose the commercial relationship between the parties.

9.   Industry-specific regulation

9.1   Gambling

The advertisement of gambling and betting is generally regulated by the applicable state and territory governments, and is covered in a variety of acts, regulations and codes of practice. The degree of regulation in each state and territory varies widely.

(a)   *Interactive gambling*

In addition to state laws, the Commonwealth regulates interactive gambling through the Interactive Gambling Act 2001 (Cth). This act makes it an offence in Australia to publish or broadcast an ad for an interactive gambling service. The prohibition extends to all forms of media, both electronic and non-electronic, and includes advertising via the Internet or via any form of broadcast.

In response to the aforementioned act, the Internet Industry Association in consultation with the internet industry and the community more generally has developed a Code for Interactive Gambling. The code provides procedures to be followed by internet service providers in relation to internet gambling content hosted outside Australia.

(b)   *Commercial Television Industry Code of Practice*

Television ads about gambling must also comply with the Commercial Television Industry Code of Practice 2015. Under the code, except for a commercial broadcast in a news, current affairs or sporting programme, an ad relating to betting or gambling must not be broadcast in G classification[1]

---

1   'G classification' stands for 'general classification' and means that the programme is suitable for all ages.

periods from Monday to Friday, or at weekends between 6:00am and 8:30am, and between 4:00pm and 7:30pm.

The code bans the promotion of live-odds betting five minutes prior to, during and five minutes immediately following the broadcast of sporting matches; and restricts generic gambling ads to breaks in play, such as half-time.

9.2   Alcohol

Australia has a quasi-regulatory system for alcohol advertising.

Advertising is regulated by the Alcohol Beverages Advertising Code Scheme (ABAC), a voluntary code that has been developed in consultation with the Australian government. Under the code, ads for alcoholic beverages must present a mature, balanced and responsible approach to the consumption of alcoholic beverages. The code is administered by a management committee of industry, advertising and government representatives, and applies to print media, billboard, internet, cinema, television and radio advertising, as well as product naming and packaging. The code covers the content of the advertising, but not its placement.

Alcohol advertising is also regulated by a number of additional codes of practice, particularly in relation to the placement of alcohol advertising, including:

- the Commercial Television Industry Code of Practice;
- the Outdoor Media Association Code of Ethics; and
- the Distilled Spirits Industry Council of Australia Statement of Responsible Practices for Advertising and Marketing.

Advertisers can have their alcohol ads checked by the Alcohol Advertising Pre-Vetting System. This is a user-pays service which pre-vets all alcohol ads against the ABAC Scheme during development.

Complaints about alcohol advertising are made to Ad Standards, which will assess the complaint under both the AANA Advertiser Code of Ethics and the Code for Advertising and Marketing Communications to Children. The complaint will also be sent to the ABAC chief adjudicator, who may assess the complaint if it raises issues under the ABAC. Prior to assessment, the advertiser is given an opportunity to respond to the complaint and this response is considered as part of the assessment.

9.3   Pharmaceuticals

In Australia, the advertisement of pharmaceuticals is subject to the requirements of:

- the Therapeutic Goods Act 1989 (Cth);
- the Therapeutic Goods Regulations 1990 (Cth); and
- the Therapeutic Goods Advertising Code, which aims to ensure that the marketing and advertising of therapeutic goods to consumers are

conducted in a manner that promotes the quality use of therapeutic goods, is socially responsible and does not mislead or deceive consumers.

'Therapeutic goods' in this context are those goods available only from a pharmacist or a medical or dental practitioner, including prescription-only medicines.

Under the Therapeutic Goods Act, prescription-only medications may not be advertised to the general public. Ads for non-prescription medicines aimed at the general public must comply with the Therapeutic Goods Act and its associated regulations, and also with the Therapeutic Goods Advertising Code.

Ads for medicinal products that are to be published in newspapers or magazines or in the form of posters or billboards, or broadcast on radio, television or film, must be approved before they are used. The Therapeutic Goods Administration administers the Therapeutic Goods Advertising Code. Complaints are heard by its Complaints Resolution Panel and may also be heard by industry complaints panels in some circumstances.

A number of codes of practice also contain provisions relating to the advertisement of therapeutic goods, including:

- the Medicines Australia Code of Conduct and supporting guidelines;
- the Australian Self-Medication Industry Code of Practice; and
- the Complementary Healthcare Council of Australia Code of Practice for the Marketing of Complementary Healthcare and Healthfood Products (at the time of writing, this is currently under review).

9.4 Financial products and services

There are a number of sources of guidance for the advertisement of financial products and services.

(a) ASIC Good Practice Guide

In November 2012, the Australian Securities and Investment Commission (ASIC) updated its *Regulatory Guide 234: Good Practice Guide* for the advertisement of financial products and services. The guidance applies to any communication whose purpose is to inform consumers about, or to promote, financial products or financial advice services. It is aimed at promoters of financial products, financial advice services, credit products and credit services, and publishers of advertising for these products and services.

The guide contains good practice guidance to help promoters comply with their legal obligations not to make false or misleading statements or engage in misleading or deceptive conduct. For example, the guidelines state that:

- ads for financial products and credit products should give a balanced message about the returns featured and the benefits and risks associated with the product;

- warnings, disclaimers and qualifications should not be inconsistent with other content in an ad, including any headline claims; and
- where a fee or cost is referred to in an ad, it should give a realistic impression of the overall level of fees and costs that a consumer is likely to pay, including any indirect fees or costs.

Other general guidance that ASIC provides with respect to specific types of media is summarised in Table 2.

Table 2. ASIC guidance for specific types of media

Medium	Summary of guidance
Mass media	Advertisers should consider the actual audience that is likely to see the ad and whether the ad is accurate, balanced and helpful for that audience. Advertising should be clearly distinguished from normal programme or editorial content.
Audio ads	Warnings, disclaimers and qualifications should be read at a speed that is comprehensible to the average listener.
Film and video ads	Information about risks and any warnings should be easily understood by the average viewer on the first viewing of an ad and not undermined by distracting sounds or images.
Internet	Advertisers should consider the overall impression created by an internet banner ad when viewed by itself for the first time. Advertisers should consider the appropriateness of using new media channels for advertising if content limitations mean that there is insufficient space to provide balanced information. Consumers should be able to keep a record of an ad, including any disclaimers or warnings.
Outdoor advertising	Advertisers should take into account the conditions under which an ad will be viewed (eg, from a distance or from a moving vehicle) when considering whether the overall impression of the ad is misleading or deceptive.

The guide should be read in conjunction with other product-specific advertising guidance provided by ASIC, including the following.

(b)   ***Regulatory Guide 156: Advertising of Debentures and Unsecured Notes***
This guide sets out the standards that ASIC expects the issuers and publishers of ads to meet when advertising debentures and unsecured notes to retail investors. For example:

- all advertisements for notes that are offered to retail investors should include a prominent statement to potential investors that there is a risk that they could lose some or all of their money; and
- ads for notes should not state or imply that the investment is suitable for a particular class of investor.

(c)   ***Regulatory Guide 45: Mortgage Schemes: Improving Disclosure for Retail Investors***
This guide sets out the standard that ASIC expects from all entities involved in the issue or advertisement of interests in mortgage schemes. For example:

- ads should include a prominent statement to the effect that investors risk losing some or all of their money; and
- ads should quote returns only if the return is accompanied by a prominent disclosure that there is a risk that the investment may achieve lower than expected returns.

(d)   ***Regulatory Guide 232: Agribusiness Managed Investment Schemes: Improving Disclosure for Retail Investors***
This guide sets out the standard that ASIC expects from all responsible entities and others involved with the issue or advertisement of interests in agribusiness managed investment schemes. ASIC has developed five benchmarks and five disclosure principles for such schemes that can help retail investors to understand the risks, assess the rewards being offered and decide whether investment is suitable for them.

(e)   ***Other regulations***
The advertisement of financial products is subject to further regulation from a number of sources, including:

- the Financial Services Reform Act 2001 (Cth), which seeks to ensure a fair, orderly and transparent market for financial products and therefore requires detailed disclosure in relation to financial products; and
- the National Consumer Credit Protection Act 2009 (Cth), including the National Credit Code, which, for example, notes that a person must not make a false or misleading representation in relation to a matter that is material to entry into a credit contract or a related transaction, or in an attempt to induce another person to enter into a credit contract or related transaction.

9.5   Food

(a)   Advertising generally

The advertisement of food and beverages in Australia is subject to both government regulation and voluntary self-regulation. Ads must comply with the various state and territory Food Acts and with the Australia New Zealand Food Standards Code; the latter contains the required standards for food produced in New Zealand and in the states, territories and Commonwealth of Australia, in relation to food sold and/or imported into both countries. The code covers everything from food processing requirements to retail sale requirements, such as packaging and labelling. The Food Acts give legal effect to the provisions of the code.

A number of self-regulatory codes and principles also apply to food and beverage advertising, and aim to ensure that advertisers maintain a high sense of social responsibility when advertising and marketing food and beverage products to Australians. For example, such codes require that advertising:

- not be misleading or deceptive;
- not undermine the importance of a healthy and active lifestyle; and
- contain only scientifically accurate claims about the health and nutritional benefits of products.

These self-regulatory codes include:

- the AANA Food and Beverages: Advertising and Marketing Communications Code; and
- the AANA Code of Ethics.

(b)   Advertising in relation to children

Advertising food to children on television is subject to a co-regulatory system. Advertisers must comply with:

- the Broadcasting Services Act 1992 (Cth);
- the Children's Television Standards (administered by the Australian Media and Communications Authority); and
- the Commercial Television Industry Code of Practice.

These regulations require that such ads:

- not promote an inactive lifestyle or unhealthy eating or drinking habits; and
- not mislead or deceive children.

In addition, a number of self-regulatory codes apply directly to ads targeting children that set out similar guidelines, including:

- the AANA Code for Advertising and Marketing Communications to

Children, which states that advertising or marketing communications to children for food or beverages must neither encourage nor promote an inactive lifestyle or unhealthy eating or drinking habits;

- the Responsible Children's Marketing Initiative of the Australian Food and Beverage Industry, which requires that advertisers not advertise food and beverage products to children under the age of 12 unless they represent healthy dietary choices; and
- the Australian Quick Service Restaurant Industry Initiative for Responsible Advertising and Marketing to Children, which seeks to ensure that only food and beverages that represent healthier choices are advertised to children.

9.6 Tobacco

In Australia, Commonwealth, state and territory laws prohibit the advertisement or promotion of tobacco products in any ad published or broadcast in Australia.

For instance, the Tobacco Advertising Prohibition Act 1992 (Cth) aims to restrict the exposure of the public to messages and images that promote, encourage or persuade people to smoke or continue smoking. This extends to e-cigarette advertising (including tobacco and nicotine free e-cigarette products).

It is an offence for a corporation to publish or broadcast a tobacco ad unless one of the limited exceptions under the aforementioned act applies. That act also makes it an offence for any person to publish tobacco advertising on the Internet or in other electronic medium in Australia – for example, via mobile phone – unless certain limited exceptions apply.

A key exception allows internet point-of-sale tobacco advertising, provided that it complies with state or territory legislation that expressly deals with internet point-of-sale tobacco advertising or, in the absence of such legislation, Australian government regulations. Under these regulations, internet point-of-sale tobacco ads must be presented in plain, text-only format, with graphic health warnings and warnings about age restrictions on tobacco sales. Accidental or incidental publication or broadcasting of tobacco ads is allowed where:

- the ad is published or broadcast as an accidental or incidental accompaniment to the publication or broadcast of other matter; and
- a person receives no direct or indirect benefit (whether financial or not) for publishing or broadcasting the ad (in addition to any direct or indirect benefit that the person receives for publishing/broadcasting the other matter).

The tobacco ad must not dominate or form a substantial feature of a broadcast programme in order to fall under this exception.

9.7 E-cigarettes

As outlined in section 9.6, the Tobacco Advertising Prohibition Act 1992 extends to e-cigarettes (including tobacco and nicotine-free e-cigarette products). Therefore, the provisions of that act will also apply to the advertisement of e-cigarettes.

The publisher acknowledges the contribution of Alison Eveleigh, Rebecca Mason and Sophie Mycock to this chapter in the previous edition.

Austria

Alexander Cizek
CIZEK I IP

1. Overview of the legal and regulatory regime for advertising

In Austria, the principal source of advertising law is the Unfair Competition Act 1984, which applies to all commercial practices. In addition, special laws apply to the advertisement of certain products (eg, pharmaceutical products) or advertising by certain occupational groups (eg, lawyers, tax advisers or doctors). Furthermore, the general provisions of the Austrian General Civil Code apply – for example, regarding tortious liability – but those provisions play only a minor role in the context of advertising law.

The Unfair Competition Act implements several EU directives, the most important of which are the Misleading Advertising Directive (2006/114/EC) and the Unfair Commercial Practices Directive (2005/29/EC).

The Unfair Competition Act aims to protect competitors, consumers and other market participants against unfair commercial practices. At the same time, it protects the interests of the public in undistorted competition. To this end, the act contains civil law prohibitions (Sections 14 and following). Individual commercial practices which are deemed particularly grave are also punishable by imprisonment or a fine (Sections 4 and 10–12).

In relation to these civil law prohibitions, the Unfair Competition Act follows the systematic structure of the Unfair Commercial Practices Directive and contains three different types of advertising prohibitions. In any case where the prohibition of advertising is under consideration, an assessment must initially be made as to whether the facts of the case fit a special rule which prevails over the more general rules of the Unfair Competition Act. In the negative, a three-step review scheme applies:

- first, the commercial practices listed in the Annex to the Unfair Competition Act – the so-called 'blacklist' – which contains particularly serious types of misleading and aggressive advertising in business-to-consumer relationships;
- second, the advertising prohibitions that are worded less narrowly than those included in the blacklist, such as 'aggressive', 'misleading' and 'comparative' advertising (Sections 1a, 2 and 2a respectively of the Unfair Competition Act); and

- third, the blanket clause in Section 1(1) of the same act on the prohibition of unfair commercial practices, which applies residually where the more specific provisions do not apply. The blanket clause applies relatively frequently.

The available remedies in case of breach of the civil law prohibitions include:
- injunctive relief;
- removal (or in certain cases revocation) of the offending material;
- publication of the judgment;
- in some instances, adequate compensation (by analogy); and
- in the event of negligence, damages and ancillary claims for the rendering of accounts, as well as certain other information.

Furthermore, certain industry associations and consumer protection associations may have standing to file actions for various types of unfair commercial practices. Preliminary (injunctive) relief is available upon request for justified claims.

Certain types of advertising are punishable as criminal offences. These include:
- wilfully misleading advertising (Section 4 of the Unfair Competition Act);
- bribery of employees and agents (Section 10);
- breach of trade secrets and industrial secrets (Section 11); and
- abuse of entrusted models or samples (Section 12).

These criminal acts carry monetary penalties of up to 180 'daily rates' or custodial penalties of up to three months' imprisonment.

Some methods of direct marketing are also punishable as administrative offences, especially:
- 'snowball' and 'pyramid' schemes (Section 27 of the Unfair Competition Act);
- violation of labelling regulations (Sections 32 and following);
- clearance sales (Section 33a); and
- geo-blocking (Section 33d).

For administrative offences, only monetary fines of up to €2,900 apply.

Besides the Unfair Competition Act, Austrian law contains other more specific codes, statutes and standards that contain provisions on advertising regulations or related restrictions. The most relevant include the following – and for the most part, their relevance within the advertising industry is described further below:

- the Advertising Tax Act 2000;
- the Audio-visual Media Services Act 2001;
- the Austrian Broadcasting Act 1984;
- the Cartel Act 2005;
- the Copyright Act 1936;
- the Data Protection Act 2000;
- the E-commerce Act 2002;
- the General Social Security Act 1955;
- the Private Radio Broadcasting Act 2001;
- the Telecommunications Act 2003;
- the Tobacco and Non-smoker Protection Act 1995;
- the Trade, Commerce and Industry Regulation Act 1994;
- the Trademark Protection Act 1970; and
- the Advertising Industry Code of Ethics.[1]

2. Comparative advertising

Comparative advertising is covered by the Unfair Competition Act, which in general allows a comparison between the advertiser's and a competitor's products provided that it is not considered unfair, which particularly includes aggressive and misleading practices. A practice is considered 'aggressive' if it could significantly impair a consumer's freedom of choice by harassment, coercion or undue influence, and cause him or her to take a transactional decision that he or she would not have taken otherwise. An ad is considered 'misleading' if:

- it deceives or has the potential to deceive the consumer to whom it is addressed; and
- by virtue of its deceptive nature, it causes or has the potential to cause the consumer to take a different transactional decision from that which he or she might otherwise have taken.

Furthermore, in order to be lawful, the comparison must be true, complete and lacking in any aggressive or impairing tendency. Comparative advertising thus must not contain any allegations about another enterprise, its directors or owners, or its products or services which are detrimental to the business or the credit standing of the enterprise or its directors or owners, unless such facts are demonstrably true.

In the course of comparative advertising, the name, registered company name or 'special designation' of an enterprise or publication that does not qualify for title protection of a copyrightable work within the meaning of Section 80 of the Copyright Act must not be used in a manner that is likely to

---

1 Available at https://werberat.at/layout/ETHIK_KODEX_1_2020.pdf.

cause confusion with a name, registered company name or 'special designation' that is rightfully used by another party. The 'special designation' of an enterprise includes business signs and other facilities designed to distinguish the enterprise from others, including the presentation of products or their packaging, which are perceived as designations of the enterprise.

Comparative advertising that directly or indirectly identifies a competitor, or products or services offered by a competitor, is permissible only if:

- in cases of comparative advertising with products identified by designations of origin, the compared products bear the same designation of origin or refer to the same origin; or
- the comparison refers to a special offer and the closing date of the special offer and, if the special offer is not yet available, the commencement date of the period during which the special price or other special conditions will apply are stated clearly and unequivocally.

According to the Austrian Supreme Court, the use of a competitor's trademark in ads promoting the advertiser's own products constitutes trademark use pursuant to Section 10 of the Trademark Protection Act. Such use in the course of comparative advertising is permissible only if:

- the trademark's reputation is not exploited unfairly; and
- the reference to the competitor's trademark is necessary and suitable to inform consumers about the pros and cons of different products or services.

The burden of proof shifts to the advertiser, which must prove the accuracy of the facts claimed within the ad.

3.   Online behavioural advertising

Section 96 of the Telecommunications Act 2003 obliges operators of public communication services (eg, access providers) and providers of 'information society services' pursuant to the E-commerce Act (eg, content providers) to inform a subscriber or user if personal data is intended to be collected, processed and transmitted, and to specify the legal basis on which and the purposes for which this will take place, as well as the duration for which the data will be stored. Further to this, the collection of personal data (eg, in the form of a cookie set on a user's device for the purposes of online behavioural advertising) is permissible only if the data subject's prior consent has been obtained. However, no consent is required for technical storage or access if the sole purpose is to perform or facilitate the transmission of a communication via a communications network, or if absolutely necessary to allow the provider of information society services to provide a service that has been explicitly requested by the subscriber or user. In reality, this exception to the requirement for consent is unlikely to apply in the case of cookies used for online behavioural advertising.

The right to information – that is, the right of access to personal data as introduced by Article 15 of the EU General Data Protection Regulation (GDPR) – is not affected and remains applicable. According to the wording of Section 96(3) of the Telecommunications Act, consent is required only where the use of cookies involves the collection, processing and transmission of personal data. In this regard, the Austrian implementation of the amendment to the e-Privacy Directive (2009/136), which contains the prior consent requirements for cookies, is narrower than the interpretations of certain other European data protection regulators of the e-Privacy Directive, which is not necessarily limited to personal data only.

4. Sales promotions

4.1 Giveaways

Before the Court of Justice of the European Union (CJEU) held in 2010[2] that a general ban under Austrian law which prevented giveaways being combined with product purchases in the business-to-consumer (B2C) sphere did not comply with the Unfair Commercial Practices Directive (2005/29/EC), Austrian law contained a general prohibition on these types of giveaways in Section 9a of the Unfair Competition Act. The implication of the CJEU ruling was the inapplicability of Section 9a to the B2C sphere; although the business-to-business (B2B) sphere was still bound by it. However, as from January 2013, giveaways are generally lawful in both the B2C and the B2B sphere, due to a change in Austrian legislation. Although giveaways are legal, the practice of adding complimentary gifts to sales may still conflict with other general provisions of the Unfair Competition Act and/or the Cartel Act 2005. Thus, under the current status of the law, giveaways remain illegal if, given the circumstances at hand, they are considered expressly unfair (especially if they involve trade practices included on the blacklist), aggressive or misleading. In particular in the B2B sphere, companies with market power should refrain from demanding complimentary gifts from suppliers, as this trade practice is likely to conflict with the prohibition of impeding competitors as well as the antitrust rules in Sections 1 and 5 of the Cartel Act, such as those prohibiting enterprises with market power from selling below cost price.

Value-adds are legal as long as the rules of the Unfair Competition Act are complied with. Hence, advertising campaigns with regard to value-adds must not be misleading, aggressive or otherwise unfair.

4.2 Sweepstakes and contests

Another common way to promote sales in Austria is through sweepstakes and

---

2   *Mediaprint Zeitungs- und Zeitschriftenverlag GmbH & Co KG v Österreich-Zeitungsverlag GmbH* (C-540/08).

similar contests. The difference between sweepstakes and games of chance is the involvement of some sort of monetary stake. The effect that this distinction has on businesses is crucial, as the operation of a game of chance is permissible only upon grant of a licence or permission by the federal government. Hence, if a sweepstake or contest is linked to the purchase of a certain product or increased prices, the sweepstake will be considered a game of chance. According to Section 28 of the Unfair Competition Act, the sale of products or services in a manner that links delivery of the product or provision of the service to the result of a contest or another form of chance is prohibited.

Sweepstakes or contests may also involve unfair trade practices – namely misleading, aggressive or otherwise unfair practices. For example, a contest will be considered misleading if the prizes which were advertised are not intended to be given away. Furthermore, a sweepstake may be considered aggressive if consumers' purchasing decisions are unduly influenced by the value of the prize. This is particularly the case where the value is so high that even an otherwise careful and critical consumer's purchasing decision is likely to be affected.

Sweepstakes and contests are subject to a tax levy of 5% of the promised prize; a tax exemption limit of €500 applies, making prize draws of up to €10,000 per year tax free.

4.3 Other activities relating to sales promotions

Price undercutting is generally lawful, as it constitutes a necessary instrument of competition. However, in exceptional cases, it may conflict with the Unfair Competition Act – particularly where the main purpose is not to further an entity's own business, but rather to drive away competitors irrespective of loss. Such practices will be considered obstructive and thus illegal as a subcategory of the general clause in Section 1 of the Unfair Competition Act.

Section 30 of the Unfair Competition Act previously prescribed that if public ads or notices announce the sale of products which stem from a bankruptcy estate, but which in truth are no longer part of it, any reference to the origin of the products from a bankruptcy estate is prohibited. However, this was repealed at the request of the European Commission in an amendment of 2015. Instead, such false statements shall be considered to fall within the general ban on misleading trade practices and, in addition, to contravene Annex I, No 7 of the EU Unfair Commercial Practices Directive (2005/29/EC), which lists as a *per se* misleading commercial practice the false statement that a product will be available for only a very limited time, or will be available on particular terms only for a very limited time, in order to elicit an immediate decision and deprive consumers of sufficient opportunity or time to make an informed choice.

It is prohibited to wrongfully attribute the holding of a qualification, authorisation or permit approved or awarded by a government authority, or to use an award or designation that makes reference to any of the above privileges, in such a way that such action is likely to deceive as to the occasion or reason for conferral of the award or the scope of the privilege.

Any public ad or notice aimed at a large group of people suggesting that a party intends to quickly clear large quantities of products and is therefore offering those products at extraordinarily advantageous conditions or prices is an 'announcement of sale'. The German-language equivalents of phrases such as 'sale', 'liquidation sale', 'clearance sale', 'quick sale', 'sale at bargain prices', 'stock clearance' and similar phrases with equal meaning are also considered to be an announcement of sale. Sections 33a to 33c of the Unfair Competition Act contain several restrictions on such announcements – in particular, a requirement to obtain prior authorisation from the competent district administrative authority. Moreover, the announcement must specify the reason for and the period during which the sale is to be held, as well as a general designation of the products to be sold. However, none of these restrictions applies to announcements concerning:

- end-of-season sales;
- seasonal clearance sales;
- stocktaking or similar sales; or
- special sales that are customary in the relevant line of business and in given seasons.

5. Ambush marketing

The term 'ambush marketing' is not defined by statute in Austria. Where ambushers refrain from using trademarks or other protected symbols for their marketing purposes, traditional IP laws are not suitable to fight ambush marketing, which is why claims based on a violation of the Unfair Competition Act generally remain the sole remedy in Austria. However, by virtue of the creativity put into new ambush marketing campaigns, the legality of such campaigns must be assessed on a case-by-case basis. The three categories of unfair competition practices that ambush marketing campaigns are likely to fall within are deception, passing off and obstructive practices.

Section 2 of the Unfair Competition Act prohibits any misleading representation if it could cause consumers to take a transactional decision that they would not have taken otherwise. Hence, any express or implied misrepresentation as to sponsorship may conflict with this provision where the message that the ambusher is an official sponsor is conveyed with a certain degree of distinctiveness. In this regard, it should also be noted that any ad which contains false information contravenes the principle of truth and is therefore considered to be *contra bonos mores* (against public morality), and thus illegal according to Section 1 of the Unfair Competition Act.

Sometimes ambush marketing campaigns may not be primarily focused on the promotion of the ambusher's products or services, but may instead try to impede a competitor which is an official sponsor. Such obstructive practices are considered unfair and thus illegal, as long as their main purpose is to impede a competitor. However, simply competing with official sponsors by promoting the advertiser's own products and services is not considered an obstructive practice.

Ambush marketing campaigns may try to exploit an event's reputation or goodwill by suggesting or creating some involvement in, or association with, the event. Such exploitation could constitute the unfair trade practice of passing off if the status of official sponsor has positive associations for consumers. Moreover, the goodwill of particular products or services which are advertised by official sponsors may also be subject to passing off if they are more positively received by consumers by virtue of being the products or services of an official sponsor.

Besides the rules of the Unfair Competition Act, the Protection of Olympic Insignia and Designations Act contains a special set of rules on the protection of the insignia of the International Olympic Committee and the Austrian Olympic Committee. In addition, the use of the German words for 'Olympiad', 'Olympia' (as long as it is not a personal given or family name) and 'Olympic' is subject to special controls, irrespective of whether those words are used alone or in connection with other words, and whether they are in German or any other language. These limitations also apply to any insignia or designations which are confusingly similar to the aforementioned items. Trademarks, business names, signs or symbols which could create the impression of an association with, or authorisation by, the International or Austrian Olympic Committee are considered to be Olympic designations.

In the context of unfair competition, Austrian law provides for several remedies, such as injunctive relief (sometimes preliminary injunctive relief), removal, damages, publication of the judgment and so on. However, with regard to the peculiarities of ambush marketing, the pursuit of an entity's rights can often encounter many obstacles, rendering the efficacy of these remedies quite doubtful. For instance, ambush marketing campaigns in general last only until the end of the corresponding event, so an injunction is therefore unlikely to be issued in time – and even preliminary injunctions may lack sufficient efficacy. Damages claims may prove similarly ineffective in this context, as the plaintiff will usually find it very hard to prove in court the amount of damages inflicted.

6.   Direct marketing

Telephone calls for the purposes of marketing ('cold calling') are prohibited pursuant to Section 107(1) of the Telecommunications Act, unless prior consent has been given by the recipient. Obtaining the recipient's consent by way of a telephone call is also prohibited, as such conduct will itself be considered cold calling. Likewise, the sending of emails and SMS texts for a similar purpose ('spamming') is prohibited pursuant to Section 107(2) of the Telecommunications Act, unless prior consent has been given by the recipient and the message is intended for the purposes of direct marketing. The requisite consent cannot be obtained if the first point of contact is made via email, as this approach will itself form part of the direct marketing. However, prior consent is not required if:

- the sender has received the contact details for the communication in the context of the sale of a product or service to its customers;
- the communication is transmitted for the purpose of promoting its own or similar products or services; and
- the customer is clearly and distinctly given the opportunity to object (free of charge and in an easy manner) to such use of his or her electronic contact details, both at the time they are collected and within each message.

However, the customer or recipient must not have generally opted out at the outset from direct marketing communications – for example, by signing up to the so-called 'Robinson List' pursuant to Section 7(2) of the E-commerce Act.

If, in the course of direct marketing, a 'periodical medium' such as a newsletter is published at least four times a year in a similar layout, it falls within the scope of the Media Act. This would necessitate an imprint of the issuing entity and disclosure in accordance with Austria's media laws. In practice, this is done by providing a link to the existing imprint of the respective corporation. Similarly, the E-commerce Act requires anyone providing an 'information society service' (including online marketing of products and services, online information offers and online advertising) to disclose its own as well as its principal's identity, as well as information as to the commercial purpose of the communication.

In the course of direct marketing, businesses may act on their own behalf or cooperate with direct marketing companies. Direct marketing companies operate an unrestricted business through which they run marketing campaigns that are directed at a select target group, or mediate client and prospective client data between the owners and users of client databases (known as 'list broking'). There are basically two options on how to cooperate with address publishers and direct marketing companies: they can be used for the marketing and distribution of promotional materials directly, or they can be used for list broking. When promotional material is distributed, it must allow for the identity of the party that initially provided the data to be traced. Usually, a printed code is used to determine the original data owner.

For the purposes of their business activities, direct marketing companies may, by virtue of the Austrian Trade Act, gather data from publicly available sources (eg, a phonebook, business directory or company register), by conducting a survey or by using another direct marketing company's client and prospective client database. The compilation of data is permissible only insofar as it is necessary for the preparation and execution of third-party marketing campaigns, including the design and distribution of promotional materials or list broking. However, without the data subjects' consent, marketing companies may gather the data only from a third-party client and prospective client database. In addition, direct marketing companies and businesses acting on their own behalf must comply with the rules of the GDPR and the Data Protection Act. In this context, it is important to note that the GDPR itself provides that the processing of personal data for direct marketing purposes constitutes a legitimate interest pursued by the controller or third party within the limits of Article 6(1)(f) of the GDPR, and is thus considered lawful processing; this means that the consent of an existing customer is not required. On the other hand, the rights of the data subject must be strictly observed – most importantly, the right to object. The customer as the data subject may object at any time, and free of charge, to the processing of his or her personal data for the purposes of direct marketing; the same is true for profiling, insofar it is connected with direct marketing activities. Where such an objection is raised, the relevant data must no longer be used for these purposes. Furthermore, the data subject must be explicitly informed, in a separate and comprehensible manner, about this right to object.

A violation of the rules of the GDPR constitutes an administrative offence and may lead to administrative fines of up to €10 million or €20 million; or, in the case of an undertaking, of up to 2% or 4% of its total worldwide annual turnover in the preceding financial year, whichever is higher. A violation of the rules of the Data Protection Act likewise constitutes an administrative offence, punishable by administrative fines of up to €50,000. A violation of Section 107 of the Telecommunications Act constitutes an administrative offence with penalties of up to €58,000. All of these offences and misdemeanours also qualify as violations of the Unfair Competition Act, which entitle competitors to file a legal action seeking injunctive relief and so on.

In the context of list broking, the Austrian Supreme Court has held[3] that the purchaser of addresses that are used for the distribution of promotional materials is liable in the event that the list broker failed to obtain the requisite declarations of consent, irrespective of whether the purchaser acted in good faith.

---

3   OGH 29 November 2005, 4 Ob 192/05x.

7.   **Product placement**

Under Austrian law, 'product placement' can be defined as any form of commercial communication (consisting of the inclusion of, or reference to, a product, service or trademark) in a programme in return for payment or similar consideration, so that it is featured within that programme.

With regard to Austrian television broadcasting law, there is a distinction between private and public broadcasting, as different rules apply to each. In terms of product placement, however, the rules until very recently used to be essentially the same, since both the Audio-visual Media Services Act and the Austrian Broadcasting Act followed the principle that product placement is generally prohibited. While this basic principle continues to apply to Austrian public television broadcasting law, as of 1 January 2021, due to a very recent amendment of the Audio-visual Media Services Act, the Austrian private television broadcasting law now assumes the opposite basic principle – that is, product placement is generally allowed (with several exceptions).

As for Austrian public television broadcasting, an exemption from this general prohibition of product placement exists for:

- cinematographic works;
- films made for television and television series;
- sports programmes; and
- light entertainment programmes, unless they are considered children's programmes or consumer programmes.

Furthermore, an exemption applies to the complimentary provision of products or services, such as production props and prizes, within a programme – although news and current affairs programmes produced by the Austrian Broadcasting Corporation (ORF) are excluded from this exemption.

If one of these exemptions applies, programmes containing product placements must comply with the following requirements:

- Content and scheduling must under no circumstances be influenced in such a way as to adversely affect the editorial responsibility and independence of the ORF or the respective private media service provider;
- Product placement must not directly encourage the purchase or rental of products or services – in particular, by making special promotional references to those products or services;
- Product placement must not give undue prominence to the product in question; and
- In order to avoid any confusion on the part of the viewer, product placement must be appropriately identified at the start and the end of a programme and when a programme resumes after a commercial break.

As for Austrian private television broadcasting, product placement is now generally permitted, with the following exceptions:

- news broadcasts;
- broadcasts of political information;
- consumer broadcasts;
- broadcasts of religious contents; and
- children's programmes.

Otherwise, programmes containing product placement must comply with the same requirements as previously and as set out above for public television broadcasting.

With regard to Austrian radio broadcasting law, product placement is similarly subject to several restrictions. In particular, when the mention of products, services, names, trademarks or activities in radio programmes is intended by the radio broadcaster to serve as advertising, but might mislead the public as to its true nature as such, it is considered 'surreptitious advertising', which is prohibited.

8. Native advertising and social media influencers

In Austria, there are no particular legal statutes pertaining to the use of social media for advertising; however, several rules contained in various legal acts regulating online trafficking do also apply to online advertising in the social media context. Thus, Austria's E-commerce Act requires anyone providing an 'information society service' (including online marketing of products and services, online information offers and online advertising) to disclose its own as well as its principal's identity, as well as information on the commercial purpose of the communication. Moreover, pursuant to the Austrian Telecommunications Act, the sending of emails or SMS messages for the purpose of direct marketing and advertising is prohibited, unless the recipient's prior consent has been obtained. Also, the data protection rules must be observed when the social media user's personal data is used; where the other legal grounds for the lawfulness of data processing laid down in Article 6, paragraph 1, items (b) to (f) of the GDPR do not apply, the use of data for marketing or advertising purposes requires the data subject's consent.

Insofar as native advertising is to be deemed as surreptitious advertising or disguised advertising, it is illegal in Austria, as every ad must be presented in such a way that its nature as such can easily be recognised by the relevant public. As a matter of Austrian statutory law, there must be a clear dividing line between promotional content and editorial contributions – for example, in all media, as well as for online vendors and providers. The mingling of editorial content and ads could easily manipulate the behaviour of market participants and consumers, as they usually accord editorial content greater credibility than commercial, promotional and advertising content; it is thus considered misleading. In case of violation, administrative penalties will apply.

As a matter of Austrian unfair competition case law, given these statutory regulations and in light of the prevailing principle of notoriousness and truthfulness in fair competition, the Austrian Supreme Court has inferred a general obligation under Austrian unfair competition law to label advertising content as such and prevent ads from being disguised as so-called 'advertorials'. Moreover, since the Unfair Competition Act was overhauled in 2007, surreptitious advertising and disguised advertising have been explicitly banned as *per se* unfair (deceitful) trade practices in Annex 11 to Section 2 of the act.

Interestingly, in a relatively recent decision, the Austrian Supreme Court[4] further distinguished editorial contributions, noting that today's more critical readership no longer assumes these to be absolutely neutral, as they frequently originate from specifically named journalists who are known to express their own opinions, and thus no longer expects them to be absolutely objective and candid. The Austrian Supreme Court thus found that an advertorial included free of charge in periodical media did not violate the general rule on labelling (paid) advertising, and was thus in line with fair competition laws. However, this decision – which exempts commercial articles that are published free of charge out of courtesy or as a favour from the rules on the labelling of advertising – has been criticised by legal commentators. And given that, in certain circumstances, a favour may also qualify as indirect consideration, and the general prohibition of misleading conduct in the Unfair Competition Act does not require consideration, it seems safest to continue marking all commercial articles as advertising.

This is also of concern to social media influencers, who significantly facilitate the dissemination of unlawful surreptitious or disguised advertising. However, user-generated content generally does not resemble editorial articles and thus is not subject to the explicit ban set out in Annex 11 to Section 2 of the Unfair Competition Act. In light of the popularity of social media in general, and the current trends and uncertainties regarding influencer marketing in particular, the Austrian Advertising Council – the self-regulatory body of the Austrian advertising industry – recently introduced to its own Advertising Industry Code of Ethics specific rules of conduct on the use of influencer marketing as a special vehicle of marketing communication, in order to encourage responsible and lawful advertising in the interests of advertisers, influencers and consumers alike.[5]

---

4   OGH, 26 September 2016, 4 Ob 60/16a.
5   See item 1.8 of the Advertising Industry Ethics Code (https://werberat.at/layout/ETHIK_KODEK
     _2_2019.pdf).

9. Industry-specific regulation

9.1 Gambling

The Gambling Act generally covers most forms of gambling, except betting and the issuance of licences to operate regional draws with gambling machines (both of which are regulated regionally).

In order to operate any game of chance which falls within the scope of the Gambling Act, a federal licence or authorisation is required. Advertising is permissible if the promoted game is not prohibited – prohibited games are games for which a federal licence or authorisation has not been granted and which are not exempt from the federal government's gambling monopoly. Thus, only entities that hold a licence can advertise draws in Austria. The same rules apply to the promotion of most forms of online gambling, which is why the advertisement of gambling on websites is prohibited if the website and the ad are directed at Austria, but the promoter has failed to obtain a licence. However, casinos in member states of the European Union or the European Economic Area (EEA) can promote visits to their foreign establishments situated in EU or EEA states if the operator of the casino has been granted an authorisation by the Austrian Tax Office.

According to Section 56 of the Gambling Act, licensees and permission holders that advertise their services must meet a certain level of responsibility. Compliance with the responsibility requirement is monitored by the relevant authority only, which is why unfair competition claims cannot be based on non-compliance.

The advertisement of regional draws with gambling machines and betting is illegal, unless a regional licence or authorisation has been granted. If an operator of online (sports) betting is based outside Austria and seeks to offer its services in Austria, it is not clear whether authorisation is required. However, in the opinion of the Federal Ministry of Finance, the offering and advertisement of sports betting via the Internet are admissible, irrespective of the server location, and do not require authorisation.

9.2 Alcohol

The advertisement of alcoholic beverages is generally permitted in Austria. However, the Audio-visual Media Services Act, the Broadcasting Act and the Private Radio Broadcasting Act contain specific restrictions on the advertisement of alcoholic beverages via television and/or radio.

The Private Radio Broadcasting Act contains a general ban on the advertisement of spirits on radio. The Audio-visual Media Services Act and the Broadcasting Act generally allow the advertisement of alcoholic beverages on television, as long as this:

- is not aimed specifically at minors (ie, those below the age of 18) and does not depict minors consuming these beverages; and

- does not encourage immoderate consumption of alcohol or present abstinence or moderation in a negative light.

Furthermore, the consumption of alcohol must not:
- be linked to enhanced physical performance or driving;
- create the impression that the consumption of alcohol contributes towards social or sexual success;
- emphasise high alcohol content as being a positive quality of the beverage; or
- claim that alcohol has therapeutic qualities or is a stimulant, a sedative or a means of resolving personal conflicts.

The Advertising Industry Code of Ethics (see section 1) also contains a brief code of general conduct with regard to alcohol advertising, including a rule that such ads not be directed towards children.

9.3 Pharmaceuticals

The advertisement of pharmaceutical products is strictly regulated in Austria and is governed by:
- the Medicinal Products Act;
- the General Social Security Act; and
- the Code of Conduct of the Pharmaceutical Industry in Austria.[6]

The Medicinal Products Act differentiates between advertising to laymen (ie, consumers) and advertising to healthcare professionals. In the context of advertising to laymen, a further distinction is made between the promotion of prescription-only and non-prescription medicines. The advertisement of prescription-only medicines to laymen is prohibited in Austria; as is the advertisement of non-prescription products that use the same name or a similar special word or scientific term as a prescription-only medicine, and the advertisement of registered homeopathic medicines.

Although the advertisement of non-prescription medicines is basically permitted, various restrictions apply. First, the ad must clearly indicate that it is an ad and the product must be clearly identified as a medicinal product. Second, the Medicinal Products Act requires that ads for medicinal products contain the following minimum information:
- the name of the medicinal product and the generic term of the active substance, if the product contains only one;
- information on the correct use of the medicinal product; and

---

6   www.pharmig.at/mediathek/downloads/pharmig-verhaltenscodex-vhc-gueltig-ab-172020-anwendbar-auf-sachverhalte-ab-1-juli-2020/?download=1&v=637281643980000000&ipignore=true.

- an express note that the product may have side effects and therefore it is recommended to read the package insert or consult a healthcare professional.

Third, the information provided must not:
- imply that the medicine has a property which exceeds its actual properties;
- mislead the consumer to expect regular results; or
- deviate from the labelling or user information rules.

In this regard, Section 53(1) of the Medicinal Products Act contains a list of elements that must not be included in ads directed at laymen.

Section 13 of the Broadcasting Act, Section 34 of the Audio-visual Media Services Act and Section 20 of the Private Radio Broadcasting Act also prohibit the broadcasting of ads for prescription-only medicines or therapeutic treatments. Ads for all other medicines and therapeutic treatments must be easily recognisable as such, and must be honest and verifiable.

If medicinal products are advertised to healthcare professionals in printed publications, through electronic media or by way of telecommunications, these ads must contain essential information about the medicinal product in line with the Regulation on the Summary of Product Characteristics for Medicinal Products. Moreover, Section 42 of that regulation sets out a list of elements that must be included in ads which are directed at healthcare professionals.

In addition to the statutory regulations discussed above, the Code of Conduct for the Pharmaceutical Industry in Austria stipulates that all advertising activities by pharmaceutical companies must be appropriate and sets out a list of rules that pharmaceutical advertising must observe.

9.4   Financial products and services

The advertisement of financial products and services is mainly regulated by:
- the Capital Market Act;
- the Investment Funds Act;
- the Real Estate Investment Funds Act; and
- the Consumer Credit Act.

The Capital Market Act generally requires the publication of an authorised prospectus prior to any public offering of securities or investments in Austria, although Section 3 of that act contains a list of exemptions to this rule. The prospectus must contain all information that, according to the characteristics of the issuer and the public offering of securities or investments, is necessary in order for the investor to assess the issuer's assets and liabilities, financial situation, profits and losses, future prospects and other matters.

According to Section 4 of the Capital Market Act, any form of advertising that refers to a public offering of investments must comply with the following requirements:

- The ad must point out that a prospectus – including any additions or amendments thereto – has been published or is about to be published. It must also indicate where this information can be accessed; and
- The ad must be clearly recognisable as such and must not contain false or misleading information. Moreover, the information must not contradict the information that is contained in the prospectus or any additions or amendments thereto.

Moreover, even if it is not for the purpose of advertising, any oral or written information about the public offer must align with the information contained in the prospectus or any additions or amendments thereto.

If the obligation to publish a prospectus does not apply, the provider's essential information must be communicated to each qualified investor or special group of investors to which the offer is directed.

Pursuant to Section 128 of the Investment Funds Act, the advertisement of shares in investment funds is permissible only if:

- reference is made to a published prospectus and to the compulsory 'consumer information document';
- the ad indicates the manner in which these documents can be accessed and the languages in which they are available;
- the ad is clearly recognisable as such;
- the ad contains no false or misleading information; and
- the ad does not contradict the information contained in the prospectus or the consumer information document.

If, in the course of advertising shares in investment funds, reference is made to a fund's past financial performance, the ad must indicate that such past performance is not a reliable source from which to infer the fund's future development.

In addition, ads must highlight:

- the fund's investment strategy, if the fund mainly invests in certain categories of investment instruments (as listed in Section 67(1), items 3–5 of the Investment Funds Act) that are not securities or money market instruments;
- any increased volatility in its net assets; and
- the authorisation of the Financial Market Authority, if the advertised fund invests solely in securities or money market instruments issued by public entities or organisations with public characteristics.

According to Section 36 of the Real Estate Investment Funds Act, the advertisement of shares in real estate investment funds (REIFs) is permissible only if reference is made to a published prospectus, including any amendments thereto, as well as the publishing entity, the publication date and the location where it can be accessed. Regarding the content and layout of ads, the above-mentioned rules on the advertisement of investments pursuant to Sections 4(2)–(4) of the Capital Market Act are explicitly declared as applicable to REIFs. If reference to a REIF's past financial performance is made in the course of advertising, the ad must indicate that such past performance is not a reliable source from which to infer the fund's future development.

The Banking Act and the Securities Supervision Act contain only several short provisions on advertising. The Banking Act restricts any association with deposit protection or investor compensation systems in ads to a statement of the respective system's name or indication and a factual description of the functionality of the system; a reference to the unlimited covering of deposits is prohibited. Under the Securities Supervision Act, doorstep selling of financial instruments and investments to consumers is permissible only upon prior invitation; moreover, the unsolicited sending of ads on financial instruments must accord with Section 107 of the Telecommunications Act.

Moreover, the Consumer Credit Act – which is based on EU Directive 2008/48/EC and entered into force on 11 June 2010 – expanded the Austrian consumer protection system and introduced new information obligations, assessments of creditworthiness and additional rights of contract rescission. The information obligations – which concern the advertisement of consumer credit agreements, the pre-contractual phase and the consumer contract agreement itself – form the core of the Consumer Credit Act.

Whenever loans, figures or values are mentioned in ads (eg, interest rates or redemption rates), a representative example must be given. Furthermore, where a loan provides for a combination of a fixed interest rate and a floating interest rate, this must also be clearly communicated in the ad. In order to prevent misleading teasers of short-term low interest rates, the advertisement of low fixed starting interest rates must also specify both the period during which that low rate applies and the subsequent floating rate (Sections 5 and 6 of the Consumer Credit Act).

9.5 Food

The advertisement of food is generally permissible in Austria, but is subject to a dual system of statutory and self-regulatory restrictions. The most important statutory provisions on the advertisement of food can be found in the Food Safety and Consumer Protection Act and in EU Regulation 1924/2006 on nutrition and health claims. Self-regulatory restrictions are set out in the Advertising Industry Code of Ethics and in the Code of Conduct for

Inappropriate Audio-visual Commercial Communication for Children's Television.

EU Regulation 1924/2006 protects consumers by prohibiting any information which is false, misleading or difficult to understand – that is, which casts doubt on the safety or nutritional adequacy of other foods, or which encourages the excessive consumption of a certain type of food by stating or suggesting, directly or indirectly, that a balanced diet does not provide all the nutrients that are needed.

The Food Safety and Consumer Protection Act prohibits the placement, advertisement and presentation of food that is misleadingly labelled in the market (eg, in relation to the product's ingredients). In the context of what consumers may typically expect in foodstuffs, the Austrian Food Codex provides an important – though not legally binding – frame of reference: it lists the qualities of foodstuffs that can generally be expected by consumers. From a legal standpoint, this may be considered as a qualified anticipated expert opinion, which in particular reflects typical consumer expectations.

Food labelling must refrain from suggesting that any foodstuff has properties that can prevent, treat or cure a human disease, or from making reference to such properties. An exemption exists for dietetic foodstuffs, to the extent only that their dietetic properties are described.

The Advertising Industry Code of Ethics, which is published by the Austrian Advertising Council, emphasises that ads for foodstuffs should refrain from being perceived as an incentive to consume or from pressurising the consumer to buy. Moreover, the Austrian advertising industry, the Austrian Broadcasting Corporation, private broadcasters and the Austrian food industry have all signed up to the Code of Conduct for Inappropriate Audio-visual Commercial Communication to Minors, which regulates the advertisement of foodstuffs to minors. For instance, ads that directly invite minors to purchase or consume products, or that contradict a healthy and active lifestyle, are prohibited.

9.6   Tobacco

As of 21 May 2016, Austria has a new tobacco law: the Tobacco and Non-Smoker Protection Act, previously known as the Tobacco Act, which implements EU Directive 2014/40/EU into Austrian law. This directive aims to:

- harmonise standards for tobacco products across the European Union;
- improve health protection; and
- prevent young people from starting smoking.

The Tobacco and Non-Smoker Protection Act regulates:

- all traditional tobacco products for smoking, snorting or chewing;
- novel tobacco products (ie, tobacco products that do not fall into any of the listed categories; and

- e-cigarettes, herbal smoking products (tobacco-free), shishas, chewing tobacco and snuff.

On 13 July 2016, the Combined Health Warning Ordinance for the manufacture, circulation and advertisement of tobacco and related products came into effect, which describes the required layout, design and form of the combined health warnings.

According to the act, advertising and sponsorship involving tobacco and related products are generally prohibited. This general ban applies in particular to advertising in information society services, in the press or in other printed publications aimed at direct or indirect sales promotion, except in the ordinary course of business. The general advertising and sponsorship ban also applies to advertising on public and private radio aimed at direct or indirect sales promotion, as well as ads that fall within the scope of the EU Audio-visual Media Services Directive (2010/13/EU). Moreover, discounted sales, free deals and inertia selling of tobacco and related products aimed at direct or indirect sales promotion are also prohibited.

There are several strictly regulated exemptions from the general advertising and sponsoring ban, such as:

- communications that are exclusively intended for and exclusively available to persons active in the tobacco trade or in a field of trade with related products, such as e-cigarettes and/or refill containers;
- press and other printed publications which are printed and published in third countries, where these publications are not principally intended for the EU market;
- the presentation of tobacco products and related products for sale, as well as price information for these and related products, at all sites authorised to sell tobacco products or related products; and
- advertising by tobacconists for tobacco products according to Section 39, paragraph 1 of the Tobacco Monopoly Act, as well as advertising for related products according to Section 1, line 1e in tobacconists and specialist shops. In the latter case, however, the ad must include a clearly legible text warning, according to Section 5, paragraph 1 or 2 of the Tobacco and Non-Smoker Protection Act, in black writing on a white background with a total size of 10% of the respective advertising material, on the harmful effects of tobacco consumption. However, there are also several counter-exceptions to this exception.

Similar restrictions are prescribed in other laws – in particular, with regard to the advertisement of tobacco on radio and television. Pursuant to Sections 13 and 16 of the Broadcasting Act, Section 33 of the Audio-visual Media Services Act and Section 19 of the Private Radio Broadcasting Act, tobacco advertising (ie, ads for tobacco and related products, including equipment designed for its consumption) on radio and television is prohibited in Austria.

The Advertising Industry Code of Ethics also contains special rules of conduct on the advertisement of addictive substances, including tobacco.

9.7 E-cigarettes

The Tobacco and Non-Smoker Protection Act also applies to e-cigarettes, which it defines as products that can be used for the consumption of nicotine-containing or nicotine-free vapour via a mouthpiece, or any component of such products, including cartridges, tanks and the device without a cartridge or tank. Consequently, the rules on the advertisement of tobacco and related products equally apply to e-cigarettes. Section 10b of the Tobacco and Non-Smoker Protection Act sets out additional rules in relation to the placement of e-cigarettes on the market.

The author would like to thank Maximilian Krautzer for his kind assistance in the preparation of this chapter.

Brazil

Paula Bezerra de Menezes
Otávio Saraiva Padilha Velasco
Soerensen Garcia Advogados Associados

1. Overview of the legal and regulatory regime for advertising

The Brazilian legal system has its origins in Roman civil law. The core rules are set out in the Brazilian Federal Constitution and are supplemented by specific codes, laws, statutes and administrative acts. These include:

- the Civil Code;
- the Consumer Protection Code;
- the Industrial Property Statute;
- the Internet and Data Privacy Statutes;
- the Taxation Code;
- the Penal Code;
- various treaties; and
- specific normative acts for each sector of the Brazilian economy.

They are described in greater detail below.

The interpretations of these rules by the courts are consolidated in a body of case law, which resembles the culture of precedents in common law.

An important player in the regulation of advertising activity in Brazil is the National Council for the Auto-Regulation of Advertising (CONAR). CONAR is a respected civil association, whose members include advertising agencies, companies, television and radio broadcasters and other representatives from the advertising sector, which seek to set rules among themselves and to prevent abuses, including unethical and illegal acts.

1.1 Relevant laws for the advertising sector

(a) Brazilian Federal Constitution

The Federal Constitution 1988 protects freedom of speech, thought and expression as a fundamental right, as long as it is not anonymous. All intellectual, artistic, scientific and communication activities can be freely expressed without the need to obtain prior approval and without any sort of censorship. However, this does not mean that people will not be held liable for violations of the rights of third parties. Moreover, everyone should have access to truthful and reliable information; and only in extreme circumstances, for professional reasons, should the source of information be kept confidential.

The freedom under the law to think, express opinions, create and/or inform (including through advertising) should not be hindered in any way. Depending on what is communicated, allegedly damaged parties are entitled to respond in an equivalent manner, and to seek material and moral damages for harm caused to their business, name and/or image.

Specific federal laws regulate entertainment activities and public events. They also determine the nature of such events and specifics such as the minimum attendance age, location, timing and similar. They also stipulate the means through which consumers can protect themselves and/or complain about television and radio programmes or advertising activities that may harm their health and/or the environment. Moreover, advertising relating to industries such as tobacco, alcohol, pharmaceuticals, therapies and agro-toxics is subject to legal restrictions; and where necessary, ads must include warnings about the harm that such products may cause.

With regard to publication, the means of communication cannot be subject to monopoly or oligopoly, either directly or indirectly. However, those involved in the media industry do not need a licence from the authorities in order to generate and publish content in general.

The specific provisions of the Federal Constitution relating to advertising can be found in Article 5 (Items IV, V, IX, and XIV) and Article 220.

(b)   Civil Code

The current Civil Code (Law 10.406/2002) is a compilation of rules that apply to the general relationships between people in society. Among other things, it governs the rights of personality, including image, in advertising. The code's most important rule is that advertising cannot use the name and/or image of third parties without proper authorisation.

The unauthorised depiction of the name and/or image of third parties may be immediately judicially prohibited, and damages may be awarded if the use is for commercial purposes and/or has in fact damaged the image or name of the third party.

The specific provisions of the Civil Code relating to advertising are set out in Articles 18 and 20.

(c)   Consumer Protection Code

The Consumer Protection Code aims primarily to protect consumers against abuses, and to ensure harmony and transparency in consumer relations. Just as the Brazilian Labour Code was introduced in order to achieve a balance in the employer-employee relationship, the Consumer Protection Code was conceived from the starting point that consumers are the weaker party in any relationship with the suppliers or advertisers of products or services.

Consumer protection is also a principle of economic order established in Article 170, Item VI of the Federal Constitution. Relationships between suppliers and targeted parties are essential in a consumer society. The better that suppliers behave in their dealings with consumers, the better this will be for the competitiveness of companies and the development of the Brazilian liberal system, which aims to ensure a decent existence for individual citizens and justice for all.

Companies should also take into account the provisions of Article 4 of the Consumer Protection Code, which reads as follows:

The National Policy for Consumer Relations seeks to contemplate consumers' needs, respect the consumer's dignity, health and safety, protect the consumer's economic interests, improve the quality of the consumer's life and also the transparency and harmony in the consumer relations… These are the principles and rules for public order and, as such, foreign companies that are engaged in activities within the Brazilian territory must comply with them.

With regard to advertising, the Consumer Protection Code states that, as a basic right of consumers, all information included in advertising should be very clear about the relevant products or services. This includes a specification of the volume, characteristics, composition, quality, price, taxes and possible risks relating to a product or service. Advertising claims cannot be abusive or untrue; while advertising methods cannot be coercive or unlawful.

Once a product or service is launched, if the supplier finds that it may present risks or danger, it must immediately arrange a recall or inform consumers of these risks through advertising and publicity. Such announcements must be made through the press, on radio and television and online, at the cost of the supplier or advertiser (as appropriate).

All sufficiently precise information advertised in connection with products and services must be respected in agreements with consumers. Companies must keep their promises. The principle of good faith is enshrined in Articles 113 and 442 of the Civil Code. The rule states that 'good faith' is considered an implied covenant of commercial agreements. The contracting parties have a duty to cooperate with each other in order to achieve specific interests that they would be unable to achieve by themselves. There is therefore a general duty of collaboration and an expectation of loyalty of the parties in the negotiation (pre-agreement), execution and termination of any agreement.

Taking into account that all agreements have a clear objective, it is reasonable to expect certain specific patterns of behaviour from each party that go well beyond the duty of no harm. Indeed, there is a legal obligation on firms and individuals to collaborate positively and take steps for the parties to achieve the desired objectives.

This principle can be invoked by consumers if what is obtained is not exactly as promised by the advertiser or supplier. If a supplier does not comply with the information as advertised, the affected consumers may:

- demand that the exact obligation be complied with;
- accept an equivalent product or service; or
- terminate the agreement and seek reimbursement plus damages.

Advertising must be clear, correct and precise. All specific important information must be set out in the Portuguese language – in particular, where it concerns the volume, composition, quality, price, taxes, warranties and possible risks relating to the product or service being offered. If the information advertised is challenged, the supplier must provide evidence that it is true – preferably through the disclosure of technical and scientific information. Furthermore, an ad will be considered untrue if:

- any information contained therein is totally or partially false; or
- the ad lacks any of the important information needed to prevent consumers from making false conclusions as to the nature, profile, volume, quality, price, origin or any other aspect of the product or service.

All advertising should be designed in a way that makes it clear to consumers that it constitutes advertising material. When advertising by telephone or mail, including email, the name of the supplier and its address should always be clearly identified. Moreover, consumers cannot be charged any of the costs incurred through advertising by telephone or mail.

Advertising will be considered abusive if the authorities decide that it:

- promotes violence;
- exploits fear or superstition;
- takes advantage of the immature judgement, understanding or experience of children;
- ignores or disrespects environmental values; or
- leads consumers to behave in a way that may harm their health and/or safety.

If a supplier allows untrue or abusive advertising, it must bear all costs of counter-advertising – that is, correcting the necessary information to clarify the understanding of consumers. The counter-advertising must have the same frequency, intensity and dimensions as the initial advertising – and should preferably be disseminated through the same media – in order to correct any misunderstanding caused.

If the above requirements are infringed by suppliers or advertisers of products or services, this can be framed not only as a civil misdemeanour, but also as a crime – with criminal sanctions applicable to those found liable.

The Consumer Protection Code adopts the principle of strict liability. This means that a consumer may seek compensation for damages from any of the companies that were involved in placing the product or service on the market (ie, the manufacturer, distributor, seller and sometimes the advertiser, as the case may be – all of which are defined in the Consumer Protection Code as 'suppliers'). In this case, the company that bears the loss caused to the consumer may proceed in court against the other parties in the supply chain that jointly concurred to cause damages. However, as mentioned, the injured consumer can proceed in court against any of these parties.

The code also sets out the circumstances in which entrepreneurs or their products or services will not be considered to have caused damage to the consumer. This will be the case where the entrepreneur can prove that:

- it did not participate in the placement of the product or service on the marketplace;
- although it placed the product or service on the marketplace, no defect in fact exists; or
- the defect results from a fault or faults that are exclusively attributable to the consumer.

These rules are based on the premise that the supplier must bear all risks that are inherent to its business; thus, in no event other than these three circumstances set out in the Consumer Protection Code may liability for indemnification be excluded.

The specific provisions relating to advertising in the Consumer Protection Code are set out in Articles 6, 10, 30, 31, 33, 35, 36, 37, 38, 60, 63, 67 and 68.

(d) *Industrial Property Law*

The Industrial Property Law (9279/96) aims, among other things, to prevent unfair competition and is very strict with regard to the use by third parties of registered trademarks and other IP rights. The law does not aim to protect consumers, but rather to protect investments – that is, to protect a business from malpractice by other businesses. Article 2 of the law states that unfair competition should be supressed.

The Industrial Property Law states that a 'trademark' is a property granted by the state after completion of a 'first to file' procedure at the Brazilian Patent and Trademark Office. Article 129 provides that the owner of a registered trademark has the exclusive right to use that mark, and is thus entitled to demand that third parties cease any unauthorised use of its mark, including any use in advertising.

The following are considered to constitute acts of unfair competition:

- the publication of false claims in order to obtain an advantage against a competitor;

- the use of a third party's marks or image in order to deceive or divert consumer attention;
- the advertisement of claims about prizes, honours or distinctions that the company, service or product has not in fact received;
- the advertisement of information obtained from third parties through illegal methods;
- the advertisement of products and services using the trade dress, visual presentation and/or packaging of third parties; and
- the advertisement of false information regarding the existence of registered marks, patents, industrial designs or similar.

The above actions can also be framed as crimes, rather than civil infringements, in relation to intellectual property.

1.2   CONAR

During the early 1970s, due to the threat of possible censorship measures by the Brazilian government, key players in the advertising sector came together to establish CONAR. To prevent the government from issuing laws that would require prior authorisation and an official certificate/seal before ads and publicity material could be released, the advertising sector proposed the introduction of a model of self-regulation. This proposal was well received and a few years later the CONAR Code was issued.

CONAR's main mission is to promote freedom of speech in advertising and to prevent abusive and deceptive advertising. The basic principles expressed in the CONAR Code are as follows:

- All ads must be ethical and honest, and respect Brazilian law;
- All ads must be designed with a sense of social responsibility and avoid exacerbating social differences;
- All ads must respect the principles of fair competition; and
- All ads must respect and not jeopardise the trust that consumers place in the advertising industry.

CONAR is not controlled by the state, and any conflicts can be directly submitted to the Brazilian courts and be subject to all measures, sanctions and remedies that they may impose. However, CONAR is also a much-respected entity in its own right and has successfully resolved a number of conflicts based on its rules (and general legislation) between companies, between advertisers, and between consumers and companies and/or advertisers.

Several important issues have been considered by CONAR's board, and many elements of case law and new rules have originated from those discussions.

2.   Comparative advertising

Comparative advertising is allowed within the Brazilian territory. However, one of the main differences between Brazil and other countries is that the exclusive rights over trademarks must be respected even in comparative advertising. Thus, the images of competitors or their trademarks cannot be used by advertisers in any circumstances.

Brazilian law treats comparative advertising in a very strict manner and regards it as a form of clarifying to consumers, in practical and scientific terms, the possible differences between competing products.

Comparative advertising should always express the truth in a sober form of communication, without the use of subjective, emotional, psychological or fictitious arguments; and the claims made in comparative advertising should always be provable. Comparative advertising should always be released together with the supporting research results. The supporting scientific data should always be mentioned or made easily accessible to consumers and competitors alike.

When developing comparative advertising strategies, the following points should be considered as reasonable 'safe harbours' to be observed:

- The use of the images, names, trademarks, trade dress and other intellectual property of third parties should be avoided.
- The information contained in comparative advertising should be precise and true, and have the sole purpose of enlightening consumers.
- Clear scientific and rational information and claims should be presented, and should be provable if challenged.
- The use of subjective, psychological or emotional arguments should be avoided.
- The information included in the comparative advertising should not deliberately damage the goodwill of competitors.

3.   Online behavioural advertising

There is no specific legislation that governs online behavioural advertising. Companies should carefully observe the Consumer Protection Code and Decree 7962/2013, which regulates e-commerce. This area of law is still developing and changes are likely in the coming years.

The Brazilian Internet Statute came into effect in 2013 and the Data Privacy Statute (13.709/2018) in September 2020. Sanctions will be in effect as from August 2021.

Anonymised data is generally exempt from the requirements of Brazilian data protection law, as long as the anonymisation cannot be reversed using reasonable efforts (eg, the cost and time required to identify individuals, available technologies and other appropriate means). As such, anonymised data can generally be monetised, traded and/or used for marketing purposes.

Brazil is seeking to frame its legislation in compliance with the following global trends:

- Customers should be clearly informed of how the information made available may be collected, treated and used (including being traded/ monetised);
- Companies should adopt the best technologies and procedures to keep data safe and anonymous, and to ensure that it cannot be linked to an individual;
- Companies should not collect, treat or use sensitive information; and
- Companies should use the necessary information in connection only with the intended purpose as notified to customers.

The following sanctions are available under the relevant laws:

- a warning;
- a fine of between BRL 1,000 and BRL 10 million;
- suspension of a specific product or service; and
- suspension of the whole activity.

4. Sales promotions

Sweepstakes or free distribution of prizes and similar contests that are used to promote the sale of products or services should be termed 'commercial promotions' in order to remain in line with the Brazilian legislation. The relevant regulations and details on such activities are mainly set out in Law 5.768/1971.

Such activities require prior authorisation, subject to a few limited exceptions – for example, where the free distribution of prizes results from a contest that is exclusively artistic, sporting or recreational, as long as participants face no risks and are not obliged to pay any amount, to purchase any products or services, to reply to research questionnaires or to provide personal data in order to participate.

Authorisation will be granted, upon request, to legal persons that:

- pay taxes regularly;
- contribute to social security; and
- either:
  - undertake commercial or industrial activities; or
  - are involved in the acquisition and sale of real estate.

Law 14.027/2020 has further relaxed these rules to allow for the authorisation of:

- broadcasting companies, including Brazilian juridical persons that belong to broadcasting groups; and
- certain non-governmental civil organisations whose social object

encompasses, for example, the promotion of culture; the conservation of historical or artistic heritage; the promotion of education; or the promotion of health. In this case, it is assumed that the free distribution of prizes will be used to collect resources for their maintenance. These non-governmental civil organisations are further prohibited from participating in party political or election campaigns.

Since the enactment of Law 13.756/2018, the Ministry of Finance has exclusive competence to assess requests for commercial promotions, to grant authorisations and to control such operations, which means that it can enforce the law and apply sanctions accordingly.

An authorisation:

- must be granted for each promotional event;
- is limited to a 12-month term; and
- will never allow for the distribution or conversion of prizes into cash, unless the law provides otherwise.

If a promotional event is run without authorisation, the organiser may be subject to a fine and a prohibition against running any commercial promotions for a period of up to two years. The same sanctions apply in case of breach of the terms set forth in the authorisation, in addition to revocation of the authorisation. Where a broadcasting company runs a promotional event in breach of an authorisation or without such authorisation, it may be prohibited from running such events for a period of up to three years.

The legal entity that organises the promotional event must:

- be registered with the Taxpayers Registry at the Ministry of Finance; and
- specify where it will run the promotion and the duration of the promotion.

Promotional events cannot aim to promote gambling or to secure excessive profit for the organisers, among other restrictions. Medicines, weapons, explosives, fireworks, alcoholic beverages and tobacco, among other things, cannot be distributed as prizes.

The authorisation request should be filed between 120 days and 40 days before the start of the promotion. The procedure, the official rules and the publicity materials must always be in Portuguese.

Only once an authorisation certificate with an individual serial number has been issued can the company start the promotion and its associated advertising. All publicity materials must include the serial number of the authorisation certificate.

Applicants for authorisation should also provide:

- the contact details of their representative;

- their updated bylaws, duly filed before the relevant local chamber of commerce;
- evidence that no taxes are outstanding in the name of the company;
- the clear and detailed rules of the promotion;
- proof of payment of the official fees; and
- their final accounting statements, with evidence that the taxes due from the promotion have been collected accordingly. These taxes will correspond to 20% of the total value of the prizes.

If a prize is not awarded because the winner has not reclaimed it within 180 days, it will be forfeited and the company running the promotion must collect the corresponding value for the National Treasury. This also applies if there is no winner of the prize.

The Control System of Commercial Promotions aims to simplify this procedure and allow applicants to request and obtain authorisations online through digital certification.

The rules on sales promotions are very well regulated in practice.

5. Ambush marketing

It is possible to combat ambush marketing through the provisions on unfair competition that are set out in:

- the Industrial Property Law;
- the Agreement on Trade-Related Aspects of Intellectual Property Rights; and
- other statutes that prohibit undue or unauthorised association with other marks, including the marks of a specific event.

6. Direct marketing

As with online behavioural advertising, there is no specific legislation that governs direct marketing in Brazil, so direct marketing companies should carefully observe the Consumer Protection Code and Decree 7962/2013, which regulates e-commerce.

Brazilian case law has confirmed that if consumers state that they do not wish to receive letters, emails, messages or any other form of direct communication, they will be entitled to seek damages if they are sent such communications after refusing or withdrawing consent.

7. Product placement

The rules on product placement are set out in the codes mentioned in section 1 above – in particular, those concerned with truthfulness and transparency towards consumers.

One key issue that suppliers and advertisers should bear in mind is that products and services – particularly those targeted at children – should always be advertised in a direct and straightforward manner.

8. Native advertising and social media influencers

There is no specific legislation that regulates native advertising and social media influencers in Brazil. Therefore, players should observe the general rules on advertising when conducting such activities.

9. Industry-specific regulation

9.1 Gambling

Lotteries and gaming can be advertised only where bets can legally occur. Moreover, it is not permitted to advertise the results of lotteries on the radio or television, in newspapers or cinemas, or anywhere else that betting is not allowed.

The main provisions concerning lotteries are set out in Articles 55, 56 and 57 of Decree 3688/1941.

9.2 Alcohol

Alcohol advertising should adhere to the principle of social responsibility, given that the consumption of this product is limited to certain groups and situations.

For example, children and teenagers cannot be targeted by such advertising; and websites and packaging must state that the product should not be consumed by underage consumers.

Alcohol advertising:

- must not encourage the excessive or irresponsible consumption of alcohol;
- must not suggest to consumers that drinking alcohol makes people more interesting;
- must not encourage teens to drink; and
- must not be broadcast on television outside the hours of 21:30pm to 6:00am.

CONAR has prepared an extensive list of basic safe harbours for alcohol advertisers, requesting that they advertise responsibly. These rules will be interpreted restrictively where a specific claim is under analysis.

Phrases such as "Drink with moderation", "This product is for adults", "Do not drink and drive" and similar should always be included in alcohol advertising.

9.3 Pharmaceuticals

Based on the Brazilian legal framework, CONAR has prepared a list of 'safe harbours' for the advertisement of pharmaceuticals. Many of these provisions are similar, due to the profiles of legal drugs.

For pharmaceuticals, advertisers should observe the governmental regulations that apply to the packaging of such products and the following principles:

- All claims in the advertising material should be based on clinical or scientific evidence;
- No claims can be made regarding a cure if medical supervision is necessary;
- No claims – particularly in promotions – should suggest to consumers that they can use more medication than is strictly necessary;
- Precise information regarding the active substance(s), quantity and similar of the product should be provided;
- All advertising should be directed to adults;
- Advertising cannot treat medicines as simple solutions for emotional or psychological problems;
- Claims should be clear and precise, and should not generate fear relating to diseases; and
- Information should be simple and clear, avoiding complex scientific wording.

All regulations on pharmaceuticals advertising – including those established by the Brazilian Food and Drug Agency (ANVISA) – must be observed at all times and interpreted in relation to each specific case. The regulations that should in particular be borne in mind in relation to pharmaceutical advertising include:

- ANVISA Board Resolutions 102/00, RDC 199/04 and 96/2008, which regulate pharmaceuticals;
- Law 6360/76, which regulates ANVISA;
- Law 9294/1996, Decree 2018/1996, Law 10167/2000 and Law 10702/2003, which impose restrictions on the advertisement of pharmaceuticals (and other products);
- Law 8069/1990 – the Children and Teenagers Code – which regulates the rights of children and teenagers;
- Federal Law 5.197/1967, which regulates the use of animals; and
- Law 5.700/1971, which regulates the use and presentation of national symbols.

9.4 Financial products and services

Ads for financial products and services should always include as much precise information as possible, without violating any confidential information from investors.

Investors must be provided with all necessary information to make a rational decision on the investment, observing the rules of the Brazilian Securities and Exchange Commission.

Any projections and/or estimates must clarify their basis, and values should take into account any applicable taxation.

Given that this is a very specific and complex issue for many, financial products claims should always seek to educate and inform.

9.5 Food

Based on the Brazilian legal framework, CONAR has prepared a list of 'safe harbours' for the advertisement of food and beverages. They include the following:

- The use of terminology such as 'diet', 'light', 'sugarless' and similar should be clear;
- Any association with pharmaceuticals should be avoided;
- Responsible eating/drinking and exercise should be encouraged;
- Statements that a specific product may replace basic meals should be avoided, unless these are evidenced and based on a medical opinion;
- Nutrition factors should be shown in a clear and simple format;
- Precise information should be provided on flavour, size, quantity, percentage of alcohol and so on;
- Exploitative claims – such as those concerning popularity, status or performance in school, sports or sexual activities – should be avoided;
- Ads should not exploit a child's environment (eg, events for children, television shows for children or similar); and
- Underweight or overweight children should not be depicted, in order to avoid harming their dignity or the dignity of third parties.

All regulations on food advertising – including regulation by ANVISA – must be observed at all times and interpreted in relation to each specific case. The regulations that should in particular be borne in mind in relation to food advertising include:

- Decree 986/1969, which sets out basic rules concerning food;
- Law 6360/76, which regulates ANVISA;
- Laws 11265/2006, 11474/2007 and 11460/2007, which regulate foodstuffs for new-borns and toddlers;
- Law 8069/1990 – the Children and Teenagers Code – which regulates the rights of children and teenagers; and
- Law 5700/1971, which regulates the use and presentation of national symbols.

9.6 Tobacco

Based on the Brazilian legal framework, CONAR has prepared a list of 'safe harbours' for the advertisement of tobacco products. They include the following:

- Tobacco advertising is authorised only inside stores and only by means of panels and posters;
- Tobacco products must not be associated with sports;
- Tobacco products must not be associated with children;
- Packaging must contain a warning message specified by the government relating to the health risks of smoking;
- Tobacco products cannot be advertised on the Internet, by direct mail or through sponsorship of cultural or sporting events; and
- The distribution of free samples of tobacco products is prohibited; no merchandising is allowed.

The regulations that should in particular be borne in mind in relation to tobacco advertising include:

- Law 9294/1996, Decree 2018/1996, Law 10167/2000 and Law 10702/2003, which impose restrictions on the advertisement of tobacco (and other products);
- Law 8069/1990 – the Children and Teenagers Code – which regulates the rights of children and teenagers; and
- Law 5700/1971, which regulates the use and presentation of national symbols.

9.7   E-cigarettes

E-cigarettes are prohibited in Brazil and consequently there are no specific regulations on the advertisement of e-cigarettes. If these sorts of products are authorised in the future, it is expected that the applicable advertising rules and limitations will be very similar to those covering tobacco products.

Canada

Jennifer McKenzie
Bereskin & Parr LLP

1. Overview of the legal and regulatory regime for advertising

1.1 Legislation and regulations

In Canada, numerous laws, regulations, guidelines and codes deal with advertising, at both the federal and provincial level. Some are product specific – such as the Food and Drugs Act[1] and the Food and Drug Regulations,[2] which regulate the advertisement of food, drugs, natural health products, cosmetics and medical devices. The advertising law with the broadest application is the Competition Act[3] – a federal statute enforced by the Competition Bureau, an independent government agency.[4] The Competition Bureau is headed by the commissioner of competition.[5]

There are two regimes for dealing with false or misleading advertising under the Competition Act: criminal and civil. Under the criminal regime, Section 52(1) of the act makes it a criminal offence to "knowingly or recklessly" make a representation to the public, by any means whatsoever, that is false or misleading in a material respect, for the purpose of promoting, directly or indirectly, the supply or use of a product or any business interest.[6] Other criminal offences include:

- the knowing or reckless inclusion of a false or misleading representation in the sender information or subject line of an electronic message (Section 52.01(1));
- deceptive telemarketing (Section 52.1);
- deceptive notice of winning a prize (Section 53(1)); and
- pyramid schemes (Sections 55 and 55.1).

Criminal matters are referred to the attorney general of Canada for prosecution. For a conviction, the elements of a criminal offence must be

1   RSC 1985, c F-27.
2   CRC, c 870.
3   RSC 1985, c C-34.
4   Competition Bureau Canada, www.competitionbureau.gc.ca/.
5   The current commissioner is Matthew Boswell who was appointed on 5 March 2019 for a five-year term.
6   RSC 1985, c C-34, s 52(1).

proven beyond reasonable doubt. If an advertiser is convicted, it is liable to pay significant fines;[7] if there is individual culpability by an officer or director, he or she might be liable to a term of imprisonment and/or to a fine.[8]

Part VII.1 of the Competition Act sets out the civil regime for deceptive marketing practices. The main section dealing with advertising is Section 74.01(1)(a). This section provides that making a promotional representation to the public that is false or misleading in a material respect constitutes reviewable conduct. It states:

A person engages in reviewable conduct who, for the purpose of promoting, directly or indirectly, the supply or use of a product or for the purpose of promoting, directly or indirectly, any business interest, by any means whatever,

(a) makes a representation to the public that is false or misleading in a material respect.[9]

Conduct that is also subject to review includes:

- unsubstantiated product claims (Section 74.01(1)(b));
- misleading price claims (Section 74.01(2));
- testimonials published without approval or permission (Section 74.02(b));
- failure to make "adequate and fair disclosure" about certain information in connection with a promotional contest (Section 74.06(a));
- the sending of a false or misleading representation in the sender information or subject line of an electronic message (Section 74.011); and
- the making of certain representations about bargain and sale prices (Sections 74.04 and 74.05).

If an advertiser is alleged to have engaged in reviewable conduct, the Competition Bureau can, depending on the issue, bring an action or application to the Competition Tribunal, the superior court of a province or the Federal Court of Canada for a determination. Each element of the reviewable conduct must be proven on a balance of probabilities. If the tribunal or court determines that the advertiser engaged in reviewable conduct, it can order the advertiser, among other things, to:

- stop engaging in the conduct;
- publish a corrective notice; or
- pay an administrative monetary penalty of up to C$750,000 for a first offence by an individual and up to C$10 million for a first offence by a corporation.[10]

---

7   RSC 1985, c C-34, s 52.1(9).
8   RSC 1985, c C-34, s 52.1(8).
9   RSC 1985, c C-34, s 74.01(1)(a).
10   RSC 1985, c C-34, s 74.1(1).

It is possible for an advertiser to consent to an order once the Competition Bureau has filed an application.[11]

In a bulletin entitled *Misleading Representations and Deceptive Practices: Choice of Criminal or Civil Track under the Competition Act*,[12] the Competition Bureau sets out some of the factors that it will consider when deciding whether to pursue the criminal or civil regime. These factors include:

- the existence of compelling evidence that the representations were made knowingly or recklessly;
- the seriousness of the representation (measured by such factors as the vulnerability of the intended audience); and
- whether criminal prosecution is in the public interest.

The Competition Bureau has published a bulletin entitled *Competition and Compliance Framework*,[13] setting out a continuum of measures that it can take to ensure compliance. The Competition Bureau's goal is to strike the right balance between voluntary compliance and enforcement through a range of tools. These tools include:

- information letters, warning letters and compliance meetings ('suasion');
- negotiated settlements, consent orders, undertakings, corrective notices and voluntary product recall ('consent'); and
- prosecutions, applications to the Competition Tribunal, product seizures, contested prohibition orders and injunctions ('enforcement').

In addition to federal law, many provinces have their own consumer protection legislation that deals with advertising and unfair practices, as well as their own enforcement regimes. For example, Part III of the Ontario Consumer Protection Act 2002[14] makes it an unfair practice to make a false, misleading or deceptive representation. Such representations include representations that "goods or services have sponsorship, approval, performance characteristics, accessories, uses, ingredients, benefits, or qualities they do not have".[15] In Quebec, the Consumer Protection Act[16] prohibits advertising directed at children under the age of 13; and the Quebec Charter of the French Language[17] mandates the use of the French language in commerce and business, including in advertising. In some media, the French language must be "markedly predominant" over any other language;[18] while in other media, French must be used exclusively.[19]

---

11   RSC 1985, c C-34, s 74.12.
12   www.competitionbureau.gc.ca/eic/site/cb-bc.nsf/vwapj/ct01181e.pdf/$file/ct01181e.pdf.
13   www.competitionbureau.gc.ca/eic/site/cb-bc.nsf/vwapj/Competition-Compliance-Framework-Bulletin-
        e.pdf/$file/Competition-Compliance-Framework-Bulletin-e.pdf.
14   SO 2013, c 30, Sched A.
15   SO 2013, c 30, Sched A, s 14(2).
16   CQLR, chapter P-40.1, s 248.
17   CQLR, chapter C-11.

1.2   Self-regulation

(a)   Ad Standards

Ad Standards (formerly Advertising Standards Canada) is a national not-for-profit advertising self-regulatory body that was constituted more than 60 years ago. Ad Standards administers a 14-clause code called the Canadian Code of Advertising Standards.[20] Many of the 14 clauses mirror the civil provisions of the Competition Act, addressing such issues as:

- accuracy and clarity in advertising (Clause 1);
- price claims (Clause 3); and
- testimonials (Clause 7).

The code goes beyond the Competition Act, however, by addressing issues such as:

- the depiction of unsafe situations in advertising (Clause 10); and
- the condonation of any form of discrimination and the disparagement of an identifiable group (Clause 14).

The code applies to 'advertising' and 'advertisement(s)', which are defined as: "any message (other than those excluded from the application of this Code), the content of which message is controlled directly or indirectly by the advertiser expressed in any language and communicated in any medium (except those listed under Exclusions) to Canadians with the intent to influence their choice, opinion or behaviour."[21]

'Exclusions' include "packaging, wrappers and labels" and "foreign media (namely media that originate outside Canada and contain the advertising in question) unless the advertiser is a Canadian person or entity".[22]

Most major advertisers and media companies are members of Ad Standards and thus have agreed to comply with the code and Ad Standards' enforcement mechanisms. Ad Standards enforces its code through two mechanisms: the Advertising Dispute Procedure and the Consumer Complaints Procedure.

Advertising Dispute Procedure: Advertisers that believe that their competitors' ads contravene the code may avail of the Advertising Dispute Procedure. On 11 February 2019, Ad Standards introduced a substantially overhauled procedure, after consulting with its own members and reviewing the dispute procedures of other agencies such as the US National Advertising Division and the UK

---

18   CQLR, chapter C-11, s 58.
19   CQLR, chapter C-11, s 89.
20   www.adstandards.ca/code/the-code-online/.
21   Canadian Code of Advertising Standards, "Definitions".
22   Canadian Code of Advertising Standards, "Exclusions".

Advertising Standards Authority.[23] There are many features to the new procedure, but key changes include the following:

- It is entirely in writing, without any oral hearing;
- A resolution meeting is no longer mandatory (but available if both parties consent);
- It is reviewed by a three-person Ad Dispute Panel, chaired by a lawyer who specialises in advertising and marketing law, rather than five persons as previously;
- There is no right of appeal; and
- It is no longer entirely confidential – Ad Standards will now publish summaries of the decision including the facts and issues at issue without naming or identifying the advertisers ('case summaries'). The case summaries are intended to "provide clarity about the kinds of advertising activity that have been found by an Ad Dispute Panel to contravene the Code in some respect or other".[24]

One of the pre-conditions of Ad Standards accepting a complaint is that it be accompanied by a written confirmation, satisfactory to Ad Standards, that the complainant has made good-faith efforts to resolve the dispute with the defendant advertiser.

If a complaint is upheld, the defendant advertiser must withdraw or amend the ad in question to Ad Standards' satisfaction within a specified timeframe. If the defendant advertiser fails to fully comply with a decision of the Ad Dispute Panel, whether or not it chooses to participate in the procedure, Ad Standards can advise the exhibiting media and the Competition Bureau of the decision. Additionally, Ad Standards may publish a summary of the Ad Dispute Panel's decision, which includes the facts and issues in dispute, the identity of the advertisers involved in the dispute and a description of the advertising.

The procedure is estimated to take between 32 and 37 business days, and the fees payable to Ad Standards for the procedure have been significantly reduced.

Consumer Complaints Procedure: The Consumer Complaints Procedure[25] is available for consumers who wish to complain in writing that ads contravene the code. Ad Standards will initially evaluate a complaint and make a preliminary determination as to whether there has been a code violation. If the complaint is accepted, the advertiser will be notified in writing and given an opportunity to respond. The complaint may be resolved at this stage or may proceed to the Standards Council, which will decide by majority vote whether

---

23   Advertising Dispute Procedure 2019, https://adstandards.ca/wp-content/uploads/Advertising-Dispute-Procedure-2019-October.pdf.
24   *Ibid*, section 4.1.
25   Consumer Complaint Procedure, https://adstandards.ca/complaints/.

there is a code violation. Generally, if the complaint is upheld, the advertiser must amend or withdraw the ad. An appeal is available. There is no threshold number of complaints that must be received by Ad Standards before it will review an ad for a potential violation of the code: one complaint is sufficient.

Certain complaints are not reviewable – for example:

- complaints that are veiled disputes between advertisers; and
- advertising that is substantially also the subject of litigation or other legal action in Canada, or under review by a Canadian court or other agency.

(b) **thinkTV**

thinkTV[26] (formerly the Television Bureau of Canada) is an association for Canadian broadcasters. On behalf of its members, thinkTV offers the thinkTV Telecaster Services, which pre-clear broadcast advertising to ensure that it complies with thinkTV's guidelines.[27] The guidelines deal with a range of topics, including:

- children's advertising;
- contests;
- sexual innuendo;
- the advertisement of personal products; and
- comparative advertising.

In connection with comparative advertising, thinkTV requires advertisers to provide an 'attestation letter' (on the advertiser's letterhead) confirming that all claims are true, together with a brief description of how the claims have been substantiated. Once a broadcast ad is approved, thinkTV issues a clearance number, which Canadian broadcasters require before the ad is broadcast.

(c) **Canadian Marketing Association**

The Canadian Marketing Association (CMA),[28] Canada's largest marketing association, maintains a Code of Ethics and Standards.[29] The CMA describes its code as "the foundation of the marketing community's self-regulation". The CMA code addresses such topics as special considerations when marketing to children and teenagers, and the protection of the environment. It also includes enforcement procedures for both members and non-members that do not comply.

---

26   https://thinktv.ca/.
27   www.thinktv.ca/wp-content/uploads/2018/05/thinktv_clearance_Telecaster_GUIDELINES.pdf.
28   www.the-cma.org/.
29   www.the-cma.org/regulatory/code-of-ethics.

2. Comparative advertising

The laws, regulations, guidelines and codes combine to require that comparative advertising:

- be truthful, fair and supported by evidence;
- not be misleading, false or deceptive, or disparaging of a product, service or business; and
- not be depreciative of a third-party registered trademark.

2.1 Unsubstantiated comparative claims

Comparative advertising is vulnerable to enforcement action by regulators. For example, the Competition Bureau can enforce against claims that are not properly substantiated. The Competition Act provides that making a representation to the public about the performance, efficacy or length of life of a product without adequate and proper testing constitutes reviewable conduct (Section 74.01(1)(b)). The act does not define what constitutes an 'adequate and proper' test; rather, this is determined on a case-by-case basis, considering factors such as the scope and nature of the claim, and whether the relevant industry provides any guidance on the manner of testing a particular product.[30] The Competition Act makes it clear that testing must be completed before the representation is made;[31] and that the burden of proving that the test is adequate and proper rests with the advertiser.

The Competition Bureau has stated that most performance claims that raise an issue under the Competition Act fall into two broad categories:

- those that are inappropriate in the context of the actual tests that were conducted; and
- those that are based on poorly designed test methodologies.[32]

2.2 Civil remedies for comparative advertising

Section 36[33] of the Competition Act provides a civil remedy to "a person who has suffered loss or damage" for conduct that is contrary to the criminal provisions of the Competition Act; but not for any of the deceptive marketing practices set out in Part VII.1 of the Competition Act. Accordingly, to give rise

---

30 See, for example, *The Deceptive Marketing Practices Digest*, www.competitionbureau.gc.ca/eic/site/cb-bc.nsf/eng/04029.html#section2_5.

31 In *Canada (Commissioner of Competition) v Chatr Wireless Inc*, 2014 ONSC 1146 post-market substantiation that proved the truthfulness of the performance claim was held to be insufficient.

32 Performance representations not based on adequate and proper tests, www.competitionbureau.gc.ca/eic/site/cb-bc.nsf/eng/00520.html.

33 This reads as follows:
   36 (1) Any person who has suffered loss or damage as a result of
   (a) conduct that is contrary to any provision of Part VI, or
   (b) the failure of any person to comply with an order of the Tribunal or another court under this Act,
   may, in any court of competent jurisdiction, sue for and recover from the person who engaged in the conduct or failed to comply with the order an amount equal to the loss or damage proved to have been suffered by him, together with any additional amount that the court may allow not exceeding the full cost to him of any investigation in connection with the matter and of proceedings under this section.

to a cause of action in civil proceedings, a party must allege the elements of the criminal offence of false or misleading advertising, including that the representation was made "knowingly or recklessly".[34]

Canada's Trademarks Act[35] contains provisions that can be implicated in the context of comparative advertising. For example, Section 7(a) states that no person shall "make a false or misleading statement tending to discredit the business, goods or services of a competitor". A claim under Section 7(a) is broader than a claim under Sections 36 and 52(1) of the Competition Act. Most notably, under the Trademarks Act, a plaintiff need not demonstrate that the misrepresentation was made knowingly or recklessly, or that the representation was false or misleading in a "material respect". In addition, under the Trademarks Act, the plaintiff can seek both damages and injunctive relief – unlike in a private civil action under Section 36 of the Competition Act, which does not expressly provide for injunctive relief.[36]

In *Maple Leaf Foods Inc v Robin Hood Multifoods Inc*,[37] the plaintiff successfully enjoined the defendant's ads for its frozen pie crusts under Section 7(a). The ads portrayed two pies side by side: one with a lattice top, under the heading "Our idea of a top crust"; and the second with an inverted bottom shell over the top, under the heading "Their idea of a top crust". There were two versions of the ads. One version referred directly to the plaintiff's trademarks, TENDERFLAKE and GAINSBOROUGH; the other version did not. The court concluded that the plaintiff was identified, even in those ads that did not specifically refer to its trademarks, given that the plaintiff had a 75% share of the frozen pie crust market in Canada. The court found the ads to be false or misleading, in that they created the general impression that the plaintiff's products could not be used to form a top crust, and that use of the plaintiff's product would result in a misshapen pie. The evidence established that a consumer could achieve a 'proper' top crust by following the directions on the plaintiff's packaging.

Section 22 of the Trademarks Act has been successfully invoked in parody cases and with mixed success in comparative advertising cases. Section 22(1) states: "No person shall use a trademark registered by another person in a manner that is likely to have the effect of depreciating the value of the goodwill thereto."

Section 22 has been the subject of very little case law in the near 70 years since its enactment. There is a decades-old decision, *Clairol International Corp v*

---

34   RSC 1985, c C-34, s 52(1).
35   RSC 1985, c T-13.
36   In the 4 August 2020 decision in *TFI Foods Ltd v Every Green International Inc*, 2020 FC 808 at para 19, Justice McHaffie noted that the Federal Court of Appeal recently confirmed that Section 36 of the Competition Act provides a statutory remedy of compensation for loss, damage and costs, but not for equitable remedies such as an accounting of profits or unjust enrichment, citing *Energizer Brands, LLC v The Gillette Company*, 2020 FCA 49 at paras 56–59.
37   1994 CarswellOnt 1032, [1994] OJ No 2165, 17 BLR (2d) 86, 58 CPR (3d) 54 (OCJ, Gen Div).

Thomas Supply & Equipment Co Ltd,[38] which enjoined a specific kind of comparative advertising; and a Supreme Court of Canada decision in *Veuve Clicquot Ponsardin v Boutiques Cliquot Ltée*,[39] which did not involve Section 22, but set clearer guidelines on when the section might be used. In between these two cases, Section 22 was occasionally used to challenge the display of competitor marks in advertising for comparison purposes, with only limited success.[40]

In *Clairol*, Revlon's Canadian distributor sold hair dye with comparative hair colour charts displaying Clairol's registered marks on the exterior of the packaging and in advertising. Clairol sued the distributor for infringement and depreciation under Section 22. The infringement claim was dismissed, as the use of Clairol's registered marks was not to distinguish the seller's products. Regarding the Section 22 claim, although the judge expressed concern that the intent of Section 22 was probably not to enjoin legitimate comparisons or criticisms, he defined 'depreciation' as:

> to reduce in some way the advantage of the reputation and connection ..., to take away the whole or some portion of the custom [trade] otherwise to be expected and to make it less extensive and this less advantageous...,
>
> through the direct persuasion and enticing of customers who could otherwise be expected to buy or continue to buy goods bearing the trade mark.[41]

The breadth of this definition made it possible to argue that even lost sales that could be attributable to comparative advertising might depreciate the goodwill of a registered mark.

The judge further analysed the word 'use' in Section 22.[42] 'Use' is defined in Section 4 of the Trademarks Act. Section 4(1) deems 'use' of a trademark in association with products (in this case, the Clairol registrations covered hair dye) to include applying the trademark on products; it does not include the display of the mark in the advertisement of products. (Section 4(2) deems 'use' of a trademark in association with services if it is used or displayed in the performance or advertisement of those services.)

Due to the definition of 'use' in Section 4 for products, the judge enjoined use of the Clairol marks on packaging material, but not use of the Clairol marks in advertising. (The corollary is that use of registered marks in advertising could be enjoined only if the registrations covered services.)

---

38 (1968), 55 CPR 176 (Exc Crt).
39 2006 SCC 23.
40 In *Future Shop Ltd v AB Sound Ltd*, (1994) 55 CPR (3d) 182 (BCSC), the plaintiff was unsuccessful in invoking Section 22. In that case the defendant used FUTURE SHOP in ads to show that its electronics were cheaper than the plaintiff's. The Supreme Court of British Columbia held that the use of another's registered trademark to capitalise on the similarities between products should be enjoined, but a comparative advertisement that "by obvious and reasonable implication stresses the differences between the advertiser's product and that of the competition does not attach itself to the competitor's goodwill in the same manner. Rather, it seeks to distance itself from that goodwill by stressing the differences".
41 *Clairol International Corp v Thomas Supply & Equipment Co Ltd* (1968), 55 CPR 176 at 199-200 (Exc Crt).
42 *Ibid* at 196.

In the years following the *Clairol* decision, it was common to caution against any display of another's registered mark, including for comparison purposes, on products and packaging *per se*; but trademark use in advertising was considered acceptable (assuming that the marks were registered for products). Over time, the practice of using another's mark on both packaging and advertising has become quite common – particularly for certain products, such as vacuum cleaner bags, electric toothbrush heads and printer cartridges, where 'fits with' or 'works with' claims that display another's mark are frequently shown on packaging. Comparative advertising for services is widespread, despite the fact that such advertising might be contrary to the *Clairol* interpretation of Section 22.

While it is the view of many that a claim for depreciation of goodwill under Section 22 should not be used to prevent truthful comparative advertising, the combination of the *Clairol* analysis and the plain language in Section 22 could still be read to make certain types of comparative advertising unlawful. The Supreme Court of Canada's *Veuve Clicquot* decision provided more guidance on what 'depreciation' means; and it and subsequent decisions have stressed that any plaintiff alleging depreciation must show how the mark is being damaged. The *Clairol* interpretation of "enticing" a consumer by displaying another's brand has not been followed; and in fact, other decisions have suggested that intellectual property should not be used to prevent competition.

The *Veuve Clicquot* case was not about comparative advertising. It was brought by a famous champagne company against a women's clothing retailer, with claims of trademark infringement, passing off and depreciation of goodwill. In this case, the language of Section 22 was being applied to argue that permitting use on unrelated services would depreciate the famous brand – thus essentially a 'dilution' argument. The Supreme Court of Canada set out four criteria for the application of Section 22:

- The plaintiff's registered trademark[43] was used by the defendant in connection with goods or services. Although the Supreme Court of Canada did not expressly clarify the longstanding debate about whether a plaintiff must demonstrate that its registered trademark has been 'used' within the meaning of Section 4 of the Trademarks Act or 'used as a trade mark' – that is, "for the purpose of distinguishing or so as to distinguish wares or services manufactured, sold, leased, hired or performed by him from those manufactured, sold, leased, hired or performed by others" – a subsequent decision assumes it is the latter;[44]
- Its mark is sufficiently well known to have significant goodwill attached to it;

---

43   In *Toys "R" Us (Canada) Ltd v Herbs "R" Us Wellness Society*, 2020 FC 682, the judge confirmed that the mark used need not be identical to the mark as registered. In that case, the registered mark was TOYS "R" US and the impugned mark was HERBS "R" US.

44   *Venngo Inc v Concierge Connection Inc*, 2015 FC 1338.

- Its mark was used in a manner likely to have an effect on that goodwill (linkage); and
- The likely effect would be to depreciate the value of its goodwill (damage).[45]

In *Veuve Clicquot*, the most important issue was the third point: the similarity between the retail store name (which was actually spelled slightly differently) and the difference in the nature of products/services made a 'linkage' unlikely.

Lastly, common law torts can also be used against comparative advertising, such as the tort of injurious falsehood and the tort of unlawful interference with economic relations.

2.3 Self-regulatory regime for comparative advertising

Ad Standards' code contains a number of provisions that deal with comparative advertising. Advertisers that believe their competitors' ads contravene the code may avail of the Advertising Dispute Procedure (see section 1.2(a)). For example, Clause 6 expressly addresses comparative advertising thus: "Advertisements must not, unfairly, discredit, disparage or attack one or more products, services, advertisements, companies or entities, or exaggerate the nature or importance of competitive differences."[46]

Other clauses that can be invoked in the comparative advertising context include Clause 1, which prohibits ads from:

- containing "inaccurate, deceptive or otherwise misleading claims, statements, illustrations, or representations"; and
- omitting relevant information in a manner that is deceptive.[47]

To help advertisers ensure that their comparative advertising does not contravene the code, Ad Standards has published Guidelines for the Use of Comparative Advertising and Guidelines for the Use of Research and Survey Data to Support Comparative Advertising Claims.[48] These guidelines recommend ways to ensure that any testing is reliable and verifiable – for example, in connection with preference claims, the guidelines recommend a minimum survey sample size of no fewer than 300 people.

---

45   *Veuve Clicquot Ponsardin v Boutiques Cliquot Ltée*, 2006 SCC 23 at para 46.
46   Canadian Code of Advertising Standards, Clause 6.
47   Canadian Code of Advertising Standards, Clause 1.
48   www.adstandards.ca/wp-content/uploads/2018/04/guidelinesCompAdvertising-en.pdf.

3. Online behavioural advertising

3.1 Regulation

Canada's federal private sector privacy law is called the Personal Information Protection and Electronic Documents Act[49] (PIPEDA) and is administered by the federal Office of the Privacy Commissioner (OPC). In general terms, PIPEDA applies to the collection, use and disclosure of 'personal information' for commercial purposes. PIPEDA is premised on meaningful consent and reasonableness – that is, even with the consent of individuals, organisations can collect, use and disclose personal information only to the extent that is reasonable to meet the purpose stated at the time of collection. The OPC has released various guidance documents[50] relating to the application of PIPEDA to online behavioural advertising. In its 2015 Policy Position on Online Behavioural Advertising,[51] the OPC stated the following:

- Data that is collected and used for online behavioural advertising is generally considered 'personal information', which is broadly defined in PIPEDA as "information about an identifiable individual", but has been held to include information that can readily identify an individual when used alone or in combination with other available data. In reaching its conclusion on the nature of collected data, the OPC noted that the very purpose of online behavioural advertising is to create profiles about individuals.

- Online behavioural advertising can be a reasonable purpose for collecting personal information under PIPEDA because it plays a "key role in providing free content on the Internet". The OPC made it clear, however, that online behavioural advertising should not be a condition of service to accessing or using the Internet generally.

- Meaningful consent is required for online behavioural advertising. The OPC has set restrictions on the use of an opt-out or implied consent. For example, to rely on opt-out consent, the OPC stipulates that organisations must be transparent about online behavioural advertising by using tools such as online banners and interactive tools that explain the purposes for collecting tracking data; burying this information in a privacy policy is not acceptable. Another restriction to using opt-out consent is that the collected information must be limited to non-sensitive information to the extent possible.

- The use of technological means of collecting data that individuals

---

49 SC 2000, c. 5.
50 The OPC's guidance documents relating to online behavioural advertising and tracking and ads are available online at www.priv.gc.ca/en/privacy-topics/technology/online-privacy-tracking-cookies/tracking-and-ads/.
51 www.priv.gc.ca/en/privacy-topics/technology/online-privacy-tracking-cookies/tracking-and-ads/bg_ba_1206/.

cannot readily disable without significant effort, such as 'zombie cookies', does not comply with PIPEDA.

- Organisations should avoid collecting personal information from children and should avoid knowingly tracking children, as well as refraining from conducting tracking activities on websites aimed at children.

PIPEDA gives the OPC the jurisdiction to investigate personal information handling practices of organisations that are subject to PIPEDA. There have been investigations into online behavioural advertising. For example, in January 2014, the OPC released its report of findings[52] following an investigation into Google's ad services. According to the report of findings, the complainant searched online, while signed into his Google account, for a medical device for sleep apnoea. A cookie was placed on his browser which caused ads for such medical devices to be displayed when he visited unrelated sites. The practice was against Google's own privacy policy, which stated that Google would not associate a cookie with certain categories of sensitive information, such as health information. The complainant took the position that he had not provided Google with consent to display his personal health information in browsers. The OPC agreed and found that, while implied or opt-out consent may be acceptable when the information is not sensitive, since the complaint related to sensitive personal health information, Google should have obtained express consent to deliver ads based on online behaviour. In response to the OPC's findings and recommended actions, Google rejected all active remarketing campaigns involving sleep apnoea devices, and increased monitoring of existing remarketing campaigns to better identify advertisers that have created campaigns for topics that may relate to sensitive categories of data.

Further, in April 2015 the OPC released its report of findings[53] following an investigation into Bell Canada's (one of Canada's three largest communications companies) Relevant Ads Program (RAP). The RAP tracked users' internet browsing activities and combined this information with existing customer account information, which Bell then used to generate detailed customer profiles. Once these profiles were created, Bell then facilitated the delivery of targeted ads by advertisers to Bell's customers. Bell did not deliver the ads directly; nor did it share the identity of its customers with the third-party advertisers. Although Bell provided customers with notifications about the RAP, the OPC was of the opinion that the notices were not sufficiently transparent. Customers were allowed to opt out of the RAP; however, as Bell had access to vast amounts of personal information, the OPC was of the opinion that the

---

52   PIPEDA Report of Findings #2014-001.
53   PIPEDA Report of Findings #2015-001.

breadth of this combined information made it more sensitive and therefore the circumstances warranted express opt-in consent. Further, when considering the reasonable expectation of the consumer, the OPC was of the view that because Bell charged for its mobile, internet, telephone and television services, customers would not expect that the personal information they provided for the primary purpose of receiving these services would then be used for the secondary purpose of delivering behaviourally targeted ads. Following the OPC's report of findings, Bell decided to withdraw the RAP and deleted all existing customer profiles.

3.2 Self-regulation

The Digital Advertising Alliance of Canada[54] (DAAC) is a not-for-profit consortium of Canadian advertising and marketing associations, including Ad Standards, the Canadian Marketing Association and the Interactive Advertising Bureau of Canada. DAAC administers a programme called AdChoices for both businesses and consumers. Businesses may elect to participate in this self-regulatory programme, in which case they will be expected to comply with the Canadian Self-Regulatory Principles for Online Behavioural Advertising[55] when engaged in online behavioural advertising. The principles set out a framework for the collection of data in connection with the delivery of online behavioural advertising, and are designed to be consistent with Canadian privacy legislation and the self-regulatory principles established by the Digital Advertising Alliance in the United States.

The principles include separate provisions for:

- 'first parties' (ie, the owner or entity that has control over the website or app);
- 'third parties' (ie, those that engage in online behavioural advertising on another entity's website, such as advertising networks); and
- 'service providers' (ie, those entities that collect and use data in the course of their activities as a provider of internet access services or client software, such as internet service providers or search engines).[56]

The principles state that consumers should be given "clear, meaningful and prominent notice" about the data collected and used during online behavioural advertising on websites and within ads, as well as a choice regarding whether and what data is collected and used for such advertising. The principles caution against collecting information from children and state that sensitive information should not be collected or used without consent.[57]

---

54   Digital Advertising Alliance of Canada, https://youradchoices.ca/.
55   https://assets.youradchoices.ca/pdf/DAAC-ThePrinciples.pdf.
56   *Ibid.*
57   *Ibid.*

Through the AdChoices programme, consumers can opt out of online behavioural advertising from registered companies. If a consumer opts out, he or she will stop receiving interest-based ads, but will continue to receive ads generally. One of the tools provided by AdChoices relates to cookies and browser controls. Businesses engaged in online behavioural advertising use cookies to help deliver ads and track their performance, and to help predict which types of ads might be of interest to users in the future. When a user chooses to opt out of online behavioural advertising, those businesses place an 'opt-out' cookie in the user's browser to tell businesses not to deliver such advertising in the future.

Businesses that have registered with AdChoices are encouraged to:

- display the 'advertising option' icon (see Figure 1) as a tool to let consumers know when information about their interests may be collected or used for online behavioural advertising; and
- list themselves on the "Consumer Opt-Out" page of DAAC's website,[58] where consumers can easily opt out of receiving online behavioural advertising from some or all participating businesses.

Figure 1. Canada's 'advertising option' icon

Ad Standards investigates, resolves and reports on consumer complaints about practices that may violate the Principles.

4. Sales promotions

Promotional contests in Canada – such as random draws and 'scratch and wins' – are regulated by provisions of the Competition Act, the Criminal Code[59] and, if offered in Quebec, the Act Respecting Lotteries, Publicity Contests and Amusement Machines,[60] which requires the contest to be registered with Quebec's provincial government, among other things. If sponsors are using personal information collected during the contest for any secondary purpose, the contest must also comply with PIPEDA and provincial privacy laws. Each law is discussed in turn below.

In relation to 'promotional contests', Section 74.06 of the Competition Act provides that the following constitute reviewable conduct:

---

58   https://youradchoices.ca/en/participating-companies.
59   RSC 1985, c C-46.
60   CQLR, ch L-6.

- A consent sponsor fails to provide adequate and fair disclosure of certain facts relating to the contest;
- The distribution of prizes is unduly delayed; or
- The prizes are not awarded on the basis of skill or chance.

Section 74.06 states:

A person engages in reviewable conduct who, for the purpose of promoting, directly or indirectly, the supply or use of a product, or for the purpose of promoting, directly or indirectly, any business interest, conducts any contest, lottery, game of chance or skill, or mixed chance and skill, or otherwise disposes of any product or other benefit by any mode of chance, skill or mixed chance and skill whatever, where

(a) adequate and fair disclosure is not made of the number and approximate value of the prizes, of the area or areas to which they relate and of any fact within the knowledge of the person that affects materially the chances of winning;

(b) distribution of the prizes is unduly delayed; or

(c) selection of participants or distribution of prizes is not made on the basis of skill or on a random basis in any area to which prizes have been allocated.[61]

The Competition Bureau has published guidelines[62] for sponsors of promotional contests to ensure that they do not fall foul of Section 74.06. These guidelines state that the following minimum amount of information – often referred to as the 'short rules' – should be disclosed to potential participants before they are "inconvenienced" into participating in the contest (eg, at the point of sale):

- the number and value of prizes;
- any regional allocation of prizes;
- the requirement to successfully answer a skill-testing question to be confirmed a winner;
- the chances or odds of winning (in some cases, a chart may simplify the explanation of the odds of winning);
- the contest closing date;
- any other facts known to the advertiser that materially affect the chances of winning; and
- how to access the full rules.[63]

The information should be readily available. For example, if it is printed on a label, the consumer should not have to buy the product or tamper with the package to read the rules.

In addition to the Competition Act, promotional contests in Canada are

---

61   RSC 1985, c C-34, s 74.06.
62   www.competitionbureau.gc.ca/eic/site/cb-bc.nsf/eng/03126.html.
63   *Ibid.*

regulated by provisions of the Criminal Code.[64] The illegal lottery provisions in the Criminal Code prohibit the disposition of property on the basis of pure chance alone.[65] The wording of this prohibition is broad enough to capture promotional contests in which prizes are given away through random draws or randomly distributed through game cards (eg, 'scratch and win' games) or any other mode of pure chance. To avoid contravening the Criminal Code, sponsors of chance-based promotional contests make prize redemption conditional on successfully answering a skill-testing question. In this way, a game of pure chance is turned into a game of mixed chance and skill. Although what constitutes a measure of skill may be debatable, a time-limited, multi-step and multi-operational mathematical question is typically used by sponsors. Contests of pure skill – such as writing contests judged by a jury according to specific criteria – do not require a skill-testing question.

Under the Criminal Code, it is also illegal to award prizes by any game of chance, or of mixed skill and chance, where the entrant must pay "money or other valuable consideration" to play.[66] For example, an entrant must not be required to purchase a product as a condition of entry. Sponsors must consider whether the contest mechanics indirectly force a purchase. This might occur if entry requires the entrant to submit a photograph with the sponsor's product. Additionally, when crafting the contest mechanics, sponsors must take care to ensure that the entrant is not required to provide consideration or something of value beyond money, such as watching a lengthy video (ie, spending time) or completing an extensive survey (ie, providing personal information). Generally, where an entrant must give up something of value or do something relatively onerous to enter a contest, there is a risk that this will be construed as consideration. A simple way to avoid the consideration prohibition is to include a 'no purchase necessary' alternative.

Quebec is the only province in Canada with contest-specific legislation, called the Act Respecting Lotteries, Publicity Contests and Amusement Machines.[57] Sponsors often exclude Quebec, believing that the requirements under this law are too onerous; but by excluding Quebec, they lose access to more than 20% of Canada's population. The biggest expense for sponsors in including Quebec is translating their rules and contest-related materials into French. Beyond that, the requirements are modest and include the following:

- including certain mandatory disclosures in the contest rules;
- filing a pre and post-contest report with the Quebec government agency that administers the act;
- paying a fee based on a percentage of the prize pool; and
- in some instances, posting security for the prizes.

---

64   RSC 1985, c C-46.
65   RSC 1985, c C-46 at ss 206-207.
66   RSC 1985, c C-46 at s 206 (1)(f).
67   CQLR, ch L-6.

Lastly, if sponsors are using personal information collected during the contest for any secondary purpose beyond administration of the contest, sponsors must also comply with Canada's federal and provincial private sector privacy laws – for example, by obtaining consent to the secondary purpose. Sponsors cannot make participation in a contest conditional upon the entrant consenting to the sponsor's secondary use of his or her personal information.

5. Ambush marketing

The first statute in Canada whose express purpose was to address ambush marketing was the Olympic and Paralympic Marks Act,[68] enacted prior to the 2010 Winter Olympic Games in Vancouver. The Olympic Act prohibited companies from running promotions in association with specifically listed marks in a manner that was likely to mislead the public into believing there was a business association with the Olympic or Paralympic Games, or approval, authorisation or endorsement by the Canadian Olympic Committee (COC).

The Olympic Act was considered somewhat superfluous to the already broad protection afforded to the COC's marks under the Trademarks Act. The COC's marks are protected as 'official marks' – that is, marks that have been adopted and used by a public authority and for which public notice of the adoption has been given in accordance with Section 9 of the Trademarks Act.[69] Once an official mark has been published as such in the *Trademarks Journal*, the Trademarks Act prohibits a person from adopting, in connection with a business, as a trademark or otherwise, any mark consisting of the official mark or so nearly resembling it as to likely be mistaken for an official mark. The test under Section 9 is resemblance, rather than the usual confusion analysis required to prove infringement.[70]

Official marks are not examined by the Trademarks Office for registrability, except to confirm that the entities giving notice of the adoption of official marks are in fact public authorities. There is a two-part test to determine whether an entity qualifies as a public authority:

- whether the appropriate government exercises a sufficient degree of control over the activities of the entity within Canada; and
- whether the entity operates for the benefit of the public and not for any private benefit.[71]

Official marks cannot be opposed or cancelled for non-use through the summary cancellation proceedings outlined in Section 45 of the Trademarks

---

68   SC 2007, c 25.
69   RSC 1985, c T-13.
70   *Ibid* at s 9.
71   *Ontario Association of Architects v Association of Architectural Technologists of Ontario*, (2002), 19 CPR (4th) 417 (FCA).

Act. There currently is no provision for invalidation of an official mark in the Trademarks Act – although they are not entirely invulnerable, as the decision to accept and publish notice of the adoption of an official mark by the registrar may be subject to an application for judicial review to the Federal Court of Canada.[72] However, on 14 December 2018, Bill C-86[73] received royal assent, which amends the Trademarks Act in several ways, including with regard to official marks. Once these amendments come into force by order in council, the prohibitions against use and registration of marks that are the same as, or that closely resemble, published official marks will not apply if the entity that requested publication of the official mark is not a public authority or no longer exists. With these amendments, the existing scope of protection for official marks will be lessened, but those which are current and otherwise adopted by public authorities will still be protected against ambush marketing.

Not all event organisers are public authorities. For example, the marks in Canada owned by FIFA (the world governing body for association football) are not official marks. In an alleged case of ambush marketing, FIFA would have to rely on passing off or infringement under the Trademarks Act or copyright infringement under the Copyright Act.[74]

There is little Canadian case law that deals with ambush marketing. The leading case is *NHL v Pepsi*.[75] In that case, the National Hockey League (NHL) granted Coca-Cola an exclusive licence to be the soft-drink sponsor of the Stanley Cup ice hockey playoffs. Coca-Cola's competitor, Pepsi, purchased broadcast time during the playoff games and broadcast its own hockey-themed ads. Pepsi further ran a contest during the playoff games called "Diet Pepsi $4,000,000 Pro Hockey Playoff Pool", which required participants to collect Pepsi bottle caps that revealed the cities/states of teams, the number of games and the words "pro hockey playoff" – all of which Pepsi admitted was intended to refer to the NHL playoffs. Hangtags on the bottles displayed the contest name and a picture of a goaltender making a save using his glove. However, the ads also included the following disclaimer: "Diet Pepsi's $4,000,000 Pro Hockey Playoff Pool is neither associated with nor sponsored by the National Hockey League or any of its member teams or other affiliates."[76]

The NHL sued Pepsi for passing off, among other things. After dismissing survey and other evidence that was adduced by the NHL to demonstrate confusion, the trial court dismissed the passing-off claim. The court held that "not every kind of connection claimed amounts to passing off";[77] and that by

---

72   See Section 18.1 of the Federal Courts Act, which requires that an application for judicial review be commenced by a party within 30 days of first communication of the decision being attacked to the party or within such further time as the court may allow.

73   The Budget Implementation Act 2018, No 2, SC 2018, c 27.

74   RSC 1985, c C-42.

75   (1992) 42 CPR (3d) 390 (BCSC), aff'd (1995), 59 CPR (3d) 216 (BCCA).

76   *Ibid* at 397.

77   *Ibid* at 402.

acquiring the right to advertise during the broadcasts, Pepsi had created a "legitimate connection"[78] with the playoffs, even though it was not the official soft-drinks sponsor. The court further found that the disclaimer dispelled any possible misconceptions.[79] The Court of Appeal confirmed that the NHL did not have some form of exclusive quasi-property right in the popularity of the playoffs.

Organisations have found ways to prevent ambush marketing in Canada when they are not otherwise protected by specific legislation or official marks, such as by providing specific terms of use on event websites. During the 2015 Pan Am games in Toronto, the games' official website, Toronto2015.org, originally prohibited any linking to the site without written permission from the organisers. The terms were subsequently revised to prohibit "use of or embedding of content" without written consent.[80] The inclusion of such terms may minimise the risk of ambush marketing by giving the organisation the option of enforcing such terms where necessary.

6. Direct marketing

6.1 Direct marketing by post

Canada's federal privacy law, PIPEDA, requires organisations to obtain individuals' consent to use their personal information in order to send them marketing materials. To determine what type of consent is required (ie, implied, negative or opt-out, or express or opt-in), organisations must assess:

- the reasonable expectations of the individuals to whom they are sending materials; and
- the sensitivity of the personal information that has been collected.

In an interpretation bulletin entitled "Form of Consent"[81] (which is currently listed on the OPC website as being "under review", which may mean that it is subject to future change), the OPC states that negative or opt-out consent may be acceptable for secondary marketing purposes, provided that the marketer satisfies certain requirements. Secondary marketing is where the use of personal information to market is secondary to the purpose of collecting personal information in the first place. Opt-out consent may be acceptable where:

- the personal information is demonstrably non-sensitive in nature and context;

---

78   *Ibid.*
79   *Ibid* at 408.
80   See, for example, "Pan Am Games Website Drops Link Ban", Toronto.com, www.toronto.com/community-story/5731594-pan-am-games-website-drops-link-ban/.
81   www.priv.gc.ca/en/privacy-topics/privacy-laws-in-canada/the-personal-information-protection-and-electronic-documents-act-pipeda/pipeda-compliance-help/pipeda-interpretation-bulletins/interpretations_07_consent/.

- the marketer's purposes are limited, well defined and stated in a clear and understandable manner; and
- the marketer has provided individuals with a convenient procedure for opting out that should take effect immediately and prior to any further use or disclosure of the personal information.

The CMA's Code of Ethics and Standards[82] supplements PIPEDA in certain respects. The code requires direct marketers to use the CMA's Do Not Mail Service to ensure that their mailing lists do not include any consumers who have chosen to have their mailing address removed from marketing mailing lists. Also, in respect of internal do not mail lists maintained by members, the code requires the prompt addition of names and addresses of customers who make such a request and the cessation of marketing to those customers. The names and addresses must be retained on the internal do not mail list for three years.

6.2 Direct marketing by electronic message

Canada's Anti-Spam Law (CASL)[83] is a federal law designed to address, in part, unsolicited electronic messages that are commercial in nature by requiring senders to obtain consent from intended recipients. CASL is far more restrictive than PIPEDA's provisions regarding commercial messages by post. Generally speaking, senders of commercial electronic messages (CEMs) must obtain express consent in writing or orally from recipients in a prescribed format for the consent to be valid. Guidelines[84] have been issued that expressly discourage:

- the use of pre-selected boxes as a means of signifying consent to the receipt of CEMs; and
- the bundling of consent to the receipt of marketing materials with consents for other purposes.

Although there are circumstances in which consent may be implied or not required altogether, these are narrowly defined and in some cases time limited.

---

82 See Section N5, "Direct Mail", www.the-cma.org/Media/Default/Downloads/Regulatory/2020/CMA-Canadian-Marketing-Code-of-Ethics-and-Standards.pdf.

83 The full name of the legislation is "An Act to promote the efficiency and adaptability of the Canadian economy by regulating certain activities that discourage reliance on electronic means of carrying out commercial activities, and to amend the Canadian Radio-television and Telecommunications Commission Act, the Competition Act, the Personal Information Protection and Electronic Documents Act and the Telecommunications Act" (SC 2010, c 23).

84 There are two sets of regulations that accompany CASL:
   • the Electronic Commerce Protection Regulations (CRTC) (SOR/2012-36); and
   • the Electronic Commerce Protection Regulations (SOR/2013-221).
   The Canadian Radio-television and Telecommunications Commission has also published two information bulletins to help interpret the Electronic Commerce Protection Regulations noted above:
   • Compliance and Enforcement Information Bulletin 2012-548 (www.crtc.gc.ca/eng/archive/2012/2012-548.htm); and
   • Compliance and Enforcement Information Bulletin 2012-549 (www.crtc.gc.ca/eng/archive/2012/2012-549.htm).
   These information bulletins provide interpretation and guidance but are not legally binding.

For example, consent is implied where there is an existing business relationship between the sender and the individual. The definition of 'existing business relationship' limits the relationship to either two years or six months from the date of sending of the CEM, depending on the activity that created the relationship. For these reasons, and given that the onus is on the sender to prove consent from each recipient of a CEM, many businesses have concluded that the default position of obtaining express consent may be the most expedient.

Further, what CASL considers to be a CEM is quite broad in scope. CEMs are messages sent by any means of telecommunication to an electronic account, such as an email account, an instant message account, a telephone account or anything similar, such as a social media account.

CASL has broad jurisdiction: it applies to most businesses that send CEMs for commercial purposes. CASL is not merely limited to Canadian businesses, but also applies to CEMs sent from foreign businesses to Canadians.

CASL not only requires consent to send CEMs, but also establishes form and content rules for CEMs themselves, which must be followed in most instances – even in those circumstances where consent is implied. For example, the sender must disclose its full name and mailing address, as well as a telephone number, email address or website address. CEMs must also include a working unsubscribe mechanism that can be "readily performed" at no cost and that removes the recipient's address from lists within 10 days. This means that it must be "accessed without difficulty or delay, and should be simple, quick and easy for the consumer to use".

CASL also contains other provisions. For example, there are rules on the alteration of transmission data in electronic messages and the installation of a computer program on another person's computer, both in the course of a commercial activity.

Three federal agencies are responsible for the enforcement of CASL:

- the Canadian Radio-television and Telecommunications Commission (CRTC), which is responsible for enforcing the consent and form and content rules under CASL;
- the Competition Bureau, which is responsible for enforcing the CASL provisions relating to false or misleading representations and deceptive marketing practices in the electronic marketplace; and
- the OPC, which is responsible for enforcing violations related to harvesting of electronic addresses and the collection of personal information through spyware and similar means.[85]

---

85   The OPC's responsibilities under CASL are set out in www.priv.gc.ca/en/privacy-topics/privacy-laws-in-canada/the-personal-information-protection-and-electronic-documents-act-pipeda/r_o_p/canadas-anti-spam-legislation/casl_faqs_2014/.

The CRTC has been the most active regulator in this area and typically enforces by:

- issuing notices of violations, setting out the alleged violations or administrative monetary penalties (AMPs); or
- negotiating formal undertakings, which can include payment of AMPs and corrective measures.

The AMPs for violating CASL range up to a maximum of C\$1 million per violation by an individual and up to a maximum of C\$10 million per violation by a corporation.[86] CASL lists the factors to be considered when determining the amount of the AMP, which include:

- the nature and scope of the violation;
- the history of the offending party; and
- the financial benefits obtained as a result of the violation.[87]

Penalties have ranged from tens to hundreds of thousands of dollars.

To facilitate investigations of violations of CASL, the federal government created the Spam Reporting Centre, which is an online system to report violations of CASL. The Spam Reporting Centre receives approximately 5,000 complaints per week.[88]

Since CASL came into force on 1 July 2014, its provisions have been swiftly implemented, with action being taken against reputable businesses for non-compliance immediately after its entry into force. While the enforcement agencies state that most enforcement is focused on traditional spam, such actions have generally gone unreported, while instances of aggressive action against reputable businesses have been highly publicised. Action has been taken not only against failure to obtain express consent (which was the focus of compliance efforts), but also against failure to comply with more nuanced aspects of the law, such as the form and content rules for CEMs, including failure to have a conspicuous and effective unsubscribe mechanism. Action has also been taken against CEMs containing false and misleading representations. Notably, offenders have faced penalties, not warnings, even where immediate steps were taken to fully comply with CASL.

The investigations under CASL to date highlight the importance of having demonstrable proof that the sender has obtained consent to send a CEM, as well as the risks of not having a workable unsubscribe mechanism that is clearly and prominently presented to recipients. It is also important to ensure that any third-party vendors are CASL compliant; and it may be prudent for any service

---

86   SC 2010, c 23 at s 20(4).
87   SC 2010, c 23 at s 20(3).
88   See "Report Spam", www.fightspam.gc.ca/eic/site/030.nsf/frm-eng/MMCN-9EZV6S.

contract to include an indemnity for failure to comply, together with robust audit and monitoring rights. Finally, in addition to ensuring that CEMs contain the prescribed information, caution should be exercised to ensure that the sender and subject lines and content are not false and misleading.

6.3 Direct marketing by telephone

The CRTC administers a set of rules specifically for telemarketers.[89] For example, telemarketers must follow the Unsolicited Telecommunication Rules, which include an obligation to register and subscribe to Canada's national Do Not Call List, and ensure that calls and faxes are not sent to those on that list. Telemarketers are also obliged to maintain and adhere to their own internal 'do not call' list. The CMA's Code of Ethics and Standards[90] also provides guidelines for direct marketing by telephone. Some of the requirements mandated by the code include the following:

- Calls must take place between the hours of 9:00am and 9:30pm on weekdays and between 10:00am and 6:00pm on weekends;
- Marketers must add phone numbers to their internal do not call list within 14 days of a request from a consumer to do so;
- Marketers must not engage in random or sequential dialling; and
- Marketers can only contact a consumer once a month at most for the same product or service, unless they have received consent to contact the consumer more frequently.

7. Product placement

There is no law in Canada that deals specifically with paid product placement or embedded marketing in audio-visual works such as movies, television shows and computer games. Furthermore, to date, the Canadian courts have not heard any cases on the issue of unauthorised product placement.

From a self-regulatory standpoint, 16 Canadian food companies have committed to a voluntary initiative – the Canadian Children's Food and Beverage Advertising Initiative[91] – which is intended to promote healthy dietary choices for children under 13. With respect to product placement, these companies have committed to the following:

- to incorporate only products that represent healthy dietary choices or include healthy lifestyle messages in interactive games primarily directed at children under 12 years of age; and
- not to pay for or actively seek to place food and beverage products in programmes or editorial content in any medium primarily directed at children.

---

89   https://crtc.gc.ca/eng/phone/telemarketing/reg.htm.
90   www.the-cma.org/regulatory/code-of-ethics.
91   https://adstandards.ca/wp-content/uploads/2018/11/CCFBAI_EN-Nov-2018.pdf.

The CMA's Code of Ethics and Standards[92] states that product placement within entertainment programming is acceptable; but product placement could nonetheless contravene other advertising and marketing laws. For example, industry-specific legislation limits the placement of alcohol and tobacco in ads, particularly if the ad could be seen by young people. Product placement that could mislead consumers about a product's attributes is also subject to the Competition Act's prohibition against false and misleading advertising.[93]

8. Native advertising and social media influencers

Native advertising and social media influencers are subject to the Competition Act and to industry guidelines developed by agencies such as Ad Standards and the Better Business Bureau (BBB).

A number of provisions in the Competition Act apply to native advertising and social influencers. As set out above, under the deceptive marketing provisions of the Competition Act, a promotional representation to the public that is false or misleading in a material respect or that is not substantiated with adequate and proper testing constitutes reviewable conduct. The Competition Bureau has said plainly that it is misleading if influencers do not make it clear that their content is advertising; and further that this is "materially misleading", given that consumers rely on influencers' opinions to make purchasing decisions.

The Competition Bureau has released *Influencer Marketing and the Competition Act*[94] and *The Deceptive Marketing Practices Digest – Volume 4: Influencer Marketing*.[95] These documents set out recommendations for both influencers and the businesses with which they work.

Regarding influencers, the documents state that influencers must disclose all "material connections" they have with the business, product or service they are promoting. Connections are defined as 'material' if they have the potential to affect how consumers evaluate an influencer's independence from a brand, and may arise if the influencer has:

- received payment in money or commissions;
- received free products or services;
- received discounts;
- received free trips or tickets to events; or
- a personal or family relationship with the brand.

If a material connection exists, the Competition Bureau advises influencers to ensure that:

---

92   www.the-cma.org/Media/Default/Downloads/Regulatory/2020/CMA-Canadian-Marketing-Code-of-Ethics-and-Standards.pdf.
93   *Ibid.*
94   www.competitionbureau.gc.ca/eic/site/cb-bc.nsf/eng/04512.html.
95   www.competitionbureau.gc.ca/eic/site/cb-bc.nsf/eng/04372.html#sec01.

- disclosures are visible, are written in clear and unambiguous language, and are contextually appropriate; and
- reviews and testimonials are based on actual experience.

As for the businesses that engage social influencers, the Competition Bureau has provided the following checklist:

- Ensure that influencers clearly disclose material connections;
- Disclose material connections in each post;
- Ensure that the representations are not false or misleading; and
- Verify that influencers are not making performance claims on businesses' behalf, unless based on adequate and proper testing.

There is also a specific provision in the Competition Act that prohibits the unauthorised use of tests and testimonials, and the mischaracterisation of such tests and testimonials.[96]

The Competition Bureau has demonstrated that it will enforce against social media posts where material connections are not disclosed, with examples of enforcement activity in October 2015[97] and December 2019.[98]

In terms of self-regulation of the advertising industry, Clause 7 of the Ad Standards' Code states: "Testimonials, endorsements or other representations of opinion or preference, must reflect the genuine, reasonably current opinion of the individual(s), group or organization making such representations, and must be based upon adequate information about or experience with the identified product or service and must not otherwise be deceptive."[99]

---

96   RSC 1985, c C-34; Section 74.02 states:
      A person engages in reviewable conduct who, for the purpose of promoting, directly or indirectly, the supply or use of any product, or for the purpose of promoting, directly or indirectly, any business interest, makes a representation to the public that a test has been made as to the performance, efficacy or length of life of a product by any person, or publishes a testimonial with respect to a product, unless the person making the representation or publishing the testimonial can establish that
      (a) such a representation or testimonial was previously made or published by the person by whom the test was made or the testimonial was given, or
      (b) such a representation or testimonial was, before being made or published, approved and permission to make or publish it was given in writing by the person by whom the test was made or the testimonial was given, and the representation or testimonial accords with the representation or testimonial previously made, published or approved.

97   In October 2015, the Competition Bureau reached a consent agreement with Bell Canada, one of Canada's largest communication companies, after encouraging employees to post positive reviews about Bell and Virgin mobile apps in various app stores without disclosing that they worked for Bell. Although Bell removed the reviews and took steps to ensure it would not happen again, the Competition Bureau took issue with the reviews while they were posted because they gave the impression of being made by independent and impartial consumers. Bell Canada agreed to pay C$1.25 million. See www.competitionbureau.gc.ca/eic/site/cb-bc.nsf/eng/03992.html.

98   In a 19 December 2019 news release, the Competition Bureau announced it had sent warning letters to over 100 brand owners and marketing agencies involved in influencer marketing. The letters urged these entities to review their marketing practices to ensure they comply with the Competition Act by clearly disclosing any material connection between the influencer and the business, product or service being promoted. See www.canada.ca/en/competition-bureau/news/2019/12/influencer-marketing-businesses-and-influencers-must-be-transparent-when-advertising-on-social-media.html.

99   Canadian Code of Advertising Standards, Clause 7.

Ad Standards has published Interpretation Guideline #5[100] to accompany Clause 7. This states that if a "material connection"[101] exists between an influencer and an entity providing a product or service, the fact and the nature of the material connection must be clearly and prominently disclosed in close proximity to the representation about the product or service.

An exception exists under the guideline where the material connection is one that a consumer would reasonably expect to exist, such as a television ad in which a celebrity publicly endorses a product or service.

Ad Standards, in collaboration with an industry panel of influencer marketing companies, has issued Influencer Marketing Disclosure Guidelines[102] to educate and provide a framework for making proper disclosures where material connections exist. The guidelines include useful channel and platform-specific disclosure guidelines for YouTube, Instagram, Snapchat, Twitter and blog posts.

The BBB's Code of Advertising[103] also sets out native advertising guidelines, including suggested language to ensure that consumers are aware when a message has been paid for. The BBB suggests that the promotion be labelled clearly and conspicuously with language such as 'paid ad', 'paid advertisement' or 'sponsored advertising content'. If an advertiser promotes content other than its own product or service, the BBB suggests including language such as 'sponsored by X' or 'brought to you by X', to avoid any misleading impression.

9. Industry-specific regulation

9.1 Gambling

The gambling laws in Canada are complex. The legality of gambling advertising in Canada is equally complex and a detailed review is necessarily beyond the scope of this chapter. The Criminal Code[104] makes certain gambling activities illegal in Canada – examples include:

- running a gaming/betting house (Section 201);
- betting and bookmaking (Section 202);
- placing bets on behalf of others (Section 203); and
- a number of other gaming activities (Section 206).

Included within the illegal acts under these sections is the advertisement of

---

100 https://adstandards.ca/interpretation-guidelines/.
101 The Interpretation Guideline defines 'material connection' as "any connection ... that may affect the weight or credibility of the representation", including "benefits and incentives, such as monetary or other compensation, free products with or without any conditions attached, discounts, gifts, contest entries, and any employment relationship".
102 https://adstandards.ca/wp-content/uploads/Ad-Standards-Influencer-Marketing-Steering-Committee-Disclosure-Guidelines_FALL2020_EN.pdf.
103 www.bbb.org/code-of-advertising.
104 RSC 1985, c C-46.

these illegal activities. However, some gambling is permitted; and what constitutes legal gambling is set out as an exception in the Criminal Code or has been sanctioned under the authority of each province and territory.

The gambling laws of each province are different. This means that different games and lottery schemes are permitted or prohibited, depending on the province. For example, casinos may be owned and operated by a provincial government, operated by private companies under contract with provincial gaming authorities or a combination of the two; and they may be for charitable or commercial purposes, depending on the province. Adding to the complexity is the fact that different operational rules may apply to casinos run by First Nations groups (which collectively refers to the Aboriginal peoples in Canada, other than the Inuit and Métis). There are currently more than 630 recognised First Nations governments or bands across Canada.

As set out in section 1.2(b), thinkTV reviews broadcast advertising for all of its members according to its own set of guidelines. In connection with gambling advertising, thinkTV requires an indemnity letter from the advertiser stating that the gambling activity and the broadcast of the ad comply with all applicable laws in the province in which the ad is to be aired. In some circumstances, thinkTV may also require the advertiser to provide a legal opinion from its lawyer.

The advertisement of 'for fun' gaming websites, rather than those for gaming or betting, is treated differently by thinkTV. For these types of services, thinkTV requires that:

- the ad comply with the section of its guidelines[105] on "Gambling Advertising"; and
- the advertiser provide an "undertaking letter" stating, among other things, that:
  - the site is for amusement only, with no opportunity to gamble for real money or money's worth;
  - there are no links to illegal sites; and
  - there will be no contact made with users to promote any illegal sites.

thinkTV also requires a Canadian legal opinion indicating "without material qualification" that the ad complies with all applicable laws.

9.2 Alcohol

Alcohol advertising is regulated both federally and provincially. Federally, the Broadcasting Act[106] enables the Radio Regulations[107] and the Television

---

105   https://thinktv.ca/wp-content/uploads/2018/05/thinktv_clearance_Telecaster_GUIDELINES.pdf.
106   SC 1991, c 11.
107   SOR/86-982.

Broadcasting Regulations[108] to regulate broadcast alcohol advertising. As per the regulations, broadcasters must adhere to the CRTC's Code for Broadcast Advertising of Alcoholic Beverages.[109] Some provinces have adopted the CRTC code.

The provisions in both the federal and provincial laws can be loosely organised under four general headings, as set out below, together with a sample of the prohibitions under each:

- Portrayal of use: Ads cannot:
    - show use or consumption, or immoderate drinking;
    - induce irresponsible drinking; or
    - claim that there are healthful, nutritive, dietary, curative, sedative or stimulating qualities to alcohol.
- Lifestyle: Ads cannot show that drinking is important for enjoying any activity, achieving social or business success, improving athletic prowess or sexual opportunity, having fun, achieving a goal or resolving a problem.
- Safety: Ads cannot show:
    - alcohol with a motor vehicle or any vehicle in motion; or
    - characters with alcohol before, in anticipation of, or involving activities demanding care, skill, attention or physical danger.
- Minors: Ads cannot refer, appeal or be directed to minors (ie, those under the legal drinking age, which is 18 or 19, depending on the province or territory). For example, ads cannot show scenes with persons who may be mistaken for minors, or use characters or personalities who appeal to minors.

Broadcasters must adhere to the CRTC code as a condition of maintaining their broadcast licence. Accordingly, at broadcasters' request, Ad Standards will review broadcast advertising for compliance with the CRTC code and issue a clearance number for compliant broadcast ads. Ad Standards also reviews broadcast, print and out-of-home advertising for compliance with the Liquor Advertising Guidelines[110] of the Alcohol and Gaming Commission of Ontario; however, such review is not mandatory. British Columbia, Nova Scotia and Quebec have mandatory pre-clearance requirements. For British Columbia, Ad Standards clears broadcast, print and out-of-home advertising for compliance with the CRTC code. Alcohol advertising in Nova Scotia is reviewed by the Nova Scotia Liquor Corporation. In Quebec, the *Régie des alcools, des courses et des jeux* reviews advertising.

---

108   SOR/87-49.
109   www.crtc.gc.ca/eng/television/publicit/codesalco.htm.
110   www.agco.ca/alcohol/guides/liquor-advertising-guidelines-liquor-sales-licensees-and-manufacturers.

Under the Broadcasting Act, if a broadcaster fails to comply with the regulations or the CRTC code, individuals can face a fine of up to C$25,000 and a corporation can face a fine of up to C$250,000 for a first offence.[111] As alcohol beverages fall within the definition of a 'food' under Canada's Food and Drugs Act[112] and Food and Drug Regulations,[113] any 'food-type' claims (eg, nutrient content claims) must comply with these laws.

9.3 Pharmaceuticals

Pharmaceutical advertising is federally regulated by the Food and Drugs Act[114] and the Food and Drug Regulations[115] (the Controlled Drugs and Substances Act[116] concerns illicit drugs). The legislation is supplemented by numerous guidelines and policy statements published by Health Canada, as well as by codes of industry associations such as:

- the Pharmaceutical Advertising Advisory Board (PAAB) Code of Advertising Acceptance;[117]
- Ad Standards' Canadian Code of Advertising;[118]
- Ad Standards' Guidelines for Consumer Advertising of Health Products;[119]
- Innovative Medicines Canada's Code of Ethical Practices;[120]
- Consumer Health Products Canada's Code of Marketing Practices;[121] and
- the Canadian Generic Pharmaceutical Association's Code of Conduct.[122]

The main prohibition in the Food and Drugs Act is Section 9(1), which states: "No person shall label, package, treat, process, sell or advertise any drug in a manner that is false, misleading or deceptive or is likely to create an erroneous impression regarding its character, value, quantity, composition, merit or safety."

There are different restrictions on advertising directed to the general public. Section 3(1) of the Food and Drugs Act prohibits the advertisement of any food, drug, cosmetic or device to the general public as a treatment, preventative or cure for any of the diseases, disorders or abnormal physical states referred to in Schedule A.1 to the act.[123] Schedule A.1 includes asthma, cancer, diabetes, depression and sexually transmitted diseases.

---

111   SC 1991, c 11 at s 34.2.
112   RSC 1985, c F-27.
113   CRC, c 870.
114   RSC 1985, c F-27.
115   CRC, c 870.
116   SC 1996, c 19.
117   www.paab.ca.
118   https://adstandards.ca/code/.
119   www.adstandards.ca/wp-content/uploads/2020/02/Consumer-Advertising-Guidelines-for-Marketed-Health-Products-2020.pdf.
120   http://innovativemedicines.ca/wp-content/uploads/2019/12/IMC-EthicalPractices-2020-web-lowres-EN.pdf.
121   www.chpcanada.ca/sites/default/files/fil_158.pdf.
122   https://canadiangenerics.ca/about-us/code-of-conduct/.
123   RSC 1985, c F-27, s 3(1).

The Food and Drug Regulations generally prohibit the advertisement of prescription drugs to the general public, with the exception of advertising that makes representations only with respect to the name, price and quantity of the drug,[124] and only after Health Canada has authorised the drug for sale.[125] The restriction applies to 'advertising'; non-promotional information about health products, including pharmaceuticals, can be communicated directly to consumers.[126]

If an ad is found to contravene the Food and Drugs Act or the Food and Drug Regulations, Health Canada will determine the health risk level of the violation and take commensurate action, such as:

- the issue of a warning letter;
- a requirement to remove the ad; or
- prosecution where necessary.

Prosecution can result in imprisonment or a fine of up to C$5 million.[127]

Health Canada encourages advertisers of pharmaceuticals to have all ads pre-cleared by one of the independent advertising pre-clearance systems.[128] Although there are a number of independent advertising pre-clearance agencies, the two main ones are PAAB and Ad Standards.

Advertising to healthcare providers can be reviewed and pre-cleared by PAAB, and consumer-directed ads can be reviewed and pre-cleared by Ad Standards. Both agencies also review communications to provide guidance on whether they constitute 'advertising' or non-promotional information, which is not subject to the same restrictions.

Ad Standards pre-clears consumer-directed advertising for non-prescription drugs (as well as medical devices, vaccines and natural health products). Ad Standards' Guidelines for Consumer Advertising of Health Products[129] were developed jointly by Health Canada and Ad Standards, and apply to advertising in all Canadian media, including social media. The guidelines provide a

---

124   CRC, c 870, s C.01.027 (1).
125   CRC, c 870, s C.08.002(1).
126   Health Canada has published guidelines to assist manufacturers determine whether communications constitute 'advertising' or non-promotional information. The guidelines are called "The Distinction Between Advertising and Other Activities" and are available at www.canada.ca/en/health-canada/ services/drugs-health-products/regulatory-requirements-advertising/policies-guidance-documents/ policy-distinction-between-advertising-activities.html. This document is in the process of being updated by a draft called "The Distinction Between Promotional and Non-promotional Messages and Other Activities for Health Products", which was presented for public consultation. The consultation period closed on 3 September 2019, and thus a new guidance document should be issued soon. The draft is available at www.canada.ca/en/health-canada/programs/consultation-guidance-promotional-non-promotional-messages-activities-health-products.html.
127   RSC 1985, c F-27, s 31.2.
128   C.01.014.21 of the Food and Drug Regulations permits Health Canada to impose terms and conditions on Class B opioids. Under this section, there have been consultations on the mandatory pre-clearance of opioid advertising to healthcare professions.
129   https://adstandards.ca/wp-content/uploads/2020/02/Consumer-Advertising-Guidelines-for-Marketed-Health-Products-2020.pdf.

framework to help manufacturers of health products comply with the Food and Drugs Act and the Food and Drug Regulations. One of the main principles in the guidelines is that advertising should be consistent with the terms of the market authorisation granted by Health Canada. The terms of market authorisation set out the claims that have been authorised by Health Canada; and although claims may be paraphrased, they cannot exceed the parameters of the marketing authorisation, either directly or indirectly. The guidelines also set out principles for comparative advertising of therapeutic and non-therapeutic claims. For example, therapeutic comparisons for products must:

- have an authorised common indication for use;
- have clinical relevance in humans;
- be substantiated by conclusive and relevant data; and
- not attack the compared product in an "unreasonable manner".

Non-therapeutic comparisons must be fair and factual comparisons of similar products, and should be based on valid, reliable, up-to-date data.

9.4 Financial products and services

In addition to the criminal and civil provisions in the Competition Act dealing with deceptive marketing practices, there are federal and provincial laws and regulations that financial institutions must follow, as well as various voluntary codes of conduct. The applicable set of rules depends on the financial institution and the financial products and services being advertised – whether for credit cards, loans, mortgages, lines of credit, consumer debit card services, pre-paid products or insurance products.

To illustrate, the federal Bank Act[130] and the Cost of Borrowing (Banks) Regulations[131] have provisions regarding the advertisement of loans for a fixed amount, lines of credit, credit cards and interest-free periods. The disclosure requirements are intended to make it easier for consumers to compare the cost of borrowing among financial institutions. For example, if an ad for a credit card makes a representation about the annual interest rate, the amount of any payment or the amount of any non-interest charge, then the ad must also disclose "at least as prominently" and "in the same manner, whether visually or aurally or both" what the annual interest rate is at the date of the ad and any "initial or periodic" non-interest charges, including any annual or monthly fees.[132] There are also rules regarding the advertisement of 'interest-free' periods, such as the mandatory disclosure of whether interest will accrue during the period and what, if any, other conditions apply to the forgiving of interest for

---

130   SC 1991, c 46.
131   SOR/2001-101.
132   SOR/2001-101, s 21.

that period.[133] If a financial institution contravenes a provision in the Bank Act or its regulations, it can be ordered to comply and may face an additional fine of up to C$1 million.[134]

The Financial Consumer Agency of Canada (FCAC) monitors federally regulated financial entities for compliance with consumer protection measures and maintains a number of voluntary codes, including the Code of Conduct for the Credit and Debit Card Industry[135] in Canada. As an example of its enforcement activities, in the early 2000s the FCAC investigated five banks in connection with ads promoting "rates as low as" or "price-to-risk" interest rates. This resulted in various findings – specifically, that each bank had violated the Cost of Borrowing (Bank) Regulations and was required to take corrective action, including amending the marketing material. The five banks involved in the investigation faced various sanctions, ranging from as little as no penalty to as large as a fine of C$30,000. More recently, the FCAC directed a trust and loan company to enter into a compliance agreement in 2010 after an individual complained that its ad for a savings product did not disclose how interest was calculated – a violation of both the Trust and Loan Companies Act[136] and the Disclosure of Interest (Trust and Loan Companies) Regulations.[137]

Advertisers are also subject to federal legislation that goes beyond the scope of financial products and services. For example, it is not uncommon for advertisers of financial products and services to want to display paper and coin currency. While not unworkable, there are provisions to be mindful of:

- The Criminal Code makes it an offence to reproduce banknotes or anything that too closely resembles them; and
- The Copyright Act gives the Royal Canadian Mint copyright in coins and the Bank of Canada copyright in banknotes.

9.5   Food

Food advertising is principally regulated by the Food and Drugs Act[138] and the Food and Drug Regulations;[139] however, certain provisions in the Safe Food for Canadians Act[140] and the Safe Food for Canadians Regulations[141] also apply to advertising. These laws are supplemented by guidelines designed to help food manufacturers comply with the legislation.

The main prohibition related to the advertising of food in the Food and

---

133   SOR/2001-101, s 22.
134   SC 1991, c 46, s 985.
135   www.canada.ca/en/financial-consumer-agency/services/industry/laws-regulations/credit-debit-code-conduct.html.
136   SC 1991, c 45.
137   SOR/92-322; FCAC Decision #111, www.canada.ca/en/financial-consumer-agency/services/industry/commissioner-decisions/decision-111.html.
138   RSC 1985, c F-27.
139   CRC, c 870.
140   SC 2012, c 24.
141   SOR/2018-108.

Drugs Act is found in Section 5(1): "No person shall label, package, treat, process, sell or advertise any food in a manner that is false, misleading or deceptive or is likely to create an erroneous impression regarding its character, value, quantity, composition, merit or safety."[142]

Section 5(2) states that any food that is not packaged or labelled according to the Food and Drug Regulations is deemed to be contrary to Section 5(1).[143]

A similar prohibition to the above is found in the Safe Food for Canadians Act.[144]

Additionally, Section 3(1) of the Food and Drugs Act prohibits the advertisement of any food (as well as any drug, cosmetic or device) to the general public as a treatment, preventative or cure for any of the diseases, disorders or abnormal physical states referred to in Schedule A.1 of the act, unless a health claim is specifically provided for in the Food and Drug Regulations.[145]

Health Canada is the government agency responsible for making policy and legislative changes with respect to food; while the Canadian Food Inspection Agency (CFIA) enforces the federal legislation relating to food. To assist companies with food labelling and advertising, Health Canada and the CFIA have created the Industry Labelling Tool,[146] which explains and illustrates how to interpret the legislation. This tool, together with the Food and Drug Regulations, sets out permitted claims with respect to food ads. The tool consolidates the regulations from across the pertinent legislation, setting out, for example:

- rules about composition claims and the use of words commonly associated with foods, such as 'true', 'pure', 'concentrated' and 'vegan';[147]
- an exhaustive list of nutrient content claims – that is, claims about the presence or absence of a nutrient, vitamin or mineral in a food. Both the compositional requirements to make the claim and the wording of the claim itself are prescribed by the Food and Drug Regulations (eg, 'low in cholesterol' and 'an excellent source of protein');[148]
- an exhaustive list of comparative claims that compare the nutritional

---

142   RSC 1985, c F-27, s 5(1).
143   *Ibid*, s 5(2).
144   SC 2012, c 24, s 6, which states:
       (1) It is prohibited for a person to manufacture, prepare, package, label, sell, import or advertise a food commodity in a manner that is false, misleading or deceptive or is likely to create an erroneous impression regarding its character, quality, value, quantity, composition, merit, safety or origin or the method of its manufacture or preparation.
       (2) A food commodity that is labelled or packaged in contravention of a provision of the regulations is considered, for the purposes of this section, to be labelled or packaged in contravention of subsection (1).
       (3) A food commodity that is advertised in contravention of a provision of the regulations is considered, for the purposes of this section, to be advertised in contravention of subsection (1).
145   RSC 1985, c F-27, s 3(1).
146   "Food Labelling for Industry", www.inspection.gc.ca/food-label-requirements/labelling/industry/eng/ 1383607266489/1383607344939.
147   "Food composition and quality claims", www.inspection.gc.ca/food-label-requirements/labelling/ industry/composition-and-quality-claims/eng/1391025998183/1391026062752?chap=2.
148   "Specific nutrient content claim requirements", www.inspection.gc.ca/food-label-requirements/ labelling/industry/nutrient-content/specific-claim-requirements/eng/1389907770176/ 1389907817577 ?chap=13.

properties of two or more foods. Both the compositional requirements and the information that must be disclosed are prescribed by the Food and Drug Regulations;[149]

- rules about claims pertaining to the place of origin of the food product. A claim that food is a 'Product of Canada' can be made only if virtually all major ingredients, processing and labour used to make the food are Canadian. A claim that food is 'Made in Canada' with a qualifying statement is permitted if the last substantial transformation of the product occurred in Canada ("Made in Canada from domestic and imported ingredients");[150]

- rules about 'function claims', meaning claims relating to the specific beneficial effects that food has on the normal functions or biological activities of the body. For example, the claim that the "consumption of 1 cup of green tea helps to protect blood lipids from oxidation" is an acceptable claim;[151] and

- an exhaustive list of the disease-reduction claims that are permitted as an exception to Section 3(1) of the Food and Drugs Act. These are claims that have been approved by Health Canada following a review of scientific evidence that has established a relationship between certain elements of healthy diets and reduced risk of developing certain diseases. The claim links a food to reducing the risk of developing a diet-related disease or condition (eg, osteoporosis, cancer or hypertension) in the context of total diet. The food product must meet specific compositional requirements to meet the claim at issue. To illustrate, one of the permitted claims links sodium and hypertension: "A healthy diet containing foods high in potassium and low in sodium may reduce the risk of high blood pressure, a risk factor for stroke and heart disease. [Product name] is low in sodium."[152]

Under the Food and Drugs Act and the Safe Food for Canadians Act, the CFIA is given broad investigatory powers, which include the power to seize products and to impose fines and imprisonment. There are a range of penalties for contravention of the Safe Food for Canadians Act, including:

- on conviction on indictment, a fine of up to C$5 million or imprisonment for a term of not more than two years, or both;

---

149 "Comparative Nutrient Content Claims", www.inspection.gc.ca/food-label-requirements/labelling/industry/nutrient-content/comparative-claims/eng/1389907986226/1389908028722.

150 "Origin claims on food labels", www.inspection.gc.ca/food-label-requirements/labelling/industry/origin-claims-on-food-labels/eng/1393622222140/1393622515592?chap=5.

151 "Acceptable Function Claims Table", www.inspection.gc.ca/food-label-requirements/labelling/industry/health-claims-on-food-labels/eng/1392834838383/1392834887794?chap=8#s13c8.

152 "Acceptable disease risk reduction claims and therapeutic claims", www.inspection.gc.ca/food-label-requirements/labelling/industry/health-claims-on-food-labels/eng/1392834838383/1392834887794?chap=0#c7.

- on summary conviction, a fine of up to C$250,000 or imprisonment for a term of not more than six months or both; and
- for a subsequent offence, a fine of up to C$500,000 or imprisonment for a term of not more than 18 months, or both.[153]

Broadcast advertising of food must be pre-cleared for compliance with federal law. The federal government has delegated its pre-clearance function to the Food and Beverage Clearance Section of Ad Standards. Canadian broadcasters require a clearance number from Ad Standards prior to broadcasting. There is no mandatory pre-clearance for printed or online advertising.

9.6 Tobacco

Tobacco and vaping products are federally regulated by the Tobacco and Vaping Products Act[154] and its various regulations, including the Promotion of Tobacco Products and Accessories Regulations (Prohibited Terms).[155] Together, they provide a legal framework to address the public health risks associated with 'tobacco products'[156] and 'vaping products'.[157] The act prohibits the promotion of these products, with limited exceptions. Provincial laws and regulations impose additional restrictions.

Under the Tobacco and Vaping Products Act, the promotion[158] of tobacco products and tobacco-related brand elements,[159] including by way of packaging, is prohibited. In addition to this broad prohibition, the act sets out further specific prohibitions, including the promotion of tobacco products:

- in a manner that is false, misleading or deceptive with respect to the

---

153   See RSC 1985, c F-27, s 31.2.
154   SC 1997, c 13.
155   SOR/2011-178.
156   "[T]obacco product means a product made in whole or in part of tobacco, including tobacco leaves. It includes papers, tubes and filters intended for use with that product, a device, other than a water pipe, that is necessary for the use of that product and the parts that may be used with the device." See SC 1997, c 13, s 2.
157   [V]aping product means
      (a) a device that produces emissions in the form of an aerosol and is intended to be brought to the mouth for inhalation of the aerosol;
      (b) a device that is designated to be a vaping product by the regulations;
      (c) a part that may be used with those devices; and
      (d) a substance or mixture of substances, whether or not it contains nicotine, that is intended for use with those devices to produce emissions.
      It does not include devices and substances or mixtures of substances that are excluded by the regulations, cannabis, as defined in subsection 2(1) of the Cannabis Act, cannabis accessories, as defined in that subsection, tobacco products or their accessories.
      See SC 1997, c 13, s 2.
158   'Promotion' is broadly defined to mean "a representation about a product or service by any means, whether directly or indirectly, including any communication of information about a product or service and its price and distribution, that is likely to influence and shape attitudes, beliefs and behaviours about the product or service". See SC 1997, c 13, s 18(1).
159   "'[B]rand element includes a brand name, trademark, trade-name, distinguishing guise, logo, graphic arrangement, design or slogan that is reasonably associated with, or that evokes, a product, a service or a brand of product or service, but does not include a colour". See SC 1997, c 13, s 2.

characteristics, health effects or health hazards of the tobacco product or its emissions (Section 20(1));

- in a manner that could cause a person to believe that the product or its emissions are less harmful than other tobacco products or their emissions (Section 20.1);
- through a testimonial or endorsement (Section 21(1));
- by the depiction of a person, character or animal, whether real or fictional (Section 21(2);
- through sponsorship – that is, in a manner that is likely to create an association between the brand element or the name and a person, entity, event, activity or permanent facility (Section 24(1));
- through the display of a brand element or the name of a tobacco product manufacturer on a facility used for sports or cultural events or activities (Section 25); and
- through sales incentives (eg, gift with purchase, giveaways) (Section 29).

The Tobacco and Vaping Products Act also prohibits the promotion of a tobacco product by means of advertising that:

- depicts, in whole or in part, a tobacco product, its packaging or a tobacco product-related brand element; or
- evokes a tobacco product or a tobacco product-related brand element.

There is a limited exception to this general prohibition for 'information advertising'[160] and 'brand-preference advertising':[161]

- in publications that are mailed directly to a named adult (those at least 18 years of age); or
- displayed on a sign where young persons (defined as persons under 18) are not legally permitted.[162]

'Lifestyle advertising'[163] – or advertising for which there are reasonable grounds to believe that it might appeal to young persons – is expressly prohibited from this limited exception for advertising.

In addition to the above forms of advertising, promotion is permitted through merchandising, subject to restrictions (Sections 26 to 28).

---

160   [I]nformation advertising *means advertising that provides factual information to the consumer about*
      (a) a product and its characteristics; or
      (b) the availability or price of a product or brand of product.
      See SC 1997, c 13, s 22 (4).
161   "[B]rand-preference advertising means advertising that promotes a tobacco product by means of its brand characteristics". See SC 1997, c 13, s 22(4).
162   SC 1997, c 13, s 22(2).
163   "[L]ifestyle advertising means advertising that associates a product with, or evokes a positive or negative emotion about or image of, a way of life such as one that includes glamour, recreation, excitement, vitality, risk or daring". See SC 1997, c 13, s 2.

9.7   E-cigarettes

The promotion of vaping products is also regulated by the Tobacco and Vaping Products Act,[164] as well as the recently enacted Vaping Products Promotion Regulations.[165] Some provincial laws and regulations impose further restrictions on the promotion of vaping products. For example, under the Tobacco and Vaping Products Act and its regulations, the definition of a 'vaping product'[166] expressly excludes 'cannabis' and 'cannabis accessories', as defined under the Cannabis Act;[167] however, certain provinces have implemented regulations on the sale of cannabis vaping devices and products.

The Tobacco and Vaping Products Act contains similar general and specification prohibitions against the promotion of vaping products to those on tobacco products (Division 2). Some additional prohibitions are specific to vaping products – for example, the Tobacco and Vaping Products Act prohibits:

- promotions relating to certain compositions (Sections 30.47 and 30.48);
- the promotion of vaping products in a manner that could cause a person to believe that health benefits may be derived from the use of the product or from its emissions (Section 30.43); and
- promotions if there are reasonable grounds to believe that the promotion could discourage tobacco cessation or encourage the resumed use of tobacco products (Section 30.44).

Advertising is permitted provided that it conveys, in the prescribed form and manner, the information required by the regulations about:

- the product and its emissions; and
- the health hazards and health effects arising from the use of the product and from its emissions (Section 30.7).

Although the Tobacco and Vaping Products Act generally prohibits the promotion of vaping products, and advertising has been restricted since its enactment, increased advertising had previously been observed on social media and other digital platforms. Consequently, on 7 August 2020, the Vaping Products Promotion Regulations[168] came into force to further restrict the promotion of vaping products (with certain provisions relating to point-of-sale display prohibitions in force as of 6 September 2020). Subject to certain limited exceptions, these regulations specifically prohibit the promotion of vaping products in a way that could be seen or heard by young persons, including the display of vaping products at the point of sale in a manner that allows them to

---

164   SC 1997, c 13, as amended.
165   SOR/2020-143.
166   SC 1997, c 13, s 2.
167   SC 2018, c 16.
168   SOR/2020-143.

be seen by young persons.[169] These regulations also prescribe the health warnings about vaping product emissions and harms.[170]

Vaping products are further federally regulated by the Canada Consumer Product Safety Act[171] and the Food and Drugs Act.[172] Vaping products that make a health claim – such as a product used to help smokers quit – are subject to the Food and Drugs Act and must receive authorisation from Health Canada before they can be advertised, sold in Canada or commercially imported. However, these vaping health products – categorised as prescription drugs, non-prescription drugs, natural health products or medical devices – are excluded from the application of the Tobacco and Vaping Products Act. Vaping products that do not make health claims are subject to the Canada Consumer Product Safety Act, which:

- prohibits the manufacture, import, advertisement or sale of any consumer product that is a "danger to human health or safety" (Sections 7(a) and 8(a));
- mandates record keeping relating to suppliers and the location and duration of retail sale of a product (Section 13); and
- mandates incident reporting (Section 14).

Health Canada administers and enforces the Tobacco and Vaping Products Act and its regulations. Inspectors monitor tobacco manufacturers, importers and retailers across Canada for non-compliance with the act and its regulations, which can result in enforcement action, including the negotiation of compliance, warning letters or the seizure of non-compliant products. Further punishment for contravening the act can include imprisonment or fines up to C$500,000.[173]

The author would like to thank Amanda Branch, Amy Dam, Anastassia Trifonova and Siobhan Doody for their assistance in the preparation of this chapter.

169   SOR/2020-143, s 2(1).
170   SOR/2020-143, s 8.
171   SC 2010, c 21.
172   RSC 1985, c F-27.
173   SC 1997, c 13, s 43.

Czech Republic

Irena Lišková
Ladislav Mádl
Randl Partners, advokátní kancelář, sro

1. Overview of the legal and regulatory regime for advertising

In the Czech Republic, advertising is regulated by multiple legal acts, both private and public, which are largely influenced by European legislation. When interpreting the general legal regulations and assessing the legality of advertising, it is essential to consider the case law of Czech and European courts, and the decisions and opinions of relevant administrative authorities, such as the Council for Radio and Television Broadcasting of the Czech Republic (CRTB) and the Office for Personal Data Protection (OPDP). The ethical standards and decisions of self-regulatory bodies also play an important role.

The basis of public law regulation is the Advertising Regulation Act.[1] This act sets out:

- the general requirements on:
  - advertising;
  - the distribution of advertising;
  - industry-specific advertising; and
  - advertising as an unfair commercial practice; and
- supervisory authorities and sanctions.

The Advertising Regulation Act implements EU regulations on various aspects of advertising law.[2] The act defines 'advertising' as an announcement disseminated mainly through communication media aimed at the promotion of business activities. The content of advertising must be legal – in particular:

- it may not be misleading, contrary to good morals or unsolicited; and
- it must not encourage behaviour that is detrimental to the health of people, the safety of people or property, or the environment.

Further applicable legal regulations can be divided into categories according to:

---

1   Act 40/1995 Coll, on Regulation of Advertising (as amended).
2   For example, Directive 97/55/EC concerning misleading advertising, the Unfair Commercial Practices Directive (2005/29/EC), the Infant Formulae Directive (2003/14/EC) and Directive 2003/33/EC on Advertising and Sponsorship of Tobacco Products.

- the recipient of the ad (ie, consumer[3] or business entity);
- the medium of advertising (eg, press,[4] radio,[5] television,[6] Internet[7] or posters); and
- the products or services that are advertised (eg, pharmaceuticals,[8] banking[9] and financial services[10] or gambling).[11]

Further national regulation is on the way in relation to video-sharing platforms such as YouTube, Instagram and TikTok, to implement the EU Audiovisual Media Services Directive. The governmental bill on video-sharing platforms services is currently being discussed in the Chamber of Deputies of the Czech Parliament.

In addition to these regulations, it is necessary to take into account the data protection regulations – in particular, the General Data Protection Regulation (GDPR) and the Personal Data Processing Act.[12]

Advertising that constitutes an unfair commercial practice is regulated from the civil law perspective by the Civil Code.[13] Sections 2976 and following of the code contain provisions on comparative advertising, misleading advertising and unsolicited advertising.

There are multiple supervisory authorities whose competence is determined by the advertised product and related industry-specific regulation. The only authorities with competence unrelated to advertised content are the CRTB and trade licensing offices. Authorities with limited competence include:

- the State Institute for Drug Control (medical drugs);
- the Central Institute for Supervising and Testing in Agriculture (fertilisers and other agriculture-related products);
- the Agriculture and Food Inspection Authority (food and tobacco);
- the customs offices (gambling); and
- the OPDP (protection of personal data and dissemination of electronic commercial marketing materials).

Municipalities may regulate the placement and distribution of advertising materials under Section 2, paragraphs 1(a) and 5 of the Advertising Regulation Act. Municipalities may specify:

---

3   Act 634/1992 Coll, on Consumer Protection (as amended).
4   Act 46/2000 Coll, Press Act (as amended).
5   Act 231/2001 Coll, on Radio and Television Broadcasting Operation (as amended); Act 484/1991 Coll, on Czech Radio (as amended).
6   Radio and Television Broadcasting Operation Act; Act 483/1991 Coll, on Czech Television (as amended).
7   Act 132/2010 Coll, on Audio-visual and Media Services on Demand (as amended); Act 127/2005, on Electronic Communications (as amended); Act 480/2004 Coll, on Certain Services of the Information Society (as amended).
8   Act 378/2007 Coll, on Pharmaceuticals (as amended).
9   Act 21/1992 Coll, on Banks (as amended).
10   Act 257/2016 Coll, on Consumer Credit (as amended).
11   Act No 186/2016 Coll, on Gambling (as amended).
12   Act 119/2019 Coll, on Processing of Personal Data (as amended).
13   Act 89/2012 Coll, the Civil Code (as amended).

- public places in which advertising is prohibited;
- certain periods during which advertising is prohibited;
- prohibited means of disseminating advertising; and
- events that are not covered by the advertising ban.

Such regulations are in place, for example, in Prague, where leaflets as a form of direct marketing are prohibited in the city centre; and in Brno, which has adopted similar regulations.

The most common sanction for violation of any of the aforementioned laws is a penalty. Under the Advertising Regulation Act, natural persons may incur a fine of between €3,800 and €77,000, and businesses a fine of up to €192,000.

If the unlawful advertising also constitutes an unfair commercial practice, the person whose rights were violated may demand remedy, adequate satisfaction, compensation for damages and/or restitution of unjust enrichment.

The supervising authority may also order that the unlawful ad be taken down, deleted or discontinued within a specified timeframe. It can also suspend the dissemination of unauthorised comparative advertising or advertising which constitutes an unfair commercial practice.

The advertiser must keep a copy of each ad for at least five years from the date on which the ad was last distributed. If an administrative proceeding is initiated pursuant to the Advertising Regulation Act before the expiry of this five-year period, the advertiser must keep a copy of the ad which is the subject of the administrative proceedings until a final decision has been issued on the matter.

The only universal advertising self-regulatory body in the Czech Republic is the Czech Advertising Standards Council (CASC). The CASC brings together clients, agencies and the media with the aim of ensuring that advertising is honest, legal, decent and truthful. Its Code of Advertising Practice sets out moral and ethical rules of advertising. The code is not a legal regulation and is binding only on the members of the CASC; however, it is widely respected. The public may submit complaints on specific ads to the CASC, which will inspect and evaluate their complaints and issue a recommendation decision. Ads depicting children in inappropriate situations, cruel treatment of animals, sexism and so on are the most common examples of unethical advertising, according to the CASC.

2.   Comparative advertising

The Civil Code and the Advertising Regulation Act define 'comparative advertising' and set out the conditions under which comparative advertising may be considered legal. Comparative advertising can be also considered a misleading practice according to the Consumer Protection Act if it targets consumers.

According to Section 2980 of the Civil Code, comparative advertising directly or indirectly identifies another competitor or its products or services. Comparative advertising is permitted if it meets the following conditions:

- It is not misleading;
- It compares products or services that satisfy the same need or are intended for the same purpose;
- It objectively compares one or several relevant, important, verifiable and typical properties of goods or services, including price;
- It compares products with a designation of origin only to products with the same designation;
- It does not disparage a competitor, its position, its activities, its results or its identification, or unfairly benefit therefrom; and
- It does not present the advertiser's products or services as an imitation or copy of trademarked products or services of a competitor, or of the competitor's name.

Comparative advertising is one of the types of unfair competition that are specified in Section 2976 of the Civil Code, which prohibits "conduct in competition which is contrary to the good morals of competition and is liable to cause harm to other competitors or customers". In order for comparative advertising to be considered unfair and illegal, it must breach one of the aforementioned conditions of Section 2980 of the Civil Code and fall under the general unfair competition clause in Section 2976 of the code.

The Czech rules on comparative advertising are significantly influenced by European regulation and may generally be considered compatible with European legislation. Where it is not compatible (there are certain discrepancies), an interpretation consistent with Article 4 of Directive 2006/114 must be adopted. In comparison to Article 4 of Directive 2006/114, which sets out eight conditions for the admissibility of comparative advertising, the Czech rules specify only six. One of the missing conditions of the directive is incorporated into another condition in the Czech version. The final missing condition is that the comparative advertising "must not create confusion among traders, between the advertiser and a competitor or between the advertiser's trademarks, trade names, other distinguishing marks, goods or services and those of a competitor". However, this corresponds in essence to the creation of a likelihood of confusion, which is prohibited under Section 2981 of the Civil Code. The creation of a likelihood of confusion is interpreted as misleading (ie, the consumer is led to believe that the product has certain qualities which it does not).

Comparative advertising is also regulated by the Advertising Regulation Act, which refers to the Civil Code and sets out special requirements regarding comparative advertising of medicinal products. Under Section 2a of the

Advertising Regulation Act, comparative advertising of medicinal products for human use or health services is permissible, provided that:

- the conditions laid down in the Civil Code are met; and
- the ad is aimed at persons who are authorised to prescribe or supply such medicinal products or to provide these health services; it cannot be targeted at the general public.

Under the Advertising Regulation Act, the supervisory authority is entitled to require the advertiser to submit evidence of the veracity of the factual statements made in the ad, where this is proportionate to the circumstances of the case or the legitimate interests of the advertiser or another person.[14] The supervisory authority is also entitled:

- to prohibit inadmissible comparative advertising as an infringement of EU Regulation 2006/2004;
- to suspend the dissemination of unauthorised comparative advertising; and
- to publish its decision and order the publication of a corrective statement.

A party whose rights have been violated by unlawful comparative advertising may demand that the advertiser refrain from unfair competition or remedy the defective state – usually by withdrawing the ad in question. Adequate satisfaction, compensation for damages and restitution of unjust enrichment can also be claimed.[15]

A fine of up to €77,000 may be imposed under the Advertising Regulation Act if the ad does not target healthcare professionals only. A fine of up to €192,000 may be imposed if the comparative advertising is considered a misleading practice under the Consumer Protection Act.

If the social harmfulness of the prohibited comparative advertising is so serious as to constitute a crime, Section 248(1) of the Criminal Code[16] may be applied (the penalty will depend in particular on the damage caused).

Supervision is undertaken by the bodies listed in the Advertising Regulation Act, depending on how the advertising is distributed and the types of products being compared.[17]

3. Online behavioural advertising

Online behavioural advertising and the tracking of online activity for the purposes of online behavioural advertising are regulated on the basis of the e-

---

14 Section 7b of the Advertising Regulation Act.
15 Under Section 2988 of the Civil Code.
16 Act 40/2009 Coll, the Criminal Code (as amended).
17 Section 7 of the Advertising Regulation Act.

Privacy Directive (2002/58/EC), as implemented by the Electronic Communications Act – and specifically its Section 89(3).

In 2009, the e-Privacy Directive was amended by Directive 2009/136/EC to require an opt-in system for cookies, rather than an opt-out system as previously. However, the Czech government has not yet responded to this change, which is thus not as yet reflected in the Electronic Communications Act. Therefore, according to the Electronic Communications Act, the prior consent of a service user to the use of cookies is not required. However, the user must be duly informed about the processing of cookies (if they are not necessary) and must be given the opportunity to refuse such processing at any time.

While the use of cookies is governed by the e-Privacy Directive, this part of the directive has not yet been implemented into Czech law. Therefore, at present, the use of cookies is regulated by various provisions on the processing of personal data. The GDPR, the Personal Data Processing Act and the opinions of data protection supervisory authorities set out the basic rules and principles on the use of cookies in the Czech Republic. These rules are summarised in the Draft Recommendation for the Processing of Cookies and Similar Means of Monitoring, which was issued by the OPDP on 25 May 2018. However, this opinion is only in draft version (it has not been confirmed by the European Data Privacy Board), and does not take into account the EU e-Privacy Regulation,[18] current opinions of the European Data Protection Board[19] and court practice.[20] In particular, the draft recommendation stipulates that in order to use cookies other than where this is necessary, it is sufficient to inform the user about the use of such cookies and offer him or her the option to refuse such processing (ie, an opt-out system), because the user's browser settings meet the requirements for user consent pursuant to the GDPR and the e-Privacy Directive. In light of developments in European law, this assessment of user consent is likely unsustainable, because under the GDPR user consent must be a freely given, specific, informed and unambiguous indication of the data subject's wishes by which he or she, through a statement or a clear affirmative action, signifies his or her agreement to the processing of his or her personal data. Therefore, the user's browser settings may not be considered to constitute valid consent under the GDPR.

The use of cookies is monitored by the Czech Telecommunication Office; if the issue also concerns the protection of personal data, the OPDP also has competence.

---

18 Proposal for a Regulation of the European Parliament and of the Council concerning the respect for private life and the protection of personal data in electronic communications and repealing Directive 2002/58/EC.

19 Such as Guideline 05/2020 on consent under Regulation 2016/679.

20 Such as the judgment of the Court of Justice of the European Union (Grand Chamber) of 1 October 2019 (request for a preliminary ruling from the *Bundesgerichtshof* – Germany) *Bundesverband der Verbraucherzentralen und Verbraucherverbände –Verbraucherzentrale Bundesverband eV v Planet49 GmbH* (Case C-673/17).

The Electronic Communications Act does not associate any sanctions with the violation of Section 89(3) of the Electronic Communications Act. In the event of a breach of the regulations on the processing of personal data, the applicable sanctions are specified in the GDPR.

4. Sales promotions

As Czech law includes no specific definition of 'sales promotions', these are regulated by the general provisions of the Advertising Regulation Act, the Consumer Protection Act and the Civil Code.

In order to be permitted, sales promotions must be fair and comply with the applicable legal regulations. In general, a commercial practice is considered to be unfair if "it is contrary to the requirements of due care and substantially distorts or is likely to substantially distort the economic behaviour of the consumer to whom it is addressed or who can be affected by it in relation to the product or service".[21] The ability to substantially distort a consumer's economic behaviour is assessed in relation to the average (fictitious) consumer to whom the seller's commercial practice is addressed. The use of unfair commercial practices is prohibited before and during the purchase decision, and after the purchase decision is made.[22]

The Consumer Protection Act[23] sets out a detailed and quite extensive list of unfair commercial practices. There are several basic principles that any advertiser should bear in mind when producing marketing communications regarding sales promotions. In particular, the Consumer Protection Act prohibits misleading advertising in general – that is, the provision of incorrect or false information, or information which is true, but which may mislead the customer in deciding to purchase. Annexes 1 and 2 of the Consumer Protection Act set out other examples of prohibited unfair practices, such as:

- bait advertising (ie, offering products or services at a certain price, even though the seller knows that it will be unable to secure the supply of those or equivalent products or services at the advertised price);
- a false declaration that the seller intends to close down or relocate; or
- an indication that a product or service is 'free of charge', 'gratis' or words to that effect.

Sections 20 and following of the Consumer Protection Act also regulate specifically organised sales or promotional events. Strict rules in this regard were introduced to the Consumer Protection Act in response to a large number of

---

21 Section 4(1) of the Consumer Protection Act.
22 Section 4(4) of the Consumer Protection Act.
23 Sections 5, 5a and 5b of the Consumer Protection Act, Annex 1 of the Consumer Protection Act – Misleading commercial practices, Annex 2 of the Consumer Protection Act – Aggressive commercial practices.

cases involving aggressive sales promotions on organised tours and trips with free lunches for seniors which also included sales events.

The Consumer Protection Act defines an 'organised event' as an event for a limited number of invited consumers during which products are sold or services are provided, promoted or offered. It is not decisive whether the event also includes the transport of participants to or from the event. A seller that intends to sell products or provide services during an organised event must file a notification with the Czech Trade Inspection, which specifies:

- the address and date of the event;
- the product or service to be sold, including the price; and
- the identity of the seller or organiser of the event.

The seller must also provide this information in advance to all invited consumers. Probably the most fundamental obligation of the seller is the prohibition on demanding or accepting consideration corresponding to the purchase price of the offered product or service, or part thereof, during the event itself or within seven days of conclusion of the purchase contract. This prohibition also applies to advance payment of the price or any other fee.

The previous law[24] restricted consumer and marketing competitions beyond the level specified by EU regulation. Currently, the situation in the Czech Republic is similar to that in other states. According to Section 2(1)(v) of the Consumer Protection Act, a consumer competition is considered to be:

- a competition, survey or other event organised for consumers that is directly connected to the promotion, offer or sale of a product or service;
- in which the seller undertakes to pay cash or non-cash prizes to participants identified at random; and
- where participation in the competition depends on:
  - the purchase of a certain product or service;
  - the conclusion of a contract with the seller; or
  - the consumer's participation in a marketing action of the seller.

Such competitions are generally permitted, as long as they do not constitute either an unfair commercial practice or gambling activity.

According to the definition set out in Section 3(1) of the Gambling Act, 'gambling' is a game, bet or lottery:

- in which the player places a bet whose return is not guaranteed; and
- where winning or losing depends in whole or in part on coincidence or chance.

If a consumer competition fulfils both of the above conditions, it will be

---

24   Act 202/1990 Coll, on Lotteries and Other Similar Games (as amended).

regarded as gambling. A competition is not considered a bet if participation is conditioned, for example, on the purchase of certain products; however, the price of such products may not exceed the usual price. If the competition operator decides to include a bet in the competition (eg, if participation is conditional on the purchase of a product whose price exceeds the usual price), it must exclude any element of coincidence or chance from the decision on the winner. This can be done, for example, by testing the creative skills or knowledge of individual competitors.

If the ad is considered to constitute an unfair commercial practice, the supervisory authority may:

- order that it be taken down or discontinued;
- where appropriate, order the advertiser or the processor of the ad to publish a corrective statement in the ad; and
- in more serious cases, impose a fine of up to €192,000.

Stricter consumer protection rules have been adopted by the EU, in particular in relation to price reductions (eg, 'Black Friday' sales) and dual quality of food. These rules should be implemented in Czech law by May 2022.

5. Ambush marketing

Ambush marketing is often used in connection with major commercial events – in particular, sports events such as the Olympic Games, the FIFA World Cup, the UEFA European Championship or the Ice Hockey World Championship. It is a great opportunity to increase market share and attract potential customers without spending a lot of money.

The term 'ambush marketing' is not defined in Czech law and there is no special legislation that prevents ambush marketing in general. Although ambush marketing is in principle entirely legal, the advertiser may commit various infringements as a result. The most common are infringements of the Civil Code provisions on competition law – in particular, infringement of the prohibition on unfair competition. 'Unfair competition' is generally considered to be conduct that is contrary to good morals and capable of causing harm to competitors or customers. A person whose rights are jeopardised or infringed by unfair competition may require the infringer to refrain from competing unfairly or remedy the defective situation. Adequate satisfaction, damages and restitution of unjust enrichment may also be claimed. Disputes arising from an infringement of the prohibition on unfair competition shall be decided by the competent courts.

In certain circumstances, ambush marketing may also lead to the misuse of visual, musical or cinematic materials created for a sports event. The Copyright Act[25] affords protection in situations where materials deemed to be copyrighted

---

25   Act 121/2000 Coll, the Copyright Act (as amended).

works are used for marketing purposes without the owner's consent. In a similar way, a breach of trademark rights may occur. As before, any disputes shall be settled by the courts and the party whose rights were breached may seek the immediate cessation of the breach, as well as reasonable satisfaction, damages and restitution of unjust enrichment, where applicable.

The Act on the Protection of Olympic Symbolism[26] is one of the few laws that specifically regulate ambush marketing in the Czech Republic. The act defines 'Olympic symbolism' to include:

- the Olympic symbols;
- the Olympic flag;
- the Olympic motto;
- the Olympic flame;
- the Olympic torch;
- the Olympic anthem;
- the Olympic emblems; and
- the terms 'Olympic' and 'Olympics'.

It further confirms that Olympic symbolism is registered in accordance with the applicable legislation and international agreements for the protection of industrial and intellectual property to which the Czech Republic is bound. The act's provisions must be observed by anyone that seeks to be associated with the Olympic movement or the Olympic Games. Any use of Olympic symbolism for commercial, advertising or other similar purposes is possible only with the prior written authorisation of the Czech Olympic Committee. This requirement also applies to any designation that comprises or incorporates Olympic symbolism. Any disputes over the rights and obligations regulated under this act will be decided by the competent court. In addition to the immediate cessation of infringing conduct, the Czech Olympic Committee or other party so entitled may claim damages, compensation for immaterial harm caused by the unauthorised use of Olympic symbolism and unjust enrichment. The Czech Olympic Committee regularly updates its Methodology for the Use of Olympic Symbolism, which briefly summarises the act and describes the current valid rules for the next Olympic Games.

In addition to the abovementioned legal instruments and the general regulations on advertising (in particular, in the Advertising Regulation Act), the ethical rules set out in the Code of Advertising Practice also have relevance.

Probably the most famous case of ambush marketing in the Czech Republic concerned Olympic symbolism. In 2006, during the Winter Olympic Games in Turin, national brewery Budějovický Budvar launched a television advertising campaign featuring two fans who had travelled to Italy for the so-called 'Hockey

---

26   Act 60/2000 Coll, the Act on the Protection of Olympic Symbolism (as amended).

Games' (in Czech, the term is '*Hokejiáda*', which may be perceived as 'Olympics in hockey').[27]

Although there is no clear strategy to prevent ambush marketing, event organisers and/or sponsors may limit the risk to some extent through:

- the registration of relevant IP rights (particularly trademarks);
- the incorporation of special terms and conditions in sponsorship contracts;
- the establishment and control of so-called 'clean zones' in the vicinity of the event;
- a strict ban on any advertising at the time and place of the event;
- the securing of exclusive television rights; and
- negotiations with broadcasters and athletes.

6. Direct marketing

The rules and principles that regulate direct marketing in the Czech Republic are based on EU law and are set out in five different acts:

- Public law regulations are set out in:
  - the Advertising Regulation Act;
  - the Information Society Act;
  - the Electronic Communications Act;
  - the Consumer Protection Act; and
  - the GDPR; and
- Private law regulations are set out in the Civil Code.

The Advertising Regulation Act sets out rules on the dissemination of unsolicited hard-copy advertising, which is prohibited if it bothers the addressee. To this end, advertising which is directed at a specific addressee shall be considered to bother the addressee where he or she has made it clear in advance, and in a comprehensible manner, that he or she does not wish to receive unsolicited advertising (eg, by placing a sign to this effect on his or her post box). The Advertising Regulation Act also stipulates that municipalities may, among other things, regulate the dissemination of advertising (both hard copy and electronic, including leaflets) in publicly accessible places, allowing them to specify:

- publicly accessible places in which advertising is prohibited;

---

27   The dispute went all the way to the Supreme Court of the Czech Republic, which confirmed that Budweiser Budvar had illegally used Olympic symbolism in its advertising campaign before and during the Olympic Games in Turin. Furthermore, due to the fact that the general partner of the Czech Olympic Committee for the Olympic Games in Torino was brewery Plzeňský Prazdroj (Pilsner Urquell), the court also characterised the behaviour of Budweiser Budvar as unfair competition. The court ordered Budějovický Budvar to pay CZK 2.25 million (€87,000) as compensation for unjust enrichment and reasonable satisfaction. The court also ordered an apology to be published in selected national newspapers.

- times during which advertising is prohibited;
- types of communication media which are prohibited; and
- events to which such prohibitions do not apply.

The Information Society Act sets out the rules on the electronic dissemination of commercial communications, stipulating that this may occur only under the conditions stipulated in the Information Society Act. Three specific rules apply in this regard:

- Contact details may be used for the electronic dissemination of commercial communications only where the recipient has given his or her prior consent;
- If a (natural or legal person) obtains the contact details of a customer in connection with the sale of a product or service according to the personal data protection requirements, it may use those contact details to disseminate commercial communications relating to its own similar products or services, provided that the customer has a clear and unambiguous opportunity to refuse consent to such use in a simple manner, free of charge or at the expense of that natural or legal person, when sending each individual message, if the customer did not initially refuse such use; and
- The dissemination of a commercial communication by electronic mail is prohibited if:
  - it is not clearly and unambiguously marked as a commercial communication;
  - it conceals or disguises the identity of the sender on whose behalf the communication is made; or
  - it is sent without a valid address to which the addressee can directly and effectively send information that he or she does not wish to receive such information from the sender.

The Electronic Communications Act also sets out rules on direct marketing by telephone. Specific rules apply to entities that gather personal data with the aim of issuing a list of subscribers, allowing subscribers to state in advance that they do not wish their personal data to be published; and it is prohibited to send marketing advertising or otherwise to offer products or services to subscribers who have stated that they do not wish their personal data to be published. The Electronic Communications Act further states that it is forbidden to use a network or electronic communications service for the purpose of direct marketing by way of automated call systems without any human participation (automated call devices), fax equipment or email if the subscriber or user in question has not given his or her prior consent to this. The act also protects the data of legal entities.

Under the Consumer Protection Act, direct marketing may qualify as an aggressive commercial practice, which is forbidden. Annex 2 of the Consumer Protection Act defines commercial practices as 'aggressive' where a seller:

- personally visits the consumer in his or her place of residence even though the consumer has asked him or her to leave and not return; or
- repeatedly makes unsolicited offers to the consumer via telephone, fax, email or other means of remote transfer (both with the exception of lawful enforcement of due obligations).

All direct marketing must also comply with the data protection legislation. This means that where personal data is processed for direct marketing purposes, the advertiser must ensure full compliance with the GDPR. In accordance with Recital 47 of the GDPR, the processing of personal data for direct marketing purposes may be considered to be carried out for a legitimate interest. To this end, the advertiser must be able to prove that its legitimate interest in direct marketing does not override the fundamental rights and freedoms of the data subjects, taking into consideration the reasonable expectations of the data subjects based on their relationship with the advertiser.

The provisions on unfair competition in the Civil Code[28] specifically address unsolicited advertising, stipulating that it includes:

- the disclosure of information about a competitor or its products or services;
- the offer of products or services by telephone, fax, email or similar means (including social media), where the recipient clearly does not wish to receive such offers; and
- advertising in which the advertiser conceals or disguises information which allow it to be identified, or which does not specify how the recipient can cease receiving the advertising without incurring extraordinary costs.

Like the Information Society Act, the code further provides that direct advertising is permitted where advertising is sent to an email address which an entrepreneur acquired in connection with the sale of its products or services.

As far as self-regulation is concerned, two codes of conduct address the issues of remote sale, telephone marketing and email marketing, among other things:

- the Code of Conduct for Telephone Sales, prepared and issued in 2009 by Telefónica O2 Czech Republic and T-Mobile Czech Republic, two of the three leading communications service providers; and
- the Code of Conduct of the Association of Direct Marketing, E-

---

28   Section 2986 of the Civil Code.

commerce and Mail Order Business, issued in 1997 and most recently updated in 2019.

Supervision is entrusted to:

- trade licensing offices (compliance with the Advertising Regulation Act);
- the Office for Personal Data Protection (compliance with the Information Society Act, the Consumer Protection Act and the GDPR);
- the Czech Trade Inspection Authority (compliance with the Consumer Protection Act in relation to repeated unsolicited offers); and
- the Czech Telecommunications Office (compliance with the Electronic Communications Act).

Sanctions will differ depending on which of these laws was violated. A penalty may be imposed for violation of:

- the Advertising Regulation Act (up to €77,000);
- the Information Society Act (up to €385,000);
- the Electronic Communications Act (up to €1.92 million for legal entities and up to €3,850 for natural persons);
- the Consumer Protection Act (up to €192,000); and
- the GDPR (up to €20 million).

In case of violation of the Civil Code, anyone whose rights have been jeopardised or violated by an act of unfair competition may:

- request the offending party to cease the relevant activity and/or remedy a defective state; and
- demand adequate satisfaction, compensation for damages and restitution of unjust enrichment.

If the offending party fails to comply, the aggrieved person may initiate court proceedings. Sanctions for violation of the Civil Code may be imposed concurrently with sanctions for violation of the Advertising Regulation Act, the Information Society Act, the Consumer Protection Act and/or the GDPR.

7. Product placement

In 2010, regulations on product placement were introduced by the Audio-visual Media Services on Demand Act, which implements the relevant European directives.[29] The provisions on product placement have been taken verbatim from the directive.

---

29   Directive 2010/13/EU of the European Parliament and of the Council of 10 March 2010 and Directive 2007/65/EC of the European Parliament and of the Council of 11 December 2007 amending Council Directive 89/552/EEC on the coordination of certain provisions laid down by law, regulation or administrative action in Member States concerning the pursuit of television broadcasting activities.

Section 2(1)(h) of the act defines 'product placement' as "any form of audio-visual commercial communication consisting of the inclusion of or reference to a product, a service or a trademark thereof so that it is featured within a programme, in return for payment or for similar consideration". Based on this amendment, an identical definition was also incorporated in the Radio and Television Broadcasting Operation Act.

According to both of these statutes, product placement is admissible only in:

- cinematographic works;
- films and series made for television broadcasting or audio-visual media services;
- sports programmes;
- light entertainment programmes, provided that these are not children's programmes; and
- cases where there is no payment, but only the provision of certain products or services free of charge – in particular, production props or prizes for competitions – with a view to their inclusion in a programme.

In addition:

- the content and, in the case of television broadcasting, the scheduling of the programme must not be influenced in such a way as to affect the responsibility and editorial independence of the media service provider;
- the programme must not directly encourage the purchase or rental of products or services – in particular, by making special promotional references to the relevant products or services; and
- undue prominence must not be given to the product in question.

In order to avoid any confusion on the part of the viewer, programmes containing product placement must be appropriately identified as such at the start and the end of the programme, as well as when the programme resumes after a commercial break or teleshopping spot (the 'PP' pictogram is used for this purpose).

Finally, there is a blanket ban on product placement of tobacco products and prescription-only medicinal products in the Czech Republic.

Compliance with these provisions is supervised by the CRTB. In addition to notifying the advertiser of the breach and specifying a timeframe rectification, the CRTB may impose a financial penalty of between €200 and €96,200.

8. Native advertising and social media influencers

Native advertising and social media influencers are relatively new phenomena and there is no specific law that regulates them so far. However, these advertising practices are at least partially covered by the Advertising Regulation Act, the Civil Code and the Consumer Protection Act. Moreover, the Audio-visual Media Services on Demand Act may apply where a provider of on-demand audio-visual media services[30] has editorial responsibility for the programme or other content.

The overarching principle that applies to native advertising and advertising by social media influencers is that it must be clear to users that the relevant content is advertising. This principle follows generally from the Advertising Regulation Act, which prohibits advertising that constitutes an unfair commercial practice. The Consumer Protection Act, which defines 'unfair commercial practices', stipulates that misleading commercial practices fall under the scope of unfair commercial practices. This includes where a seller uses editorial space in communications media for the paid promotion of its products or services, without consumers being able to clearly identify from the content, images or sounds of the communication that it is actually an ad (ie, subliminal advertising).

Further self-regulatory principles and rules on native advertising have been set out by the CASC and the Association for Internet Progress (AIP).

One section of the CASC Code of Advertising Practice is dedicated to the identification of advertising that resembles editorial content. The code also sets out rules on personal recommendations in advertising (widely used by social media influencers), which provide as follows:

- Ads must not include false personal recommendations or statements in favour of the advertised product – any personal recommendations or favourable statements must be based on the genuine personal experience of the referee;
- Personal recommendations must not include statements or opinions that are incompatible with the Code of Advertising Practice, and must not be used in a manner that might be potentially misleading to the consumer; and
- Personal recommendations must not include any statements regarding the positive effects of the advertised products, unless there is sufficient reliable evidence of such.

The AIP is an association established under Czech law in the same way as the CASC and has been active in the field of internet advertising since 2000. It has issued:

- a Code of Conduct for Taking Over and Use of Extraneous Content on the Internet; and

---

30   According to the Audio-visual and Media Services on Demand Act, on-demand audio-visual media services are information society services whose provider has editorial responsibility and whose main purpose is to provide programmes to the public for information, entertainment or education, and which allow programmes to be watched at a time chosen by the user and at the individual request of the user on the basis of a programme catalogue drawn up by an on-demand audio-visual media service provider (eg, a television channel).

- two supplements to this code:
  - the Rules for Native Advertising; and
  - the Recommended Rules for a Cooperation of Influencer and Advertiser.

The Rules for Native Advertising cover only in-feed units (ie, Category 1 of the Interactive Advertising Bureau categorisation) as follows:

- A newsroom or editorial office must generate its own content. If a topic is proposed by an external advertiser, the relevant content itself must be generated independently by the newsroom or editorial office (sponsored content); and
- In order to preserve the transparency and credibility of the media, it is mandatory to distinguish any type of PR article or sponsored content that resembles content generated by the newsroom or editorial office – for example, by including the phrase 'commercial attachment', 'sponsored' or similar.

These rules are accompanied by several model cases which stipulate, among other things, that the following also fall within the scope of native advertising:

- cases where a company or editor is invited by company X to travel abroad to an event (eg, to a trade fair) in exchange for writing an independent article about the event (ie, sponsored content); and
- cases where a newsroom or editorial office receives finished text from company X or the publisher's sales department, and publishes it as is or with only minimal edits (ie, a PR article).

In such cases, the AIP sets out recommendations on how such pieces should be labelled – for example:

- "The visit took place thanks to the assistance of company X";
- "Products for testing were donated by company X";
- "Commercial annex"; or
- "This article is sponsored by company X".

In relation to social media influencers, the Recommended Rules for Cooperation of Influencers and Advertisers provide as follows:

- If there is a paid business cooperation between the influencer and the contracting authority, the influencer must include textual or aural information on the business cooperation in the content created for these purposes.
- If the influencer receives money or other consideration for the promotion of products and services, or the possibility to keep or use the tested products or services free of charge, he or she must include

information to this effect in an agreed manner. All of these circumstances fulfil the characteristics of a paid business cooperation and oblige the influencer to follow the following rules:

- Information on the business cooperation must be provided at the beginning of the published content, in a clear and comprehensible manner, so that everyone can recognise that it is paid advertising;
- The influencer must adapt the form of communication to the intended target group (labelling cannot be avoided by listing only the hashtags #ad, #sponsored, #advertising and so on, as these are difficult for consumers to understand and may be misleading);
- The influencer must not lie about or conceal his or her actual experience with the relevant product or service;
- The influencer must ensure that the manner in which the business cooperation information is announced is appropriate to the platform on which the communication is posted – for example, in the case of video platforms (eg YouTube), the influencer must ensure that the business collaboration information is included for long enough for everyone to read it;
- The influencer or the advertiser must comply with the AIP's warning of any violation of these rules and must take the recommended steps to remedy this; and
- The influencer and the advertiser must take particular care when advertising to target groups where at least one-third of the intended audience is expected to be under the age of 18, or when advertising products or services listed in the Advertising Regulation Act (eg, tobacco products, alcohol, medicinal products for human use) – in this case, they must follow the regulations set out in the applicable laws.

The AIP rules are recommendations and serve as a template to be adapted as appropriate by the individual creators of the relevant content.

Sanctions are imposed only for a violation of law and will depend on which of the acts was violated. Public law regulations include the Advertising Regulation Act and the Consumer Protection Act (in both cases, penalties of up to €192,000 may be imposed). Further sanctions are available under private law regulation – in particular, the Civil Code and its provisions on unfair competition (anyone whose right has been jeopardised or violated by an act of unfair competition may request the offending party to cease the relevant activity and/or remedy a defective state; and demand adequate satisfaction, compensation for damages and restitution of unjust enrichment).

Violations of soft law (ie, the rules and codes of self-regulatory bodies) are not sanctioned; but these rules are binding on members of these bodies and are widely respected by all other major players.

9. Industry-specific regulation

General rules applicable to advertising in specific industries are stipulated in:

- the Advertising Regulation Act;
- the Civil Code (unfair competition); and
- the Consumer Protection Act (consumer protection and prohibition of unfair commercial practices).

The Radio and Television Broadcasting Operation Act stipulates common rules for broadcasting operators. The Audio-visual and Media Services on Demand Act stipulates common rules for providers when advertising on audio-visual media services. Certain self-regulatory rules are also set out in the Code of Advertising Practice, although they are not legally binding.

The following specific industries (with the exception of financial products and services) are regulated by individual provisions of the Advertising Regulation Act; these provisions are detailed or accompanied by industry-specific provisions of the Code of Advertising Practice (again, not legally binding). The advertisement of certain products – such as tobacco products, medicines and alcohol – is also further regulated by other laws (eg, the Radio and Television Broadcasting Operation Act; the Audio-visual Media Services on Demand Act).

The competence of the supervisory authorities is determined based on either:

- the communication means used to disseminate the advertising; or
- the advertised product or service.

9.1 Gambling

The advertisement of gambling is regulated by Section 5j of the Advertising Regulation Act. Three main principles apply to gambling advertising:

- It must not suggest that participation in gambling may be a source of income in a similar way as earning money from dependent, individual or other activity;
- It must not be targeted at persons under the age of 18 – in particular, by depicting such persons or using elements, means or actions that predominantly address such persons; and
- It must contain a statement prohibiting persons under the age of 18 from gambling and a visible and clear warning in the following wording: "The Ministry of Finance warns: participation in gambling may lead to addiction!"

A special provision of the Gambling Act stipulates that no ads, communications or other forms of marketing may be placed on a building or a publicly accessible part of a building in which gaming premises are located.

The Code of Advertising Practice also includes a special chapter entitled "Lotteries, Betting and Gaming", which sets out the applicable self-regulation rules. Among other things, these provide that advertising in this field should be socially responsible and should not encourage excessive betting. There are also several rules relating to minors, which provide that advertising should not be targeted at or depict minors, and should not be placed in media intended primarily for minors.

Supervision in this field is entrusted by law to customs offices, which may impose sanctions of up to €192,000 on both natural and legal persons who disseminate, place or process advertising in this field.

9.2   Alcohol

The advertisement of alcohol is not prohibited in general, but numerous restrictions apply. The advertisement of alcohol in general is regulated by Section 4 of the Advertising Regulation Act, which provides that such advertising must not:

- encourage the immoderate use of alcohol or portray abstinence or chastity negatively or ironically;
- be targeted at persons under the age of 18. In particular, it must not depict such persons – or persons who look as though they are under the age of 18 – consuming alcoholic beverages, or use elements, means or actions that predominantly address such persons;
- associate the consumption of alcohol with enhanced performance or with driving a vehicle;
- give the impression that the consumption of alcohol contributes to social or sexual success;
- claim that alcohol has medicinal properties or a stimulating or calming effect, or that it is a means of solving personal problems; or
- emphasise the alcohol content as a positive feature of the beverage.

Section 52 of the Radio and Television Broadcasting Operation Act regulates commercial communications about alcoholic beverages and sets out similar requirements to those listed above. The advertisement of alcohol is also regulated by the Audio-visual and Media Services on Demand Act.

The Code of Advertising Practice additionally includes a chapter on alcohol advertising, with specific sections addressing:

- irresponsible consumption of alcohol;
- adolescents;
- driving;
- dangerous activities;
- health aspects;
- alcohol content;

- performance and sexual success;
- sales support; and
- dignity and religion.

Supervision in this field is entrusted to several authorities, depending on the medium, and sanctions of up to €77,000 may be imposed.

9.3 Pharmaceuticals

The advertisement of pharmaceuticals is governed by Sections 2a and 5 to 5c of the Advertising Regulation Act. These provisions relate to medicinal products for human use, and the regulations vary depending on whether the advertising is targeted at the general public or experts. In general:

- only properly registered medicinal products for human use may be advertised;
- any information contained in an ad must correspond to the information listed in the approved product summary of the medicine; and
- the ad must support the rational use of the medicine by objectively introducing it without overstating its properties.

Comparative advertising of medicinal products for human use and healthcare services is allowed where:

- it meets the conditions set out in the Civil Code; and
- it is targeted exclusively at experts.

Only medicinal products for human use which, according to their composition and purpose, can be used without diagnosis, prescription or treatment by a general practitioner or on the advice of a pharmacist may be advertised to the general public. Further conditions are set out on the content of such ads. The advertisement of prescription-only medicines and medicines containing narcotic drugs or psychotropic substances is prohibited.

Advertising targeted at experts may be disseminated only in communications intended mainly for such experts (eg, professional non-periodical publications, professional periodicals, professional audio-visual programmes). Further conditions on the content of such ads are also imposed.

The following are also considered to constitute advertising:

- visits by commercial agents to persons who are entitled to prescribe, supply or dispense medicines;
- the supply of samples of medicinal products for human use;
- support in the prescription, dispensation or sale of medicinal products for human use by way of donation, consumer competition, offer or promise of any benefit or financial or material reward;

- the sponsorship of meetings attended by experts to support the prescription, sale, dispensation or consumption of medicinal products for human use; and
- the sponsorship of scientific congresses for experts and the payment of travel and accommodation costs relating to such attendance.

Advertising that promotes the donation of human tissues or cells, or that highlights the need for or availability of human tissues or cells, with the purpose or result of financial profit or comparable advantage, is prohibited.

Further rules on the advertisement of pharmaceuticals are set out in the Radio and Television Broadcasting Operation Act and the Audio-visual Media Services on Demand Act, which generally prohibit the advertisement of prescription-only medicines or medicinal procedures.

The advertisement of medicines is also subject to self-regulation – in particular, Part II, Chapter V of the Code of Advertising Practice. These provisions also apply to the advertisement of medical devices.

Supervision in this field is entrusted to the State Institute for Drug Control, which may impose penalties of up to €77,000.

9.4 Financial products and services

The advertisement of financial products and services is regulated by specific provisions included in the Banking Act, the Consumer Credit Act, the Collective Investments Act and the Supplementary Pension Insurance Act.

The Consumer Credit Act in particular contains quite detailed regulations on the advertisement of consumer credit. In general, it stipulates that when communicating with a consumer, a provider or intermediary may not use unclear, false, misleading or complex information. If an offer of consumer credit or its intermediation provides details of the cost, it must include a representative case containing specific information specified in the Consumer Credit Act. Breach of these rules may incur a penalty of up to €385,000.

Supervision in this field is entrusted to the Czech National Bank, which can ultimately impose quite severe sanctions (especially on the administrators of collective investment funds under the Collective Investments Act).

9.5 Food

The advertisement of food is regulated by Sections 5d to 5f of the Advertising Regulation Act. The first provision of Section 5d stipulates that nutrition and health claims may be included in food advertising only in accordance with the provisions set out in EU Regulation 1924/2006.

Under the Advertising Regulation Act, food advertising must comply with:

- the Food Act – and in particular, with the specific conditions of the term 'Czech Food';

- EU Regulation 1169/2011 on the provision of food information to consumers; and
- EU Regulation 1151/2012 on quality schemes for agricultural products and foodstuffs.

Ads for food supplements and food for particular nutritional uses must include, in clear and readable (in case of print advertising) text, the terms 'food supplement' or 'food for particular nutritional uses'. There are also special provisions for the advertisement of infant and follow-on formula.

Further rules on the advertisement of food are set out in the Radio and Television Broadcasting Operation Act and the Audio-visual Media Services on Demand Act, which prohibit commercial communications that suggest that the country of origin is the Czech Republic if the conditions set out in the Food Act are not met. A special provision in the Consumer Protection Act also prohibits the offer of products that are dangerous due to their interchangeability with food.

The Code of Advertising Practice sets out further rules on the advertisement of food in general, as well as specific rules for advertising targeted at children. Among other things, advertising may not:

- support the excessive consumption of food or cast doubt on the benefits of a healthy and balanced diet;
- undermine the role of parents in determining a suitable diet for their children; or
- exploit a child's imagination (eg, through animation or fantasy features) to promote unhealthy eating habits.

Supervision in this field is entrusted to the Czech Agriculture and Food Inspection Authority. Fines of up to €77,000 may be imposed for failure to comply with the above rules.

9.6 Tobacco

The advertisement of tobacco is primarily regulated by Section 3 of the Advertising Regulation Act, which provides in general that the following are prohibited:

- tobacco advertising;
- tobacco sponsorship;
- the free distribution of tobacco products; and
- any business communication whose direct or indirect effect is the advertisement of tobacco products.

This prohibition also includes advertising which does not explicitly mention a tobacco product, but which uses the trademark, emblem or other characteristic hallmark of a tobacco product.

Section 48 of the Radio and Television Broadcasting Operation Act further prohibits commercial communications about cigarettes and other tobacco products.

However, the prohibition on tobacco advertising does not apply to:

- ads targeted at experts in the tobacco business;
- ads placed in specialised shops or on displays or signs in such shops;
- the sponsorship of motor sport competitions and sponsorship communications in venues for such competitions (if those competitions do not take place in other EU member states); and
- publications printed and published in third countries (if not particularly intended for the internal EU market).

However, such ads must:

- not be targeted at persons under the age of 18;
- not encourage the take-up of smoking; and
- include a special warning, details of which are specified in the Advertising Regulation Act.

Further rules are also stipulated in the Audio-visual and Media Services on Demand Act, which prohibits the advertisement of tobacco products.

The Code of Advertising Practice further stipulates that:

- ads for tobacco products:
  - should not be targeted at minors, encourage minors to consume tobacco products or depict scenes or situations that minors might find particularly attractive;
  - should not feature minors, but only persons who are or seem to be older than 25;
  - should not be placed in communications media aimed primarily at minors, or on billboards installed in the vicinity of schools, children's playgrounds or other facilities primarily frequented by minors;
  - should not suggest that the consumption of tobacco products may enhance sexual, entrepreneurial or sporting success; and
  - should not suggest that the consumption of tobacco products may help people to relax or concentrate;
- tobacco product brands and logos:
  - should not be placed on goods intended primarily for children; and
  - should be placed on clothes of adult sizes only;
- promotions and other sales support of tobacco products should be directed solely to adults;
- tobacco product-related contests and competitions should be limited to adult participants; and

- ads for tobacco products should include special images and text pursuant to the respective laws.

Violations of the Advertising Regulation Act may incur fines of up to €77,000. Supervision in this field is entrusted to the Czech Agriculture and Food Inspection Authority, the CRTB and regional trade licensing offices.

9.7 E-cigarettes

The advertisement of e-cigarettes is regulated by Section 3a of the Advertising Regulation Act, which prohibits:

- ads whose aim or direct or indirect effect is to promote e-cigarettes or their refills, disseminated by various means (an exception is made for publications dedicated to professionals involved in the e-cigarette trade, where such publications are not primarily targeted at the internal EU market); and
- any form of event sponsorship whose aim or direct or indirect effect is the promotion of e-cigarettes and their refills, if the event is held in several EU member states or if it otherwise has a cross-border effect.

Further rules on the advertisement of e-cigarettes and refills are set out in the Radio and Television Broadcasting Operation Act and the Audio-visual Media Services on Demand Act, which prohibit the advertisement of e-cigarettes and their refills.

Violations of the law may incur fines of up to:

- €77,000 (under the Advertising Regulation Act or the Audio-visual Media Services on Demand Act); or
- €96,000 (under the Radio and Television Broadcasting Operation Act).

Compliance with the above rules is supervised by regional trade licensing offices or the CRTB, depending on the medium through which the ad is disseminated.

Denmark

Carina Hyldahl
Kenneth Kvistgaard-Aaholm
Gorrissen Federspiel

1. Overview of the legal and regulatory regime for advertising

1.1 Marketing Practices Act

Advertising in Denmark is mainly governed by the Marketing Practices Act,[1] which sets out important general provisions that apply to all kinds of marketing activities. The Marketing Practices Act applies to private business activities and to public activities to the extent that products are offered on the Danish market.[2] The term 'advertising' is not defined in the Marketing Practices Act. However, 'commercial practices' are defined as all acts, omissions, courses of conduct, representations and commercial communications, including advertising and marketing, by a trader in relation to the promotion, sale or supply of a product to consumers. Pursuant to the legislative history, 'advertising' and 'commercial practices' cover the same activities. Thus, the act generally covers all commercial representations that promote the supply of products or services. The Marketing Practices Act is largely based on harmonised EU directives.[3]

The Marketing Practices Act contains two general provisions: one in Section 3 relating to fair marketing practice and one in Section 4 relating to fair commercial practice.

Section 3(1) of the Marketing Practices Act states that businesses covered by the act must comply with 'fair marketing practice' with reference to consumers, other traders and the public interest. To the extent that consumers' financial interests are affected, special provisions apply. The term 'fair marketing practice' is a legal standard that changes over time and must therefore be interpreted in accordance with recent case law and opinions of the Danish Consumer Ombudsman.[4] In other words, while the standard is broad in scope and not very specific, it is very flexible and is always intended to reflect the 'current' position of society.

---

1 Consolidated Act 426 of 3 May 2017 on Marketing Practices.
2 Special restrictions apply to financial companies.
3 Such as Directive 2005/29/EC on unfair commercial practices, Directive 2006/123/EC on services in the internal market and Directive 1999/44/EC on certain aspects of the sale of consumer goods and associated guarantees.
4 See www.consumerombudsman.dk.

Section 3(2) of the Marketing Practices Act concerns marketing activities directed at children and young people. It stipulates that marketing aimed at children and young people must be designed with specific reference to their natural credulity and lack of experience and critical sense, making them readily influenced and easy to impress. This section is supplemented by Section 11 of the Marketing Practices Act, which specifically regulates commercial practices directed at children and young people under the age of 18. It provides, among other things, that commercial practices may not:

- directly or indirectly incite children or young people to violence or other dangerous or inconsiderate behaviour;
- make unwarranted use of violence, fear or superstition in order to influence them; or
- mention or include images of or references to intoxicants, including alcohol.

The Act on Radio and Television Broadcasting[5] and a ministerial order issued under this act[6] contain additional regulations concerning radio and television ads directed at children under the age of 14. Among other things, they include:

- a prohibition on the use of children in television ads unless children are a natural part of the surroundings or necessary in order to demonstrate the use of the product in question;
- an absolute prohibition on product placement (see section 7); and
- a prohibition on children recommending products or services.

Pursuant to Section 3(3), marketing relating to the financial interests of consumers is subject to the specific rules on fair commercial practice within the Marketing Practices Act. These rules include a general provision which sets out the standard of 'fair commercial practice' (Section 4 of the Marketing Practices Act). 'Fair commercial practice' is defined as the standard of special skill and care that a trader may reasonably be expected to exercise towards consumers, commensurate with honest marketing practice and the general principle of good faith in the trader's field of activity. Furthermore, pursuant to Sections 5 and 6 of the act, the rules on fair commercial practice provide that the trader's commercial practice must not:

- contain false information or in any way deceive or be likely to deceive the average consumer, even if the information is factually correct; or
- mislead by omitting or hiding essential information, or by providing essential information in an unclear, unintelligible, unambiguous or

---

5   Consolidated Act 1350 of 4 August 2020 on Radio and Television Broadcasting.
6   Ministerial Order 1155 of 18 June 2020 on Advertising and the Sponsoring of Radio and Television Programs and On-demand Audiovisual Media Services and Entering into Partnerships.

untimely manner. Whether a statement is misleading depends on how it is understood by the recipients.

These provisions are especially relevant in relation to sales promotions (see section 4), products 'on sale' and indications of certain savings or similar advertising. In this respect, the Danish Consumer Ombudsman has issued a detailed set of guidelines[7] on the use of prices in marketing. Moreover, a trader may not use harassment, unlawful coercion, force or undue influence that is likely to significantly impair the consumer's freedom of choice with regard to a product (Section 7 of the Marketing Practices Act). Marketing that is misleading or aggressive, or that exposes the consumer to undue influence, is included within this prohibition. To breach the rules on fair commercial practice, the commercial practices in question must materially distort or be likely to materially distort the economic behaviour of the average consumer, or the average member of the group if the practices are directed to a group of consumers (Section 8 of the Marketing Practices Act). It is sufficient if the commercial practice could result in the average consumer making a transactional decision (as defined in the Marketing Practices Act) which he or she would not otherwise have made – it is not decisive that the economic behaviour was in fact distorted.

The legal standards regarding misleading commercial practices also apply in business-to-business (B2B) relations (Section 20 of the Marketing Practices Act). The Consumer Ombudsman does not handle B2B marketing issues and it is thus reasonable to believe that the courts will generally adopt a more restrictive approach when interpreting the Marketing Practices Act in a consumer-related matter. Hence, they may find that certain advertising measures conflict with (for example) fair marketing practice in a business-to-consumer (B2C) marketing scenario, but not in a B2B marketing scenario. Furthermore, several of the more specific regulations apply only in relation to B2C advertising (eg, guarantees, invitations to purchase, price information, purchase on credit, fees, organised discounts and credit agreements).

1.2 Supervision

The Danish Consumer Ombudsman plays an important role in the interpretation of, and supervision of compliance with, the Marketing Practices Act. The ombudsman publishes guidelines[8] on marketing issues and comments on specific cases; and although formally the opinions of the ombudsman have no legal effect, the role of the ombudsman is *de facto* substantial. The guidelines

---

7   Available in Danish at www.forbrugerombudsmanden.dk/media/49800/retningslinjer-for-prismarkedsfoering.pdf.
8   Some of the guidelines are available in English at www.consumerombudsman.dk.

are widely used by practitioners as an explanatory and detailed tool in interpreting and understanding the Marketing Practices Act.

Besides the supervision conducted by the Consumer Ombudsman, the Radio and Television Board[9] (among other functions) monitors whether private and public broadcasters are fulfilling their legal obligations, and ensures that the content and form of television and radio advertising comply with the marketing regulations.

1.3 Other regulatory measures

Some of the sector-specific legislation on advertising is outlined in section 9. Often, such legislation sets out the general requirement of fair marketing practice and the prohibition against misleading marketing, along with additional sector-specific provisions (eg, an absolute prohibition on the advertisement of tobacco products and specific information requirements applicable to ads for pharmaceuticals).

The Code on Advertising and Marketing Communication Practice[10] issued by the International Chamber of Commerce (ICC) may be used by Danish advertisers as a means of self-regulation. The code is not legally binding, but it corresponds to a significant extent with the general requirement of fair marketing practice under the Marketing Practices Act. In this regard, the Consumer Ombudsman has specifically stated that he will take the code into account when interpreting the requirement of fair marketing practice; and presumably the Danish courts will do the same.

1.4 Infringement and penalties

Advertisers must ensure that their ads do not infringe the IP rights of third parties, including in particular Danish and EU trademarks. In this respect, the advertiser will be held liable if the products in an ad infringe the IP rights of third parties, even if the advertiser is merely reselling the products. Moreover, other businesses may assert the protection afforded under the Marketing Practices Act against an advertiser – for instance, if the ad constitutes an unfair marketing practice against that other business. In relation to both IP infringements and violations of the Marketing Practices Act, the advertiser may be obliged to pay damages and/or reasonable compensation. Furthermore, the Danish courts may issue an injunction against illegal advertising, including a preliminary injunction.

If a matter is considered by the Consumer Ombudsman, the initial legal risk is the negative publicity generated by any criticism issued by the ombudsman. In severe cases, or if negotiations with the advertiser fail, the ombudsman may initiate court proceedings and in some cases issue an enforcement order against

---

9   See https://english.kum.dk/policy-areas/media/.
10   www.codescentre.com/index.php/icc-code.

the marketing activities, which the ombudsman must subsequently bring before the courts if requested to do so by the business in question.

The Consumer Ombudsman's powers to initiate court proceedings include the ability to initiate actions for damages on behalf of individual third parties that have suffered loss due to illegal marketing. Moreover, the ombudsman can issue administrative fines in straightforward cases where there are no evidential challenges – most likely, these will be cases regarding electronic bulk messaging (spamming) and similar violations where there is clear case law to support the level of a fine and other aspects.

The violation of an injunction – including a preliminary injunction – an enforcement order issued by the Consumer Ombudsman or an agreement with the ombudsman may lead to criminal liability, most likely in the form of a fine.[11] The violation of certain provisions of the Marketing Practices Act and the sector-specific legislation may also lead directly to criminal liability – these include, for example:

- the prohibition against misleading marketing;
- the prohibition against spam;
- the regulations on marketing targeted at children and young people; and
- the prohibition against tobacco advertising.

However, the mere violation of the general provision on fair marketing practice cannot by itself lead to criminal liability.

2.   Comparative advertising

Comparative advertising is regulated by Section 21 of the Marketing Practices Act. This provision defines 'comparative advertising' as any advertising that, explicitly or by implication, identifies a competitor or its products or services.

Comparative advertising is permitted if the following cumulative (EU directive-based)[12] conditions are met:

- It is not misleading;
- It compares products or services that meet the same needs or are intended for the same purpose;
- It objectively compares one or more material, relevant, verifiable and representative features of these products and services, which may include price;

---

11   There are no official guidelines regarding the size of such a fine. According to case law, the size of the fine is determined with regard to the gravity and extent of the infringement and the obtained or intended financial profit, including whether the violation was intentional. Most often the fine is in the range of DKK 10,000 to DKK 500,000 (approximately €1,350 to €67,000), depending on the aforementioned criteria. Regarding violation of the spam prohibition, case law seems to impose a fine of minimum DKK 10,000 for up to 100 violations; if there are more than 100 violations, each violation warrants a fine of DKK 100 (approximately €13.50).
12   Directive 2006/114/EF concerning misleading and comparative advertising.

- It does not create confusion among traders, between the advertiser and a competitor, or between the advertiser's trademarks, trade names, other distinguishing marks, products or services and those of a competitor;
- It does not discredit or denigrate the trademarks, trade names, other distinguishing marks, products, services, activities or circumstances of a competitor;
- For products with a designation of origin, it relates in each case to products with the same designation;
- It does not take unfair advantage of the reputation of the trademarks, trade names or other distinguishing marks of a competitor, or of the designation of origin of competing products; and
- It does not represent products or services as imitations or replicas of products or services bearing a protected trademark or trade name.

An ad that directly or indirectly refers to a competitor or its products constitutes comparative advertising. An indirect reference is made where it is nonetheless possible to identify the competitor or its products even though the competitor or its products are not directly mentioned in the ad. For example, a reference to an entire industry may constitute an indirect reference if the industry referred to is delimited and identifiable. Case law shows that very little is required for a comparison to be considered at least implied and thereby covered by the regulations. This is illustrated by the Maritime and Commercial High Court's decision in Case U 1989.322 S. In this case, a description of a health product as 'extra strong' was considered to be a reference to a competing product, and to conflict with the marketing legislation in force at that time. However, at the time this decision was issued, the two products in question were the only ones available on the market. If the comparison concerns a non-competing product, the provisions do not apply. However, such advertising is still subject to the general requirements, especially on fair marketing practice. If a claim regarding a product or service is mere puffery, such as 'the world's best', it will not be considered comparative.

Regarding comparative advertising in television and radio ads, the Radio and Television Board seems to have adopted a rather restrictive practice – presumably because it is difficult for competitors to respond quickly with a counter-campaign (ie, retaliation), especially on television. In this regard, a general principle of 'justified retaliation' applies: while a company that is the target of an unfair campaign is not permitted to commit acts of unfair competition, case law shows that a company that strikes back with means that would otherwise be considered to conflict with the requirement of fair marketing practice will often not be found liable.

Special legislation has been adopted with regard to pharmaceuticals, as described in section 9.3.

3. Online behavioural advertising

The main issue with regard to online behavioural advertising concerns the extent to which it is permitted to store, access and process information about a user's online behaviour. Applicable in this regard is the Danish Data Protection Act,[13] which supplements the General Data Protection Regulation (GDPR);[14] and the Ministerial Order on Cookies,[15, 16] which implements Article 5(3) of the e-Privacy Directive.[17] In addition, the Danish Business Authority and the Danish Data Protection Agency have issued guidelines on the Ministerial Order on Cookies.

Before storing or accessing information in an end user's system, Section 3 of the Ministerial Order on Cookies requires that the end user:

- be provided with comprehensive information about the storage and accessing of any information, whether personal or not; and
- consent to such storage or access, after having received said information.

To meet the 'comprehensive information' requirement, the information must satisfy the following requirements:

- It appears in clear, precise and easily understood language;
- It contains details of the purpose of the storage of, or access to, information in the end user's system;
- It contains details that identify any natural or legal person that arranges for the storage of, or access to, the information;
- It contains a readily accessible means by which the end user can refuse to consent or can withdraw consent to the storage of, or access to, the information, as well as clear, precise and easily understood guidance on how the end user can avail of this right; and
- It is immediately available to the end user by being communicated fully and clearly to him or her. In addition, when the storage of, or access to, information takes place through an information and content service, the information provided to end users must be directly and clearly marked and accessible at all times in relation to the information and content service in question.

The Ministerial Order on Cookies defines 'consent' as any freely given,

---

13 Consolidated Act 502 of 23 May 2018 on the Protection of Data.
14 Regulation EU 2016/679 of 27 April 2016 on the protection of natural persons with regard to the processing of personal data and on the free movement of such data, and repealing Directive 95/46/EC.
15 Ministerial Order 1148 of 9 December 2011 on Information and Consent Required in the Case of Storing or Accessing Information in End-User Terminal Equipment.
16 The ministerial order is not limited to cookies, but covers all similar technologies. Furthermore, the regulation is applicable to all types of electronic media, including personal computers, smartphones, tablets and so on.
17 Directive 2002/58/EC, as amended by Directive 2009/136/EC, on Privacy and Electronic Communications.

specific and informed indication of the end user's wishes, by which the end user signifies his or her agreement to the storage of information or the gaining of access to information stored on his or her system.

The Danish Business Authority's cookie guidelines stipulate that end users can no longer consent to cookies merely by browsing a website. Thus, consent must be given actively; and the former practice whereby consent could be obtained by pre-ticked boxes or by active use of a service has been abandoned.

According to the Danish Business Authority's guidelines, the following requirements for consent apply:

- The user must be able to give or refuse consent to the use of cookies;
- The user must be able to revoke consent;
- The user must be able to easily find information about the use of cookies on the website; and
- The consent must be linked to the purpose of storing or accessing information.

In practice, consent is often obtained through use of a cookie banner, which presents the end user with information on the website's use of cookies and allows the end user either to accept or reject the use of cookies.

Two exceptions apply to the consent requirements. Most notably, consent is not required if the storage of, or access to, information is necessary in order for the provider of an information society service explicitly requested by the end user to provide this service (ie, technical cookies). This exception applies, for instance, to online shops where cookies are necessary to keep items in the user's shopping basket as he or she navigates from one page to another. However, if the cookies are also stored for other purposes (eg, behavioural advertising), the user's consent must be obtained.

The rules on cookies regulate only the storage or accessing of information on the end user's system. In the event of any further processing of any personal data, the data protection legislation must be observed. This means that the controller must, at the time the personal data is obtained, inform the end user of matters such as:

- the identity of the controller;
- the purpose of the processing of the personal data; and
- the categories of recipients of the personal data (Article 13 of the GDPR).

Violation of the Ministerial Order on Cookies or the data protection legislation may be sanctioned by a fine. According to Article 83(5) of the GDPR, infringements of the end user's rights under Article 13 of the GDPR are subject to administrative fines of up to €20 million or, in the case of an undertaking, up to 4% of its total worldwide annual turnover in the preceding financial year, whichever is higher. If the information or data is legally obtained and processed, online behavioural advertising is generally allowed – but subject to the general requirements of the Marketing Practices Act, and especially the requirement on fair marketing practice and the prohibition against spam.

4. Sales promotions

While the Marketing Practices Act previously contained a separate section on sales promotions, these rules are only implicitly expressed in the current version of the act.

Sales promotions aim to promote the sale of a product – for example, by indicating that the consumer will obtain some sort of additional benefit (often in financial terms). Such marketing includes, among other things:

- a discount in the form of price reductions;
- additional amounts of the purchased products or services;
- coupons and bonus schemes;
- gifts; and
- competitions.

Often, sales promotions are used in connection with the advertisement of certain products or services, although broader sales promotions aimed at increasing sales in general are covered by the same regulations.

A sales promotion must:

- comply with fair commercial practice;
- not contain misleading information or omit or hide essential information; and
- not use harassment or aggressive practices.

The use of sales promotions is allowed if the terms of the offer are transparent and easily accessible to consumers. This implies that all applicable conditions in order to obtain the benefit of the sales promotion must be stated clearly and unambiguously. Any potential restrictions must appear as clearly as all other conditions. However, this does not mean that all conditions must be included at all times in the marketing of a specific sales promotion, but only that the conditions must be 'easily accessible'. This requirement will differ depending on the medium and what could reasonably be required in the given situation. Thus, if the sales promotion appears in a written publication or in a television or radio ad, it may be sufficient to explain the main terms, together with an indication that the full conditions can be obtained by contacting the advertiser or visiting a website or a store. If the sales promotion appears online or in an email, it may be sufficient if the conditions can be accessed by following a link. If the sales promotion appears in a store, the conditions should be accessible in direct connection with the offer – for instance, in hard copy. If the conditions are comprehensive, they may all be included on a leaflet (for example). What is decisive is that the conditions are made available to the consumer in a reasonable format.

Apart from the requirement to state the value of additional products or services offered as part of a promotion, the Marketing Practices Act does not define the exact information that must be supplied. Overall, the consumer must be given sufficient information to assess the offer – for instance, including the duration of the offer and any additional payments needed to obtain a certain benefit. With this in mind, the extent of the information and requirements on clarity must be assessed on a case-by-case basis.

If products or services are offered at a certain price, and the advertiser has reason to believe that it will be unable to accommodate demand in a fair quantity, considering the offer and the extent of the marketing, a reservation in this regard must be made in the ad for the sales promotion.

With regard to the use of discounts, there is an overlap with the Consumer Ombudsman's rather detailed position on price marketing/indications, which is based on an interpretation of the prohibition against misleading information.[18]

5. Ambush marketing

Ambush marketing mainly arises in relation to sporting events, when companies that are not official sponsors of the event or a certain team attempt to free ride on some of the publicity and goodwill generated by the event or team.

Ambush marketing is not regulated under Danish law. As with all other marketing, ambush marketing is subject to the Marketing Practices Act, and particularly the general requirement of fair marketing practice.

The Danish courts have not publicly ruled on whether ambush marketing *per se* conflicts with Danish law. Further, given that the issues arising from ambush marketing are mainly B2B related, the Consumer Ombudsman has made no statements on the matter.

In general, it is legal to market a business in a way that creates associations with (for instance) a sporting event, even if the advertiser has no formal connections to that event, as long as this is done in a fair manner and does not involve the provision of false or misleading information. Thus, it is reasonable to assume that ambush marketing as a concept is legal from a marketing law perspective. However, ambush marketing could easily be considered to conflict with the Marketing Practices Act if it is combined with information that – contrary to the truth – indicates a connection with (for example) a sports team or its official sponsor, or free rides on the goodwill of the event or similar. Other risks, such as trademark infringement, may also be an issue.

---

18   Available in Danish at www.forbrugerombudsmanden.dk/media/46455/20170703-prisretningslinjer-fo.pdf.

6.   Direct marketing

Together with the Danish Act on Consumer Agreements,[19] the Marketing Practices Act imposes restrictions on direct marketing in Denmark.

Pursuant to Section 10(1) of the Marketing Practices Act, a trader must not approach anyone – whether consumers or other traders – by means of electronic mail (eg, emails and text messages), an automated calling system or a fax machine for the purpose of direct marketing, unless the recipient has given prior consent (ie, the provision regulates the prohibition against spam).

The purpose of this provision is to prevent consumers, traders and public authorities from being overloaded with unsolicited inquiries.

This provision applies to direct marketing forwarded to a specific consumer or trader. The forwarding of newspapers, ads and similar to an indefinite group of potential buyers will not be characterised as direct marketing. As regards consent, the Consumer Ombudsman holds that this must be the expression of a freely given, specific and informed indication of intent (ie, an opt-in solution). The trader must also allow the free and easy revocation of such consent.

An exception to this prohibition is set out in Section 10(1) of the Marketing Practices Act, which provides that a trader that has received a customer's electronic contact details (eg, email address) in connection with the sale of products may market its own similar products to that customer by electronic mail. However, the customer must:

- be informed that he or she will receive electronic marketing; and
- be given the opportunity of declining to receive (ie, opting out of) such marketing – both when providing his or her contact details at the initial purchase of products and in all subsequent communications.

In addition, the contact details must be given in connection with the sale of products; thus, a potential customer who has shown interest in a product, but has not purchased it, is not covered by the exception in Section 10(2).

Further, the exception relates only to the trader's own similar products. What this exactly covers will depend on the customer's expectations; thus, it is not decisive how the trader understands its 'own similar products'.

Section 10(3) sets out the conditions that must be fulfilled where a trader, for the purpose of direct marketing, addresses someone by electronic mail. For example:

- the marketing must be clearly identifiable as such;
- it must be clear to the recipient that the intention is to promote the marketing; and
- the conditions of promotions (eg, discounts, gifts) must be clearly presented.

---

19   Consolidated Act 1457 of 17 December 2013 on Consumer Agreements.

Unlike for electronic communications, direct marketing by regular (postal) mail is allowed without the prior consent of the recipient. However, businesses may not direct their marketing by regular mail to natural persons who have requested not to receive such marketing. A request to opt out can be specifically directed to certain businesses or advertisers, or made generally to the Civil Registration System in Denmark, which holds an opt-out list of persons who have generally opted out of direct marketing (the so-called 'Robinson list').[20] Businesses must acquaint themselves with the Robinson list when it is published every quarter.

The first time that a business directs advertising towards a natural person, it must provide information on the possibility to opt out of direct marketing.

The right to opt out of direct marketing, including via the Robinson list, does not cover unaddressed marketing materials, such as leaflets distributed door to door, free weekly newspapers and so on. However, consumers may place a "No thanks" sticker on their mailboxes. It is arguably in conflict with the requirement of fair marketing practice if businesses do not respect such a sticker.

Direct marketing always involves the processing of personal data and must thus comply with the data protection legislation (see section 3). Such processing requires a sufficient legal basis under the GDPR. If the strict requirements for direct marketing under the Marketing Practices Act are fulfilled, in most cases personal data can be processed for this purpose on the basis of legitimate interest in accordance with Article 6(1), lit f of the GDPR. However, a trader cannot pass on information about a consumer to another trader for direct marketing purposes without the consumer's consent.

Finally, the Consumer Agreement Act stipulates that businesses cannot contact consumers by telephone or in person (eg, door-to-door sales) for the purpose of entering into an agreement, including all types of sales, unless previously requested by the consumer. While the prohibition against door-to-door sales is absolute, an organisation can contact consumers by telephone for the purpose of selling certain listed products and services (eg, insurance, books and newspapers), unless the consumer has requested not to be contacted – either specifically or through the Robinson list.

7. Product placement

Product placement in radio and television is governed by a ministerial order issued under the Radio and Television Broadcasting Act and supplemented by the requirements of the Marketing Practices Act. Other types of product placement are merely governed by the Marketing Practices Act.

As a general rule, product placement in radio, television and similar on-demand services is prohibited. However, product placement is permitted under

---

20   See https://cpr.dk/kunder/kundeadgang/ (Danish).

certain circumstances in television and on-demand audio-visual media services where:
- the purchased programme contains product placement produced abroad; and
- the programme falls within a specific genre, including films, documentaries, television series, sport programmes and entertainment shows.

Specific requirements must further be met. For example:
- the programme must not encourage the purchase of the product by making special promotional references or give undue prominence to the product;
- the programme must not include product placement of tobacco and e-cigarettes, refill containers and the like, or prescription-only medicines;
- the product placement must not damage respect for human dignity or promote discrimination, encourage behaviour that could be damaging to health or safety, harm minors morally or physically, or encourage them to purchase a product due to their lack of experience;
- where the product placement relates to alcohol, it may in no event be aimed at minors; and
- no product placement may be included in programmes aimed at children under the age of 14.

Certain additional regulations apply in relation to DR (the national Danish broadcaster) and TV2 (a major state-owned Danish broadcaster). Both DR and TV2 can broadcast films and documentaries containing product placement, provided that these programmes are produced by and for others, and are covered by the general exceptions referred to above.

The prohibition against product placement does not prevent product sponsorship if:
- the product, service or trademark shown has no significant value; and
- no relevant media service provider or related person has received payment in relation to the product placement.

The Marketing Practices Act further requires that advertising be clearly identifiable as such, regardless of its form and the medium used. Hence, Danish law prohibits hidden advertising, including product placement. When assessing whether the use of products constitutes unlawful hidden advertising, it must in particular be considered whether the use of the product in question can be characterised as being an ad or whether it is a natural part of the surroundings. It is not necessarily decisive if the placement of the product has been paid for or if the product is a free sample; however, such particulars may be weighty indications.

Further, there are no requirements regarding form and the advertiser is free to decide how to make the product placement distinguishable as advertising. If it is clear from the product placement that it constitutes advertising activity, this will suffice. The identification as an ad does not need to be positioned within the programme itself; it may also suffice to notify viewers or listeners about the product placement at either the beginning or the end of the broadcast.

Even where product placement does not conflict with the regulations applicable to television broadcasters and is not prohibited as hidden marketing, it is also necessary to ensure that it does not conflict with other regulations – in particular:

- the requirement of fair marketing practice;
- the prohibition against misleading marketing; and
- the additional considerations required for marketing directed towards children and young people.

8.   Native advertising and social media influencers

8.1   Native advertising

Native advertising is regulated by the Marketing Practices Act, supplemented by guidelines issued by the Consumer Ombudsman[21] on marketing on social media.

Native advertising is subject to the rules on hidden advertising. These require that the relevant business clearly provide information about the commercial intention behind a post – in this case, advertising. When ads are tailored for certain media, there may not be enough space to describe all necessary conditions relating to the offer or proposal; to this end, the Consumer Ombudsman has stated that it is sufficient to refer to the conditions elsewhere, as long as the ad outlines the offer or proposal in a clear, true and well-balanced way.

Furthermore, native advertising often includes promotional measures (eg, giveaways, participation in a competition or trial periods). Such initiatives are specifically subject to the provisions on sales promotions (see section 4).

As native advertising is triggered by the user's activities – that is, what he or she 'likes', follows or shares – such ads may also give rise to considerations regarding unsolicited communications. However, for these rules to apply, the communication must take place by electronic message, automatic calling system or fax machine.

---

21   www.forbrugerombudsmanden.dk/media/46472/2016-standpunkt-til-nordisk-standpunkt-for-markedsfoering-via-sociale-medier.pdf (Danish).

8.2 Social media influencers

Social media is often used for marketing by private individuals (influencers), who are paid by businesses in order to market products or services through their own social media profiles.

This subject matter is regulated by the Danish Marketing Practices Act, the Danish E-commerce Act[22] and a set of guidelines issued by the Consumer Ombudsman regarding advertising on social media.[23]

These rules require the influencer to clearly state that the post, or a reference within the post, is advertising; and to indicate clearly who the advertising is on behalf of. The guidelines issued by the Consumer Ombudsman contain specific examples of how such posts should be sufficiently marked – for example, by using the word 'advertisement' together with the company name; whereas the words 'sponsored by' or 'ad' will be insufficient.

If an influencer receives a gift from a business, any post regarding that gift must be marked so that it is clearly apparent that the post concerns a gift, as it is presumed that the gift has been sent in order to obtain marketing value. However, reviews of books, movies, music, theatre performances and similar are not considered to be advertising if the gift received was merely the relevant book, CD, theatre ticket or similar.

Furthermore, if the advertising is directed towards children or young people, there is an even greater need for clarity. Additionally, if a business sends gifts to an influencer under the age of 18, this may conflict with the general provision on fair marketing practice, depending on:

- the age of the influencer;
- the influencer's target group of followers; and
- whether there has been advance contact with the influencer's parents.

Failure to comply with the above provisions may trigger the imposition of a fine both on the influencer and on the business.

9. Industry-specific regulation

9.1 Gambling

Although gambling is strictly regulated in Denmark, the advertisement of gambling is not covered in great detail in the Gambling Act.[24]

The Gambling Act provides that the chances of winning must be presented in a transparent and balanced way, in order to avoid giving the impression that they are higher than they in fact are. Furthermore, the ad must present

---

22   Consolidated Act 227 of 22 April 2002 on services in information society.
23   www.forbrugerombudsmanden.dk/media/46472/2016-standpunkt-til-nordisk-standpunkt-for-markedsfoering-via-sociale-medier.pdf (Danish).
24   Consolidated Act 1303 of September 2020 on Gambling.

gambling as an entertainment proposition, and must by no means be directed towards children or young people under the age of 18. Celebrities are specifically not allowed to imply, contrary to the truth, that gambling has contributed to their success (for people other than celebrities, such marketing would arguably conflict with the general requirement of fair marketing practice and/or the prohibition on misleading marketing). Additionally, ads must not present gambling as a solution to financial troubles or a means of imputing social status to the gambler.

Any marketing that violates the Gambling Act will arguably also amount to a violation of the Marketing Practices Act. However, given the broad scope of the generally applicable Marketing Practices Act, it also prohibits certain marketing measures relating to gambling that are not covered by the Gambling Act. Most important are the requirements of fair marketing practice and the prohibition against misleading marketing. Other relevant provisions of the Marketing Practices Act include those on the regulation of sales promotions, the prohibition of spam and comparative advertising.

On 1 July 2020, new rules on the marketing of consumer loan companies and credit agreements to consumers came into force which prohibit their marketing in connection with the marketing of games or gambling providers. This means that a consumer loan company cannot market itself – for example, its name, logo or other identifying features – or consumer credit agreements if this is done in connection with the marketing of games or gambling providers.

9.2 Alcohol

Denmark has no general prohibition against the advertisement of alcohol. However, Section 11 of the Marketing Practices Act provides that marketing towards children and young people (under the age of 18) must not:

- directly or indirectly encourage the consumption of alcohol; or
- mention, contain pictures of or make references to alcohol.

Alcohol advertising must observe the general provisions of the Marketing Practices Act, especially the requirement of fair marketing practice.

The Alcohol Advertising Board supervises the marketing of alcohol in Denmark. In collaboration with several professional organisations and public bodies, the board has issued a set of guidelines concerning the marketing of alcohol.[25] In cases where there has been a breach of the guidelines, the board may express criticism. The board cannot impose any legal remedies itself, although in severe cases it may hand the matter over to the Consumer Ombudsman. The guidelines may be used by either the Consumer Ombudsman

---

25   See https://alkoholreklamenaevn.dk/retningslinjerne/retningslinjerne/ (Danish).

or the Danish courts to interpret the fair marketing practice requirement of the Marketing Practices Act.

By way of example, the guidelines provide that the marketing of alcohol must not:

- give the impression that alcohol may be healthy, lead to success or enhance the consumer's psychological or mental capacity;
- connect alcoholic beverages to active sporting activities; or
- show the intake of alcoholic beverages in workplaces or educational institutions.

As regards the advertisement of alcohol on radio or television, specific restrictions apply pursuant to Section 13 of the Ministerial Order on Advertising and the Sponsorship of Radio and Television Programmes.

9.3 Pharmaceuticals

The advertisement of pharmaceuticals is mainly governed by the Medicines Act,[26] the Ministerial Order on Advertising for Pharmaceuticals[27] and the Ministerial Order on the Dispensing of Pharmaceutical Samples.[28]

Additionally, the Danish Medicines Agency has issued a set of guidelines on the advertisement of pharmaceuticals, based on the aforementioned regulations.[29]

The Medicines Act defines 'medicinal products' as all types of products that:

- are presented as a suitable product for the treatment or prevention of diseases; or
- may be used to restore, change or modify physiological functions by exerting a pharmacological, immunological or metabolic effect, or to make a medical diagnosis, regardless of whether the purchase of the product requires a prescription or whether it is a herbal medicine.

General dietary supplements are not covered by the Act. The Medicines Act covers both human and animal pharmaceuticals.

The regulations distinguish between advertising directed towards the 'general public' and that directed towards healthcare personnel (eg, doctors, nurses, dentists, veterinarians). The following mainly relates to advertising directed towards the general public.

Ads for pharmaceuticals must:

- be objective;

---

26 Consolidated Act 99 of 16 January 2018 on Pharmaceuticals.
27 Ministerial Order 1153 of 22 October 2014 on the Advertising for Pharmaceuticals.
28 Ministerial Order 1244 of 12 December 2005 on the Dispensing of Pharmaceutical Samples.
29 Guideline 10356 of 29 December 2014 on Advertising of Pharmaceuticals. See https://laegemid delstyrelsen.dk/en/licensing/supervision-and-inspection/guidelines-on-advertising/~/media/ 2F54F95366514C508D77B7DF0D4F136F.ashx.

- contain sufficient information; and
- not exaggerate the effect of the pharmaceutical product or be misleading in any other way.

When applying these general conditions, broader considerations – such as the objective of limiting the unnecessary consumption of pharmaceuticals – can be taken into account.

Ads for pharmaceuticals must be clearly identifiable as advertising and must make clear that the product in question is a pharmaceutical product. All information in the ad must correspond to the approved product summary of the pharmaceutical product; however, the wording does not need to be identical. Among other more specific requirements with regard to advertising directed towards the general public, it is not permitted to:

- advertise pharmaceuticals that are prescription-only or that are otherwise unfit for use without prior medical attention;
- advertise pharmaceuticals that cannot legally be sold in Denmark;
- hand out pharmaceuticals free of charge (eg, samples);
- indicate that it is unnecessary to seek professional medical assistance;
- indicate that a person's general wellbeing can be improved by using the pharmaceutical product or, alternatively, impaired if the pharmaceutical product is not used; or
- direct the marketing at children;

The regulations require that certain minimum information be provided in ads for pharmaceuticals. The requisite information will differ depending on the medium: more requirements apply if the ad is placed in a magazine compared with on television, radio or outdoors (eg, a billboard at a bus stop). The common information requirements applicable to all such ads include:

- the name of the pharmaceutical;
- the effect of the pharmaceutical;
- any side effects; and
- an explicit invitation to read the information in the patient information leaflet.

Pursuant to the Ministerial Order on Advertising for Pharmaceuticals, specific requirements apply with regard to the comparative advertising of pharmaceuticals:

- It must be clearly indicated which pharmaceuticals are included in the comparison; and
- The comparison must only be between pharmaceuticals that are objectively comparable – that is, medicines with the same scope – and must be based on the information of the authorised product summary.

The Danish Medicines Agency and the Danish Ministry of Health supervise compliance with the legislation. To the extent not covered by the special legislation on pharmaceuticals, the Marketing Practices Act applies. However, the Consumer Ombudsman has stated that in his opinion, the special legislation is adequate and thus does not expect to interfere in the marketing of pharmaceuticals.

9.4 Financial products and services

The advertisement of financial products and services is primarily regulated by the Financial Business Act[30] and the Ministerial Order on Good Practice for Financial Businesses.[31]

Generally, the Financial Business Act requires financial businesses to be operated in accordance with honest business principles and good practice within their field of activity. The Ministerial Order on Good Practice for Financial Businesses states that the commercial practices of financial businesses must not:

- contain incorrect information; or
- by virtue of their form of production or otherwise, mislead or be capable of misleading the average consumer, regardless of whether the information is factually correct.

The advertisement of financial products and services is mainly supervised by the Danish Financial Supervisory Authority. However, the Consumer Ombudsman has the power to handle consumer-related matters within the financial sector in some cases. According to the Marketing Practices Act, the general requirement of fair marketing practice does not apply to financial businesses, to the extent that the aforementioned special regulations apply. However, the Consumer Ombudsman may initiate court proceedings in consumer-related matters regarding violation of the requirement of honest business principles and good practice following from the Financial Business Act. In other instances in which the Marketing Practices Act applies, the Consumer Ombudsman is competent to handle potential violations (in consumer-related matters).

9.5 Food

The advertisement of food is primarily regulated by the Foodstuffs Act,[32] the Ministerial Order on the Labelling of Food[33] and the Marketing Practices Act.

The Foodstuffs Act provides that advertising, labelling, packaging and

---

30   Consolidated Act 705 of 6 September 2019 on Financial Businesses.
31   Ministerial Order 330 of 7 April 2016 with amendments, on Good Practice for Financial Businesses.
32   Consolidated Act 999 of 2 July 2018 on Foodstuffs.
33   Ministerial Order 1355 of 27 November 2015 on the Labelling of Food.

similar must not be misleading. This general condition is supplemented by the Marketing Practices Act, especially in terms of the requirement of fair marketing practice. The ministerial order mainly regulates labelling requirements in relation to ingredients, place of origin, shelf life and so on.

As regards advertising as such, it is not permitted to indicate that a food product has certain qualities if those qualities are required by law (eg, the ad should not specify that the product does not contain a specific substance if that substance is already prohibited by law), or if all similar products have the same qualities. Further, advertising must not state that food products may prevent, ease or have a positive effect on diseases or symptoms of diseases.

In relation to television and radio commercials, the Act on Radio and Television Broadcasting stipulates that it is not permitted to indicate that chocolate, other sweets, snacks and soft drinks may replace regular meals.

9.6   Tobacco

The Act on Prohibition against Advertising for Tobacco[34] explicitly prohibits all forms of advertising for tobacco and products used in connection with tobacco, including products such as pipes and cigarette papers; in practice, this has been extended to prohibit the marketing of items such as humidors. The act defines 'advertising' as all commercial measures aimed at advancing tobacco sales. In addition, the Act on Radio and Television Broadcasting also prohibits the advertisement of tobacco products.

A few exceptions apply to the prohibition against tobacco advertising. For instance, it does not cover communications between professionals within the tobacco business. Tobacco products may also be advertised to customers at the point of sale in certain types of speciality stores relating to tobacco products; and it is generally permitted to place tobacco products close to checkout counters, bars and so on without placing actual tobacco ads there as well. It is expected that upcoming legislation will require tobacco products to be hidden at points of sales – that is, it will be possible to sell them on request, but they cannot be visibly displayed.

9.7   E-cigarettes

The advertisement of e-cigarettes – both with and without nicotine – and refillable containers is regulated by the Act on Electronic Cigarettes.[35] The content of this act corresponds to that of the Act on Prohibition against Advertising for Tobacco.

---

34   Consolidated Act 964 of 26 August 2019 on Prohibition Against Advertising for Tobacco.
35   Consolidated Act 426 of 18 May 2016 on electronic cigarettes.

Finland

Johanna Flythström
Mikael Segercrantz
Verna Syrjänen
Roschier

1. Overview of the legal and regulatory regime for advertising

Advertising is primarily regulated in Finland by law. The legal statutory framework consists of consumer protection laws, including the Consumer Protection Act (38/1978), which regulates advertising to consumers. The purpose of the Consumer Protection Act is to protect consumers from inappropriate advertising, unfair advertising practices and unreasonable agreement terms, among other things. In addition, business-to-business advertising is governed by unfair business practices legislation, such as the Unfair Business Practices Act (1061/1978). The Unfair Business Practices Act aims to prohibit advertising practices which may be harmful for other companies by, for example, regulating comparative advertising. The act also generally prohibits inappropriate business practices as well as false and misleading marketing.

Under the Act on Competition and Consumer Authority (661/2012), prohibitions of advertising in violation of the Consumer Protection Act are issued by the Consumer Ombudsman. They may be challenged before the Market Court. The Act on Certain Competences of the Consumer Protection Authorities (566/2020) was also recently adopted for the purposes of implementation of the EU Consumer Protection Cooperation Regulation[1] in Finland. The act extends the investigatory powers of competent authorities and enables the issuance of penalty payments in case of non-compliance.

In recent years, following the adoption of the General Data Protection Regulation (2016/679) (GDPR),[2] data protection has become increasingly important – especially in relation to direct advertising, advertising to minors and advertising through electronic channels. Sector-specific laws regarding the advertisement of certain products or services (eg, tobacco, alcohol, gambling and pharmaceutical products) and media-specific laws (eg, radio and television legislation) complement the general framework.

---

1   Regulation (EU) 2017/2394 of the European Parliament and of the Council of 12 December 2017 on cooperation between national authorities responsible for the enforcement of consumer protection laws and repealing Regulation (EC) No 2006/2004.
2   Regulation (EU) 2016/679 of the European Parliament and of the Council of 27 April 2016 on the protection of natural persons with regard to the processing of personal data and on the free movement of such data, and repealing Directive 95/46/EC.

In addition to the statutory framework, IP laws such as the Copyright Act (404/1961) and the Trademarks Act (544/2019) must be considered in advertising that contains copyright-protected works and trademarks.

Advertising is also regulated by self-regulatory codes. The main self-regulatory system followed in Finland is the International Code of Advertising Practice published by the International Chamber of Commerce (ICC). The ICC code is not a legally binding instrument as such, but its principles complement the statutory framework. Self-regulatory bodies may issue statements on whether advertising activities comply with the ICC code. Under the Finnish Central Chamber of Commerce, the Council of Ethics in Advertising issues statements to consumers and companies on ethical aspects of specific ads or advertising practices.

The Board of Business Practice, acting under the Finnish Central Chamber of Commerce, handles advertising-related disputes between companies. A company may request a statement from the board on whether certain activities carried out by another business violate good business practice or are otherwise inappropriate, or whether advertising activities carried out by another company violate the ICC code. The matters are decided based on written documents and no hearings are held. The proceedings generally last about three months and in many cases may prove to be more cost efficient for the parties than dispute resolution through other means. If the Board of Business Practice decides that good business practice has not been followed in advertising, the party in breach must rectify its conduct. If a decision of the Board of Business Practice is not complied with, the statement may be published upon request. The board does not handle disputes regarding agreements, IP rights or violations of competition law.

Different industries also have their own self-regulatory codes. As an example, Pharma Industry Finland (PIF) has issued its own Code of Ethics which contains rules on the targeting of pharmaceutical advertising and information at consumers and healthcare professionals. The key principles are that:

- prescription-only medicines may be targeted only at professionals; and
- only self-care medicines available without prescription may be marketed to consumers.

A pharmaceutical company can inform consumers about diseases and their prevention, diagnosis and treatment, and must guide the consumer towards additional information on health promotion and the treatment of the disease. Sailab (MedTech Finland) also has its own Code of Ethics with extensive guidance geared at enabling the development of medical technology and enhancing security and impactfulness, among other things.

The Council of Mass Media in Finland follows the Guidelines of Journalism issued by the Union of Journalists. The guidelines contain provisions on:

- the professional status of journalists;
- the obtainment and publication of information;
- the rights of interviewers and interviewees;
- the correction of mistakes and the issue of opinions; and
- publicity and privacy.

The Ethical Committee for Premium Rate Services has also issued its own set of norms for providing premium electronic services. Its advertising principles concern, among other things:

- the content of advertising;
- the protection of minors; and
- price announcements.

2. Comparative advertising

Comparative advertising is regulated in Finland in Section 2a of the Unfair Business Practices Act, which implements the Comparative Advertising Directive.[3] Consistent with the definitions set forth in the Comparative Advertising Directive, 'comparative advertising' is defined in the Unfair Business Practices Act as "advertising which, either explicitly or by implication, identifies a competitor or a product offered by a competitor". Such advertising is allowed, assuming that it meets the following criteria:

- It is not misleading;
- It compares products that meet the same needs or are intended for the same purpose;
- It objectively compares one or more material, relevant, verifiable and representative features of the products;
- It does not create confusion between the advertiser and a competitor or between their trademarks, company names or other distinguishing features or products;
- It does not discredit or denigrate a competitor's trademark, company name or other distinguishing features or products, actions or circumstances;
- It does not take unfair advantage of the reputation of a competitor's trademark, company name or other distinguishing features, or the designation of origin of a product advertised by a competitor; and
- It does not present products as imitations or replicas of products bearing a protected trademark or name.

Comparative advertising that is not consistent with the Unfair Business

---

3   Directive 2006/114/EC of the European Parliament and of the Council of 12 December 2006 concerning misleading and comparative advertising.

Practices Act may also lead to claims under trademark and copyright legislation. Furthermore, Section 2 of the Unfair Business Practices Act prohibits false or misleading expressions that concern one's own or another party's business and that might affect the demand or supply of a product or damage another's business. It also prohibits the use of expressions that are inappropriate in their form or manner of presentation, or that include irrelevant matters.

In cases of unlawful comparative advertising, the Market Court may prohibit the company from continuing such advertising and reinforce this order with a conditional fine. The prohibition can also be issued on an interim basis. The Market Court may also order that rectifying measures be undertaken where this is necessary due to obvious harm caused by the ad. The order can be reinforced with a conditional fine.

At the request of the applicant, the Market Court may also order that information pertaining to the prohibition order be published in one or several newspapers or magazines (information on interim orders may not be ordered to be published).

Unlawful comparative advertising may also lead to liability for damages under the Damages Act (412/1974). Moreover, under Section 9 of the Unfair Business Practices Act, intentional or grossly negligent violation of the above rules may be punishable as a competition method offence.

3. Online behavioural advertising

The tracking of internet users' online activity for the purposes of online behavioural advertising is regulated in the Act on Electronic Communication Services (2014/917), which implements the e-Privacy Directive[4] as well as the GDPR. The Data Protection Act, however, includes no provisions on cookies or profiling.

The admissibility of processing of non-essential cookie data has recently been under discussion in Finland. Under Section 205 of the Act on Electronic Communication Services, the storage of cookies that track the use of services and the use of such data by the service provider is allowed if:

- the user has given his or her consent; and
- the service provider provides the user with understandable and comprehensive information on the purpose of the storage or use of the data.

Whereas previously, the Finnish Transport and Communications Agency (Traficom) interpreted Section 205 to allow the processing of non-essential cookie data based on consent given through browser settings, without the use

---

4   Directive 2002/58/EC of the European Parliament and of the Council of 12 July 2002 concerning the processing of personal data and the protection of privacy in the electronic communications sector.

of a separate pop-up banner, the Finnish Data Protection Authority held in May 2020[5] that instructing a website user to manage browser privacy settings does not constitute sufficiently active and explicit consent under the GDPR for processing non-essential cookie data.

Traficom has also issued guidelines on the sufficiency of information that is provided to users.[6] According to the guidelines, information on cookies and their purpose, as well as usage data, must be provided to users in a clear and comprehensive manner. In light of the October 2019 *Planet49* ruling of the Court of Justice of the European Union,[7] Traficom has also confirmed that information on the duration of the operation of cookies and whether third parties may have access to cookies must also be provided.

If data collected through cookies constitutes personal data (ie, it relates to an identified or identifiable natural person), the provisions – including sanctions – set out in Chapter 8 of the GDPR apply. Under Section 349 of the Act on Electronic Communication Services, non-compliance with these provisions may constitute a data protection violation in electronic communications, punishable by a fine. It may also lead to criminal liability under Chapter 38, Section 3 of the Penal Code (39/1889), on the basis of message interception.

4.   Sales promotions

4.1   Promotional games

In Finland, the provisions on sales promotions – such as promotional lotteries, discounts, combined offers and giveaways – are mainly set out in Chapter 2, Section 13 of the Consumer Protection Act. Accordingly, if advertising is associated with lotteries, promotional competitions or games, the terms and conditions relating to participation must be clear, understandable and easily accessible. Chapter 2, Section 4 of the Consumer Protection Act applies to promotional lotteries and provides that advertising must make clear its commercial purpose, as well as on whose behalf it is carried out.

The Consumer Ombudsman has also issued Guidelines on Promotional Games[8] that further substantiate the requirements set forth for promotional games. According to these guidelines, when marketing is conducted in the form of promotional lotteries, the following aspects should be clearly stated in connection with the marketing materials:

---

5   https://tietosuoja.fi/-/apulaistietosuojavaltuutettu-maarasi-yrityksen-muuttamaan-tapaa-jolla-se-pyytaa-suostumusta-evasteiden-kayttoon?languageId=en_US.

6   The guidelines are available at www.kyberturvallisuuskeskus.fi/en/our-activities/regulation-and-supervision/confidential-communications.

7   Case C-673/17, *Bundesverband der Verbraucherzentralen und Verbraucherverbände – Verbraucherzentrale Bundesverband eV v Planet49 GmbH.*

8   The guidelines are available at www.kkv.fi/en/decisions-and-publications/publications/consumer-ombudsmans-guidelines/by-subject/promotional-games/.

- who is organising the draw or competition;
- when the draw or competition begins and ends;
- what criteria are used to determine the winner in a competition based on knowledge or skills;
- when the draw will take place; and
- how winners will be informed about winning and receiving the prize.

The guidelines also set out requirements on this information, which should be formulated in a way that is clear and understandable. First, the offer letter may not, for example, mislead the consumer into thinking that it is an announcement of a draw that has already taken place and that he or she has already won a prize. Further, the rules of the promotional game must be presented in all advertising material so that they are clear and readily available to the consumer. If information on a draw is provided in a way that does not enable the consumer to take part in it immediately – for example, in television ads – it is sufficient that the advertising material explains clearly where consumers can find instructions, such as by providing a link to a website. Finally, information on the prizes must be sufficiently detailed.

Promotional lotteries or games should not dominate marketing communications compared to the product offered. Moreover, lavish prizes and a notably high probability of winning are factors that will be considered when assessing whether a lottery may induce the consumer to make a purchase decision that he or she would not have made without the hope of winning. In evaluating dominance, the overall presentation of the material is considered and each part of the campaign is evaluated separately. Promotional lotteries are not considered to be suitable for all products. The advertisement of some product groups requires factuality and greater than normal reliability – for example, credit, health and medical services and products. For example, ads that promised a chance to win an eye operation were deemed to be against good practice. The prizes of promotional games should not be inappropriate – for example, guns or live animals should not be used as prizes.

Under the general provisions of the Consumer Protection Act, advertising must not be misleading. In connection with promotional lotteries, this has been interpreted to mean, for example, that consumers should not be given the impression that they must buy a product in order to be able to participate in a lottery with the opportunity to win a chance-based prize if it is also possible to participate free of charge. Moreover, the use of aggressive marketing methods is prohibited. Therefore, lotteries should not be used for the purposes of advertising products that the consumer (eg, a minor) would not be able to use for one reason or another.

Promotional lotteries are assessed in a stricter manner when they are targeted at minors. Competitions in which consumers can participate by buying a product should not be targeted at minors under the age of 15. Minors can enter into transactions without representation by their guardians only if those transactions are usual and of little significance. Therefore, a minor under the age of 15 cannot effectively give consent to direct advertising and thus a prize draw in which permission is requested for direct advertising cannot be marketed to minors. Such activities should not be used when targeting 15 to 17-year-olds if they involve products that minors cannot purchase independently. Further, if promotional games are targeted at minors, the prizes must be suitable for the target group. The prize should not consist of a product that is prohibited for children, such as a movie or video game that is rated suitable only for adults.

4.2 Discounts

The use of discounts in advertising is regulated in Chapter 2, Section 11 of the Consumer Protection Act. Accordingly, the discount rate should be calculated on the basis of the price that the company has previously charged for the product in question. The Consumer Ombudsman has issued Guidelines on Discount Terminology used in advertising.[9] The main rule is that any type of price comparison is permitted, as long as it is neither untrue nor misleading.

The term 'discount sale' should not be used to describe the affordability of the company's prices in relation to competitors or the overall price level, as the comparison prices must be based on its original prices. Further, a distinction should be made between discount sales and special offers. In this regard, the Consumer Ombudsman's guidelines highlight that a discount sale differs from a special offer in that:

- special offers usually relate to a smaller number of products than discount sales;
- special offers are usually valid for a shorter timeframe than discount sales; and
- special offer price reductions are usually smaller than those in discount sales.

The basis of the discount sale must be the price normally charged by the company in question before the price is reduced. The discount must be calculated on the price at which consumers were able to purchase the product from the marketed place of sale prior to the discount sale. The price of the product may not be declared to be reduced if the price has not in fact been reduced and the price advantage obtained by the consumer is not real. Repeat discount sales are considered inappropriate, as they blur consumers' perceptions of normal price levels at the place of sale and the actual advantage gained from the discount.

---

9   The guidelines are available at www.kkv.fi/en/decisions-and-publications/publications/consumer-ombudsmans-guidelines/by-subject/discount-terminology-used-in-marketing/.

4.3 Giveaways

Combined offers and giveaways are regulated in Chapter 2, Section 12 of the Consumer Protection Act. If such measures are used as part of marketing, the marketing must clearly announce the content and value of the offer, as well as the separate prices of the products offered, unless the price of the giveaway is less than €10. In addition, the conditions of use of the offer – in particular, its duration and quantitative and other limitations – must be stated. The Consumer Ombudsman has noted that consumers are entitled to demand that an advertised free gift be available during the campaign and are not obliged to accept an alternative product instead of the advertised giveaway.

The Consumer Ombudsman has also emphasised the position of children as a special group of consumers, noting that children cannot assess the value of a free gift in the same way as adults. Therefore, a free toy of insignificant monetary value may be more tempting to a child than the product itself. As this makes giveaways an easy way to influence purchase decisions, the advertisers of products that may be of interest to children must ensure in particular that the presentation of a free gift is not the central focus of an ad or packaging.

4.4 Sanctions

Under the Act on Competition and Consumer Authority, the Consumer Ombudsman may prohibit unlawful sales promotions and reinforce this prohibition with a conditional fine. The use of aggressive methods and the unlawful use of giveaways in advertising may also lead to a penalty payment issued by the Market Court at the request of the Consumer Ombudsman. While the amount of this penalty payment is assessed on a case-by-case basis, the maximum amount is 4% of the company's turnover in the fiscal year preceding the violation.

5. Ambush marketing

In Finland, there are no specific legal provisions that prohibit ambush marketing as such. However, depending on the circumstances in each individual case, ambush marketing may be regarded as an unfair business practice or be prohibited as an infringement of IP rights.

In many cases, ambush marketing is conducted either through dilution or as indirect ambush marketing. In such case the provisions on advertising may support a defence against ambush marketing.

Under Section 1 of the Unfair Business Practices Act, fair business practice may not be violated and practices that are otherwise unfair to other entrepreneurs may not be used in business. Further, the commercial purpose of the advertising and the party on whose behalf the ad is distributed must be clearly apparent from the ad.[10] However, the Unfair Business Practices Act includes no specific provisions that expressly refer to ambush marketing.

Ambush marketing is also rarely invoked in Finnish legal practice and there is no established case law on ambush marketing.

However, guidance on questions relating to ambush marketing may be sought through the ICC code.[11] While not legally binding, the ICC code does have an impact on the interpretation of acceptable and prohibited practices.[12]

The ICC code sets the baseline for the assessment of ambush marketing. It requires, among other things, that all advertising communications be legal, decent, honest and truthful.[13] Furthermore, advertising communications should not make unjustifiable use of the name, initials, logo and/or trademarks of another firm, company or institution.[14] Moreover, advertising communications should in no way take undue advantage of the goodwill of another firm, company or institution in its name, brands or other intellectual property; or take advantage of the goodwill earned by other advertising campaigns without prior consent.[15]

The ICC code also includes specific provisions on ambush marketing, which provide that no party should seek to give the impression that it is a sponsor of an event or is providing media coverage of an event, whether sponsored or not, if it is not in fact an official sponsor or providing media coverage. Furthermore, the sponsor and the event organisers should each take care to ensure that any actions taken by them to combat 'ambush marketing' are proportionate and do not damage the reputation of the event or impact unduly on members of the general public.[16]

Unlawful ambush marketing may be prohibited on the basis of either the Unfair Business Practices Act or relevant IP legislation, such as the Copyright Act or the Trademark Act. Liability for damages may also apply.

6. Direct advertising

In Finland, electronic advertising requires prior active consent (opt-in) if it is targeted at a specific natural person. Under Section 200 of the Act on Electronic Communication Services, electronic direct marketing – that is, direct marketing by means of automated calling systems, fax machines or email, text, voice, sound or image messages – may be directed only at natural persons who have given their prior consent.

---

10   See Section 1 of the Unfair Business Practices Act. However, for a business practice to be considered unfair, it is not required to establish that there would have been actual risk of confusion. See, for example, Decision 121/12 of the Market Court.
11   The ICC International Code of Advertising Practice is available at www.iccwbo.org.
12   According to the Government Bill for the Unfair Business Practices Act (HE 1978:114), practices adopted in the commerce may be taken into account when interpreting what constitutes fair business practice on advertising communication. See Government Bill HE 1978:114, p 19, which refers to the practices adopted in commerce (eg, the ICC code). This is also confirmed by Finnish case law – see, for example, Decision 121/12 of the Market Court.
13   See ICC Code (2018), Article 1.
14   See ICC Code (2018), Article 15.
15   See ICC Code (2018), Article 15.
16   See ICC Code (2018), Rule B4.

However, electronic direct marketing is permitted in relation to existing customers where it relates to a previous sale of a product. If a service provider or product seller obtains the contact information (email, text, voice, sound or image messages) of an individual customer in the context of the sale of a product or service, it may use this contact information for direct marketing of its own products in the same product group and of other similar products or services. The customer must have the opportunity to reject this use of his or her contact information, easily and at no charge, both at the time it is collected and in connection with any email, text, voice, sound or image message. The service provider or product seller must notify the customer clearly of the possibility to do so.

Direct marketing other than electronic direct marketing to an individual discussed above is allowed if the individual has not specifically prohibited it. Postal direct advertising that is not addressed to a specific person is permitted, unless a person expressly forbids it. In practice, people can opt out of unaddressed postal direct advertising by placing a sign on their mailbox stating that they do not wish to receive advertising – for example, "No advertising mail" or similar. This ban on unaddressed advertising applies to all unaddressed marketing materials, as the restriction cannot be applied only to specific ads or advertising types. However, it is not possible to prevent official communications and advertising supplements being placed inside newspapers or magazines.

Further, the marketing provisions of the Consumer Protection Act should be taken into consideration, as direct marketing conducted without consent may be considered an aggressive practice within the meaning of Chapter 2, Section 9 of the act. The Consumer Ombudsman, which supervises compliance with the Consumer Protection Act, considers that:

- consumers must be offered an active method to indicate consent to the receipt of electronic marketing messages; and
- companies may not use automatically checked checkboxes, for example, to obtain consent.

In addition, from a data protection law perspective, personal data may not be used for direct marketing if this was not made clear to the consumer at the time of the collection of his or her data. The provisions of the GDPR must be considered when the personal data of a data subject is processed for direct marketing purposes. For example, the controller must:

- duly inform the data subject of the processing of his or her personal data for direct marketing purposes; and
- ensure that the data subject's rights are observed. The data subject has the right, at any time, to object to the use of his or her personal data for direct marketing purposes and the data may no longer be processed for this purpose after such objection has been made.

The Data Protection Ombudsman supervises compliance with both the data protection legislation and the electronic direct marketing provisions of the Act on Electronic Communication Services.

A breach of electronic direct marketing rules may lead to various sanctions. Pursuant to Sections 330 and 332 of the Act on Electronic Communication Services, the Data Protection Ombudsman may issue a remark, which may be reinforced by conditional fine, threat of performance and threat of suspension. In addition, a breach may lead to sanctions under the Act on Certain Competences of the Consumer Protection Authorities. Under Section 15 of that act, a penalty payment may be imposed on a trader that, to the detriment of consumers, intentionally or through negligence, breaches the direct marketing provisions of the Act on Electronic Communication Services. Moreover, under Section 13, breach of the prohibition of aggressive practices set forth in the Consumer Protection Act may also lead to a penalty payment.

7. Product placement

Product placement is regulated in Chapter 26 of the Act on Electronic Communication Services, which contains provisions on marketing in audio-visual and radio programmes in accordance with the Audio-visual Media Services Directive.[17] 'Product placement' is defined in Section 220 of the Act on Electronic Communication Services as any form of inclusion of, or reference to, a product, service or trademark in an audio-visual programme in return for payment or for similar consideration.

In Finland, product placement is permitted only in the following types of programmes, as set out in Section 220 of the Act on Electronic Communication Services:

- cinematographic works;
- films and series made for audio-visual content services;
- sports programmes; and
- light entertainment programmes.

However, product placement is never permitted in children's programmes. The provision of products or prizes for an audio-visual programme free of charge is also considered to be product placement if they are of significant value.

Section 221 of the Act on Electronic Communication Services contains further provisions on product placement. The implementation of product placement is subject to certain limitations. It may not:

17   Directive 2010/13/EU of the European Parliament and of the Council of 10 March 2010 on the coordination of certain provisions laid down by law, regulation or administrative action in Member States concerning the provision of audio-visual media services.

- influence the content of programmes or how they are placed in the programme;
- encourage the purchase or rental of products or services;
- constitute advertising or otherwise refer to products; or
- give undue prominence to the products.

There are also restrictions on the kinds of products that may be marketed by means of product placement. Product placement of tobacco products and products from undertakings whose principal activity is the manufacture or sale of cigarettes and other tobacco products is prohibited. In addition, product placement of specific medicinal products or medical treatments available only on prescription is prohibited.

The use of hidden marketing methods is prohibited in general. This is stated in the general principles applicable to marketing set out in Section 214 of the Act on Electronic Communication Services, according to which marketing must be readily recognisable as such. Section 221 of the Act on Electronic Communication Services contains rules on how such identification should be implemented in product placement. Viewers must be clearly informed that a programme contains product placement by means of text or a sign that is used uniformly by all audio-visual content service providers. Further, programmes containing product placement must be appropriately identified at the start and the end of the programme, and when the programme resumes after a commercial break. The identification need not take the form of advertising. However, product placement need not be identified if:

- the programme in question has been neither produced nor commissioned by the content service provider itself or an undertaking affiliated with the content service provider; and
- knowledge of the product placement could not be obtained with reasonable effort.

Traficom supervises marketing on radio and television and in video-on-demand services. Traficom has issued guidance on the identification of product placement. Traficom considers that the existence of product placement should be identified using text stating that the programme contains product placement or by a product placement logo. In practice, product placement is identified using a common logo placed in the corner of the screen.[18]

---

18 According to Traficom, the four largest commercial television broadcasters in Finland use this common logo for product placement. More information is available on Traficom's website at www.traficom.fi/en/communications/tv-and-radio/marketing-sponsorship-and-product-placement and in Traficom's guidelines on product placement and sponsorship at www.traficom.fi/sites/default/files/media/regulation/Ohje-tuotesijoittelusta-ilmoittamisesta-ja-sponsoritunnisteiden-sisallosta.pdf.

Figure 1. Common logo for product placement

Supervision decisions and coercive measures are regulated in Chapter 42 of the Act on Electronic Communication Services. If these provisions are violated, Traficom may issue a complaint and order that the error be remedied within a specified reasonable timeframe. Traficom can also order an interim decision. A conditional fine, a threat of termination or a threat of taking action at the defaulter's expense may be issued in support of such obligations. Further, under Section 334 of the Act on Electronic Communication Services, a penalty payment may be imposed on a television or radio broadcaster that violates Chapters 25 and 26 (eg, the rules on product placement), and that fails to rectify its actions within a specified timeframe having been requested to do so. In determining the penalty payment, regard must be had to the nature, extent and duration of the relevant action. As a rule, the minimum penalty payment is €1,000 and the maximum is €1 million.

8.   Native advertising and social media influencers

The most interesting legal issues relating to influencer marketing pertain to where the distinction lies between marketing and editorial content in social media – that is, the kinds of activities on social media that constitute marketing and how marketing should be identified in order to distinguish it from other content.

In Finland, there are no specific rules on social media marketing; the same rules and regulations apply to influencer marketing as to other types of marketing, both online and offline. Both the Consumer Protection Act and the Unfair Business Practices Act contain provisions on the identification of marketing. According to Section 4, Chapter 2 of the Consumer Protection Act, marketing must clearly indicate its commercial nature and the entity on whose behalf the marketing is conducted. According to Section 1 of the Unfair Business Practices Act, the commercial purpose of the marketing and the party on whose behalf the marketing is conducted must be clearly apparent from the marketing. Special attention must be paid to marketing targeted to minors, as children are less capable of recognising advertising than adults. In addition, the marketing itself must be consistent with generally accepted marketing practices.

In 2019, the Consumer Ombudsman issued Guidelines on Influencer Marketing in Social Media,[19] which clarified how commercial content should be

---

19   The guidelines are available at www.kkv.fi/en/decisions-and-publications/publications/consumer-ombudsmans-guidelines/by-subject/influencer-marketing-in-social-media/.

identified on social media. 'Influencer marketing' is defined in the guidelines as commercial cooperation between companies and influencers in order to promote the sale of a company's products or raise its brand profile. While the same principles and rules apply to all social media platforms, the features of those platforms vary, so the guidelines provide examples of good identification methods on the most common platforms. The marketing must be clearly recognisable, regardless of whether the consumer is using a computer or a mobile device.

The guidelines provide that at the beginning of every influencer marketing post, it should be clearly stated that the post is an ad for a company or other recognisable commercial name. If the company's official name is not used in consumer marketing, but rather another commercial name, a trademark that is more widely recognised by consumers may be used to indicate the company behind the marketing. The Consumer Ombudsman recommends that the expression 'advertisement' (in Finnish: 'mainos') be used. Alternatively, the wording 'commercial cooperation' (in Finnish: 'kaupallinen yhteistyö') may be used. Therefore, the identification may be presented in the form: "Advertisement with Company X" or "Commercial cooperation with Brand Y". The text should be written in the same language that is used for the content – for example, if the caption of an Instagram post is written in Finnish, the wording should not be in English. The consumer must be able to identify the post as marketing at a quick glance, which means that all marketing posts should be identified as such at the very beginning of the post and not, for example, at the end of a long blog post or at the end of a video.

In addition, Article 7 of the ICC code includes a requirement on identification and transparency, which corresponds to the national rules. In recent years, the Council of Ethics in Advertising has issued several non-binding statements on influencer marketing on various social media platforms. Most of these decisions relate to the identification of marketing. The council has paid detailed attention to, for example, the placement of labels and the graphic implementation, such as the font and colour of the text and background. Even though its decisions are non-binding, they are widely complied with in the industry and thus help to shape how influencer marketing is conducted in practice. They also provide valuable guidance for the industry, as so far, no influencer marketing cases have been tried before the Market Court.

A company is always responsible for its marketing, regardless of the party that it partners with on its marketing efforts; and ultimate responsibility for compliance rests with the company on behalf of which the influencer marketing is conducted. Under the Consumer Ombudsman guidelines, a company in practice fulfils its obligations of marketing identification when it instructs the influencer to act in a way that ensures no hidden advertising is engaged in. Therefore, it is important that companies agree with influencers on, for example, the labelling of commercial posts. Under the Consumer Protection Act, if a non-compliant company cannot be persuaded to cease the unlawful activity voluntarily, the Consumer Ombudsman can refer the issue to the Market Court for resolution. The court may order a prohibition, reinforced with a conditional fine. In addition, the Act on Certain Competences of the Consumer Protection Authorities provides for the imposition of a penalty payment for breach of the identification requirement set out in the Consumer Protection Act.

9.   Industry-specific regulation

9.1   Gambling

In Finland, state-owned Veikkaus Oy has a monopoly for gambling services. The advertisement of gambling is regulated in Section 14b of the Lotteries Act (1047/2001). Accordingly, Veikkaus Oy may advertise gambling if the ad does not promote gambling that causes economic, social or health-related harm and relates only to gambling conducted under the Lotteries Act. Such ads may not be directed at minors, among other things; and the advertisement of gambling is prohibited on television and radio and in cinemas in connection with broadcasts directed at minors. Gambling ads should not depict substantial gambling in a positive light, or non-gambling or reasonable gambling in a negative light. The advertisement of gambling outside the monopoly (ie, by anyone other than Veikkaus Oy) is banned under the Lotteries Act.

The National Police Board monitors compliance with the Lotteries Act. It has competence to prohibit any advertising that violates the above rule. The prohibition may also be reinforced with a conditional fine. A violation of the advertising ban may also be punishable as a lotteries offence under the Criminal Code.

9.2   Alcohol

The advertisement of alcohol is regulated in Chapter 7 of the Alcohol Act (1102/2017). It is prohibited to advertise strong alcoholic beverages – that is, beverages with more than 22% alcohol by volume (ABV). Moreover, the Alcohol Act contains several restrictions with regard to the advertisement of mild alcohol beverages – that is, beverages with a maximum of 22% ABV. These restrictions aim to protect minors and the public at large from the harmful effects of alcohol consumption. The marketing of alcohol may not, for example:

- be targeted at minors under 18 years old;
- contain lotteries or competitions;
- link the consumption of alcohol to driving a vehicle;
- emphasise the alcohol content of the beverage as a positive quality;
- depict abundant alcohol consumption in positive terms or moderate consumption in negative terms; or

- suggest that alcohol increases functional capacity or social or sexual success; has medical or therapeutic effects; or refreshes, calms or helps to settle conflicts.

Further, consumer-generated content cannot be used or shared on online platforms in connection with alcohol marketing, and materials cannot be provided for sharing through such platforms to consumers.

The Regional State Administrative Agencies and the National Supervisory Authority for Welfare and Health (Valvira) monitor compliance with the alcohol advertising legislation. Valvira has also published guidance on the advertisement of alcohol.[20] The Federation of the Brewing and Soft Drinks Industry (Panimoliitto) also sets out good practices in its guidelines,[21] which extend beyond the requirements of legislation.

9.3 Pharmaceuticals

The advertisement of pharmaceuticals is regulated in the Medicines Act (395/1987) and the Medicines Decree (693/1987). The guiding principles are that the advertisement of prescription pharmaceuticals to the public is not allowed and ads should not induce the unnecessary use of pharmaceuticals.

The Finnish Medicines Agency (Fimea) has also issued guidance on the advertisement of pharmaceuticals.[22] The advertisement of pharmaceuticals is also covered in the Code of Ethics of PIF.[23]

Fimea may prohibit non-compliant ads and reinforce this prohibition with a conditional fine. Non-compliant advertising may also be punishable by a fine as a medicinal product offence. PIF also has competence to issue a penalty fine of between €1,000 and €100,000 on members that violate its Code of Ethics.

9.4 Financial products and services

The marketing of credit institutions is regulated in the Credit Institutions Act (610/2014). Chapter 15, Section 2 of the act provides that in its marketing, a credit institution must provide the customer with all information on the product that may be of significance in making decisions on the product. Moreover, the institution may not include false or misleading information in its marketing, or otherwise follow a procedure that is unfair from the point of view of the customer or contrary to good practice. Marketing which does not convey the necessary information from the point of view of the customer's financial security is always deemed unfair. The same marketing requirements apply to

---

20   The guidelines are available in Finnish at www.valvira.fi/documents/14444/221693/Alkoholin_markkinoinnista.pdf/ac0ffcc8-1719-50d1-f7e5-f078c15a40a2.
21   The guidelines are available in Finnish at https://panimoliitto.fi/vastuullisuus/markkinoinnin-itsesaately/alkoholimainonta/.
22   See www.fimea.fi/web/en/supervision/advertising_of_medicinal_products.
23   The Code of Ethics is available at www.pif.fi/media/tiedostot/pif-code-of-ethics-2019.pdf.

payment institutions and are set forth in Chapter 6, Section 32 of the Payment Institutions Act (297/2010).

In addition, the advertisement of consumer credit is regulated in Chapter 7, Section 8 of the Consumer Protection Act, which sets out requirements on the information to be provided when advertising consumer credit. For example, the ad should indicate the actual annual percentage rate of charge if it refers to the interest rate of the credit or any other figure describing the cost of the credit, and other information concerning the terms of the credit agreement. This information must be indicated in a clear, visible and concise manner, and must comply with the credit terms normally offered by the lender.

Moreover, Section 13 on good lending practice prohibits a credit institution from advertising credit in a way that could clearly impair the consumer's ability to consider carefully whether to avail of the credit. This provision supplements the other provisions of Chapter 7, among others.

Under Chapter 7, Section 50 of the Consumer Protection Act, a prohibition on the continuation of actions in breach of Chapter 7 may be issued. The Act on Certain Competences of the Consumer Protection Authorities also allows for the imposition of a penalty payment.

In addition, the Consumer Ombudsman has issued Guidelines on the Provision of Consumer Credit,[24] which provide guidance on the application of the consumer credit rules of Chapter 7 of the Consumer Protection Act.

9.5   Food

In Finland, the marketing of food is regulated in the Food Act (23/2006). The general requirements on information about foods are set out in Section 9 of the Food Act. On food packaging, in presentations and advertising, and otherwise in connection with marketing, information about food must:

- be truthful and sufficient;
- not be misleading; and
- not present the food as having properties related to the prevention, treatment or cure of human diseases or refer to such information, unless otherwise provided elsewhere in the law.

Article 16 of the General Food Regulation also prohibits the provision of misleading information.[25] Further provisions in this regard are issued by decree

---

24   The guidelines are available in Finnish at www.kkv.fi/ratkaisut-ja-julkaisut/julkaisut/kuluttaja-asiamiehen-linjaukset/aihekohtaiset/kuluttajaluottojen-tarjoaminen/.

25   Regulation (EC) No 178/2002 of the European Parliament and of the Council laying down the general principles and requirements of food law, establishing the European Food Safety Authority and laying down procedures in matters of food safety.

26   The guidelines, set out in Chapter 12, are available in Finnish at www.ruokavirasto.fi/globalassets/tietoa-meista/asiointi/oppaat-ja-lomakkeet/yritykset/elintarvikeala/elintarvikealan-oppaat/elintarviketieto_opas_fi.pdf.

of the Ministry of Agriculture and Forestry. Moreover, the Food Safety Authority has issued a guide on foodstuff information, which contains a chapter on marketing.[26]

Chapter 7 of the Food Act contains provisions on administrative coercive measures, which may be reinforced by conditional fine, threat of performance and threat of suspension. Under Section 65 of the Food Act, the Food Safety Authority may prohibit a food business operator from continuing to conduct marketing that violates the food regulations or from resuming such or similar marketing. This prohibition may also be temporary. If the marketing may cause a serious health hazard or is essentially incorrect or misleading, the Food Safety Authority may take additional measures until the marketing has been revised to comply with the regulations. Further, when imposing a marketing prohibition, the Food Safety Authority may oblige the food business operator to submit a correction of marketing.

The provisions on marketing set out in the Consumer Protection Act and the Unfair Business Practices Act also apply to the marketing of food. The Consumer Ombudsman has issued guidelines on the marketing of foodstuffs to children, which require a careful approach to the advertisement of unhealthy products and the avoidance of emotional means of advertising.[27]

9.6   Tobacco

The marketing and display of tobacco products are banned in Finland. According to Section 68 of the Tobacco Act (549/2016), the marketing of tobacco products, tobacco substitutes, smoking accessories, tobacco imitations, e-cigarettes and nicotine-containing liquids is prohibited. Further, according to Section 71 of the Tobacco Act, as a rule, it is prohibited to display tobacco products, tobacco substitutes, e-cigarettes, nicotine-containing liquids and the trademarks thereof in the retail sale of tobacco products, tobacco substitutes, e-cigarettes and nicotine-containing liquids.

Both municipalities and Valvira supervise compliance with the marketing and display prohibitions. A municipality may prohibit actions that violate the Tobacco Act and may cancel a retail licence if the licence holder breaches the marketing and display prohibitions despite the issue of a written warning or a criminal sanction by the municipality or another supervisory authority. Moreover, if tobacco products are marketed in violation of the marketing ban in more than one municipality, Valvira can issue a marketing ban. Pursuant to Section 99 of the Tobacco Act, Valvira may prohibit the party that commissioned or executed the marketing activity, as well as its employees, from continuing or resuming the non-compliant activity. Further, according to

---

27   The guidelines are available at www.kkv.fi/en/decisions-and-publications/publications/consumer-ombudsmans-guidelines/by-trade/children-and-foodstuffs-marketing/.

Section 101 of the Tobacco Act, Valvira may order that the product be withdrawn from the market at the expense of the manufacturer or importer. In addition, under Section 102 of the Tobacco Act, if the non-compliance with the marketing prohibition is of such a nature or significance that its continuation or resumption must be urgently prevented, Valvira may issue a temporary prohibition before reaching a final decision on the matter.

Pursuant to Section 219 of the Act on Electronic Communication Services, companies whose principal activity is the manufacture or marketing of tobacco products are prohibited from sponsoring programmes, audio-visual content services or radio broadcasts.

In addition, the Act on Electronic Communication Services provides that the product placement of tobacco products is prohibited; and that tobacco companies cannot sponsor audio-visual or radio programmes.

9.7   E-cigarettes

The marketing of e-cigarettes is regulated in the same way as the marketing of tobacco products. Therefore, the marketing and display prohibitions and related sanctions under the Tobacco Act as set out in section 9.6 also apply to e-cigarettes; as do the sponsorship and product placement bans set out in the Act on Electronic Communication Services.

France

Emmanuelle Jardin-Lillo
TGS France Avocats

1.   Overview of the legal and regulatory regime for advertising

1.1   Definition

In France, advertising is not a subject that is specifically codified. There is no existing advertising code and no legal definitions. However, 'advertising' has been defined by case law as "any information intended to allow a potential client to get an opinion about the characteristics of products or services offered to him/her".[1]

In this context, the various advertising practices are governed by existing laws and codes, such as the Consumer Code, the Civil Code and the IP Code in particular; as well as by further rules – either explicitly specified or interpreted by way of ethics – set out by advertising professionals.

1.2   Legal framework

Notwithstanding the fact that advertising is not specifically codified in French law, and as a result of increasing pressure from the industry, certain steps have been taken to protect consumers against deceitful information and professionals whose legitimate interests can suffer from some of their competitors' unfair behaviour.

(a)   Protecting consumers

The offence of deceptive advertising was first introduced in Act 63-628 of 2 July 1963, before being extended under Act 73-1193 of 27 December 1973, incorporated into the Consumer Code under Articles L121-1 and following. Later, when EU Directive 2005/29 of 11 May 2009 on unfair commercial practices was transposed into French law, the offence of deceptive advertising was replaced by the offence of deceptive commercial practices. (In fact, after Acts 2008-3 of 3 January 2008 and 2008-776 of 4 August 2008 came into force, which were intended to transpose EU Directive 2005/29 into French law, the European Commission issued summonses on France on 25 June 2009 stating

---

1   Cass Crim, 14 October 1998.

that the French laws did not meet European requirements. A new Act 2001-525 of 17 May 2011 completed the transposition, but was still found to be lacking by the commission.)[2] Under this legislation, unfair (ie, deceptive or aggressive) commercial practices – that is, any practices that do not meet professional diligence requirements and that substantially alter or are likely to materially alter consumers' economic behaviour – are prohibited.

Advertising which is deceptive, misleading or likely to mislead is considered a deceptive commercial practice, incurring criminal penalties of up to two years' imprisonment and a fine of up to €300,000 for natural persons (€1.5 million for corporations), which may increase up to 50% of the advertising costs or to 10% of the average annual turnover, calculated based on the annual turnover figures for the last three years known at the date of the facts.

'Aggressive' commercial practices – that is, pressurising or coercing consumers to influence their choice – are punished by up to two years' imprisonment and a fine of up to €300,000 for natural persons (€1.5 million for corporations). The amount of the fine may be increased, in proportion to the benefits derived from the offence, to 10% of the average annual turnover, calculated based on the annual turnover figures for the last three years known at the date of the facts. Under French law, this is a new offence which groups together some older offences, such as 'abuse of a state of weakness'.

Furthermore, Act 94-665 of 4 August 1994, known as the Toubon Act (replacing Act 75-1349 of 31 December 1975 on the use of French, which is not enforced much), provides that all written, spoken and audio-visual advertisements intended for French consumers must be in French. Breach of this requirement may be subject to criminal penalties (a fine of up to €750 for natural persons and of up to €3,750 for corporations, charged as many times as there are recorded offences). However, the relevant advertising copy may be made available with a translation into one or more foreign languages as well as French.

Additionally, specific provisions are applicable in commercial areas that are considered particularly sensitive (eg, alcohol, tobacco and pharmaceuticals), requiring that consumers be specially protected. These special regulations are described sector by sector in section 9 of this chapter.

(b)   *Protecting competitors*
Case law has established various rules in order to prevent unfair advertising between competitors.

Unfair competition actions generally follow the same rules as standard civil liability suits (Articles 1382 and 1383 of the Civil Code). Proof must therefore be provided that the competitor committed an offence and that damage was suffered as a result of the offence.

---

2   A reasoned opinion was given by the European Commission on 29 September 2011.

Thus, denigrating advertising – that is, discrediting competitors by spreading malicious information about them or their products or services – is punished as an act of unfair competition and anyone who commits it will be held liable. Through unfair competition actions, it may also be possible to protect an advertising concept and punish any imitation likely to create confusion in consumers' minds, and any parasitism.

Reproducing a trademark, an object or a slogan protected by IP rights in an ad without the owner's consent is considered a counterfeiting offence, punishable by three years' imprisonment and/or a fine of up to €300,000. Advertising slogans, pictures and photographs used for an advertising campaign can also be protected by copyright.

1.3 Supervision

In France, there are two independent administrative authorities with the power to monitor and rule on advertising:

- The *Commission National de l'Informatique et des Libertés* (CNIL) is in charge of monitoring and governing the use and processing of personal data; and
- The *Conseil Supérieur de l'Audiovisuel* (CSA) is in charge of guaranteeing the freedom of audio-visual communication.

Moreover, many professional organisations and associations exercise a kind of self-regulation, with recommendations and ethics rules applicable to the content of advertising messages. These are not legally binding, but they may be referred to in court to help judges interpret the texts.

These professional organisations and associations provide legal and practical advice to advertisers and advertising agencies, to help them manage their communication strategies. Particularly well-known organisations include the *Autorité de Régulation Professionnelle de la Publicité* (ARPP) and the *Union Française du Marketing Direct et Digital* (UFMD).

2. Comparative advertising

For a long time in France, comparative advertising met with serious cultural opposition. It was often seen as a disparaging practice, aimed at discrediting competitors or their products or services, and was condemned by the courts. But in Act 92-60 of 18 January 1992 on improving the protection of consumers, the French legislature finally accepted the practice of comparative advertising, which was codified under Articles L122-1 and following of the Consumer Code.

The transposition of the EU Comparative Advertising Directive (97/55/EEC) into French law by way of Order 2001-741 of 23 August 2001 required no significant changes to French legislation; just a few adjustments.

Today, the regulations on comparative advertising are applicable to all advertising that involves a comparison of products or services, and that implicitly or explicitly identifies a competitor or its products or services.

Only commercial advertising is covered, and a distinction must be drawn between comparative advertising and comparative information. Press articles, political campaigns, comparative studies and tests from consumer organisations, among other forms of data comparison, are not included within the scope of the comparative advertising regulations.

2.1 Validity conditions

In France, comparative advertising is allowed only subject to certain limited conditions.

The 'positive' conditions that apply are as follows:

- Comparative advertising must be truthful – that is, it must not be deceptive or likely to be misleading;
- The advertising must concern products or services that meet the same needs or that are intended for the same purpose, substitutable and available to consumers; and
- The advertising must objectively compare one or more essential, relevant, verifiable and representative characteristics of the products or services, without including any subjective comments.

The 'negative' conditions include the following:

- The advertising must not take undue advantage of the good name of a brand, the trade name or other distinctive sign of a competitor, or the designation of origin or protected geographical indication of a competing product;
- The advertising must not discredit or disparage the brands, trade names, other distinctive signs, products or services of a competitor;
- The advertising must not cause any confusion between the advertiser and a competitor, or between the brands, trade names, other distinctive signs, products or services of the advertiser and those of a competitor;
- The advertising must not present the products or services as an imitation or reproduction of any products or services sold under a brand or protected trade name;
- Ads for products sold under a designation of origin or protected geographical indication may include a comparison only with products or services that hold the same designation or indication; and
- Comparative advertising must not be displayed on media such as packaging, invoices, transport tickets, means of payment or tickets giving access to shows or places open to the public.

Although there is no longer any obligation to inform a competitor about comparative advertising involving that competitor before it is published, the advertiser must be able to prove promptly the substantive accuracy of the claims made in the relevant ad.

Where an ad conveys facts that are reasonably considered as truthful, a critical comparison should be tolerated. Nevertheless, the words used in such advertising are important and there is a risk that they may be considered intentionally malicious. This will be true of an ad that only presents negative aspects of a competitor's product.[3]

Rating systems may be used in ads that compare the performance of products, but only provided that the advertiser is in a position to let any interested party know, from the creation of the advertising message, where and how to easily find details of the rating scale used and how it works, in order to check its accuracy.[4]

Comparative advertising on prices is allowed to mention a product range sold by competitors, provided that the products included in a given assortment:

- are identified or designated;
- represent the most common purchases; and
- meet the same needs by being interchangeable.[5]

2.2 Penalties

An advertiser on whose behalf an ad is published is the party responsible for comparative advertising. The professionals who contribute to the design and creation of the advertising message (eg, an advertising agency) may be held civilly or criminally liable together with the advertiser when a breach of the regulations occurs.

French law does not provide for any specific penalties concerning comparative advertising. Instead, the standard penalties provided by law apply for breaches of the regulations:

- civil penalties – action for damages, compensation, cessation of unfair competition practices; and/or
- criminal penalties – court proceedings related to the offence of misleading commercial practices (see section 1) or trademark infringement.

Infringements of the rules on comparative advertising may also be detected and prosecuted by General Directorate for Competition Policy, Consumer Affairs and Fraud Control (DGCCRF) officials, who may, after an adversarial procedure, order the advertiser to cease the unlawful comparative advertising practice within a reasonable timeframe. If, at the end of this period, the

---

3   Cass Comm, 25 September 2012, *Sté Bodum v Sté Nestlé Nespresso.*
4   Opinion 09-14 of 9 December 2009 by *Commission d'examen des pratiques commerciales.*
5   Cass Crim, 4 March 2008.

advertiser has not complied with the DGCCRF's injunction, the DGCCRF may impose an administrative fine on the advertiser, up to a maximum of €3,000 for a natural person and €15,000 for a legal person. DGCCRF officials can also act before the civil court to ask the judge to order the cessation of the practice, after notifying the public prosecutor.

2.3 Online comparators: an exception to the rule?

Comparative advertising presupposes that there is a competitive situation between the operators whose products or services are being compared. In the absence of a competitive relationship between the operators, the court will refuse to accept the classification as comparative advertising. This is the case for online comparison websites where there is no competitive link between the organiser of the website and the compared operators.[6]

However, the competitors whose products or services are compared must be identified, explicitly or implicitly. Since 1 January 2018, online platforms offering comparison tools must also include on their website a specific section dedicated to the methods of comparison used, so that consumers can be informed in the best possible way. For example, if a comparator obtains remuneration from a company in order to position its product at the top of the results, the word 'advertisement' must be expressly mentioned. And since 1 January 2019, online comparators with at least 5 million internet users must now disseminate 'best practices' for the sake of transparency and clarity.

3. Online behavioural advertising

3.1 Issues of principle

Online behavioural advertising has raised some ethical issues in France, arising mainly from the intrusion into the private lives of internet users that results from the gathering and storage of behavioural information, through which the activities of individuals are monitored and a detailed profile of their interests is compiled.

This technique raises issues of principle arising from:
- the nature of the information being collected (often through the use of cookies and similar technical devices);
- the respect due to consumers and their private lives; and
- potential connections with their personal data.

In France, as early as February 2009, the CNIL took an interest in this subject and published a document entitled *La publicité ciblée en ligne* (*Targeted Online Advertising*), which stated as follows:

---

6   Paris Court of Appeal, 22 January 2013, *Sté Concurrence v Google*.

- Online targeted advertising is governed by the rules applicable to the protection of personal data;
- The analysis of online behaviour is allowed only if the internet user has been informed about it and can simply and quickly oppose it; and
- Professionals must be encouraged to adopt good practice codes.

3.2   Legal framework

Through the transposition into French law of the Telecoms Package (consisting of Directive 2009/136/EC of 25 November 2009 amending Directive 2002/22/EC, Directive 2002/58/EC and EU Regulation 2006/2004 on electronic communications) and the implementation of the General Data Protection Regulation (2016/679), it has been possible to define and provide a framework for targeted advertising by recasting Act 78-17 of 6 January 1978, known as the Data Protection Act.

French Governmental Order 2011-1012 of 24 August 2011 on electronic communications provides that cookies can be placed on an internet user's browser only if:

- the user has been informed beforehand of the purpose of those cookies and of the manner in which he or she can opt out; and
- his or her prior consent has been obtained (often referred to as 'opting in').

Under French and EU law, therefore, advertisers that use cookies must comply with two obligations:

- Inform the internet user that advertising cookies are being placed on his or her browser, the purpose of the cookies and the possibility to opt out. Explanations must be clear and clearly displayed. To obtain the internet user's consent, an icon can be used containing a link to a notice or dedicated site, a banner at the top of a page, a consent request area, a tick box or other similar means.
- Allow the internet user to express his or her choice on whether to receive targeted advertising through the placement of cookies on his or her browser. The internet user's prior consent must be clearly and accurately requested. Users must be provided with simple ways to accept or refuse – in general or in particular, permanently or only once – the placement of the advertiser's cookies on their devices.

Failure to comply with these fairness and transparency rules towards internet users may entail:

- penalties from the CNIL of up to €20 million or, in the case of an undertaking, up to 4% of its total worldwide annual turnover in the preceding financial year, whichever is higher; and

- criminal penalties of up to five years' imprisonment and/or a fine of up to €300,000.

The prior consent and information rules do not apply to a cookie:
- whose sole purpose is to allow or facilitate electronic communication (eg, flash cookies to operate an audio or video medium player);
- which is strictly required to supply an online communication service at the user's express request (eg, 'user session' cookies); or
- which is exempt under certain circumstances defined in the CNIL Guidelines of 4 July 2019 on cookies and other trackers (eg, trackers intended for authentication with a service or trackers intended to save the contents of a shopping cart on a merchant site).

Where a systematic and extensive evaluation of personal behaviour of a natural person takes place based on automated processing, including profiling, and decisions are taken based on that processing which have legal effects for the natural person or similarly significantly affect him or her, a data protection impact assessment is required. An evaluation of the impact of the envisaged processing operations on the protection of personal data is mandatory under French law and according to a CNIL decision of 11 October 2018 regarding processing operations that are subject to the requirement of a data protection impact assessment.

3.3   Self-regulation

For several years now, the industry has been working on the implementation, in France and in Europe more widely, of self-regulatory rules that facilitate the development of targeted advertising in an atmosphere of trust and respect for internet users. By as early as 2009, several French professional associations had drawn up good practice rules that promote:
- transparency;
- respect for internet users' private lives;
- increased protection for some categories of internet users; and
- the safe handling and storage of information that is collected.

In 2010 a recommendation, entitled *La publicité ciblée sur Internet*, was adopted by the *Forum des droits sur l'Internet* for the better identification of online behavioural advertising, to implement a system that allows internet users to opt out (although not in a manner that is consistent with the 'opt-in' system referred to above), and to prohibit the targeting of children under 13 in such advertising.

An ethics charter (*Charte sur la publicité ciblée et la protection des internautes*) was then signed by the French government and 10 professional associations.

This charter includes recommendations on:

- internet users' information;
- the exercise of their rights with regard to online targeted advertising;
- connections between browsing data and personal data;
- location-based advertising;
- the right to erase cookies;
- the protection of children under 13; and
- the control (ie, capping) of exposure to advertising.

In 2012, as an extension of the ethics charter, some professional associations drew up a Good Practice Guide on the Use of Advertising Cookies, which in particular suggests typical ways to inform internet users on the use of cookies for advertising purposes.[7]

3.4 The key role of the CNIL

In 2019 and 2020, the CNIL decided to make targeted advertising a priority. After consulting with various stakeholders (professional associations and civil society) in Autumn 2019, the CNIL circulated a draft Recommendation on Cookies and Other Tracers in January 2020, which it submitted for public consultation for several weeks.

Moreover, in a decision of 19 June 2020, the *Conseil d'État* essentially validated the guidelines on cookies and tracers adopted by the CNIL on 4 July 2019. The guidelines explain the rules resulting from the GDPR on the collection of consent to cookies. The guidelines also make a number of recommendations. The protection of the personal data of internet users is also strengthened.

As part of its action plan on targeted advertising and in order to take into account the entry into force of the GDPR, the CNIL released amending guidelines and a recommendation regarding the use of cookies and other tracking devices on 17 September 2020 (published on 1 October 2020).

The CNIL aims to give internet users more control over the use of their data for advertising purposes and has reminded them of two main principles:

- Internet users must be clearly informed of the purposes of cookies; and
- It must be as easy for internet users to refuse cookies as to accept them.

The CNIL also asked players to comply with the rules as clarified, confirming that the period of adaptation should not exceed six months.

On 7 December 2020, the CNIL's restricted committee, which is responsible for imposing sanctions, fined:

---

[7] This guide is accessible on the website of the *Union Française de Marketing Direct & Digital* and on the sites of participating associations.

- Amazon Europe Core €35 million for placing advertising cookies on users' computers through the amazon.fr website without obtaining prior consent and without providing adequate information; and
- Google LLC and Google Ireland Limited a total of €100 million for placing advertising cookies on the computers of users of search engine google.fr without obtaining prior consent and without providing adequate information.

Although these decisions concerned breaches of obligations that existed before the GDPR came into force, and thus did not relate to the new guidelines and recommendation of the CNIL, they demonstrate the importance of this matter to the CNIL.

4. Sales promotions

The French legal provisions on promotional operations such as lotteries, sales with bonuses and tied sales were amended in May 2011, in order to comply with the EU Directive on Unfair Commercial Practices (2005/29/EC).

However, the transposition of this directive was incomplete and the French legal system still had specific features. In light of the case law of the Court of Justice of the European Union, the French legislature was forced to rethink the transposition and go further towards harmonising its national regulations with the EU regime. Thus, Law 2014-1545 of 20 December 2014 relating to the simplification of business life completed the transposition of the directive; while Order 2016-301 of 16 March 2016 completely overhauled the French Consumer Code accordingly.

Such practices are now punishable by two years' imprisonment and a fine of €300,000 for natural persons and €1.5 million for legal entities, which may be increased to 10% of average annual turnover, calculated based on the annual turnover figures for the last three years known at the date of the facts, or to 50% of the advertising expenditure incurred.

4.1 Promotion through price

(a) Price reductions

A price reduction on a product or service to encourage purchase may be implemented by way of an immediate or deferred discount voucher. This technique involves:

- offering, for the purchase of a given product, an immediate reduction coupon against the purchase of another product; or
- granting to anyone who purchases a given product a discount against the subsequent purchase of another product, whether this product is identical to or different from the original purchase.

Initially, in order to be authorised, this practice had to comply with the provisions of the Decree of 31 December 2008 on the advertisement of price reductions to consumers, and could not involve selling at a loss. This decree was repealed by Decree of 11 March 2015, which now provides that any advertisement of price reductions is lawful provided that it does not constitute an unfair commercial practice.

In practice, the terms and conditions remain the same. It is preferable to ensure that the price reduction offer is clearly formulated and detailed, with an indication of the amount of the reduction, the product concerned, the name and references of the issuer, the period of validity and so on.

(b)   Refund offers

Refund offers involve offering consumers a refund of the price of their purchase against proof of purchase, through either a coupon found on the product itself or any proof of purchase. This promotion technique allows consumers to obtain, against submission of a given number of proofs of purchase, a refund of the cost of a product.

The price may be refunded in full or in part, and for the sale of one or more identical products, in which case proofs of purchase are often collected through a single medium (eg, a loyalty card). Where the offer is for a full refund, the operation may be considered a gift or a sale with a bonus. Where the offer is for a partial refund, the operation is considered a price reduction governed by the regulations concerning price reduction notices and sale at a loss. In that case, the terms of the operation must be clearly displayed and accurately described on the product itself, for fear of the advertiser or vendor being charged with misleading advertising. The same goes for any restriction or obligation that consumers must comply with in order to be entitled to a refund.

In addition to the legal and regulatory provisions applicable to promotional operations, the technique of promotion through price is expected to comply with some ethics rules set forth in a recommendation entitled *Publicité de prix* and drawn up by the ARPP concerning price presentation and any references linked to the price.

4.2   Promotion through product showcasing

(a)   Tied sales

Tied sales include two types of practices:
- related sales, in which a product or service is provided subject to the purchase of another product or service; and
- batch sales, where several products, whether similar or not, are sold in the same package.

The regulations applicable to tied sales were relaxed in 2011 to comply with European requirements on the authorisation of tied sales, subject to the following conditions:

- Consumers are free to purchase separately the products being sold in a batch; and
- Products sold in a batch are complementary and serve the same purpose (eg, a set of saucepans).

In 2014, in order to ensure full transposition of the EU regulations, the French legislature went even further by simplifying the legal framework for tied sales. Henceforth, making the sale of a product conditional on the purchase of a fixed quantity or on the concomitant purchase of another product or service, and making the provision of a service conditional on the provision of another service or on the purchase of a product, are prohibited where such conditions constitute an unfair commercial practice (Article L121-11 of the Consumer Code).

(b) Sales with a bonus

Sales with a bonus attract consumers by offering them the prospect of obtaining, in consideration for the purchase of a product or service, another product or service provided free of charge or at a low cost.

In 2011, the regulations on sales with a bonus were relaxed slightly, in order to comply with European requirements. Sales with a bonus are legal if:

- they are not found to be unfair; and
- the value of the bonus being offered does not exceed 7% of the sale price of the main product.

The bonus must be marked with the name, brand or logo of the relevant party, provided that such labelling complies with the rules on advertising.

In 2014, in order to ensure full transposition of the EU regulations, the French legislature went even further by simplifying the legal framework for sales with a bonus in the following way: "any sale or offer for sale of products or products or any provision or offer for provision of services made to consumers giving entitlement, whether free of charge, immediately or in the future, to a premium consisting of products, goods or services shall be prohibited where the practice in question is unfair" (Article L121-19 of the Consumer Code).

4.3 Promotions by way of games

(a) Prize draws

The legal framework for prize draws has also been relaxed in order to comply with European requirements.

In 2011, prize draws were permitted, provided that they did not require a financial contribution from participants and were not unfair in any manner. In 2014, the French legislature went further in order to harmonise the regime with the European requirements. Now, any commercial practice in the form of promotional activity that aims to confer a prize or advantage of any kind by means of a prize draw, through whatever means or through the intervention of a random element, is prohibited if this practice is unfair (Article L121-20 of the Consumer Code).

In practice, the specific presentation rules previously required to avoid misleading consumers still apply. Among other requirements, these rules require that the following information be provided:

- a list of the prizes on offer, including their nature, exact number and market value;
- the specific wording *"Le règlement des opérations est adressé, à titre gratuit, à toute personne qui en fait la demande"* ("The rules of the game shall be sent, free of charge to anyone requesting them"); and
- the name and details of the public officer (a bailiff who is responsible for ensuring that the draw meets all legal requirements) with whom these rules have been filed.

(b) Competitions

As opposed to lotteries and prize draws, which rely on chance, competitions rely on the shrewdness, skill or intelligence of participants, who then win prizes according to their ranking.

There are no specific penalties as far as competitions are concerned, but penalties may be incurred on the grounds of deceptive or misleading advertising. In this context, it is better to provide specific presentation rules about the existence and/or value of prizes in particular, and to file these rules with a bailiff.

4.5 The special case of food products

Law 2018-938 of 30 October 2018 on the balance of commercial relations in the agricultural and food sector and healthy, sustainable and accessible food for all (known as the EGALIM Law), supplemented by Order 2008-1128 of 12 December 2018 and Decree 2018-1304 of 28 December 2018, introduced new rules on sales promotions and the threshold for resale at a loss of foodstuffs and products intended for pet food. The application of these provisions is limited to two years.

For example:

- the threshold for resale at a loss is raised by 10%;
- the use of the word 'free' is now prohibited; and
- promotions are capped twice:

- in value (capped at 34% of the selling price); and
- in volume (capped at 25% of the forecast turnover of the reference concerned).

On 5 February 2019, the DGCCRF published guidelines to help operators in the agri-food sector to implement the thresholds capping promotions and the ban on the use of the term 'free' for foodstuffs. These guidelines on the framework for promotions were updated on 16 January 2020.

The current experiment of raising the threshold for resale at a loss and the framework for promotions for foodstuffs was recently extended by Law 2020-734 of 17 June 2020, which relaxed the volume framework for foodstuffs with a marked seasonal character.

Law 2020-1525 of 7 December 2020 on accelerating and simplifying public action (known as the ASAP Law) has reaffirmed the conditions for raising the threshold for resale at a loss and the framework for promotions, in terms of value and volume, for relevant foodstuffs and other products until 15 April 2023. The ASAP Law provides for a specific derogation from the volume-based promotion framework (25%) for certain seasonal foodstuffs or categories of foodstuffs, a list of which will be determined by ministerial order. These provisions are applicable to contracts in progress as at the date of entry into force of the ASAP Law.

As a reminder, the resale or announcement of resale of a product in its current state at a price that is lower than the actual purchase price is notably punishable by a fine of €75,000 for a natural person and €375,000 for a legal entity. Failure to comply with the regulations on the supervision of promotions by a supplier or distributor will be punishable by an administrative fine of €75,000 for a natural person and €375,000 or half of the advertising expenses incurred as a promotional advantage for a legal entity.

5. Ambush marketing

Ambush marketing – referred to as '*marketing à l'embuscade*', '*marketing sauvage*' or '*marketing pirate*' – is not yet a well-known practice in France. Ambush marketing was first used in France during the 2007 Rugby World Cup: the DIM Company sat young girls in the *Stade de France* who undressed during matches to reveal underwear manufactured by the company. The 'DIM DIM Girls' created a worldwide buzz at the time.

In a 10 February 2012 decision, the Paris Court of Appeal defined 'ambush marketing' as activity by "a company to get public visibility during a sports or cultural event in order to associate its image with that event, while avoiding paying anything to the organisers and becoming an official supporter".

In itself, the technique of ambush marketing is not illegal in France. It often consists of the following:

- purchasing advertising space close to an event or during its broadcasting on television;
- referring to signs or brands that have been registered by the event organiser and other symbols or images relating to the event;
- purchasing tickets or official products in order to give them away, either directly or through promotional operations, in favour of one's own products or services; or
- organising activities, competitions or similar in parallel with the main event.

The different ways to deter ambush marketing include the following.

5.1 Event marketing rights

In France, sports federations and organisers of sports events own the marketing rights for the events that they organise (Article L333-1 of the Sports Code). This ensures that they can control any marketing action in connection with the event. So, for instance, the publication of photographs taken during the event must be authorised by the organiser.

However, the Court of Cassation stated in a 20 May 2014 decision that an infringement of the ownership of exploitation rights of sports federations and sports event organisers over the sports events or competitions that they organise presupposes an appropriation or exploitation of those sports events or competitions. This decision therefore opens the door to controlled and lawful ambush marketing, which involves the use of sports news without infringing the monopoly of the federations that organise the relevant sports events.

Moreover, the exercise of such marketing rights is restricted by the obligation to respect freedom of expression. Sports federations and organisers of sports events cannot, as owners of the marketing rights, impose on the athletes who take part in an event any obligation that may infringe their freedom of expression (Article L333-4 of the Sports Code).

5.2 *Ad hoc* laws

While ambush marketing practices find fertile ground in all events that are widely covered by the media, they are particularly prominent during major sports competitions, because of the media impact. In this context, the rules of the game are becoming increasingly complex, incorporating *ad hoc* legislation adopted on the recommendation of the organiser (eg, the International Olympic Committee or UEFA) by the host states of the event. These rules are binding and sometimes even derogate from internal standards.

For a few years now, the organisers of major sports events, in partnership with the cities hosting these events, have lobbied for the adoption of legal measures, such as those enacted for the London Olympic Games in 2012. These special laws are innovative because they are the first to expressly deal with ambush marketing; but their scope is limited in both time and space. The purpose of such *ad hoc* laws is often to protect the signs and images relating to the relevant sports event; they may also serve to regulate advertising within and around the event. Apart from specific regulations on the Olympic Games (see below), to this day such measures have never been adopted in France.

In the same way, media and marketing regulations for the FIFA World Cup clearly prohibit ambush marketing, which is defined as any attempt by any entity to gain an unauthorised commercial association with the competition itself, or to exploit the goodwill and publicity generated by the competition or FIFA in a manner that is not expressly authorised by FIFA.

5.3 The classic legal framework

More generally, 'parasitism' is often claimed before French courts to condemn ambush marketing practices. Anything that a company does to take advantage of another company's efforts without paying for it may be considered as parasitism. However, in order to file a claim for unfair or parasitic competition, a number of conditions must be met:

- An actual competition must exist;
- An offence must have been committed; and
- Damage and causality must be linked.

Proving all of these can be problematic.

Trademark laws may provide appropriate protection to sports event organisers that register expressions and signs related to the event as trademarks. Moreover, in France, the French National Olympic and Sports Committee owns national Olympic emblems, the Olympic motto, hymn and symbol, as well as the terms 'Olympic Games' and 'Olympiad'. It is also strictly prohibited for anyone to file as a trademark, reproduce, imitate, display, delete or change these signs without the prior consent of the French National Olympic and Sports Committee (Article L141-5 of the Sports Code).

6. Direct marketing

6.1 Legal framework

Under French law, 'direct marketing' is defined in Article L34-5 of the Post and Electronic Mail Code as "direct prospecting by way of automated calling or communication systems, telefaxes or electronic mail, using contact information of natural persons". Direct marketing regulations therefore concern only operations aimed at natural persons; professionals and corporations are not protected by French law.

Insofar as direct marketing relies on the contact information of natural persons which allows for their identification, this information is regarded as personal data. Direct marketing must therefore comply with the rules on the protection of personal data and especially the Data Protection Act, as amended by Act 2018-493 of 21 June 2018, as well the GDPR.

There are further requirements under the data protection legislation on the creation of databases containing personal data. The details of these requirements are beyond the scope of this chapter, but the requirements include:

- giving appropriate notices;
- obtaining consent in certain circumstances; and
- generally collecting and processing personal data fairly and lawfully, and for specific, explicit and legitimate purposes.

The CNIL is competent to control and audit all data controllers and/or processors.

Upon failure to comply with applicable provisions of the aforementioned regulations, the CNIL may issue a warning (considered as a penalty), or impose financial penalties of up to €20 million or, in the case of an undertaking, up to 4% of the total worldwide annual turnover in the preceding financial year, whichever is higher. Criminal penalties may also be imposed (up to five years' imprisonment and a maximum fine of €300,000), pursuant to Article 226-16 and subsequent articles of the French Criminal Code.

The French Consumer Code requires companies conducting direct marketing by telephone to compare their prospecting files with a national list – known as BLOCTEL – containing the telephone numbers of consumers who do not wish to be solicited by telephone. Otherwise, the rental or sale of files that contain telephone data and the contact details of one or more consumers who are registered on the BLOCTEL list is prohibited. Any professional that enriches or makes available to other professionals a commercial prospecting file must use the BLOCTEL service before making the file available, to ensure that it complies with the list.

At the same time, several professional organisations and associations organised together under the UFMD have drawn up an email charter entitled *Code relatif à l'utilisation de coordonnées électroniques à des fins de prospection directe*. This code is intended for professionals who use direct marketing techniques for commercial purposes, and reasserts the need to comply with the fundamental principles of personal data protection.

6.2 Opting in and opting out

Direct marketing operations are subject to compliance with the data protection legislation, as they involve the use of personal data such as names, postal addresses, email addresses and telephone numbers. The basic principle is that anyone may object, free of charge and without justification, to his or her data being used for marketing purposes. However, the rules differ depending on the type of direct marketing operation, as follows:

- Direct marketing by fax, email, text or multimedia messaging: Advertising is possible provided that the person has expressly consented to be contacted (via a checkbox) at the time of collection of the email address, phone number or fax number. This is an 'opt-in' system, involving prior consent. However, there are two exceptions to this rule:
  - if the prospect is already a client or if the advertising is for products or services which are similar to those already provided to the prospect by the company; or
  - if the advertisement is not commercial in nature (eg, for a charity).

  In both cases, at the time of collection of the contact information, the prospect must be informed and given the opportunity to oppose (via a checkbox) the use of his or her personal data for marketing purposes. This is an 'opt-out' system, relying on the right of the data subject to oppose the processing.
- Direct marketing by post or telephone: Advertising is possible provided that the person contacted has been informed and given the opportunity to oppose (via a checkbox) the use of his or her address or telephone number at the time of collection of the personal data. This is an 'opt-out' system, also known as an opposition right.

In December 2018 the CNIL stated its position on data transfers to (commercial) partners:

- The data subject must give valid consent prior to any data transfer to partners. Therefore, the data subject must be informed about partners and data recipients on the collection form: either an exhaustive and up-to-date list of partners must be included on the collection form, or the full list must be accessible through a link to updated privacy and/or cookie policies.
- The data subject must be informed whenever the list is revised or modified.
- Each new partner that receives data must, when communicating for the first time with the data subject and at the latest within one month, inform the data subject of the processing activities made with its data.
- The consent collected by a data controller on behalf of its partners is valid only with regard to those partners.

7. Product placement

Long regarded as 'surreptitious' advertising, product placement was not allowed in French television programmes until 2010. In movies, however, the use of this practice dates back to the end of the 19th century, without being regulated.

In France, product placement generally relies on an agreement under which an advertiser pays a certain sum of money to have its product shown on screen. The agreement may also involve loaning equipment or providing services during filming.

7.1 Legal framework

Product placement in movies has historically been tolerated and is subject to no specific legal framework.

In relation to television, the EU Audio-visual Media Services Directive (2007/65/EC) – which was transposed into French law by Act 2009-258 of 5 March 2009 on audio-visual communication – officially recognised the existence of product placement as an audio-visual commercial communication and established a legal framework for it. The directive established a principle for the prohibition of product placement – although member states may allow it, under certain conditions, for cinematographic works, films and series made for audio-visual media services, sports and entertainment programmes.

French law officially allows product placement on television and gives the CSA the authority to supervise it, while ensuring compliance with the following rules:

- The content of programmes, including product placement, must not be influenced in any manner that affects the publisher's editorial responsibility and independence;
- The programmes must not directly encourage people to purchase the products or include promotional references;
- The programmes must not unjustifiably highlight the product; and
- Television viewers must be clearly informed of existing product placement at the beginning and the end of the relevant programmes, as well as upon their resuming after a commercial break.

In its Deliberation 2010-4 of 16 February 2010, completed by Deliberation 2012-35 of 24 July 2012, the CSA stated as follows:

- Product placement is allowed only in cinematographic works, audio-visual works of fiction and music videos, excluding those aimed at children. It is prohibited in all other programmes.
- Product placement is not allowed for products for which advertising is prohibited or strictly controlled for public health or safety reasons (eg, spirits, tobacco, medicines, firearms).
- Programmes including product placement must be clearly identified with the pictogram 'P' (see Figure 1) appearing for one minute at the beginning of the programme, after each commercial break and during the whole length of the credits at the end of the programme. For music videos, the pictogram must be permanently displayed. Television

services must regularly inform television viewers by displaying a banner saying: "This programme includes product placement."

Figure 1. Pictogram to be shown in programmes that include product placement

7.2 Recent developments

Today, product placement is often also included in non-audio-visual media, but without any real regulation.

Product placement in video games – also known as in-game advertising – is increasingly common. New technological opportunities are also increasing the use of product placement, such as augmented reality and 'click to buy'.

Above all, the real proliferation of product placement is to be found on social networks. Whether on Instagram, Facebook, YouTube or Snapchat, influencers are increasingly taking advantage of their fame to highlight the products of certain brands in their publications (eg, videos, stories, photos and articles). Digital product placement has become a very powerful communication tool.

In this context, the ARPP has completed its Digital Advertising and Marketing Communications Code, which focuses on influencers' communications with brands. Because an influencer can intervene in collaboration with a brand in order to publish content (eg product placement, participation in content production, publication of commercial content), influencers must disclose to consumers the existence of a commercial relationship with the advertiser (see section 8).

8. Native advertising and social media influencers

Native advertising and social media influencers are digital communication techniques that are increasingly evolving without any clear and adapted legal framework, although digital advertising and marketing communications must comply with rules based on the principles of the International Chamber of Commerce.

In its recommendation entitled *Communication Publicitaire Digitale* (*Digital Advertising Communication*), the ARPP recently adopted new provisions on native advertising (October 2015) and communications between influencers and brands (June 2017), in order to reflect the current realities of the market.

8.1   Native advertising

Native advertising covers all advertising formats that adopt or are closely integrated within the design and appearance of the website on which they are displayed.

In this context, the ARPP considers that the commercial nature of such advertising must be identified unambiguously and in a clear and immediate way, with a clear note such as 'advertising', 'sponsored by...' or 'in partnership with...'. This note must be readable or audible and legible, in order for the commercial nature of this material to be immediately understood.

Given the editorial appearance of such advertising, special attention should be paid to the truthfulness and fairness of the content.

8.2   Social media influencers

Influence marketing is a communication strategy that allows a brand to disseminate information through influential people online and/or through social networks. The aim is to improve the image or fame of the brand through targeted communications to a qualified audience.

The ARPP has analysed communications from influencers to define their specificities. An influencer (or blogger, vlogger or similar) – that is, an individual expressing a point of view or giving advice – may act within a purely editorial framework, which is outside the scope of professional regulation of advertising, or in collaboration with a brand for the publication of content.

According to the ARPP, the existence of a commercial collaboration between an influencer and an advertiser for the publication of content must be made known to the public. This can be done by any means. It is generally considered acceptable to insert a statement such as 'in partnership with...' or 'sponsored by...' on communications. The functionalities integrated into social networks now make it possible to directly and easily identify these partnerships. On Instagram, for example, the phrase 'paid partnership with...' appears under the name of the influencer.

If no mention is made, the communication will be considered as a misleading commercial practice pursuant to Articles L121-2, 3° and L121-4 of the French Consumer Code.

The nature of the influencer's statement as advertising is established when the following criteria are met:

- The influencer receives benefits as a result of the creation of the content, whether financial remuneration or advantage or consideration in any form whatsoever – in particular, the delivery of products or services in his or her favour;
- The advertiser or its representatives exercise preponderant editorial control (in particular, by including mentions or scenarios) and validation of the content; and
- The influencer's speech is aimed at promoting the product or service.

In this case, the content of the message published by the influencer is regarded as advertising. It must then comply with the ARPP's ethical rules and the applicable legislation on advertising.

8.3 A 'first global legislative initiative'

The French legislature recently decided to fill the legal void concerning child influencers. Law 2020-1266 of 20 October 2020 regulates the commercial exploitation of the images of children under the age of 16 on online video platforms (eg, YouTube, TikTok, Instagram); it will come into force six months after its publication, in April 2021. The aim is to respond to the growing phenomenon of child 'YouTubers', whether they are active within the context of an employment relationship or outside it.

Child influencers whose activities are considered as work now benefit from the protection of the Labour Code; as do child models, performers and advertisers. Before filming their children or broadcasting videos of their children, parents must request individual authorisation or approval from the administration.

For those grey areas of the Internet where the activities of child influencers are not part of an employment relationship, protection is also provided. A declaration of activity must be made where certain thresholds (relating to the duration or volume of content, or the income earned from its distribution) are met.

Furthermore, video sharing platforms are encouraged to adopt charters to combat the illegal commercial exploitation of the images of children under 16. The objectives are:

- to encourage users to be informed;
- to encourage reporting;
- to take useful measures in the event of a report;
- to improve the detection of situations that present a risk to minors; and
- to facilitate the right of minors to erase data.

The CSA is in charge of promoting the signature of these charters.

Nevertheless, contrary to what was proposed in the original text, the responsibility of the platforms remains theoretical, as no binding mechanism has been put in place thus far. Consequently, it remains unclear whether the law of 19 October 2020 provides a response that is commensurate with the issues at stake.

9. Industry-specific regulation

Specific provisions on advertising apply in many sectors of the French economy, including the following.

9.1 Gambling

Various industry bodies have drawn up ethics rules on gambling – in particular, the *Jeux d'argent* recommendations published in July 2009 by the ARPP. The advertisement of gambling is also regulated by Act 2010-476 of 12 May 2010 (amended by Act 2012-354 of 14 March 2012) and Decree 2010-624 of 8 June 2010, which sets forth two principles:

- Any advertising must include a warning against excessive and pathological gambling, and a message referring to an information and assistance system; and
- Special protection is provided for minors, and ads for gambling are strictly prohibited in any publication, audio-visual programme or website that is specifically intended for minors.

When the majority of the capital of *La Française Des Jeux* was transferred to the private sector, the French government took the opportunity to amend the legislation on gambling and games of chance.

Order 2019-1015 of 2 October 2019 reforming the regulation of gambling and games of chance recast the regulations by codifying the general principles of gambling and hazard law in the Internal Security Code (Articles L320-1 and following of the Internal Security Code). In particular, this order strengthened the framework for commercial communications in favour of gambling and hazard games, and introduced a requirement to provide information to players on the risks associated with excessive or pathological gambling by means of a warning message. A fine of €100,000 may be imposed in the event of non-compliance. This order also created, on 1 January 2020, a new independent administrative authority, the National Gaming Authority. Decree 2020-199 of 4 March 2020, completed by Decree 2020-1349 of 4 November 2020, specifies the methods of operation and organisation of the authority, as well as its powers of control and sanction.

9.2 Alcohol

The advertisement of alcoholic beverages is governed by Articles L3323-2 and following of the Public Health Code, arising from Act 91-32 of 10 January 1991 on tobacco and alcohol control, known as the *loi Evin*. This law deals with the direct and indirect advertising of alcohol (among other things). 'Indirect' advertising is defined as advertising for any activity or product other than an alcoholic beverage which, through its graphics, design or use of a trademark or advertising sign, is reminiscent of an alcoholic beverage.

The law also includes an exhaustive list of permitted advertising media and the content of permitted advertising for alcoholic beverages. 'Permitted media' include:

- the press (except publications for young people);
- radio (during specific time slots);
- posters, leaflets and items inside drinking establishments;
- trade circulars;
- catalogues and brochures; and
- the Internet.

'Permitted content' includes:

- the origin, name and composition of a product;
- the preparation method, sales method and consumption method of a product;
- its area of production;
- any prizes and awards obtained;
- the labels of origin or other geographic indications; and
- the colour and characteristics pertaining to aroma and taste.

Anything that is not expressly allowed in the *loi Evin* is strictly forbidden.

Any alcohol advertising must include a health warning in the following form: *"L'abus d'alcool est dangereux pour la santé. A consommer avec moderation"* ("Excessive drinking is dangerous for your health. Drink in moderation").

Illegal advertising of alcoholic beverages is punishable by a fine of up to €75,000 for natural persons (€375,000 for corporations), which may be increased to 50% of the sum disbursed to finance the advertising campaign.

In addition to the legal requirements for alcohol advertising, various industry bodies have drawn up ethics rules – in particular, the recommendation entitled *Alcool*, published in June 2010 by the ARPP.

9.3   Pharmaceuticals

Advertising for medications is strictly governed by Articles L5122-1 and following of the Public Health Code, which relate to all forms of information, prospectuses and incentives intended to promote the prescription, delivery, sale or ingestion of medications.

The advertisement of medications to the public is limited to medications that:

- need not be prescribed by a doctor;
- are not refunded by mandatory health insurance schemes; and
- have obtained full marketing authorisation.

Such ads must not be misleading or detrimental to public health protection, and must objectively describe medications and encourage their proper use. Fines ranging from €3,750 to €37,500 may be imposed for any illegal advertising.

Ads are subject to prior control by the *Agence Nationale de Sécurité du Médicament et des produits de santé* (ANSM), which issues 'advertising visas' as appropriate and provides marketing authorisations for medications.

In March 2014 the ANSM published a charter on the communication and promotion of health products (medicines and medical devices) online and in e-media. The charter aims to help operators to design their websites and digital offerings in compliance with the regulations, by distinguishing what qualifies as advertising, and is hence covered by the provisions laid down by the Public Health Code, from what qualifies as information or online sales.

On 2 October 2019 the ARPP and the National Council of French Medical Associations signed a partnership agreement with the aim of defining good practices and a common doctrine in the field of health communication.

9.4 Financial products and services

Governed by the Monetary and Financial Code and the general rules of the *Autorité des Marchés Financiers* (AMF), advertising for financial products must, broadly speaking, comply with standards of clarity, accuracy and consistency. It must be well balanced and mention any potential risks that may be involved, as well as the corresponding benefits.

If these regulations are not adhered to, measures may be ordered by the AMF or a court action for deceptive advertising may be initiated. The AMF's Enforcement Committee may take disciplinary measures against professionals (a warning, reprimand or temporary or permanent ban on some or all of the services being provided) and/or financial penalties, in an amount that may not exceed €100 million or 10 times the profits that may have been made.

Law 2016-1691 of 9 December 2016 (known as the Sapin II Law), relating to transparency, the fight against corruption and the modernisation of economic life, regulates the advertisement of certain categories of financial contracts. Since 1 January 2017, direct or indirect advertising sent by electronic means to non-professional clients relating to the provision of investment services concerning speculative and high-risk financial contracts has been prohibited (new Article L533-12-7 of the Monetary and Financial Code and Article L222-16-1 of the Consumer Code). Any sponsorship or patronage of investment services relating to financial contracts is also prohibited (Article L222-16-2 of the Consumer Code). In the event of non-compliance with these prohibitions, all players involved in the dissemination of advertising may incur an administrative fine of up to €100,000.

The AMF and industry bodies have also drawn up guides and recommendations for investment service providers. In October 2017 the ARPP adopted three new recommendations on financial advertising for:

- financial and investment products and services;
- leveraged financial products and contracts, providing exposure to forex, stock market indices, commodity prices and binary options; and
- so-called 'atypical investments' and related services.

Specific regulations also apply to the advertisement of consumer credit, property loans, interest-free credit or revolving credit, and even reverse mortgage loans. However, these aspects are beyond the scope of this chapter.

9.5 Food

The advertisement of food is governed by all general provisions on deceptive advertising and labelling discussed earlier in this chapter. Such advertising must therefore:

- be clear and accurate;
- not mislead consumers about the characteristics of the foodstuff concerned; and
- not claim to provide any protection, treatment or cure.

With regard to processed food and drinks with added sugar, salt or artificial sweeteners, ads must include a health warning, such as:

- *"Pour votre santé, mangez au moins cinq fruits et légumes par jour"* ("For your health, you should eat at least five fruit and vegetables per day"); or
- *"Pour votre santé, pratiquez une activité physique régulière"* ("For your health, you should take regular physical exercise").

The content of this information and the manner in which it is publicised will depend on the relevant medium (eg, press, posters, radio, television, cinema or Internet). The requirements are governed by the Order of 27 February 2007 setting out the terms concerning health messages that must be included in advertising or promotional messages in favour of some foodstuffs and beverages. Failure by advertisers to comply with this information obligation is punishable by a fine of €37,500, which may be increased to 30% of the advertising expenditure.

In October 2018 the *Direction Générale de la Santé* referred to *Santé Publique France* (the national public health agency, established in May 2016) proposed changes to the health messages set out in the Order of 27 February 2007 that accompany ads for certain foods and beverages. On 24 June 2020, *Santé Publique France* published the results of a survey on the exposure of children and adolescents to advertising, according to which:

- it recommended that priority be given to regulating commercial communication and promotion of brands on television and on the Internet, and in particular that advertising, product placement and television sponsorship for fatty, sweet and savoury products and associated brands be banned during the time slots when the greatest number of children and adolescents watch television; and

- it proposed that the system of health messages be adapted so that these fully play the role of behavioural incentives and are thus dissociated from the advertising content.

Various industry bodies, in collaboration with the French government, have also drawn up specific ethics rules to promote dietary habits and physical activity that are beneficial for people's health in programmes and ads that are broadcast on television. In addition, the ARPP has published various recommendations – in particular, *Comportements alimentaires* (modified in June 2014) – setting forth ethics rules in favour of a balanced diet.

9.6   Tobacco

The advertisement of tobacco and tobacco products is governed by Articles L3511-1 and following of the Public Health Code, arising from the *loi Evin*.

Any direct or indirect advertising for tobacco or tobacco products is thereby strictly prohibited. This even extends to any use of a trademark or advertising sign that might be reminiscent of tobacco or any tobacco product. There are some exceptions to this general rule, relating to signs for tobacco outlets, posters inside tobacco outlets, specialist professional publications and so on. However, any such advertising must include health warnings such as "*Fumer tue*" ("Smoking can kill you") or "*Fumer provoque des maladies graves*" ("Smoking can make you seriously ill").

9.7   E-cigarettes

The advertisement of e-cigarettes is banned in France under Order 2016-623 of 19 May 2016, which transposed Directive 2014/40/EU of 3 April 2014 on the manufacture, presentation and sale of tobacco and related products. The order prohibits propaganda or advertising, whether direct or indirect, for e-cigarettes. However, advertising posters may still be installed in establishments that sell e-cigarettes, provided that these are not visible from the outside. The ban on advertising also does not apply to publications and online communication services published by professional organisations, or to specialised professional publications.

Illegal advertising of tobacco is punishable by a fine of up to €100,000 for natural persons (€500,000 for corporations), which may be increased to 50% of the advertising costs.

Germany

Susan Kempe-Müller
Latham & Watkins LLP

1. Overview of the legal and regulatory regime for advertising

In Germany, advertising law is governed by the Unfair Competition Act, which applies to all commercial practices. In addition, special laws apply to the advertisement of certain products (eg, medicinal products) and advertising by certain occupational groups (eg, lawyers or doctors). Furthermore, the general provisions of the Civil Code – for example, regarding tortious liability – apply; but they play only a minor role.

The Unfair Competition Act implements several EU directives, the most important of which are the Misleading Advertising Directive (2006/114/EC) and the Unfair Commercial Practices Directive (2005/29/EC).

Pursuant to its Section 1, the Unfair Competition Act aims to protect competitors, consumers and other market participants against unfair commercial practices. At the same time, it protects the interests of the public in undistorted competition (see the civil law prohibitions under Sections 3–7 of the act). Individual commercial practices which are deemed particularly reprehensible are also punishable by imprisonment or a fine (Sections 16–20 of the act). These aspects of the legal framework are described in the remainder of this section.

1.1 Civil law prohibitions

The Unfair Competition Act follows the systematic structure of the Unfair Commercial Practices Directive and contains three different types of advertising prohibitions:

- All commercial practices listed in the Annex to the act, the so-called 'blacklist', are illegal under Section 3(3) of the act. The blacklist includes particularly serious types of misleading and aggressive advertising in business-to-consumer relationships.
- There are advertising prohibitions that are worded less narrowly than those included in the blacklist, and for these there is more room for interpretation. The prohibitions cover other types of aggressive (Section 4a), misleading (Sections 5 and 5a) or disturbing (Section 7) advertising. Moreover, comparative advertising (Section 6) and acts against a competitor (Section 4) are also regulated.

- Sections 3(1) and 3(2) of the act contain blanket clauses on the prohibition of unfair commercial practices which apply residually when the more specific provisions do not apply. The blanket clauses are applied relatively rarely.

Claims for removal may be asserted under the Unfair Competition Act against anyone who engages in an unfair commercial practice. If there is a risk that an impermissible practice is to be used for the first time or if there is a risk of recurrence, claims for injunctive relief may be asserted against the advertiser (Section 8(1)). Not only competitors are entitled to make such claims, but also, for example, certain industry associations (Section 8(3)). In Germany, justified claims for injunctive relief may be enforced by a court within a few days through a preliminary injunction.

Moreover, under Section 9 of the act, anyone who, with intent or negligently, engages in an unfair commercial practice is obliged to compensate the competitor for damages.

1.2 Criminal law prohibitions

Certain types of advertising are punishable as criminal offences. These include, in particular, misleading advertising using false information in communications directed at a wider audience (eg, newspaper ads) with the intent of creating the impression of a particularly favourable offer (Section 16(1) of the Unfair Competition Act). For instance, the Federal Court of Justice convicted mail order retailers for sending catalogues of products to numerous consumers together with incorrect prize notifications. The retailers had informed consumers about valuable gifts they would receive if they ordered an item from the catalogue. However, the promised gifts were never awarded.[1]

Under Section 16(2) of the Unfair Competition Act, some methods of direct marketing are also punishable as criminal offences, especially 'snowball' and 'pyramid' schemes. Indeed, anyone that advertises by means of a telephone call made to a consumer without the latter's prior express consent commits an administrative offence under Section 20 of the act.

2. Comparative advertising

Section 6 of the Unfair Competition Act defines 'comparative advertising' as well as the requirements for its permissibility.

'Comparative advertising' is defined in Section 6(1) of the act as "any advertising which explicitly or by implication identifies a competitor or the goods or services offered by a competitor". For a long time, it was controversial

---

1   BGH, *Gewerblicher Rechtsschutz und Urheberrecht* (GRUR) 2008, 818: *strafbare Werbung im Versandhandel* (punishable advertising in mail order business).

whether the mere recognisability of a competitor's products or services was sufficient for advertising to be deemed comparative or whether a comparison contrasting the products was required. Today, the Federal Court of Justice upholds the latter view.[2] Comparative advertising is deemed to exist only where offers are presented as alternatives to consumers. Merely criticising a competitor, alluding solely to its reputation or making an invitation to compare products will not suffice to bring the activity within the comparative advertising regime.

Section 6(2) of the act governs the permissibility of comparative advertising. According to Section 6(2), item 1, a comparison is permissible if it relates to products or services that meet the same needs or are intended for the same purpose – a "sufficient degree of exchangeability" is required.[3] According to Section 6(2), item 2, a comparison is also not deemed unfair if it objectively relates to material, relevant, verifiable and representative features or the price of the products or services. The comparison must not lead to a risk of confusion between the advertiser and a competitor, or between the products or services offered by them (Section 6(2), item 3).

The comparison must not:

- take unfair advantage of, or impair the reputation of, a distinguishing mark used by a competitor (Section 6(2), item 4); or
- discredit or denigrate the products offered by a competitor (Section 6(2), item 5).

However, the mere contrasting of the advantages and disadvantages of the products compared is inherent to comparative advertising and is not deemed to discredit the products within the meaning described above. A comparison is discrediting only if special circumstances arise that make the comparison appear unreasonably derogative, deprecatory or non-objective.[4] Humorous or ironic comparative advertising can be permissible even if it is not restricted to fine humour or subtle irony. Such comparative advertising constitutes an impermissible deprecation only when it mocks or ridicules the competitor or is taken literally, and thus seriously, by the audience to whom the advertising is addressed.[5]

Moreover, pursuant to Section 6(2), item 6 of the act, the offer made by the advertiser must not be an imitation of products or services sold under a protected distinguishing mark (the so-called 'perfume clause').

Section 6 of the Unfair Competition Act does not, however, conclusively

---

2   BGH, GRUR 2012, 74, margin no 19: Coaching newsletter.
3   ECJ, ECR 2007, I-3115-3184, GRUR 2007, 511, 514: *De Landtsheer v CIVIC*; ECJ, ECR 2006, I-8501-8558, GRUR 2007, 69, 72: *LIDL Belgium v Colruyt*.
4   BGH, GRUR 2008, 443, margin no 18: *Saugeinlagen* (absorbent food pads).
5   BGH, GRUR 2010, 161, margin no 20: *Gib mal Zeitung* (Gimme the paper).

regulate comparative advertising; the other provisions of the act also apply to such marketing techniques – for instance:

- the prohibition against misleading consumers (Section 5); and
- the prohibition against asserting or disseminating untrue facts which are likely to cause harm to a competitor's business operations (Section 4, item 2).

Individual cases of comparative advertising are regulated in other laws – for example, comparative advertising of medicinal products targeting any other audience than health professionals is governed by Section 11(2) of the Healthcare System Advertising Act.

The use of a trademark in comparative advertising may constitute trademark infringement. This, however, does not apply to comparative advertising permitted by Section 6 of the Unfair Competition Act. It is an intrinsic characteristic of comparative advertising that it identifies a competitor or its products or services (under the definition of Section 6(1)); consequently, the reference to a competitor's trademark or other distinguishing mark may be indispensable for effective comparative advertising and, provided that the requirements for the permissibility of comparative advertising (as outlined above) are observed, such reference does not constitute an infringement of the competitor's right of exclusivity.[6] If, however, the use of the trademark is unfair within the meaning of the Unfair Competition Act, it may also constitute trademark infringement.[7]

3. Online behavioural advertising

When engaging in online behavioural advertising, data privacy must be considered. At a European level, the most relevant legislation in this context is the e-Privacy Directive.[8] However, the e-Privacy Directive has not been implemented into German law. The federal government saw no need to transpose the directive, arguing that the relevant provisions already existed under Sections 12–15 of the Telemedia Act. In fact, provisions on the handling of personal data on the Internet can be found in Sections 11–15a of the Telemedia Act. 'Telemedia' in this context is defined in Section 1(1) of the act as electronic information and communication services excluding telecommunication services and broadcasting.

The question of which law governs data privacy in relation to telemedia and online behavioural advertising became the subject of debate with the

---

6   Recitals 14 and 15 of Directive 97/55/EC; Recitals 14 and 15 of the Misleading Advertising Directive 2006/114/EC; BGH, GRUR 2008, 628, margin no 15: *Imitationswerbung* (imitation advertising); ECJ, C-533/06, GRUR 2008, 698, margin nos 39 *et seq*: *O2 v O2 (UK)*.

7   For further detail see Köhler/Bornkamm/Feddersen, *Gesetz gegen den unlauteren Wettbewerb UWG: Kommentar*, 38st edn, 2020, Section 6, margin nos 34 *et seq*.

8   Directive 2009/136/EC, amending Directive 2002/28/EC.

enforcement of the General Data Protection Regulation[9] (GDPR) in 2018. Article 95 of the GDPR states that the provisions of the e-Privacy Directive are given precedence over the GDPR under certain circumstances.[10] Subsequently, this raised the question of whether the respective provisions of the Telemedia Act also take precedence over those of the GDPR. The Conference of the Independent Data Protection Authorities of the Federal Government and the German States takes the stance that the regulations of the GDPR apply first and foremost, as the e-Privacy Directive was not transposed into the Telemedia Act. Furthermore, there is no room to apply the e-Privacy Directive directly.[11]

This topic became particularly controversial following the Court of Justice of the European Union's (CJEU) 2019 ruling on the use of cookies in advertising.[12] In relation to cookies, Article 5(3) of the e-Privacy Directive requires the user's prior consent to store cookies for that user ('opt in'); whereas Section 15(3) of the Telemedia Act stipulates that cookies for advertising purposes and market research may be stored without the user's active consent, as long as the data stored is pseudonymised and the user does not object ('opt out'). Under the opt-out option, websites frequently used pre-ticked checkboxes in order to ensure users' consent to store advertising and tracking cookies. However, the CJEU ruled that this does not constitute valid consent for cookie storage, regardless of whether the cookie contains personal data. Subsequently, the Federal Court of Justice concurred with the decision, arguing that Section 15(3) of the Telemedia Act must be interpreted in conformity with the e-Privacy Directive.[13]

Thus, considering the ongoing debate and the fact that the long-awaited e-Privacy Regulation is still in the drafting phase at the EU institutions, uncertainties regarding this topic remain. To give a broad overview of all relevant law, the respective stipulations of both the Telemedia Act and the GDPR are outlined below.

Pursuant to Sections 12(1) and 12(2) of the Telemedia Act, the collection and use of personal data are permissible only if legally permitted or if the user has given his or her consent.[14]

In collecting data, a distinction is made in Germany between 'inventory data' and 'usage data'. 'Inventory data' is the basic personal data of the contractual relationship, such as the name, address and classification of the agreed service. Such data may be collected and used to the extent that it is

---

9   Regulation (EU) 2016/679.
10   Conrad/Hausen in Auer-Reinsdorff/Conrad, *Handbuch IT- und Datenschutzrecht*, 3rd edn, 2019, Section 36, margin no 7.
11   See p 6 of "Guidance from the Supervisory Authorities for providers of telemedia:, www.datenschutzkonferenz-online.de/media/oh/20190405_oh_tmg.pdf.
12   ECJ, GRUR 2019, 1198: *Planet49*.
13   BGH, ruling of 28 May 2020 - I ZR 7/16: *Cookie-Einwilligung II* (cookie consent II).
14   The Telemedia Act is not applicable to user profiles that are fully anonymised from the outset – for example, the type and duration of a website visit without reference to the individual user – as these profiles cannot be attributed to specific individuals.

required for the creation, content design or amendment of a contractual relationship on the use of telemedia between the service provider and the user (Section 14(1) of the Telemedia Act). 'Usage data' is data that inevitably accrues during and as a result of the telemedia usage, such as data identifying the user or data on the type of individual use of the Internet (eg, browsing beginning and end points, and websites visited). Some data constitutes both inventory and usage data (eg, a user's name).[15]

Under Section 15(1) of the Telemedia Act, usage data may be collected and used only to the extent that this is necessary in order to facilitate or invoice for the utilisation of telemedia. This necessity must be interpreted in a narrow sense.[16] The use of data for online behavioural advertising is generally not considered necessary because internet services can also be offered without such advertising and/or without any personalised advertising; the advertising is merely a secondary aspect of the internet service.[17] Consequently, under Sections 12(1) and 12(2) of the Telemedia Act, personal data may be used for personalised advertising only with the user's consent.

It is also prohibited to consolidate a user's usage data on the utilisation of various telemedia, except for invoicing purposes (Section 15(2)). The use of profiles for any purposes other than those mentioned in the law is not permissible. Consequently, the transmission of usage profiles to third parties is in particular not permitted.

Under the GDPR, a number of provisions must be observed when storing cookies that contain personal data. 'Personal data' (Article 4(1) of the GDPR) means any information relating to an identified or identifiable natural person, such as his or her name, email address or IP address.[18] Data must be processed in accordance with the general principles outlined in Article 5 of the regulation, such as lawfulness, transparency, data minimisation, storage limitation and accountability of the data controller. Furthermore, data processing is considered lawful only if the requirements of Article 6 of the GDPR are met. In relation to cookies, the most relevant instances include:

- consent (Article 6(1)(a));
- execution or preparation of a contract (Article 6(1)(b)); and
- presence of a legitimate interest (Article 6(1)(f)).[19]

Additionally, the data subject must be provided with the information listed in Article 13 of the GDPR, including:

---

15   Regarding content data and connection data, see Schmitz in Spindler and Schmitz (eds), *Telemediengesetz: Kommentar*, 2nd edn 2018, Section 15, margin nos 42, 75; and Bauer, *MMR 2008*, 435, 436.

16   *Ibid*, margin no 42.

17   Bauer, *MMR 2008*, 435, 436.

18   CJEU, *Neue Juristische Wochenschrift (NJW)*, 2016, 3579, margin no 49.

19   See p 7 of "Guidance from the Supervisory Authorities", www.datenschutzkonferenz-online.de/media/oh/20190405_oh_tmg.pdf.

- the purpose of the data processing;
- the contact details of the data controller;
- the period for which the data will be stored; and
- the users' privacy rights, such as the right to be forgotten (Article 17) or the right to object (Article 21).

If these provisions are violated, the data subject has the right to lodge a complaint with a supervisory authority (Article 77) and may be entitled to compensation for material or non-material damages suffered as a result of an infringement.

Personalised online advertising must also be in line with the provisions of the Unfair Competition Act. Particularly important are cases in which a user fails to recognise advertising as such as a result of personalisation, as this type of concealed advertising is unfair under Section 5a(6) of the Unfair Competition Act.

4.   Sales promotions

The typical forms of promotional measures in Germany are premiums (gifts made conditional on the purchase of products or the use of services), discounts, loyalty programmes, gifts, prize competitions, promotional contests and special product or price guarantees. They are used at all levels of the distribution chain and may be directed at consumers, retailers or even sales personnel.

Up until the 2015 version of the Unfair Competition Act, very strict standards had applied in Germany in relation to sales promotions. Some promotional measures were prohibited entirely. A number of these restrictions were removed with the amendment of the Unfair Competition Act in 2015. However, a few restrictions still apply and some sales promotions are explicitly banned by law. All other promotional measures must align with the general provisions of Sections 3–7 of the Unfair Competition Act regarding advertising, meaning that they must not:

- be conducted in an aggressive or misleading way;
- violate professional diligence; or
- represent an obstruction of a competitor or of the market in general.

In all cases, the promotional measures must not be misleading (Sections 5 and 5a of the Unfair Competition Act), meaning that the conditions of the sales promotion must be stated clearly and unambiguously at the time of the promotion. These conditions include all circumstances restricting the possibility of consumers obtaining the benefit which they could not anticipate beforehand.[20] The conditions must also be easily accessible. This is not the case

---

20   BGH, GRUR 2010, 247, margin no 13: *Solange der Vorrat reicht* (while stocks last); BGH, GRUR 2009, 1064, margin nos 33: *Geld-zurück-Garantie II* (money-back guarantee II).

if, for instance, the conditions are printed only on the underside of a label of a yoghurt drink that customers cannot see until they buy the drink and open it.[21]

The blacklist set out in the Unfair Competition Act explicitly mentions a number of prohibited means of sales promotion. For example, it is prohibited:

- to create a false impression that the consumer has won a prize when such a prize does not in fact exist or when the possibility of obtaining a prize is subject to the consumer paying money (Annex to the Unfair Competition Act, item 17); or
- to offer a promotional contest without awarding the prospective prizes or a reasonable equivalent (Annex, item 20).

Moreover, consumers must not be provided with false information suggesting that a product is available only for a short amount of time in order to force consumers into making a purchase (Annex, item 7). Lastly, a product must not be labelled 'for free' or 'free of charge' if there are actually costs associated with it that are not considered inevitable costs (Annex, item 21).

So-called 'combined offers' – meaning the granting of gifts, guarantees and chances of winning in addition to the main service – were deemed unfair under the Unfair Competition Act prior to 2015. Now, combined offers are generally not considered unfair practices. Businesses may offer their products separately or with combined offers, meaning that they are also free to decide whether the additional services or products are of lower or higher value than the promoted product.[22] In a number of cases, however, combined offers are explicitly banned by law – for example, under Section 24(1) of the Tobacco Tax Act or Section 7(1) of the Healthcare System Advertising Act. Furthermore, a combined offer is considered to be misleading if consumers are not provided with clear and unambiguous information regarding the availability and features of the additional services or products or the fact that they can be acquired only upon purchase of the promoted product.[23] Combined offers must also not deliberately target vulnerable consumers such as children and adolescents, migrants or sick people. Otherwise, they will be deemed a violation of professional diligence under Section 3(2) of the Unfair Competition Act.[24]

Discounts are another type of sales promotion that is generally considered permissible under the Unfair Competition Act. To avoid being considered misleading, information must be provided stating, in particular:

---

21 BGH, GRUR 2009, 1064, margin nos 30 *et seq*: *Geld-zurück-Garantie II* (money-back guarantee II).
22 BGH, GRUR 2002, 967, 978: *Kopplungsangebot I* (combined offer I); Köhler in Köhler/Bornkamm/ Feddersen, *op cit*, Section 3, margin no 8.21.
23 BGH, GRUR 2010, 247, 248: *Solange der Vorrat reicht* (while stocks last); OLG Stuttgart, GRUR-RR 2007, 361, 362; BGH, GRUR 2002, 967, 978: *Kopplungsangebot I* (combined offer I); Sosnitza in Piper/Ohly/Sosnitza (eds), *Gesetz gegen den unlauteren Wettbewerb: Kommentar*, 7th edn, 2016, Section 5a, margin no 33.
24 BGH, GRUR 2002, 967, 979: *Kopplungsangebot I* (combined offer I); GRUR 1998, 1041, 1042.

- the time limits on the offer;
- the limitations to the group of participants; and
- the minimum and maximum order quantities.[25]

However, it is generally permissible to add 'while stocks last' as a condition.[26] A ban on discounts exists for retailers with regard to the sale of new books, as book prices are fixed by law and must not be altered (Section 3 of the Fixed Book Price Act).

Businesses may also try to boost sales by way of loyalty or pay-back programmes for their customers. Unlike discounts and premiums, which are usually given out as a one-time offer, there is a risk that loyalty programmes may generate a 'pulling effect' on members. This may lead to customers focusing solely on that business due to their membership of the loyalty programme, to the effect that they disregard other businesses and their products. Depending on the extent of the pulling effect, the loyalty programme may be considered an aggressive advertising practice (Section 4(a) of the Unfair Competition Act), especially if customers are forced to make purchases in order to avoid their bonus points expiring after a unreasonably short period of time.[27] Also, loyalty programme members must not be given misleading information (Section 5(1)) suggesting that bonus points constitute a certain price advantage or that they may be paid out in cash to the customer.[28]

Promotional gifts may also be used by business as an incentive for customers. Unlike premiums, gifts are products or services which are given out free of charge and regardless of the purchase of the business's products, in order to encourage customers to buy products of that business in general. In order not to be considered misleading, customers must be informed of:

- who is giving out the gift;
- what actions are required to receive it; and
- possible subsequent costs that may arise from accepting the gift.[29]

With regard to participation in a promotional contest or prize competition, the relevant conditions of participation must be stated clearly and unambiguously, and must be made easily accessible to the participants, so as not to be deemed misleading (Section 5a(2)). However, this does not include the obligation to provide information about the actual chances of winning, the number of prizes and the amount of tickets given out. If this information is supplied, on the other hand, it must not be misleading.[30]

---

25   BGH, GRUR 2009, 1064, margin no 28: *Geld-zurück-Garantie II* (money back guarantee II).
26   BGH, GRUR 2010, 247, 248: *Solange der Vorrat reicht* (while stocks last).
27   OLG Jena, GRUR-RR 2002, 32, 33 *et seq.*
28   Köhler in Köhler/Bornkamm/Feddersen, *op cit*, Section 3, margin no 8.55.
29   *Ibid*, Section 3, margin nos 8.61 *et seq.*
30   *Ibid*, Section 3, margin no 8.78.

Moreover, before 2015, the Unfair Competition Act provided that a combined offer of tying a promotional contest or prize competition to the purchase of products or the use of a service was generally deemed unfair. However, the CJEU ruled in 2010 that such a prohibition, which does not consider the circumstances of any individual case, runs counter to the Unfair Commercial Practices Directive and is thus contrary to EU law.[31]

Following the CJEU, the Federal Court of Justice decided that such a combined offer is considered unfair only if, in the individual case, it constitutes a misleading business practice or conflicts with the requirements of professional diligence.[32] A practice may be deemed to be misleading if consumers are misled about the chances of winning or insufficiently informed about the conditions for participation or the possibilities of winning. With regard to professional diligence, the Federal Court of Justice has left the question undecided as to whether a violation may exist if a combined offer in a prize competition constitutes such a strong incentive that it destroys the rationality of the average consumer's demand decision.[33] Following the case law, it can be expected that prize competitions and promotional contests tied to sales transactions will in future be prohibited only in individual cases.

Irrespective of the above, these concerns are relevant from a legal perspective only if a prize competition exists separately from the sales transaction. It is not relevant if the price for products or services is subject to a certain event – for example, where the rate of interest of a cash investment depends on the outcome of a sporting event, or when every hundredth purchase in a supermarket is free.[34]

Lastly, prize competitions, raffles and similar contest are banned when advertising medicinal products, procedures, drugs and similar outside the health professionals market (Section 11(1), sentence 1, item 13 of the Healthcare System Advertising Act; see section 9.3).

5. Ambush marketing

German law generally does not provide for any exclusive right of an organiser to the publicity effect of an event. It is generally permitted to report on an event, to use the existing public interest in it and to advertise in the surroundings of the event; moreover, advertising measures placed deliberately in the physical proximity of a competitor's advertising cannot be objected to as a hindrance to that competitor.[35]

31   ECJ, C-304/08, GRUR 2010, 244, margin nos 49–51: *Plus Warenhandelsgesellschaft* (Plus trading company).
32   BGH, GRUR 2011, 532, margin no 25: *Millionen-Chance II* (chance in a million II).
33   BGH, NJW 2014, 2279, margin no 23: *Goldbärenbarren* (Geld Bear Bars); GRUR 2011, 532, margin no 26: *Millionen-Chance II* (chance in a million II); further examples of violations and non-violations of professional diligence given by Köhler in Köhler/Bornkamm/ Feddersen, *op cit*, Section 3, margin no 8.29.
34   BGH, GRUR 2009, 875, margin nos 9 *et seq*: Jeder 100. *Einkauf gratis* (every 100th purchase is free); GRUR 2007, 981, margin nos 29 et seq: 150% *Zinsbonus* (150% interest bonus).
35   Ohly in Piper/Ohly/Sosnitza, *op cit*, Section 4, margin no 4/66.

However, limits on advertising measures are imposed by the general provisions of copyright, trademark, work title and competition law, as well as by an event organiser's 'householder' rights. 'Householder' rights (Sections 858 and following, 903 and 1004 of the Civil Code) enable an organiser to eliminate undesired advertising measures directly at the event location.

Advertising outside the premises of an event must be in line with the Unfair Competition Act. If a non-sponsor expressly claims to be a sponsor, this constitutes a false statement prohibited by the act's blacklist (Section 3(3) in conjunction with Annex, item 4).[36] If a non-sponsor does not expressly claim to be a sponsor, but still creates this impression, this constitutes misleading advertising under Section 5(1), sentence 2, item 4 of the act. The replication of a sponsor's advertising concept may also be unfair under Section 4, item 3b of the act. If elements protected by trademark rights, design rights or copyrights are used by the non-sponsor, this may constitute a violation of the corresponding rights of exclusivity.

The Unfair Competition Act can be used against 'indirect' ambush marketing[37] only to some extent. If the advertising is not misleading within the meaning of Section 5 of the Unfair Competition Act, the only other possibility of suppressing the activity is under Section 4, item 4 when the advertising deliberately obstructs competitors. An advertising campaign is deemed to deliberately obstruct competing businesses when, based on an objective assessment of the circumstances, it is deemed to be primarily designed to impair the competitive development of a competitor and not to promote the advertiser's own competitive position.[38]

German legislation contains special protection for the Olympic Games through the adoption of the Olympic Protection Act in 2004. The act grants the national committee and International Olympic Committee exclusive rights to use the Olympic rings and the designations 'Olympics', 'Olympiad' and 'Olympic' (each on its own or in combination). Under Section 3 of the act, protected elements must not be used in advertising to label products and/or services or to designate a business or an event if:

- this could give rise to the risk of confusion, including the risk of association; or
- such use would take unfair advantage of, or be detrimental to, the reputation of the Olympic Games without due cause.[39]

---

36 Körber/Mann, GRUR 2008, 737, 738 *et seq.*
37 For example, when an advertising campaign is shown immediately before a televised broadcast of a major event but no false statements are made claiming that the advertiser is a sponsor.
38 BGH, GRUR 2008, 621, margin no 32: *Akademiks*; GRUR 2007, 800, margin no 23: *Außendienstmitarbeiter* (field staff); and GRUR 2005, 581, 582: *The Colour of Elégance*.
39 Regarding the restrictive interpretation of the Olympic Protection Act and the Federal Court of Justice's ruling on the validity of the statute, see Adolphsen/Berg, GRUR 2015, 643 and Röhl, GRUR-RR 2012, 381 with further references.

6. Direct marketing

Under Section 7 of the Unfair Competition Act, 'disturbing' advertising is not permitted. It is 'disturbing', for instance, to advertise by means of a telephone call made to a consumer without his or her prior express consent, or made to another market participant without at least the latter's presumed consent (Section 7(2), item 2). Advertising using an automated calling machine, a fax machine or electronic mail without the addressee's prior express consent is also not permitted (Section 7(2), item 3). 'Electronic mail' in this context comprises emails, text messages and multimedia messages. Express consent can be given orally or in writing. Presumed consent exists when the advertiser can expect, based on specific circumstances, the addressee's interest in the call.[40]

In addition, it constitutes a disturbance if advertising using a means of communication:

- conceals or keeps secret the identity of the sender on whose behalf the communication is transmitted (Section 7(2), item 4a of the Unfair Competition Act);
- refers to a website that does not contain the necessary information, which includes the party that commissioned the website and the terms and conditions of presents or prize competitions (Section 7(2), item 4b of the Unfair Competition Act, or in connection with Section 6(1) of the Telemedia Act); or
- contains no valid address to which the recipient can send an instruction to terminate transmission of communications of this kind without costs arising by virtue thereof, other than basic transmission costs (Section 7(2), item 4c of the Unfair Competition Act).

Under the GDPR, further provisions regarding direct marketing apply. Recital 70 and Article 21 of the GDPR explicitly mention direct marketing measures, stating that where personal data is processed for direct marketing purposes, the data subject has the right to object to the data processing.

The GDPR provisions are particularly relevant with regard to the express consent required under Section 7(2), item 3 of the Unfair Competition Act, which must be interpreted in accordance with the GDPR. Article 4, item 11 of the GDPR offers a legal explanation of 'consent'. It is defined as any freely given, specific, informed and unambiguous indication of the data subject's wishes, by statement or by a clear affirmative action. In order to comply with the GDPR's transparency provisions (Articles 12(1) and 13(1)(c)), 'informed' means that the consumer must be made aware of:

- the kind of advertising used (eg, email, telephone, text message);

---

40 BGH, GRUR 2010, 939, margin no 20: *Telefonwerbung nach Unternehmenswechsel* (telephone advertising after company change).

- the products or services promoted; and
- the business responsible for the advertising.[41]

'Freely' given consent means, pursuant to Recital 42, sentence 5 of the GDPR, that the data subject has a genuine or free choice, or can refuse or withdraw consent without detriment. It is subject to debate whether consent is not freely given if the performance of a contract (which does not require the data to be processed) is conditional on that consent (Article 7(4) of the GDPR). Consent may be considered as freely given in the case of a prize competition in which the participant consented to advertising by eight explicitly named businesses and was informed adequately about the area of work of the business running the advertisement.[42]

'Pyramid' and 'snowball' schemes, as well as 'progressive canvassing', are all illegal under Section 3 of the Unfair Competition Act, in connection with the Annex to that act, item 14, or under Section 16(2) of that act. Criminal prosecution as well as civil action may be taken against the persons responsible.

7. Product placement

Product placement is subject to the general standards set forth in Sections 3 and 5a(6) of the Unfair Competition Act, pursuant to which a person that conceals the advertising nature of commercial practices is acting unfairly.

7.1 Placement in radio and television broadcasts

Product placement during radio and television broadcasts is governed by the special provisions of the Interstate Broadcasting Treaty,[43] which implemented the Audio-visual Media Services Directive into German law.[44] 'Radio and television broadcasts' include television and radio productions transmitted by public and private stations and channels.

Section 2(2), item 11 of the Interstate Broadcasting Treaty legally defines 'product placement' as "the identified mention or representation of products, services, names, trademarks or activities of a manufacturer or service provider in broadcasts, in return for payment or similar consideration, with the aim of increasing sales. The provision of goods or services free of charge constitutes a product placement if the relevant goods or services are of significant value".

Under Section 7(7), sentence 1 of the Interstate Broadcasting Treaty, product placement is generally not permitted. A person that places products in the course of a commercial practice will be deemed to be acting unfairly under

---

41 Conrad/Treeger in Auer-Reinsdorff/Conrad, *op cit*, section 34, margin no 501.
42 OLG Frankfurt, Wettbewerb in *Recht und Praxis (WRP)* 2019, 1489, 1490, margin no 9.
43 Interstate Treaty on Broadcasting and Telemedia (Interstate Broadcasting Treaty) in the version of the Twenty-second Interstate Treaty on the Modification of Interstate Treaties on Broadcasting Law of 15-26 October 2018, in effect since 1 May 2019.
44 Directive 2007/65/EC amended by Directive 2010/13/EU and Directive (EU) 2018/1808.

Section 5a(6) of the Unfair Competition Act. However, the Interstate Broadcasting Treaty provides for exceptions for public sector broadcasts (Section 7(7), sentence 2 and Section 15) and for private sector broadcasts (Section 7(7), sentence 2 and Section 44) if, among other things, the following conditions are met:

- The editorial responsibility and independence of the broadcaster regarding the content and time slot are not affected (Section 7(7), sentence 2, item 1);
- The product placement does not constitute a direct invitation to purchase, rent or lease the products or services (Section 7(7), sentence 2, item 2); and
- The product is not singled out too prominently (Section 7(7), sentence 2, item 3).

The promoted products or services must also be adequately identified at the beginning and end of a broadcast and after commercial breaks (Section 7(7), sentences 3 and 4).

These exceptions do not apply to children's broadcasts, where product placement is prohibited in all cases (Section 15, sentence 1, item 1 and Section 44, sentence 1, item 1 of the Interstate Broadcasting Treaty).

On the basis of the Interstate Broadcasting Treaty, the supervisory authorities for radio and television programmes and telemedia of the German federal states have developed joint guidelines for product placement on television,[45] in which the requirements of the Interstate Broadcasting Treaty are specified in more detail. In addition, the Association of Commercial Broadcasters and Audio-visual Services in Germany, the German Producers Alliance and the Central Association of the German Advertising Industry have together developed a code of conduct regarding product placement.[46]

7.2 Placement in movies and computer games

Motion pictures are not governed by the Interstate Broadcasting Treaty, but only by the Unfair Competition Act. In two judgments from 1995, the Federal Court of Justice ruled that product placement in motion pictures is not generally prohibited,[47] but the advertising nature of the placement must not be concealed. If props are used in a motion picture that have been made available by an advertiser for reasonable integration into the plot, this need not be clarified, because such props can and should be expected to feature in an entertainment

---

45   "Joint guidelines of the *Landesmedienanstalten* for advertising, product placements, sponsorships and teleshopping on the television"; last amended on 18 September 2012.

46   See www.produzentenallianz.de/die-produzentenallianz/ergebnisse/inhalte-ergebnisse/verhaltenskodex-produktplatzierungen-von-produzentenallianz-vprt-sendern-und-zaw.html.

47   BGH, NJW, 1995, 3177, 3180: *Feuer, Eis & Dynamit* I (Fire, Ice & Dynamite I); and BGH, NJW 1995, 3182: *Feuer, Eis & Dynamit II* (Fire, Ice & Dynamite II).

medium of a commercial nature. If, however, payments or payments in kind of some significance are made by a company in consideration for itself or its products featuring in the picture in any way, this must be pointed out.[48]

Similar general principles apply to product placement in computer games. Anything that might constitute concealed advertising is not permitted in computer games.[49]

7.3 Unfair product placement

The person responsible for unfair product placement is, on the one hand, the producer of the broadcast, movie or computer game (as the case may be). On the other hand, the advertiser whose products are being promoted is also considered to be responsible in accordance with the principles of joint liability[50] if it has wilfully arranged for concealed advertising.

8. Native advertising and social media influencers

Modern forms of advertising pose new legal challenges. Among those is native advertising, which is the subtle embedding of advertising in a familiar text environment such as blogs or social media platforms, so that it appears to be part of that environment.[51] A common format of native advertising is content marketing, which is characteristically designed in such a way that the user initially cannot tell the difference between advertising and editorial content.[52] The use of social media influencers to promote sponsored content has become increasingly important. Thanks to their personal approach, influencers enjoy high credibility with their followers, which has a positive effect on the promoted products.[53]

Under German law, native advertising and influencer advertising using telemedia must be disclosed in order to protect consumers (Section 58(1) of the Interstate Broadcasting Treaty and Section 6(1), item 1 of the Telemedia Act). The means of disclosure may include labels such as 'advertisement', as long as the consumer can perceive them easily and immediately. Labels that might be overlooked are insufficient, such as the use of hashtags ('#ad') or the addition of 'sponsored content' or 'paid partnership' within or at the end of a social media post, if these labels are not visible at first sight.[54] To assist in the correct labelling of advertising on social media, the supervisory authorities of the

---

48 BGH, NJW 1995, 3177, 3180: *Feuer, Eis & Dynamit I* (Fire, Ice & Dynamite I).
49 Köhler in Köhler/Bornkamm/Feddersen, *op cit*, Section 5a, margin no 7.86.
50 BGH, GRUR 2007, 890, margin no 21: *Jugendgefährdende Medien bei eBay* (youth endangering media on eBay).
51 Ahrens in Gloy/Loschelder/Danckwerts, *Handbuch des Wettbewerbsrecht*, 5th edn 2019, section 70, margin no 98; Gerecke, GRUR 2018, 153, 154.
52 Wiebe/Kreutz, *WRP* 2015, 1053,1055.
53 Ahrens in Gloy/Loschelder/Danckwerts, *op cit*, section 70, margin no 99.
54 LG Hamburg, MMR 2020, 130, margin no 76 *et seq*; OLG Celle, GRUR 2017, 1158, margin no 10 *et seq*: Hashtag #ad; Köhler in Köhler/Bornkamm/Feddersen, *op cit*, Section 5a, margin no 7.80a.

German federal states for radio and television programmes and telemedia have published a set of guidelines.[55]

Failure to disclose advertising as such can also be considered unfair under the Unfair Competition Act. Pursuant to Section 5a(6) of the act, unfairness occurs where the commercial intent of a commercial practice (as defined in Section 1, item 1) is not identified, causing consumers to take a transactional decision which they would not have taken otherwise. Although it is debatable whether an influencer's acceptance of a product free of charge and promotion of it constitutes a 'commercial practice', this is definitely considered a commercial practice if the influencer receives payment or similar advantages for that promotion.[56] A further indication of a commercial practice may be a link from the influencer's social media post to the promoted product's website, even if the influencer points out that he or she purchased the product himself or herself, or that the link serves only informational purposes. Pursuant to Section 5a(6) of the Unfair Competition Act, a disclosure as advertising is not necessary if the commercial intent is directly apparent from the context. This might be the case, for instance, if an influencer's account is verified by a 'blue tick' badge on Instagram and has thousands of followers, as users might expect these accounts to exist primarily for commercial and brand building purposes.[57]

If influencers fail to disclose advertising as such, they might be sued to have the advertising taken down and, in the event of recurrence, to cease and desist (Section 8(1) of the Unfair Competition Act). They may also be obliged to compensate competitors for damages therefrom if competitors can demonstrate damages (which is difficult) (Section 9). In certain circumstances, claims to cease and desist as well as takedown under Section 8(1) may also apply to the business that commissioned the advertising.

9.   Industry-specific regulation

9.1   Gambling

Under German law, 'gambling' means any game where winning or losing in accordance with the game's rules depends not to a material degree on the knowledge, skill or attention of the participants, but mostly on chance.[58] In contrast to a mere prize competition, gambling requires the participants to pay a stake that is not insignificant.[59] 'Insignificant' in this context means requiring

---

55   www.die-medienanstalten.de/fileadmin/user_upload/Rechtsgrundlagen/Richtlinien_Leitfaeden/Leitfaden_Medienanstalten_Werbekennzeichnung_Social_Media.pdf.

56   KG, GRUR-RR 2018, 155, margin no 9; KG, MMR 2018, 98 margin no 14; Köhler in Köhler/Bornkamm/Feddersen, *op cit*, Section 5a, margin no 7.71.

57   LG Munich, GRUR-RR 2019, 332, margin no 45.

58   BGH, *Neue Zeitschrift für Strafrecht* (NStZ) 2003, 372, margin no 3: Oddset-Wetten (Oddset bets); GRUR 2002, 636: *Sportwetten* (sports bets); and NJW 1987, 851, 852 with further references.

59   BGH, NJW 1987, 851, 852 with further references.

a participation fee of no more than €0.50.[60] If the person organising or operating the gambling activity has failed to obtain the necessary licence from the authorities, any related advertising is also punishable under Section 284(4) of the Penal Code.

Special types of gambling include lotteries and raffles. Any person organising, operating or advertising a lottery or raffle publicly without the necessary licence from the authorities also becomes liable to criminal prosecution under Section 287(1) or 287(2) of the Penal Code. A 'lottery' exists if a number of persons have the possibility of obtaining a chance, based on a fixed lottery plan and for a fixed fee, of winning a random amount of money.[61] A 'raffle' exists if the prize to be won is not money, but other movable or immovable property.

Besides being punishable under criminal law, ads for unlicensed gambling, lotteries and raffles are also prohibited under advertising law. They are unfair pursuant to Section 3a of the Unfair Competition Act.[62]

The German Advertising Standards Council has issued a code of conduct governing the commercial communication of gambling,[63] which is addressed to gambling operators. The code of conduct is intended to prevent, among other things, gambling ads from being mistaken as an inducement to problematic gambling behaviour or from targeting children and minors. Anyone can submit a complaint and the Advertising Standards Council can itself instigate proceedings against the alleged offending party. An advertiser which is subject to a complaint is given the opportunity to respond. Subsequently, if the complaint is upheld by the Advertising Standards Council, the advertiser is notified and asked to modify or discontinue the advertising. If the advertiser is not willing to follow the council's recommendation, the council issues a reprimand and makes the case public.[64] In so doing, it will appeal in particular to the media to stop carrying the relevant ad. The Advertising Standards Council cannot force the advertiser to withdraw an offending ad. However, if a breach of law is suspected, the council can pass the case to the responsible authorities.

Breaches of codes of conduct do not in themselves constitute a violation of the Unfair Competition Act. Unfairness within the meaning of Section 3(1) of that act may be deemed to exist only if the degree of unfairness of the activity corresponds to the practices set out in the examples in Sections 4 and following of the act.[65]

---

60   BGH, GRUR 2012, 193, margin no 69: *Sportwetten im Internet II* (sports bets on the internet II); and GRUR 2012, 201, margin no 66: *Poker im Internet* (poker on the internet).
61   Fischer, Strafgesetzbuch: Kommentar, 67th edn, 2020, Section 287, margin no 2.
62   Cf BGH, GRUR 2012, 193, margin no 19: *Sportwetten im Internet II* (sports bets on the internet II).
63   www.werberat.de/werbekodex/gluecksspiel.
64   The rules of procedure of Germany's Advertising Standards Council may be accessed (in German) at www.werberat.de/content/verfahrensordnung-des-deutschen-werberats.
65   BGH, GRUR 2011, 431, margin nos 13 *et seq*: FSA-Kodex (FSA code).

9.2 Alcohol

Alcohol advertising is subject to the general provisions of the Unfair Competition Act. In contrast to tobacco, there is no specific duty in Germany to include warnings relating to alcohol.

Section 6(5) of the Interstate Treaty on the Protection of Minors from Harmful Media contains a provision aimed specifically at alcohol advertising, pursuant to which advertising for alcoholic beverages must not:

- be aimed at children or adolescents;
- specifically appeal to children and adolescents through its presentation; or
- show children or adults consuming alcohol.

Whether an advertising campaign addresses children or adolescents must be determined from the viewpoint of the targeted consumers. Important criteria in this regard include:

- the presentation of the ad;
- the manner of speech; and
- associations with the lives of adolescents.

If, based on these criteria, it is deemed that the ad is aimed at minors, it is usually not enough just to issue a formal notice that the ad should be directed at adults instead[66] – a solitary formal notice cannot change the overall objective pursued by the ad and turn it into an ad aimed at adults. Further action must be taken.

Under Section 7(10) of the Interstate Broadcasting Treaty, radio or television ads for alcoholic beverages must not promote the excessive consumption thereof. The same prohibition applies to ads in audio-visual on-demand media services (eg, video-on-demand services) under Section 58(3) of the treaty in conjunction with Section 7(10) of the treaty.

Alcohol ads during public film screenings, such as in cinemas, may be broadcast only after 6:00pm, in accordance with Section 11(5) of the Protection of Young Persons Act.

The code of conduct on commercial communications for alcoholic beverages issued by Germany's Advertising Standards Council contains detailed requirements on the permitted content of ads for alcoholic beverages.[67] The code of conduct sets forth principles for commercial communication in relation to the following:

- abusive consumption;
- minors;
- athletes;

---

66   OLG Hamm, Lebensmittelrecht Rechtsprechung (LMRR) 2006, 70.
67   See www.werberat.de/werbekodex/alkoholhaltige-getranke.

- safety;
- health claims;
- alcohol content;
- anxiety;
- loss of inhibition;
- personal conflicts;
- performance; and
- the age of the depicted individuals.

The code of conduct is addressed to producers, distributors and importers of alcoholic beverages.

9.3 Pharmaceuticals

In Germany, the advertisement of pharmaceuticals is governed by the Healthcare System Advertising Act, which applies to ads for medicinal products, medical devices, plastic surgery without medical necessity (aesthetic surgery), and other medicines, procedures, treatments and products.[68] The act applies only to the extent that an advertising claim relates to the diagnosis, removal or alleviation of diseases, conditions, bodily injury or pathological complaints in humans or animals (so it includes, for example, disease claims regarding cosmetics).

The Healthcare System Advertising Act distinguishes between ads directed at healthcare professionals and ads directed to the general public. 'Healthcare professionals' as defined in Section 2 of that act include:

- all members of health professions or the health industry;
- institutions that serve the health of humans or animals; and
- other persons who legally trade in medicinal products, medical devices, procedures, treatments, products or other medicines, or who use them in the exercise of their profession. These include, in particular, physicians, pharmacists, wholesalers, nurses and carers.

Medicinal products that are subject to regulatory authorisation must not be advertised before authorisation has been granted. This also applies to indications for which a medicinal product has not (yet) been authorised by the relevant regulatory authority (Section 3a of the Healthcare System Advertising Act). For example, a medicinal product authorised for use by adults must not be advertised for use with children.

Under Section 10(1) of the Healthcare System Advertising Act, medicinal products that are subject to prescription may be advertised only to physicians, dentists, veterinarians, pharmacists and distributors of medicinal products.

Non-prescription medicinal products can be advertised to non-

---

68   Hereinafter jointly referred to as 'remedies'.

professionals, subject to a number of restrictions. For example, it is not permitted to compare medicinal products (Section 11(2)) or to hand out samples of medicinal products (Section 11(1), item 14). To report a medical history of a patient is also prohibited if it could induce incorrect self-diagnoses by the addressees of the ad (Section 11(1), item 3).

Section 3 of the act has the greatest practical relevance, as it prohibits misleading advertising; in particular, pharmaceuticals must not be ascribed an effect that they do not have. A claim regarding effects may be included only where the effect has been scientifically proven. In this regard, the advertiser may rely on the content of its regulatory authorisation for the pharmaceutical and the official summary of product characteristics.[69] In the opinion of the Federal Court of Justice, the effect is deemed to be scientifically proven if it has been confirmed in a randomised, placebo-controlled, double-blind study with adequate statistical evaluation and subsequent publication.[70] It depends on the circumstances of the individual case whether studies conducted subsequently based on existing study data in the course of a subgroup analysis or studies conducted by way of a meta-analysis summarising several scientific tests can support an advertising claim. In this context, it depends on whether the scientific rules applicable to these studies have been complied with. As to the question of whether the respective ad is misleading, it is important to decide whether the ad points out sufficiently explicitly the particularities of the type, conduct or evaluation of the study and, where applicable, the restrictions made in the study itself regarding the validity and significance of the findings. If a study has only limited scientific validity, the addressees of the ad must be made aware of this fact.[71]

Anyone that wilfully violates the prohibition on misleading advertising is liable to criminal prosecution under Section 14 of the Healthcare System Advertising Act. Other violations of the act can be deemed administrative offences and are punishable under Section 15 by the imposition of a fine.

The statutory provisions on advertising have been specified and developed further by the Voluntary Association for the Self-regulation of the Pharmaceutical Industry (FSA). Many German pharmaceutical companies and German subsidiaries of foreign pharmaceutical companies are members of the FSA. The FSA has issued a number of internal codes of conduct, two of which are relevant with regard to advertising:

- the FSA Code of Conduct on Collaboration with Healthcare Professionals;[72] and
- the FSA Code of Conduct on Collaboration with Patient Organisations.[73]

---

69   BGH, WRP 2013, 772, 776: *Basalinsulin mit Gewichtsvorteil* (basal insulin with weight advantage).
70   *Ibid*, p 775.
71   *Ibid*.
72   See www.fsa-pharma.de/de/kodizes/zusammenarbeit/fachkreise.
73   See www.fsa-pharma.de/de/kodizes/zusammenarbeit/patientenorganisationen.

9.4 Financial products and services

The advertisement of investment services offered by investment services providers within the meaning of the Securities Trading Act is governed by the rules of conduct set forth in Sections 63 and following of the act. These rules are based on the EU Markets in Financial Instruments Directive.[74]

All information in this sector, including marketing communications to customers, must be fair, clear and not misleading (Section 63(6), sentence 1 of the Securities Trading Act). Moreover, marketing communications must be clearly identifiable as such (Section 63(6), sentence 2).

In order to counter undesirable developments with regard to the advertisement of investment services, under Section 92(1) of the Securities Trading Act, the Federal Financial Supervisory Authority (FFSA) may prohibit certain types of advertising. A similar rule exists under Section 23 of the Banking Act with regard to advertising by credit institutions and financial services providers. Based on the former of these two regulations, in 1999 the FFSA prohibited advertising by so-called 'cold calling',[75] unless such contact was established as a result of a prior invitation extended by telephone directly to the investment services provider.

Advertising for capital management companies and externally managed investment companies is subject to Section 33 of the Capital Investment Code, which replaced the Investment Act. Section 33 of that act refers to Section 23 of the Banking Act, as the same provisions apply.

Furthermore, Section 7 of the Securities Prospectus Act sets out special rules on the advertisement of public offers of securities or admission to a listing on an organised market. However, with the Prospectus Regulation[76] effective since 2019, the (very similar) provisions of Article 22 of the regulation relating to advertising override those of Section 7 of the Securities Prospectus Act.

9.5 Food

German food law contains a specific prohibition against making misleading statements, which can be found in Section 11 of the Food and Feed Code. This provision refers to Articles 7 and 36 of EU Regulation 1169/2011, which regulates food labelling in the European Union. Section 11(1), item 1 of the Food and Feed Code prohibits the placement on the market of foodstuffs with, among other things, a misleading name, format, packaging, specification, amount, expiration date or origin. For instance, a cream cheese container whose contents constituted less than half of the volume of the outer packing was ruled to be deceptive.[77]

---

74 Directive 2014/65/EU.
75 See www.bafin.de/SharedDocs/Veroeffentlichungen/DE/Aufsichtsrecht/Verfuegung/vf_990727_cold calling.html.
76 EU Regulation 2017/1129.
77 OLG Karlsruhe, GRUR-RR 2015, 253, margin no 15.

Moreover, under this section, foodstuffs must not be advertised by claiming that they have slimming, slimness-promoting or weight-reducing properties – for example, the slogan "Slim while you sleep" for bread with high levels of protein.[78]

Foodstuffs must also not be presented as a medicine product or promoted as having the ability to prevent, treat or cure a disease (Section 11(1), item 2).

In Germany, special regulations that apply to many foodstuffs set out further requirements regarding labelling and, in some cases, other forms of advertising. Examples include:

- the Butter Regulation;
- the Fruit Juice Regulation;
- the Honey Regulation;
- the Coffee Regulation;
- the Cocoa Regulation;
- the Cheese Regulation;
- the Jam Regulation;
- the Drinking Milk Regulation;
- the Milk Products Regulation;
- the Mineral Water Regulation;
- the Sugar Regulation;
- the Dietary Supplement Regulation; and
- the Regulation on Foods for Special Dietary Uses.

A discussion of these specific regulations is beyond the scope of this chapter.

In addition to its codes of conduct in relation to gambling and alcohol, Germany's Advertising Standards Council has issued a code of conduct on commercial communications for foods and alcoholic beverages.[79]

9.6   Tobacco

Tobacco advertising is governed by the Unfair Competition Act and the Tobacco Products Act.[80] The latter covers tobacco products and related products, including electronic cigarettes, refill containers and herbal products for smoking (Section 2, items 1 and 2).

There is a general prohibition on tobacco advertising on the radio (Section 19(1)), in the press and other print publications (Section 19(2)), on the Internet (Section 19(3)) and on television (Section 20). The prohibition on tobacco advertising in the press also applies to advertising in which a cigarette manufacturer presents its company by referring to its product, without directly

---

78   OLG Schleswig, LMRR 2012, 45.
79   See www.werberat.de/werbekodex/lebensmittel and www.werberat.de/werbekodex/alkoholhaltige-getranke.
80   The Tobacco Products Act implements the provisions of Directive 2014/40/EU into German law.

promoting its product sales (ie, in image campaigns).[81] The only exceptions to this prohibition apply to:

- publications aimed at persons working in the tobacco trade (Section 19(2), sentence 2, item 1); and
- publications printed and published outside the European Union that are not primarily intended for the EU market (Section 19(2), sentence 2, item 2).

However, outdoor advertising for tobacco products will also be heavily restricted in the future. A newly added Section 20a of the Tobacco Products Act provides for an outdoor ban on the advertisement of:

- tobacco products (starting January 2022);
- heated tobacco products (January 2023); and
- e-cigarettes and refill containers (January 2024).

An exception will be made for advertising on outdoor surfaces of specialised tobacco trade business premises.

Under Section 11(6) of the Protection of Young Persons Act, tobacco advertising during public film screenings (ie, in cinemas) may be broadcast only at movies that are suitable for an audience aged 18 or older.

Tobacco advertising, just like advertising for all products in general, must not be misleading. With regard to tobacco products and related products, the information given will be misleading in particular if tobacco products are ascribed certain effects that are not scientifically proven or not supported by sufficient scientific evidence (Section 18(2), sentence 2, item 1 of the Tobacco Products Act). This provision also applies to herbal products for smoking; the packaging must also not promote the fact that the product is free of additives or flavourings (Section 18(5), sentence 2).

Section 21(1) of the act contains further provisions applicable to the content of tobacco ads, pursuant to which such ads must not:

- claim that tobacco products are non-hazardous to health or suitable for exerting a favourable influence on bodily functions, performance capability or wellbeing;
- cause or encourage young people or adolescents to consume tobacco;
- present smoking as being exemplary; or
- claim that tobacco products are completely natural or free from additives.[82]

Any sponsorship of radio programmes and cross-border events promoting the sale of tobacco products is prohibited under Sections 19(4) and 19(5) of the act.

---

81   BGH, GRUR 2017, 1273 margin nos 17 *et seq*; GRUR 2011, 631, margin nos 9 *et seq*: *Unser wichtigstes Zigarettenpapier* (our most important cigarette paper).
82   This prohibition also applies to expressions with the same meaning, such as 'organic' (BGH, GRUR 2011, 633, margin nos 13 *et seq*: *Bio Tabak* (organic tobacco)).

Under Section 12, items 1 and 2 of the Tobacco Products Regulation, packaged tobacco products placed on the market must bear the warning "Smoking kills" and the information "Tobacco smoke contains over 70 substances that have been proven to cause cancer". With regard to herbal products for smoking, the products must carry the warning "Smoking this product is harmful to your health" (Section 30(1)).

9.7 E-cigarettes

The advertisement of e-cigarettes is governed by the Tobacco Products Act (see section 9.6). Under Section 2, item 2 of the act, e-cigarettes are considered related tobacco products to which the provisions of the act apply.

Section 18(1) on the prohibition of misleading advertising also applies to e-cigarettes and refill containers (Section 18(4)) (see section 9.6). Furthermore, the ad must not suggest that e-cigarettes are less harmful than other tobacco products or aim to reduce the harmful components of tobacco smoke (Section 18(2), sentence 2, item 2). In this context, a court ruled that the slogan "e-Cigarettes save lives – switch now!" was not permissible.[83] Furthermore, the promotional information must not relate to taste, smell, flavourings or other additives, or refer to their absence (Section 18(2), sentence 2, item 3).

Regarding the advertisement of e-cigarettes, Sections 19 and 20 of the Tobacco Products Acts apply, imposing a general ban on the advertisement of e-cigarettes in print media and on the radio, television and the Internet (see section 9.6). This also includes ads for e-cigarettes in an email newsletter sent out by an online shop if the newsletter registration is open to the general public.[84] As from January 2024, the outdoor advertisement of e-cigarettes will be restricted to the premises of specialised tobacco trade businesses.

Pursuant to the Tobacco Products Regulation, the packaging of e-cigarettes must carry information about all chemicals contained and the nicotine content, among other things; as well as a warning that the product must not be placed in the hands of children or adolescents (Section 27(1), sentence 2, items 1, 2 and 4 of the regulation).

The author would like to thank Pia Sösemann, attorney with Latham & Watkins LLP, for her assistance with this chapter.

---

83   LG Trier, ruling of 22 May 2020, case file 7 HK O 30/19, becklink 2016406; decision not yet final.
84   OLG Koblenz, GRUR-RR 2020, 165, margin nos 21 *et seq.*

Greece

George A Ballas
Theodore J Konstantakopoulos
George Ch Moukas
Vasileios A Xynogalas
Ballas, Pelecanos & Associates LPC

1.　Overview of the legal and regulatory regime for advertising

The applicable regulatory framework for advertising in Greece is outlined below.

1.1　Consumer Protection Law

Law 2251/1994 (as codified by Ministerial Decision 5338/2018) on Consumer Protection and Unfair Commercial Practices ('Consumer Protection Law') is the main statute in this field, which implements the relevant EU consumer protection directives referenced (ie, Directive 93/13/EEC on unfair contract terms; Directive 2011/83 amending Directive 93/13/EEC and repealing Directive 97/7/EC on distance selling; and Directive 2005/29/EC on unfair commercial practices). The Consumer Protection Law includes rules on advertising and unfair business practices. The definition of 'business practices' in this context includes all kinds of commercial communications, including advertisements, and all marketing practices that are linked to the promotion or sale of products or services.

The Consumer Protection Law rules on advertising include detailed guidelines on comparative advertising, and prohibit television broadcasting of ads for children's toys from 7:00am to 10:00pm every day. Unfair marketing/promotional practices include misleading and/or aggressive advertising that distorts consumers' economic behaviour and impairs their ability to make informed decisions. Examples include:

- the provision of untrue information regarding the specifications or price of a product;
- the exertion of psychological pressure on children to buy a product; and
- the use of threatening or abusive language.

Article 13A of the Consumer Protection Law provides for fines for breaches of the legislation, which start at €1,500 and may reach €1 million for suppliers (including advertisers). For repeat offenders, further sanctions include the doubling of these fines as well as the temporary suspension of business operations for up to one year. The Consumer Protection Law also entitles consumers or consumer groups to request from the court the discontinuance of unfair marketing/promotion practices. Furthermore, consumers can claim for damages, and class actions are also envisaged if the relevant legal requirements are met.

1.2 Regulation of television/video broadcasting

With regard to traditional television broadcasting and video-on-demand services, according to Presidential Decree 109/2010 implementing EU Directives 2010/13/EC and 2007/65/EC (on audio-visual media services, including audio-visual commercial communication, sponsorships and product placement), audio-visual commercial communications provided by media service providers in Greece:

- must be readily recognisable as such – surreptitious audio-visual commercial communications are prohibited;
- must not use subliminal techniques;
- must not prejudice respect for human dignity or include or promote discrimination based on sex, racial or ethnic origin, nationality, religion or belief, disability, age or sexual orientation; and
- must not encourage behaviour that is prejudicial to health or safety or grossly prejudicial to the protection of the environment.

1.3 Unfair Competition Law

The Unfair Competition Law (146/1914) defines as 'unfair' "any act made in commercial, industrial or agricultural transactions for purposes of competition which is contrary to moral principles". The provisions of this law often apply to advertising, since advertising practices may qualify as unfair (especially comparative and/or misleading advertising).

The law provides for a series of rights and remedies for claimants, such as filing of a preliminary injunction – which can be followed by a main action (regular lawsuit) – requesting a 'cease and desist' order in relation to the unfair practice. Further sanctions of a criminal/penal nature are also set out in the Unfair Competition Law, but their application often depends on the filing of a complaint on behalf of an injured party.

1.4 Greek Code of Advertising and Communication

The Greek Code of Advertising and Communication is a self-regulatory code (and therefore is not legally binding), which is nonetheless enforced by the Council for Communication Control. The code is the main self-regulatory mechanism in this field and applies to all industries.

According to the principles included in the code, marketing communications must:

- be lawful, decent, truthful, candid and in line with the principles of fair competition and proper commercial practices;

- have a sense of social responsibility and be based on the principles of good faith; and
- not be immoral or undermine human decency and integrity.

In addition to these general good practice guidelines, the code includes sector-specific rules.

1.5 Supervision

The competent regulatory authorities for monitoring compliance with the Consumer Protection Law are the Hellenic Consumers' Ombudsman (an independent authority) and the General Secretariat for Trade and Consumer Protection (under Greece's Ministry of Development). The National Council for Radio and Television (NCRTV), which is an independent authority, oversees and regulates the radio and television market. The Council for Communication Control has competence for applying the Greek Code of Advertising and Communication.

2. Comparative advertising

The definition and the conditions of admissibility of comparative advertising are stipulated in Article 9(2) of the Consumer Protection Law. Defined as "any advertisement that aims at or implies, directly or indirectly, a specific competitor or the products and/or services that such competitor offers", comparative advertising is permissible only if:

- it is not misleading;
- it compares products or services corresponding to the same needs or the same purposes;
- it objectively compares one or more characteristics that are substantial, relevant, verifiable and representative of the compared products and services, including the price;
- it does not result in the discrediting or denigration of a competitor's trademarks, trade names, other distinctive signs, products, services, activities or circumstances;
- in relation to products with a specific designation of origin, it compares only products with the same designation of origin;
- it does not take unfair advantage of the reputation of a competitor's trademark, trade name or other distinctive sign, or of the designation of origin of the competitive products;
- it does not present products or services as imitations or replicas of products or services bearing a trademark or a trade name; and
- it does not create confusion among traders, between an advertiser and a competitor, or between the advertiser's trademarks, trade names, other distinctive signs, products or services and those of a competitor.

Complementarily to the foregoing, the provisions of the Unfair Competition Law also apply in the context of consumer protection, given that comparative advertising may qualify as unfair if, for example, it features or refers to a competitor's products or services (even without explicitly naming the competitor) in a way that denigrates or discredits them, or in a way that demonstrates an intention to denigrate them, in order to maximise the features and/or quality of the advertised products or services.

Moreover, the relevant provisions of the Greek Code of Advertising and Communication stipulate that comparisons included in ads should be presented in a non-misleading way and according to the principles of fair competition – that is, any comparison should be based on elements that can be proven and that have not been chosen in order to be used in bad faith and/or in a biased way.

According to the provisions on comparative advertising set out in the Consumer Protection Law, the use of a competitor's trademark, trade name, distinctive title or similar is in principle permissible. As a rule, a registered trademark confers on the owner exclusive rights therein, entitling it to prevent all third parties from using the mark in the course of trade without authorisation. Nevertheless, a trademark does not entitle the owner to prohibit a third party from using it in the course of trade in accordance with honest practices in industrial or commercial matters, among other requirements. In particular as regards the issue of misleading and comparative advertising, such (comparative) advertising is permitted where:

- it does not create confusion in the marketplace between the advertiser and a competitor, or between the advertiser's trademarks, trade names, other distinguishing marks, products or services and those of a competitor;
- it does not discredit or denigrate the trademarks, trade names, other distinguishing marks, products, services, activities or circumstances of a competitor;
- it does not take unfair advantage of the reputation of a trademark, trade name or other distinguishing mark of a competitor, or of the designation of origin of competing products; and
- it does not present products or services as imitations or replicas of products or services bearing a protected trademark or trade name.

Therefore, the inclusion of a competitor's trademark in comparative advertising which meets the above conditions in relation to Article 9 of the law is not considered unauthorised use of that trademark, as defined in the Trademark Law (4679/2020), which would create a right of action for the trademark owner. However, if comparative advertising uses a competitor's trademark in order to mislead consumers or in a way that enhances or establishes a risk of confusion, and/or presents products and/or services that imitate those of a competitor, the provisions on the protection of trademark rights will come into play, along with additional provisions regarding the infringer's civil and criminal liability – especially if the comparison includes elements that discredit the competitor. Furthermore, any unlawful use of the trademark of a competitor will entail liability under the Unfair Competition Law and under the respective provisions on unfair competition included in the Trademark Law, given that the infringer is likely to gain unfair profit from the competitor's economic and promotional business efforts, and/or from the trademark's reputation (in cases involving a notorious trademark).

3. Online behavioural advertising

There is currently no specific legislation in Greece that addresses online behavioural advertising as such. However, the general principles of advertising laid down under the Consumer Protection Law and the Greek Code of Advertising and Communication apply, along with the general provisions and sanctions of the General Data Protection Regulation (2016/679) (GDPR) and the Data Protection Law (4624/2019), which introduced supplemental measures for the application of the GDPR.

Guidelines from the Hellenic Data Protection Authority (DPA) are also relevant here. The DPA Guidelines basically adopt Opinion 2/2010 dated 22 June 2010 of the Article 29 Working Party[1] for online behavioural advertising, and Opinion 16/2011 dated December 8 2011 of the European Advertising Standards Alliance/Interactive Advertising Bureau Best Practice Recommendation on Online Behavioural Advertising. According to the guidelines, advertising network providers should comply with the obligations that arise from the Greek data protection legislation, notably with respect to rights of access, rectification, erasure and retention. In addition, and taking into account that publishers may share certain responsibility for the data processing that takes place in the context of behavioural advertising, the guidelines call upon publishers to share with advertising network providers the responsibility for providing the requisite information to individuals.

Although there is currently no legislation in Greece which addresses online behavioural advertising specifically, the use of cookies for the purposes of online behavioural advertising, among other things, is regulated. The use of cookies is regulated by Article 4 of Law 3471/2006 (as amended by Law 4070/2012), which transposed the Cookies Directive[2] of the European Union. Broadly speaking, this provides that the storage of information on or the access to information already

---

1   The Article 29 Working Party is an independent body made up of representatives of the various European data protection regulators.
2   Directive 2009/136/EC.

stored (eg, through the use of a cookie) on the device of a user is permitted only if the user has provided his or her informed consent. Article 4 also states that such consent can be expressed using the appropriate settings of a browser or other application. These requirements do not apply to the use of cookies that are necessary for the provision of an online service; however, it is unlikely that this exception would apply to any cookies used for the purposes of online behavioural advertising.

The DPA Guidelines on this matter (published in July 2012) make special reference to 'web analytics' cookies and 'online advertising' cookies, clarifying that prior consent is required for their use. According to the guidelines, prior consent can be provided via pop-ups or using a web browser that, by default, rejects all third-party cookies and requires the active acceptance of cookies by the user ('opting in'). Implied consent is not acceptable in this context.

4.   Sales promotions

In Greece, the umbrella term 'sales promotion' mainly covers sales, combined sales, discounts, gifts, incentive offers, prize draws and competitions. The legal framework for sales promotions includes statutory and self-regulatory provisions.

Focusing mainly on the Unfair Competition Law, the Consumer Protection Law and Law 4177/2013 (as well as Ministerial Decisions 56885/2014 and 91354/2017) setting out merchandise purchase price regulations, the legal framework for sales promotions is completed and reinforced by the Greek Code of Advertising and Communication. Depending on the types of products or services on offer, specific legislative provisions may also be relevant, such as the legislation on the promotion of games of chance and the promotion of sales.

In the absence of specific legislative definition, and although not expressly defined in the Greek Code of Advertising and Communication, all marketing methods and techniques that render products more attractive through the provision of additional advantage to the consumer or that create the expectation of receiving such an advantage are considered 'sales promotions' in Greece. Moreover, the Greek Code of Advertising and Communication specifically defines the term 'offer' as "any presentation or promotion of products with the intent to sell [them]".

As derived from the applicable legislation, and also confirmed by the Greek Code of Advertising and Communication, all sales promotions should:

- be fair towards consumers and other competitors;
- be conducted in a way that avoids unnecessary disappointment to consumers;
- be administrated promptly and efficiently (also with regard to the obligations arising from them); and
- be transparent to participants.

Furthermore, promoters, intermediaries and other parties should avoid bringing sales promotions into disrepute.

Prize draws and skill-based competitions used in combination with sales promotion practices are further defined by the Greek Code of Advertising and Communication as 'promotion incentives'. Although these are permitted in principle, such advertising practices shall, according to the code, be considered:

- misleading if consumers are not clearly informed that no purchase is needed for their participation; and
- unfair if, for example, participation in such prize draws or competitions requires the purchase of a specific product, thus altering consumers' choice/purchase criteria, or if the benefits of the prize draw or competition are disproportionately high in comparison with the price of the advertised product, thus enticing consumers to participate.

With regard to incentive offers, consumers must be fully informed and able easily and clearly to identify and understand the conditions of each offer, including those terms that may finally persuade them not to purchase a product. In addition, the presentation of any incentive offer or sales promotion should not be misleading. Furthermore, the value of the supplementary offered product should not be exaggerated, hidden or disguised in relation to the main product's value; and words such as 'free' or 'gift' ('δωρεάν' or 'δώρο' in Greek) may be used only if no obligation and no disproportionate delivery/transport charges are entailed, and if the price of the main product has not been increased in order to cover all or part of the cost of the offer.

As one of the most popular types of sales promotion, price discounts are also considered to be most likely to mislead consumers in Greece. Untrue or non-existent promotional materials on the duration of the discount offer or the quantities and availability of products within the advertised timeframe for the duration of the discount will thus likely be considered misleading and unfair under the respective provisions of the Consumer Protection Law and the Unfair Competition Law.

Sales promotions are further regulated by Law 4177/2013 (as well as the provisions of Ministerial Decisions 56885/2014 and 91354/2017) on merchandise purchase price regulations – which, for example, require that an indication be included on written labels on items that are subject to a sales promotion (via a price discount), and that an indication be provided of their prices before and after the reduction. For 'outlet' or 'stock' stores, there is a similar requirement to indicate the price before and after the reduction in a way that shows the clear distinction between the two prices.

Non-compliance with the provisions on sales promotions entails liability as provided for by the Consumer Protection Law and the Unfair Competition Law (see section 1 for details of the relevant penalties). Furthermore, illegal actions with regard to sales promotions may incur liability in accordance with the basic provisions of the Greek Civil Code (mainly regarding torts) and the Greek Penal Code.

5. Ambush marketing

There is currently no legislation in Greece that regulates ambush marketing, apart from Law 2598/1998 relating to the Olympic Games (see below). However, the general principles of advertising laid down under the Consumer Protection Law and the Greek Code of Advertising and Communication apply to ambush marketing, along with the provisions and sanctions of the trademark and unfair competition legislation.

The only law that has been enacted with regard to ambush marketing is Law 2598/1998 on the organisation of the Olympic Games in Athens in 2004. This law regulated unauthorised commercial associations with the Athens 2004 Olympic Games. Article 3 governed the protection and registration of the various names, marks, slogans and symbols associated with the Athens 2004 Olympic Games, and specified the penalties and enforcement procedures for infringing uses of the Olympic symbols, including a fine of not less than €586.94 and a minimum of three months' imprisonment.

6. Direct marketing

In general, direct marketing must comply with:

- the general provisions of the GDPR;
- the Data Protection Law;
- Article 11(3) of Law 3471/2006 on the protection of personal data and privacy in the electronic telecommunications sector;[3]
- decisions and guidelines issued by the DPA;
- Article 6 (on unsolicited commercial communication) of Presidential Decree 131/2003;[4] and
- Article 4 (on distance selling) of the Consumer Protection.

Direct marketing by email and text messaging requires opt-in consent. An exception applies if the recipient's contact details have been lawfully obtained in the course of the sale of a product or a service or other 'transaction' – in which case emails and text messages can be sent for direct marketing of the sender's own similar products or services, even where the recipient has not provided his or her prior consent, as long as the recipient is given a clear and simple means to object (opt out), free of charge, to such collection and use of his or her electronic contact details both when the electronic contact details are

---

3   Implementing EU Directive 2002/58/EC.
4   Implementing the EU E-commerce Directive (2000/31/EC).

being collected and on the occasion of each subsequent relevant communication.

The GDPR has reinforced the requirement that consent be informed. Providing information to recipients prior to obtaining their consent is essential in order to enable them to make informed decisions, understand what they are agreeing to and exercise their right to withdraw their consent, for example. At least the following information must be provided in order for marketers to obtain valid consent:

- the controller's identity;
- reference to the purpose of the data processing operations for which consent is sought (ie, marketing activities);
- the (type of) data that will be collected and used;
- the existence of the right to withdraw consent;
- as applicable, information on the use of the data for automated decision making; and
- information on the possible risks of data transfers due to the absence of an adequacy decision and of appropriate safeguards.

With regard to the second and third bullets above, the Article 29 Working Party has noted that where the consent sought is to be relied upon by multiple (joint) controllers, or where the data is to be transferred to or processed by other controllers that wish to rely on the original consent, these organisations should all be named. The other information that must be provided to data subjects according to the GDPR (Article 13), while not typically needed for the validity of consent, must also still be provided (eg, by reference to a relevant privacy notice).

When providing this information, marketers should use clear and plain language. Consent must be clear and distinguishable from other matters, and be provided in an intelligible and easily accessible form. That said, a declaration by the user that he or she has been informed (eg, by ticking a relevant box) will not suffice where notice is not actually easily accessible (eg, this would be the case where the notice is accessible only via a hyperlink leading to another page). According to the Article 29 Working Party, layered and granular information can be an appropriate way of dealing with the twofold obligation of being precise and complete on the one hand, and understandable on the other; the same applies with regard to mobile interfaces. Further, according to DPA guidance, when consent is provided via a website, notice can be provided by, for example:

- making the user read the notice (via a pop-up window) before being able to provide consent; or
- placing the notice in a special field of adequate size and making the user scroll down through the text before being able to provide consent.

Marketers can use JavaScript code to control and prove that the user has actually read the notice prior to the provision of consent.

The GDPR clearly outlines the explicit obligation of the controller (in this case, the marketer) to demonstrate the data subject's consent; the burden of proof rests with the controller. It is up to the controller to prove that valid consent has been obtained from the data subject and to this end the controller is free to develop methods to comply with this provision in a way that is fitting in its daily operations. According to WP29, as long as a data processing activity (in this case, marketing) lasts, the obligation to demonstrate consent exists. Once the processing activity ends, proof of consent should be kept for no longer than is strictly necessary to comply with a legal obligation or for the establishment, exercise or defence of legal claims. According to the DPA, consent declaration (and withdrawal of consent) must be retained for up to six months as of the last communication activity or withdrawal of consent.

Postal marketing (via printed promotional material) can be addressed only to recipients:

- who have provided their prior consent (via a so-called 'opt-in') to such kind of communication;
- where the marketer has obtained the recipient's contact details in the course of a previous business transaction with the recipient; or
- where the recipient's contact details have been collected from a legitimate source (eg, telephone directories).

In both the second and third cases above, the marketer must ensure that the recipient has not previously objected to such communication (ie, the recipient is not included on a so-called 'Robinson list' or 'Article 13 register', which is an opt-out list of people who do not wish to receive postal marketing communication).

Direct marketing by telephone (with human intervention) is permitted unless the recipient has opted out of such communication. However, direct marketing by telephone without human intervention (via automated calls) requires prior informed opt-in consent.

Given the absence of specific penalties for breaches of the direct marketing provisions, the provisions and sanctions set out in the GDPR and the Data Protection Law will apply. Those penalties will depend on the severity and particular circumstances of each case.

7. Product placement

Article 12 of Presidential Decree 109/2010 (see section 1.2) establishes the conditions for the admissibility of product placement. The provisions of that presidential decree are complemented by the NCRTV Guidelines (Directive 1 of 12 July 2011).

'Product placement' is defined in Article 2(13) of the presidential decree as "any presentation of or reference to a product, service or trademark featured within a specific programme, in return for payment or for similar consideration". Product placement is permitted in cinematographic works, films and series made for audio-visual media services, sports programmes and light entertainment programmes (eg, music programmes, music videos, comedies, reality shows, travel programmes), as long as the following requirements are met:

- Their content and, in the case of television broadcasting, their scheduling in no way affect the responsibility and editorial independence of the media service provider;
- They do not directly encourage the purchase or rental of products or services, in particular by making special promotional references to those products or services; and
- They do not give undue prominence to the product in question.

Permission is also granted where there is no payment, but only the provision of certain products or services free of charge (eg, production props and prizes) with a view to their inclusion in a programme, as long as the conditions outlined above are also met.

Product placement is prohibited:

- if any of the aforementioned programmes, works and so on are addressed to minors;
- for tobacco products or cigarettes, and from undertakings whose principal activity is the manufacture or sale of cigarettes and other tobacco products;
- for specific medicinal products or medical treatments that are available in Greece on prescription only;
- for products, services or trademarks of entities whose main activity is the organisation and operation of gambling activities or games of chance;
- in any other case where, under Greek law, televised advertising is prohibited (eg, news, political programmes, documentaries and programmes with religious content); and
- between 7:00am and 10:00pm, with regard to the placement of children's toys.

Viewers must be clearly informed of the existence of product placement. Programmes containing product placement must be appropriately identified as such at the start and end of the programme and when it resumes after a commercial break, in order to avoid any confusion on the part of the viewer, with the exception of programmes that have been neither produced nor commissioned either by the media service provider itself or by a company affiliated to the media service provider.

Product placement should therefore take effect in a uniform way for all broadcasters as follows:

- At the beginning of a programme, for at least 10 consecutive seconds, the phrase "This programme contains product placement" should appear (in Greek) on the screen; this phrase should also be aurally reproduced.
- During a programme, the Greek letters 'ΤΠ' (standing for 'Τοπ οθέτηση Προϊόντος' – 'product placement 'in Greek) should clearly appear on the upper or lower part of the screen for at least 10 consecutive seconds after every commercial break or other break of the programme. This indication should also appear for the duration of the transmission of a music video with product placement.
- At the end of a programme, for at least 10 consecutive seconds, the phrase "This programme contained product placement", along with the names of the products and/or services placed, should appear (in Greek) on the screen.

The letters 'ΤΠ' should also be placed next to the names of the respective programmes as indicated in electronic programme guides. The inclusion of those letters (for five consecutive seconds) is also obligatory at the beginning of any trailer by a broadcaster if some of the trailed programmes contain product placement.

The following practices with regard to product placement are also prohibited:

- surreptitious product placement;
- thematic placement of products or services upon which the content of a programme depends;
- direct promotion or incitement to buy a product or hire a service (eg, by promoting its price or availability); and
- excessive promotion of a product and/or service (eg, by insisting on the service's advantages or the product's characteristics).

The correct application and control of the legal provisions relating to product placement are the responsibility of the NCRTV, the competent authority under the law in this context. The NCRTV, *ex officio* or following a complaint, will rule on an alleged infringement of the product placement legislation. It may accordingly impose sanctions of an administrative, civil and/or penal nature for any proved offence, mainly in line with Law 2328/1995 (on private television and local radio) or Law 2644/1998 (on pay television).

Presidential Decree 109/2010 (see section 1.2) also provides for the possibility of self-regulation, such as through certain codes of conduct drafted or adhered to by broadcasters.

8. Native advertising and social media influencers

There is currently no legislation in Greece that specifically addresses native advertising and advertising by social media influencers. However, the general principles of advertising under the Consumer Protection Law and the Greek Code of Advertising and Communication apply, along with Presidential Decree 131/2003 (Article 5) and in particular the rules on product placement. Covert advertising is prohibited. Importantly, such commercial communications must be clearly identifiable as such, clearly distinguished from other (editorial) content, to avoid engaging in misleading conduct. Most prominent social media platforms have introduced and enforce rules on promotion by influencers.

9. Industry-specific regulation

9.1 Gambling

The advertisement of gambling is addressed by the Gambling Law (4002/2011). Article 35 of that law provides for specific restrictions on 'commercial communications' relating to gambling.[5] Such communications (including advertising communications) must include reference to the participation requirements (ie, individuals must be over the age of 21 and hold an 'individual player card'), and must also make reference to hotlines and support services for rehabilitation from excessive gambling; direct or indirect reference to offers of credit to participate in games of chance is prohibited. Such commercial communications must not advertise the provision of gambling services by unlicensed providers and entities that provide credit to players. Furthermore, the content of such communications must comply with the principles laid down in the Regulation for Gaming Operation and Control (at the time of writing, the drafting of this regulation is pending).

Further guidance is provided in Decision 163/2015[6] of the Hellenic Gaming Commission (HGC) and in HGC Directive 1/2017, as follows:

- Commercial communications relating to games of chance are permitted only based on relevant approval by the HGC. The providers of games of chance must file with the HGC a specific commercial communication plan for approval.[7]
- Before taking any of the abovementioned actions, the provider of

---

5   A 'commercial communication' is "(a) any form of communication for the direct or indirect promotion of products, services or image of undertakings, organisations or any person conducting activity relevant with games, (b) any information enabling direct access to activity relevant with games, (c) communications regarding products or services of an undertaking operating in the field of games".
6   The Regulation of Issues of Commercial Communication of Games of Chance, as in force and also supplemented by HGC Decision 251/2017.
7   Guidance on the drafting of a commercial communication plan has been published by the HGC.

advertising services[8] must examine and confirm whether the provider of games of chance is a lawful provider.[9]

- Special provisions are in place for the protection of minors, including a prohibition on the promotion of games of chance on websites targeting minors.
- Covert advertising or indirect advertising is prohibited. Commercial communications must be clearly identified as such, regardless of their form or the means used for the promotion.
- Commercial communications on websites via pop-up windows are prohibited.
- All commercial communications must include certain minimum information (eg, a reference to the regulator, age limit, hotlines). If there is insufficient space to fit all required information, use of a pop-up window is possible (however, age restrictions must still be included in the main body of the communication).

According to Article 52(2) (on penal sanctions) of the Gambling Law, a marketer can be found liable for advertising games of chance that are carried out by non-licensed entities. Penal sanctions include between two and five years' imprisonment and a fine ranging from €100,000 to €200,000.

9.2 Alcohol

The advertisement of alcohol should conform to the general principles of advertising laid down under the Consumer Protection Law (see section 1.1) and the relevant provisions of Presidential Decree 109/2010 (see section 1.2).

According to Article 10(4) of the decree, audio-visual commercial communications for alcoholic beverages must not be aimed specifically at minors and must not encourage immoderate consumption of such beverages.

Furthermore, under Article 22 of the decree, television advertising and teleshopping for alcoholic beverages must comply with the following criteria:

- They must not be aimed specifically at minors or, in particular, depict minors consuming these beverages;
- They must not link the consumption of alcohol to enhanced physical performance or to driving;
- They must not create the impression that the consumption of alcohol contributes towards social or sexual success;

---

8   That is, the person appointed to organise, perform, promote and/or present actions of commercial communication for games of chance.
9   Sufficient proof of the legality is the existence of a HGC decision approving a commercial communication plan of the provider (previously filed for approval by the HGC). Upon the advertiser's request, the provider must promptly provide this plan to the advertiser. In case of doubt regarding the legality of the provider, the advertiser can file a relevant inquiry with the HGC.

- They must not claim that alcohol has therapeutic qualities or that it is a stimulant, a sedative or a means of resolving personal conflicts;
- They must not encourage the immoderate consumption of alcohol or present abstinence or moderation in a negative light; and
- They must not place an emphasis on high alcoholic content as being a positive quality of such beverages.

The sanctions that can be imposed by the Council for Communication Control for breach of the decree include:
- a warning, with an order to comply;
- a fine ranging from €14,673.54 to €1,467,354.14; and/or
- a temporary or permanent prohibition to broadcast.

Moreover, the general sanctions for breach of the Consumer Protection Law (as described in section 1.1) could also apply in this case.

Further to the above legislative framework, the following self-regulation instruments apply:
- the Greek Code of Advertising and Communication (Annex VI); and
- the Code of Self-Regulation of the Union of Alcoholic Drinks Enterprises (UADE).

The former includes an annex dealing with alcoholic beverages. It expressly mentions that all commercial communications relating to alcoholic drinks (including promotions, sponsorship and communications through all media, including the Internet) must conform with the provisions of the code. This essentially means that a commercial communication relating to alcoholic beverages must:
- be lawful, decent, truthful, candid and in line with the principles of fair competition and proper commercial practices;
- have a sense of social responsibility and be based on the principles of good faith; and
- not be immoral or undermine human decency and integrity.

The UADE Code has been signed by the legal representatives of the enterprises that are members of the UADE and witnessed by representatives of the Greek Ministry of Health. The basic principles of the UADE Code include:
- the avoidance of alcohol ads addressed to minors;
- the avoidance of minors' and celebrities' participation in alcohol promotion campaigns;
- the dissociation of ads from sexual, social and/or professional success;
- the discouragement of uncontrollable alcohol consumption, especially

connected with activities requiring high levels of concentration, such as driving; and

- the prohibition of alcohol ads during sports events involving the participation of minors.

Special provisions apply for online commercial communications – for example, such ads should not be placed on online media where at least 70% of the visitors are "reasonably expected" to be over 18 years old.

9.3   Pharmaceuticals

Over and above the general legal framework established by the Consumer Protection Law, there are other regulations that apply to the advertisement of medicinal products. The applicable legal framework and the implications for manufacturers, advertisers and consumers are outlined below.

In general, medicinal products cannot be advertised before marketing authorisation has been obtained. Furthermore, all parts of an ad of a medicinal product must comply with the particulars listed in the summary of product characteristics. In addition, under Legislative Decree 96/1973 on the marketing of pharmaceutical dietary and cosmetic products, advertising is prohibited for medicinal products that are available on medical prescription only, or that contain psychotropic or narcotic substances.

According to Ministerial Decree 22261/2002 on the advertisement of non-prescription medicinal products and Joint Ministerial Decision 32221/2013 implementing Directive 2001/83/EC on the Community code relating to medicinal products for human use, the advertisement of a medical product to the general public must be set out in such a way that it is clear that the message is an ad and that the product is clearly identified as a medicinal product. It must further contain a minimum amount of information regarding the specific product – more specifically:

- the name of the medicinal product, as well as the common name if the medicinal product contains only one active substance;
- the information necessary for correct use of the medicinal product; and
- an express, legible invitation to read carefully the instructions on the package leaflet or on the outer packaging, as the case may be.

Furthermore, according to Circular 16251/2019 of the National Organisation for Medicines, an ad for medicinal products should be accompanied by a sign reading: "ΤΟ ΥΠΟΥΡΓΕΙΟ ΥΓΕΙΑΣ ΚΑΙ Ο ΕΘΝΙΚΟΣ ΟΡΓΑΝΙΣΜΟΣ ΦΑΡΜΑΚΩΝ ΣΥΝΙΣΤΟΥΝ: ΔΙΑΒΑΣΤΕ ΠΡΟΣΕΚΤΙΚΑ ΤΙΣ ΟΔΗΓΙΕΣ ΧΡΗΣΗΣ- ΣΥΜΒΟΥΛΕΥΤΕΙΤΕ ΤΟ ΓΙΑΤΡΟ Ή ΤΟ ΦΑΡΜΑΚΟΠΟΙΟ ΣΑΣ" (which translates as: "THE MINISTRY OF HEALTH AND THE NATIONAL ORGANISATION FOR MEDICINES RECOMMEND: READ CAREFULLY THE

INFORMATION LEAFLET – CONSULT YOUR DOCTOR OR YOUR PHARMACIST").

Moreover, an ad for a medicinal product aimed at the general public must not contain any material that:

- gives the impression that a medical consultation or surgical operation is unnecessary, in particular by offering a diagnosis or by suggesting treatment by mail;
- suggests that the effects of taking the medicine are guaranteed, are unaccompanied by adverse reactions or are better than, or equivalent to, those of another treatment or medicinal product;
- suggests that the health of the subject can be enhanced by taking the medicine;
- suggests that the health of the subject could be affected by not taking the medicine (this does not apply to vaccination campaigns);
- is directed exclusively or principally at children;
- refers to a recommendation by scientists, health professionals or persons who are neither of the foregoing but who, because of their fame, could encourage the consumption of medicinal products;
- suggests that the medicinal product is a foodstuff, cosmetic or other consumer product;
- suggests that the safety or efficacy of the medicinal product is due to the fact that it is natural;
- could, by a description or detailed representation of a case history, lead to erroneous self-diagnosis;
- refers in improper, alarming or misleading terms to claims of recovery; or
- uses in improper, alarming or misleading terms pictorial representations of changes in the human body caused by disease or injury, or of the action of a medicinal product on the human body or parts thereof.

For the purposes of ensuring that the foregoing regulatory framework is followed by regulated entities, the National Organisation for Medicines may take any necessary action to prohibit an ad or impose fines or other sanctions provided by law (Law 1316/1983 on the creation and competences of the National Organisation for Medicines).

In addition to the above legislative framework, the Hellenic Association of Pharmaceutical Companies – a professional non-profit association of legal entities involved in the manufacture, trade and promotion of medicinal products in Greece – has issued a self-regulatory code, the Code of Practice on the Promotion of Prescription-only Medicinal Products. This code of practice sets out rules relating to the promotion of pharmaceutical products for human use, based on professional responsibility, ethics and transparency. The code includes a procedure (of first and second degree) for overseeing its implementation, and the relevant review committees can impose certain sanctions for non-compliance, including fines of up to €50,000.

9.4 Financial products and services

The advertisement of financial products and services is governed by Joint Ministerial Decision Z1-699/2010, implementing EU Directive 2008/48/EC.

According to Article 4 of this decision, any ad concerning credit agreements which indicates an interest rate or any figures relating to the cost of the credit to the consumer must include standard information, including the borrowing rate, the total amount of credit, the annual percentage rate of charge, the total amount payable by the consumer and the amount of the instalments, among other things.

Article 20 of the decision, referring to credit intermediaries, obliges any such intermediary to indicate, in advertising and documentation intended for consumers, the extent of his or her powers and in particular whether he or she works exclusively with one or more creditors or as an independent broker.

Joint Ministerial Decision Z1-699/2010 also refers to the provisions in the Consumer Protection Law relating to unfair trade practices. The provisions in Article 4θ of the Consumer Protection Law on the distance selling of financial services refer to the provisions of Article 11 of Law 3471/2006 on electronic communications, as described in detail in section 6.

The general sanctions included in the Consumer Protection Law (see section 1.1) will apply in case of breach of the provisions of Joint Ministerial Decision Z1-699/2010.

Also applicable, in addition to the above legislative framework, is the Code of Banking Ethics – a self-regulatory code prepared by the Hellenic Banking Association, which is a non-profit legal entity of private law that represents Greek and foreign credit institutions operating in Greece. The Code of Banking Ethics includes a chapter on the promotion of banking services and outlines the basic rules that apply to the promotion and marketing of banking products and services, as follows:

- All bank advertising must be lawful, decent, true and within the limits of fair competition.
- Uniform banking terminology should be used, if possible, to allow customers to compare similar products or services that are offered by different banks.
- Comparative data should be based on accurate facts that can be established and are as complete as good-faith and business ethics dictate, in order to provide accurate and objective information to the target public.
- Consumers should be encouraged to search for additional information on each product or service ad from the credit institution, to make it clear that the ad does not include all the information needed.

9.5 Food

Further to the general legal framework set out in the Consumer Protection Law, and with regard to food in particular, the main regulatory text applicable is Ministerial Decision 1100/1987 on the Code of Foodstuffs, Beverages and Objects of Common Use ('Food Code'), which includes general and product-specific provisions. Articles 10 and 11 of the code specifically refer to food advertising and labelling.

Breaches of the advertising provisions of the Food Code will be treated as misleading advertising and the sanctions included in the Consumer Protection Law may be enforced.

Moreover, EU Regulation 1924/2006 is also applicable and provides that nutrition and health claims included in ads should not:

- be false, ambiguous or misleading;
- give rise to doubt about the safety and/or the nutritional adequacy of other foods;
- encourage or condone excessive consumption of a food;
- state, suggest or imply that, in general, a balanced and varied diet cannot provide appropriate quantities of nutrients; or
- refer to changes in bodily functions which could give rise to or exploit fear in the consumer.

According to Article 10(3) of Presidential Decree 109/2010 (see section 1.2), audio-visual commercial communications addressed to minors should not encourage them to excessively consume foods or beverages containing nutrients and substances such as fats, trans-fatty acids, salt/sodium or sugars. Reference should also be made to Annex V of the Greek Code of Advertising and Communication, which specifically refers to food advertising in relation to the protection of minors.

9.6 Tobacco

Further to the general legal framework set out in the Consumer Protection Law and the Greek Code of Advertising and Communication, certain additional regulations apply with regard to tobacco products. These are described below.

As a general rule, and in accordance with Ministerial Decree 81348/2005, the advertisement of tobacco products in printed media and in so-called 'information society' services is not permitted. An exception applies for printed advertising included in publications intended exclusively for professionals in the tobacco trade and in publications that are published in third countries where those publications are not principally intended for the EU market. This exception also extends to online advertising.

That same ministerial decree introduced a total ban on radio advertising of tobacco; while Law 1730/1987 imposed a total ban on television advertising of tobacco. Article 10 of Presidential Decree 109/2010 (see section 1.2) provides for a total ban of all forms of audio-visual commercial communications for cigarettes and other tobacco products. Law 3730/2008 prohibits the projection of tobacco product advertising in cinemas.

Moreover, Article 2 of Law 3730/2008 introduced a ban on outdoor tobacco advertising, and also prohibits indoor advertising of tobacco products, including in cinemas, theatres, military units, courtrooms, hotels, other accommodation units, trade stores, educational institutions and health institutions. However, certain exceptions apply.

Annex II of the Greek Code of Advertising and Communication deals specifically with tobacco products and introduces best practice guidelines, including a ban on ads for tobacco products on television and radio.

Breach of Article 2 of Law 3730/2008 could lead to a fine ranging from €500 to €10,000. Ministerial Decree 81348/2005 provides for penal sanctions for breaches of the tobacco advertising regulations, combining up to six months' imprisonment with fines of up to €29,300. The sanctions imposed by the Council for Communication Control for breach of Presidential Decree 109/2010 include:

- a warning, with an order to comply;
- a fine ranging from €14,673.54 to €1,467,354.14; and
- a temporary or permanent prohibition on broadcasting.

9.7 E-cigarettes

Law 4419/2016 has implemented Directive 2014/40/EU on the manufacture, presentation and sale of tobacco and related products, and regulates commercial communications regarding e-cigarettes and refill containers, among other things.

According to Article 18 of Law 4419/2016, commercial communications online, in the press and in other printed publications with the aim or direct or indirect effect of promoting e-cigarettes and refill containers are prohibited (exceptions apply); the same applies for television and radio. Also prohibited is any form of public or private contribution to radio and television programmes with the aim or direct or indirect effect of promoting e-cigarettes and refill containers.

The prohibitions of Article 2 of Law 3730/2008 regarding indoor and outdoor advertising (as described in section 9.6) also apply to e-cigarettes and refill containers. Audio-visual commercial communications to which Presidential Decree 109/2010 (implementing Directive 2010/13/EU) applies are also prohibited for e-cigarettes and refill containers.

The publisher acknowledges the contribution of Nicholas I Gregoriades and Maria E Spanos to this chapter in the previous edition.

Hong Kong

Charmaine Koo
Kelley Loo
Deacons

1. Overview of legal and regulatory regime for advertising

Hong Kong has no comprehensive statute regulating advertising or trade practices. Instead, advertising is regulated by many applicable laws, including the common law (eg, misrepresentation, the tort of deceit and defamation), IP laws and consumer protection laws. In addition, certain business sectors are regulated by specific ordinances and regulations, and by industry codes of practice – including the advertising industry itself. It is not possible to cover every statute in detail; therefore, this chapter aims to provide a general but non-exhaustive overview of the advertising regime in Hong Kong.

1.1 Common law

The content of an ad is subject to regulation by the law on misrepresentation. This is where A makes a false statement of fact to B with the object of inducing B to enter into a contract or a legally binding transaction with A. In addition, a party may be liable for the tort of deceit where it makes a false statement (knowing it to be untrue or being reckless as to its accuracy), intending another party to act in reliance on it, and the other party does rely on it and suffers loss. However, as there must be proof of fraud, an action for the tort of deceit is very difficult to sustain. Advertisers should be aware of the potential legal risks under the defamation laws in Hong Kong if an ad contains any material that may be regarded as damaging to the reputation of another.

1.2 Intellectual property

The IP rights most likely to be relevant to advertising are trademarks and copyright. These are protected in Hong Kong under the Copyright Ordinance (Cap 528) and the Trade Marks Ordinance (Cap 559) as well as the common law tort of passing off. The Copyright Ordinance protects original works including literary, dramatic, musical, artistic works, sound recordings, films, broadcasts and cable programmes. The acts of copyright infringement are specifically defined in the Copyright Ordinance and include the following offences that may be relevant to advertising:

- making an unauthorised reproduction;

- issuing or making available infringing copies to the public;
- making an adaptation (which includes a translation);
- broadcasting; and
- exhibiting and distributing infringing copies in the course of, or in connection with, any trade or business.

Under the Trade Marks Ordinance, a trademark owner is entitled to prevent other traders from using a mark which is identical or similar to its registered mark, in relation to the same or similar products or services covered by the registration (where, in the case of a similar mark or products/services, such use results in a likelihood of confusion), without its consent. There are certain exceptions to trademark infringement under the ordinance, including use for the purpose of identifying a competitor's goods or services, provided that such use accords with honest practices in industrial and commercial matters (see section 2).

Passing off is a common law action that can be used to protect both registered or unregistered trademarks, trade names, an individual's name or reputation and the design or look of a particular product, including its packaging. Passing off can be used to prevent all kinds of misrepresentations that cause confusion and damage to a plaintiff. The categories of potentially actionable misrepresentations are not exhaustive. In order to establish passing off, it is necessary to show that:

- the plaintiff has a reputation or goodwill in Hong Kong in the trademark, name, products, services or other elements sought to be protected;
- a misrepresentation is being made by a trader in the course of trade which will confuse the public into believing that its business, products or services are those of the plaintiff's, or are somehow associated with the plaintiff's; and
- the misrepresentation is likely to cause damage to the business or goodwill of the plaintiff.

It is sufficient if there is an overall impression that the defendant's business is related to the plaintiff's business. This will include a belief that the plaintiff has approved or licensed the defendant, or its products or services, in some way. Each case must be assessed on a case-by-case basis and will turn on its own facts, and all relevant circumstances will be taken into account.

1.3 Consumer protection

The main statute is the Trade Descriptions Ordinance, which prohibits false and misleading trade descriptions of products and services, including in ads. The Trade Descriptions Ordinance also prohibits misleading omissions, aggressive commercial practices, bait advertising and bait-and-switch tactics. 'Bait advertising' is where traders advertise goods at exceeding attractive prices, but the product is actually not available or is available only for an unreasonably short timeframe or in unreasonably small quantities. 'Bait and switch' is the practice of promoting products at bargain prices and very favourable terms, but then switching to more expensive products once the consumer has been lured into the shop.

A 'trade description' is any direct or indirect indication, by whatever means given, in relation to products or services or any part thereof. It includes anything containing information on the products or services or any part thereof, in whatever form (eg, statements, ads or display notices) and communicated through whatever means (eg, any form of media, including electronic, oral and visual means and even conduct). The provision of false, misleading or incomplete information may constitute an offence under the Trade Descriptions Ordinance, which could result in a fine of HK$500,000 and imprisonment for five years. In addition, the person convicted of such offence may also be ordered by the court to compensate any victims' financial loss resulting from that offence.

Under the Trade Descriptions Ordinance, the chief executive in Council may by order require that any description of advertisement of any products specified in the order contain or refer to information (whether or not amounting to or including a trade description) relating to such products and, subject to the provisions of the ordinance, impose requirements regarding the inclusion of that information or of an indication of the means by which it may be obtained. (The chief executive is the chief representative of the Hong Kong Special Administrative Region and the head of the government in Hong Kong. She is assisted in policy making and the administration of the government by the Executive Council, which is the formal body of advisers to the chief executive.)

Consumer contracts are subject to other relevant statutes, such as the Unconscionable Contracts Ordinance, which protects consumers against unfair terms in standard contracts.

1.4   Industry regulations

Certain industries or products may be subject to specific ordinances or regulations, such as:

- the Undesirable Medical Advertisements Ordinance;
- the Public Health and Municipal Services Ordinance;
- the Estate Agents Practice (General Duties and Hong Kong Residential Properties) Regulation; and
- the Banking Ordinance.

Certain business sectors have formulated their own practice codes. For example, the Federation of Beauty Industry (HK) and the Cosmetics and Perfumery Association of HK have formulated their own codes of practice recommending best practices for adoption by practitioners, so as to enhance self-regulation within the local beauty industry.

The Hong Kong Association of the Pharmaceutical Industry also has its own Code of Practice covering advertising, promotion and other marketing activities relating to pharmaceutical products.

1.5 Advertising codes of practice

There are also various codes of practices which regulate or recommend best practices as regards the contents of ads in Hong Kong. For example, the Hong Kong Communication Authority has issued various general codes of practice relating to advertising, including:

- the Generic Code of Practice on Television Advertising Standards (GCPTAS);
- the Generic Code of Practice on Television Programme Standards (GCPTPS);
- the Radio Code of Practice on Advertising Standards (RCPAS); and
- the Radio Code of Practice on Programme Standards (RCPPS).

The principle of these codes is that all advertising should be legal, clean, honest and truthful. These codes provide that ads which are broadcast should not contain any descriptions, claims or illustrations which are untrue or misleading; and that advertising matter should not contain claims intended to disparage competitors or competing products. Special care must be taken in respect of advertising that may be viewed by children or adolescents. There are specific guidelines on products such as alcohol, tobacco, medical preparations and nutritional or dietary products; and in certain sectors, such as financial services and real estate.

The Communication Authority may issue warnings or directions requiring a broadcaster to take such action as the authority considers necessary. It may also impose financial penalties or suspend or revoke the offending broadcaster's licence. However, there is no authority responsible for policing and preventing misleading advertising published in the non-broadcast or print media.

The Association of Accredited Advertising Agencies of Hong Kong (HK4As) has its own Code of Practice to regulate the conduct of its members. The general principle of the standards is that "all advertising shall be legal, decent, honest and truthful". Any member found guilty of contravention or non-compliance with the standards will be penalised in accordance with the relevant rules of the association.

The Hong Kong Consumer Council has also issued two general guidelines – the *Good Corporate Citizen's Guide* and the *Good Corporate Citizen's Guide II – Rules* – to provide a general reference on the recommended standards of business ethics and best practices, which the business community in Hong Kong is encouraged to observe.

2. Comparative advertising

In Hong Kong, comparative advertising is permitted in principle, provided that certain requirements are met. Where the comparative advertising names a competitor's brand or product, the Trade Marks Ordinance provides a defence for use of a competitor's registered mark for the purpose of identifying goods and services as those of the owner of the mark, provided that such use accords with honest practices in industrial and commercial matters. This is intended to allow product and service providers to inform consumers about the relative merits of competing products, provided that the advertising is honest. This generally means that the claims are true and accurate, and supported by evidence. The advertising should also be aimed at informing the consumer rather than denigrating the competitor.

In deciding whether the use is honest, the court may consider such factors as it considers relevant, including whether:
- the claim is true;
- the use takes unfair advantage of the trademark;
- the use is detrimental to the distinctive character or repute of the trademark; or
- the use is such as to deceive the public.

Such issues are not always easy to determine. In *PCCW-HKT Datacom Services Limited v Hong Kong Broadband Network Ltd*,[1] the Court of First Instance held that the average consumer in Hong Kong is used to hyperbole, puffery and colourful or sensational language, such that use of the words "bloated fees" and "big eater or gluttonous" (which were the words that the plaintiffs had complained of) had no derogatory meaning in Hong Kong and could be used in comparative advertising. While the court acknowledged that the concept of 'unfair advantage' does not fit easily into the context of comparative advertising, because it is expected that an advertiser will not paint its competitor's goods in a favourable light, it is said that if the ad is substantially true and not misleading, any advantage taken will not be unfair.

HK4A's Code of Practice specifies that comparative advertising is permissible provided that:
- what is being compared is clear;
- the comparisons are fair and reasonable; and
- the comparisons are substantiated and supportable by research or other statistical evidence.

---

1   [2018] HKCFI 2037.

Disparaging advertising – that is, advertising which seeks to compare a product or service to similar products or services in a way which is misleading, derogatory or false in implication or in fact by its members – is not allowed by HK4A's Code of Practice.

Although it is in principle allowed, comparative advertising can raise other legal issues involving not just intellectual property, but also misrepresentation, defamation, potential breaches of advertising codes of practice and the breach of laws or regulations that apply to specific industries or products. For example, copyright law may be relevant where another party's distinctive logo, packaging or trade dress is reproduced in a comparative advertising campaign. Also, the Hong Kong Association of the Pharmaceutical Industry (HKAPI) Code of Practice sets out rules for comparative claims between pharmaceutical products and provides that a competitor product brand name should be used only with written consent from that company.

3. Online behavioural advertising

There is no specific law regulating online behavioural advertising in Hong Kong. However, online behavioural tracking raises privacy concerns and the Hong Kong Privacy Commissioner has published an information leaflet which sets out guidelines for businesses on the use of online behavioural tracking. These are simply best practice guidelines, but the Privacy Commissioner is extremely vigilant in ensuring compliance with the law, and is known to initiate compliance checks even without receiving any complaints. The guidelines are available on the Office of Privacy Commissioner's website at www.pcpd.org.hk/english/publications/files/online_tracking_e.pdf.

Organisations that deploy online tracking on their websites, resulting in the collection of the 'personal data' of website users, must observe the six Data Protection Principles set out in the Personal Data (Privacy) Ordinance (Cap 486), governing:
- the purpose and manner of collection;
- the accuracy and duration of retention;
- the use of personal data;
- the security of personal data;
- the general availability of the information; and
- access to personal data.

Under the ordinance, 'personal data' is any data:
- that relates directly or indirectly to a living individual;
- from which it is practicable for the identity of the individual to be directly or indirectly ascertained; and
- in a form in which access to or processing of the data is practicable.

Organisations are strongly advised to adopt fair and transparent practices as outlined in the Privacy Commissioner's guidelines, including the following:

- Inform users of:
  - what information is being collected or tracked by them;
  - the purpose of collecting the information;
  - how the information is collected (including what tools are used);
  - whether the information will be transferred to third parties (and if so, the classes of such third parties and purpose of the transfer); and
  - how long the information will be retained.
- Inform users whether any third party is collecting or tracking their behavioural information. Users should be informed of:
  - the class of such third parties;
  - the purpose and means of collection;
  - the retention period; and
  - whether such information collected will be transferred to other parties by the third party.
- Offer users a way to opt out of the tracking and inform them of the consequences of opting out. If it is not possible to opt out of tracking while using the website, explain why, so that website users can decide whether to continue using the website.

If online tracking information is collected for direct marketing purposes, data users must follow the requirements of the Personal Data (Privacy) Ordinance. The law regulating the use of personal data in direct marketing activities has very stringent requirements including, among other things, obtaining the explicit consent of the data subject (see section 6).

4.   Sales promotions

Sales promotions are not regulated by a single law in Hong Kong, but will be affected by a variety of legal provisions and codes of practice, depending on the activity.

Activities will be subject to contract law and advertisers should be aware that certain sales promotion schemes may create binding contracts with members of the public (eg, the offering of free gifts for customers who purchase a certain value of products).

Consumer protection provisions will also apply, including the Trade Descriptions Ordinance, which prohibits misleading price information and bait advertising.

To the extent that the sales promotion activity consists of a competition or scheme that involve an element of chance (eg, lucky draws or scratch cards), the activity will be regulated under the Gambling Ordinance (Cap 148). The Gambling Ordinance provides that all 'gambling' and 'lotteries' are unlawful, unless specifically permitted under the ordinance. 'Gambling' includes "gaming, betting and bookmaking". Organising or participating in unauthorised gambling or lotteries is an offence. Payment for entry is not a deciding factor. A 'game' is defined as a game of chance and a game of chance and skill combined. The ordinance is not concerned with pure games of skill (eg, chess); but any game of skill that has an element of chance will be governed by the ordinance.

In order to organise and conduct a trade promotion competition which involves a game of chance in Hong Kong, a trade promotion competition licence must be obtained from the Office of the Licensing Authority of the Home Affairs Department. Licensees must comply with the terms and conditions imposed by the licence.

Certain products are subject to specific regulation in the context of sales promotions. For example, under the GCPTAS and the RCPAS, the presentation of tobacco products as a prize or gift for contests is not permitted; and the presentation of alcohol as a prize or gift in isolation is prohibited. The codes also provide that no ad for a medical preparation or treatment may contain any reference to a prize competition or promotional scheme such as gifts, premium offers or samples.

The GCPTAS and the RCPAS also set out rules for contests included in a television or radio programme or ad, including the following:

- All contestants must be offered an opportunity to win on the basis of skill or knowledge, and not purely by chance;
- All rules and conditions of contests must be clearly and fully announced at the beginning of the contest; and
- Where a contest is included in a programme, references to prizes must not be made in such a way as to amount to advertising.

The codes cover only contests included in a programme or an ad appearing on domestic free and domestic pay television programme services and sound broadcasting services licensed under the Telecommunications Ordinance. Contests that are not broadcast (eg, appearing in print media) are governed by the general law, including the Gambling Ordinance. The general law and the Gambling Ordinance also apply to contests broadcast on television and radio.

Under the HK4As Code of Practice, except where the law prohibits use of the word 'free' in advertising, products or services offered without cost or obligation to the recipient may be unqualifiedly described as 'free'. However, where 'free' means that the offer requires the recipient to purchase some other item, the term can be used only conditionally, as long as:

- the terms and conditions are accurately and conspicuously disclosed in conjunction with the term 'free'; and
- the products or services required for purchase are not increased in price or decreased in quality or quantity.

If the so-called 'free' item is an essential part of the product sold as a complete unit and not an accessory, extra or duplicate, then the term cannot be described as 'free' in the ad.

Certain industries may have to be particularly careful when offering gifts and promotions. For example, the HKAPI code provides rules on promotional items that may be given away and on the sponsorship of conferences or other promotional or educational programmes. In some situations, the offering of free gifts or other advantages may be subject to the Prevention of Bribery Ordinance (Cap 201) – for example, this ordinance prohibits the offering of an 'advantage' to an agent in the conduct of its principal's affairs or business without the permission of the principal. The definition of 'advantage' is very wide and encompasses any gift, reward or property, service or favour, including gifts or free attendance at seminars or conferences.

5.   Ambush marketing

Ambush marketing is not specifically regulated in Hong Kong, but may infringe trademark, copyright or other IP rights in relation to an event. A false or misleading association with an event may also constitute passing off or a breach of the Trade Descriptions Ordinance or various codes of practice, depending on exactly how it is made. Each case will therefore turn on its own facts.

When major events are held, countries commonly introduce special laws to give the event organisers and sponsors additional protection by making it unlawful to carry out certain ambush marketing activities which might otherwise be permitted under the general law. For example, as a part of China, Hong Kong hosted the equestrian events during the 2008 Beijing Olympics and shared the guidelines on marketing and promotions established by the Beijing Olympic Committee to protect the IP rights associated with the Olympic symbols, including the names, abbreviations, emblems and mascots of the Beijing Games.

6.   Direct marketing

In Hong Kong, the collection, use and/or transfer of individuals' personal data for direct marketing purposes is regulated under the Personal Data (Privacy) Ordinance and a data user must comply with the Data Protection Principles imposed under the ordinance (see section 3).

In addition, the ordinance includes stringent requirements in relation to direct marketing. In particular, the law provides that:

- data subjects must give their explicit consent or an explicit indication of no objection to the use of their data in direct marketing; and
- data users must provide detailed information so that data subjects can make an informed choice.

A data user must also comply with the following notification requirements, among others, prior to using personal data in direct marketing:

- inform the data subject that:
  - it intends to use the personal data for direct marketing purposes; and
  - it may not use the personal data unless it has received the data subject's consent to do so;
- provide information on the kinds of personal data to be used and the classes of marketing subjects (eg, cosmetic products or telecommunications network services) in relation to which the data is to be used; and
- notify the data subject when using personal data in direct marketing for the first time.

The penalty on conviction of each offence is a fine of HK$500,000 and imprisonment for up to three years.

In addition to data privacy considerations, electronic marketing messages promoting products or services that can be sent as text or pre-recorded voice messages to telephones, fax machines or email addresses are governed by the Unsolicited Electronic Messages Ordinance (Cap 593) and the Unsolicited Electronic Messages Regulation. The Communications Authority is empowered under the ordinance to approve codes of practice to provide further practical guidance. The Communications Authority's guidelines are available at www.ofca.gov.hk/filemanager/ofca/common/uemo/uemo_industry_guide_e.pdf.

The Unsolicited Electronic Messages Ordinance regulates the sending of all forms of commercial electronic messages (CEMs) with a Hong Kong link. A 'CEM' is defined as an electronic message:

- offering to supply, or advertising or promoting, products, services, facilities, land or an interest in land; or
- advertising or promoting a supplier or prospective supplier of products, services, facilities, land or an interest in land.

The ordinance sets out the rules for sending CEMs, such as providing accurate sender information and unsubscribe facilities, and provides for the establishment of 'do not call' registers. It also prohibits professional spamming activities, such as:

- the use of unscrupulous means to gather or generate recipient lists for sending CEMs without the recipients' consent; and
- fraudulent activities relating to the sending of multiple CEMs.

The following types of messages are exempt from the application of the ordinance:

- person-to-person interactive calls;

- messages sent in response to the recipient's specific request, such as fax-on-demand;
- messages such as invoices or receipts to confirm a commercial transaction that the recipient has previously agreed to enter into with the sender; and
- sound broadcasting services and television programme services.

The Hong Kong Direct Marketing Association also has a voluntary Code of Ethics and a Code of Practice on Person-to-Person Marketing Calls.

7. Product placement

There is no specific law or regulation governing product placement in Hong Kong. However, in the case of promotions broadcast on the television or radio, the GCPTPS and the RCPPS provide that, as a general rule, ads should be recognisably separate from programmes.

Generally, indirect advertising in television programmes is permitted, with the exception of:
- news programmes;
- current affairs programmes (though product or service sponsorship is allowed, provided that care is exercised in the choice of sponsor, to safeguard the credibility and integrity of such programmes);
- children's programmes;
- educational programmes; and
- religious service and other devotional programmes.

According to the GCPTPS, the placement of advertising material should be confined to commercial breaks. Indirect advertising on television – that is, the mingling of programme and advertising material or the embedding of material within programme content – must be controlled, because viewers should not be confused as to whether they are watching a programme or a paid ad.

However, exceptions do apply, such as the following:
- An exception may be made if an extract or reference from a particular ad is necessary in a news or factual programme for reference purposes; and
- A television programme may refer to or use extracts from ads, provided that the choice and range of ads are subject only to the editorial requirements of the programme and are not influenced by advertising considerations.

Pre-July 2018, the GCPTPS and RCPPS provide that no undue prominence should be given in any television or radio programme to a product, service, trademark, brand name or logo of a commercial nature, or a person identified with the above, so that the effect of such reference amounts to advertising.

However, since July 2018, the Communications Authority has relaxed the regulations for indirect advertising in television programmes. In particular, the GCPTAS now provides that a licensee may include one or more products or services within a television programme in return for payment or other valuable consideration, provided that the following requirements are met:

- Their exposure or use is presented in a natural and unobtrusive manner, having regard to the programme content and genre, and there is no direct encouragement to purchase or use the products or services;
- The sponsor for the product or service featured is clearly identified in the opening and/or end sponsor credits of the programme. The GCPTAS also provides specific rules on the form of the sponsor identification and how sponsor credits and identifications should appear in the content of the opening and/or end sponsor credits;
- An announcement containing the wording "The following programme contains indirect advertising" is made to clearly inform viewers of the inclusion of sponsorship in the programme before the programme starts; and
- The product or service featured in the programme is not unacceptable for advertising under the GCPTAS.

The advertising standards set out in other chapters of the GCPTAS shall apply to sponsorship where appropriate, including the provisions on the substantiation of factual claims and disparagement of competitors.

Indirect advertising in radio programmes is also generally allowed. However, the RCPPS's rules on indirect advertising have yet to be amended. Therefore, the current rules still prohibit radio programmes from giving undue prominence to a product, service, trademark, brand name or logo of a commercial nature, or a person identified with the above, so that the effect of such reference amounts to advertising. Such references must be limited to what can clearly be justified by the editorial requirements of the programme itself or what is of an incidental nature.

While specific regulations govern product placements in movies, advertisers and promoters should ensure that they comply with the general laws, such as those on misrepresentation or defamation, consumer protection laws such as the Trade Descriptions Ordinance, and any relevant codes of practice. In particular, products such as alcohol and tobacco are subject to additional regulatory restrictions (see section 9).

8. Native advertising and social media influencers

There is no specific law or regulation governing native advertising or advertising activities carried out by social media influencers. However, the Trade Descriptions Ordinance will still be relevant, such that an advertiser must still comply with the requirements of the Trade Descriptions Ordinance, including not omitting or hiding:

- material information regarding the commercial intent of the native advertising; or
- where social media influencers are engaged, the connection between the social media influencers and the advertiser (eg, if the social media influencer has been paid by the advertiser, this should be disclosed).

Similar to traditional advertising, native advertising and social media advertising must also comply with other provisions of the Trade Descriptions Ordinance, including not providing false and misleading trade descriptions of products or services in ads.

Social media influencers will also likely be subject to the Trade Descriptions Ordinance as a 'trader' if they receive payment or other remuneration. A 'trader' is defined as any person (other than an exempt person)[2] who, in relation to a commercial practice, is acting or purporting to act for purposes relating to the person's trade or business. A 'commercial practice' is defined as any act, omission, course of conduct, representation or commercial communication (including advertising and marketing) by a trader which is directly connected to the promotion of a product to consumers.

As with traditional advertising, advertisers and influencers must also comply with IP laws and other general laws, such as those on misrepresentation or defamation.

9. Industry-specific regulation

9.1 Gambling

In Hong Kong, gambling activities and lotteries are strictly controlled by the Gambling Ordinance and the Betting Duty Ordinance (Cap 108), and subsidiary legislation. Under the Gambling Ordinance, all gambling activities are illegal, except those which are:

- expressly authorised by the government under the Betting Duty Ordinance – that is, authorised horse racing, authorised football betting and the Mark Six Lottery;
- licensed by public officers appointed by the secretary for home affairs (eg, *mah-jong* parlours); or
- exempted under Section 3 of the Gambling Ordinance (mainly social gambling).

---

2   'Exempt persons' under the Trade Descriptions Ordinance include certified public accountants, registered dentists, barristers, solicitors, registered medical practitioners and other professionals, which activities are all governed by other applicable laws.

Subject to a very limited scope of statutory exceptions and exemptions, all gambling activities and lotteries are unlawful in Hong Kong. Under the Gambling Ordinance, ads to promote or facilitate bookmaking and betting-related services are prohibited. The advertisement of unlawful gambling activities and unlawful lotteries is also prohibited.

The advertisement of authorised fixed odds and *pari mutuel*[3] betting on horse races and football matches, and authorised lotteries is regulated by the Betting Duty Ordinance. This specifies that any advertising or promotional activity for authorised/licensed gambling activities must not:

- target juveniles;
- exaggerate the likelihood of winning; or
- expressly or impliedly suggest that betting is a source of income or a viable way to overcome financial difficulties.

The Betting Duty Ordinance also requires that a notice be conspicuously displayed on any website through which bets for such authorised/licensed gambling activities are accepted, warning of the seriousness of the problems caused by excessive gambling and providing information on the services and facilities available in Hong Kong to problem gamblers and pathological gamblers.

After the legalisation of football betting, the government issued the Codes of Practice for the Conduct of Football Betting and Lotteries in 2004 to provide guidance on compliance with the licensing conditions for football betting and lotteries. Under the codes, licensees should not:

- advertise the conduct of football betting and lotteries in, or in close proximity to, educational and training institutions for juveniles (defined in the Betting Duty Ordinance as persons under 18 years); or
- place ads or promotional materials on billboards or other outdoor displays that are directly adjacent to such institutions.

Gambling advertising is also regulated by the GCPTAS and the RCPAS. Under these codes, ads for lotteries, football and horse race betting which are authorised under the Betting Duty Ordinance and for horse racing are allowed, provided that they do not encourage betting or contain any references to betting tips. No ads for such activities should be shown within or in proximity to children's programmes. In addition, the licensee must ensure that ads:

- are not shown between 4:00pm and 8:30pm each day on domestic free television programme services or at times when television programmes, in the opinion of the Communication Authority, target young persons under the age of 18;

---

3   This is a system of betting where the winners divide the total amount of the bet.

- target only an adult audience and do not feature children or adolescents;
- do not feature any personality who has particular appeal to children or adolescents;
- do not state or imply praise for those who participate in lotteries/football/horse race betting or denigrate those who abstain;
- do not mislead or exaggerate one's likelihood of winning;
- are instructional in nature or unduly exhort the public to bet;
- do not feature excessive or reckless betting; and
- do not present lotteries/football/horse race betting as an alternative to work or a way out of difficulties.

9.2 Alcohol

The advertisement of alcoholic beverages is specifically regulated under the GCPTAS and the RCPAS. The specific conditions relate to the advertisement of 'liquor' or 'alcoholic liquor', defined by the Dutiable Commodities Ordinance (Cap 109) as any liquid which contains more that 1.2% of ethyl alcohol by volume, except denatured spirits or any such liquid that is an ingredient in any goods, if that liquid cannot be converted to pure ethyl alcohol or to an intoxicating liquor, or if such a conversion would not be economical. The ordinance contains detailed definitions of different kinds of alcoholic beverages.

The GCPTAS provides that ads for alcoholic beverages:
- must target adults only and must not feature the participation of children or adolescents. The codes also refer to young persons under the age of 18, but 'adolescents' can include young people over the age of 18, according to the normal understanding of the term;
- Ads must not be shown in proximity to children's programmes or those targeting young persons under the age of 18;
- For domestic free television programme services, ads must not be shown between the hours of 4:00pm and 8:30pm. For domestic pay television programme services, the code also provides that alcoholic beverages should not be presented as desirable in programmes or channels targeting children.
- Ads must not attempt to prevent drinking as a desirable new experience or portray drinking as indispensable to popularity or success; and
- Ads must not suggest that a drink is more preferable because of its higher alcohol content or intoxicating effect.

Similar provisions are set out in the HK4A Code of Practice.

9.3 Pharmaceuticals

Under the Public Health and Municipal Services Ordinance (Cap 132), it is an offence for anyone to issue a label or to publish an ad which falsely describes any food or drug or is likely to be misleading as to the nature, substance or quality of any food or drug, unless it can prove that it did not know, and could not with reasonable diligence have ascertained, the false character of the label. The maximum penalty for breach is a fine of HK$50,000 and imprisonment for six months.

In addition, the Undesirable Medical Advertisements Ordinance (Cap 231) aims to protect public health by prohibiting or restricting the publication of ads for medicines, surgical appliances or treatments that may induce the improper management of certain health conditions set out in Schedules 1 and 2 of the ordinance. Anyone who is guilty of an offence under the ordinance shall be liable to a fine of HK$50,000 and imprisonment for six months upon first conviction; and upon a second or subsequent conviction for an offence under the same section, to a fine of HK$100,000 and imprisonment for one year. Additional guidance can be found in the Guidelines on the Undesirable Medical Advertisements Ordinance (Cap 231) issued by the Department of Health.

As the Public Health and Municipal Services Ordinance covers many areas relating to public health, it is enforced by the relevant government departments – for example, false labelling and the advertisement of food fall under the remit of the Food and Environmental Hygiene Department; whereas the management of public swimming pools falls under the remit of the Leisure and Cultural Services Department. The Undesirable Medical Advertisements Ordinance is enforced by the director of health.

An 'advertisement' is defined under the Undesirable Medical Advertisements Ordinance as "including any notice, poster, circular, label, wrapper or document, and any announcement made orally or by any means of producing or transmitting light or sound", which is very broad. This includes ads published:

- in newspapers and magazines;
- in leaflets;
- on the radio, television or Internet; and
- on the label of a container or package that contains any medicine, surgical appliance, treatment or orally consumed product.

A 'medicine' is defined as including "any kind of medicament or other curative or preventive substance, and whether a proprietary medicine, a patent medicine, a Chinese herbal medicine, a proprietary Chinese medicine, or purported natural remedy".

Schedules 1 and 2 of the Undesirable Medical Advertisements Ordinance set out specific categories of diseases in respect of which the advertisement of medicines, surgical appliances or treatments is restricted or banned, depending on the type of disease involved. Pharmaceutical advertising for major diseases or conditions (eg, tumours, sexually transmitted diseases or diseases of the heart or cardiovascular system) aimed directly at the general public through the mainstream media is prohibited. The advertisement of treatments for minor diseases or conditions (eg, common colds, coughs, influenzas, rhinitis, indigestions, headaches, dry skin) is permitted.

In the case of pharmaceutical advertising through broadcast media, the GCPTAS and the RCPAS will be relevant. According to these codes, ads for certain unacceptable products or services – such as treatments for smoking cessation, clinics for the treatment of hair and scalp and pregnancy testing services – are prohibited on broadcast media. In addition to the kinds of diseases and conditions for which treatments may be advertised, the design and the contents of pharmaceutical ads are strictly controlled.

It is also prohibited to give the impression of professional advice and support from doctors or other medical professionals. Presentations of a patient undergoing treatment, appeals to fear, dramatisation of ailments and offensive descriptions of the illness are also banned. Ads should not make exaggerated claims with superlative and comparative adjectives, such as 'the most successful' or 'quickest.'

Pharmaceutical advertising must also comply with relevant industry codes of practice – in particular, the HKAPI Code of Practice, which covers advertising, promotion and other marketing activities relating to pharmaceutical products.

9.4   Financial products

This is a highly regulated and complex area in Hong Kong. Different types of financial products and financial services require approval from the relevant authorities, and are regulated by specific ordinances and regulations which govern licences and the advertisement of financial products and services, including:

- the Companies Ordinance (Cap 32);
- the Banking Ordinance (Cap 155);
- the Insurance Companies Ordinance (Cap 41);
- the Securities and Futures Ordinance (Cap 571); and
- the Mandatory Provident Fund Schemes Ordinance (Cap 485).

In addition to specific rules set out in the ordinances and regulations, different products and services are overseen by the relevant regulatory bodies, which may have additional rules and guidelines, such as the Securities and Futures Commission (SFC), the Hong Kong Monetary Authority, the Mandatory Provident Schemes Authority and the Insurance Authority. These bodies also have guidelines and codes of conduct which will affect how products are advertised, including:

- the Code on Unit Trusts and Mutual Funds;

- the Code on Investment-linked Assurance Schemes;
- the Code on Pooled Retirement Funds;
- the Code on Immigration-linked Investment Schemes; and
- the SFC Code on MPF Products.

The advertisement of consumer credit merits particular mention. Hong Kong has no specific legislation or regulations governing this issue. However, the advertisement of consumer credit will be affected by the following:

- the non-statutory Code of Banking Practice with respect to 'authorised institutions' within the meaning of the Banking Ordinance; and
- the Money Lenders Ordinance (Cap 163) with respect to non-authorised institutions within the meaning of the Banking Ordinance.

Authorised institutions are subject to the non-statutory Code of Banking Practice, which was issued jointly by the Hong Kong Association of Banks and the DTC Association, which represents restricted licensed banks and deposit-taking companies. The code is endorsed and governed by the Hong Kong Monetary Authority. The advertisement of consumer credit falls within the code's provisions on 'bank marketing' and 'direct mailing'. These require authorised institutions to ensure that all advertising and promotional materials:

- are fair and reasonable;
- do not contain misleading information; and
- comply with all relevant legislation, codes and rules.

Where benefits are subject to conditions, such conditions should be clearly displayed in the advertising materials wherever practical. Where there are limitations as to space (eg, on poster ads and television ads), the ads should include reference to the means by which further information may be obtained.

In any advertising and promotional material for a banking service that includes a reference to an interest rate, the advertiser should also indicate the annualised percentage rate (where relevant) and other relevant fees and charges, and also that full details of the relevant terms and conditions are available on request.

Unauthorised institutions are subject to the Money Lenders Ordinance. Consumer credit is a form of money lending and the ordinance governs the acts of 'money lenders', defined as a "person whose business (whether or not he carries on any other business) is that of making loans or who advertises or announces himself or holds himself out in any way as carrying on that business". Authorised institutions under the Banking Ordinance are expressly excluded.

The Money Lenders Ordinance provides generally that in any ad, circular, business letter or other similar document, the name of the money lender, as specified in its licence, must be shown in such manner as to be not less conspicuous than any other name. Any ad must also clearly show the words "Money Lender's Licence No", immediately followed by the number.

Where any ad purports to indicate the terms of interest on which a loan may be made, the ad must show the interest proposed to be charged as an annual percentage rate and in such manner as to be not less conspicuous than any other matter mentioned in the ad.

Advertisers must also comply with the Codes of Practice issued by the Communication Authority (for ads broadcast on television or radio) and the advertising industry's own codes of practice, including the HK4A's Code of Practice. The GCPTAS and RCPAS include detailed provisions on the advertisement of financial products and services, but also make clear that the licensee is responsible for ensuring that ads comply with all of the relevant legal and regulatory requirements.

9.5 Food

Under the Public Health and Municipal Services Ordinance, it is an offence for any person to issue a label or to publish an ad which falsely describes any food or drug or is likely to mislead as to the nature, substance or quality of any food or drug, unless it proves that it did not know, and could not with reasonable diligence have ascertained, that the label was of such a character as aforesaid.

Food ads must comply with general law and consumer protection laws such as the Trade Descriptions Ordinance. Also, depending on the food product in question, the advertisement of specific products may be subject to additional requirements imposed by the relevant subsidiary legislation. For example, for milk products, the Milk Regulation (Cap 132AQ) contains additional provisions setting out restrictions on the sale, advertisement and so on of milk or milk beverages imported from Hong Kong.

The Undesirable Medical Advertisements Ordinance is relevant to the advertisement of health food and supplements, and includes regulations which are similar to those relating to pharmaceutical products.

Food ads and promotions broadcast on the television or radio that include claims relating to nutrition or dietary effects should adhere to the rules and guidelines listed in the GCPTAS and RCPAS, which contain detailed provisions on claims relating to nutrition and dietary effects, including the following:

- Specific claims on the nutritional value of foods must be supported by sound scientific evidence and must not give a misleading impression as to the nutritional or health benefits of the food as a whole;
- Ads for dietary supplements, including vitamins or minerals, should not state or imply that they are necessary as additions to a balanced diet to avoid dietary deficiency or that they are the only means to enhance normal good health; and

- Ads for food products aimed at achieving weight loss or reduction of body fat must make it clear that the product can assist weight loss only as part of a calorie-controlled diet. Such ads must not be addressed to persons under the age of 18 or suggest that being underweight is acceptable or desirable.

9.6 Tobacco

The Smoking (Public Health) Ordinance (Cap 371) regulates all matters related to smoking, including tobacco advertising. The ordinance prohibits tobacco advertising in printed publications, in public places, in film, on the radio and online. Breach of the ordinance is punishable on summary conviction to a fine of HK$50,000 and, in the case of a continuing offence, to a further penalty of HK$1,500 for each day that the offence continues. The sole exceptions relate to:

- printed publications published for the tobacco trade and any 'in-house' magazine of a company engaged in the trade of tobacco; and
- any ads that are displayed in or on the premises of a manufacturer or wholesaler of tobacco products and are not visible from outside the premises.

Further, no person may, for the purpose of promotion or advertising, give a cigarette, tobacco, cigar or pipe tobacco to any person.

A 'tobacco advertisement' is an ad which:

- contains any inducement, suggestion or request to buy or smoke a tobacco product;
- aims, expressly or impliedly, to promote or encourage the use of a tobacco product; or
- illustrates or mentions smoking or tobacco products or their packaging or qualities.

The GCPTAS and RCPAS make clear that all relevant provisions of the Smoking Ordinance must be complied with. The presentation of tobacco products as prizes or gifts for radio or television contests is not permitted. Any ad for certain tobacco-related products – such as cigarette holders, tobacco filters and other smoking accessories – should:

- target adults only;
- not feature children or adolescents; and
- not be shown in proximity to children's programmes or programmes which target persons under 18.

The ordinance also requires that the tobacco packaging contain a health warning (in a prescribed form and manner) and specify the tar and nicotine yields. An offence is committed if the packaging, or anything attached to or printed on the packaging, of a tobacco product falsely misleads, deceives or likely create an erroneous impression about the characteristics, health effects, hazards or emissions of the product, or creates a false impression that it has less harmful effects than other comparable products. The penalty on a summary conviction is HK$50,000.

The HK4A's Code of Practice also contain similar provisions targeted at tobacco advertising, and refers to the Smoking Ordinance and the GCPTAS.

9.7 E-cigarettes

At present, there is no specific legislation governing e-cigarettes in Hong Kong. The current Smoking Ordinance does not expressly cover e-cigarettes. The ordinance was last substantively amended in or around 2006, before e-cigarettes became prevalent.

The Hong Kong government has introduced the Smoking (Public Health) (Amendment) Bill 2019, which aims, among other things:

- to impose a blanket ban on the import, manufacture, sale and distribution of alternative smoking products; and
- to prohibit the advertisement of alternative smoking products.

However, the work on this bill ceased in June 2020[4] and therefore the bill did not become law. Despite this, there are still a few provisions in the Smoking Ordinance which are arguably broad enough[5] to regulate e-cigarettes to some extent, such as the prohibition on smoking in designated non-smoking areas. Similarly, ads for e-cigarettes could arguably also be prohibited by the current definition of a 'tobacco advertisement' (see section 9.6).

Meanwhile, according to the Pharmacy and Poisons Regulations,[6] nicotine is categorised as Part 1 poison in the Poisons List.[7] Therefore, any e-cigarettes containing nicotine must be registered with the Pharmacy and Poisons Board before sale in Hong Kong. Otherwise, possession of Part 1 poisons is prohibited and the penalty on conviction is HK$100,000 and two years' imprisonment.

The publisher acknowledges the contribution of Winne Yue to this chapter in the previous edition.

---

4 The Smoking (Public Health) (Amendment) Bill 2019 was introduced by the Sixth Legislative Council (serving from 1 October 2016 to 1 October 2020) and also ceased by the Sixth Term.
5 For example, 'smoking' is defined as the inhalation and expulsion of the smoke of tobacco or other substances, and thus arguably could cover the smoking of e-cigarettes.
6 As provided in Schedule 10 of the Pharmacy and Poisons Regulations (Cap 138A).

Hungary

Anikó Keller
Szecskay Attorneys at Law

1. Overview of the legal and regulatory regime for advertising

The Hungarian regulatory regime includes both statutory and self-regulatory bodies.

1.1 Statutory regulation

The most important roles are played by three statutory bodies:

- the Hungarian Competition Authority (HCA);
- the consumer protection authorities, which comprise:
  - the local government offices acting as consumer protection authorities in the first instance; and
  - the Government Office of County Pest acting as second instance consumer protection authority (collectively, 'the consumer protection authority'); and
- the Hungarian National Bank (HNB), acting as financial supervisory authority.

The statutory rules on advertising are set out in:

- Act XLVII of 2008 on the Prohibition of Unfair Business-to-Consumer Commercial Practices ('Unfair Commercial Practices Act');
- Act XLVIII of 2008 on the Basic Requirements and Certain Restrictions of Commercial Advertising Activities ('Advertising Act'); and
- Act LVII of 1996 on the Prohibition of Unfair and Restrictive Market Practices ('Competition Act').

These acts implement the EU legislation that is relevant in connection with advertising.[1]

The overarching principles of the legislation applied by the above statutory bodies are as follows:

---

1   The relevant EU legislation comprises Directive 2006/114/EC concerning misleading and comparative advertising, Directive 2003/33/EC relating to the advertising and sponsorship of tobacco products, Directive 89/552/EEC concerning the pursuit of television broadcasting activities, and Directive 2005/29/EC concerning unfair business-to-consumer commercial practices in the internal market (the Unfair Commercial Practices Directive).

- Commercial communications, including ads, should be fair;
- The practices applied should comply with the requirements of professional diligence and should not distort the economic behaviour of consumers; and
- The practices used should not mislead consumers and business partners or be aggressive.

(a) Unfair Commercial Practices Act

The Unfair Commercial Practices Act also contains a blacklist of market practices that should be considered as unfair by their very nature, which basically mirrors Annex I of the Unfair Commercial Practices Directive[2] and includes, among other things:

- claiming in a commercial practice to offer a competition or prize promotion without awarding the prizes described or a reasonable equivalent; and
- describing a product as 'gratis', 'free', 'without charge' or similar if the consumer has to pay anything other than the unavoidable cost of responding to the commercial practice and collecting or paying for delivery of the item.

In unfair market practice cases, the consumer protection authority will start the proceedings, unless the commercial practice is capable of influencing competition, in which case the HCA shall proceed. The HNB has competence regarding commercial practices related to activities that it supervises. Proceedings may start *ex officio* or on the basis of a notification or complaint.

As a general rule, the authorities have the competence to:

- declare an act as illegal, order the termination of such illegal conduct and prohibit the continuation of any illegal conduct;
- order the publication of a statement of correction in connection with any misleading information;
- accept commitments undertaken by the infringing party; and
- impose a fine.

The fine shall be determined with regard to all relevant circumstances of the case, in particular:

- the gravity and duration of the illegal conduct;
- the advantage gained by such conduct;
- the market position of the offenders;
- their degree of responsibility; and
- any cooperation given in the investigation.

---

2   Annex I of the Unfair Commercial Practices Directive (2005/29/EC) lists commercial practices that are in all circumstances considered unfair.

Repeat offending should also be taken into account.

In HCA cases, the maximum amount of the fine is 10% of the previous business year's net turnover of the group involved in the infringement. For consumer protection authority and HNB cases, the maximum amount of the fine is 5% of the net turnover, but at most Ft2 billion (around €5.8 million).

Furthermore, the authorities may start a class action on behalf of consumers to enforce their civil law claims against an undertaking that has infringed the Unfair Commercial Practices Act or the Competition Act, where activities infringing the provisions of one of those acts by an undertaking concern a large group of consumers that can be defined based on the circumstances of the infringement, even though the identity of the individual consumers is not known.

(b) Unfair competition and IP infringement

The Competition Act includes rules relating to the prohibition of unfair competition. Among such rules, there is a Hungarian passing-off rule, pursuant to which it is prohibited to manufacture, distribute or advertise products or services without the consent of a competitor where such products or services have the same typical outside appearance, packaging or labelling (including designation of origin), or where they use a name, mark or designation by which a competitor or its products or services are usually recognised. In legal terminology, this is called 'infringement of the characteristic appearance', or 'slavish imitation'.

According to the same act, the denigration or discrediting of competitors is prohibited – that is, it is prohibited to infringe or jeopardise the good reputation or credibility of a competitor by:

- communicating or disseminating untrue facts;
- misrepresenting true facts with any false implication; or
- any other practices.

The protection against the discrediting or denigration of competitors aims to protect goodwill, which also includes reliability and trustworthiness.

Where violations occur under the Competition Act without any trademark infringement, the injured party is entitled to enforce similar claims to those established in the Trademark Act (see section 1.1(c)).

Other risks to be considered by advertisers in Hungary include the infringement of IP rights if the advertising unlawfully uses or otherwise infringes the IP rights of others.

The civil courts are competent to deal with IP infringement and unfair competition cases.

(c) Trademark infringement

In the event of trademark infringement, the injured party is entitled to enforce claims pursuant to Act XI of 1997 on the Protection of Trademarks and Geographical Indications ('Trademark Act'). In its claim, the injured party may demand:

- a court ruling establishing that trademark infringement has occurred;
- cessation of the trademark infringement or threat of infringement, and a prohibition on further infringement;
- the provision by the infringer of information on parties that participated in the manufacture of and trade in infringing products or the performance of infringing services, as well as on business relationships established for the use of the infringer;
- that the infringer make amends for its actions, by declaration or in some other appropriate manner, and if necessary due publicity of such measures by and at the expense of the infringer;
- restitution of the economic gains achieved through infringement of the trademark; and/or
- seizure of those assets and materials used exclusively or primarily in the infringement of the trademark, as well as of the infringing products or their packaging, or the delivery of those assets or materials to a particular person, their recall and withdrawal from commercial circulation, or their destruction.

There might also be criminal liability for trademark infringement. If this is the case, the basic punishments are imprisonment for up to two years, community service or a pecuniary penalty. In qualified cases (depending on the amount of damage caused or the professional nature of the conduct), the punishment may be increased to imprisonment for between two and eight years.

1.2 Self-regulation

The significance of self-regulation is growing; however, it plays only a supplementary role in the regulatory system in Hungary. The most well-known self-regulatory bodies that generally deal with advertisers – irrespective of their business field – are the Self-Regulatory Advertising Board and the Hungarian Advertising Association. In terms of advertising ethics, both bodies apply the same requirements, as set out in the Hungarian Code of Advertising Ethics, which is itself modelled on the International Chamber of Commerce Code.

The ethical rules mirror the statutory rules relating to advertising. The Self-Regulatory Advertising Board provides copy advice (ie, on whether an ad complies with advertising ethical rules) upon the request of advertisers, agencies or the media. Complaints in respect of ads may be filed with both bodies, by both consumers and competitors. Sanctions applied by the bodies include a request for the removal or amendment of unethical advertising. However, sanctions imposed by the bodies bind the parties involved in the complaints procedure only if they are members of the respective body. Non-compliance with decisions of the bodies may result in the termination of membership, but compliance is otherwise unenforceable.

2. Comparative advertising

The Competition Act includes provisions that comply with EU Directive 2006/114/EC, thus establishing certain negative and positive conditions separately. According to the positive conditions laid down in Section 10 of the act, comparative advertising:

- must compare only products that are similar in terms of purpose and function;
- must objectively compare one or more features of the goods in question which are definitive and typical, and which can be confirmed;
- must objectively exhibit the prices, where applicable; and
- must pertain to products of the same origin, where it pertains exclusively to products with a designation of origin.

Section 6/A of the same act further provides that comparative advertising must not:

- injure the reputation of another company or the name, merchandise, brand name or other marking of such a company;
- lead to any confusion between the advertiser and another company or the name, merchandise, brand name and other marking of such a company;
- result in any unfair advantage derived from the reputation of another company or the name, merchandise, brand name and other marking of such a company; or
- violate Section 6 of the Unfair Competition Act regarding the prohibition on imitating the merchandise of another company or the characteristics of such merchandise.

An ad does not qualify as comparative advertising within the meaning of the Competition Act if the consumer cannot – directly or indirectly – recognise one or more specifically identifiable undertakings or products other than those promoted in the ad. Where the use of a superlative to express market superiority or absolute priority in an ad implies an element of comparison, but without specific competitors or products being identifiable, the ad shall not be considered as comparative advertising. However, the provisions on comparative advertising shall apply if the number of operators on the market is low and the consumer can identify the competitor to which the advertiser's assertions are directed.

If the publisher of a survey is unrelated to the producers of the products involved in a published test or comparison, in such a way that the publisher does not have an interest in producing the goods, the publication of the results is not deemed to promote the marketing of the products. Thus, the publication of the survey results does not qualify as commercial advertising and consequently does not fall within the scope of the regulations. These rules apply if the results of an independent survey are used by a commercial undertaking in its own advertising; and in this case, the advertiser shall be liable, not the person carrying out the product comparison test. The advertiser cannot plead that the comparison was not its own, but rather that of an independent third party, and that as such, the advertiser was unable to control the method of comparison.

The separation of the rules on business-to-business and business-to-consumer relationships in Hungary means that the misleading character of comparative advertising addressed to consumers is governed by the Competition Act and the Unfair Commercial Practices Act. In case of a violation of the positive conditions, the HCA may commence proceedings; while in case of a violation of the negative conditions, the injured party (the competitor) may enforce its claims for dismissal before the court.

If the comparative advertising contains a competitor's trademark and does not comply with the above requirements, the trademark holder may enforce claims for trademark infringement, provided that the unlawful comparative advertising violates the functions of the trademark. The claims that can be enforced on the basis of unfair market practice and trademark infringement are almost identical.

For details regarding sanctions, see section 1.

3.   Online behavioural advertising

Online behavioural advertising is regulated by rules included in Act C of 2003 on Electronic Communications ('Electronic Communications Act') and the General Data Protection Regulation (2016/679) (GDPR).

The Electronic Communications Act regulates the tracking of internet users' online activity (eg, the use of cookies). According to the act, it is prohibited to store information on an internet user's device or to gain access to information on an internet user's device, unless the user is provided with clear and comprehensive information (including the purpose of the data processing) about the storage of, or access to, the information, and has provided his or her explicit and well-informed consent. In practice, this means that the user must:

- be informed prior to the application of a cookie in respect of its application;
- provide his or her well-informed consent; and
- have the possibility of opting out.

The GDPR also applies if the data collected includes personal data. In such circumstances, the data subject's well-informed consent must be obtained in respect of data processing. This means that, prior to data processing, the data subject must be clearly and comprehensively informed of all aspects concerning the processing of his or her personal data, such as:

- the purpose for which his or her data is required;
- the legal basis for the data processing;
- the person entitled to control the data and to carry out the processing;
- the duration of the proposed processing operation; and
- the persons to which his or her data may be disclosed.

Information must also be provided on the data subject's rights and remedies. Implied consent is not acceptable.

These rules are enforced by the National Media and Infocommunications Authority and the Hungarian National Authority for Data Protection and Freedom of Information.

In respect of self-regulation in this area, the scope of the Hungarian Code of Advertising Ethics extends to all advertising; thus, if online behavioural advertising is unlawful, this will also be considered an infringement of the ethical rules of the Code of Advertising Ethics.

Sanctions include heavy fines – in particular, in case of infringement of the rules on the processing of personal data, where fines can be imposed of up to 4% of annual worldwide turnover of the preceding financial year or €20 million (whichever is the higher).

4. Sales promotions

Apart from the general rules that prohibit advertisers from misleading consumers with respect to any aspects of a product, there are no specific provisions included in the Unfair Commercial Practices Act or the Advertising Act on sales promotions. However, the Hungarian Code of Advertising Ethics contains rules applicable to sales promotions.

In the course of a sales promotion, justified disappointment of consumers must be avoided. This means that equal treatment of consumers must be applied and any claims or complaints of consumers must be dealt with quickly and efficiently.

According to the Hungarian Code of Advertising Ethics, when advertising a sales promotion, the conditions of such a promotion must be communicated unambiguously. The value of the promised gift or other advantage must not be exaggerated and the price of the product which must be bought in order to participate in the sales promotion must be clear.

If, in the sales promotion, a gift is offered together with the purchase of a product, a reasonable stock of such a gift must be available. In the case of limited stock, it is advisable to use the disclaimer "as long as stocks last"; however, this does not exempt the business from a violation of consumer protection laws if the amount of stock was not reasonable in the first place.

As regards communications about sales promotions, according to the Hungarian Code of Advertising Ethics, these must include, among other things:

- the conditions of participation in the promotion and the availability of the promotion rules;
- the significant characteristics of the offered gift;
- the term of the promotion;
- any applicable restrictions; and
- the relevant data of the business.

If the promotion is a promotional game, it must first be decided whether Act XXXIV of 1991 on Gambling Operations ('Gambling Act') applies. According to that act, a prize draw may be organised by a business supplying products and/or services on a regular basis in its own name. A 'prize draw' in this sense is a promotion in which a customer who purchased goods has a chance to win prizes if the ticket received at the time of the purchase is drawn during a public draw. If all of the foregoing conditions are met, the promotion qualifies as a prize draw under the Gambling Act, which means that:

- the prizes must be handed over to the winners within 90 days of the draw date;
- specific rules apply with regard to substitute winners;
- a public notary must be present at the draw;
- game tax must be paid on prizes that were not claimed;
- the promotional winning game must be reported to the tax authority; and
- an administrative service fee must be paid.

However, if any conditions of the Gambling Act are not met, the provisions of the Gambling Act will not apply and the business need only comply with the general consumer protection and advertising rules.

A 'promotional game' is not qualified as a prize draw if, to mention a few examples:

- the game is skills based; or
- entry to the game is made online or via a basic-fee text message and the winners are not identified by an actual draw of tickets (in fact, generally the receipts for the tickets sold), but by other methods (eg, by uploading a number from the receipt and then making the draw from among such numbers).

Irrespective of whether a game falls under the scope of the Gambling Act, according to the Hungarian Code of Advertising Ethics, consumers must be informed about, among other things:

- the detailed rules of participation in the prize promotion;
- any costs associated with participation other than the usual ones;
- the nature, value and number of the prizes;
- the selection procedure for the award of prizes;
- when and how the results will be made available; and
- the time period during which prizes may be collected.

5. Ambush marketing

Hungarian law and self-regulatory codes do not include specific rules relating to ambush marketing. However, ambush marketing at a particular event might infringe a number of statutory rules and requirements of the Hungarian Code of Advertising Ethics.

There is also a potential risk of unauthorised use of a trademark where the name, slogan or similar of the event is a trademark. Even if those identifying marks of the event are not protected by trademark registration, the Hungarian passing-off rule may apply (see section 1).

Common ways to prevent ambush marketing in Hungary include restrictive ticket terms and conditions that prohibit participants from taking unofficial marketing materials into the event.

6. Direct marketing

The relevant provisions on direct marketing are included in the Advertising Act. According to Section 6 of that act, the sending of direct marketing materials is subject to the express prior consent of the recipient, so Hungarian law thus applies an 'opt-in' system (except for a type of postal marketing (below) and telemarketing if carried out through non-automated telephone calls).

A statement of consent may be made out in any way or form, on condition that it contains the name of the person providing it and, if the ad to which the consent pertains may be disseminated only to persons of a specific age, his or her place and date of birth, together with any other personal data authorised for processing by the person providing the statement, including an indication that it was given freely and when in possession of the necessary legal information.

This statement of consent may be freely withdrawn at any time, free of charge and without any explanation. In this case, all personal data of the person who has provided the statement must be promptly erased from the records, and all ads must be stopped.

In direct marketing materials, a clear and prominent statement must be inserted to inform the recipient about the address and other contact information to which the statement on withdrawal of consent for receiving such ads must be sent (in emails, this in practice means a link to unsubscribe).

The notice of withdrawal may be transmitted by post or by electronic mail, with facilities to ensure that the person sending the notice is clearly identifiable.

Direct marketing by mail is subject to the prior explicit consent of the data subject (Section 6(1) of the Advertising Act), unless the marketing letter qualifies as a so-called 'addressed marketing parcel' – that is, a communication consisting solely of advertising, marketing or publicity material and comprising an identical message, except for the addressee's name, address and other data that does not alter the nature of the message, which is sent to at least 500 addressees (Sections 6(4) and (9) of the Advertising Act). In such case the message may be sent even in the absence of consent; although the advertiser must ensure that the data subject can object to the receipt of such message at any time, in which case no such further message may be sent. Furthermore, if the ad is sent by post, the first ad material sent by the advertiser must contain a return envelope to allow notice to unsubscribe to be sent in the form of registered mail with pre-paid postage and with notice of delivery. Once the recipient has unsubscribed, such unsolicited advertising materials may not be sent by way of direct marketing to the person affected.

Advertisers, advertising service providers and publishers of ads must maintain records on the personal data of persons who provided a statement of consent.

The handling of personal data must also comply with the relevant provisions of the GDPR, including those relating to the contents of the respective privacy policy regarding such data processing and the requirements of consent itself.

These restrictions apply to natural persons only, irrespective of whether the relationship is business-to-consumer or business-to-business.

7. Product placement

According to the relevant sections (particularly Sections 30 and 31) of Act CLXXXV of 2010 on Media Services and the Mass Media ('Media Act'), product placement in media services is generally allowed. However, product placement is prohibited in:

- news programmes and political information programmes;
- programmes made specifically for minors under the age of 14;
- programmes reporting on the official events of national holidays;
- programmes dealing with consumer matters; and
- programmes with religious content.

Programmes in which product placement is generally allowed may not contain product placement with respect to the following types of products:

- tobacco products, cigarettes or other products from companies whose principal activity is the manufacture or sale of cigarettes and other tobacco products;

- products that may not be advertised pursuant to the Media Act or other legislation;
- pharmaceutical products, therapeutic products or processes available only on prescription; and
- gambling services provided without the state tax authority's authorisation.

Programmes that contain product placement must meet the following requirements:

- Their content and, in the case of a linear media service, their scheduling must not be influenced in such a way as to affect the responsibility and editorial independence of the media service provider;
- They must not directly encourage the purchase or rental of goods or services;
- They must not give undue prominence to the product in question, which does not otherwise stem from the content of the programme; and
- Viewers must be clearly informed of the existence of product placement, such that programmes containing product placement are appropriately identified, using optical or acoustical means, at the start and the end of the programme and when a programme resumes after a commercial break.

Because product placement is a commercial communication, it must also meet further general requirements – for instance, it must not violate human dignity, must not discriminate and so on.

8.   Native advertising and social media influencers

8.1   Native advertising

The HCA identifies native advertising as fundamentally a legitimate business practice. However, it also emphasises that if an ad is significantly similar to the platform content, the consumer may not perceive it as an ad.

Therefore, according to the Hungarian Code of Advertising Ethics, an ad must be clearly identifiable as such, regardless of its place of publication and the technical method used to publish or disseminate it. In media containing both news and editorial material, advertising material must be easily and clearly identifiable and the advertiser and/or brand must also be identifiable. These general provisions are of increased importance when it comes to native advertising.

Native advertising often takes the form of advertorials. The Unfair Commercial Practices Act sets out a blacklist of unfair commercial practices. The use of editorial content in printed or electronic media to promote the sale or other form of use of a product where a business entity has paid for the promotion without making this clear in the content or by images or sounds clearly identifiable by the consumer (ie, an advertorial) is considered as an unfair commercial practice. If a commercial communication is considered to be advertising that is disguised as editorial content, this will be considered an unfair commercial practice irrespective of whether the information provided is objective and true.

In the case of paid search results (eg, Google AdWords), the search results link through to a landing page on the advertiser's website. According to the case law of the HCA, this landing page must be clear, explicitly informative and not advertisement-like in order to supplement the information which was referred to, but not described. Otherwise, this will be considered to be capable of misleading consumers under the Unfair Commercial Practices Act.

8.2   Social media influencers

In late 2017 the HCA issued guidelines on influencer marketing. The HCA has also conducted several investigations in connection with influencer marketing.

Influencer marketing is not unlawful if the direct economic interest between the advertiser and the promoter is obvious to consumers. It is important that consumers can distinguish independent content from paid content. Otherwise, the publication of such online content may be considered to be an unfair commercial practice and may be subject to a competition investigation procedure of the HCA.

The content of influencer marketing is considered to constitute a commercial practice through which a product or service is advertised if there is a relationship between the influencer and the manufacturer or distributor of the product or service.

The consideration that the influencer receives for the posts may be financial; but it also can be some other incentive for which one would normally pay consideration (eg, products or services), or even the mutual provision of services to one another (barter).

The undertaking which has an interest in the sale of a certain product is considered responsible for publication of this content. This means that not only influencers, but also manufacturers and distributors and cooperating agencies and offices may be held liable for this commercial practice.

In order to comply with the relevant rules, three requirements must be met:
- The nature of the communication (ie, an ad) must be identified;
- The relationship between the influencer and the party whose product or service is advertised must be transparent, identifiable and clear; and
- The claims published in connection with the product or service must be true and substantiated.

In connection with the first and second requirements above, the guidelines provide that the post should indicate that it is an ad in a clear, noticeable, easily understandable and emphasised way. The different ways in which the post will appear on different tools used by the consumer (eg, smartphones, tablets and PCs) should be taken into account in this regard. The indication that the post is an ad should clearly appear to consumers without any need to conduct a search or to take other action (eg, scrolling down or clicking on a link).

The use of hashtags is very common on certain social media platforms (eg, Instagram and Facebook). In such cases, the following marks should be sufficient: #Advertisement, #Advertising and #Paid content. The advertised product or company should also be tagged.

The hashtag #Advertisement, #Advertising or #Paid content should be placed before every other hashtag. It is not necessary to indicate the exact registered name of the company whose product or service is advertised; it is sufficient to clearly identify the product or service by way of its trademark or commercial name.

However, hashtags such as #Thankyou #Partner and #Promotion are unlikely to make the existence of a business relationship clear for consumers, and thus are not sufficient to comply with the law. This is also the case where the business relationship or the fact that the post is advertising is presented in a hidden form – for example, in footnotes or in other parts of the text which are unlikely to be read by consumers. Likewise, merely including a link to the website of the advertiser or mentioning the name of the company is not sufficient.

Finally, advertisers should prepare terms of contract, systems and programmes to ensure that influencers with whom they enter into a business relationship familiarise themselves with the legal requirements in this regard, as they may be held liable for such posts if they have participated in creating their content and form. A monitoring and reporting system should also be considered.

9. Industry-specific regulation

9.1 Gambling

Generally, the Advertising Act allows the advertisement of gambling; however, there are several restrictions. Most importantly, it is prohibited to invite children (ie, those under the age of 14) or juveniles (ie, those between the ages of 14 and 18) to participate in gambling. It is also prohibited to include an ad for gambling in any medium that is addressed primarily to children or juveniles; and children may not participate in ads on gambling.

The Gambling Act does not allow the advertisement of any gambling activity that is organised without the permission of the tax authority.

According to the Hungarian Code of Advertising Ethics, an ad must not suggest that gambling is a solution to personal or professional problems, especially depression, personal or social failures, or loneliness. Also, it must not imply that gambling may be a solution to financial problems. Further, the ad may not be misleading with respect to the chances of winning.

9.2 Alcohol

Alcoholic products may be advertised; however, several restrictions are provided for in the Advertising Act and in the Hungarian Code of Advertising Ethics.

The advertisement of alcohol must not be addressed to children (under the age of 14) or juveniles (between the ages of 14 and 18), and they must not participate in such ads. The ad must not urge immoderate alcohol consumption and must not connect alcohol consumption with enhanced physical performance or driving. It must not be suggested that alcohol helps to achieve social or sexual success, has therapeutic effect or helps to solve personal conflicts.

Alcohol ads must not appear on the outer cover page of an advertising medium or on the home page of a website. They also must not be published in theatres or cinemas before 8:00pm or, in the case of programmes addressed to children or juveniles, just before, during or just after such a programme.

Ads for alcoholic products must not appear:

- on toys or on their packaging;
- in educational and medical institutes; or
- within 200 metres of the entrance of such institutes in the case of outdoor media.

9.3 Pharmaceuticals

The advertisement of pharmaceuticals is specifically regulated by:

- Act XCVIII of 2006 on the General Provisions Relating to the Reliable and Economically Feasible Supply of Medicinal Products and Medical Aids and on the Distribution of Medicinal Products ('Medicines Supply Act'); and
- Decree 3/2009 of the Minister of Health.

In addition, four Hungarian pharmaceutical associations have jointly adopted the Code of Ethics of Pharmaceutical Communications, which is a self-regulatory instrument.

As far as pharmaceuticals-related commercial practices are concerned, the legal regulation differentiates between practices aimed at the general public ('advertising') on the one hand, and practices aimed at healthcare professionals ('detailing') on the other. 'Healthcare professionals' are defined as persons authorised to order or distribute pharmaceuticals (doctors, pharmacists, manufacturers and distributors). Generally speaking, the content of ads for pharmaceuticals is regulated more strictly than that of detailing.

The most important rule is that ads for a pharmaceutical product must always be based on the summary of product characteristics (SPC) and the patient information leaflet (PIL) of the specific pharmaceutical that is approved by the regulatory authority. There are several other specific requirements and prohibitions as to the content of ads – for example, mandatory warnings must be included in each ad, with the exact wording prescribed by law.

The ad must also comply with the general rules on advertising and thus must not be misleading.

Prescription-only pharmaceuticals must not be advertised.

As far as detailing is concerned, the legal regulations aim to prevent any undue influence on healthcare professionals (HCPs). Thus, it is prohibited to give any kind of gifts to them whose total annual value exceeds 60% of the monthly statutory minimum wage. Gifts must always be in connection with the HCP's professional activities and cannot be purely monetary. While it is not prohibited to organise events to promote pharmaceuticals to HCPs, the amount that may be spent on hospitality is strictly limited. Only persons with a detailing authorisation are entitled to carry out the detailing of pharmaceuticals. The content of detailing is somewhat less strictly regulated than that of advertising: claims can be communicated even if they are not included in the SPC or the PIL if they do not contradict those sources of information and are sufficiently supported by scientific evidence.

Pharmaceuticals-related commercial practices are supervised by a number of authorities, depending on the types of communication and the rules being applied – namely, consumer protection agencies, the National Institute of Pharmacy and Nutrition and the HCA. In supervising the rules on detailing, the National Institute of Pharmacy and Nutrition may carry out a so-called 'dawn raid' – an on-site search of premises without prior warning – based on prior authorisation from the public prosecutor.

Sanctions for breach of the legal rules on pharmaceuticals-related commercial practices are severe and may include, depending on the circumstances of the case:

- the imposition of fines;
- a prohibition on further detailing; and
- a suspension of the company's contract to include its pharmaceuticals in the social subsidy system.

9.4 Financial products and services

Hungarian legislation does not contain many express rules on the advertisement of financial products or services.

According to Act CCXXXVII of 2013 on Credit Institutions and Financial

Enterprises ('Bank Act'), ads on behalf of credit institutions, acting in their capacity as advertisers, which invite minors to place money on deposit, borrow or use other financial services must be published in at least two national daily newspapers generally, and in at least one local newspaper and one national newspaper when transmitted on behalf of credit institutions set up as cooperative societies. The Bank Act also stipulates that draws, except for prize draw deposits, may not be advertised.

According to legislation on consumer loans, ads for consumer loans must always specify the annual percentage rate in a clear and distinctive manner. If there are any further numbers indicated in the ad pertaining to additional interest, fees, commissions or expenses, such detailed information must be indicated in a short, distinctive and clear manner, together with a representative example to facilitate the interpretation.

The main applicable rules may be derived from the general principles of advertising law, such as the prohibition on misleading consumers and the requirement for clear and unambiguous information. The latter requirement gained significant importance in recent years due to the ongoing negative effects of the 2008 financial crisis and its severe impact on consumers, particularly those suffering the consequences of applying for foreign-currency loans.

As a result, the HNB has issued several guidelines and rules of conduct regarding the policies and principles that are expected to be followed by financial institutions when contacting consumers. Such guidelines mainly focus on the need to provide clear and complete information regarding the offered products and services – for example, by meeting the following requirements:

- ensuring transparency;
- reducing informational asymmetry;
- providing information on the pros and cons of each service; and
- making a clear comparison of the offered products and services of the service provider.

According to the Unfair Commercial Practices Act, the HNB has general jurisdiction in connection with any infringement of the provisions relating to the commercial advertising of activities supervised by the HNB and of the related codes of conduct; while the HCA has jurisdiction if the commercial practices in question exert a material influence upon competition.

9.5   Food

Food advertising is regulated by Act XLVI of 2008 on the Food Supply Chain and on the Control and Supervision of the Food Supply Chain ('Food Supply Chain Act') and EU Regulation 1924/2006 on nutrition and health claims made on foods.

The overarching principle of the legislation is the prohibition against misleading consumers:

- with regard to the characteristics of the foodstuff and, in particular, with regard to its nature, identity, properties, composition, quantity, durability, origin or provenance, or method of manufacture or production;
- by attributing to the foodstuff effects or properties that it does not possess; or
- by stating or suggesting that the foodstuff possesses special characteristics when in fact all similar foodstuffs possess such characteristics.

An important rule is that the food advertising must not attribute to any foodstuff the property of preventing, treating or curing a human disease, or refer to such properties.

Some special rules set forth in Decrees 36 and 37 of 2004 of the Minister of Health, Social and Family Affairs[3] apply to foodstuffs intended for particular nutritional uses and to foodstuffs that qualify as food supplements.

No specific statutory rules apply to children in connection with the advertisement of foodstuffs, so there are no statutory rules regarding the advertisement to children of food products that are high in sugar or fat. However, the rules of the Hungarian Code of Advertising Ethics apply, and this code has a chapter on with food advertising that includes a number of rules relating to children, as follows:

- In ads for food and drinks, claims referring to nutritional and health advantages must have a firm and justifiable basis. Such claims may be communicated in accordance with the nature and extent of their proof, providing the consumer with supportable information.
- Ads for food and drinks must not encourage excessive consumption; portion sizes must be proportionate to the scenario of the ad.
- Ads for food and drinks must not undermine the importance of a well-balanced diet or of a healthy, active lifestyle.
- Where the product is presented as part of a meal in the ad, other elements of the meal should also reflect the principle of balanced nourishment.
- Text, as well as vocal and visual elements, used in the ad must truthfully reflect important product characteristics presented in the ad, such as taste, size, content, nutritional or health-related advantages, and must not be misleading to consumers as regards any of the foregoing characteristics.

---

3   These decrees implement Directive 2009/39/EC on foodstuffs intended for particular nutritional uses and Directive 2002/46/EC on the approximation of the laws of the member states relating to food supplements.

- Food products that are not suitable substitutions for whole meals must not be presented as such.
- Nourishment and health-related comparisons must be based on foundations that can be proved and supported objectively, and that are clearly understandable.
- Advertisers of food and non-alcoholic beverages must pay special attention, in the case of ads aimed at children, not to use personalities (real or animated) from radio, television or printed media to the trading of products, gifts or services in a manner that makes it difficult to differentiate between the edited content and the commercial promotion.
- While fantasy, including animation, is acceptable in communications targeted at both younger and older children, special care must be taken not to exploit children's imaginations in a manner that would be misleading concerning the dietary advantages of the product in question.
- Ads for food and non-alcoholic beverages that feature renowned characters from children's programmes cannot be broadcast in the environment of the same programme.
- Food and drink ads that address children cannot encourage them to eat or drink immediately at or before bedtime.
- Ads for food and non-alcoholic beverages must not mislead consumers about the possible positive health effects, other advantageous characteristics or positive physiological or social effects of consuming the advertised product. In ads targeted at children or the young, the same applies to hinting at status in a community, popularity within a certain age group, school or sporting success or increased intelligence.
- Ads for food and non-alcoholic beverages must not undermine the role of parents and other adults responsible for the wellbeing of a child in terms of guidance in diet and lifestyle choices.
- Food and drink ads targeted at children must not create an impression of urgency or disproportionate price reduction – for instance, by using the expressions 'now' or 'only'.

As for sanctions and enforcement, please see section 1.

9.6 Tobacco

The advertisement of tobacco products is completely forbidden by the Advertising Act, even indirectly.

'Indirect' advertising refers to:

- ads which do not refer specifically to a tobacco product, but which seek to advertise a tobacco product by using any other mark or trademark relating to the tobacco product in question;

- ads that present a tobacco product under the name, mark or trademark of another product; and
- ads that present another product under the name, mark or trademark of a tobacco product.

This prohibition does not apply to professional ads addressed exclusively to distributors of tobacco products.

9.7 E-cigarettes

As from 1 January 2020, the advertisement of e-cigarettes falls under the same regime as that applicable to traditional tobacco products under the Advertising Act; therefore, the advertisement of e-cigarettes is completely prohibited. In addition, the internal rules of social media advertising platforms usually prohibit the advertisement of tobacco products and related products, thus including e-cigarettes and refills.

The author would like to thank Zoltán Kovács, Dávid Kerpel, Gábor Faludi Jr and Gusztáv Bacher for their invaluable assistance in the preparation of this chapter.

Ireland

Patricia McGovern
DFMG Solicitors LLP

1. Overview of the legal and regulatory regime for advertising

'Advertising' is defined in general terms by the Advertising Standards Authority for Ireland (ASAI) in its Code of Standards for Advertising and Marketing Communications in Ireland ('ASAI Code')[1] as including, but not being limited to, "a form of marketing communication carried by the media, usually in return for payment or other valuable consideration or in a space that would generally be provided for in return for payment". The ASAI Code also defines a number of other relevant key concepts:

- A 'marketing communication' is defined as including, but is not limited to, advertising, as well as other techniques such as promotions, sponsorships and direct marketing, and should be interpreted broadly to mean any form of communication produced directly by, or on behalf of, advertisers intended primarily to promote products, to influence the behaviour of and/or to inform those to whom it is addressed.
- An 'advertiser' includes anyone that disseminates marketing communications, including promoters and direct marketers. References to 'advertisers' should be interpreted as including intermediaries and agencies, unless the context indicates otherwise.
- A 'product' can encompass goods, services, facilities, opportunities, fundraising, prizes and gifts.
- A 'consumer' is anyone who is likely to see or hear a particular marketing communication, whether in the course of business or not.
- A 'claim' can be direct or implied, written, verbal or visual. The name of a product can constitute a claim.
- 'Promotional marketing practices', including sales promotions, are marketing techniques which involve the provision of direct or indirect additional benefits, usually on a temporary basis, designed to make goods or services more attractive to purchasers.

---

1 Advertising Standards Authority for Ireland, Code of Standards for Advertising and Marketing Communications in Ireland, seventh edition, effective from 1 March 2016.

- A 'promoter' is any person or body through which a sales promotion is initiated or commissioned.
- An 'intermediary' is any person or body, other than the promoter, responsible for the implementation of any form of sales promotional activity.

All of this means that the code has a very wide ambit.[2]

The legal and regulatory framework relating to advertising and marketing communications in Ireland consists of legislation bolstered by the rules and standards of a number of independent, industry-specific, self-regulatory bodies. These bodies are set up by statute or are administered and financed by stakeholders of a specific industry to promote minimum standards in marketing and advertising communications that are appropriate for each industry.

1.1   Industry/regulatory bodies

Bodies such as the ASAI, the Competition and Consumer Protection Commission, the Broadcasting Authority of Ireland and the Commission for Communications Regulation all have a stake in promoting high standards in advertising and marketing communications.

The ASAI is an independent self-regulatory body set up and financed by the advertising industry and briefed with promoting high standards of marketing communications in the public interest under the headings of advertising, promotional and direct marketing. The ASAI is involved in administering the ASAI Code. It is involved in enforcing the provisions of the ASAI Code through the cooperation of advertisers, agencies and the media. Its members are required to abide by the ASAI Code and not to publish an ad or conduct a promotion in contravention of it. The ASAI also provides copy advice and monitoring services, and performs a complaints function; complaints are investigated free of charge. While the ASAI is not an arbitration service for disputes between commercially interested parties, an intra-industry complaint may be investigated by the ASAI where the interests of consumers are involved. The ASAI Code does not prejudice consumers' or advertisers' rights under law. A marketing communication which contravenes the provisions of the ASAI Code must be amended or withdrawn. In the case of a sales promotion, the promoter may be requested to make the necessary changes to the way the promotion is communicated or conducted and, where appropriate, may also be asked to recompense any consumers who have been adversely affected. The media should refuse to publish a marketing communication which fails to conform to ASAI Code requirements. A member that does not accept ASAI decisions may be disciplined by the board

---

2   These definitions are contained in Section 1 of the ASAI Code.

of the ASAI and may be subject to penalties, including fines and/or suspension of membership.[3]

The Broadcasting Authority of Ireland (BAI) was established on 1 October 2009 under the Broadcasting Act 2009, with the remit of regulating content across all broadcasting arenas. The BAI assumed the roles previously held by the Broadcasting Commission of Ireland and the Broadcasting Complaints Commission. The 2009 act sets out a range of general and specific objectives for the BAI, one of which is the preparation and revision, where necessary, of broadcasting codes that govern the standards and practices to be observed by broadcasters.[4] The BAI has put in place a number of codes and standards, such as the General Commercial Communications Code ('BAI Code'),[5] codes relating to advertising to children and the BAI Rules on Advertising and Teleshopping. The BAI Code provides[6] that all commercial communications must comply with applicable Irish and European legislation, which includes, but is not limited to, the 2009 act, the Audiovisual Media Services Directive (2010/13/EU) as implemented[7] and the European Communities (Audiovisual Media Services) Regulations 2010.[8]

The BAI also performs a complaints function. Viewers and listeners who believe that a commercial communication[9] does not comply with the BAI Code are entitled to make a complaint. The complaint should be made, in the first instance, to the broadcaster. If the broadcaster does not respond to the complaint or the complainant is not satisfied with the response, the complaint may be referred to the BAI. In case of non-compliance by broadcasters, the BAI Compliance and Enforcement Policy may be invoked.

---

3   See the Appendices to the ASAI Code, in particular Appendix 1.
4   Section 42(1) of the Broadcasting Act 2009.
5   The BAI Code became effective on 1 June 2017.
6   Section 1 of the BAI Code.
7   Directive 2010/13/EU, with the exception of Articles 4(3) and 4(4), has been transposed into Irish law in a piecemeal fashion by the following pieces of Irish legislation:
    • the European Communities (Television Broadcasting) Regulations 1999 (SI 313/1999);
    • the European Communities (Audiovisual Media Services) Regulations 2010 (SI 258/2010);
    • the European Communities (Audiovisual Media Services) (Amendment) Regulations 2012 (SI 247/2012); and
    • the Broadcasting Act 2009 (the television elements).

8   In January 2020, the Irish government published the General Scheme of the Online Safety and Media Regulation Bill 2019. Its aim is to regulate harmful content and to implement the revised Audiovisual Media Services Directive.
9   Defined in Section 2 of the BAI Code as:
    Images with or without sound and radio announcements which are designed to promote, directly or indirectly, the goods, services or image of a natural or legal entity pursuing an economic activity. Such images and radio announcements accompany or are included in a programme in return for payment or for similar consideration or for self-promotional purposes. Forms of commercial communication include, among other things:
        – advertising,
        – sponsorship,
        – teleshopping, and
        – product placement.
    Public service announcements and charity appeals broadcast free of charge are not commercial communications.

1.2 Advertising law in Ireland: legal considerations

A number of legal considerations arise when examining the implications of advertising in Ireland. Two of particular note are as follows.

(a) Intellectual property

Business names, brands, logos, product names, slogans, domain names and other signs used in advertising may be protected as trademarks under the Trademarks Act 1996 (as amended). Logos may also be protectable as registered and unregistered designs under the Industrial Designs Act 2001 (as amended). Written material, photographs, art and graphics may all be protected by copyright under the Copyright and Related Rights Act 2000 (as amended). In their marketing communications, advertisers should bear in mind their legal requirement not to abuse the IP rights of others.

(b) Defamation

Advertisers should also be conscious of the Defamation Act 2009 when advertising their products and/or services. An ad may be deemed defamatory if it could injure the reputation of a person or a business in the eyes of reasonable members of society. Advertisers should be particularly careful when making implications and innuendos in their ads. An ad may also give rise to a liability in tort for injurious falsehood if statements contained in an ad were made maliciously and are calculated to injure a person in his or her trade. Furthermore, an ad may give rise to a liability in tort for negligent misstatement where it causes injury to a person in his or her trade, but no malicious intent existed.

2. Comparative advertising

In Ireland, Section 13 of the Trademarks Act 1996 grants the owner of a registered trademark the exclusive right to use that trademark in Ireland in respect of the goods and/or services for which it is registered. However, the act also provides that nothing will prevent the use of a registered trademark by any person for the purpose of identifying goods or services as those of the proprietor or licensee of the registered trademark. This use must:

- be in accordance with honest practices in industrial or commercial matters; and
- not without due cause take unfair advantage of, or be detrimental to, the distinctive character or reputation of the trademark.[10]

The Comparative Advertising Directive[11] codifies the law on comparative

---

10   Section 14(6) of the Trademarks Act 1996.
11   Directive 2006/114/EC.

advertising at an EU level. Article 4 of the directive sets out, in detail, the conditions that must be met for comparative advertising to be permitted. The directive is given effect in Ireland by the Misleading and Comparative Advertising Regulations.[12] These regulations substantially repeat the provisions of Article 4 of the Comparative Advertising Directive.

Regulation 2 of the Misleading and Comparative Advertising Regulations provides that a 'comparative marketing communication' means any form of representation made by a trader that explicitly or by implication identifies a competitor of the trader or a product offered by such a competitor.

Regulation 4(1) provides that a trader must not engage in a prohibited comparative marketing communication. A comparative marketing communication is prohibited if the comparison:[13]

- is misleading under Regulation 3 of the Misleading and Comparative Advertising Regulations;
- is a misleading commercial practice under any of Sections 43 to 46 of Ireland's Consumer Protection Act 2007;
- does not compare products that meet the same needs or are intended for the same purpose;
- does not objectively compare one or more material, relevant, verifiable and representative features of those products, which may include price;
- discredits or denigrates the trademarks, trade names, other distinguishing marks, products, activities or circumstances of a competitor;
- for products with a designation of origin, does not relate in each case to products with the same designation;
- takes unfair advantage of the reputation of a trademark, trade name or other distinguishing marks of a competitor or of the designation of origin of competing products;
- presents goods or services as imitations or replicas of goods or services bearing a protected trademark or trade name; or
- creates confusion among traders – either between the trader that made the comparative marketing communication and a competitor, or between the trademarks, trade names, other distinguishing marks, goods or services of the trader that made the comparative marketing communication and those of a competitor.

Regulation 3 of the Misleading and Comparative Advertising Regulations provides that a marketing communication is misleading if in any way

---

12 The European Communities (Misleading and Comparative Marketing Communications) Regulations 2007 – SI 774/2007.
13 Regulation 4(2) of the Misleading and Comparative Advertising Regulations.

(including its presentation) it deceives or is likely to deceive the trader to which it is addressed or which it reaches in relation to any matter set out in Regulation 3(4), such as:

- the existence or nature of the product;
- its main characteristics or its price; or
- the nature, attributes and rights of the trader that made the marketing communication.

Broadly speaking, the Consumer Protection Act 2007 provides that a commercial practice is misleading if it:

- includes false information in relation to certain matters and that information would be likely to cause the average consumer to make a transactional decision that he or she would not otherwise make;[14]
- is likely to cause the average consumer to be deceived or misled in relation to certain matters;[15] or
- is likely to cause the average consumer to make a transactional decision that he or she would not otherwise make.[16]

The same act provides that a commercial practice involving marketing or advertising is misleading if it would be likely to cause the average consumer to confuse a competitor's product with the trader's product, or a competitor's trade name, trademark or some other distinguishing feature or mark with that of the trader. A practice is also misleading if it would be likely to cause the average consumer to make a transactional decision that he or she would not otherwise make.[17] In determining whether a commercial practice is misleading, it must be considered in its factual context, taking account of all of its features and the circumstances.

A commercial practice is also considered misleading if it involves a representation that the trader abides or is bound by a code of practice and the representation would be likely to cause the average consumer to make a transactional decision that he or she would not otherwise make, and the trader fails to comply with a firm commitment – that is, one that is not merely aspirational, but is capable of being verified – in that code of practice.[18]

A trader or other person (including a brand owner) may, upon giving notice of the application to the trader against which the order is sought, apply to the Irish Circuit Court or the Irish High Court under the Misleading and Comparative Advertising Regulations for an order prohibiting that trader from

---

14   Section 43(1) of the Consumer Protection Act 2007.
15   *Ibid*, Section 43(2).
16   *Ibid*.
17   Section 44(1) of the Consumer Protection Act 2007.
18   *Ibid*, Section 45(1).

engaging in or continuing to engage in a misleading marketing communication or a prohibited comparative marketing communication.[19] If in bringing such an application the truth of a factual claim in a representation is an issue, and the trader against which the order is sought does not establish on the balance of probabilities that the representation is true, then the representation shall be presumed to be untrue.[20] The court will consider all interests involved and, in particular, the public interest when dealing with such an application.[21]

The court may make an order without proof of any actual loss or damage on the part of the person making the application, or any intention or negligence on the part of the trader against which the order is sought.[22] Moreover, the court may impose in the order terms or conditions that it considers appropriate, including a requirement that the trader publish a corrective statement, at the trader's own expense and in any manner that the court considers appropriate, in respect of matters that are the subject of the order.[23]

A number of provisions set out in the ASAI Code require that comparisons be fair and that there be no likelihood of the consumer being misled.

3.   Online behavioural advertising

Online behavioural advertising is essentially activities that companies engage in to collect information about online activity, with that information then being used to show the user targeted advertising or content.

In Ireland, the legislation most relevant to online behavioural advertising includes:

- the European Communities (Electronic Communications Networks and Services) (Privacy and Electronic Communications) Regulations 2011 ('Electronic Privacy Regulations')[24] which implement the e-Privacy Directive (2002/58/EC, as amended by EU Directive 2009/136/EC);
- the General Data Protection Regulation[25] (GDPR); and
- the Data Protection Act 2018, which supplements the GDPR in Ireland.

The various relevant pronouncements and guidelines issued by the Irish Data Protection Commission and the European Data Protection Board (EDPB) must also be considered.

Broadly speaking, Regulation 5(3) of the Electronic Privacy Regulations prohibits the storing of information (eg, a cookie used for online behavioural advertising) or the gaining of access to information already stored on a user's

---

19   Regulation 5(1) of the Misleading and Comparative Advertising Regulations.
20   *Ibid*, Regulation 5(2).
21   *Ibid*, Regulation 5(3).
22   Regulation 5(4) of the Misleading and Comparative Advertising Regulations.
23   *Ibid*, Regulation 5(5).
24   SI 336 of 2011.
25   EU Regulation 2016/679.

device (referred to as 'terminal equipment' in the legislation) (eg, a cookie used for online behavioural advertising), unless the user has given his or her consent to that use and has been provided with clear and comprehensive information about the collection of such information in accordance with data protection legislation. The information should be prominently displayed and easily accessible, and should include, without limitation, the purposes of the processing of the information.

The Electronic Privacy Regulations do not provide any guidelines on how such information should be provided to the user or how the user's consent is to be obtained, other than stating that the methods of providing information and giving consent should be as "user-friendly as possible".[26] The Office of the Irish Data Protection Commissioner has issued a Guidance Note on Cookies and other Tracking Technologies,[27] which confirms that the Electronic Privacy Regulations require consent in order to gain access to information stored on the terminal equipment of a subscriber or user, or to store any information on the person's device. Hence, consent is necessary to store or set cookies, regardless of whether the cookies or other tracking technologies contain personal data. Consent for the setting of cookies must be of the standard defined in Article 4(11) of the GDPR, which provides that the 'consent' of the data subject means any "freely given, specific, informed and unambiguous indication of the data subject's wishes by which he or she, by a statement or by a clear affirmative action, signifies agreement to the processing of personal data relating to him or her". Any information whose sole purpose is to facilitate the transmission of a communication is exempt from the consent requirement. Likewise, information that is strictly necessary to provide a service that has been explicitly requested by the user is not subject to the consent requirement. According to the Data Protection Commissioner's guidance note, "Cookies related to advertising are not strictly necessary and must be consented to".[28] The following should also be noted:

- Consent may not be bundled for multiple purposes.
- There should be a first layer of communication outlining that consent to the use of cookies is being requested for specific purposes.
- There should then be a second layer to provide more detailed information about the types of cookies used, with options to opt in or accept.
- Pre-checked boxes, sliders or other tools set to 'on' by default are not permitted.
- A user must be able to withdraw consent as easily as it is given.

---

26   Regulation 5(4) of the Electronic Privacy Regulations.
27   www.dataprotection.ie/sites/default/files/uploads/2020-04/Guidance%20note%20on%20cookies%20 and%20other%20tracking%20technologies.pdf.
28   *Ibid*, p6.

- If a cookie is used to store a record, consent must be reaffirmed after six months.
- If a banner or pop-up is used, there must not be an interface which nudges the acceptance of cookies over their rejection.

Section 18 of the ASAI Code specifically deals with online behavioural advertising. The rules require that third parties provide clear and comprehensive notice about the collection and use of web-viewing behaviour data for the purposes of online behavioural advertising on their own website, including how a web user can opt out from having web-viewing behaviour data collected and used for this purpose. The notice should link to a relevant mechanism that allows the consumer to opt out of the collection and use of web-viewing behaviour data for online behavioural advertising purposes by that third party and other third parties.

Third parties must also provide a clear and comprehensive notice that they are collecting and using web-viewing behaviour data for the purposes of online behavioural advertising, either in or around the display ad delivered using online behavioural advertising. The notice should link to a relevant mechanism through which the web user can opt out of the collection and use of web-viewing behaviour data for the purposes of online behavioural advertising.

Interest segments specifically designed for the purpose of targeting online behavioural advertising at children aged 12 or under must not be created; and online behavioural advertising segments relying on the use of sensitive personal data must not be created or used without obtaining a web user's prior explicit consent.

3.1 Online political advertising

On 8 January 2021, the General Scheme of the Electoral Reform Bill 2020[29] was published. This bill outlines a wide range of reforms, including:

- the establishment of a statutory, independent Electoral Commission;
- the modernisation of the electoral registration process; and
- provisions intended to assist the holding of electoral events when COVID-19 restrictions are in place.

Of particular relevance are the provisions dealing with online political advertising.

An 'online political advertisement' is defined as including a button, icon, tab or hyperlink with the text "Political Advert", in a position where the viewer will readily see it, which links to a page clearly displaying a transparency notice.[30]

---

29   www.gov.ie/en/publication/34cf6-general-scheme-of-the-electoral-reform-bill-2020/.
30   Head 121.

A 'transparency notice' is a notice that displays, in a clear and conspicuous manner:

- the name, postal address, email address and, where applicable, the website address of the buyer who paid for the online political ad;
- confirmation of whether micro-targeting was applied in the placement, display and promotion of the online political ad and, where applicable, a description of the criteria used for any such micro-targeting;
- confirmation of whether the target audience contains a lookalike targeting list and, where applicable, a description of the characteristics of the target audience;
- the total amount paid for the online political ad, including the amounts paid for content creation and for online placement, display and promotion;
- the number of days during which the online political ad will be placed, displayed and promoted on the online platform, and the start and end date of the online advertising campaign; and
- the number of user impressions that the online political ad is intended to reach and the number of active engagements by user.[31]

Information specified in a transparency notice must be maintained in real time by the online platform and must be notified to the Electoral Commission as soon as may be after it is displayed. An online platform must establish and maintain an online archive or library of online political ads and the accompanying transparency notices commissioned for placement, display or promotion on that online platform.

At the expiration of the period of the online advertising campaign, the online platform must:

- transfer each online political ad and its accompanying transparency notice to the online archive; or make reasonable arrangements – either itself or with such person or persons as it chooses – to ensure that public access to the online archive or library is maintained in the public interest and for the purpose of research relating to the holding of elections and referendums and on matters connected therewith; and
- retain in the online archive or library each online political ad and its accompanying transparency notice for a period of not less than seven years after the expiration of the period of the online advertising campaign.

If an online platform is about to be wound up, dissolved or cease trading, it must transfer the online archive or library, including the associated online

---

31   *Ibid.*

political ads and their accompanying transparency notices, to the Electoral Commission to ensure that it continues to be maintained in the public interest and for the purpose of research.

The bill also provides for the appointment by an online platform of a responsible person to assume responsibility for, and undertake, the customer due diligence measures that will apply to the buyers of online political ads.[32] The responsible person must ascertain the identity of a buyer and take such measures as are necessary to verify the identity of the buyer and the information to be provided for the purpose of placing, displaying or promoting an online political ad. These verification procedures must, in the main, be undertaken prior to accepting the buyer's business and prior to placing the political ad online.[33] The responsible person must also determine whether the buyer of an online political ad, or a person connected with the buyer, is residing in a place outside of the Republic of Ireland.[34] He or she must take appropriate action to examine the source of funding behind such ads to ensure, in the public interest, that there is no undue foreign influence arising.[35] There are also obligations on the buyer of online political ads to provide the required information.[36]

4. Sales promotions

Sales promotions are provided for in Section 5 of the ASAI Code, which contains a non-exhaustive list of what are considered sales promotions in Ireland, including:

- premium offers;
- reduced-price and free offers;
- the distribution of vouchers, coupons and samples;
- personality promotions;
- charity-linked promotions; and
- prize promotions.

4.1 Gaming and Lotteries Act 1956

When a promoter is embarking on the design and commissioning of a sales promotion in Ireland, the first legal requirements that should be considered are found in the Gaming and Lotteries Act 1956, as amended. Failure to bear this act in mind could result in a promotion being considered an illegal lottery. The act and the considerations arising therefrom are in addition to any consumer protection considerations.

'Lotteries' are defined in Section 2 of the Gaming and Lotteries Act 1956 as "all competitions for money or money's worth involving guesses or estimates of

---

32	Head 122.
33	Head 123.
34	Head 124.
35	*Ibid.*
36	Head 127.

future or past events the results of which are not yet ascertained or are not yet generally known".

In general, if a promotion is to fall outside the ambit of the 1956 act, it must be:

- a promotion where no purchase is necessary – by the foregoing definition, the existence of a payment of any kind (including the purchase of a product at its normal price) will bring the promotion within the scope of the 1956 act;
- a promotion that is operating under a charity licence; or
- a promotion that includes a test of skill, which must be more than a mere means to avoid the prohibition on illegal lotteries (eg, a single question with an obvious answer may not be sufficient). At least one independent party (unrelated to the promoter) must be involved in determining the winner or winners of a test of skill.

Even where a competition or promotion states that no purchase is necessary, the promoter must ensure that there are no hidden charges for entry to the competition. Furthermore, the details of the promotion must be made available to the public generally, rather than only on promotional packaging for products.

However, the Gaming and Lotteries (Amendment) Act 2019 has relaxed the above rules somewhat. While it does not change the definition of a 'lottery' outlined above, it has introduced a limited exception for certain product promotions. Essentially, a promotion that would otherwise fall within the definition of a 'lottery' will be exempt from the requirement to be licensed where it is conducted in conjunction with the sale or marketing of a particular product and:

- the total value of the prizes does not exceed €2,500; and
- there is no charge for taking part in the lottery other than the purchase of the product concerned (if required), and there is no additional charge for redemption of the prize.

'Marketing' is defined as any form of commercial communication that is intended to increase or has the effect of increasing the recognition, appeal or consumption of a particular product. 'Sell' is defined as selling by retail or wholesale and includes:

- offering or exposing for sale;
- inviting the making by a person of an offer to purchase;
- distributing free of charge; and
- supplying for any of these purposes (whether or not for profit).

'Product' is not defined, so it is unclear whether this term is confined to goods or also includes services.

4.2   ASAI Code

A promoter must also pay attention to Section 5 of the ASAI Code. This sets out a number of requirements that must be adhered to when considering a sales promotion, selected examples being as follows:

- Consumers should be told before entry if participants may be required to become involved in any of the promoter's publicity or advertising, whether it is connected with the promotion or not. Prize winners' interests should not be compromised by the publication of excessively detailed information.
- Promoters should not offer promotional products that would be likely to cause offence.
- The following points should be explained to the targets of the promotion:
  - how to participate, including conditions and costs;
  - the promoter's full name and business address;
  - the closing date for entry to the competition, prominently displayed (and listed separately from the closing date for the purchase of promoted products where different dates apply);
  - any proof-of-purchase requirements;
  - any geographical or personal restrictions;
  - any necessary permissions, including parental consents;
  - any limits on the number of applications;
  - any limits on the number of promotional products available or limits on the number of prizes that one household may win; and
  - any other factor that is likely to influence consumers' decisions or understanding of the promotion.
- The following should be specified in the entry requirements:
  - the closing date;
  - any age, eligibility or geographical restrictions;
  - any restrictions on the number of entries for a prize;
  - any requirements for proof of purchase; and
  - any permissions required (eg, from parents).

4.3   Promotions directed at persons under 18 years of age

Promotions that are aimed at children (ie, persons under the age of 18) must offer prizes that are age appropriate. Section 7 of the ASAI Code contains specific rules on promotions aimed at children, which provide that marketing communications that are addressed to children should:

- not offer promotional products that are unsuitable for distribution to children;
- be carried out responsibly, taking into account the location in which the promotion is conducted;

- make it clear that parental permission is required if expensive and/or inappropriate prizes and incentives might cause conflict between children and their parents – examples include animals, bicycles, outings, concerts and holidays; and

- not exploit children's susceptibility to charitable appeals.

5.   Ambush marketing

There are no specific provisions under Irish law to protect event organisers or to secure the legitimate interests of sponsors that have paid for exclusivity. The only protections that currently exist for organisers and sponsors are found in the existing Irish IP regime[37] or in the contractual provisions of any sponsorship agreements, where applicable.

In Ireland, organisers and brands need to rely on trademark law, copyright and design law and the tort of passing off to protect their rights. The Misleading and Comparative Advertising Regulations and the Consumer Protection Act 2007 may also be called in aid. It is vital that any and all registrable intellectual property is registered, including event names and designs. Copyright should be claimed where appropriate and companies should ensure that any brands, signs, logos and designs are adequately registered.

6.   Direct marketing

Direct marketing has been described by the Irish Data Protection Commission[38] as an organisation (the marketer) attempting to promote a product or service or attempting to get someone to request additional information about a product or service by targeting him or her as an individual. Direct marketing may include emails, texts, fax messages, telephone calls and mail, all of which are discussed below. Direct marketing may be unsolicited.

There are a number of legal protections for consumers targeted by direct marketing, including the GDPR as supplemented by the Data Protection Act 2018 and the Electronic Privacy Regulations. While the Electronic Privacy Regulations are applicable (via Regulation 13) only to marketing delivered by email (including text messaging), fax, automatic calling machines and telephone, the provisions contained in the GDPR potentially apply to all forms of communication targeted at a consumer.

The consent of the target is of paramount importance where there is use of personal data for direct marketing. This consent must be to the use of personal data for direct marketing purposes. The minimum level of consent is the right

---

37   The Trademarks Act 1996 (as amended); Council Regulation 2007/1001 on the EU Trademark; the Madrid Protocol; the Copyright and Related Rights Act 2000 (as amended); the Industrial Designs Act 2001 (as amended); and the tort of passing off.

38   www.dataprotection.ie/en/news-media/blogs/direct-marketing-what-you-need-know-about-direct-marketing#.

to refuse such use of personal data both at the time the data is collected (a so-called 'opt-out') and, in the case of direct marketing by electronic means, on sending every subsequent marketing message.[39] Marketing materials should always include a valid address to which an unsubscribe or opt-out notice can be sent.

In relation to other mediums (eg, post), individuals are entitled under Article 21 of the GDPR to object, on written request and free of charge, to the use of their personal data for marketing purposes. Article 12(5) of the GDPR further provides that the opt-out right must be free of charge. Where the Office of the Data Protection Commissioner forms the opinion that a data controller has contravened or is contravening a provision of the GDPR, it may use the enforcement powers conferred on it.

There are, however, some exceptions to the requirement for consent. Regulation 13(11) of the Electronic Privacy Regulations permits direct communication without the necessity of consent where certain conditions are met. The consumer in question must be an existing customer of the data controller which is responsible for the electronic direct marketing communication. The following conditions must then be complied with:

- The product or service being marketed must be the organisation's own product or service;
- The product or service being marketed must be of a kind similar to that supplied to the customer in the context of the original sale;
- The customer must have been clearly and distinctly given the opportunity to object to the use of his or her details at the time those details are collected, as well as each time the organisation sends an electronic marketing message to the customer; and
- The initial direct marketing communication must be sent within 12 months of the date of the original sale to the customer.[40]

6.1 Direct marketing by telephone and fax

The use of any publicly available electronic communications service to make an unsolicited telephone call for the purpose of direct marketing is prohibited where the subscriber or user has notified the person that he or she does not consent to such calls or the relevant information is recorded with the National Directory Database.[41] The use of any publicly available electronic communications service to make an unsolicited communication for the purpose of direct marketing by means of a telephone call or automated calling machine to the mobile telephone of a subscriber or user is prohibited, unless the subscriber or user has confirmed

---

39   Regulation 13(3) of the Electronic Privacy Regulations.
40   See also www.dataprotection.ie/en/organisations/rules-electronic-direct-marketing#.
41   Regulation 13(5) of the Electronic Privacy Regulations.

that he or she consents to the receipt of such communications on his or her mobile telephone or has consented to receiving such communications and the consent is recorded on the date of such communication in the National Directory Database.[42, 43] This applies to both individuals and businesses, and this preference must be noted in the National Directory Database.

If the communication is sent by fax for the purpose of direct marketing to the line of an individual (as opposed to a company), the line of the individual on which the fax operates must be used solely for domestic/personal purposes. It is not permitted to send a fax for the purpose of direct marketing to the line of an individual, unless he or she has previously consented to the receipt of such communications. If the line is used (in any part) to run a business, that line will be treated as a business line and not a residential line. If the line is used by a business for business purposes, it is not permitted to send a fax for marketing purposes to it if that business has recorded its preference not to receive marketing calls in the National Directory Database.[44]

6.2   Direct marketing by electronic mail

The Electronic Privacy Regulations define 'electronic mail' as any text, voice, sound or image message, including an SMS message, sent over a public communications network which can be stored on the network or on the recipient's device (referred to as 'terminal equipment' in the legislation) until it is collected by the recipient.[45]

A person that obtains a customer's contact details for electronic mail in the context of the sale of a product or service must not use those details for direct marketing without the customer's prior consent, unless:

- the product or service being marketed is the person's own product or service;
- the product or service is of a similar kind to that supplied to the customer in the context of the sale by the person;
- the customer is clearly and distinctly given the opportunity to object, in an easy manner and without charge, to the use of those details at the time the details are collected or, if the customer has not initially refused that use, each time the person sends a message to the customer; and
- the sale of the product or service occurred not more than 12 months prior to the sending of the direct marketing communication or, where applicable, the contact details were used for the sending of electronic mail for the purposes of direct marketing within that 12-month period.[46]

---

42   *Ibid*, Regulation 13(6).
43   www.comreg.ie/consumer-information/home-phone/unsolicited-contacts-national-directory-database-2)
44   Regulation 13(6) of the Electronic Privacy Regulations.
45   *Ibid*, Regulation 2(2).
46   *Ibid*, Regulation 13(11).

If a subscriber fails to unsubscribe using the cost-free means provided by the direct marketer, he or she will be deemed to have remained opted in to the receipt of such electronic mail for a 12-month period from the date of issue to him or her of the most recent marketing electronic mail. If an individual is not a customer, it is not permitted to use electronic mail to send a marketing message to his or her contact address unless the prior consent of that individual to the receipt of such messages has been obtained. Consent can be withdrawn at any time. In the case of business contacts, it is not permitted to use electronic mail to send a marketing message to a business contact address or telephone number if the subscriber has notified the sender that it does not consent to the receipt of such communications.[47]

6.3 Direct marketing by post

Postal marketing which involves the use of personal data is governed by the GDPR. Prior to any use of personal data for postal marketing, the entity engaging in the direct marketing must notify the targets of the direct mail campaign that their data will be used for this purpose and in doing so must give them an opportunity to refuse such use.

If the personal data has been collected for future use, consent should be given by the data subject at the time of collection – generally by providing a tick-box on the form seeking the data. If the data has been obtained from a third party, including a source of information that is publicly available, the targeted individuals must be given the opportunity to refuse such inclusion; this must be done before any marketing material is sent. In any instance where a targeted individual objects to the use of his or her personal data, such data can no longer be used for the purposes of direct marketing. The individual may withdraw his or her consent to direct marketing at any time.[48]

It is permitted to use names and addresses drawn from the Edited Electoral Register[49] for postal marketing. This register comprises individuals who, when registering to vote, did not object to their personal data being used for marketing or other non-statutory purposes. It is incumbent on the user of this data to ensure that the most up-to-date version of the Edited Electoral Register is used.

---

47   Regulation 13(1) of the Electronic Privacy Regulations.

48   Article 7(3) of the GDPR.

49   Every local authority in Ireland is responsible for compiling and publishing a list of voters in its area. This is called the Register of Electors or the Electoral Register. The published Register of Electors contains each voter's name, address, polling station and category of voter. Local authorities publish two versions of the Register of Electors: the Full Register and the Edited Register. The Full Register lists everyone who is entitled to vote. Once the Full Register has been published, it can be used only for an electoral or other statutory purpose. The Edited Register contains the names and addresses of those voters who have indicated that their details can be used for other purposes (eg, for direct marketing by a commercial company or other organisation); www.citizensinformation.ie/en/government_in_ireland/elections_and_referenda/voting/registering_to_vote.html#l8c508.

The Data Protection Commission has issued guidelines on canvassing and elections.[50] Information on the Electoral Register may be used to communicate with voters. The Data Protection Act 2018 modifies the right to object to direct marketing in the course of electoral activities so there is no right to object to electoral direct marketing by post. In the context of canvassing, you can only be subject to electronic direct marketing if you have consented. Transparency is required in the context of online political advertising. Data protection rights must, however, be balanced against the public interest to ensure the effective operation of a democratic society – for example, to facilitate the functioning of the electoral system.

7.   Product placement

The Broadcasting Authority of Ireland, in Section 2 of the BAI Code, defines 'product placement' as any form of commercial communication on television consisting of the inclusion of or reference to a product, a service or the trademark thereof so that it is featured within a programme. The decisive criterion distinguishing product placement from sponsorship is the fact that in product placement, the reference to a product or service is built into the action of the programme. In contrast, sponsor announcements or references may be shown during a programme, but are not part of the plot or narrative of the programme. The display of logos or branding in programme content (and outside of sponsorship announcements or references) is considered product placement if it meets the definition of 'product placement'. The BAI Code goes on to distinguish two types of product placement:

- 'paid product placement', defined as where a third party provides products and services for inclusion within a television programme for payment or similar consideration to the broadcaster; and
- 'prop placement', defined as where a third party provides products and services for inclusion within a television programme free of charge and the total value of all the products and services featured in a single scheduled episode of a programme is of significant value. Products and services are deemed of significant value where the total value of all products and services featured in a single episode of a programme exceeds €1,000. The BAI reserves the right to amend this interpretation of significant value from time to time as it sees fit, and such amendments will be published on the BAI's website at www.bai.ie.

The BAI Code goes on to provide that where products and services are featured within a television programme free of charge, and where the total value of all products and services featured within a single scheduled episode of

---

a programme is not of significant value, this does not constitute product placement. However, where the featuring of such products and services is unduly prominent, is not editorially justified and/or could be construed as a commercial communication, the BAI may rely on the provisions of the code prohibiting surreptitious commercial communications.

Product placement is prohibited, save to the extent set out in the BAI Code. It is permitted only in cinematographic works, television films, sports programmes, dramas (including one-off dramas), drama series and serials (excluding docudramas) and light entertainment programmes (excluding talk/chat shows that regularly include 20% or more of news and current affairs content).[51] Prop placement is permitted in all programmes, but must not affect the integrity of such programmes – in particular, news and current affairs programmes. However, prop placement in children's programmes is not permitted in the case of products or services that may not feature in children's programmes (eg, alcohol).[52]

Sponsors of programmes are permitted to place their products and services in the programmes that they sponsor.[53] Product placement for tobacco is prohibited;[54] as is product placement for products or services that are not permitted to be promoted under the BAI Code.[55]

The BAI Code contains a number of requirements that programmes containing permitted product placement must meet. By way of example:

- the programme's content and scheduling must not be influenced in such a way as to affect the responsibility and editorial independence of the broadcaster; and
- the placement therein must be editorially justified and not give undue prominence to the product or service in question.

Programmes must not directly encourage the purchase or rental of products or services by making special promotional references to those products or services. Audiences must be clearly informed of the existence of product placement. This does not apply when broadcasting television programmes have been neither produced nor commissioned by the broadcaster or a company affiliated to the broadcaster.[56]

8.   Native advertising and social media influencers

'Native advertising' can be described as a type of advertising that matches the form and function of the platform upon which it appears. It may function like

---

51   Section 10.2 of the BAI Code.
52   *Ibid*, Section 10.3.
53   *Ibid*, Section 8.
54   *Ibid*, Section 10.9(a).
55   *Ibid*, Section 10.9(c).
56   *Ibid*, Sections 10.5 to 10.8.

an advertorial and manifest as a video, article or editorial. The problem that it gives rise to is that the consumer may not in fact recognise it as an ad because it is blended into the native content of the platform. The ASAI has produced a guidance note on the issue of the recognisability of marketing communications.[57] Key factors include the following:

- The ASAI Code applies to all commercial marketing communications, regardless of the medium in which they appear.
- Consumers must be able to easily recognise when they are being addressed by a marketing communication, so that they can make an informed decision about their engagement with the content.
- A marketing communication should be designed and presented in such a way that it is clear that it is a marketing communication.
- Marketing communications should not misrepresent their true purpose.
- The identity of the advertiser, product or service should be apparent and, where appropriate, contact information should be included.
- Advertisers should not exploit the credulity, inexperience or lack of knowledge of consumers.
- Advertisers' own posts or tweets are marketing communications when they relate to their brand or products.
- Where celebrities are sponsored by brands or paid directly to promote a brand's products, it must be clear that their posts are marketing communications.
- The context of the post or accompanying hashtag may make it clear that it is a marketing communication. However, where the context or accompanying hashtag does not make this clear, it is incumbent on the advertiser to ensure that clear guidance is given so that clear 'flags' are used (eg, #ad).
- Materials created by individuals – user-generated content – are not considered to be marketing communications, even where they reference or review advertisers' products or services. If, however, an advertiser has paid the reviewer (directly or in kind) and has significant control over the content of the review, is likely that the material will be considered a marketing communication.
- When a blogger enters into a commercial arrangement with an advertiser to promote the company's products or services through his or her blog, he or she is effectively acting as a publisher and has a responsibility to indicate to readers what materials constitute marketing communications.
- Disclaimers should be visible for consumers to see before they interact with or read the relevant material.

---

57 www.asai.ie/wp-content/uploads/ASAI-Guidance-Note-on-Recognisability-in-advertising-V1-Nov-16.pdf.

- I: a brand sponsors a blogger, but has no control over the materials that he or she produces, these are unlikely to constitute marketing communications; but good practice would suggest that the commercial relationship should be disclosed.
- I: an advertiser provides free products to a blogger (reviewer or vlogger) on condition that this leads to a positive review, this review will be considered to be a marketing communication and should be identified as such.
- I: the product is offered free, but with no expectation that there be a review or that there be a positive review (ie, the advertiser has no control over any subsequent content), then the material is not a marketing communication for the purposes of the ASAI Code.

The Consumer Protection Act 2007 and in particular Section 46 is also relevant as it provides that the withholding, omission or concealment of material information is a misleading commercial practice.

9.   Industry-specific regulation

9.1   Gambling

(a)   General provisions
Gambling in Ireland falls into two main categories:
- betting, which is governed primarily by the Betting Act 1931, as amended; and
- gaming and lotteries, which are governed by the Gaming and Lotteries Act 1956, as amended.[58]

Section 20 of the 1931 act imposes certain restrictions on retail bookmakers, including a prohibition on maintaining in or around the shop any attraction (other than the mere carrying on of business) which causes or encourages, or is likely to cause or encourage, persons to congregate.

The BAI Code includes a specific section on gambling.[59] Commercial communications for remote bookmaking operations carried on by someone who does not hold a bookmaker's licence are not permitted. Commercial communications that seek to promote services to those who want to bet are acceptable. However, commercial communications of this nature must not contain anything that could be deemed as a direct encouragement to gamble.

---

58   The 1956 act (as amended) was discussed earlier in this chapter, describing the considerations that a sales promoter must take into account when commencing any promotional activities.
59   Section 2C of the BAI Code.

Information detailing special offers, free bets as prizes in competitions, discounts, inducements to visit any betting establishment (including those accessible online) or any promotional offer intended to encourage the use of services of this nature is not permitted.[60] Portrayals of gambling in commercial communications must not:

- encourage behaviour that is socially irresponsible or that could lead to financial, social, psychological or emotional harm;
- suggest that gambling can be a solution to personal or professional problems or financial concerns, or that it can enhance personal qualities or contribute towards sexual attraction and success or social success;
- depict or feature children gambling; or
- contain material which is directed exclusively or principally at children, or be broadcast in or around children's programmes.[61]

(b) Gambling Control Bill 2013

It has long been recognised that gambling laws in Ireland need a radical overhaul. On 15 July 2013, the Irish minister for justice, equality and defence announced that the Irish government had approved the General Scheme of the Gambling Control Bill 2013. The general scheme contains proposals for the licensing and regulation of gambling in Ireland. However, since then, there has been little progress. For that reason, the general scheme is not discussed here.

9.2   Alcohol

The advertisement of alcohol in Ireland is regulated and controlled through a combination of legislation and industry codes and standards. The principal means of control, and the implications thereof, are described below.

(a) Public Health (Alcohol) Act 2018

The purpose of the Public Health (Alcohol) Act 2018 is to reduce the consumption of alcohol in Ireland. It introduced significant new rules on the advertisement of alcohol. These include a prohibition on the advertisement of alcohol in certain places, such as on public service vehicles, at transport stations and within 200 metres of a school, a playschool or a local authority playground. On 12 November 2020, restrictions on the visibility of alcohol in stores were introduced. From 12 November 2021, prohibitions will be introduced on alcohol advertising and sponsorship at sporting events and events aimed at children or events at which most attendees are children. Further restrictions were introduced on 11 January 2021.[62] These prohibit:

---

60   *Ibid*, Section 20.4.
61   *Ibid*, Sections 20.5–20.6.
62   The Public Health (Alcohol) Act 2018 (Sale and Supply of Alcohol Products) Regulations 2020 (SI 4/2020).

- the award or use of bonus or loyalty card points in relation to the sale of alcohol products; and
- the sale of alcohol products at a reduced price for a limited period or because they are being sold with another product or service.

The act also contains a number of additional measures which are yet to be commenced. These include minimum unit pricing and requirements in relation to the labelling of alcohol products.

(b)   ASAI Code

The ASAI Code requires that marketing communications for alcoholic drinks (ie, those that exceed 1.2% alcohol by volume):
- be socially responsible;
- not exploit the young or immature; and
- not encourage excessive drinking or present abstinence or moderation in a negative way.[63]

Even if the main product marketed in the ad is not an alcoholic drink, the ad may still fall within the scope of these rules if it depicts or refers to alcohol or to a specific alcohol brand or company.[64] Marketing communications for alcohol should include a message to drink alcohol responsibly.[65]

Marketing communications may refer to the social dimension or refreshing attributes of a drink, but should not state, depict or imply that:[66]
- alcohol can improve physical performance or personal qualities or capabilities;
- the presence or consumption of alcohol can contribute to social, sporting or business success or distinction;
- those who do not drink are less likely to be accepted or successful than those who do; or
- the consumption of alcohol can contribute towards sexual success or make the drinker more attractive.

Advertisers should take account of public sensitivities regarding coarseness and sexual innuendo, and should not portray drinking alcohol as a challenge or depict or imply that those who drink are brave, daring or tough. The presence or consumption of alcohol should not be linked to aggressive, unruly, irresponsible or anti-social behaviour.[67]

---

63   ASAI Code, Section 9.1.
64   *Ibid*, Section 9.2.
65   *Ibid*, Section 9.4.
66   *Ibid*, Section 9.5.
67   *Ibid*.

The ASAI Code refers specifically to children and requires that marketing communications for alcoholic drinks should not be directed at children or in any way encourage them to start drinking. Anyone depicted in an alcohol marketing communication should be aged over 25 and should appear to be over 25; and aspects of youth culture and treatments that are likely to appeal to children should not be used. This rule may not apply if the marketing communication shows an image of people attending an over-18s ticketed event which appears either on the advertiser's own media (eg, its own website) or on the advertiser's social media page, provided that:

- such media are accessed through a secure and appropriate age verification system; and
- the person depicted:
  - appears to be clearly over 18 years of age;
  - is not playing a significant role;
  - cannot be seen consuming alcohol; and
  - does not appear to be under the influence of, or to have consumed, alcohol prior to the events depicted in the marketing communication.[68]

Marketing communications should not feature personalities or characters (real or fictitious) that would have a particular appeal to children; and alcohol marketing communications should not be placed in media primarily intended for children.[69]

(c)   CopyClear

All campaigns by drinks manufacturers solely or mainly for alcohol carried in Irish media must carry the approval of CopyClear[70] (formerly Central Copy Clearance Ireland).[71] This body provides a service for all advertising of alcoholic drinks in Ireland and all media types. In 2013, its remit was extended to include all non-paid-for space online which is under the control of advertisers or their agents, including advertisers' own websites. Ads are pre-vetted against, among other things, the BAI Code and the ASAI Code; and unless an ad conforms and acquires an approval number from CopyClear, no Irish media owner should accept it.[72]

---

68   ASAI Code, Section 9.7.
69   *Ibid*, Section 9.5.
70   https://copyclear.ie/. The Central Copy Clearance Ireland Limited was established in February 2003 and is now known as CopyClear. It is jointly run by the Institute of Advertising Practitioners in Ireland and the Association of Advertisers in Ireland on behalf of the advertising industry. It is funded by the drinks industry.
71   ASAI Code, Section 9.12.
72   Department of Health and Children, Alcohol Marketing, Communications and Sponsorship Codes of Practice; rinksireland.ie/Sectors/DI/DI.nsf/vPagesDI/Responsibilities~Advertising~alcohol-marketing-communications-and-sponsorship-code-of-practice/$File/Alcohol+Marketing,+Communications+and+Sponsorship+Codes+of+Practice.pdf

(d)   Voluntary codes

The advertisement of alcohol is also subject to the requirements set out in the voluntary codes agreed among the Department of Health and Children, the drinks industry and the media in relation to television, radio, cinema and outdoor media, print media and digital (non-broadcast) media advertising.[73] These codes provide as follows, among other things:

- Alcohol advertising is not permitted unless the relevant medium has an adult audience profile of 75% or greater; and
- Where permissible under audience profiling, a weight ceiling will apply across all media and sponsorships whereby alcohol advertising will be limited to no more than 25% of available space on any occasion.

These voluntary codes apply to all alcohol advertising purchased in any medium based in the Republic of Ireland and/or aimed at the Irish marketplace.

The codes also specify that there should be no sponsorship by alcohol brands of sporting events for participants under 18 or where their audience (attending or viewing via broadcast) has a profile of less than 75% of adults. There is also a prohibition on the sponsorship of individuals, teams, bands or acts, or concerts featuring them if they are below the legal drinking age.[74]

(e)   Responsible Retailing of Alcohol in Ireland

The Irish retailing industry has established a company called Responsible Retailing of Alcohol in Ireland Limited (RRAI), whose objectives are to:

- implement the RRAI Voluntary Code of Practice on the Display and Sale of Alcohol Products in Mixed Trading Premises;
- communicate the code to all relevant stakeholders;
- support participating retailers with relevant information and training products;
- measure compliance with the code by means of an independent retail audit; and
- establish a credible and effective customer complaint procedure regarding the code.[75]

(f)   Broadcasting Authority of Ireland

The BAI Code provides a list of rules regulating commercial communications for specific products and services. The BAI Code has a number of provisions similar to the ASAI Code concerning the promotion of alcohol in broadcast media. For example, commercial communications for alcoholic drinks must not:

73   Ibid.
74   Ibid, p19.
75   www.rrai.ie/.

- encourage immoderate consumption of alcohol;
- present abstinence or moderation in a negative light; or
- claim that alcohol has therapeutic qualities, or that it is a stimulant, sedative, tranquilliser or a means of resolving personal conflicts.[76]

Commercial communications for drinks that have an alcohol content of 25% and above by volume (eg, vodka, whiskey, tequila) are not permitted.[77] Broadcasters must ensure that commercial communications for alcoholic drinks are not broadcast in or around children's programmes, and must take account of the age profile of viewers to ensure that the ads are communicated in or around programmes with an adult audience profile of 75% or greater.[78] Commercial communications for alcopops and products of a similar nature are not permitted.[79]

(g)   MEAS Code of Practice

Mature Enjoyment of Alcohol in Society Limited (MEAS) was established in August 2002 by the alcohol manufacturers, distributors and trade associations of Ireland as an independent not-for-profit company with no commercial purpose.[80] MEAS has published the MEAS Code of Practice on the Naming, Packaging and Promotion of Alcoholic Drinks, and provides a complaints function whereby members of the public who consider that an alcoholic drink, promotional activity or sales practice is in breach of the MEAS Code of Practice can contact MEAS on an anonymous basis and have the matter investigated.

9.3   Pharmaceuticals

The advertisement of medicinal products is governed by a combination of legislation and self-regulatory codes of practice. The principal legislation is the Medicinal Products (Control of Advertising) Regulations 2007 ('Medicinal Products Regulations').[81] The Medicinal Products Regulations enact Directive 2001/83/EC[82] as amended by Directive 2004/27/EC[83] relating to medicinal products for human use. The Health Products Regulatory Authority (HPRA) is the body responsible for monitoring the advertisement of medicinal products and enforcing the regulations. It has published its own guide.[84]

---

76   See BAI Code, Section 11.2.
77   *Ibid*, Section 11.3(a).
78   *Ibid*, Section 11.6.
79   *Ibid*, Section 11.3 (b).
80   www.meas.ie/.
81   SI 541/2007.
82   Directive 2001/83/EC of the European Parliament and of the Council of 6 November 2001 on the Community code relating to medicinal products for human use.
83   Directive 2004/27/EC of the European Parliament and of the Council of 31 March 2004 amending Directive 2001/83/EC on the Community code relating to medicinal products for human use.
84   www.hpra.ie/docs/default-source/tracked-changes-documents/sur-g0025-guide-to-advertising-compliance-v4-changes-tracked.pdf?sfvrsn=2.

In addition, the Irish Pharmaceutical Healthcare Association (IPHA) administers a number of codes of practice.[85] These codes set out detailed guidance to assist pharmaceutical companies in complying with the Medicinal Products Regulations. The objective of the codes is to ensure the highest possible standards in the promotion and advertisement of medicines. Observance of the provisions of the codes is a condition of membership of the IPHA.

The Medicinal Products Regulations expressly prohibit the advertisement of medicinal products that are not the subject of a marketing authorisation or certificate of traditional use registration. A 'certificate of traditional use registration' is a certificate of traditional use registration which is for the time being in force and which has been granted by the Irish Medicines Board under the Medicinal Products (Control of Placing on the Market) Regulations 2007 in respect of a traditional herbal medicinal product.[86] A 'marketing authorisation' is defined as an authorisation which is for the time being in force and which has been granted by the Irish Medicines Board in accordance with the Medicinal Products (Control of Placing on the Market) Regulations 2007 (as amended). It includes a product authorisation, a parallel import licence and authorisations granted by the European Commission under various European Council regulations.[87]

An ad for a medicinal product must not be issued unless:

- all parts of the ad comply with what is set out in the summary of product characteristics for the product;
- the ad encourages the rational use of the product by presenting it objectively and without exaggerating its properties; and
- the ad is not misleading.[88]

An ad must not be issued in respect of any medicinal product that, by virtue of the Medicinal Products (Prescription and Control of Supply) Regulations 2003 (as amended), may not be sold except in accordance with a prescription.[89] An ad must not be issued in respect of any medicinal product that is a controlled drug under Section 2 of the Misuse of Drugs Act 1977.[90]

9.4 Financial products and services

The advertisement of financial products and services is specifically regulated and controlled by Section 13 of the ASAI Code and the Central Bank Consumer Protection Code 2012.

---

85   The principal two are the Code of Standards of Advertising Practice for the Consumer Healthcare Industry – Revision 5.2 and the Code of Practice for the Pharmaceutical Industry – Edition 8.4.
86   (see Regulation 3 of these Regulations).
87   Council Regulation (EEC) 2309/93 of 22 July 1993, as amended.
88   Medicinal Products Regulations, Regulation 7.
89   *Ibid*, Regulation 9.
90   *Ibid*, Regulation 10.

(a)   ***ASAI Code***

Section 13 of the ASAI Code, which specifically applies to financial services and products, provides that the advertisement of financial services and products should be prepared with care, and with the conscious aim of ensuring that members of the public fully grasp the nature of any commitment into which they may enter as a result of responding to a marketing communication. Advertisers should not take advantage of people's inexperience or gullibility.[91]

A marketing communication should indicate the nature of the contract being offered and provide information on:

- any limitations on eligibility;
- any charges, expenses or penalties attached; and
- the terms on which withdrawal may be arranged.

Alternatively, where a marketing communication is short or is general in its content, free explanatory material giving full details of the offer should be made available, or should be readily accessible, before a binding contract is entered into.[92]

Any ad for a financial product or service should make it clear in a prominent manner that the value of investments is variable and, unless guaranteed, can go down as well as up. If the value of the investment is guaranteed, details should be included in the marketing communication.[93] The ad should specify that past performance or experience is not necessarily a guide for the future. Any examples used should not be unrepresentative.[94]

(b)   ***Central Bank Consumer Protection Code 2012***

The Central Bank Consumer Protection Code 2012 (CPC)[95] was created pursuant to Section 117 of the Central Bank Act 1989; the most recent iteration of the CPC came into effect on 1 January 2012. It contains a list of rules that regulated entities (eg, banks, insurers and insurance intermediaries in Ireland) must comply with in their dealings with consumers. Its main aims include:

- increasing standards of service to consumers;
- ensuring that consumers are provided with financial products that are suitable for them; and
- ensuring greater transparency for the consumer.

The Central Bank of Ireland has the power to administer sanctions for a contravention of the CPC under Part IIIC of the Central Bank Act 1942. Any

---

91   ASAI Code, Section 13.1.
92   *Ibid*, Section 13.3.
93   *Ibid*, Section 13.5.
94   *Ibid*, Section 13.6.
95   www.centralbank.ie/docs/default-source/regulation/consumer-protection/other-codes-of-conduct/unofficial-consolidation-of-the-consumer-protection-code.pdf?sfvrsn=7.

contraventions of the CPC may be subject to the imposition of administrative sanctions under Part IIIC as amended by Section 10 of the Central Bank and Financial Services Authority of Ireland Act 2004. These sanctions include:

- a caution or reprimand;
- a direction to refund or withhold all or part of an amount of money charged or paid, or to be charged or paid, for the provision of a financial service;
- a monetary penalty (not exceeding €5 million in the case of a corporate and unincorporated body, and not exceeding €500,000 in the case of a person);
- a direction disqualifying a person from being concerned in the management of a regulated financial service provider;
- a direction to cease the contravention if it is found that a contravention is continuing; and
- a direction to pay all or part of the costs of the investigation and inquiry.

The CPC provides that a regulated entity must ensure that:

- the design, presentation and content of an ad are clear, fair, accurate and not misleading;
- an ad does not seek to influence a consumer's attitude to the advertised product or service or the regulated entity, whether by ambiguity, exaggeration or omission; and
- the nature and type of the advertised product or service are clear.

Also, a regulated entity must ensure that:

- key information is prominent and not obscured or disguised in any way;
- small print or footnotes are used only to supplement or elaborate on the key information in the main body of the ad; and
- the information is of sufficient size and prominence to be clearly legible.

9.5 Food

The advertisement of and provision of information about food is regulated through the EU (Provision of Food Information to Consumers) Regulations 2014 (as amended)[96] and the ASAI Code. The regulations define 'food information' as information concerning a food and made available to the end consumer by means of a label, other accompanying material or any other means, including modern technology tools or verbal communications.

Regulation 5(2) of the 2014 regulations makes it an offence to advertise food in a manner which:

- is misleading, inaccurate, unclear or not easy to understand for the consumer;

---

96   SI 556/2014.

- is subject to derogations provided for by EU law applicable to natural mineral waters and foods for particular nutritional uses; or
- attributes to the food, or refers to, the property of preventing, treating or curing a human disease.

Regulation 25 dictates that food business operators that breach the 2014 regulations may be required to recall food and may be liable for a fine.

Ads that make nutrition or health claims about a food product must comply with EU Regulation 1924/2006 on nutrition and health claims made on foods. Article 3 of this regulation requires that claims made, through ads or otherwise, not:

- be false, ambiguous or misleading;
- give rise to doubt about the nutritional adequacy of other foods;
- encourage or condone excess consumption of a food;
- state, suggest or imply that a balanced and varied diet cannot provide appropriate quantities of nutrients in general; or
- refer to changes in bodily functions that could exploit fear in the consumer, either textually or through pictorial, graphic or symbolic representations.

Section 8 of the ASAI Code requires that marketing communications for food and non-alcoholic beverages not encourage or condone excess consumption, or encourage an unhealthy lifestyle or unhealthy/unbalanced eating or drinking habits.[97]

An ad representing any material characteristics of a food product, including size and content, should be accurate and should not mislead consumers concerning any of those characteristics or the intended use of the product.[98]

Nutritional and health benefit claims should be supported by documentary evidence substantiating that they meet the conditions of use associated with the relevant claim.[99]

9.6 Tobacco

The advertisement and sale of tobacco products are heavily regulated. A number of acts (collectively the Public Health (Tobacco) Acts 2002 to 2015) effectively prohibit any and all tobacco advertising, including the advertisement of tobacco products where they are sold. This legislation is supplemented by a large number of regulations which also regulate advertising promotion and sponsorship.

---

97 ASAI Code, Section 8.4.
98 *Ibid*, Section 8.7.
99 *Ibid*, Section 8.9.

In conjunction with the National Tobacco Control Office, the environmental health officers of the Health Service Executive (HSE) enforce most of the tobacco control legislation in Ireland.

Cigarettes must be sold in packs containing no fewer than 20 cigarettes. It is an offence to sell confectionery aimed at children that has been manufactured in such a way as to resemble a tobacco product.

Cigarettes sold in Ireland, including those imported from abroad, must carry health warnings in both the Irish and English languages, in addition to graphic health warnings. The following additional requirements apply:

- No advertising or display of tobacco products is permitted in a retail premises that sells tobacco products.
- Tobacco products must be stored out of view, within a closed container or dispenser which is accessible only by retail staff.
- The retailer may use a pictorial list (in accordance with regulations) to inform a member of the public aged 18 years or older who intends to purchase a tobacco product as to the products that are available.
- Retailers must display a sign at their premises informing the public that tobacco products may be sold at those premises to those over 18 years of age.
- Self-service vending machines are prohibited, except in licensed premises and registered clubs, and must be operated in accordance with regulations.
- All retailers of tobacco products must register with the HSE.[100]

The European Communities (Audiovisual Media Services) Regulations 2010[101] prohibit sponsorship of on-demand audio-visual media services or programmes by manufacturers or sellers of tobacco products.[102] It also prohibits product placement of tobacco products.[103] All forms of audio-visual commercial communications for cigarettes and other tobacco products are prohibited.[104] 'Audio-visual commercial communications' include, among other things, television advertising, sponsorship, teleshopping and product placement.[105] Tobacco advertising is specifically prohibited on radio,[106] in most printed media[107] and in 'information society services'[108] (ie, any service normally

100   www.hse.ie/eng/services/list/1/environ/tobacco-control.html.
101   SI 258/2010 which gives effect to Council Directive 89/552/EEC of 3 October 1989 as amended by Directive 2007/65/EC.
102   Regulation 7(4).
103   Regulation 9(a).
104   Audio-visual Media Services Directive, Article 9(1)(d).
105   Directive 2010/13/EU, Article 1(h).
106   Directive 2003/33/EC, Article 4.
107   *Ibid*, Article 3.
108   *Ibid*, Article 3.

provided for remuneration, at a distance, by electronic means and at the individual request of the recipient).[109]

The Public Health (Tobacco) (Amendment) Act 2004 (as amended) prohibits sponsorship or the giving of financial or other assistance in relation to an event or activity as consideration for the promotion of tobacco products, tobacco manufacturers or tobacco trademarks. The act also prohibits the supply of promotional gifts, tokens, trading stamps, coupons or any other thing given as consideration for the purchase of a tobacco product.[110] All commercial communications concerning cigarettes and tobacco are not acceptable under Section 4 of the BAI Code.

The Public Health (Standardised Packaging of Tobacco) Act 2015 specifies that all tobacco products manufactured for sale in Ireland from 30 September 2017 must be in standardised retail packaging. A grace period of one year was permitted for the sale of non-compliant products; however, since 30 September 2018, all tobacco products on retail sale in Ireland must comply with this requirement.

'Standardised packaging' means that all forms of branding – including trademarks, colours and graphics – are removed from the packaging. Any brand names must be presented in a uniform typeface with all packs in a plain neutral colour.

9.7   E-cigarettes

(a)   Legislation

The European Union (Manufacture, Presentation and Sale of Tobacco and Related Products) Regulations 2016 (SI 271 of 2016) came into force on 20 May 2016, and implemented the rules on nicotine-containing e-cigarettes and refill containers set out in the Tobacco Products Directive (2014/14). They were amended in June 2017 (SI 252/2017), April 2018 (SI 132/2018) and September 2018 (SI 365/2018). Certain sections of the Public Health (Standardised Packaging of Tobacco) Act 2015 transpose in part Articles 13 and 14 of the Tobacco Products Directive. Those sections were also commenced on 20 May 2016 by means of the Public Health (Standardised Packaging of Tobacco Act 2015) Commencement Order 2016 (SI 270 of 2016).

The European Union (Manufacture, Presentation and Sale of Tobacco and Related Products) Regulations 2016 (SI 271/2016) contain a number of

---

109   'Information society services' are defined in Article 2(d) of Directive 2003/33/EC as meaning "services within the meaning of Article 1(2) of Directive 98/34/EC of the European Parliament and of the Council of 22 June 1998 laying down a procedure for the provision of information in the field of technical standards and regulations and of rules on information society services within the meaning of Article 1(2) of Directive 98/34/EC".

110   Section 38(9) of the Public Health (Tobacco) Act 2002, as amended by Section 9 of the Public Health (Tobacco) (Amendment) Act 2004.

requirements which must be complied with in relation to the placing of tobacco products, including e-cigarettes, on the market. These include requirements concerning:

- information and labelling on e-cigarettes and refill containers;
- product presentation for e-cigarettes; and
- commercial communications relating to e-cigarettes and refill containers.

Overall, they provide for the following, among other things:

- mandatory safety and quality requirements;
- obligatory health warnings;
- obligatory listing of ingredients; and
- the prohibition of promotional elements.[111]

The content of websites must not have the aim or the direct or indirect effect of promoting e-cigarettes.

While the majority of e-cigarettes are sold as consumer products, medicine licences may also be sought.

(b)   ASAI Code

Section 17 of the ASAI Code regulates the advertisement of e-cigarettes. It defines an 'electronic cigarette' as "a product that is intended for inhalation of vapour via a mouth piece, or any component of that product, including but not limited to cartridges, tanks or e-liquids". Marketing communications for e-cigarettes should:

- be socially responsible;
- not contain anything which promotes any design, imagery or logo style that might reasonably be associated with a tobacco brand;
- not promote the use of tobacco products or show their use in a positive light;
- make clear that the product is not a tobacco product;
- not contain medical or health claims unless so authorised; and
- not be directed to people under 18 or be likely to appeal to them. People shown using e-cigarettes or playing a significant role in such communications should neither be nor appear to be under 25.

---

111   www.hse.ie/eng/about/who/tobaccocontrol/tobaccoproductdirective/guidance-electronic-cigarettes-and-or-refill-containers.pdf.

Italy

Daniela Ampollini
Trevisan & Cuonzo

1. Overview of the legal and regulatory regime for advertising

1.1 Applicable legal framework

General advertising law in Italy is contained in two decrees:

- Legislative Decree 206/2005 – known as the Consumers' Code – which sets out all general rules concerning business-to-consumer commercial practices, including misleading advertising; and
- Legislative Decree 145/2007, which regulates business-to-business advertising, including misleading and comparative advertising.

In addition, an Advertising Standards Code has been in force in Italy for many decades, preceding the entry into force of the legislation on advertising. The Advertising Standards Code was adopted by the Advertising Standards Institute and was last amended in March 2020. Although binding on a voluntary basis only (ie, only in respect of those subjects that have committed to comply with it, including by becoming members of associations that recognise the code[1] or by accepting standard clauses contained in advertising contracts), the code has been broadly accepted by the industry and the decisions of the authority in charge of its application (the *Giurì* – see section 1.4) represent the most relevant body of case law on advertising matters in Italy.

Other statutes govern advertising in specific sectors of industry and commerce in which particularly high communication standards or specific regulations are needed, due to the nature and features of the products advertised, the target group to which the advertising is addressed or the medium used. These are described in section 9.

The adoption of certain advertising practices may constitute unfair competition under Article 2598 of the Italian Civil Code. This prohibits the adoption of any commercial practice that:

- might create confusion with the products or services of a competitor;

---

[1] A list of the associations that recognize the Advertising Standards Code can be found at www.iap.it/conoscere-iap/associati/.

- might disparage or denigrate a competitor or its activity; or
- is unfair and capable of causing harm to a competitor.

According to the established case law of the Italian Supreme Court, an advertising practice that is in breach of the Advertising Standards Code constitutes an act of unfair competition under Article 2598 of the Civil Code.[2]

1.2 Definition of 'advertising'

Italian law sets out a rather broad definition of 'advertising', which includes "any message that is disseminated, in whatever manner, in the framework of a commercial, industrial, craft or professional activity for the purpose of promoting the sale of goods or services or the acquisition or transfer of rights or obligations thereupon".[3] Furthermore, the packaging of products is expressly included in the definition of 'advertising' included in the Consumers' Code and the Advertising Standards Code.

As far as the provisions of the Consumers' Code are concerned, the concept of advertising is encompassed by the broader definition of 'commercial practices' – these being (Article 18) "all actions or omissions carried out by a company vis-à-vis consumers before, during or after a commercial operation".

1.3 Principles of Italian advertising law

The main principle behind Italian advertising law is that advertising must be transparent, truthful and fair.[4] This principle is mainly expressed in the prohibition of misleading advertising: that is, all types of commercial communications that – even by omission, ambiguity or exaggeration that is not obviously hyperbolic – may induce consumers into error. This includes circumstances in which an advertising communication is disguised and does not appear as such in the eyes of the public.[5]

Furthermore, under Article 20 of the Consumers' Code, commercial practices as defined above are unfair (ie, either aggressive or misleading in their nature) if they are contrary to the requirements of professional diligence and materially distort, or could materially distort, the economic behaviour of the average consumer whom they reach or to whom they are addressed, or of the average member of the group in the case of commercial practices directed towards particular groups of consumers.

A number of specific obligations and prohibitions are further provided for

---

2   Supreme Court, 15 February 1999, 1259, in Riv dir ind, 1999, 3, 196; Court of Venice, 28 September 2010, in Nuova Giur Civ, 2011, 4, 1, 275; Court of Appeal of Milan, 28 June 2006, in Giur.It, 2007, 7, 1703; Court of Turin, 24 January 2006, in Dejure.
3   Article 2 of Legislative Decree 145/2007.
4   *Ibid*, Article 1(2) and Article 1 of the Advertising Standards Code.
5   Article 2 of the Advertising Standards Code; see also Article 2 of Legislative Decree 145/2007 and Articles 21–23 of the Consumers' Code.

(especially by the Advertising Standards Code), which ultimately reconcile with this main principle. For instance, it is explicitly provided that:

- scientific or technical terminology or statistics must be used in an appropriate manner;
- endorsements by third parties are allowed only if they are clear about their promotional nature and are responsible and verifiable;
- warranties may be referred to, but only in a rigorous and precise manner;
- the risks for health, safety and the environment must be highlighted in respect of certain products;
- ads stating or evoking environmental or ecological benefits must be based on truthful, relevant and scientifically verifiable data, and must clearly indicate the aspect of the advertised product or activity to which the claimed benefits relate;
- comparative advertising is allowed only within specific limits;
- advertising must not exploit superstition or fear, or make use of violence, vulgarity or indecency; and must not offend morality or religion, or harm minors (ie, persons under the age of 18); and
- advertising must not imitate that of others, especially where this could create confusion, and must avoid denigrating third parties.

1.4 Advertising litigation

There are three main ways to complain about or bring a claim in relation to an unlawful advertising practice:

- via the Antitrust Authority;
- via the *Giurì*; and
- direct to the courts.

The three paths are not mutually exclusive.

(a) Antitrust Authority

Italy's Antitrust Authority[6] is competent to hear complaints from consumers or competitors against advertising practices that, under the provisions of the Consumers' Code and Legislative Decree 145/2007, result in misleading or unlawful comparative advertising.

The procedure follows an administrative path, during which the addressee of the complaint is invited to produce written pleadings and documents in defence. The Antitrust Authority has ample powers of inspection and in principle, the burden of proof lies with the authority. However, where the authority believes this to be justified by the specific circumstances of the case, the advertiser must provide evidence of the truthfulness of the facts connected

---

6   https://en.agcm.it/en/.

to the advertising practice. If such evidence is not provided or is considered to be insufficient, the facts will be considered untrue.

As regards sanctions, if the Antitrust Authority finds that the advertising practice is unlawful, it will order an injunction and apply a financial sanction of between €5,000 and €5 million; and if dangerous products are involved or if the practice may threaten – even indirectly – the safety of minors, the minimum sanction is €50,000. Publication of the decision may be ordered and additional sanctions are possible in case of non-compliance with the authority's decision.

(b)   Giurì

Consumers and competitors alike can bring a case before the *Giurì*, the body set up by the Advertising Standards Institute to enforce the Advertising Standards Code. The *Giurì* will retain jurisdiction only if the respondent has accepted it.

The procedure starts with the filing of a complaint, indicating the allegedly unlawful advertising practice and the grounds on which it is allegedly unlawful, along with the relevant documentation. The complaint and the relevant documentation are then notified to the defendant, which is granted a period of eight to 12 days to file observations. An oral hearing is then held approximately three weeks after filing of the complaint; and at the end of the hearing, a decision on the merits of the case is immediately issued. It is a well-established principle of the Advertising Standards Code that the burden of proving that the facts conveyed in the advertising are true and that therefore the advertising practice is not misleading lies with the advertiser.

If the *Giurì* finds that the advertising practice is in breach of the Advertising Standards Code, it will issue an injunction. The *Giurì* has no power to issue administrative sanctions or award damages. Publication of the decision may also be ordered if the injunction is not complied with. 'Phase-out' periods are generally allowed where the unlawful advertising practice concerns the appearance or packaging of products.

Besides the *Giurì*, the Advertising Standards Institute has also established a Control Committee with the power to initiate investigations of advertising campaigns which are deemed to be non-compliant with the Advertising Standards Code. The injunctions of the Control Committee may be appealed to the *Giurì*. Furthermore, the Control Committee exercises advisory powers: in particular, it may express opinions concerning specific advertising communications before these are made public, and may request that any parts that are deemed non-compliant with the relevant provisions be changed before launch.

(c)   *Courts*

Competitors may bring unlawful advertising practices to the attention of the ordinary courts under Article 2598 of the Civil Code. Preliminary injunction proceedings are available, which may generally take between one and two months – although this can be reduced to four to six days where the court agrees to issue an *ex parte* injunction. Merits proceedings may then be instituted that are aimed at obtaining a final injunction and damages. The average timing of the full process is two or three years.

2. Comparative advertising

Under Legislative Decree 145/2007 (implementing Article 14 of Directive 2005/29/EC), 'comparative advertising' is "any advertising which explicitly or implicitly identifies a competitor or the products or services offered by a competitor". Comparative advertising is allowed, provided that the following are complied with:

- It is not misleading;
- It concerns products or services that meet the same needs or are intended for the same purposes;
- It objectively compares one or more material, relevant, verifiable and representative features of those products and services, which may include price;
- It does not create confusion among traders, between the advertiser and a competitor or between the advertiser's trademarks, trade names, other distinguishing marks, products or services and those of a competitor;
- It does not discredit or denigrate the trademarks, trade names, other distinguishing marks, products, services, activities or circumstances of a competitor;
- For products with a designation of origin, it relates in each case to products with the same designation;
- It does not take unfair advantage of the reputation of a trademark, trade name or other distinguishing mark of a competitor or of the designation of origin of competing products; and
- It does not present products or services as imitations or replicas of goods or services bearing a protected trademark or trade name.

So-called 'indirect comparative advertising' (in which the advertising message refers to competitors in general without identifying them) and 'superlative advertising' (in which the advertised product is presented as the best product as compared with all competitors), absent any (albeit implicit) identification of the comparison reference, are excluded from the definition of 'comparative advertising' in Legislative Decree 145/2007. These practices are thus not subject to the above restrictions, although they must still conform to the general principles of advertising law and unfair competition.

All types of comparative advertising – including indirect and superlative advertising – are included in the definition of 'comparative advertising' set out in the Advertising Standards Code. According to Article 15 of the code, comparative advertising is allowed where it is useful to illustrate, from a technical or economic point of view, the features and advantages of the products in question by objectively comparing essential, pertinent and technically verifiable characteristics of competing products or services that meet the same needs or are intended for the same purposes. The comparison activity must:

- be fair and not misleading;
- not generate confusion or be derogatory to competitors; and
- not gain the advertiser undue advantage from the notoriety of others.

3.   Online behavioural advertising

The main issue peculiar to online behavioural advertising concerns the intersection of personal data collected through different online services available to users and the use of cookies and other online identifiers to target consumers.

The provisions governing personal data processing for online profiling under Italian law were amended by Legislative Decree 101/2018 (implementing the EU General Data Protection Regulation (2016/679) (GDPR)) and Law 160/2019, which came into force on 19 September 2018 and 1 January 2020, respectively. As a result, Title X of the Italian Data Protection Code (Legislative Decree 196/2003) relating to 'electronic communications' has been aligned with the GDPR. In particular, Article 122 of the Data Protection Code now provides that online processing of personal data is allowed only if a user has given his or her prior informed consent (ie, an 'opt-in').

To obtain such consent, the use of a simplified notice regarding the processing of data via cookies is allowed. The requirements for such a simplified notice and the procedure for obtaining the user's consent are described in the Simplified Information Arrangements issued by the Italian Data Protection Authority (DPA) on 8 May 2014. According to these rules, the consent request to the use of cookies must be included in an overlay banner on the website's home page (or on any other landing page), which displays an initial short information notice. If the user wishes to access additional information or make specific choices with regard to the individual cookies stored by the website, he or she can access other website pages containing the extended information notice.

Merely 'technical' or 'strictly necessary' cookies – which are defined as "technical storage or access to stored information where they are aimed exclusively at carrying out the transmission of a communication on an electronic communications network, or insofar as this is strictly necessary to the provider of an information society service that has been explicitly requested by the contracting party or user to provide the said service" – are always allowed, irrespective of whether consent has been given. However, it is unlikely that any cookies used for online behavioural advertising would fall within this definition.

In addition, on 19 March 2015 the DPA published guidelines on the processing of personal data for online profiling, which apply to any service provider using electronic communication networks and which specifically address the intersection of data collected through different online services and the processing of data collected via an online identifier (eg, fingerprinting). The guidelines essentially provide as follows:

- The automatic processing of personal data in relation to the use of an email service does not normally require prior consent, except in case of profiling purposes other than those strictly related to the email service itself; and

- The intersection of data collected through different online services and the use of online identifiers to determine specific behaviour patterns are allowed only with prior informed consent.

4. Sales promotions

Sales promotions in Italy are regulated by Presidential Decree 430/2001 and by Circular Letter 1/AMTC of 28 March 2002, which together set out the legal framework for certain kinds of promotional activities that involve the winning of prizes – activities that take place under the supervision of the Ministry of Economic Development.

In addition, Article 21 of the Advertising Standards Code explicitly provides that, in any ads for sales promotions relating to competitions or operations with prizes, the advertiser must make the public clearly and easily aware of the conditions for participation, the applicable terms, the expiry dates and the prizes being offered.

Two types of promotions are regulated under Italian law:

- competitions with prizes, in which a prize is awarded, with or without the purchase of the promoted product, based on random chance or the ability/skill of participants; and

- so-called 'operations with prizes', in which a prize is assigned to all customers who qualify by taking a specific action (eg, purchasing a certain amount of the promoted product).

In both cases, although there is no legal limit on the value of the prizes to be offered, it is not permitted to offer cash, company shares or life insurance policies as prizes. Participation must be free of charge, although it is possible to include a requirement that the promoted product be purchased as a prerequisite for participation.

According to the guidelines of the Ministry of Economic Development (last updated on 13 February 2020), if the promoter launching a competition or operation with prizes is established in an EU member state and the competition does not require the purchase of a product in Italy, there is no need for a legal presence in Italy and the law of the member state in which the promoter is based will apply. On the contrary, if the promoter launching such a promotion is established outside the European Union, it will need to appoint a legal entity in Italy and Italian law will apply.

4.1 Competitions with prizes

These types of sales campaigns can have a maximum duration of one year. At least 15 days before the start of the campaign, a communication must be sent to the Ministry of Economic Development by completing and submitting a specific form accessible through the ministry's website.[7] A copy of the terms and conditions for participation in the competition and proof of issuance of an appropriate guarantee (see below) must also be attached. Another form must be sent to the ministry once the campaign has ended.

The terms and conditions must contain details of:

- the promoter;
- the term of the campaign;
- its territorial scope;
- the mechanism to be used for prize distribution;
- the nature and indicative value of each prize that will be distributed;
- the prize delivery period; and
- details of a not-for-profit organisation to which any prizes that are not claimed or allocated after the end of the campaign will be donated. This is required by law.

In the advertising material, the promoter must at least refer to the conditions for participation, the term of the campaign and the overall value of the prizes to be won, as long as the full terms and conditions are referred to and are made available on demand.

In order to guarantee that the promised prizes are in fact awarded, the promoter must deposit with the Ministry of Economic Development a sum, or provide a guarantee by a bank or insurer, that is equal to the overall value of the prizes. This amount will be returned and the guarantee released after the end of the campaign.

Specific formalities apply to the procedure for the allocation of prizes. In particular, the draw must take place in the presence of a notary public or an officer of a consumer protection association enrolled at the Chamber of Commerce, who must verify the regularity of the draw procedure and draft the

---

7   www.impresa.gov.it/.

minutes thereof. Where the draw is operated electronically or using computer software, a sworn statement by a technical expert must be enclosed, explaining how the electronic draw works and attesting that randomness/impartiality is guaranteed.

A specific tax and value added tax regime applies for promotions, but a discussion is beyond the scope of this chapter.

4.2 Operations with prizes

Operations with prizes are regulated less strictly than competitions with prizes and in a less onerous manner. In particular:

- a campaign may last up to five years;
- no copy of the terms and conditions need be sent to the Ministry of Economic Development, as long as it is preserved by the promoter;
- the guarantee need cover only 20% of the value of the prizes; and
- there is no obligation to designate a not-for-profit organisation for the donation of unclaimed prizes.

A list of sales promotions that are exempt from the applicable requirements is set out in Article 6 of Presidential Decree 430/2001. Finally, Article 8 of the same decree sets out the circumstances in which no sales promotions are allowed.

5. Ambush marketing

In Italy, ambush marketing is regulated by Law Decree 16/2020, issued on 11 March 2020, in light of the upcoming ATP Finals 2021–2025 in Turin and the 2026 Winter Olympic Games in Milan-Cortina. Unlike the previous temporary laws on ambush marketing (eg, Law 167/2005), the new law is of a permanent nature and has general application.

In particular, Articles 10 and 11 prohibit parasitic advertising activities that are carried out on the occasion of sporting events or exhibitions of national or international significance, which are not authorised by the organisers and are aimed at gaining an economic or competitive advantage. These restrictions apply for up to 180 days after the end of the event.

A sanction of between €100,000 and €2.5 million applies in case of violations, subject to administrative proceedings within the jurisdiction of the Antitrust Authority, in accordance with the procedural provisions of Legislative Decree 145/2007.

6. Direct marketing

Direct marketing – that is, the sending of advertising communications directly to potential customers through post, telephone, fax, email, text or multimedia messaging – is regulated from multiple points of view under Italian law.

First, particularly insistent marketing practices could potentially fall under the notion of 'aggressive commercial practices' (Articles 24 to 26 of the Consumers' Code), which are defined as "commercial practices... that limit or are capable of limiting the average consumer's freedom of choice and behaviour in relation to the product, and that, therefore, induce or are capable of inducing the average consumer to make a commercial decision he/she would not otherwise have made". In fact, according to Article 26 of the code, repeated unsolicited commercial solicitations by telephone, fax, email or other means of distance communication are considered aggressive practices.

Second, from a privacy law perspective and pursuant to Article 130 of the Italian Data Protection Code, direct marketing through automated means without the intervention of an operator (eg, emails or text messages) is allowed only where it is based on prior consent (ie, an 'opt-in' applies). However, email direct marketing is allowed if:

- the email address was provided to the advertiser by the interested person within the framework of the sale of a product or service similar to the promoted one; and
- the interested person, once appropriately informed, has not exercised the right to opt out.

Direct marketing made through post or telephone is allowed unless the recipient of the marketing activity has opposed it (ie, opted out) by notifying the Public Registry of Opt-outs.[8]

In any event, under Articles 12, 13, 14, 17 and 21 of the GDPR, the controller must provide the data subject (ie, in the above cases, the recipient of the marketing communications) with a specific privacy notice; and the data subject has the right to request the controller to erase his or her personal data without undue delay, and to object at any time to the processing of his or her personal data for direct marketing purposes.

Email direct marketing is further regulated by the legislation on e-commerce. Under Articles 8 and 9 of Legislative Decree 70/2003, the advertiser has specific notification obligations in relation to the recipient of the communication, who must (among other things) be clearly informed of the communication's promotional nature, the advertiser's identity and the right to opt out of future similar communications.

7.   Product placement

The general principle on product placement, which is allowed subject to specific restrictions and requirements, is that it must not result in disguised advertising.

In particular, product placement in films is regulated by the Ministerial

---

8   www.registrodelleopposizioni.it.

Decree of 30 July 2004 and is allowed on condition that the film's final credits contain an appropriate notice concerning the advertised brands and products, and specifically referencing the advertisers. In any event:

- the brand must be integrated into the narrative context without interrupting the same; and
- the placement must comply with the general principles of advertising law and particularly those of fairness, transparency and truthfulness.

Product placement in television programmes is governed by Article 40*bis* of Legislative Decree 177/2005. More specifically, placement is allowed as long as:

- it does not compromise the responsibility and editorial independence of the media services provider;
- it does not directly encourage the purchase of the products placed; and
- no undue prominence is given to the products placed.

In the case of programmes produced or commissioned by the media services provider itself, viewers must be clearly informed of the existence of the product placement through announcements at the beginning and end of the programme and after all commercial breaks. More generally, no product placement is allowed in programmes targeted at children; and no placement is permitted for tobacco products (including the products of companies whose main activity is the sale of tobacco products) or for medicinal products or medical therapies that are subject to medical prescription.

8.   Native advertising and social media influencers

In addition to the general principles established by Legislative Decree 145/2007, the Consumers' Code and the Advertising Standards Code, online advertising is specifically regulated by the Digital Chart Regulation of 29 April 2019, which is now an integral part of the Advertising Standards Code and which specifically aims to establish the criteria to clearly identify the promotional nature of online marketing communications.

Article 1 of the Digital Chart provides that where the measures indicated therein are adopted, the fundamental requirement of 'marketing communication recognisability' is deemed to have unequivocally been satisfied.

In particular, an influencer (eg, a celebrity, blogger or similar internet user whose actions might potentially influence the commercial choices of the public) who accredits a product or a brand within his or her own content as a form of marketing communication must insert one of the following labels or hashtags at the beginning of the online message and/or within the first three hashtags:

- '*Pubblicità*'/'Advertising'; '*Promosso da* [brand]'/'Promoted by [brand]'; '*Sponsorizzato da* [brand]'/'Sponsored by [brand]; or '*in collaborazione con* [brand]'/'In partnership with [brand]'; or

- *#Pubblicità*/#Advertising; *#Sponsorizzato da* [brand]/#Sponsored by [brand]; or #ad together with #brand.

As regards videos and live streams, disclaimers referring to their promotional nature must also be inserted either in the opening scenes or when the specific product/brand features are in shot.

However, if the relationship between the influencer and advertiser involves the advertiser occasionally sending the influencer its products free of charge or for modest consideration, or invitations to participate in an event, the latter may simply feature a disclaimer stating, "Product sent by [brand]" (or equivalent) or inform the audience that he or she is attending the event at the advertiser's invitation.

In these two particular cases, "the advertiser must clearly and unequivocally inform the influencer when sending the product of the obligation to insert this disclaimer".

As regards native advertising, the Digital Chart requires the promotional nature of in-feed units, paid search units and recommendation widgets to be clearly visible through the insertion of labels and specific descriptors, or through the adoption of any other suitable practice. Furthermore, the chart establishes that the marketing nature of in-app advertising and/or advergames must be appropriately stated.

9. Industry-specific regulation

9.1 Gambling

Pursuant to Article 9 of Law Decree 87/2018, as from 1 January 2020, any form of advertisement for gambling carried out in any way and by any means is forbidden, including:

- during sporting, cultural and artistic events;
- on television and radio shows;
- in daily and periodical newspapers and publications in general;
- on billboards; and
- on the Internet.

Only national and local lotteries may be advertised.

9.2 Alcohol

The advertisement of alcoholic beverages and spirits is regulated in a number of statutes. Provisions are included in:

- the Advertising Standards Code (Article 22);
- Law 125/2001 on alcohol and alcohol-related problems (Article 13);
- the Consumers' Code (Article 21(3));

- Legislative Decree 177/2005 on the general law relating to television transmissions (Articles 37 and 39); and
- the Code of Conduct on Television and Minors (Article 4).

The implications of each of these provisions are described further below.

(a) *General legal obligations*

Article 22 of the Advertising Standards Code provides that marketing communications concerning alcoholic beverages should not conflict with the obligation to depict styles of drinking behaviour that project moderation, wholesomeness and responsibility in such a way as to protect the primary interests of the population in general, and of children and the young in particular, in a family, social and working environment safeguarded from the negative consequences of alcohol abuse. Article 22 also illustrates specific restrictions that apply to marketing communications concerning alcoholic beverages.

Article 13 of Law 125/2001 contains a general prohibition against:

- attributing to the advertised alcoholic beverage an efficacy or therapeutic indication that has not been expressly recognised by the Italian Ministry of Health;
- depicting minors drinking alcohol; and
- representing the consumption of alcohol in a positive manner.

Article 21(3) of the Consumers' Code imposes a general obligation whereby all commercial practices (including advertising) concerning products that are capable of endangering the health or safety of consumers must appropriately inform consumers of this fact, so that consumers are not induced to disregard normal rules of caution and carefulness. This provision may be considered to be the legal basis for the practice of including phrases such as "Drink responsibly" in alcohol advertising in Italy.

(b) *Television and radio advertising*

Law 125/2001 (Article 13) and the Code of Conduct on Television and Minors (Articles 4.2 and 4.4) provide that it is forbidden to place ads for alcoholic beverages:

- in television or radio programmes addressed to minors, as well as in the 15 minutes preceding and following the transmission of these programmes;
- in locations that are mainly frequented by minors;
- on television between 4:00pm and 7:00pm;
- in daily or periodical newspapers that are addressed to minors; and
- in cinemas when films targeted at minors are being shown.

Legislative Decree 177/2005 on television transmissions (Article 39) further provides that television and radio programmes or programmes distributed through any other medium (including all types of digital media) cannot be sponsored by entities whose main activities consist in the production or sale of spirits.

9.3 Pharmaceuticals

Based on the provisions of Legislative Decree 219/2006 (the Pharmaceuticals Code), advertising to the public is allowed only for pharmaceuticals that, considering their composition and therapeutic objective, are aimed at being used without the intervention of a medical doctor for the purposes of diagnosis, prescription or surveillance in the course of treatment, or without the necessary advice of a pharmacist.

The distribution to the public of pharmaceuticals for promotional purposes is forbidden. It is also forbidden to depict or present pharmaceuticals in the press, radio or television in a context that would favour the consumption of the product, even if this is done in messages that do not in themselves constitute advertising (eg, press articles that are of an informative nature).

It is expressly provided that pharmaceutical advertising must:

- be absolutely transparent as regards the advertising nature of the message;
- clearly indicate the name of the product and that of the active substance (unless the product contains a combination of active substances, in which case the name of the product is sufficient);
- indicate all information necessary for the product's consumption; and
- invite the public to consult the indications set out in the packaging leaflet (or on the packaging, where applicable).

In addition, a number of explicit restrictions apply, including that advertising must not:

- suggest that it is not necessary to consult a doctor;
- be misleading or shocking as regards the effects of taking or not taking the product;
- liken the product to foodstuff, cosmetics or other consumer goods;
- suggest that the product has no undesired effects;
- compare the efficacy of the advertised product with that of another treatment or pharmaceutical;
- include recommendations by scientists, health operators or famous persons;
- directly address children; or
- suggest that the efficacy or safety of the advertised product derives from the fact that it is 'natural'.

In any event, where allowed, pharmaceutical advertising can be carried out only with prior authorisation (in the form of a licence) from the Ministry of Health, which will provide approval after consulting a committee of experts (and in some cases a specific committee of the Advertising Standards Institute). Each licence lasts for 24 months and concerns a specific advertising message. As an exception, no licence is required for insertions in daily or periodical newspapers insofar as these are limited to the reproduction of the information contained in the package leaflet with only the addition of a picture of the packaging of the product; nor is a licence required for posters concerning non-prescription products affixed in pharmacies, upon prior notice to the Ministry of Health.

The Advertising Standards Code also contains general principles on the advertisement of pharmaceuticals. Article 25 provides that pharmaceutical advertising must:

- take into account the particular importance of this subject matter;
- be realised with the maximum sense of responsibility possible;
- conform with the technical characteristics of the product;
- call the attention of the consumer to the need for careful use of the product;
- contain a clear and explicit invitation to read the warnings contained in the package leaflet; and
- not induce any improper use of the product.

9.4 Financial products and services

The advertisement of financial products and services is regulated by Legislative Decree 58/98 ('Unified Code on Financial Services'). This sets out a number of principles which apply in this regard, as follows:

- A product cannot be advertised before the publication of its prospectus (ie, the disclosure document that describes the financial security for potential buyers, as provided for by the EU Prospectus Directive (2003/71/EC)), with the sole exception of 'community financial instruments' (eg, shares in closed-end funds).
- All advertising must be transparent and recognisable as such. The message must be precise and not misleading as to the characteristics, nature or risks of the products and the relevant investment.
- The advertising message must indicate that a prospectus was or will be published, as well as where it can be found, and must not contain information that does not conform to that reported in the prospectus.
- If the message refers to the financial return expected from the proposed investment, it must:
  - specify the relevant reference period;

- represent in a clear manner the risk profile associated with the return;
- compare the return with the reference parameter indicated in the prospectus for representing the risk-return profile or, in the absence of such a parameter, with a parameter that is coherent with the investment policy described in the prospectus;
- indicate such returns after taxes or, where this is not possible, specify that the indicated returns are before taxes; and
- include the warning "Past returns are not indicative of future returns".

- If statistics, studies or data elaborations are indicated (or however referred to), the relevant sources must be mentioned.
- All advertising messages must state in an easily perceivable manner "Before accepting, read the prospectus". This warning must at least be given orally when advertising through audio-visual media.

The advertisement of financial products is also subject to notification to the National Commission for Companies and Stock Exchange (CONSOB). CONSOB has also issued a communication (11021864/2011) concerning the advertisement of non-equity financial products (which is beyond the scope of this chapter).

The advertisement of financial products is also contemplated by the Advertising Standards Code. Article 27 provides that all marketing communications aimed at soliciting or promoting financial transactions, banking services in general and insurance services, where it is necessary to emphasise the investment aspect, must supply clear and comprehensive information to avoid misleading consumers and to ensure that the following are identified:

- the promoter;
- the nature of the proposal;
- the quantity and characteristics of the goods or services being offered; and
- the terms of the transaction and the relevant risks, to ensure that recipients of the message – even if inexperienced in this field – can make informed choices about the use of their resources.

In particular, such communications must:

- avoid, when referring to yearly interest rates, using terms such as 'income' and 'return' to indicate the sum total of unearned income plus increases in property values;
- refrain from suggesting that consumers must make commitments and pay deposits without appropriate guarantees; and

- not project future performance on the basis of past performance, or communicate returns based on calculations over periods that are not sufficiently representative with reference to the particular nature of the investment and to the fluctuations in results.

Marketing communications relating to real estate transactions must be set out in such a way as to avoid deception by passing off financial investments for real estate investments or by focusing on the financials of a real estate property without making clear that the investment actually involves securities.

9.5 Food

EU Regulation 1169/2011 concerns the provision of food information to consumers and, among other things, sets out the principles that govern the advertisement of foodstuffs. Article 7 of this regulation establishes in particular that food advertising must not mislead consumers:

- as to the characteristics of the food, its nature, identity, properties, composition, quantity, durability, country of origin or place of provenance, method of manufacture or production;
- by attributing to the food effects or properties which it does not possess;
- by suggesting that the food possesses special characteristics when all similar foods possess such characteristics – in particular, by specifically emphasising the presence or absence of certain ingredients and/or nutrients; or
- by suggesting – by means of the appearance, the description or pictorial representations – the presence of a particular food or ingredient in the product, where in reality a component naturally present or an ingredient normally used in that food has been substituted with a different component or ingredient.

Article 7 further provides that:

- food advertising must be accurate, clear and easy to understand for the consumer; and
- subject to derogations applicable to natural mineral waters and foods for particular nutritional uses, food advertising must not attribute to any product the property of preventing, treating or curing a human disease, or refer to such properties.

Legislative Decree 231/2017 establishes the applicable sanctions for breach of the regulatory provisions – for instance, providing that breach of so-called 'fair information practices' under Article 7 of EU Regulation 1169/2011 is subject to a financial sanction of between €3,000 and €24,000. As regards health claims, the general principle is that only claims specifically approved by the

European Commission, upon scientific consultation with the European Food Safety Authority, are allowed, under EU Regulation 1924/2006. A list of generally approved claims is contained in EU Regulation 432/2012.

Finally, Article 7 of Legislative Decree 169/2004 and Article 23*bis* of the Advertising Standards Code regulate the advertisement of food supplements and dietary products. Among other things, such advertising must refrain from claiming properties that the products do not possess or referencing medical recommendations or claims. Further provisions concerning the advertisement of food supplements are contained in the Regulation on Marketing Communication of Food Supplements adopted by the Advertising Standards Institute.

9.6   Tobacco

Based on Legislative Decree 165/1962 and Legislative Decree 300/2004, the advertisement of tobacco is forbidden. As regards television advertising, Ministerial Decree 425/1991 specifies that it is forbidden to carry out any form of television advertising of cigarettes or other tobacco products. The decree explicitly states that this ban encompasses indirect advertising through the use of names, trademarks, symbols or other elements that are characteristic of tobacco products or of companies whose main activity consists in the production and sale of such products, where, due to the forms, modalities and means used, or any other unambiguous element, such use could constitute the advertisement of such products. To this end, when establishing the 'main activity' of a company, account must be taken of turnover made in the national territory from its various activities, in order to determine its main activity.

9.7   E-cigarettes

Under Article 21 of Legislative Decree 6/2016, all marketing communications concerning e-cigarettes and refill containers aimed at, or having the direct or indirect effect of, promoting e-cigarettes and refill containers are forbidden. This ban applies to marketing communications carried out through information society services, audio-visual media and/or radio, in the press and in printed publications, and on the occasion of public or private events, with just two exceptions:

- publications that are exclusively intended for professionals in the e-cigarettes and refill containers sector; and
- publications that are printed and published in non-EU countries, if not mainly destined for the EU market.

Japan

Toshiya Furusho
Mizuki Kanno
Yuki Kuroda
Takamitsu Shigetomi
Oh-Ebashi LPC & Partners

1. Overview of the legal and regulatory regime for advertising

1.1 Administrative law

Japan has adopted various administrative laws to regulate advertising, comprising general administrative laws and special laws to regulate advertising in certain business sectors.

(a) General administrative laws

The general administrative laws that are relevant to the field of advertising are:

- the Act against Unjustifiable Premiums and Misleading Representations ('Misleading Representations Act'); and
- the Act on Prohibition of Private Monopolisation and Maintenance of Fair Trade ('Anti-monopoly Act').

Misleading Representations Act: Originally, the Misleading Representations Act of 1962 was categorised as one of the special acts relating to the Anti-monopoly Act for which the Japan Fair Trade Commission (JFTC) was responsible. In 2009, however, the Japanese government launched the Consumer Affairs Agency (CAA) to regulate consumer-related administrative affairs and transferred jurisdiction and authority for overseeing the Misleading Representations Act to the CAA.

Reflecting this change, the Misleading Representations Act was revised to make the purpose of this act the protection of the interests of general consumers. Specifically, Article 1 of the Misleading Representations Acts provides that: "The purpose of this Act is to protect the interests of general consumers by providing for limitations and the prohibition of acts that are likely to interfere with general consumers' voluntary and rational choice-making in order to prevent the inducement of customers by means of unjustifiable premiums and misleading representations in connection with the transaction of goods and services."

Table 1. Outline of the Misleading Representations Act

Purpose	Protection of the interests of general consumers	Article 1
Prohibition/ restriction	Prevention of the unjustifiable inducement of customers	Article 1
	Premiums (eg, maximum value, total amount)	Article 4
	Misleading representations	Article 5
Administrative sanctions/ measures against violation	Governmental orders (eg, cease orders)	Article 7
	Payment order for surcharge	Article 8

Under this act, 'representations' are defined as ads or any other representations which an entrepreneur makes as a means to induce customers to purchase the products or services which the entrepreneur supplies, or the trade terms or any other particulars concerning the transaction, and which are designated by the prime minister in the public notice as such.[1] As the list of representations in this public notice is broad, including online and oral communications,[2] almost all methods which entrepreneurs use as a means of inducing customers are considered as representations.

Article 5 of the Misleading Representations Act is of particular importance in relation to advertising and provides as follows:

No entrepreneur shall make such representation as provided for in any one of the following items in connection with transactions of goods or services which he supplies:

(1) Any representation by which the quality, standard or any other matter relating to the content of goods or services are shown to general consumers to be much better than the actual one or much better than that of other entrepreneurs who are in a competitive relationship with the entrepreneur concerned, contrary to fact and thereby which tends to induce customers unjustly and to impede voluntary and reasonable choice by general customers;

(2) Any representation by which price or any other trade terms of goods or services

---

1   Misleading Representations Act, Article 2(4).
2   See the JFTC Notification 3 of 30 June 1962.

will be misunderstood by general consumers to be much more favourable to the general consumers than the actual one or than those of other entrepreneurs who are in a competitive relationship with the entrepreneur concerned, and thereby which tends to induce customers unjustly and to impede voluntary and reasonable choice by general customers; or

(3) *In addition to what are listed in the preceding two items, any representation by which any matter relating to transactions of goods or services is likely to be misunderstood by general consumers and which is designated by the Prime Minister as such, finding it likely to induce customers unjustly and to impede voluntary and reasonable choice by* general customers.

In relation to Article 5(3), the subject matter that is restricted by the prime minister includes:

- representations on soft drinks that do not contain fruit juice;
- representations on country of origin;
- representations on the cost of consumer credit;
- bait-and-switch advertising generally; and
- representations on nursing homes whose residents must pay for services.

The Misleading Representations Act applies to foreign entrepreneurs as long as such entrepreneurs make representations (including through a website) to general consumers in Japan and sell products to general consumers in Japan.

In the event of a violation of Article 5 of the Misleading Representations Act, the prime minister has the power to order the entrepreneur to:

- cease the infringing act;
- take the necessary measures to prevent a recurrence of the violation; and
- take any other measures – including notification to the public – that are necessary to deal with the matter.[3]

In 2016 the act was revised to introduce a surcharge system in relation to misleading representations. The prime minister may order an entrepreneur to pay the national treasury a surcharge equivalent to 3% of the proceeds from the sale of products or services relating to the conduct that is subject to the surcharge (ie, misleading representations) in the period during which such representations were made.[4] If any sales of the relevant products or services are made after the date on which the conduct that is subject to the surcharge was discontinued, the period that is subject to the surcharge will be extended to the date of the last transaction within six months of the date of discontinuation. According to Article 33 of the Misleading Representations Act, the prime minister is to delegate the authority under the act to the secretary general of the

---

3   Misleading Representations Act, Article 7.
4   *Ibid*, Article 8.

CAA. Consequently, in practice, the abovementioned orders are issued by the secretary general of the CAA.

Anti-monopoly Act: The JFTC has the authority to regulate advertising based on the Anti-monopoly Act.

Article 19 of that act provides that no entrepreneur should adopt unfair trade practices. Article 2(9)(6)(ha) provides that certain acts by an entrepreneur which the JFTC has designated as constituting the unjust inducement or coercion of customers of a competitor to deal with that entrepreneur are unfair trade practices. These acts are as follows:

- General Designation 8 – unjustifiable acts to induce a competitor's customers to trade with the entrepreneur by misleading them in a way that suggests that the quality, trade terms or other characteristics of its own products or services are better or more favourable than those of the competitor; and
- General Designation 9 – acts to induce a competitor's customers to trade with the entrepreneur by unjustifiable profit, considering normal trade practices.

The differences in the scope of application of the Misleading Representations Act and the Anti-monopoly Act are as follows:

- The Anti-monopoly Act applies to unjustifiable representations regardless of whether the relevant customers are general consumers; and
- The Anti-monopoly Act deals not only with misrepresentation, but also with inducement.

If an entrepreneur violates the Anti-monopoly Act, the JFTC may order it to:

- cease and desist from engaging in the infringing act;
- delete clauses from a contract; or
- take any other measures necessary to eliminate the infringement.[5]

(b) ***Special laws to regulate advertising in certain business sectors***
In addition to the general administrative laws described above, there are various special laws that regulate advertising and/or representations in certain sectors. The major laws are outlined below and are explained in detail in section 9, where relevant.

---

5   Anti-monopoly Act, Article 20.

Act on Securing Quality, Efficacy and Safety of Products Including Pharmaceuticals and Medical Devices ('Pharmaceutical Affairs Act'): This act:

- prohibits the advertisement of a medical drug or medical device before it has received government approval;[6]
- prohibits false or excessive advertising;[7]
- prohibits advertising that assures consumers of the efficacy of a medical drug;[8]
- obliges pharmaceuticals manufacturers to include the term 'toxin' on the packaging, containers and so on of drugs that contain poisonous substances;[9] and
- prohibits the advertisement of certain designated medical drugs (eg, cannabis and other stimulants).[10]

Importantly, the Pharmaceutical Affairs Act was revised in 2019 to introduce a new system to order the payment of a surcharge in case of violations of Article 66(1) of the Pharmaceutical Affairs Act restricting advertising. The revision is expected to take effect on 1 August 2021.

Food Labelling Act: The Food Labelling Act was enacted in 2013 and came into force in 2017. The Food Labelling Act sets out comprehensive rules and regulations to ensure proper food labelling by establishing standards and specifying other necessary information regarding the labelling of food that is intended for sale. Originally, three statutes – the Food Sanitation Act, the Act on Standardisation of Agricultural and Forestry Materials and the Appropriate Quality Labelling and Health Promotion Act – individually regulated food labelling in Japan. The Food Labelling Act was enacted to integrate these acts in a single statute.

In light of the important role that food labelling plays in ensuring the safety of food and helping consumers to make autonomous and rational choices in this regard, the act aims to establish standards and specify other necessary information regarding the labelling of food that is intended for sale (including its assignment other than by sale to unspecified or numerous persons), in order to:

- promote the interests of general consumers;
- protect and promote the health of the people;
- ensure the smooth production and distribution of food; and
- promote food production in response to consumer demand.[11]

---

6   Pharmaceutical Affairs Act, Article 68.
7   *Ibid*, Article 66(1).
8   *Ibid*, Article 66(2).
9   *Ibid*, Article 44.
10   *Ibid*, Article 76(5).
11   Food Labelling Act, Article 1.

Food Sanitation Act: The Food Sanitation Act empowers the prime minister to set forth the necessary criteria for the labelling of apparatus or containers and packaging for which such standards have been established under the act, with input from the Consumer Commission.[12] Apparatus or containers and packaging for which labelling criteria have been established pursuant to Article 19(1) of the Food Sanitation Act may not be sold, displayed for marketing purposes or otherwise used in business without labelling that conforms to such criteria.[13] False or exaggerated labelling or advertising that may cause harm to public health in relation to food, additives, apparatus or containers and packaging may not be used.[14]

Health Promotion Act: The Health Promotion Act was enacted in 2002 and contains provisions that oblige entrepreneurs to obtain the prime minister's approval to include on their food products any representation which suggests that the product is suitable for special use for a baby, child, pregnant woman or patient; and other matters as set forth in the Cabinet Office Ordinance.[15] According to the ordinance, such special use includes food used for specified health purposes, such as dietary supplements. The Health Promotion Act prohibits the inclusion of significantly false and/or misleading labelling on foods with regard to their efficacy for health promotion.[16]

Act on Japanese Agricultural Standards: The Act on Japanese Agricultural Standards regulates the labelling of agricultural and forestry products, excluding food and drinks. Based on this act, Japanese Agricultural Standards (JAS) was established to establish standards for the grading of agricultural and forestry products.[17] JAS conducts grading tests for such products and the JAS mark may be included on the labelling of products that pass the test.

1.2 Civil law

(a) Civil Code and Anti-monopoly Act

Consumers who suffer as a result of misleading representations may seek damages under Article 709 of the Civil Code, which provides for damages in tort. Consumers may also seek damages under this article against unfair business practices that violate the Anti-monopoly Act.

In addition, under Article 24 of the Anti-monopoly Act, anyone whose interests are infringed or likely to be infringed by unfair business practices and

---

12   *Ibid*, Article 19(1).
13   *Ibid*, Article 19(2).
14   *Ibid*, Article 20.
15   Health Promotion Act, Article 43(1).
16   *Ibid*, Article 65(1).
17   Act on Japanese Agricultural Standards, Article 3.

who thereby suffers or is likely to suffer extreme damage is entitled to seek the suspension or prevention of any such infringement.

(b) *Consumer Contract Act*

The Consumer Contract Act provides for civil and contractual remedies against misleading representations made by an entrepreneur. As regards contractual remedies, the act provides the right to rescind the manifestation of an intention to enter into a contract if misleading representations are made. For example, Article 4(1) of the act provides as follows:

> *A consumer may rescind the manifestation of his/her intention to offer or accept a Consumer Contract if either of the actions listed in the following items in which the Entrepreneur engaged when soliciting the Consumer to enter into such a Consumer Contract caused the Consumer to be under the mistaken belief listed in the relevant item, based on which the Consumer manifested the intention to offer or accept the relevant Consumer Contract:*
>
> *(i) Misrepresentation as to an Important Matter: Mistaken belief that said misrepresentation is true; or*
>
> *(ii) Providing conclusive evaluations of future prices, amounts of money that a Consumer should receive in the future and other uncertain items subject to future change with respect to goods, rights, services and other matters that are to be the subject of a Consumer Contract: Mistaken belief that the content of said conclusive evaluations is certain.*

As regards civil remedies, the Consumer Contract Act sets out a so-called 'consumer organisation action system', which allows qualified consumer organisations to seek injunctive relief from an entrepreneur that engages in, or is likely to engage in, acts such as those proscribed by Article 4(1).[18] This system allows for the establishment of consumer organisations, on behalf of individual consumers, to seek to prevent misleading representations made by entrepreneurs.

(c) *Unfair Competition Prevention Act*

Article 2(1)(20) of the Unfair Competition Prevention Act prohibits:

- the inclusion of misrepresentations on products or services, and in advertising and other communications used in transactions relating to such products or services, in a manner that is likely to mislead the public as to:
    - the place of origin, quality, content, manufacturing process, use or quantity of such products; or
    - the quality, content, purpose or quantity of such services; and
- the assignment, delivery, display for the purpose of assignment or

---

18   See Article 12 of the Consumer Contract Act.

delivery, export, import or provision through an electronic telecommunications line of products or services with such an indication.

Anyone whose business interests are infringed or are likely to be infringed by unfair competition may seek injunctive relief and damages against the infringer or potential infringer.[19]

1.3 Criminal law

Traditionally, a seller that deceives a consumer and obtains property from him or her will be punished under Article 246 of Japan's Penal Code, which stipulates that: "A person who defrauds another of property shall be punished by imprisonment with work for not more than ten years." The Unfair Competition Prevention Act also provides for a criminal penalty of imprisonment with labour for up to five years, a fine of up to ¥5 million or both in relation to acts that fall under Article 2(1)(20).[20]

Furthermore, each administrative act that regulates a specific industry usually provides for the imposition of criminal penalties for prohibited representations. For example, Article 72(1) of the Food Sanitation Act stipulates penal penalties of imprisonment with labour for up to two years or a fine of up to ¥2 million for violations of Article 19(2)[21] or Article 20.[22]

1.4 Self-regulation

The Japan Advertising Review Organisation (JARO) is one of the major self-regulatory bodies for advertising in Japan. JARO handles complaints and enquiries from consumers, competitors and others. The Japan Advertising Agencies Association (JAAA) – in which more than 150 advertising firms in Japan participate – has voluntarily established a Code of Ethics and a Creative Code.[23] In addition, many industry associations have established their own regulations and associated guidelines to be followed by members, and a procedure for handling consumer complaints.

In addition, each industry has established a Fair Competition Code based on Article 31 of the Misleading Representations Act. Each code generally sets out labelling obligations, prohibitions and other penalties for misleading representations. A member that violates its respective Fair Competition Code

---

19   See Articles 3 and 4 of the Unfair Competition Act.
20   See Article 21(2)(1) and (5) of the Unfair Competition Act.
21   Article 19(2) of the Food Sanitation Act provides that: "Apparatus, or containers and packaging for which the criteria for labelling have been established pursuant to the provisions of [Article 19(1)] shall not be sold, displayed for the purpose of marketing, nor used in business, without labelling which conforms to such criteria."
22   Article 20 of the Food Sanitation Act stipulates that: "False or exaggerated labelling or advertising, which may cause harm to public health regarding food, additives, apparatus, or containers and packaging, shall not be used."
23   These codes are available in English at www.jaaa.ne.jp/en/about/about5/.

may find imposed upon it a monetary penalty as stipulated in the code. Each industry establishes a Fair Trade Commission to enforce the Fair Competition Code.

2. Comparative advertising

Comparative advertising is regulated by the Misleading Representations Act. Specifically, Article 5(1)(1) applies where an entrepreneur makes representations in comparative advertising which suggest that the quality, standard or other characteristics of its products or services are significantly superior to those of competitors, in a manner which is likely to unjustly induce customers and to interfere with their ability to make autonomous and rational choices in this regard. Article 5(1)(2) applies where an entrepreneur makes representations in comparative advertising which suggest that a price or any other trade terms of the products or services it is offering for sale are significantly more advantageous than those of its competitors, in a manner which is likely to unjustly induce customers and to interfere with their ability to make autonomous and rational choices in this regard.

In order to clarify the standards for determining the legality of comparative advertising, the JFTC published its Comparative Advertising Guidelines in 1987. Under the guidelines, it is generally considered that the following requirements must be met in order to ensure the legality of comparative advertising:

- The subject matter articulated in the ad (eg, regarding the quality of the products or services) must be objectively proved, with corroborating evidence;
- The numbers and facts presented in relation to the content or terms of products or services must be objectively proved by corroborating evidence, and precisely and appropriately cited in the ad; and
- The method of comparison must be fair.

One of the major court decisions relating to comparative advertising was issued on 19 October 2004 by the Tokyo High Court.[24] The court found that an ad issued by a home electronics mass retailer stating, "We are always setting, and will set, cheaper prices than [a named competitor]" was not contrary to Article 5 of the Misleading Representations Act, because the retailer succeeded in proving the legality of this comparative advertising.

3. Online behavioural advertising

There are no specific laws and regulations on online behavioural advertising, or on the use of cookies or web beacons.

However, the Act on the Protection of Personal Information might apply in

---

24   Tokyo High Court, *Heisei* 16 (*Ne*) No 3324 (Judgment of October 19 2004), *Hanrei-Jihō* 1904, p128.

certain situations. Generally speaking, advertising identifiers such as the Identifier for Advertising or the Google Advertising ID, cookies and web beacons are not regarded as personal information, except where they can be readily collated with other information and thereby identify a specific individual.[25] If such information falls within the definition of 'personal information', the entrepreneur must abide by the act's relevant provisions,[26] such as the obligation not to acquire such information through deception or other wrongful means.

There are also industry-specific guidelines for online behavioural advertising. The Japan Interactive Advertising Association, which obtained a licence from the Interactive Advertising Bureau in 2017, has published Guidelines on Behavioural Targeting Advertisements[27] and Guidelines on Privacy Policies.[28] These cover so-called 'informative data' such as advertising IDs, cookies, location data, browsing history and purchase history, where these do not meet the definition of 'personal information' under the Act on the Protection of Personal Information. They require relevant organisations to satisfy various obligations, including ensuring transparency and offering individuals the opportunity to opt out.

In addition to restrictions under the Act on the Protection of Personal Information, the gathering of personal data may constitute an invasion of privacy under the theory of tort; in such circumstances, an entrepreneur risks being held liable for compensation for damages.

4. Sales promotions

The Misleading Representations Act includes provisions that restrict the use of benefits (so-called 'premiums') for the purpose of sales promotions.

Under this act, the term 'premiums' includes any item, money or other kind of economic gain offered as a means to induce customers – irrespective of whether the method is direct or indirect, and irrespective of whether a lottery method is used – in connection with a transaction involving products or services that the entrepreneur supplies (including transactions relating to real estate), and which are designated as such by the prime minister.[29]

Where he deems this necessary in order to prevent the unjust inducement of customers, the prime minister:

- may restrict:
  - the maximum value of a premium;
  - the total amount of premiums;

---

25   Article 2(1) of the Act on the Protection of Personal Information.
26   See Articles 15–35 of the Personal Data Protection Act, setting forth duties of an entrepreneur dealing with personal information.
27   www.jiaa.org/gdl_siryo/gdl/bta/ (in Japanese).
28   www.jiaa.org/gdl_siryo/gdl/privacy/ (in Japanese).
29   Misleading Representations Act, Article 2(3).

- the kinds of premiums offered;
- the method of offering a premium; or
- any other matter relating thereto; or
- may prohibit altogether the offering of a premium.[30]

There are two main types of restrictions:
- the provision of a premium by way of offering a prize; and
- the provision of a premium without offering a prize.

The CAA has imposed restrictions on each type of premium. For example, "the restriction of matters regarding the provision of premiums by way of offering a prize"[31] provides that the maximum value of a premium may be no more than 20 times the sales price of the product being offered in the promotion. Specific restrictions apply in the following sectors:
- newspapers;
- magazines;
- real estate; and
- medical drugs, medical devices and hygiene inspection stations.

In 2001 the JFTC published a policy on offering prizes online. This provides that the restrictions set out in the Misleading Representations Act will apply in cases where:
- consumers cannot apply for a sweepstake plan unless they purchase a product or service on an e-commerce site; or
- consumers cannot easily apply for a sweepstakes plan online (eg, if they cannot find out the correct answer to a quiz question without purchasing a product or service).

As regards premiums by way of offering a prize, no representations may be made that could be misunderstood by general consumers as being significantly more advantageous to them than is actually the case.[32]

5. Ambush marketing

There is no law or rule that specifically prohibits ambush marketing in Japan; however, ambush marketing may be regulated through the Trademark Act, the Unfair Competition Prevention Act, the Copyright Act and other legislation.

Where the name, logos and/or emblems of an event have been registered as trademarks, no party can use them for its own products or services without the

---

30   *Ibid*, Article 4.
31   This restriction was published by the JFTC in 1977.
32   Misleading Representations Act, Article 5(1)(2).

authorisation of the trademark owner. Any unauthorised use constitutes trademark infringement and is subject to damages and/or an injunction.

The Unfair Competition Prevention Act provides that the following actions constitute unfair competition, and are subject to damages and/or an injunction:

- creating confusion with a third party's products or business by using an indication of products or business that is identical or similar to that of the third party, which is well known among consumers or other purchasers, or by assigning, delivering, displaying for the purpose of assignment or delivery, exporting, importing or providing through an electronic telecommunications line products or services that include such an indication;[33] and
- using as one's own an indication of products or business that is identical or similar to a third party's famous indication of products or business, or assigning, delivering, displaying for the purpose of assignment or delivery, exporting, importing or providing through an electronic telecommunications line products or services that include such an indication.[34]

Remedies under the Unfair Competition Prevention Act are available with or without trademark registrations. Therefore, even if an event organiser has never registered its name of similar as a trademark, it may be able to prevent the unauthorised use of its name, logos, emblems or similar by ambushers under the Unfair Competition Prevention Act where these are well known or famous. Furthermore, where an ambusher uses the name, logos and/or emblems of an international organisation (eg, the United Nations or the International Olympic Committee) as its trademark, such use is prohibited under Article 17 of the Unfair Competition Prevention Act.

Additionally, where the logos or emblems fall within the definition of a 'work'[35] set out in the Copyright Act, the author of that work or a copyright holder which has obtained copyright from the original author can take steps to prevent the work from being copied or adapted without authorisation.

Moreover, where an ambusher uses a celebrity's image for its products or services without authorisation, such use may constitute a violation of the celebrity's right of publicity. Although there is no statutory provision that recognises this right in Japan, the Supreme Court has ruled that the unauthorised use of the images of celebrities may constitute an infringement of the right of publicity under tort law.[36] Damages and injunctions may be granted against such infringements.

---

33   Unfair Competition Prevention Act, Article 2(1)(1).
34   *Ibid*, Article 2(1)(2).
35   Article 2(1)(1) of the Copyright Act defines a copyrightable 'work' as "a production in which thoughts or sentiments are expressed in a creative way and which falls within the literary, scientific, artistic or musical domain".
36   See Supreme Court, *Heisei* 21 (*Jyu*) 2056 (Judgment of 2 February 2012), *Minshu⁻* Vol 66 No 2, p 89.

6.   Direct marketing

The Act on the Protection of Personal Information includes no specific provisions on direct marketing. However, an entrepreneur conducting direct marketing will be subject to the general data processing rules set out in the Act on the Protection of Personal Information, such as the following:

- An entrepreneur handling personal information must not acquire personal information through deception or other wrongful means;[37]
- At the time of collection of personal information, the entrepreneur must promptly notify the data subject of the purposes of collection or publicly announce them (except where it has already publicly announced those purposes);[38] and
- In principle, the entrepreneur must obtain the consent of customers to disclose their data to a third party.[39]

Two laws – the Act on Regulation of Transmission of Specified Electronic Mail and the Act on Specified Commercial Transactions – are particularly relevant to direct marketing. The former regulates all email marketing activities, including business to business. The latter applies only to certain types of business-to-consumer (B2C) activities and provides more comprehensive protection to consumers, including stricter advertising and email regulations. An entrepreneur must satisfy the requirements of both laws.

The Act on Regulation of Transmission of Specified Electronic Mail regulates the sending of so-called 'specified electronic mail' – that is, email sent as a means of advertising for the sender's own sales activities or for those of others.[40] To send specified electronic mail, an entrepreneur must in principle obtain consent from the recipient. However, several exceptions allow the entrepreneur to send emails without consent in certain cases, such as where it has already entered into commercial transactions with the recipient.[41] The act also requires the entrepreneur:

- to maintain a record of consent; and
- to offer the opportunity to opt out and include a specific notice in specified electronic mail.[42]

The Act on Specified Commercial Transactions regulates several types of B2C activities that are considered as high risk for consumers. One of these is 'mail order sales',[43] including e-commerce. The regulations on mail order sales include provisions on advertising and emails.

---

37   Article 17(1) of the Act on the Protection of Personal Information.
38   *Ibid*, Article 18(1).
39   *Ibid*, Article 23(1).
40   Article 2(2) of the Act on Regulation of Transmission of Specified Electronic Mail.
41   *Ibid*, Article 3(1).
42   Articles 3(2), 3(3) and 4 of the Act on Regulation of Transmission of Specified Electronic Mail.

Where a seller or service provider advertises terms and conditions under which it sells products, rights or services through mail order sales, it must include in the ad relevant information concerning the transaction, such as the following:

- the price of the products, rights or services (including any delivery charges);[44]
- the timing and means of payment for the products, rights or services;[45]
- the time at which the products will be delivered or the rights or services will be provided;[46] and
- information on the withdrawal from, or cancellation of, an offer for a sales contract for the products, rights or services.[47]

Where a seller or service provider advertises the terms and conditions under which it is willing to sell products, rights or services through mail order sales, it must make no representations – whether about the content or performance of the products, rights or services; the withdrawal from, or cancellation of, an offer for a sales contract for the products, rights or services; or anything else specified by ordinance of the competent ministry with respect to mail order sales – that differ significantly from the truth or that could mislead people into believing that the offer is significantly better or more advantageous than it actually is.[48]

To send email marketing to a consumer, the seller or service provider must first obtain the recipient's consent. The Act on Specific Commercial Transactions sets out several exceptions to this requirement, but these are narrower than those under the Act on Regulation of Transmission of Specified Electronic Mail.[49] The act also requires the seller or service provider to maintain a record of consent and to offer an opportunity to opt out.[50]

7. Product placement

There are no specific laws or regulations in Japan that govern product placement. Thus, the general regulations set out in section 1 are primarily applicable.

---

43   Article 2(2) of the Act on Specified Commercial Transactions. 'Mail order sales' are defined as the sale of products or designated rights or the provision of services for which the seller or service provider has received an offer for a sales contract or service contract by post or by any other means specified by ordinance of the competent ministry, and that does not fall under the category of Telemarketing Sales.
44   Article 11(1) of the Act on Specified Commercial Transactions.
45   *Ibid*, Article 11(2).
46   *Ibid*, Article 11(3).
47   *Ibid*, Article 11(4).
48   *Ibid*, Article 12.
49   *Ibid*, Article 12-3(1).
50   *Ibid*, Article 12-3(2)(3).

8. Native advertising and social media influencers

There are no specific laws or regulations in Japan on native advertising or social media influencers, and stealth marketing itself is not prohibited. However, such types of advertising are regarded as 'representations' under the Misleading Representations Act. The Misleading Representations Act will apply to an entrepreneur if:

- the entrepreneur has a third party, such as an advertising company or a social media influencer, post articles or comments (ie, representations) regarding the substance of the products or services which it supplies or the trading terms of its transactions; and
- the entrepreneur is involved in decisions on the content of such representations.

Thus, the general regulations of the Misleading Representations Act set out in section 1.1(a) will apply.

9. Industry-specific regulation

9.1 Gambling

Pachinko gambling in Japan is one of the types of amusement business that are regulated under the Act on Control and Improvement of Amusement Business, etc. Article 16 of the act stipulates that amusement entrepreneurs must not advertise their business in a way that is likely to harm public morals near their places of business.

In July 2012 the National Police Agency circulated a notice[51] which reinforced the regulation of *pachinko* gambling parlour advertising. This provides that the following types of advertising will be considered likely to harm public morals:

- indications implying that the parlour has installed amusement machines through which customers can win prizes;
- indications implying the win rate for big prizes on amusement machines, which rate may be adjusted;
- indications implying that the parlour is involved in awarding prizes;
- indications representing, directly or indirectly, the purchase rate at ball exchanges by showing the amount of *pachinko* balls that customers have been awarded;
- indications implying that customers can easily obtain a significantly large number of *pachinko* balls;
- indications representing, directly or indirectly, that activities will be

---

51   See Notification 102 dated 13 July 2012, issued by the director of Safety Division, Community Safety Bureau, National Police Agency.

conducted that violate any regulation on the charge for *pachinko* games; and

- indications implying that the parlour disregards the view that the result of a *pachinko* game might differ depending on the individual customer's skill.

The notice also confirms that announcements on the location of a *pachinko* parlour, the charge for *pachinko* games or the variety of prizes awards must not violate the advertising regulations.

9.2   Alcohol

The Act Concerning Liquor Business Associations and Measures for Securing Revenue from Liquor Tax sets out statutory standards on labelling for alcohol products in Japan.

Producers or sellers of alcoholic beverages must include the following information on the labels of their products an easily distinguishable way:

- their name or brand name;
- the location (address) of the place of production; and
- the volume of the container and the content of the product.[52]

The minister of finance may further specify:

- the manner in which producers or sellers of alcoholic beverages must label their alcoholic beverage containers with details on the manufacturing process or the quality of the alcohol used, and other matters similar thereto; and
- how the labelling must help to prevent underage drinking.[53]

Based on these provisions, four standards – including the Labelling Criteria Concerning the Prevention of Underage Drinking – have been enacted.

In addition to statutory requirements, fair competition codes for certain alcoholic beverages have been established based on Article 31 of the Misleading Representations Act. These fair competition codes work by means of self-regulation.

9.3   Pharmaceuticals

The Pharmaceutical Affairs Act regulates the advertisement of pharmaceuticals in Japan and sets out the following requirements, among others:

---

52   Article 86-5 of the Act Concerning Liquor Business Associations and Measures for Securing Revenue from Liquor Tax and Article 8-3 of the Order for Enforcement of the Act Concerning Liquor Business Associations and Measures for Securing Revenue from Liquor Tax.

53   Article 86-6 of the Act Concerning Liquor Business Associations and Measures for Securing Revenue from Liquor Tax and Article 8-4 of Order for Enforcement of the Act Concerning Liquor Business Associations and Measures for Securing Revenue from Liquor Tax.

- Article 68 provides that no one may advertise the name, manufacturing process, effects, efficacy or performance of pharmaceutical products or medical devices before they have received approval under Article 68 of the act;
- Article 66(1) prohibits advertising that describes or circulates false or exaggerated information with respect to the name, manufacturing process, effects, efficacy or performance of pharmaceutical products, cosmetics or medical devices; and
- Article 66(2) of the act prohibits advertising that describes or circulates false or exaggerated information that could mislead consumers into thinking that a doctor or other person has certified the effects, efficacy or performance of pharmaceutical products, cosmetics or medical devices.

Article 44 sets out the requirements for the labelling of poisonous drugs and harmful drugs. With respect to poisonous drugs, white lettering depicting the name of the product and the word 'toxin' must be positioned on a black background, and the immediate container or capsule must be framed in white.[54] With respect to harmful drugs, red lettering depicting the name of the product and the word '*geki*' (meaning 'harmful') must be positioned on a white background, and the immediate container or capsule must be framed in red.[55] Article 76-5 of the act prohibits the advertisement of designated substances (ie, psychotoxic substances and substances which could cause health and hygiene hazards if used in the human body), except in newspapers or magazines directed at medical industry professionals concerned with medical and pharmaceutical matters or natural science, or in other media principally targeted at those who use such designated substances for medical purposes.

The Pharmaceutical Affairs Act was revised in December 2019 to provide for the imposition of:

- administrative cease and desist orders in case of violations of Article 66(1) or 68 of the act;[56] and
- administrative surcharge payment orders in case of violations of Article 66(1) of the act.[57]

These revisions will take effect on 1 August 2021.

In addition to statutory regulations set out in the Pharmaceutical Affairs Act, the Standards for Fair Advertising Practices concerning Medicinal Products etc – a notice by the chief of the Pharmaceutical Bureau of the Ministry of Health, Labour and Welfare – regulates the advertisement of pharmaceuticals.

---

54 Pharmaceutical Affairs Act, Article 44(1).
55 *Ibid*, Article 44(2).
56 *Ibid*, Article 72-5, which will take effective on 1 August 2021.
57 *Ibid*, Article 75-5-2(1) of the Pharmaceutical Affairs Act.

9.4 Financial products and services

The Financial Instruments and Exchange Act lays down statutory regulations on ads for financial products and services. Article 37(1) of the act provides:

A financial instruments entrepreneur, etc shall indicate the following matters pursuant to the provisions of a Cabinet Office Ordinance when advertising the contents of his/her financial instruments business or conducting any similar acts specified by a Cabinet Office Ordinance:

- *the trade name or name of said financial instruments entrepreneur, etc.;*
- *the fact that said financial instruments entrepreneur, etc. is a financial instruments entrepreneur, etc., and his/her registration number; and*
- *the matters concerning the contents of the financial instruments business conducted by said financial instruments entrepreneur, etc., which are specified by a Cabinet Order as important matters that may have an impact on customers' judgment.*[58]

Furthermore, Article 37(2) prohibits a financial instruments entrepreneur or similar entity from giving any indication that is significantly contradictory to known facts or seriously misleading with regard to the projected profits from a financial instrument transaction or other matters specified by Cabinet Office ordinance, when advertising its financial instruments business or conducting similar activities.

The banking industry has established its own Fair Competition Code based on Article 31 of the Misleading Representations Act; while the Life Insurance Association of Japan has also developed Guidelines for Appropriate Representation of Life Insurance Products.

9.5 Food

(a) Food Labelling Act

As explained in section 1.1(b), the Food Labelling Act sets out comprehensive rules and regulations to ensure proper food labelling by establishing standards and specifying other necessary information regarding the labelling of food that is intended for sale. Originally, three statutes – the Food Sanitation Act, the Act on Standardisation of Agricultural and Forestry Materials and the Appropriate Quality Labelling and Health Promotion Act – individually regulated food labelling in Japan. The Food Labelling Act was enacted to integrate these acts in a single statute.

---

58   Under the Order for Enforcement of the Financial Instruments and Exchange Act, a financial instruments entrepreneur must include information on issues such as the following:
- fees;
- the risk that the customer may incur a loss due to fluctuations in the exchange rate, the value of currencies, quotations on the Financial Instruments Market and other indicators; and
- the risk that this loss may exceed the amount of a customer's margin or any other security deposit specified by a Cabinet Office ordinance as payable by the customer.

The prime minister must establish standards for the labelling of food that is intended for sale for each category of food and each category of person engaged in food-related business or similar, which help to ensure consumers' safe ingestion of food and autonomous and rational decision making in this regard (Food Labelling Standards).[59] The standards specify:

- the information that persons engaged in food-related business should display when selling food, including name, allergen information, preservation method, expiration date, ingredients, additives, nutritional value and caloric value and country of origin; and
- the labelling method and other information that persons engaged in food-related business should comply with when displaying the information set forth in the preceding bullet.

Persons engaged in food-related business must not sell food that is not labelled according to these standards.[60]

If a person engaged in food-related business sells food (excluding liquor) without displaying the information set forth in Article 4(1)(i) of the Food Labelling Act and as specified by the Food Labelling Standards, or fails to comply with the requirements of Article 4(1)(ii) and as specified by the Food Labelling Standards with regard to food that is intended for sale, the prime minister or the minister of agriculture, forestry and fisheries may instruct such person to display the labelling information or otherwise to comply with those requirements.[61]

The Food Labelling Standards include provisions on 'foods with health claims', which are allowed to indicate their function. This is the generic term used for food products containing ingredients that help to maintain and improve health. There are three labelling systems under the standards, as follows.

Foods for specified health uses (Article 2(1)(9)): The labels of such foods can include claims about specific health improvements that may be expected, such as "Helps to keep your digestive system healthy". To launch such products, permission must be obtained from the CAA once the government has evaluated the claimed effects and the safety of the product.

Foods with function claims (Article 2(1)(10)): This system was introduced in 2015 in order to make more products available with clear labelling on certain nutritional or health functions, to help consumers make more informed choices in this regard. Before marketing such products, food producers must submit the

---

59   Food Labelling Act, Article 4(1).
60   *Ibid*, Article 5.
61   *Ibid*, Article 6(1).

necessary information to the secretary general of the CAA, including scientific evidence of the safety and effectiveness of the product. Unlike for foods for specified health uses, the CAA does not evaluate the safety and effectiveness of foods with function claims in advance, and the producer need not obtain permission from the CAA to include function claims on food labels. However, the producer must make appropriate function claims based on scientific evidence for which they are responsible, obtained from clinical trials or systematic literature reviews. To make function claims, a pre-market notification must be submitted and the packaging must be labelled in accordance with the Food Labelling Standards pursuant to the Food Labelling Act, as well as the Guidelines on Notification of Foods with Function Claims.

Foods with nutrient function claims (Article 2(1)(11)): These can be used to supplement or complement daily nutrients (vitamins/minerals) that tend to be insufficient in everyday diets. If a food product contains certain amounts of nutrients whose function meets the Food Labelling Standards, the label can include a nutrient function claim as prescribed by the standards, without any need to submit a notification to the government.

(b) Act on Japanese Agricultural Standards

The Act on Japanese Agricultural Standards deals with the labelling of the quality of agricultural and forestry products, excluding food and drinks.

Article 59(1) of the act empowers the prime minister to enact standards for the labelling of the quality of agricultural and forestry products.[62] If an entrepreneur does not comply with the criteria set out in Article 59(1), the prime minister or the minister of agriculture, forestry and fisheries may instruct it to comply.[63]

(c) Food Sanitation Act

The Food Sanitation Act deals with food advertising. Under Article 19(1) of the act, the prime minister may establish the necessary criteria for the labelling of apparatus or containers and packaging for which such standards have been established under the act, with input from the Consumers' Commission. Furthermore, under Article 19(2), apparatus or containers and packaging for which labelling criteria have been established pursuant to Article 19(1) may not be sold, displayed for marketing purposes or otherwise used in business without labelling which conforms to those criteria.

In addition, Article 20 prohibits false or exaggerated labelling or advertising regarding food, additives, equipment, containers or packaging which may cause harm to public health.

---

62   Japanese Agricultural Standards, Article 60.
63   *Ibid*, Article 61(1).

(d)   Health Promotion Act

The Health Promotion Act regulates the labelling of food for special dietary uses (FOSDUs). FOSDUs are foods for which claims can be made about special purposes of use, such as support for infant growth and the health or recovery of pregnant or lactating women, patients with dysphagia and other patients. A producer that wishes to indicate that a food is suitable for one of these special dietary uses must obtain labelling permission from the prime minister.[64]

Under Article 43(6) of the act, anyone that intends to indicate special dietary uses and has obtained labelling permission under Article 43(1) must indicate the items in accordance with criteria stipulated by Cabinet Office ordinance. Under Article 65, no one can include an indication on a label that substantially differs from the declared content of the product or is likely to cause consumer confusion with respect to the effects of the product on health maintenance or promotion.

9.6   Tobacco

The Tobacco Industries Act sets out the statutory regulations on tobacco advertising in Japan.

According to Article 39(1) of the act, Japan Tobacco Inc – which is the sole manufacturer of tobacco products in Japan – or a wholesaler of imported tobacco must include on the product packaging the wording prescribed by ministerial ordinance, to attract attention to the relationship between tobacco consumption and potentially harmful effects on consumers' health. Under Article 36(4)(1) of the Ordinance for Enforcement of the Tobacco Industries Act, certain wording specified in the ordinance must be clearly displayed on the two dominant sides of tobacco packaging, using more than 50% of the surface area of each.

Article 36-2 of the ordinance provides that when Japan Tobacco Inc or a wholesaler uses on its packaging wording such as 'low tar', 'light', 'ultra-light' or 'mild' – which may lead some consumers to misunderstand the relationship between the consumption of manufactured tobacco products and health – the company must indicate that this wording does not mean that such products are less harmful to health than others.

Article 40 of the act further provides that anyone that advertises manufactured tobacco products must:

- take due care to prevent underage smoking;
- make clear the relationship between tobacco consumption and health; and
- endeavour to avoid excessive advertising of tobacco products.

---

64   Article 43(1) of the Health Promotion Act.

In addition to the statutory regulations mentioned above, the Tobacco Institute of Japan has established its own standards on tobacco advertising and sales promotions, and requires members to comply with those standards.

9.7   E-cigarettes

Under the Pharmaceutical Affairs Act, e-cigarettes which use liquid solutions containing nicotine are categorised as medical devices and such liquid solutions are categorised as medical drugs. Those e-cigarettes are not distributed in Japan. The regulations of the Pharmaceutical Affairs Act discussed in section 1.1(b) apply to the advertisement of such products.

Heated tobacco products, which use a special device to heat tobacco sticks, are popular in Japan. The tobacco sticks are categorised as 'tobacco products' under the Tobacco Industries Act and thus the regulations discussed in section 9.6 apply. In addition, the Tobacco Institute of Japan has established its own standards on tobacco advertising and sales promotions, which include provisions on heated tobacco products.

By contrast, the devices used to consume heated tobacco products are not categorised as 'tobacco products' under the Tobacco Industries Act. The standards of the Tobacco Institute of Japan include rules on such devices and members must comply with them.

Latvia

Pauls Ančs
Sarmis Spilbergs
Edvijs Zandars
Ellex Klavins

1.   Overview of the legal and regulatory regime for advertising

Advertising in Latvia is regulated generally through:

- the Advertising Law;[1]
- the Consumer Rights Protection Law;[2]
- the Unfair Commercial Practice Prohibition Law;[3] and
- the Law on Information Society Services.[4]

Additional rules on specific sectors or certain parties can be found in the Electronic Mass Media Law,[5] the Personal Data Processing Law,[6] the Competition Law[7] and other sector-specific legislation as described in section 9 of this chapter.

Many of the applicable rules are similar to those in other EU countries, since the Advertising Law and the Unfair Commercial Practice Prohibition Law encompass a multitude of provisions from the EU Comparative Advertising Directive (2006/114/EC) and the Unfair Commercial Practices Directive (2005/29/EC); while provisions of the Audio-visual Media Services Directive (2010/13/EU) have (among other things) been transposed into the Electronic Mass Media Law. Likewise, the E-commerce Directive (2000/31/EC), the General Data Protection Regulation (2016/679) (GDPR) and other advertising-related provisions of EU law have been transposed into Latvian laws and regulations, or are directly applicable.

The general principles encompassed in the Advertising Law and applicable to all ads require that advertising be lawful, truthful and objective, and accord with fair advertising practices. The Advertising Law also expressly prohibits discrimination, defamation, infringements of IP rights and the exploitation of the lack of experience of children and other persons or any effects created by fear and superstition.

---

1   *Latvijas Vēstnesis*, 10 January 2000, No 7 (1918).
2   *Latvijas Vēstnesis*, 1 April 1999, Nos 104/105 (1565/1565).
3   *Latvijas Vēstnesis*, 12 December 2007, No 199 (3775).
4   *Latvijas Vēstnesis*, 17 November 2004, No 183 (3131).
5   *Latvijas Vēstnesis*, 28 July 2010, No 118 (4310).
6   *Latvijas Vēstnesis*, 4 July 2018, No 132 (2018/132.1).
7   *Latvijas Vēstnesis*, 23 October 2001, No 151 (2538).

Several industry groups (eg, traders, brewers and pharmaceutical companies) have, as advertisers, developed self-regulatory codes with more detailed ethical behaviour rules. Members of the Latvian Advertising Association have also developed their own self-regulatory code, the Latvian Advertising Professionals' Code of Ethics, which contains rules on advertising that are mostly line with the provisions of law, but in some cases are more specific.

According to the Unfair Commercial Practice Prohibition Law, such industry codes are binding on companies and persons that have undertaken to observe them. Adverse actions that are contrary to the principles established in the specific code, if they have the potential to cause harm to consumers, are considered to be misleading commercial practices and may be punished with a fine of up to 10% of the trader's net revenue in the last financial year, but in any case of not more than €100,000. Thus, the approach to self-regulatory codes should be serious, not careless – incorrectly assuming that compliance is voluntary and that breaches are of no consequence could result in sanctions.

An 'ad' under the Advertising Law is defined as a "communication or endeavour in any form or means associated with economic or professional activity, intended to promote the popularity of or demand for goods or services (including immovable property, rights and obligations)". Accordingly, anything done to directly or indirectly promote certain products or services will typically qualify as advertising. Also, the practice of the local regulatory authority with responsibility for the protection of consumer rights and interests and supervision of the market, the Consumer Rights Protection Centre (CRPC), demonstrates that this definition is interpreted very broadly – for example, extending to the use of trademarks in sponsorship.[8] Sector-specific rules must also be observed in the dissemination of ads through different advertising platforms (eg, e-marketing, online journals, cookies, email marketing, radio, television).

In Latvia, issues with advertising usually arise due either to non-compliance with and breach of regulatory provisions or to violation of IP rights. The CRPC proactively enforces the Advertising Law and the Unfair Commercial Practice Prohibition Law. Violations of the advertising rules may result in fines of up to €14,500; however, the typical fine applied in practice is usually around one-tenth of that.

Competitors that believe their rights have been violated by a competitor's advertising may lodge an unfair competition claim in the Latvian courts and claim damages; enforcement authorities such as the CRPC or the Competition Council will not usually review disputes between two competitors. In limited cases, the CRCP will initiate a case upon the application of a company if it takes

---

8   Consumer Rights Protection Centre's Decision E03-PTU-K82-24 of 7 June 2012; and Consumer Rights Protection Centre Decision E03-PTU-K194-48 of 1 November 2012.

the view that the collective interests of consumers are affected; but mainly enforcement authorities will act only upon either their own initiative or a complaint by a consumer. There have been only a few civil law cases in the Latvian courts under unfair competition rules between two competitors. This is probably due to the length of such proceedings and the difficulty of proving the actual damage suffered. The interpretation of advertising rules mainly derives from the decisions of the regulatory authorities and from court decisions where the penalised advertiser has tried to challenge the decisions of the relevant authorities.

Possible infringements of IP rights via advertising may take several forms. The Latvian courts have previously ruled on the prohibition of using identical or highly similar claimants' trademarks in the defendant's advertising materials.[9] In a recent case, JC Bamford Excavators Limited successfully protected its family of registered trademarks, which includes the word mark JCB, against Latvian company SIA "JCB AGRI". The defendant had not only included the sign JCB in its registered name, but also used it in its business in relation to identical products and services. In addition, SIA "JCB AGRI" used the applicant's corporate colours in its advertising materials, such as booklets, cups, stationery and business cards. The courts of all instances recognised infringement of the exclusive rights of JC Bamford Excavators Limited and, among other things, prohibited SIA "JCB AGRI" from using the name JCB in its business documents and advertising.[10]

In a similar case, the court also found trademark infringement in the activities of the defendant's subsidiaries. Along with the court's decision prohibiting the defendant from using the trademark VIA 3L in the course of business, the use of this mark was prohibited in business documents and advertising.[11]

IP infringements are also often linked to unfair competition. For instance, in *Nestlé v Sara Lee Baltics*,[12] the court found that the use of a red cup in ads and campaigns where these cups were gifted to customers by Sara Lee Baltics not only infringed Nestlé's exclusive rights, based on its well-known red cup trademark, but also constituted unfair competition.

In Latvia, infringements of IP rights in advertising may also occur where a work protected by copyright is used in an ad without proper authorisation. The use of ideas and concepts contained in the ads of one telecommunications

---

9   Chamber of Civil Cases of the Supreme Court of the Republic of Latvia, Ruling PAC-739/2012 of 16 October 2012; Chamber of Civil Cases of the Supreme Court of the Republic of Latvia, Ruling PAC-0156 of 20 March 2012. See also Riga District Court ruling of 27 September 2004 in Case C-3471/2.
10   Supreme Court of the Republic of Latvia, Ruling SKC-103/2018 of 4 June 2018.
11   Chamber of Civil Cases of the Supreme Court of the Republic of Latvia, Ruling SKC-337/2017 of 28 December 2017.
12   Chamber of Civil Cases of the Supreme Court of the Republic of Latvia, Ruling PAC-739/2012 of 16 October 2012.

operator in ads for its rival is one example of such an occurrence.[13] A breach of copyright was also found to result from the unauthorised use of a song on a television broadcast and its ads; the claimants were awarded a total of LVL 25,000 (approximately €36,000) in damages.[14]

In another dispute, the Ethics Board of the Latvian Advertising Association declared the advertisement of a political party, which was created on the basis of publicly distributed and well-known Apple advertisements, unethical. The Ethics Board acknowledged once again that the use (including imitation, adaptation or borrowing) of an advertising idea or concept by another advertising professional violates the standards and ethical requirements of the advertising industry.[15] Although the Ethics Council is not competent to assess copyright infringement, such conduct would very likely also infringe copyright.

2. Comparative advertising

The Advertising Law defines 'comparative advertising' as "any type of advertising which uses a comparison that directly or indirectly refers to either a competitor or products or services offered by a competitor".

The meaning of 'indirect reference' was explained in a case[16] involving an ad containing the message: "Do not entrust your cartridges with anyone else but Baltic Office Service." Although the claimant competitors argued that they were being referenced indirectly, the court found that the ad was not comparative, since neither a direct nor an indirect reference was made towards other competitors. The claim was too general to allow anyone to identify any of the competitors of the Baltic Office Service as being those who "could not be entrusted with the cartridges".

In order to determine whether a general reference constitutes comparative advertising, the particular product or service market should be analysed. It should be considered whether the ad allows the average consumer to identify a particular competitor in the particular market. For example, in markets with very few operators (eg, mobile telecommunications), 'anyone else' would clearly mean the other few operators; whereas in saturated markets (eg, office supply providers), the average consumer would not know all other suppliers and so would be unable to associate 'anyone else' with a particular supplier. In a case concerning one of the biggest beer producers in Latvia, the court held that, given the wide recognition of this beer producer, a general reference towards 'beer producers' as such was enough to enable the average consumer to identify this producer through the particular ad.[17]

---

13   Ethics Board of the Latvian Advertising Association, Decision 02/2012 of 30 August 2012.
14   Chamber of Civil Cases of the Supreme Court of the Republic of Latvia, Ruling of 27 March 2008.
15   Ethics Board of the Latvian Advertising Association, Decision 01/2018 of 17 October 2018.
16   Administrative Regional Court, judgment of 14 December 2009 in Case A4264370.
17   Supreme Court judgment of 26 November 2004 in Case SKA-155.

Comparative advertising in general is permissible under the Advertising Law, as long as it complies with the following:

- It is not misleading;
- The comparison is made between products that are the same or that can be used for the same kinds of purpose;
- The comparison is objective;
- The comparison concerns material, typical, verifiable and related characteristics of the products;
- The ad does not discredit the competitor or its product;
- The ad does not make unfair use of any designation mark concerning the competitor or the reputation of the country of origin of the product; and
- The ad does not present products as being an imitation of other products that bear a registered trademark.

The regulatory authorities have dealt with issues of whether the particular products can be compared and whether the comparison is objective.[18] Whether the products may be compared is determined by taking into account characteristics of the product such as its use, as well as the charges that a consumer must bear in order to obtain the product.[19] If the compared products may be used for the same purposes, they will be considered as comparable. However, if the charges that the consumer must bear to obtain each product differ considerably, the products will not be considered comparable, even if the use of each product is similar. For example, the CRPC found that, although the use of two types of digital television services was similar, the fact that one provider charged extra for its digital video recording service while the other did not proved that the services were not comparable.

As regards the objectivity criterion, this is met if the information presented in the ad is genuine. This means that as long as the ad contains true facts about the characteristics of the competitor's product, the ad is objective.[20]

3. Online behavioural advertising

Following the implementation of the e-Privacy Directive (2009/136/EC) in May 2011 by the addition of new provisions to the Law on Information Society Services, there are rules on the legitimate use of cookies and similar technologies that are used, among other things, in relation to online behavioural advertising. At the time of writing, there is no case law or decisions of a regulatory authority in this area.

According to Article 71 of the Law on Information Society Services, the

---

18   Consumer Rights Protection Centre, Decision 4-nk of 7 July 2010; and Consumer Rights Protection Centre, Decision 21-06/552-K-161 of 22 January 2013.
19   Consumer Rights Protection Centre, Decision 21-06/552-K-161 of 22 January 2013.
20   Consumer Rights Protection Centre, Decision 21-06/552-K-161 of 22 January 2013.

storage of information or the acquisition of access to information stored on a user's device is permitted if the relevant person has provided his or her consent after receiving clear and comprehensive information regarding such storage or access. Consent is not necessary if the storage or acquisition of access to the information is necessary to provide a service requested by the person (necessary cookies); however, this exception will not apply in the case of cookies used for online behavioural advertising. This means that, in respect of cookie use for online behavioural advertising, prior informed consent is needed.

Thus far, the relevant regulatory authority – the Data State Inspectorate – has not issued any recommendations or guidance as to the actual means through which to obtain the consent referred to above. However, the Article 29 Working Party (an independent European working party that dealt with issues relating to the protection of privacy and personal data until the entry into force of the GDPR) has issued guidance on obtaining consent for cookies;[21] and recent judgments of the Court of Justice of European Union[22] have further clarified what is considered as lawful consent for cookies. According to the respective guidance and the case law, a requirement to use internet browser settings (ie, setting a browser in a mode where cookies are either permitted or not for all possible sites) or consent through the mere use of the website will not suffice in this regard and active consent from the user of the device must be obtained. This means that the individual must be informed about the use of cookies (eg, through cookie banners), and must have an option to choose the types of cookies that he or she wishes to accept (ie, before the cookies are saved on the device, the user must accept the cookies by ticking a checkbox or similar means). Consent must be active, meaning that checkboxes for the saving of cookies cannot be pre-ticked – the individual must tick them himself or herself if he or she so chooses.

Furthermore, the operator of the website which is responsible for the use of cookies must inform visitors to the website about:

- the purposes of each cookie;
- how long the cookies will be saved on the device; and
- whether and which third parties may access the information stored by the cookies.

Any processing of personal data in relation to online behavioural advertising (including arising from the use of cookies) is subject to the general rules on data protection stipulated by the GDPR – for example:

- the processing of personal data must have a legal basis (Article 6 of the GDPR); and

---

21   29 Working Party Working Document 02/2013 adopted on 2 October 2013.
22   Court of Justice of European Union Cases C-673/17 (*Planet49*) and C-40/17 (*Fashion ID*).

- relevant information about the data processing must be provided to the individual (Article 13 of the GDPR).

The general data protection principles stipulated in Article 5 must also be observed – for example:
- the data processing should not go beyond what is necessary for the aforementioned purpose of data processing;
- the data processing must be lawful, fair and transparent;
- the data must be accurate; and
- the integrity and confidentiality of the personal data must be ensured.

4. Sales promotions

The main sources of law that govern sales promotions are the Consumer Rights Protection Law and Cabinet Regulation 178 on procedures for displaying prices of products and services, adopted on 18 May 1999. Furthermore, according to Article 9 of the Unfair Commercial Practice Prohibition Law, the unfair use of sales promotions also falls within the scope of a misleading commercial practice. An advertiser that is found guilty of a misleading commercial practice may be subject to a financial penalty.

According to these laws, the use of the word 'sale' and similar terms in sales promotions is permissible only when:
- the sale concerns all or some of the products advertised;
- the sale is limited to a specified timeframe; and
- the prices have been reduced (with the original price and the price after reduction clearly displayed).

Wording such as 'discount', 'reduced prices' and similar may be used only in regard to products that the seller sells on a continuous basis, when the price reduction takes place within a specified timeframe and the prices have actually been reduced.

Some additional rules on sales promotions can be found in the Latvian Advertising Professionals' Code of Ethics, though this code is binding only on members of the Latvian Advertising Association. These rules stipulate, for example, that when advertising a product discount, the ad must show the actual reduction in price as compared with the original price of the product. Where discounts apply, the ad should also indicate all conditions affecting use of the discount. Moreover, as regards any offers of free merchandise, the code provides that a product can be advertised as being 'free of charge' only in those cases where the consumer need only pay normal delivery charges.

In one of its decisions,[23] the CRPC established that a product discount ad

---

23   Consumer Rights Protection Centre, Decision E03-PTU-K39-27 of 14 June 2012.

was misleading when the original price was lower than that indicated in the ad. In this particular case the product was not sold in Latvia, although it could be purchased in Latvia via the Internet. In order to determine the relevant price, the CRPC took into account the entire price range for this product on the Internet. In doing so, the CRPC established that the particular product could be purchased for a price lower than that indicated in the ad.

In another decision,[24] the CRPC established that a sales promotion which related to a special offer on digital television provision was misleading as it did not specify all conditions of the offer. When addressing the objections of the operator that it was not possible to include all information regarding the offer in the ad, the CRPC pointed out that the particular media used for the ad in this particular case – namely, a website and a printed brochure – did not preclude the inclusion of information regarding the nature of the contract. The CRPC noted, nevertheless, that there are cases in which the inclusion of all information is not possible and this will depend on the particular form of the ad.

The CRPC has also decided that another form of misleading practice in regard to sales promotions is the provision of incorrect information on the timeframe during which the particular offer is valid. For example, one case dealt with by the CRPC[25] concerned two ads issued within an interval of one week, which related to the same offer but contained different end dates for the offer. The CRPC found that this was unlawful.

Prize draws and competitions as a means of sales promotion may be advertised only if they have been confirmed with the Lotteries and Gambling Supervisory Inspection (LGSI). On top of the general advertising requirements, such ads must always mention the lottery permission number, as well as the location from which the terms and conditions of the campaign may be obtained. These rules apply to instances where a person must purchase a product or service in order to be eligible for a prize. If a contest is organised without requiring any purchase in order to participate, it does not qualify as a product or services lottery that must be confirmed with the LGSI.

5. Ambush marketing

At the time of writing, there is no law in Latvia that directly addresses ambush marketing. Neither the legislature nor any professional associations have provided any regulations or guidance in this regard.

Ambush marketing nonetheless exists in Latvia. Most often, operators have tried to associate their products with events such as the Nationwide Latvian Song and Dance Festival or popular sports events such as the Ice Hockey World

---

24   Consumer Rights Protection Centre, Decision E03-PTU-K60-37 of 19 July 2012.
25   Consumer Rights Protection Centre, Decision E03-PTU-K46-16 of 10 May 2012.

Championships. In practice, in Latvia – as in other countries – it is up to the event organisers to define the applicable rules for items that can be brought into events, and typically for security personnel to enforce these rules. Furthermore, in some instances violations of IP rights can be tied to ambush marketing, as well as unfair competition or unfair commercial practices, as possible tools in the prevention or penalisation of ambush marketing.

6. Direct marketing

Direct marketing is regulated in the Law on Information Society Services (which applies to electronic communications only), the GDPR and the Advertising Law (which apply to all forms of direct marketing).

Latvia follows the 'opt-in' and 'soft opt-in' principles with respect to email marketing directed towards individuals. This means that:

- the consent of the individual must be obtained before sending email messages to him or her (the opt-in principle); or
- the company may use email addresses that it has acquired in earlier transactions with individuals, provided that:
  - during these earlier transactions the individual did not object to email marketing;
  - the products advertised are similar to those that were offered during the earlier transactions; and
  - in each message the individual is informed about the possibility to unsubscribe (the soft opt-in principle).[26]

In relation to direct marketing campaigns directed towards individuals by using other electronic means (eg, by SMS or voice calls), only the opt-in principle applies, meaning that explicit consent must be acquired from the individual before any message is sent to him or her.[27]

In relation to any direct marketing sent to companies, only the opt-out principle applies. This allows email marketing without prior consent, but the sender must always allow and respect requests to unsubscribe.

Non-electronic marketing sent to individuals is not specifically regulated under Latvian law and therefore only the general advertising and data protection rules apply.

Consent obtained in the opt-in scenarios must comply with the requirements of the GDPR. The consent should be explicit. Accordingly, a pre-ticked website box will not be regarded as a means of valid consent in Latvia; but if the person has actively ticked the box, this will be acceptable. Even where

---

26   Law on Information Society Services, Article 9.
27   *Ibid* and Recommendation of the Data State Inspectorate, entitled "Transmission of Commercial Communication"

valid consent is obtained, in all subsequent marketing communications an 'unsubscribe' (ie, opt-out) option should be provided. Furthermore, according to the recommendation of the Data State Inspectorate entitled "Transmission of Commercial Communication", consent that is vague and too general will not suffice. For example, agreeing to a proposition such as "Do you agree to receive commercial mailings?" will not be regarded as valid consent, due to the vague nature of the proposition.[28] The individual must be informed about how his or her data will be processed, who will process it and the types of commercial mailings to which he or she has consented.

Non-personalised marketing via the postal service is not regulated in Latvia, although numerous companies and organisations have signed a self-regulatory memorandum undertaking to respect a recipient's wish not to receive non-addressed mail, where this wish is expressed through a corresponding sticker on mailbox. It is thus not prohibited to place marketing materials in mailboxes irrespective of the recipient. There are currently no official 'do not mail' or 'do not call' registers in Latvia.

7. Product placement

Product placement in Latvia is regulated by the Electronic Mass Media Law, which closely mirrors the provisions of the Audio-visual Media Services Directive (2010/13/EU). As in that directive, the Electronic Mass Media Law defines 'product placement' as "any form of audio-visual commercial communication consisting of the inclusion of or reference to a product, a service or the trademark thereof so that it is featured within a programme, in return for payment or for similar consideration". And as in the directive, the Electronic Mass Media Law allows product placement only in limited cases, when specific criteria are followed.

The Electronic Mass Media Law allows product placement in films and series made for audio-visual media services, sports programmes and light entertainment programmes, except for children's programmes. Product placement is also allowed where there is no payment, but only the provision of certain products or services free of charge, such as production props and prizes, with a view to their inclusion in a programme.

Programmes that contain product placement must meet the following requirements:

- Their content and scheduling can under no circumstances be influenced in such a way as to affect the responsibility and editorial independence of the media service provider;

---

28   Recommendation of the Data State Inspectorate, entitled "Transmission of Commercial Communication"; and Consumer Rights Protection Centre, Decision E03-PTU-K8-8 of 29 March 29 2012.

- They must not directly encourage the purchase or rental of products or services – in particular, by making special promotional references to those products or services;
- They must not give undue prominence to the product in question; and
- Viewers must be clearly informed of the existence of product placement.

Programmes containing product placement must be appropriately identified at the start and end of the programme and when a programme resumes after a commercial break, in order to avoid any confusion on the part of the viewer. There are currently no specific regulatory requirements on how product placement should be identified; but according to current practice, wording such as "Product placement is used in the programme" will suffice.

8. Native advertising and social media influencers

There are no specific, legally binding regulations in Latvia on social media influencers; however, they are subject to the requirements of all regulatory instruments that regulate advertising. The CRPC has indicated that the authors of digital content are performers of commercial practices; they are thus also subject to the Unfair Commercial Practices Prohibition Law and may be subject to sanctions for non-compliance with the regulatory requirements – for example, by providing false information or creating a false impression that they are acting for purposes unelated to economic or professional activities, or are representing themselves as consumers,[29] by not disclosing that their content is in fact advertising.

The CRPC has indicated that in communications with consumers, content creators must disclose the commercial nature of such communications – for example, through a hashtag or other means that signals that content has been created within the framework of, or has been influenced by, advertising, sponsorship or business cooperation.

The Association of Latvian Bloggers and Influencers, which was established in 2018, has developed guidelines in cooperation with the CRPC on the activities of influencers in relation to advertising. The guidelines set out principles on how consumers should be informed about advertising and explain when it is appropriate to use each specific hashtag. The content creator is free to indicate advertising in either Latvian or English.

Furthermore, the Association of Latvian Bloggers and Influencers has developed its own Code of Ethics, which states, among other things, that a content creator should provide references if the information is posted on behalf of a third party or the influencer is being rewarded. This code is not legally binding; however, each member of the association must sign the code, thus

---

29   Unfair Commercial Practices Prohibition Law, Article 11(22).

confirming that he or she will abide by it in good faith. Violations of the code of Ethics are reviewed by the board of the Association of Latvian Bloggers and Influencers.

A new Directive 2019/2161 has been adopted that amends the Unfair Commercial Practices Directive. The amendments extend the list of commercial practices which in all circumstances are considered unfair by supplementing this list with Point 23c, which states that submitting or commissioning another legal or natural person to submit false consumer reviews or endorsements, or misrepresenting consumer reviews or social endorsements, in order to promote products will be considered an unfair commercial practice. This could greatly affect social media influencers, who often review and endorse products. The provisions of Directive 2019/2161 will become effective on 28 May 2022.

9. Industry-specific regulation

9.1 Gambling

Gambling in Latvia is regulated by the Gambling and Lotteries Law. This law stipulates that the advertisement of gambling in Latvia is strictly prohibited outside the premises on which gambling is organised. Furthermore, only the name of the gambling location and the trademark of the gambling organiser can be indicated on the premises – no other form of advertising is permitted.

Given the rather general ban on the advertisement of gambling in Latvia, the industry has often tried to find creative ways to circumvent this restriction. Even so, the supervisory bodies – the LGSI, the National Electronic Mass Media Council (NEMMC) and the CRPC – proactively enforce the general ban, which has resulted in some interesting and useful court and regulatory guidance.

The concept of 'premises' is of general importance. The courts have defined 'premises' as any place where a person can access gambling services, including physical and virtual casinos and their respective websites.[30] In one decision the court regarded a gambling website as 'premises' on which gambling was organised under the Gambling and Lotteries Law.[31] Both 'bricks and mortar' and online gambling organisers have been fined by the relevant authorities for the dissemination of prohibited advertising in various forms and through various

---

30 Administrative Regional Court, Decision of 4 October 2013 in Case A420685510, para 10.
31 Administrative District Court, Decision of 30 January 2012 in Case A420685510 (1-125-12/6), para 7.
32 Administrative District Court, Decision of 28 May 2008 in Case A42559606, para 10.
33 Decision of the National Electronic Mass Media Council of 14 March 2013; www.neplpadome.lv/lv/sakums/padome/padomes-sedes/sedes-sadalas/par-azartspelu-reklamesanu-neplp-uzliek-tv3-6000-latu-naudas-sodu.html.
34 Consumer Rights Protection Centre, Decision E03-KREUD-32 of 10 June 2010.
35 Consumer Rights Protection Centre, Decision E03-PTU-K34-11 of 12 April 2012; and Consumer Rights Protection Centre, Decision E03-PTU-K64-19 of 31 May 2012.
36 Consumer Rights Protection Centre, Decision E03-PTU-K8-8 of 29 March 2012; and Administrative District Court Decision A420544312 of 13 March 2013.

channels, including newspapers,[32] electronic mass media,[33] websites,[34] cinemas,[35] direct marketing[36] and even a tent for football fans.[37]

Even the mere display of the trademark(s) of a gambling organiser is regarded as the advertisement of gambling. To illustrate, the Administrative District Court has previously found the display of a gambling organiser's trademark, when supplemented with the address of its premises and a visual image of cards, to constitute the advertisement of gambling.[38] Likewise, the CRPC has found the placement of an online gambling organiser's trademark together with its slogan on a tent set up for football fans during the UEFA Euro 2012 tournament to constitute the advertisement of gambling, as it undoubtedly promoted interactive gambling and the demand for it, as well as promoting the website that hosted the interactive gambling.[39] The NEMMC, in turn, has even regarded the advertisement of a bar that was owned by and operated under the same trade name as a well-known gambling organiser to constitute indirect advertising of the gambling organiser.[40]

The advertising ban is problematic from an enforcement perspective in the online environment. As many online betting and gambling sites that are legally available in Latvia are not established and licensed in Latvia, the LGSI finds it burdensome to enforce Latvian laws against such operators. Thus, fines are imposed on the local disseminators of such ads (ie, the media), not the advertiser, which – in line with general principles – should be responsible for the legitimacy (or otherwise) of the material. For example, a popular news website in Latvia was fined for hosting an ad for a website which allowed users to make their forecasts (bets/sweepstakes) on the outcome of certain events; although no gambling as such occurred on the advertised site, users were redirected to a gambling site whose advertisement was not permitted.

Finally, the LGSI may only effectively control '.lv' top-level domains, even though gambling advertising often appears on '.com' or '.net' sites which are popular among Latvian users.

9.2 Alcohol

The advertisement of alcoholic beverages in Latvia is regulated by the Handling of Alcoholic Beverages Law. The specific requirements of that law and other requirements relating to alcoholic beverages apply only to beverages that contain more than 1.2% alcohol by volume (ABV), or more than 0.5% ABV for beer.

The Handling of Alcoholic Beverages Law prohibits the advertisement of alcohol:

---

37   Consumer Rights Protection Centre, Decision E03-PTU-K134-45 of 11 October 2012.
38   Administrative District Court, Decision of 28 May 2008 in Case A42559606, para 10.
39   Consumer Rights Protection Centre, Decision E03-PTU-K134-45 of 11 October 2012.
40   Decision of the National Electronic Mass Media Council of 14 March 2013; www.neplpadome.lv/lv/sakums/padome/padomes-sedes/sedes-sadalas/par-azartspelu-reklamesanu-neplp-uzliek-tv3-6000-latu-naudas-sodu.html.

- in educational and healthcare institutions and on buildings and structures of such institutions;
- on mail correspondence and postal packages;
- on covers of books, magazines, newspapers and their attachments;
- on public transport vehicles and inside them; and
- in environmental advertising. Although 'environmental advertising' is not defined in the Handling of Alcoholic Beverages Law, the CRPC understands it to mean any advertising that is displayed in or moved to public spaces. In one decision the CRPC imposed a penalty of LVL 300 on a wine trader who had put price reduction posters showing wine bottles in the display windows of his shop. The CRPC argued that alcohol ads that are placed in publicly visible display windows have an effect equivalent to more common forms of environmental advertising, such as ads that are placed on stands in public places.[41]

The general requirement stipulated by the Handling of Alcoholic Beverages Law regarding the advertisement of alcoholic beverages is that all ads for alcoholic drinks must contain information that warns against the negative effects of alcohol consumption and informs about the prohibition to sell or give alcoholic drinks to minors, or to purchase alcoholic drinks for them. At least 10% of the content of the relevant ad must be allocated to this information. Furthermore, according to the Handling of Alcoholic Beverages Law, it is prohibited in an alcoholic beverage ad to:
- depict persons consuming alcoholic beverages;
- utilise state symbols of Latvia;
- express an opinion regarding alcoholic beverages as a means of medical treatment;
- associate alcoholic beverage consumption with sports activities or driving a means of transport;
- express views that alcoholic beverages have stimulant or sedative effects or help to solve personal problems;
- present abstinence or moderation in alcohol consumption in a negative light; or
- create an impression that consumption of alcoholic beverages ensures social or sexual success.

Irrespective of the purpose of an ad, the depiction of an individual consuming an alcoholic beverage is prohibited by the Handling of Alcoholic Beverages Law. The practice of the CRPC and the Administrative District Court has established that the consumption of an alcoholic beverage is depicted where

---

41   Consumer Rights Protection Centre, Decision E03-PTU-K10-2 of 30 June 2015.

the physiological process of consumption or tasting is demonstrated in a manner that clearly indicates the consumption of an alcoholic beverage, regardless of inclusion of the image of a person's mouth touching the liquid involved. In one case the CRPC fined an advertiser whose ads showed people standing around a table holding cognac glasses. The CRPC argued that although the persons were not explicitly shown consuming alcohol, the ad created an impression that consumption would immediately follow and therefore the ad infringed the prohibition on depicting persons consuming alcoholic beverages. The CRPC's position was later upheld by courts at two instances.[42]

The Electronic Mass Media Law prescribes that only beer and wine may be advertised in audio and audio-visual commercial communications. Among other things, these ads cannot feature or be targeted at minors. In addition, the advertisement of alcoholic beverages may not be associated with the development of physical capabilities or with driving a vehicle.

The Latvian Advertising Professionals' Code of Ethics[43] provides that advertising for alcoholic beverages must comply with the following requirements:

- Any self-regulatory regimes of companies involved in the manufacture and advertisement of alcoholic beverages must be followed;
- The ad must be placed on a platform where and at a time when it may be presumed that at least a majority of viewers have reached the minimum age to be eligible to purchase alcoholic beverages, should this be technologically and technically measurable;
- The use of objects, images, characters and so on that primarily attract the attention of persons under the minimum age to be eligible to purchase alcoholic beverages is prohibited; and
- Only persons aged 25 or older may take part in the ad.

The advertisement of alcohol-related trademarks of manufacturers of alcoholic beverages can also be viewed as the advertisement of alcoholic beverages. In one decision, the CRPC found an ad for a musical event that encompassed the verbal trademark of a well-known alcoholic beverage manufacturer to infringe the Handling of Alcoholic Beverages Law, as it did not contain the requisite warning. The local regulatory authority concluded that the trademark could only be associated with consumption of alcoholic beverages of the manufacturer and, thus, the placement of the trademark on the ad was considered to constitute the advertisement of its alcoholic beverages.[44] In another case the CRPC also considered the placement of the trademark of a beer

---

42   Regional Court, judgment of 24 March 2014 in Case 130067613.
43   www.lra.lv,webroot/file/uploads/files/Etikas_kodekss_10122014.pdf.
44   Consumer Rights Protection Centre, Decision E03-PTU-K82-24 of 7 June 2012.

manufacturer on a tent set up for football fans to constitute the advertisement of an alcoholic beverage.[45]

There are no specific legal provisions regarding the advertisement of alcoholic beverages online. According to case law, the advertisement of a website that allows the purchase of alcoholic beverages in itself does not qualify as the advertisement of alcoholic beverages. However, should the ad, in promoting a website that allows the purchase of alcoholic beverages, depict alcoholic beverages (and/or a particular brand), it could under certain circumstances be viewed as an ad for the alcoholic beverage.

9.3   Pharmaceuticals

The advertisement of pharmaceuticals is specifically regulated by the Pharmaceutical Law,[46] the Electronic Mass Media Law and Cabinet Regulation 378 adopted on 17 May 2011 under the title "Procedures for Advertising Medicinal Products and Procedures by Which a Medicinal Product Manufacturer is Entitled to Give Free Samples of Medicinal Products to Physicians". All measures that have the purpose of promoting sales of medicines qualify as advertising. For example, letters sent to pharmacies offering to sell certain medicines at a discount will be recognised as advertising.[47] Under Latvian law, only medicinal products with marketing authorisations that are valid in Latvia can be advertised.

The advertising regime differs depending on whether the ad is aimed at the general public or medical professionals. It is permitted to advertise to the general public over-the-counter (OTC) (ie, non-prescription) medicines at all times, and vaccines only during a vaccination campaign (when state authorities encourage vaccination in cases of emergency such as an unexpected outbreak of a disease). No other advertisement of pharmaceuticals to the general public is allowed. Prescription medicines may be advertised only to healthcare professionals and such communications should not be made available to the general public. The distribution of medical product samples to the general public for advertising purposes is not permissible; whereas a maximum of 1,000 samples per company per year can be distributed to healthcare professionals.

Ads targeted towards the general public, regardless of their form, must always contain:

- the name of the product;
- information on the correct use of the product;
- an invitation to read carefully the relevant information on the packaging;

---

45   Consumer Rights Protection Centre, Decision E03-PTU-K134-45 of 11 October 2012.
46   *Latvijas Vēstnesis*, 10 April 1997, No 103 (818).
47   Administrative District Court, judgment of 10 May 2012 in Case 1-1016-12/26.

- an invitation to consult a physician or pharmacist on the use of the medicinal product; and
- a warning (taking up no less than 10% of the total space of the ad) that the unnecessary use of medicinal products is harmful to health.

Cabinet Regulation 378 lists information that cannot be included in ads targeted at the general public. This prohibition includes statements that imply that:

- treatment may be provided via mail or in other similar ways; or
- diagnosis can be given without consulting a physician.

It is also prohibited to imply that:

- the product has no side effects; or
- use of the product will significantly improve the overall health of the person or the health of the person may deteriorate if the relevant product is not used (this does not apply to vaccine ads).

Also, ads cannot contain improper, alarming or misleading descriptions on possible recovery from negative outcome of a condition.

Lately, there have been instances in which the regulatory authority (the Health Inspectorate) has tried to fine magazines for publishing articles in which doctors recommended or described specific OTC medicines, even though these seemingly had no promotional purpose. The Health Inspectorate considers that the mention of medicines by name in such articles to also constitutes advertising, based on the broad definition of 'advertising of medicinal products', as provided in Article 86(1) of Directive 2001/83/EC on the Community code relating to medicinal products for human use. Whether this interpretation is correct will have to be decided by the courts.

As regards advertising targeted at medical professionals, the rules on the content are not as detailed as those relating to advertising targeted at the general public. The ad must contain at least:

- the most essential information that conforms to the description of the medicinal product;
- information on whether the product is a prescription medicine or an OTC medicine; and
- the date on which the ad was most recently reviewed.

The most important rule in the relationship between the pharmaceutical industry and healthcare professionals is that no material stimulus should be provided as an inducement to prescribe certain products. Thus, detailed codes of ethics have been drafted for interaction between the pharmaceutical industry and the healthcare industry and patient organisations.

9.4 Financial products and services

The main sources of regulation for the advertisement of consumer credit services is the Consumer Rights Protection Law and Cabinet Regulation 691 on the regulation on consumer credit, adopted on 25 October 2016. The Consumer Rights Protection Law prohibits the advertisement of consumer credit services, unless:

- the advertising is conducted by a credit services provider or a credit intermediary on the premises in which it carries out its economic activities;
- the advertising is conducted through a website or online system of the credit services provider or credit intermediary, which the consumer uses after receiving authorisation to use the service;
- the advertising is conducted by the credit services provider or credit intermediary through a mobile app which the consumer uses after receiving authorisation to use the service;
- the advertising is conducted by individually addressing the potential client on site or by telephone, where the consumer has provided his or her consent;
- the advertising is conducted by mail or email, where the consumer has provided his or her prior unambiguous consent; or
- in the case of the advertisement of products or services that are unrelated to credit (except on television or radio), a person other than the credit services provider or credit intermediary provides information on the possibility of financing payment through a credit agreement.

These restrictions have been criticised by the industry – and even by government institutions[48] – as excessive. The original aim was to restrict the advertisement of payday loans; but due to a poor legislative process, the advertisement of almost any type of credit service is now prohibited. For this reason, these restrictions are likely to be relaxed at some point in the future.

This prohibition does not apply to the advertisement of the logos of credit services providers. However, the advertisement of such logos (including sponsorship) is prohibited on radio or television in publicly procured programmes that are financed by state or municipal budgets.

Cabinet Regulation 691 sets out detailed requirements on the advertisement of credit services. According to Chapter III, ads must not encourage irresponsible borrowing or provide information on the possibility for people with a poor credit history to obtain credit.

As regards the content of ads, where an ad contains information on the

---

48   www.lsm.lv/raksts/zinas/ekonomika/neplp-ludz-saeimu-parskatit-kreditesanas-reklamas-ierobezo jumus.a360359/.

charges relating to the credit (eg, an interest rate), the following information must be included:

- the borrowing rate (fixed, variable or both), together with information on the applicable charges included in the total cost of the credit to the consumer;
- the total amount of credit;
- the annual interest rate of charge;
- the duration of the credit agreement, if applicable;
- in the case of credit in the form of deferred payment for specific products or services, the price of the products or services and the amount of any initial payment;
- the total amount payable by the consumer and the amount of the instalments, where possible; and
- the obligation to conclude a contract for ancillary service related to the credit agreement, if the conclusion of such a contract is compulsory in order to obtain the credit or to obtain it on the advertised terms and conditions, and the cost of that service cannot be determined in advance.

This information must be presented on certain occasions in the form of a clear and representative example. This rule applies to ads concerning:

- overdraft credit;
- credit for immovable property;
- credit that requires the deposit of security; and
- short-term credit.

The overall impression of the ad should also be considered. In one instance, an ad for credit read, in large, red letters, "Loan without monthly interest"; but at the bottom of the ad, in small, white letters, was a description of additional payments due to obtain the loan. The CRPC found this to be misleading advertising – a decision which was subsequently confirmed by the regional court. The court found that the ad as a whole was misleading, because although descriptive text on the additional payments had been included, it was visually inconspicuous and the average consumer could only be expected to pay attention to the large, visually prominent text.[49]

9.5 Food

In addition to the harmonised requirements of EU acts, such as Regulation (EU) 1169/2011 on the provision of food information to consumers and Regulation (EC) 1924/2006 on nutrition and health claims, the advertisement of specific

---

[49] Administrative Regional Court, judgment of 1 June 2017 in Case A420163016.

categories of food is regulated by specific provisions encompassed in regulations of the Cabinet of Ministers. For example, special provisions on the advertisement of food supplements were introduced as a result of the implementation into Latvian law of Articles 6 and 7 of Directive 2002/46/EC on the approximation of the laws of the member states relating to food supplements. These prescribe that advertising must not:

- attribute to food supplements the property of preventing, treating or curing a human disease, or refer to such properties; or
- include any mention or implication that, in general, a balanced and varied diet cannot provide appropriate quantities of nutrients.

Specific to Latvia is a provision that only food supplements which are included in the Register of Food Supplements maintained by the Food and Veterinary Service can be advertised. Additionally, the ad must be accompanied by the declarations "Food supplement" and "Food supplement does not replace a complete and balanced diet", which must also take up at least 5% of the space of the ad. These provisions are among the most commonly infringed by players in the food advertising industry in Latvia.

The CRPC recently found that an ad broadcast on television breached the rules on the advertisement for food supplements because it misled consumers into thinking that a certain food supplement could treat cancer.[50] The CRPC has also found certain specific health claims used in advertising to be contrary to the health claims registered in the Register of Food Supplements, and to be misleading as suggesting that the food supplement could cure diseases.[51]

Latvia has also implemented special requirements on energy drinks. The Law on the Handling of Energy Drinks prohibits the advertisement of energy drinks in educational institutions and on buildings and structures of such institutions. The advertisement of energy drinks (as well as audio and audio-visual commercial communications relating to energy drinks) may not be targeted at persons under the age of 18 and it is prohibited to depict such persons in ads for energy drinks or audio and audio-visual commercial communications relating to energy drinks. Audio and audio-visual commercial communication relating to energy drinks are prohibited in broadcasts of electronic mass media which are targeted at persons under the age of 18, and before or after such broadcasts. Also prohibited is advertising in press publications whose target audience is persons under the age of 18.

In cases of permitted advertising, the Law on the Handling of Energy Drinks requires that at least 10% of the ad space be allocated to a warning about the

---

50   Consumer Rights Protection Centre, Decision 1-pk of 23 March 2012.
51   Consumer Rights Protection Centre, Decision E03-PTU-K42-32 of 5 July 2012; Consumer Rights Protection Centre, Decision E03-PTU-K83-36 of 19 July 2012; and Consumer Rights Protection Centre, Decision E03-PTU-K56-43 of 6 September 2012.

negative effects of excessive consumption of energy drinks. Additionally, the ad must not create the impression that energy drinks should be used:

- when participating in sports competitions or performing individual or organised activities for the preservation or improvement of health, or to quench thirst when participating in such activities; or
- together with alcoholic beverages.

9.6 Tobacco

According to the Law on the Handling of Tobacco Products, Herbal Products for Smoking, Electronic Smoking Devices and Their Liquids ('Tobacco Law'), 'advertising' is:

any form of commercial communications (for example, printed work, posters, adhesives, advertising images on walls, radio broadcasts and television broadcasts, clips, films, and videos), as well as an activity with the objective to directly or indirectly promote the purchase or consumption of tobacco products, electronic smoking devices, or refill containers, including placement of products in retail outlets, using different effects promoting consumption [for example, words (slogans), forms, shapes, images, colours, light and sound effects].

This definition is very broad and basically covers any action which seeks to promote the consumption of tobacco products.

The advertisement of tobacco products in Latvia is generally prohibited, except in:

- publications which are intended strictly for professionals in the tobacco trade engaged in the sale of such products; and
- publications that are printed and published in third countries, where those publications are not principally intended for the EU market.

This permitted type of advertising must not be made accessible to Latvian consumers.

According to the Tobacco Law and the Advertising Law, it is prohibited to:

- manufacture or trade in sweets and snacks, toys or other articles in the form of smoking products, such that they might attract the attention of minors (persons under the age of 18);
- depict minors in ads for tobacco products or target such ads at minors;[52]
- depict persons smoking in any ads, whether for tobacco products or otherwise;
- include misleading or false information, or otherwise misinform consumers in a manner that might create an erroneous impression of the characteristics of such products, their effect on health, the risks

---

52   This requirement is stipulated in Article 5(3) of the Advertising Law. For the avoidance of doubt, the Tobacco Law imposes a general ban on the advertisement of tobacco products to consumers.

associated with their consumption and the substances to which consumers are exposed when consuming these products;

- distribute tobacco products free of charge for advertising purposes; or
- place on the unit pack or any outer packaging of tobacco products a depiction of the symbols of the state of Latvia, images of natural persons (other than the natural persons depicted in the combined health warnings) or cartoons.

In practice, the CRPC strictly enforces the general ban on the advertisement of tobacco products. It has previously found that the use of the trademark of a tobacco manufacturer in an ad on various platforms that sought to raise awareness of the dangers of smuggled cigarettes constituted the advertisement of tobacco products because, in the CRPC's view, the promotion and dissemination of a tobacco manufacturer's name and/or trademark cannot be seen to have any purpose other than promoting sales of its products.[53] The placement of specific tobacco products separate from other tobacco products – for example, in order to emphasise a special discount price – has also been held to constitute the advertisement of tobacco products.[54]

Since 20 October 2020, it is prohibited to display tobacco products at retail points of sale, with the following exceptions:

- duty-free shops;
- on ships engaged on international voyages; and
- in specialised shops for tobacco products and their accessories that are situated in constructively separate premises that have their own entrance, as long as the products and their trademarks are not visible from the outside.

New products were recently introduced to the Latvian market which could appeal to the consumers of tobacco products. One such product is a tobacco-free nicotine pouch which is basically the same product as tobacco snus, except it does not contain tobacco. This product is not as yet directly regulated by any legislative acts regulating tobacco products; however, the Parliament is working on amendments to the Tobacco Law which would regulate these new products under the product category "tobacco substitute product". When finally adopted, the amendments will become part of the law and the general advertising ban will also apply to these products. What is more, the competent authority has issued an opinion on this kind of product which suggests that until it is directly regulated under the Tobacco Law, some requirements set out

---

53   Consumer Rights Protection Centre, Decision E03-PTU-K59-29 of 14 July 2012.
54   Consumer Rights Protection Centre, Decision E03-KREUD-45 of 12 August 2010; and Consumer Rights Protection Centre, Decision E03-KREUD-34 of 17 June 2010.

in the Tobacco Law may be applied to it by analogy. Although the competent authority has not directly mentioned the advertising ban set out in the Tobacco Law as among those requirements that are already considered applicable to such products, it has suggested that once the product is regulated under the Tobacco Law, the advertising ban will also likely apply to this kind of product. Thus, there is a risk that the competent authority may apply the general advertising ban to such products until the amendments to the Tobacco Law become effective.

9.7   E-cigarettes

E-cigarettes in Latvia are regulated by the Law On the Handling of Tobacco Products, Herbal Products for Smoking, Electronic Smoking Devices and Their Liquids (see section 9.6). The same advertising ban that applies to tobacco products also applies to e-cigarettes.

The CRPC recently imposed a fine of €2,000 on a retailer of electronic smoking devices for placing an ad for e-cigarettes next to its sales point. The CRPC concluded that this constituted advertising, as its purpose was to promote the sale of this kind of product; and further that the ad misinformed consumers about the harm associated with the consumption of such products.[55]

What is more, public opinions and legislative proposals issued by the competent authorities suggest that the advertisement of heated tobacco products is not directly regulated under the Tobacco Law and does not fall under the general advertising ban. However, pursuant to the amendments to the Tobacco Law discussed in section 9.6, they will be regulated under the amended legislation and the general advertising ban will thus also apply to these products once the amendments have been adopted on their final reading in Parliament.

The authors would like to thank Anna Marta Nordmane, Kaspars Olševskis and Mikijs Zīmecs for their invaluable assistance in the preparation of this chapter.

The publisher acknowledges the contribution of Zane Akermane to this chapter in the previous edition.

---

55   Consumer Rights Protection Centre, Decision 6-pk of 8 June 2020.

Mexico

Carlos Dávila-Peniche
Marina Hurtado-Cruz
Baker McKenzie Mexico

1. Overview of the legal and regulatory regime for advertising

Advertising in Mexico is regulated under many different laws and standards set by different authorities. There is no specific statute that covers all aspects of advertising law. The applicable regulations may vary considerably, depending on the product or service, the medium and the type of advertising. The main regulations and regulatory include the following.

1.1 Federal Consumer Protection Law

The Federal Consumer Protection Agency (PROFECO) is responsible for enforcing the Federal Consumer Protection Law in Mexico.

The Federal Consumer Protection Agency regulates the advertisement of all products and services in general, excluding professional services derived from employment relationships, corporate transactions and financial services. It also regulates promotions, offers, door-to-door and online sales, and warranties.

The Federal Consumer Protection Law and PROFECO internal guidelines require that all information relating to a product or service advertised in any medium be truthful and verifiable, meaning that it must be supported by technical or scientific evidence where appropriate – even when the product displays text indicating the approval or recommendation of a professional association. Even if it is truthful, advertising cannot be misleading due to the inclusion of inaccurate, false, exaggerated or partial information. The use of categorical terms (ie, that affirm or deny something absolutely) can be considered potentially misleading. In addition, it is prohibited to discredit competitor establishments, products, services or brands by means of false or misleading information.

In addition, PROFECO has the power to:

- publish information relating to products or services that do not comply with the law;
- provide information to consumers or authorities about defective or harmful products;
- recall products in the interest of public safety;
- destroy products that put consumers' lives or health at risk; and
- provide non-binding reviews of ads prior to launch (copy advice).

Compliance with the Federal Consumer Protection Law is enforced by PROFECO through proceedings that can be initiated *ex officio* or pursuant to third-party complaints. Further evidence and information are gathered through an inspection carried out by PROFECO, including verification of labelling, prices, quantities, quality, warranties, contents and advertising. If there is sufficient evidence of non-compliance with the Federal Consumer Protection Law, PROFECO may impose precautionary measures and will initiate sanction proceedings. These precautionary measures may include:

- seizure of products;
- suspension of the commercialisation of products or services;
- removal from the market of products or services; and
- orders to suspend advertising.

Based on the information provided by the parties and obtained by PROFECO in the proceeding, a decision will be issued. Sanctions will be determined on the basis of:

- the damage caused to consumers;
- the intentional nature of the offence; and
- the economic condition of the infringer.

The sanctions range from fines of up to approximately $250,000 to prohibitions on the commercialisation of products or services. In case of recidivism, an additional fine of up to 10% of the annual gross income obtained through the commercialisation of the relevant products or services in the last fiscal year in which the offence was committed may be imposed.

Fines are directly imposed by PROFECO. If the infringer pays the fine within 30 business days of service of the fine, a 50% discount will apply, as long as the fine is not challenged.

1.2 General Health Law and Health Advertisement Regulation

The Commission for the Protection of Sanitary Risks (COFEPRIS) is responsible for enforcing the General Health Law and its various regulations, including the Health Advertisement Regulations.

The General Health Law and the Health Advertisement Regulations regulate the advertisement of:

- over-the-counter (OTC) drugs;
- drugs restricted to health professionals;
- homeopathic drugs;
- herbal remedies;
- food supplements;
- medical devices;
- psychotropic substances and narcotics;

- food and non-alcoholic beverages;
- alcoholic beverages and tobacco;
- cleaning and beauty products and related services;
- pesticides and fertilisers; and
- health services in general.

The information contained in ads relating to the quality, origin, purity, conservation or nutritional properties of regulated products must be verifiable; and ads must include instructional and educational content.

The prior authorisation of COFEPRIS is required to advertise certain products, such as OTC drugs and alcoholic beverages. Prior notification of COFEPRIS is required to advertise other products, such as food and cosmetics; while for other products, it is necessary only to comply with the General Health Law and regulations.

Before advertising any product or service, it is important to determine whether a prior permit is required to commercialise the product, since advertising information may be subject to restrictions stated in the sanitary permit. The table on the following page is a short list of examples; however, the list is not exhaustive.

COFEPRIS has the power to order the suspension of advertising that may contravene the General Health Law and regulations. Those responsible for the advertising must suspend the ad within 24 hours in the case of radio, film or television advertising, or ads on public roads. If the advertiser does not comply, COFEPRIS may directly request the relevant dissemination channel to suspend the ad within the following 24 hours, by sending a suspension notice together with a copy of the notification issued to the advertiser.

Failure to comply with the General Health Law and regulations can result in:

- warnings;
- fines of up to $50,000;
- provisional or definitive closures; and
- arrest for up to 36 hours.

Sanctions are determined by COFEPRIS on the basis of:

- the damage caused to consumers;
- the seriousness of the infringement;
- the economic situation of the infringer; and
- the benefit obtained by the infringer.

During the proceedings, COFEPRIS can perform verification checks and impose preliminary measures, such as preventing media outlets from specific advertising that may infringe the law and imposing sanctions if they do not comply.

Table 1. Commercialisation and advertising requirements for specific products

Product/service	Commercialisation requirement	Advertising requirement
OTC drugs (sold to the general population)	Marketing authorisation	Prior advertising authorisation
Prescribed products (sold to health professionals only)	Marketing authorisation	Advertising notification
Medical devices	Marketing authorisation	Prior advertising authorisation
Herbal remedies	Notification	Prior advertising authorisation
Food supplements	Consultation to classify the product	Prior advertising authorisation
Cosmetics	Notification	Advertising notification per brand
Alcoholic beverages	None	Prior advertising authorisation
Food and non-alcoholic beverages	None	Advertising notification. Advertisers of some high-calorie food and beverages may require authorisation to advertise their products on television and movie theatres during restricted schedules.

1.3 Industrial property law

The Mexican Industrial Property Act (MIPA), in full force and effect since 1991, as well as the recently published Federal Industrial Property Protection Act (FIPPA), which replaced MIPA as from 5 November 2020, protect a number of IP rights (eg, patents, industrial designs, trademarks, slogans, non-traditional trademarks and trade dress), and further aim to prevent unfair competition. This legal framework includes administrative infringement actions for the following unlawful activities:

- generic unfair competition acts relating to IP rights;
- confusing, misleading or deceptive actions in commerce, such as suggesting that:
  - an association exists between the advertiser's establishment and that of a third party; or
  - products or services are manufactured according to specifications, licences or authorisations from a third party; and
- actions that seek to or successfully denigrate the products, services, industrial or commercial activity or establishment of another party, as well as tendentious, false or exaggerated comparative advertising, under the terms set out in the Federal Consumer Protection Law. This infringement action is independent and separate from a Federal Consumer Protection Law action.

The Mexican Institute of Industrial Property (IMPI) is competent to hear such cases in the first instance. The plaintiff has the burden of proving that an infringement exists. IMPI will assess the evidence and arguments filed by the parties and issue a resolution declaring whether the plaintiff has demonstrated the existence of an infringement, through the evidence filed. Once IMPI has issued a resolution, the affected party can challenge its validity before the federal courts on two occasions, before the resolution becomes definitive. If the federal courts confirm the infringement, the affected party can bring a damages claim against the infringer. The plaintiff can file this claim either as a civil claim before a federal court or with IMPI directly, through a specific instrument under FIPPA. In any case, the plaintiff must present sufficient evidence to show the actual damages and lost profits caused as a direct consequence of the infringement.

Additionally, the plaintiff can request IMPI to apply certain remedies as a preliminary injunction during the infringement proceedings. MIPA provides for the following remedies:

- the withdrawal from circulation or a ban on the distribution of infringing merchandise;
- the withdrawal from circulation of infringing advertising materials, tags, paperwork and similar infringing articles;
- the seizure of implements or instruments intended or used for the manufacture, preparation or production of infringing materials;
- an immediate prohibition on the marketing or use of the infringing products or services;

- the seizure of infringing products;
- the suspension or discontinuation, by the infringer or third parties, of infringing acts; and
- the suspension of service or closure of an establishment, where all other remedies are insufficient.

To be granted such measures, the plaintiff must prove the following to IMPI:
- ownership of its rights; and
- either:
  - the provision of sufficient security to cover any damages that may be suffered by the party against which the measure is sought; or
  - the provision of the necessary information to identify the infringing products, services or establishments.

Where infringement is proved, IMPI may apply one or more of the following sanctions:
- a fine of up to $86,000;
- a daily fine of up to $2,170 for each day on which the infringement persists;
- the temporary closure of an establishment for up to 90 days;
- the definitive closure of an establishment; and
- arrest for up to 36 hours.

Finally, under FIPPA, the domestic environment for unfair competition enforcement has become more stringent.

1.4 Copyright law

The Federal Copyright Law, in full force and effect since 1996, and as most recently amended in July 2020, sets out the legal framework for the protection of original forms of expressions, including literary and artistic works, audio-visual works, musical compositions, databases, software and folklore. The law also protects other types of rights, such as:
- neighbouring rights for interpreters, executioners, phonogram publishers and broadcasting organisations; and
- traditional rights.

The Mexican copyright system is based on a civil law system, rather than the US copyright model. Following the international treaties, the Federal Copyright Law provides protection derived from the moral and economic rights of authors, copyright and neighbouring rights titleholders. With regard to moral rights, the law protects:
- the right to disclose the work or keep it unpublished;

- the right of paternity;
- the right of integrity;
- the right of modification;
- the right to withdraw the work from commercial trade;
- the right of attribution; and,
- the right against false attribution.

With regard to economic rights, the law protects:
- the right of reproduction;
- the right of communication to the public;
- the right of broadcast or transmission;
- the right of distribution; and
- the right of adaptation.

While moral rights endure for the author's lifetime, the typical duration of economic rights is the author's life plus 100 years thereafter. The typical duration of neighbouring rights is 75 years from:
- the first fixation of the interpretation or execution in a phonogram;
- the first interpretation or execution of a work not fixated in a phonogram; or
- the first transmission on radio, television or any other means.

The Federal Copyright Law also protects the following rights relating to advertising:
- a person's self-image, which is akin to publicity rights (see section 1.5), derived from its hybrid regulation in the Mexican legal system;
- the *reserva de derechos*, which is exclusive to the Mexican copyright system and provides exclusive rights for the following types of creative expressions for a five-year period:
  - certain types of advertising promotions which constitute new methods to promote and offer products or services, with the additional incentive of offering another product or service under more favourable conditions than the usual conditions;
  - the names and physical or psychological characteristics of characters with human traits, or fictional or symbolic characters; and
  - persons or groups dedicated to artistic activities;
- with regard to the use of music compositions, the synchronisation right, which grants the publisher the right to authorise or prohibit the use of a musical composition as a simultaneous incorporation, whether total or partial, of a musical work with a series of images, producing a sensation of movement. Advertisers commonly obtain the right to use a musical composition as part of an audio-visual ad; and

- traditional indigenous rights, which apply to literary and artistic works and popular art derived from popular culture or expressions of traditional culture, or based on the multicultural composition of the Mexican state, as manifested in the cultural and identity of indigenous peoples and communities.

The law envisages certain defences for unauthorised copyright use, such as the following:
- a quote, provided that it is not a simulated and substantive reproduction of the work;
- the reproduction of published works relating to current events, unless explicitly prohibited by the title holder;
- the reproduction of part of a work for scientific, literary or artistic critique or investigation;
- private copying; and
- the reproduction, communication and distribution of works visible from public spaces, including drawings, paintings, photographs and audio-visual works.

In connection with copyright infringement, the Federal Copyright Law provides for a hybrid enforcement system, including a conciliation procedure, in addition to civil, administrative and criminal remedies and actions. Typically, copyright titleholders tend to rely on civil and administrative remedies to enforce their rights. The approach will vary depending on the right infringed and the litigation strategy. The affected party may choose between:
- filing a civil claim before a judge for contractual breach and damages resulting from unauthorised copyright use and exploitation; and
- pursuing an administrative copyright infringement action with IMPI.

Additionally, the National Copyright Institute has jurisdiction to hear cases relating to the infringement of moral rights. Finally, the Federal Copyright Law and the Federal Criminal Code recognise offences relating to the intentional unauthorised reproduction and exploitation of copyright on a commercial scale.

1.5   Publicity rights

Mexican law regulates self-image rights, akin to publicity rights, in two separate and independent instruments, which require appropriate clearance for use to avoid potential claims due to unauthorised use. On the one hand, the Federal Copyright Law expressly regulates an individual's portrait. On the other hand, state civil codes protect an individual's image as part of his or her personal traits which are subject to human rights, increasing the commercial risks involved where a third party uses or exploits personal traits – including the right to image and voice – without authorisation.

Under the Federal Copyright Law, the right to exploitation of an individual's portrait is usually invoked to enforce the self-image rights of models and celebrities. However, the scope of this protection is not limited to such individuals; anyone can raise an infringement action based on this right. A specific administrative infringement claim may be brought against such unauthorised use, which must be filed with IMPI, which has jurisdiction over this type of infringement.

In parallel, subject to the regulation and requirements of each state's civil code, an individual can take action against any unauthorised use of his or her personal image or likeness, including his or her voice, through the appropriate civil actions foreseen under each state's civil code, which usually relate to moral damages. This approach is independent from administrative infringement under the Federal Copyright Law. An affected party can file a civil action and an administrative infringement in parallel for the unauthorised use of his or her image, which increases the importance of obtaining appropriate clearance of such rights for use in advertising.

1.6 Federal Law of Telecommunications and Broadcasting

The Federal Law of Telecommunications and Broadcasting is enforced by the Federal Institute of Telecommunications (IFT). The purpose of this law is to regulate:

- the use and exploitation of the radio electric spectrum, public telecommunications networks, orbital resources, satellite communications and broadcasting services of general interest;
- the rights of users and audiences; and
- competition and free participation in these sectors.

The Federal Law of Telecommunications and Broadcasting contains some specific provisions on advertising. It states that in order to avoid the transmission of misleading advertising, without affecting freedom of expression, the transmission of publicity or propaganda presented as journalistic or news information is forbidden. In addition, the advertisement of products or services on restricted television that is not available in the Mexican market must include visual or sound resources that indicate this fact. Television operators must include this provision in their respective agreement with programmers. In relation to the advertisement of lotteries or draws, a prior permit from the Ministry of the Interior is required. Likewise, advertising relating to the practice of medicine and controlled healthcare products requires the prior authorisation of COFEPRIS.

Under the Federal Law of Telecommunications and Broadcasting, the IFT ensures that programming directed at children respects the values and principles, health regulations and guidelines established by the IFT. Furthermore, advertising directed at children must not:

- promote illegal or violent behaviour, through either real or animated characters;
- present children or adolescents as sexual objects;
- exploit the immaturity of children to persuade them of the benefit of products or services;
- incite children to buy or request the purchase of a product;
- promote or incite bullying; or
- contain subliminal messages.

The IFT has the power to verify and order the suspension of advertising that could violate the law. Where the IFT finds that advertising contravenes the law, it will notify COFEPRIS, PROFECO or the Ministry of the Interior, which will exercise powers of sanction.

1.7   Self-regulatory bodies

In Mexico, the various industries of the private sector commonly have their own self-regulatory bodies, which issue good practice guidelines and codes of conduct for members. Most of these bodies have ethical codes that regulate advertising. Compliance with these codes is mandatory for members. Many of these bodies have entered into agreements with the authorities to help ensure compliance with the applicable law.

The objective of these self-regulatory bodies is to create mechanisms that promote responsible commercial expression. Their ethical codes include additional rules to those that are legally binding. In most cases, these bodies provide members with advertising copy advice services, as well as advertising dispute resolution proceedings, which may be cheaper and faster than going to the corresponding authorities.

One of the main self-regulatory bodies is the Self-Regulation National Council (CONAR), which enforces its ethical code on advertising in general and advertising addressed to children. If a party is found to be in breach of the code, CONAR may issue an order to modify or suspend advertising through any medium. Failure to comply can lead to the member's suspension or expulsion. Another relevant self-regulatory body is the National Chamber of the Personal Care and Home Industry, which again has a specific code of conduct for these industries and has similar proceedings. Even though the decisions of self-regulatory bodies are not binding on non-members, they do prompt authorities such as COFEPRIS and PROFECO to initiate legal proceedings.

The pharmaceutical industry has similar self-regulating provisions. The Council for Ethics and Transparency of the Pharmaceutical Industry (CETIFARMA) has a Code of Good Promotional Practices. CETIFARMA is an internal body of the National Chamber of the Pharmaceutical Industry in Mexico. A Code of Interaction with Healthcare Professionals has also been issued by the Mexican Association of Innovative Industries of Medical Devices.

2. Comparative advertising

In Mexico, comparative advertising is allowed as long as it is truthful. However, it is important to ensure that other rights, such as IP rights, are not affected. The main laws that regulate comparative advertising are outlined below.

2.1 Federal Consumer Protection Law

The Federal Consumer Protection Law regulates advertising in general and establishes that all information relating to a product or service advertised on any medium should be truthful and verifiable, meaning that it must be supported by technical or scientific evidence where appropriate. Even if it is truthful, advertising cannot be misleading by means of inaccurate, false, exaggerated or partial information. The same rules apply to comparative advertising of the same or different brands.

In addition, the Guidelines for the Analysis and Verification of Advertising, published in the *Official Journal of the Mexican Federation* on 24 July 2012, provide that comparative advertising must be objective and truthful, and must avoid discrediting the products, services, business, brands or trademarks of other persons or corporations by means of false affirmations.

PROFECO's Guidelines for Performing Prices Comparative Advertising were published in the *Official Journal of the Federation* on 19 October 2009. These guidelines are addressed to stores or supermarkets that compare their prices to those charged by other supermarkets for the same products. These guidelines establish the rules that must be followed, which include the following:

- The prices being compared must relate to the same products, brand and presentation;
- The prices must be indicated in numbers, rather than percentages; and
- The prices must appear in recent purchase tickets.

PROFECO is responsible for hearing any proceedings arising from comparative advertising pursuant to the Federal Consumer Protection Law.

2.2 Industrial property law

FIPPA regulates unfair competition acts relating to IP rights and sanctions misleading actions in commerce, such as alleging that:

- a relationship exists between one establishment and that of a third party; or
- products or services are manufactured according to specifications, licences or authorisations issued by a third party.

FIPPA likewise sanctions the denigration or attempted denigration of the products, services, industrial or commercial activity or establishment of a third party, where the comparative advertising is tendentious, false or exaggerated, under the terms set out in the Federal Consumer Protection Law.

All proceedings involving comparative advertising pursuant to the Industrial Property Law will be heard in the first instance by IMPI. The sanctions are the same as those set out in section 1.3.

2.3 Civil actions/copyright

Typically, actions relating to unlawful or deceptive comparative advertising will fall within the spectrum of unfair competition infringements under FIPPA. The affected party must file an unfair competition action with IMPI, which has jurisdiction to hear unfair competition actions. However, if the comparative advertising includes other types of IP rights – such as copyright or a *reserva de derechos* – or affects the company's reputation, the affected party may consider preparing a civil action derived from the illicit behaviour; although in practice, these actions are typically prosecuted through administrative remedies at IMPI.

3. Online behavioural advertising

The Federal Consumer Protection Law states that companies that use consumer information for advertising or marketing purposes must inform consumers on request, free of charge, of:

- the information that they keep about them;
- the third parties with which information has been shared and the information that has been shared with them; and
- the recommendations that they have implemented.

The company must respond within 30 days of the request.

Consumers may directly demand that specific suppliers and companies that use their information for marketing or advertising purposes not disturb them at their home address or workplace, by email or by any other means in order to offer products or services; and that they not send them advertising. Likewise, consumers may demand that such suppliers and companies not share their information with third parties, except where this has been ordered by a judicial authority.

In accordance with the Federal Consumer Protection Law, suppliers and companies are prohibited from using information about consumers for marketing or advertising purposes, and from sending advertising to consumers who have expressly expressed that they do not wish to receive it. In addition, suppliers are prohibited from sending advertising information to consumers that have registered with the public registry administered by PROFECO. This public registry contains information of registered consumers who do not want to receive advertising. Suppliers that are subject to advertising are jointly responsible for managing consumer information when such advertising is disseminated through third parties. PROFECO will impose sanctions in case of non-compliance, including fines of up to $90,000.

Additionally, under the Federal Law on the Protection of Personal Data held by Private Parties and its implementing regulations, the use of personal data – understood as the use, transfer, storage, management, collection or deletion of any information concerning an identified or identifiable individual – is regulated in Mexico. The National Institute for Transparency, Access to Information and Personal Data Protection is responsible for enforcing this law, which also applies to online activities; this is expected to become a hot topic for supervision in the near future. The law requires that the data subject provide:

- consent for the use of personal data; and
- explicit consent for sensitive personal data, such as data relating to racial or ethnic origin, political opinions, religious or philosophical beliefs, trade union membership, genetic data, health, medical information, sex life or sexual orientation or criminal convictions.

Typically, consent is granted through a privacy notice, which must include information such as the following:

- key information that the data subject should understand in order to grant informed consent;
- details of how to withdraw consent;
- information on the categories of personal data concerned;
- the intended purposes of the data processing; and
- the data subject's rights.

The standard for granting authorisation for direct marketing activities is prior opt-in consent; this applies to email marketing, SMS/text message marketing and online behavioural advertising/ad personalisation marketing. This consent should be expressly obtained from the data subject when informing him or her about the processing activities that will take place upon receiving consent. Best practice is to include such information and authorisation at the time of providing the privacy notice, with a specific opt-in authorisation checkbox to comply with the law's standards.

4. Sales promotions

'Promotions' are defined in the Federal Consumer Protection Law as commercial practices involving the offer of products or services to consumers together with:

- the incentive of providing an additional product or service, or additional content, either free of charge or at a single or reduced price;

- the incentive to participate in sweepstakes, contests or similar activities; or
- the inclusion of promotional information on the labels or packaging of the products, in addition to the mandatory labelling or packaging information.

The supplier or company must provide consumers with clear and complete information about the promotion, including the terms and conditions, and the validity period or the number of products or services offered. If there is no indication of the validity period or the number of products or services offered, it is presumed that this is indefinite until a public revocation notice is issued through the same media used to advertise the promotion. Any consumer who meets the promotion requirements will be entitled to purchase during the validity period or as long as the products or services are available.

It is not necessary to file a notification or obtain authorisation from PROFECO to carry out promotions; however, exceptions or limitations may apply to promotions involving certain products or services that are also regulated by other applicable laws, such as medicines, tobacco and alcohol.

If the supplier or company does not comply with the terms of its offer, the consumer may choose to enforce compliance or accept another equivalent product or service. In any case, the supplier or company should pay the consumer the difference between the price at which the product or service was offered in the promotion and its normal price.

5. Ambush marketing

Ambush marketing is not specifically regulated under Mexican law. However, this does not mean that remedies are unavailable to affected parties where there are grounds to believe that such marketing is illegal. Similarly, parties can put in place adequate protection before an event through an appropriate contractual framework. The challenge lies in the fact that ambush marketers often adopt a very creative and strategic approach to design campaigns that avoid falling under the scope of the unfair competition regulations, resulting in a sophisticated legal battle in a relatively unexplored field.

First, as there are no specific regulations on the different types of direct and indirect ambush marketing, a rights holder and its commercial partners must secure adequate protection in advance which could help to prevent ambush marketing, defend its exclusivity and challenge parasitic advertising. Practical recommendations that sponsors and rights holders can implement include the following:

- Establish a comprehensive portfolio of trademarks and copyrights well in advance of the event, with sufficiently broad protection for key and ancillary products and services.

- Avoid generic contractual provisions to prevent and deter unfair competition. It is key to ensure that individuals and organisations that are related to the event understand:
  - their duty of care deriving from exclusive sponsorship;
  - the importance of fair practices; and
  - their obligations and responsibilities relating to advertising within a specified timeframe before and after the event.

  This is especially true today, given the ever-growing prominence of social media and influencers.
- Liaise with law enforcement agencies to train and educate them to help prevent ambush marketing in the relevant venues and online.
- Establish a sponsor cohort or taskforce to plan coordinated strategies in advance and develop a consolidated approach to present a united front against deceptive ambush marketing.
- Before the event, be proactive in sending out notices providing details of the sponsorship and warning that action will be taken against acts of unfair competition in order protect and enforce IP rights in accordance with domestic law.
- Develop policies and guidelines to train athletes on acceptable conduct rules and inform them of applicable sanctions in case of breach.

The federal courts have held that ambush marketing can be a form of unfair competition under the general framework set forth under MIPA and continued under the new FIPPA. Generally speaking, the federal courts consider that ambush marketing will constitute an act of unfair competition where two agents have concurrent market competition, either by themselves or through third parties with which they have commercial relationships, based on a particular and specific circumstance. The case in question involved a sports event, but the findings can be extended to other types of events on a case-by-case basis, including an assessment of the relevant grounds and evidence that can be used to demonstrate the existence of unfair competition. Such acts can include risk of association, trademark infringement, passing off or other practices relating to parasitic advertising. Finally, the rights holder can request one or more of the injunctive relief measures available under MIPA or the new FIPPA.

Additionally, the affected party may seek remedies through other courses of action, such as those available under civil or commercial law and criminal law. From a civil or commercial law perspective, the affected party might have grounds to file a claim based on illegitimate enrichment or damages derived from non-contractual civil liability. In practice, this type of sophisticated claim requires careful preparation and a higher threshold of evidence – especially as most civil judges are not specialised in these matters. On the other hand, from a criminal law perspective, the affected party could have grounds to file a complaint based on deceptive advertising as available under the Federal Consumer Protection Law.

6. Direct marketing

Direct marketing is regulated by the Federal Consumer Protection Law. This law requires that any advertising sent to consumers through any means indicate the name, address and telephone number or email address of the supplier.

Consumers may directly demand that specific suppliers and companies that use their information for marketing or advertising purposes not disturb them at their address, workplace, email address or by any other means, to offer products or services, and not send them advertising. Likewise, consumers may demand that such suppliers and companies not transfer their information to third parties, except where this has been ordered by a judicial authority.

In accordance with the Federal Consumer Protection Law, suppliers and companies are prohibited from using consumers' information for marketing or advertising purposes, and from sending advertising to consumers who have expressly expressed their wish not to receive it. In addition, suppliers and companies are prohibited from sending advertising information to consumers who are registered in the public register administered by PROFECO. This register contains the details of registered consumers who not want to receive advertising. Suppliers and consumers that advertise to consumers are jointly responsible for the management of consumer information where such advertising is conducted through third parties.

The standard for granting authorisation for direct marketing activities is prior opt-in consent; this applies to email marketing, SMS/text message marketing and online behavioural advertising/ad personalisation marketing. This consent should be expressly obtained from the data subject when informing him or her about the processing activities that will take place upon receiving consent. Best practice is to include such information and authorisation at the time of providing the privacy notice, with a specific opt-in authorisation checkbox to comply with the law's standards.

7. Product placement

The inclusion of products or brands in television programmes, movies and other audio-visual materials is increasingly common in Mexico. Although there are no specific regulations on product placement, the existing regulations on advertising and intellectual property will apply.

8. Native advertising and social media influencers

There are no specific regulations on native advertising and social media influencers in Mexico, and the Mexican courts and PROFECO have yet to address this issues in case law, as it is quite a novel field. Consequently, there are no specific guidelines that advertisers must observe with regard to informing consumers about native advertising and endorsements. In the absence of a specific set of regulations, the applicable framework is comprised of best practices and the general rules set forth in the Federal Consumer Protection Law, the Federal Civil Code, MIPA and the new FIPPA. Additional rules, and regulatory surveillance and enforcement, may apply if the product or service that is advertised relates to a particular field.

Advertising and marketing agencies, trademark owners and agencies commonly enter into commercial agreements with social media influencers to promote their products and brands. The contractual framework allows the parties to define the limits and responsibilities arising from social influencers' activities, and the potential ramifications and risks that might arise in practice, informed by a sophisticated business understanding and assignment of risk. This approach is relevant because there is a risk that the advertiser and the social media influencer may have shared liability derived from such advertising campaigns.

The starting point should be to conduct thorough due diligence and obtain sufficient background information on the other contracting party. The substance of the agreement should include:

- an appropriate description and details of the social media influencer's activities;
- the frequency with which such activities will be conducted;
- clear disclosures;
- content originality; and
- proper clearance to avoid infringement, including in relation to data privacy, confidentiality, trademark and copyright issues.

Similarly, the agreement should include guidelines to avoid making false, dishonest, deceptive or misleading information or representations, including statements, narratives, images or audio-visual content, including user-generated videos. Another recommendation is that brand owners create, develop and implement social media policies together with the influencer, as this will assist in showing that reasonable and appropriate measures were taken to ensure the adequacy of advertising and endorsements in social media. This shifts the responsibility to the influencer, who should be aware of his or her legal obligations.

While PROFECO thus far has not played an active role in enforcement in this space, given the increasing importance of native advertising and social media influencers, it is reasonable to assume that enforcement will likely increase in the near future. As such, the applicable penalties set out in the Federal Consumer Protection Law, as well as in MIPA and the new FIPPA, will apply.

9. Industry-specific regulation

9.1 Gambling

The Ministry of the Interior is in charge of regulating the Federal Gaming and Sweepstakes Law and its implementing regulations in Mexico.

The Federal Gaming and Sweepstakes Law states that games and gambling are forbidden in Mexico with the exception of those expressly authorised, such as board games, bowling, sports, racings and sweepstakes. 'Sweepstakes' are defined under the law as:

> any activity in which the owners or holders of a ticket, by means of the previous selection of a number, combination of numbers or any other symbol, obtain the right to participate, freely or by payment, in a procedure previously established and approved by the Ministry of the Interior, pursuant to which a number, combination of numbers, symbol or series of symbols is determined randomly, which generates one or more winners of a prize.

The Federal Gaming and Sweepstakes Law recognises the following types of sweepstakes:

- Sweepstakes for commercial propaganda: These aim to promote the products or services of a company, with consumers offered the possibility to participate without fulfilling the conditions associated with the payment or acquisition of another product. The tickets must include the legend: "Free ticket with no purchase condition."
- Sweepstakes with ticket sales: Consumers buy a ticket to participate in the sweepstake.
- Instant sweepstakes (also known as 'instant lotteries'): Participants immediately learn of the results by removing or scratching hidden numbers or symbols on the ticket. The winners can claim prizes in accordance with the procedure outlined on the ticket or proof of entry.
- Sweepstakes without ticket sales: Consumers obtain the right to participate in the sweepstake free of charge by acquiring a product or service, or a ticket to participate.

Before promoting and conducting sweepstakes, a permit from the Ministry of the Interior is required. The regulation on the matter is very strictly applied; as a result, many companies prefer to hold contests or other events that do not involve chance.

Permits to carry out sweepstakes can be granted only to persons of Mexican nationality or companies incorporated under Mexican law. A foreign company thus cannot obtain a permit to carry out a draw or sweepstake in Mexico. Many corporate documents and details about the dates and stages of the draw must be provided. For example, a bond that covers the amount of the prizes must be filed with the application, along with invoices for the prizes. The identification of the winners and award of the prizes must take place in Mexico in the presence of an inspector on a fixed date. If the winners are decided randomly by electronic means, the software must have previously been approved by the Ministry of the Interior, among other requirements.

Unlike sweepstakes, in contests where winners are decided based on knowledge or skills, a permit from the Ministry of the Interior is not required. The contest need only be notified to PROFECO and comply with Mexican Official Standard NOM-020-SCFI-2007.

Failure to comply with the Federal Gaming and Sweepstakes Law may result in economic fines or closure of the business.

9.2 Alcohol

The advertisement of alcoholic beverages is specifically regulated by the General Health Law and its Regulations. The Federal Consumer Protection Law is also applicable. The regulation of alcohol advertising is very strict in Mexico and prior authorisation from COFEPRIS is required. In accordance with the law, 'alcoholic beverages' are those containing from 2% to 55% of ethyl alcohol by volume.

The advertisement of alcoholic beverages can be targeted only at adults of 18 years and over. The use of precautionary legends such as "The abusive consumption of this product is harmful to health" is required for the packaging of alcoholic beverages, as well as for print, online, radio and television advertising. Likewise, the hours in which alcohol advertising can be broadcast on radio and television are restricted. In the case of cinema, ads may be transmitted only during films targeted at adults. Regarding online advertising, there must be access controls to ensure that it is accessible only to adults.

With regard to the content of alcohol advertising, many rules must be followed in order for the advertising to be authorised. For example, advertising will not be authorised if it:

- promotes the excessive consumption of alcohol;
- is associated with activities or characteristics that are attributable to young people under 25 years of age;
- is associated with ideas or images of fame, success, prestige or enhanced masculinity or femininity;
- is associated with civic, religious, sports or work activities;
- features prominent sports people or people with sports equipment; or
- depicts people who are actually or apparently consuming the product – only scenes in which the product is served without the presence of people may be depicted.

With respect to sponsorship, companies that produce or distribute low-alcohol beverages may sponsor sports activities and creative events; while those that produce or distribute medium and high-alcohol beverages may sponsor creative events only. Only brands, emblems and logos can be used in sponsorship activities. In addition:

- ads and sponsorship messages must not include imperative messages associated with the product;
- the product must not be related to the athlete, artist or event to be sponsored;
- images of alcoholic beverages or tobacco must not be included in the ads or sponsorship messages; and
- testimonies of athletes or public figures must not be included in the ads or sponsorship messages.

The use of brands, emblems and logos on sportswear is allowed for only low-alcohol products. The trademark can be incorporated on the back of shirts in a size no greater than one-sixth of the area of the shirt back.

Alcohol products cannot be promoted through sweepstakes, contests or collectibles targeted at those under 18 years of age.

Finally, the penalties for infringing the General Health Law and its Regulations include fines of up to $40,000. In addition, COFEPRIS may order the suspension of the advertising. PROFECO can also impose the sanctions indicated in section 1.1.

9.3   Pharmaceuticals

The General Health Law and the Health Advertisement Regulation regulate the advertisement of pharmaceuticals. The competent authority is the Ministry of Health through its agency COFEPRIS. The Federal Consumer Protection Law enforced by PROFECO is also applicable to pharmaceuticals.

For prescription-only products, advertising must be targeted to health professionals and prior notification must be filed with COFEPRIS. The advertisement of these products must be based on the information to prescribe and must be disseminated through specialised channels, such as dictionaries of pharmaceuticals and drug guides.

Non-prescription products, such as over-the-counter drugs and herbal remedies, can be advertised to the general public, but prior authorisation from COFEPRIS is required. Ads for these products must be tailored to any requirements specified by COFEPRIS when it authorised the product and consistent with the specification of the marketing authorisation. Ads should include the message, "Consult your physician", as well as a warning if any danger is associated with use of the product.

COFEPRIS will not authorise ads for medicines and herbal remedies if they:

- present the product as a definitive solution to the prevention, cure or rehabilitative treatment of a specific disease;

- promote consumption of the product by means of sweepstakes, contests or in exchange for any other product or service; or
- include statements that may be misleading, not verifiable or not duly supported.

The statements in ads for herbal remedies must be limited to the symptomatic effect based on the information expressed on the label and must not claim curative properties. The label must include a warning message determined by COFEPRIS or, in its absence, the following statement: "This product has not been scientifically shown to have preventive or curative properties."

With regard to medical devices, ads will be authorised by COFEPRIS according to the characteristics and purposes for which they have been registered on a case-by-case basis, and will be subject to the indications or uses approved by COFEPRIS. The marketing authorisation will specify whether the product must be advertised to healthcare professionals only or may be advertised to the general population.

COFEPRIS and the IFT have the power to order the media to suspend any ads that were not previously authorised, are misleading or may affect health. Furthermore, COFEPRIS may impose a fine of up to $40,000; while PROFECO may impose the sanctions indicated in section 1.1.

9.4 Financial products and services

The Mexican legal framework sets forth specific regulations on the advertisement and promotion of financial products and services, including fintech. The applicable rules are set out in:

- the Act for Protection and Defence of the User of Financial Services Financial Services;
- the Act for Transparency and Ordering of Financial Services; and
- the Law to Regulate Financial Technology Institutions.

Following the guidelines and legal requirements described in these rules, the competent authorities for the analysis, supervision and enforcement of advertising activities in this field are the National Commission for the Protection and Defence of Users of Financial Services (CONDUSEF) and the Federal Consumer Protection Agency.

In particular, the Act for Protection and Defence of the Users of Financial Services prohibits financial institutions from using information in a consumer database to send direct marketing and advertising to clients who have expressed that they do not wish to receive this type of information. For this purpose, CONDUSEF maintains a User Register, in which users can specify whether financial service providers are permitted to use their personal data for marketing or advertising purposes. The User Register, in combination with the Financial Services Providers Register, constitutes an extensive database that is useful for surveillance and enforcement purposes. CONDUSEF is a moderately active regulator, which can impose fines ranging from $2,000 to $10,000.

Similarly, the Act for Transparency and Ordering of Financial Services imposes additional rules on advertising and marketing both for financial entities and for commercial entities. 'Financial entities' include:

- credit institutions;
- regulated and unregulated multiple-purpose financial companies;
- popular financial companies;
- community financial companies;
- savings and loan cooperatives;
- financial entities that act as trustees in trusts granting credits, loans or financing to the public;
- credit unions; and
- fintech institutions.

'Commercial entities' are defined as societies that regularly grant credits, loans and financing plans to the public. These entities, in addition to financial services providers, are bound to comply with the advertising requirements established by CONDUSEF in connection with their active and passive operations, as well as their services. CONDUSEF regularly publishes and updates the administrative regulations that set out these referred requirements, which address transparency issues, best practices and the prevention of deceptive advertising and unfair competition. Finally, CONDUSEF has the authority to:

- temporarily block or suspend any illegal advertising; and
- impose fines ranging from $9,000 to $22,500 due to lack of information or transparency, unfair competition or deceptive advertising.

Finally, as per the Act for Transparency and Ordering of Financial Services, PROFECO has jurisdiction to investigate and supervise compliance with the administrative requirements for advertising and marketing activities in the financial services field. In practice, CONDUSEF and PROFECO coordinate their investigations, supervision and enforcement activities, to the benefit of the consumers and users of financial services. Derived from the importance and impact that financial services have on general consumers, both agencies work together to create and deliver educational campaigns and promote greater transparency in the financial services field.

9.5 Food

The advertisement of food is specifically regulated by the General Health Law and the Health Advertisement Regulation, which are enforced by the Ministry of Health through COFEPRIS. The Federal Consumer Protection Law enforced by PROFECO is also applicable.

Prior authorisation is not required to advertise food; however, prior notification should be filed with COFEPRIS.

Food advertising shall include warning messages about the condition of the product, as well as messages promoting a balanced diet or health habits. In addition, advertising should not:

- be misleading;
- affirm that the product fulfils the nutritional requirements of a human being;
- compare the product with natural foods in a denigrating way;
- express or suggest that the product provides extraordinary features or skills to consumers;
- associate the product with the consumption of alcoholic beverages or tobacco; or
- state that the produce prevent or cure a disease.

Furthermore, in 2014 the Guidelines on the Nutritional and Advertising Criteria that Advertisers of Food and Non-Alcoholic Beverages Must Observe to Advertise their Products on Open and Restricted Television as well as in Movie Theatres were published in the *Official Journal of the Federation*. In accordance with these guidelines, high-calorie food and non-alcoholic beverages, as well as confectionery, chocolates and chocolate-like products, may be advertised only according to the following schedules and conditions:

- On open and restricted television:
  - Monday to Friday from 12:00am to 12:30pm, and from 7:30pm to 11:59pm;
  - Saturday and Sunday from 12:00am to 7:00am, and from 7:30pm to 11:59pm; and
  - during the transmission of soap operas, sports, newscasts and series whose official or origin classification is not considered suitable for minors; and
- in movie theatres, during the screening of films whose official classification is not suitable for minors

Permission from COFEPRIS is required to advertise high-calorie products in schedules and programming categories other than those indicated above.

On 27 March 2020 an amendment to Mexican Official Standard NOM-051-SCFI/SSA1-2010 was published in the *Official Journal of the Federation*. This amendment introduces changes with regard to the front labelling of pre-packaged food and non-alcoholic beverages, and is the result of recent reforms to the General Health Law in relation to obesity and labelling. The revised standard represents a significant shift in public labelling policies.

Warning logos must now be displayed on products based on their nutritional content. If a product displays a warning logo or contains sweeteners or caffeine labels, images such as children's characters, animations, celebrities, cartoons, athletes, mascots and any other symbols that encourage its consumption must not be used. The words '*tipo*' ('type') and '*estilo*' (style) can no longer be used to relate to a similar product. Instead, the generic name of the product should be used, preceded by the word '*IMITACIÓN*' ('Imitation').

The regulations on complementary nutritional information (logos and labels) took effect on 1 October 2020; while other related regulations are effective from 1 April 2021.

Failure to comply with the General Health Law, the Regulations or the Mexican Official Standards relating to food may incur fines of up to $40,000.

With regard to advertising addressed to children, the Federal Law on Television and Broadcasting tasks the IFT with ensuring that the programming directed to children respects the values and principles, health regulations and guidelines it has established. Furthermore, advertising aimed at children must not:

- promote illegal or violent behaviour;
- present children or adolescents as sexual objects;
- exploit their immaturity to persuade them of the benefit of products or services;
- incite them to buy or request the purchase of a product;
- promote or incite bullying; or
- contain subliminal messages.

The IFT can order the suspension of advertising that may violate the law.

In addition, self-regulatory body CONAR promotes and enforces the Self-regulatory Code for Food and Non-Alcoholic Beverage Advertising Targeted at Minors. This code sets out the self-regulatory advertising standards applicable to the food and non-alcoholic beverage industry in relation to products aimed at those under 18 years of age.

9.6   Tobacco

The advertisement and promotion of tobacco products is forbidden in Mexico, aside from three specific exceptions:

- in adult magazines;
- in direct personal communication by mail; and
- in establishments where access is restricted to adults.

The General Act for Tobacco Control explicitly prohibits the promotion of these products by means of any mass communication medium, which is understood to include videos, photos and content uploaded to social media.

The act sets forth the following prohibitions on the advertisement, promotion and sponsorship of tobacco products,

- The commercialisation of tobacco products to minors (ie, under the age of 18) is prohibited;
- No natural or legal person may promote tobacco products on radio, television, cinema or the Internet. Advertising is limited exclusively to:
  - adult magazines;
  - direct personal communication by mail; and
  - establishments where access is restricted to adults.
- Tobacco product promotions are prohibited.
- The sponsorship of sports and cultural activities by a tobacco company, any of its related companies or brands is prohibited, either directly or indirectly.
- It is prohibited to use any type of incentive to encourage the purchase of a tobacco product. Similarly, the act prohibits the distribution, commercialisation or gift, direct or indirect, of a promotional article that bears a word mark or design mark of a tobacco-related product.

Enforcement and supervision are conducted by the Health Ministry.

The penalties for infringing these restrictions are harsh and should be taken seriously, as the Mexican Health Ministry considers tobacco products to be some of the most harmful products on the market. The fines that the Ministry can impose range from $18,000 to $45,000.

9.7 E-cigarettes

In February 2020, the Mexican Health Ministry published a decree prohibiting the import and commercialisation of e-cigarettes and vaping, including advertising activities.

Netherlands

Manon Rieger-Jansen
Roelien van Neck
Bird & Bird

1. Overview of the legal and regulatory regime for advertising

In the Netherlands, legislation regarding advertising is laid down in the Dutch Civil Code. The advertising rules are part of the more general provisions of tort (unlawful acts).

Articles 6:194 to 6:196 of the Civil Code contain provisions on misleading and comparative advertising and, in principle, forbid misleading advertising and lay down the rules for comparative advertising.[1] Where a breach of these provisions occurs, a civil court (in summary proceedings) can:

- prohibit the ad;
- order rectification of the unlawful ad; and
- in rare cases, order the advertiser to pay damages.

Other sanctions such as recall and destruction of the advertising materials are also possible.

Article 6:194 of the Civil Code, which prohibits misleading advertising, is applicable only in business-to-business (B2B) situations. Unfair business-to-consumer (B2C) commercial practices are governed by Articles 6:193a to 6:193j of the Civil Code.[2] A consumer who is misled by an ad can rely on these provisions; class actions by associations of consumers are also possible. Furthermore, the Authority for Consumers & Markets (ACM) can impose sanctions under administrative law – including fines of up to €900,000 per breach or 1% of the turnover of the advertiser – based on the Enforcement of Consumer Protection Act.

Apart from the legislative framework for advertising law in the Civil Code, the Netherlands also has a self-regulatory regime laid down in the Dutch Advertising Code.[3] The body that deals with this self-regulatory regime is the Advertising Code Foundation (ACF); and the Advertising Code Committee (ACC) has the authority to deal with complaints from consumers and

---

1   See EU Directive 2006/114/EC on misleading and comparative advertising.
2   Implementing EU Directive 2005/2019/EC.
3   For more details see www.reclamecode.nl.

businesses. The ACC is an independent body consisting of members appointed by advertisers' organisations, an association of communication consultancies, media organisations, the Dutch Consumers' Association and an independent chairman with a legal background.

The overarching principles of the Dutch Advertising Code are that ads should conform to the law, the truth and the requirements of good taste and decency. Ads must not:

- be misleading or dishonest;
- contravene the public interest, public order or morality; or
- be gratuitously offensive or constitute a threat to mental and/or physical public health.

The code consists of a general part – which applies to all ads, irrespective of the medium used – and a number of special advertising codes for specific products and services and industries, such as alcoholic beverages, tobacco products, telemarketing and games of chance and social media. There is also a special advertising code on advertising aimed at children and youths.

If a private person or company is of the view that an ad violates the Dutch Advertising Code, a complaint can be lodged with the ACC. The complaints procedure is easily accessible for everyone and a complaint can be filed by submitting details online through a specific complaint form. The advertiser can file a response to the complaint and a hearing may be held. The ACC will render a decision regarding the ad's compliance with the Dutch Advertising Code. A decision can be appealed to the Board of Appeal.

If the ACC decides that the ad violates the Dutch Advertising Code, it will issue a recommendation that the advertiser no longer advertise in such a manner. Depending on the circumstances – for instance, in case of repeat violations by the advertiser – the ACC may bring the decision to the attention of the public by means of a press release.

Within the ACF, the Compliance Department examines whether advertisers comply with decisions of the ACC; if not, details of these advertisers can be published on the ACC website. This way, non-compliance is brought to the attention of the public, but also of the government regulators. Furthermore, the ACF has concluded a cooperation protocol with the ACM, governing their mutual cooperation and consistency of approach in terminating unfair commercial practices.

Advertisers that are members of the ACF and pay the annual contribution can seek voluntary clearance advice from the ACC. The advice given is confidential and non-binding. However, this clearance system is not frequently used.

For linear and non-linear audio-visual media services, rules on advertising are laid down in the Media Act.[4] The act in particular contains provisions on broadcasting times, sponsorship and product placement. The Dutch Media Authority is the supervising authority. Under the Media Act, media institutions are obliged to associate themselves with the ACF and are bound to discontinue any ad that the ACC or the Board of Appeal has found to violate the Dutch Advertising Code.

Advertisers should further be careful with the IP rights of others. Ads that copy material from third parties may constitute copyright infringement under the Copyright Act. When trademarks of third parties or signs that are confusingly similar thereto are used in ads, the trademark rights of those third parties might be infringed under the Benelux Convention on Intellectual Property or the EU Trademark Regulation.[5]

2. Comparative advertising

In the Netherlands, the rules on comparative advertising are laid down in Article 6:194a of the Civil Code. This article implements EU Directive 2006/114/EC[6] into Dutch law and stipulates that 'comparative advertising' means any advertising that, explicitly or by implication, identifies a competitor or products or services offered by a competitor.

Article 6:194a of the Civil Code permits comparative advertising where the following conditions are met:

- It is not misleading or an unfair trade practice within the meaning of Articles 6:193c to 6:193g of the Civil Code;
- It compares products or services that meet the same needs or that are intended for the same purpose;
- It objectively compares one or more material, relevant, verifiable and representative features of those products and services, which may include price;
- It does not create confusion in the marketplace between the advertiser and a competitor, or between the advertiser's trademarks, trade names, other distinguishing marks, products or services and those of a competitor;
- It does not discredit or denigrate the trademarks, trade names, other distinguishing marks, products, services, activities or circumstances of a competitor;
- For products with a designation of origin, it relates in each case to products with the same designation;
- It does not take unfair advantage of the reputation of a trademark, trade name or other distinguishing marks of a competitor, or of a designation of origin of competing products; and

---

4   This act was revised on 10 December 2009 to implement the EU Audio-visual Media Services Directive (2007/65/EC).
5   See EU Regulation 2017/1001.
6   See n 1 above.

- It does not present products or services as imitations or replicas of products or services bearing a protected trademark or trade name.

Furthermore, any comparison referring to a special offer must:
- indicate clearly and unambiguously the end date of the offer and, should the special offer not yet apply, the beginning of the period during which the special price or other specific conditions will apply; or
- state that the special offer is subject to the availability of the products or services.

If comparative advertising is not in line with the conditions set out in the Civil Code, a case can be brought before a civil court (in summary proceedings). The court can:
- prohibit the ad;
- order rectification of the unlawful ad;
- in rare cases, order the advertiser to pay damages; and
- impose other sanctions, such as recall and destruction of the advertising materials.

In principle, an advertiser may use the trademark of a competitor in comparative advertising if all conditions for comparative advertising have been met. A trademark owner can prevent the use of a sign that is identical or similar to its trademark in comparative advertising if that use does not satisfy all of the conditions for comparative advertising.[7] If an identical or similar sign is used in a manner that is likely to cause confusion, the conditions as set out above will not be satisfied, the comparative ad will not be lawful and the trademark owner can then sue the advertiser for trademark infringement. When copyrighted materials are used in the comparison, the advertiser risks a claim for copyright infringement.

A similar provision on comparative advertising is laid down in the Dutch Advertising Code. Complaints about comparative advertising can be made to the ACC, as further set out in section 1 of this chapter.

3. Online behavioural advertising

Online behavioural advertising is governed by:
- the EU General Data Protection Regulation (2016/679) (GDPR);
- the Act Implementing the GDPR (*Uitvoeringswet AVG* (UAVG)); and
- the Telecommunications Act.

Article 11.7a of the Telecommunications Act stipulates that websites must

---

7   Court of Justice of the European Union (CJEU), Case C-533/06, *O2 v Hutchison 3G*, 12 June 2008, now enshrined in Article 9(3)(f) of EU Regulation 2017/1001 and Article 10(3)(f) of Directive 2015/2436.

inform visitors (internet users) and ask for their consent before storing any information (eg, cookies) on the visitor's device or gaining access to such information on such device. Such consent should meet the requirements of the GDPR, meaning that the consent must be freely given, specific, informed and unambiguous. Typically, visitors are asked (eg, via a banner) on their first visit to the website to consent to the placement of cookies. Information on the cookies is often provided through a banner that links through to a document or page (eg, a cookie notice) that provides further information on the different types of cookies and how to delete them.

Not all uses of cookies are subject to these obligations, as the law acknowledges that cookies can be a legitimate and useful tool to ensure that internet and other telecommunications services function properly. For example, where websites store information or gain access to information on devices for the sole purpose of facilitating communication, this is exempt, as it is understood to be part of the process of (tele)communication. Further to this, cookies that are used to facilitate an information society service explicitly requested by the subscriber or user are also exempt. An example of the latter is the use of cookies to play a video which the user has specifically requested or to remember a user's log-in credentials and prior authentication over multiple pages. The primary supervisor of the cookie rules is the ACM. While the ACM actively enforces the cookie rules, it has not imposed any fines so far. The ACM's supervision typically takes the form of sending emails and letters to companies in which it highlights identified violations of the cookie rules. In most cases, such correspondence and investigations are not made public (eg, by means of publication of an investigative report), although ACM enforcement actions against the Dutch public broadcaster, NPO, and the largest Dutch railway operator, NS, have been made public.

In addition to the ACM, the Dutch Data Protection Authority (DDPA) is a secondary supervisor of the cookie rules. This is because cookies are often used as a means to link data and online behaviour to an individual. This could be to store log-in details or preferences, but also (and often highlighted in the discussions on cookies) to build profiles of individuals. It is this particular use that is of specific interest (and to some extent, concern) to data protection authorities such as the DDPA.

The link with data protection is made even more explicit in Article 11.7a of the Telecommunications Act, as it contains a burden of proof for so-called 'tracking cookies'. These are cookies that are used to collect, combine or analyse data relating to various information society services such as websites, so that the user may be treated differently – for example, through targeted advertising. This burden of proof effectively makes it easier for the DDPA to supervise the use of cookies for advertising, as it will be for the website or advertising network to prove that such use does not constitute the processing of personal data. Due to the broad definition of 'personal data' under the EU and national data protection laws, this is no easy task.

Finally, since the introduction of the GDPR, a new round of discussions – and more recently, enforcement – involving cookies has emerged. In particular, the requirement of 'freely given consent' is hotly debated, with the DDPA being of the opinion that websites cannot require individuals to consent to a website in order for them to be able to access the website (so-called 'cookie walls' or 'forced consent solutions').

4.   Sales promotions

The Betting and Gaming Act contains a general prohibition on conducting a competition for prizes or premiums if the winners are selected by any form of chance without a licence issued by the Betting and Gaming Authority. It is irrelevant whether a monetary fee is required to participate. Promotional games of chance are nonetheless tolerated (ie, no action will be taken against the organiser), even without a licence, if they meet the criteria set out in the Code of Conduct for Promotional Games of Chance 2014.

The main criteria set out in the code are as follows:

- The total value of the prizes per promotional game cannot exceed €100,000 (excluding any taxes) per year;
- Participation must be free of charge (other than communication costs, with a maximum of €0.45 for that element);
- The organiser may offer only one promotion per year per product, service or organisation;
- During the promotional period, there can be no more than 20 draws;
- Minors (ie, persons under the age of 18) can participate only with the permission of their parents; and
- The organiser must draw up general conditions and make these conditions known to the participants.

If the total value of the prizes of a promotional game of chance amounts to €4,500 at most (so-called 'small promotional games of chance'), some of the above criteria do not apply.

If a promotion does not meet the above criteria, it will be unlawful according to the Betting and Gaming Act (especially since it is unlikely that a licence would be obtainable for the promotion). Enforcement has taken place under the Betting and Gaming Authority since April 2012. The Betting and Gaming Authority has powers under administrative law and can, among other things, demand termination of a game under threat of periodic penalty payments and impose penalties of up to €870,000 or 10% of the annual turnover of the relevant operator, whichever is the higher.

5.   Ambush marketing

In the Netherlands, there is no specific legislation on ambush marketing. Some forms of ambush marketing can be prevented under IP laws or general tort law.

For major events, the event organisers will typically have registered the names, logos and other features of the event as trademarks. These trademarks can be used in the course of trade only where a proper licence has been granted, for which the official sponsors pay considerable amounts. If an ambush marketer makes unauthorised use of these registered trademarks, the event organisers can bring a claim for trademark infringement. Also, the ambush marketer should refrain from using copyright-protected works (eg, logos and characters), whose use might lead to a copyright infringement claim.

With ambush marketing, the ambush marketer typically takes advantage of the goodwill vested in the event, but without using the registered trademarks or copyrights of others, often by promoting its own trademark. In that case, it will often be very hard – or even impossible – to bring any action against the ambush marketer. The ambush marketer has considerable scope to benefit from the goodwill vested in an event. From the standard case law of the Dutch Supreme Court, it follows that taking advantage of the achievement of another is not prohibited as such – even where this is to the detriment of the other party (in the case of ambush marketing, the event organisers or a competitor that is an official sponsor).[8] However, if the ambush marketer creates the wrongful impression that it has a relationship with the event organiser or is an official sponsor, this will constitute tort under Dutch law.

Some types of ambush marketing can be stopped through the control of access to stadiums. People bringing unauthorised promotional materials (typically of a competitor of the official sponsor) can be refused access to the stadium, provided that prior notice of this policy is given. An injunction against handing out unauthorised promotional materials within a certain distance of the stadium has been ordered in Dutch case law where the ambush marketing campaign was intended to circumvent the restrictions on marketing actions by non-sponsors within the stadium and was thus considered tortious.[9]

Organisations such as the International Olympic Committee and FIFA require countries that want to be a candidate for the Olympic Games or the FIFA World Cup to enact special laws that provide both adequate trademark protection and protection against ambush marketing. There is currently no such legislation in place in the Netherlands. When bidding for the 2018/2022 FIFA World Cup to be held in the Netherlands (and Belgium), the Dutch government denied FIFA's request to introduce specific legislation on ambush marketing, declaring: "There is no specific 'ambush marketing law' in Dutch

---

8   Dutch Supreme Court, 27 June 1986, *Decca v Holland Nautic*; Dutch Supreme Court, 23 October 1988, *KNVB v NOS*; and Dutch Supreme Court, 23 May 2003, *KNVB v Feyenoord*.
9   Amsterdam Court of Appeal, 23 November 2006, *Bavaria v KNVB*.

legislation. We consider 'ambush marketing' to be covered by a) intellectual property laws, more specifically the copyright and trademark law, b) unfair competition law, more specifically misleading and comparative advertising law and the unfair commercial practices Law and c) general tort law."[10]

6. Direct marketing

A series of regulations govern various types of direct marketing in the Netherlands. A starting point is the GDPR and UAVG; in addition, the Telecommunications Act governs commercial communications by email and telephone. Various self-regulatory codes – all part of the general Dutch Advertising Code – also apply and are generally worded similarly to the relevant legislation.

Under the GDPR, the processing of personal data must be fair and lawful. Data subjects must be given information on the purpose of data collection and must also be given the opportunity to opt out of the use of their data for direct marketing purposes.

Under Article 11.7 of the Telecommunications Act, different rules apply to different means of communication:

- Article 13, paragraphs 1–4 provide for a (strict) opt-in regime for unsolicited electronic communications using automatic calling systems, fax and electronic messages (including email and SMS); and
- pursuant to Article 13, paragraphs 5–12, in principle, a (less strict) opt-out regime applies to the use of other means of electronic communications for commercial, ideological or charitable purposes such as telemarketing.

Pursuant to Article 11.7, paragraph 1 of the Telecommunications Act, the main rule is that the use of email and similar electronic communications is prohibited, unless the sender can demonstrate that the recipient has consented to such communications prior to approaching him or her through these means for direct marketing purposes. Companies should be aware that the term 'sender' is interpreted broadly and applies not only to the actual sender, but also to the advertising company and other parties that play a decisive role in sending direct marketing communications.

Companies should also note that the opt-in regime applies regardless of whether the recipient is a consumer (B2C communications) or a corporate user (B2B communications). There is a specific exemption for electronic messages sent to corporate recipients, pursuant to which an opt-in is not required if contact details are used which are specifically communicated for that purpose (eg, 'promotions@companyname.com') or if the subscriber is located outside the European Economic Area and the locally applicable requirements are met.

---

10   Government Guarantee 8.

An important exemption to the opt-in regime for sending direct marketing emails and other electronic communications applies to existing customers (both B2B and B2C). Pursuant to Article 11.7, paragraph 4 of the Telecommunications Act, electronic contact details which were obtained in the context of the sale of a product or service may be used for direct marketing purposes, provided that:

- the customer could opt out at the time the contact details were obtained;
- the contact details are used only to send messages about the company's own and similar products and/or services; and
- an easy opt-out is offered in each message.

In each direct marketing message, companies must inform the recipients of the communications in each message about the actual identity of the person on whose behalf the communication is sent. The communication must also contain contact details to which the recipient can send a request to terminate such communications. In practice, this requirement is usually implemented by including an opt-out/unsubscribe link in each message.

As indicated above, pursuant to Article 11.7, paragraphs 5–12 of the Telecommunications Act, the main rule for other means of communication is that subscribers can be approached unless they have opted out. This is in particular relevant for telemarketing.

Pursuant to Article 11.7, paragraphs 9 and 10 of the Telecommunications Act, companies engaged in telemarketing (ie, telemarketing companies and their clients) are prohibited from approaching subscribers who are registered on the Do-Not-Call Register, and must check the Do-Not-Call Register and remove any registered phone numbers from their call files before using these files. Furthermore, pursuant to Article 11.7, paragraph 12 of the Telecommunications Act, they must offer subscribers on each call the option to opt out of any future unsolicited calls from the calling company and to register their phone number on the Do-Not-Call Register. Most companies have implemented this by using an interactive voice response application which starts directly after the call itself has finished.

Article 11.7, paragraph 11 of the Telecommunications Act contains an exemption for existing customers which is similar to the existing customer exemption to the opt-in regime described above. Existing customers may be approached even though they are registered on the Do-Not-Call Register if their contact details were obtained in the context of the sale of a product or service, provided that:

- the customer could opt out at the time the contact details were obtained;
- the contact details are used only for communication about the company's own and similar products and/or services; and
- an easy opt-out is offered in each call.

The rules on telemarketing apply only to subscribers who are natural persons (B2C); but in practice, corporate users that have registered their phone numbers on the Do-Not-Call Register are also protected, because these numbers must also be removed from the call files for the telemarketing campaign before the start of the campaign.

Compliance with Article 11.7 of the Telecommunications Act is actively enforced by the ACM on the basis of complaints. The ACM regularly imposes fines ranging from several tens of thousands of euros to sometimes more than €1 million for a number of related violations of the rules relating to spam and telemarketing. These fines are generally also published by the ACM and can thus give rise to considerable reputational damage. More recently, enforcement by the ACM has slowed down somewhat, although the DDPA has stepped up enforcement in the area of direct marketing and has issued its first fines for violations of the GDPR and UAVG concerning the use of personal data for direct marketing purposes.

A bill is now pending that would amend the Telecommunications Act to introduce, among other things, an opt-in regime for direct marketing telephone calls to natural persons.

7. Product placement

Under the relevant Dutch regulations, 'product placement' is defined as including or making reference to a product, service or brand in the course of a programme or similar offering, for monetary or similar compensation. The EU Audio-visual Media Services Directive (2007/65/EC) has been implemented in the Media Act and is relevant here.

Specific rules on product placement apply to public broadcasters and commercial broadcasters. For public broadcasters, a ban on product placement generally applies. For commercial broadcasters, a ban on product placement also applies, although product placement is permitted in certain categories of programmes, including films, series, sports broadcasts and light entertainment. Where product placement is permitted, certain limitations apply, including the following:

- Product placement may not be a direct stimulus to purchase the product;
- Product placement for certain categories of products (eg, medical treatments, tobacco and pharmaceuticals) is completely prohibited; and
- Product placement for alcohol is prohibited for public broadcasting channels and for commercial television channels between 6:00am and 9:00pm (see section 9.2).

The Dutch Media Authority is the supervisory authority and has powers under administrative law to issue substantial penalties for breaches of the regulations. An amended Media Act, implementing the new Audio-visual Media Services Directive (2018/1808/EU), entered into force in September 2020. Under the amended Media Act, product placement is generally permitted for commercial broadcasters, but certain exceptions apply (ie, news programmes and programmes regarding consumer matters).

8. Native advertising and social media influencers

The self-regulatory Dutch Advertising Code requires that ads be recognisable as such by virtue of their layout, presentation, content or otherwise, taking into account the public for which they are intended. Specifically, with regard to native advertising (ie, paid editorial content used to advertise a product), both the Dutch Civil Code (Article 6:193g(k)) and the Dutch Advertising Code stipulate that it should always be made clear to the consumer that the editorial is a paid ad. This should be done either in the text of the editorial or in easily identifiable images or sounds. Otherwise, such editorial will be regarded as misleading advertising under the Civil Code and the Dutch Advertising Code.

The rules on social media influencer marketing and user-generated content are mainly based on two types of self-regulation. Advertising on social media is covered by the Dutch Advertising Code on Social Media and Influencer Marketing. In addition, several YouTube vloggers have created *De Social Code*, a voluntary self-regulatory code set up by and for YouTubers, which provides guidance on when and how to identify that a video has been sponsored. There are no sanctions for non-compliance with this code.

The main requirements of the Dutch Advertising Code on Social Media and Influencer Marketing are as follows:

- Ads must be identified as such where there has been any compensation, whether in cash or in kind;
- Children under 12 years old may not be encouraged to advertise products or services on social media; and
- The advertiser is responsible for ensuring that the influencer follows these rules.

The Advertising Code on Social Media and Influencer Marketing also contains a specific provision on children and influencer marketing, which confirms that children may not be directly encouraged to advertise products and services on social media. The general rules on clearly identifying advertising on social media will still apply to advertising aimed at children.

This code can be enforced by submitting a complaint to the ACC. The ACC can issue a warning and keeps a 'name and shame' list of parties that do not comply with such warnings. After the implementation of the new Media Act, as referred to above, influencers' online video channels will also be covered by the Media Act and will be subject to the same substantial fines as already apply to advertising on television.

9. Industry-specific regulation

9.1 Gambling

Gambling is regulated under the Betting and Gaming Act. Entities that do not possess a Dutch betting and gaming licence under the act cannot provide any opportunity to participate in betting and gaming; nor are they allowed to encourage (including advertising for) participation in such games (Article 1(1) of the Betting and Gaming Act). Consequently, ads for gambling operations by or for unlicensed entities are not permitted.

Under the Betting and Gaming Decree on Advertising and Addiction Prevention, specific information must be provided in any publicity for games of chance offered by licence holders, including the costs of participating and the statistical chance of winning a prize (Article 5(1) of the decree). Licence holders may not advertise via linear broadcasting between 6:00am and 7:00pm, with the exception of neutral sponsorship messages (Article 3(4) of the decree).

Particular commercial promotions and promotional games of chance where consumers can win a prize (eg, when they buy a product) are allowed and may be advertised, as long as they meet the conditions of the Code for Promotional Games of Chance. This code includes regulations on maximum prize value, number of draws and maximum participation costs.

The Betting and Gaming Authority monitors compliance with the Betting and Gaming Act and the Code for Promotional Games of Chance. It has the power to impose administrative sanctions, such a penalty of up to €870,000 or 10% of the (net) annual turnover of the infringer, whichever is the higher.

See also section 4 on the use of games of chance in sales promotions.

9.2 Alcohol

Alcohol advertising is mainly governed by self-regulation under the Advertising Code for Alcoholic Beverages, which is part of the Dutch Advertising Code. This code applies to advertising for alcoholic beverages, and non-alcoholic beverages when these are recommended for consumption together with alcoholic beverages. The rules also apply to digital marketing and social media.

The code focuses on the responsible consumption of alcohol and stipulates that ads must not show, suggest or encourage the excessive or otherwise irresponsible consumption of alcohol. Furthermore, claims are prohibited that refer to the disinhibiting effects of alcoholic beverages, such as the reduction or elimination of fears and feelings of inner or social conflict. Claims may not suggest health benefits, improved physical or mental performance, or enhancement of sporting or professional performance by consuming alcohol. Furthermore, alcohol advertising must not create the impression that there is a link between alcohol consumption and social or sexual success. Alcohol advertising must not be aimed at pregnant women or minors.

The Foundation for Responsible Alcohol Consumption (STIVA), which represents producers and importers of alcoholic beverages, has also agreed on rules for alcohol advertising. In case of non-compliance with the code, the ACC or the Board of Appeal can impose a penalty of up to €50,000. Furthermore, members of STIVA must register alcohol promotions with STIVA prior to the event and advertisers risk a fine of up to €5,000 for any breach observed by STIVA. Finally, STIVA maintains a compulsory prior clearance system for all television, radio and cinema alcohol ads.

There is no Dutch legislation that regulates the content of alcohol advertising. However, the Media Act contains a number of provisions on the broadcasting of alcohol advertising – in particular, stipulating that alcohol advertising is not allowed on radio and television from 6:00am to 9:00pm. Sponsorship is allowed between those times, but only by a mere mention of the name or trademark of the sponsor.

9.3 Pharmaceuticals

Pharmaceutical advertising is governed by Chapter 9 of the Medicines Act,[11] which is enforced in the Netherlands by the Healthcare Inspectorate; and by a number of self-regulatory codes.

The Medicines Act distinguishes between advertising to the general public and advertising to healthcare professionals. As general principles, advertising must be in accordance with the summary of product characteristics and must not be misleading. Additionally, advertising that does not promote the rational use of a pharmaceutical product is prohibited. Prescription-only medicines may not be advertised to the general public, but only to healthcare professionals. Furthermore, it is not permitted to undertake any form of advertising for an unregistered pharmaceutical product.

The Healthcare Inspectorate will forward complaints to the self-regulating authorities – the Foundation for the Code for Pharmaceutical Advertising (CGR) or the Inspection Board for the Advertising of Medicinal Products to the General Public (KOAG) – on the basis of working arrangements between the Healthcare Inspectorate, the CGR and the KOAG. In cases of very serious violations of the Medicines Act, the inspectorate will handle the complaint itself. Where a violation of the advertising rules under the Medicines Act has occurred, the Healthcare Inspectorate can impose a fine of up to €150,000 per violation.

Apart from the Medicines Act, further rules for pharmaceutical advertising directed towards healthcare professionals are laid down in self-regulatory codes – in particular, the Code on Advertising for Medicinal Products, which covers (among other things) hospitality, sponsorship and the distinction between advertising and information. Complaints about violations of the code can be

---

11   Implementing EU Directive 2001/83/EC relating to medical products for human use.

filed with the CGR, which can prohibit the use of an ad or part thereof, or order a rectification or recall. Decisions can be appealed. If the decision of the CGR is not complied with, the CGR can make public the non-compliance ('naming and shaming') and inform the Healthcare Inspectorate; civil proceedings are also possible.

Advertising to the general public is regulated in the Code for Advertising Medicine to the General Public, which is part of the Code on Advertising for Medicinal Products. All advertising to the general public for medicines must be approved in advance by the KOAG.

The KOAG also monitors (on its own initiative, but also in response to complaints) compliance with the Code for Advertising Medicine to the General Public.

9.4   Financial products and services

Under the Financial Supervision Act, specific regulations apply in the Netherlands to the advertisement of financial products and services.

Ads for specific financial products, including credit facilities, must include certain mandatory language and/or standard warning signs, depending on the product offered. Advertising for complex financial products must include a so-called 'risk meter' and warning sentence ("Do not run unnecessary risks. Read the financial information leaflet" (in Dutch, *Loop geen onnodig risico. Lees de Financiële Bijsluiter*")). Ads for credit facilities must include the costs of the loan and the highest applicable interest; they must also include a warning sentence ("Please note! Borrowing money costs money" (in Dutch, *Let op! Geld lenen kost geld*")) and a warning symbol. More generally, ads for financial products should be clear and accurate, and should not be misleading in any way.

There are no specific rules with regard to the advertisement of general banking services, general investment services and general insurance. Language used in ads should nonetheless be clear and accurate, and should not be misleading in any way.

The competent regulator is the Financial Markets Authority. In the event of a breach of the abovementioned regulations, the Financial Markets Authority has the power to impose fines, which can also be made public.

9.5   Food

Food advertising is mainly governed by self-regulation, under the Advertising Code for Food Products and the Confectionery Code, both of which are part of the Dutch Advertising Code. These codes were partly introduced to promote healthy eating patterns; however, no distinction between healthy and unhealthy food is made in the Advertising Code for Food Products. The codes further impose restrictions on food advertising aimed at children, as advertising aimed at children under seven years of age is prohibited.

In addition to these codes, food advertising is regulated by the Dutch Commodities Act, which forbids the promotion of food and drink products by claiming that they can prevent, treat or cure diseases. Food advertising is also regulated via EU Regulation 1924/2006 on nutrition and health claims made for food products.

All permitted nutrition claims and authorised and non-authorised health claims are entered in a community register of nutrition and health claims. The Netherlands Food and Consumer Product Safety Authority can intervene and take measures in response to violations of the Commodities Act, such as issuing warnings or imposing administrative fines.

9.6   Tobacco

Tobacco advertising is regulated in the Netherlands by the Tobacco Act. The main rule is that tobacco advertising is prohibited, except in tobacco shops or in a tobacco sales stand with a lockable door in a store, which is clearly separated from the rest of the store.

On 1 July 2020, a display ban entered into force, meaning that supermarkets must hide their tobacco products from view. Since 1 January 2021, other stores have followed suit. The display ban also applies to web shops, which since 1 January 2021 are no longer allowed to show pictures of the products or to link to webpages showing pictures of the products.

The Netherlands Food and Consumer Product Safety Authority enforces the provisions of the Tobacco Act and can impose administrative fines of up to €450,000 on players in the tobacco industry for breaches of the law.

The Dutch Advertising Code also contains a special Advertising Code for Tobacco Products that applies to advertising and sponsorship insofar as they are permitted under the Tobacco Act and are consumer-oriented.

Since 1 October 2020, all cigarettes are now sold in neutral, blank packaging (besides the current warning texts and dissuasive photos and the name of the manufacturer).

9.7   E-cigarettes

The general prohibition on advertising also applies to e-cigarettes. Advertising is thus prohibited on the basis of the Tobacco Act, except for advertising in tobacco shops or in a tobacco stand with a lockable door in a store, which is clearly separated from the rest of the store. Furthermore, the display ban in both physical stores and online web shops also applies to e-cigarettes.

It is expected that in 2022, e-cigarettes will be sold in neutral packaging, similar to the packaging of regular cigarettes.

The authors would like to thank their colleagues Berend van der Eijk, Lisette den Butter and Hester Borgers for their valuable contributions to this chapter.

Norway

Simen Blaker Strand
Ida Gjessing
GjessingReimers

1. Overview of the legal and regulatory regime for advertising

Good business practice is an overarching legal standard under Norwegian commercial law, and this applies as much to advertising as to any other area of business. Norway's Marketing Control Act of 2009 implemented EU law within this field and replaced similar legislation from 1972. The legal standard for good business practice has a long and well-established tradition in Norwegian legislation and case law, as well as in administrative practices for advertising law and related fields.

Chapter 1 of the Marketing Control Act sets forth the general purposes of the act, including the principle that marketing should not conflict with good marketing practice. This is a normative standard, taking into consideration ethical and moral views and whether the marketing employs offensive means. There is a special prohibition against marketing conduct that conflicts with the equality of the sexes.

Commercial practices that affect consumers are dealt with in Chapter 2 of the act, including provisions that prohibit unfair commercial practices, misleading acts and omissions, and aggressive commercial practices, as well as provisions ensuring clear pricing.[1] Chapter 3 imposes restrictions on particular forms of marketing, such as by telephone, postal mail and electronic mail, and other forms of unsolicited marketing.[2]

Chapter 4 sets out special provisions for the protection of children. These provisions are quite strictly interpreted and leave little room for advertising directed at children. Even if advertising is not directed especially at children, care should be taken in cases where the ad or the product itself is likely to influence children. Direct purchase requests aimed at children are in any event prohibited.

Section 25 of Chapter 6 of the Marketing Control Act sets forth the general principle that: "No act shall be performed in the course of trade which conflicts with good business practice among traders."[3] This general legal standard is

---

1   Chapter 2 implemented EU Directive 2005/29/EC on unfair commercial practices into Norwegian law.
2   Chapter 3 implemented EU Directive 97/7/EC on the protection of consumers in respect of distance contracts into Norwegian law.
3   All translations of the code are taken from the website of the Consumer Authority, www.forbrukerombudet.no.

further reflected in other provisions of Chapter 6 of the Marketing Control Act, which all refer to conduct between traders: topics covered include misleading marketing, insufficient guidance and the copying of other entities' marks, products, catalogues, advertising materials and so on. Although Chapter 6 is directed towards the conduct of professional parties, it involves considerations of the effect of marketing and advertising conduct on consumers and other purchasers.

Compliance with the Marketing Control Act, apart from Chapter 6, is monitored by the Consumer Authority, which may refer cases to the Market Council.

Private entities and persons are obliged to disclose documents and to give other information to the Consumer Authority and the Market Council upon request. The investigators may be assisted by the police in order to enforce this obligation.

However, the work of the Consumer Authority is based on a negotiation model. The Consumer Authority may, on its own initiative or at the request of third parties, take initiatives in order to ensure compliance. In doing so, the Consumer Authority will endeavour to obtain the voluntary settlement of any alleged infringements.

The Consumer Authority may take a decision on the matter itself if:

- a settlement is not reached;
- awaiting a decision of the Market Council would be inconvenient or damaging; or
- the act is substantially identical to an act that was previously prohibited by the Market Council.

The Consumer Authority and the Market Council may:

- impose fines;
- issue an injunction; or
- take other steps, or prompt the courts to take steps, to stop or remedy illegal advertising – including, in certain limited cases, ordering third parties to remove content or to restrict access to an online interface.[4]

Infringement of Chapter 6 pertaining to practices among traders is mostly enforced by private actions, either within the ordinary court system or by referring the case to the Norwegian industry and commercial enterprises dispute resolution panel (NKU). The NKU is composed of members designated by the major industry and advertising players, and is a vehicle for the out-of-court

---

4   Incorporation of EU Regulation 2017/2394 of the European Parliament and of the Council of 12 December 2017 on cooperation between national authorities responsible for the enforcement of consumer protection laws.

resolution of disputes under Chapter 6 of the Marketing Control Act. The NKU may not issue injunctions or impose sanctions. However, its opinions are considered to be normative and private parties usually adhere to them. Parties in dispute may also decide in advance that the case shall be finally resolved by the NKU.

Infringement of the Marketing Control Act may be sanctioned by fines or even imprisonment for up to six months. In the event of infringement of certain sections of Chapter 6, private parties may claim injunction and compensation based on the damage and loss incurred, a reasonable licence fee or the reimbursement of profits made, depending on the circumstances.

Special provisions for advertising by way of broadcasting apply. Pursuant to Chapter 3 of the Broadcasting Act of 4 December 1992,[5] advertising directed at children is prohibited; as is political or religious advertising. Advertising must be clearly understood to be a commercial communication, and may not be surreptitious or use subliminal techniques. Furthermore, product placement is prohibited unless certain conditions are fulfilled. Restrictions apply to the advertisement of certain commodities. There are certain limits and slots for the broadcasting of commercials. Sponsorship of broadcasting programmes is generally allowed on certain conditions and with some limited exceptions. Compliance with the Broadcasting Act is overseen by the Norwegian Media Authority, which has the power to impose fines in case of breach of the regulations.

2. Comparative advertising

'Comparative advertising' is any advertising that directly or indirectly compares the advertiser's products or services to those of a competitor.

Pursuant to Section 7 of the Marketing Control Act, comparative advertising is considered to be misleading towards consumers if it creates confusion with the product or trademark, trade name or other distinguishing mark of a competitor. Such misleading advertising is subject to sanctions from the Consumer Authority and the Market Council as set out above.

More detailed regulations are set out with regard to misleading advertising constituting breach of good business practices among traders. Comparative advertising will be accepted only if certain cumulative conditions are fulfilled. These are set forth in Regulation FOR-2000-12-19-1653 on comparative advertising[6] and are based on Section 26 of the Marketing Control Act, which prohibits misleading representations that are likely to influence the demand for or the supply of products, services or other products. A representation may be

---

5   Chapter 3 of the Broadcasting Act implemented EU Directive 2010/13/EU, the Audio-visual Media Services Directive, into Norwegian law.

6   Regulation FOR-2000-12-19-1653 implemented EU Directive 2006/114/EC concerning misleading and comparative advertising into Norwegian law.

made in any form – orally, in writing or otherwise – and also includes the packaging of a product.

Comparative advertising is authorised only if the following criteria are fulfilled:

- It is not misleading;
- It compares products or services that meet the same needs or are intended for the same purpose; ,
- It objectively compares one or more material, relevant, verifiable and representative features of those products or services, which may include price;
- It does not discredit or denigrate the trademarks, trade names, other distinguishing marks, products, services, activities or circumstances of a competitor;
- For products with a designation of origin, it relates in each case to products with the same designation;
- It does not take unfair advantage of the reputation of a trademark, trade name or other distinguishing marks of a competitor, or of the designation of origin of competing products;
- It does not present products or services as imitations or replicas of products or services bearing a protected trademark or trade name; and
- It does not create confusion among traders, between the advertiser and a competitor, or between the advertiser's trademarks, trade names, other distinguishing marks, products or services and those of a competitor.

Comparative advertising affecting traders may be referred to the ordinary courts or to the NKU. There are several court decisions and legal opinions of the NKU within this area, following which the criteria are quite strictly observed. This is in line with the tradition within Norwegian marketing law, as comparative advertising was even more strictly limited prior to implementation of the EU Comparative Advertising Directive.

The courts may order an injunction as well as compensation in civil dispute resolution, or even penalties or imprisonment in public prosecution.

3. Online behavioural advertising

Privacy and data protection are generally governed by Norway's Personal Data Act of 15 June 2018, which implemented in its entirety by reference the EU General Data Protection Regulation (2016/679) into Norwegian law. The Electronic Communications Act[7] of 4 July 2003 governs the use of cookies on the Internet through its Section 2-7b.

---

7   The Electronic Communications Act Section 2-7b implemented Article 5(3) of Directive 2002/58/EC (the e-Privacy Directive) into Norwegian law.

The use of cookies is allowed only if the user is clearly and comprehensively informed about:
- the information stored or accessed;
- the purposes of the processing of the information; and
- the entity which is responsible for the processing.

The user must provide his or her prior consent in respect of the use of cookies. This does not prevent the technical storage of or access to information that is made for the purpose of transmission of communications via an electronic communications network, or to the extent necessary in order to provide an information society service following a request by the user. However, it is highly unlikely that any of these exceptions would apply in respect of cookies used for online behavioural advertising.

If personal data is collected, through the use of cookies or otherwise, all provisions of the Personal Data Act and thus also the GDPR must be complied with. Such provisions include, among other things:
- an obligation to use the information for explicitly stated purposes only;
- provisions pertaining to data security and quality; and
- an obligation to ensure that consent used as the basis for the processing of personal data is a freely given, specific, informed and unambiguous indication of the data subject's wishes by which he or she, through a statement or by a clear affirmative action, signifies agreement to the processing of personal data relating to him or her; and that it meets the further conditions set out in Article 7 of the GDPR.

The Personal Data Act is overseen by the Norwegian Data Protection Authority; whereas the Norwegian Communications Authority monitors compliance with the Electronic Communications Act.

Advertising on the Internet must further be in line with the provisions of the Marketing Control Act.

4. Sales promotions

Misleading advertising is prohibited, and this also applies to misleading sales promotions. Pursuant to Section 7 of the Marketing Control Act,[8] a commercial practice is considered misleading if it contains "false information and is therefore untruthful, or if it is otherwise likely to deceive consumers in relation to … the price of the product or how the price is calculated, or the existence of a price advantage".

Under Section 8 of the act, omissions may be considered to be misleading and therefore illegal – for instance, if information is presented in an "unclear,

---

8   Implementing EU Directive 2005/29/EC, the Unfair Commercial Practices Directive.

unintelligible, ambiguous or unsuitable manner". An invitation to purchase must include clear information about the price and applicable taxes. If the price cannot be given in advance, clear information about how the price is calculated must be provided. Any additional costs must also be presented, such as those for freighting, delivery or postage.

It follows from Section 10 of the act that, in connection with the sale of products, services or other things to consumers, price information must, where practically possible, be presented in such a way that it can be easily seen by customers. Special regulations apply to the proper provision of information about the prices of certain products and services, including an obligation to provide prices of products that are calculated by uniform measures such as weight and volume. Also, Section 9 of the Electronic Commerce Act (on direct marketing by electronic means) states that price information must be clear and complete.

Many cases referred to the Consumer Authority pertain to wrong or misleading price information. If a sales promotion communicates that the products or services are sold at a reduced price, the advertiser must be able to document that the genuine earlier price was applied before the sale period. As a rule of thumb, the Consumer Authority maintains that:

- at least three items must have been sold at the earlier price; and
- those sales must have been made no earlier than six weeks before the sale period commenced.[9]

Furthermore, any sales offers must be real – that is, the number of products available at the promoted price must not be too limited. If there are any limitations with respect to the number of items that are available for purchase by customers, such information must be clearly communicated in the advertising.

Slogans such as 'cheapest', 'best price' and so on are difficult to convey legally. Such communications will be considered misleading if the advertiser cannot document that no other similar offer will be available on the market at a lower price.[10]

The use of additional gifts is no longer forbidden, but the conditions under which such gifts are distributed must be clearly communicated. Section 18 of the Marketing Control Act provides that traders offering consumers an additional advantage – for example, by way of rebates, gifts or participation in competitions or draws – must ensure that the conditions for profiting from the offer are clearly and easily available to consumers. The same applies to

---

9   "Guidelines for Price Advertising", Consumer Authority, June 2009.
10   See, for example, the Consumer Authority communication of 29 January 2013 pertaining to mobile service provider One Call.

marketing by way of direct electronic means (see Section 9 of the Electronic Commerce Act). Care should be taken not to tailor any prize draws or competitions in such a way that the advertising may be deemed to be a lottery being contingent upon governmental authorisation. If a stake or premium is necessary in order to take part in a draw, this will likely be deemed to be a lottery requiring authorisation (see Sections 1, 4c and 6 of the Lottery Act of 24 February 1995).

5.   Ambush marketing

Branding and official products of events such as music festivals and sports events may enjoy protection against ambush marketing by way of:
- registration of trademarks or designs; or
- bilateral agreements with accredited persons, participants or other cooperating entities and persons.

The audience may, upon purchasing tickets, be requested to accept prohibitions against the marketing and use of unofficial products at the arena. The proprietor of the arena or other premises where an event takes place may, by virtue of this arrangement, request people engaged in ambush marketing to leave the premises.

However, the Marketing Control Act might also be a basis for an injunction against the marketing and sales of unofficial products. Pursuant to Section 30 of that act, the marketing and sale of a copy of a product, marketing material or distinguishing mark are prohibited if:
- they might cause a risk of confusion in the marketplace; and
- the product, distinguishing mark or marketing material is used in such manner or under such circumstances that it is considered to be an unfair exploitation of a third party's efforts or results.

Even if there is no risk of confusion, such marketing and sale can be considered to be contrary to Section 25 of the Marketing Control Act, which prohibits acts that conflict with good business practice among traders.

There is a risk that logos and distinguishing names and marks may derogate through widespread authorised as well as unauthorised commercial use, and also by generic use by the public. To overcome this problem, a provisional law was issued during the XVII Winter Olympic Games at Lillehammer, Norway, in 1994, establishing protection for the Olympic rings, as well as certain other symbols and logos, including the official logo shown in Figure 1.

Figure 1. Official logo for the Lillehammer Winter Olympic Games

6. Direct marketing

Direct marketing is governed by the Marketing Control Act. Direct marketing by telephone or postal mail to consumers is allowed, unless the consumer has chosen to opt out of receiving such communications, by notifying a central direct marketing opt-out register or the trader directly (see Sections 12, 13 and 13(a) of the Marketing Control Act). Advertisers using this kind of direct marketing must consult the register before approaching a consumer for the first time and thereafter at monthly intervals.

When approaching consumers by way of unsolicited direct marketing, the trader is obliged to present itself, the marketing nature of the communication and the possibility for the consumer to opt out of the process. In the case of unsolicited marketing by telephone or addressed mail, the trader must disclose who has provided the personal information that led to the inquiry (see Section 16 of the Marketing Control Act). Direct marketing by way of telephone calls from traders to consumers may take place only on working days between 9:00am and 9:00pm, and may not be made from a hidden or unregistered telephone number (see Section 14 of the Marketing Control Act).

If there is an existing customer relationship, a trader may contact that customer by direct marketing even though the customer is registered in the direct marketing opt-out register, provided that the communication relates to the trader's own products or services that are similar to those with which the customer has already engaged. The trader must, however, simultaneously provide the customer with an option to opt out of such customer-specific direct marketing.

Under Section 15 of the Marketing Control Act, certain forms of direct marketing towards physical persons are prohibited unless prior positive consent is obtained. This pertains to the use of electronic mail, fax and automated calling machines, or other electronic means allowing individual communication. An exception applies with respect to the use of electronic mail if the addressee is already a customer and the customer has provided the electronic address to the trader in connection with a sale. At the time of the communication, the customer shall be given the opportunity to freely opt out of future direct communications.

The provisions stated above in Chapter 6 also apply to electronic communications directed at customers from information services providers pursuant to Section 9 of the Electronic Commerce Act, which refers to the provisions of the Marketing Control Act.

7. Product placement

As a starting point, hidden marketing in broadcasting, as well as product placement, is prohibited. However, pursuant to Sections 3-6 and 3-7 of the Broadcasting Act,[11] product placement in broadcast films, fiction series, sports programmes and light entertainment programmes is permitted, subject to the fulfilment of certain conditions.

The placement of products, services or trademarks against consideration and where the placement is made for marketing purposes is considered to be product placement. The delivery of free products of insignificant value is not considered to be product placement. Product placement is in all circumstances forbidden if the programme involved is directed at children.

Product placement must be clearly marked at the beginning and end of the programme, as well as following commercial breaks in the programme. This obligation does not apply to product placement in programmes that have not been made or ordered by the service provider (ie, the broadcaster).

The content and scheduling of a programme must not be affected in a way that influences editorial responsibility and independence. A direct invitation to purchase or rent products or services – including special sales promotional references to such products or services – is not allowed. In addition, product placement must not give the relevant products or services an unduly prominent role.

Programmes produced or ordered by service providers under Norwegian jurisdiction or their affiliated entities cannot include product placements for:

- products or services that are of special interest to children; or
- weapons, weapon models or toy weapons.

Such entities further may not engage in product placement paid by political organisations.

The Norwegian Media Authority is responsible for ensuring compliance with the Broadcasting Act. In certain circumstances infringements may be penalised by fines and even imprisonment for a maximum period of six months.

8. Native advertising and social media influencers

Advertising in social media, often incorporated in editorial content, is increasingly common. There is no specific legislation directed towards such advertising; however, the Marketing Control Act and other trade-specific

---

11   Implementing Directive 2010/13/EU, the Audio-visual Media Services Directive.

legislation will apply. Pursuant to Section 3 of the Marketing Control Act, all advertising must be made and presented in a form that makes it clear to the audience that the communication is commercial marketing.

Unsolicited expressions by influencers and others are not considered to be advertising. However, if the influencer is given consideration for the activities – whether by payment, services or free access to products – it will no longer be considered an independent expression. Linking or other references to editorial content for commercial purposes will also be considered as a marketing activity and the professional party linking to such editorial content will be responsible.

If the commercial advertising is not clearly visible from the content itself, any such advertising must be expressly marked as advertising. The guidelines of the Consumer Authority require such markings to be prominently positioned and in a sufficiently visible font to be immediately noticed by the reader. The Consumer Authority has imposed fines for hidden advertising in the form of photos and expressions promoting a supplier or its products in social media by influencers. Through its administrative practice, the Consumer Authority has held that:

> being able to differentiate advertising from other content is a fundamental requirement for the consumers' ability to make an informed decision. The use of influencers is a popular marketing strategy exploiting the influential force of social media. Hence, it is important that such marketing is not disguised as personal recommendations, but rather expressly appears as advertising.[12]

Depending on the circumstances, an influencer may have contributory liability for the advertising; thus far, however, administrative practice has been directed solely towards the trader.

9.   Industry-specific regulation

9.1   Gambling

Lotteries and monetary gambling are prohibited by the Lottery Act of 24 February 1995 and by the Gaming Scheme Act of 28 August 1992, unless special provision is provided to the contrary (see Section 2 of the Gaming Scheme Act and Section 4c of the Lottery Act).

With respect to monetary gambling, only governmental companies are authorised gambling operators; and their revenues are allocated to the funding of sports and cultural activities, or other humanitarian or social purposes.

Traditional lotteries and bingo games may be arranged by other entities with individual authorisation. The revenues may be used only for social and humanitarian purposes. Certain limited exceptions to the requirement for authorisation apply with respect to gaming activities involving small-value

---

12   Consumer Authority Decision FOV-2020-507, Sports nutrition.

prizes (see Section 7 of the Lottery Act). Subject to special authorisation, the installation of prize and entertainment machines may also be allowed.

The Gaming Authority is the surveillance authority in Norway. The Gaming Authority may order rectifications and impose administrative fines if the provisions of the law are breached. Infringement of the Gaming Scheme Act may be sanctioned with fines or imprisonment for up to three months; whereas infringement of the Lottery Act may be sanctioned with fines or imprisonment for up to three years, depending on the circumstances.

The marketing of foreign gambling operators directed at Norwegian customers is illegal. The Gaming Authority aims to stop online gambling directed at Norwegian customers, in part by way of blocking payments.[13]

9.2   Alcohol

The advertisement of alcoholic beverages to consumers is prohibited in Norway under Section 9-2 of the Alcohol Act. Beverages containing 2.5% or more alcohol by volume are considered to be alcoholic beverages. The prohibition extends to the marketing of ingredients suitable for use in alcoholic drinks, as well as equipment for the brewing or other making of alcoholic beverages.

Pursuant to a Supreme Court decision of 24 June 2009, the prohibition was held not to be contrary to the European Economic Area Agreement. The Supreme Court considered the prohibition to be suitable in order to maintain a reduced intake of alcohol and to be a necessary precaution that could not be substituted by other means.

The advertisement of a trademark that is used for alcoholic beverages as well as for other products is also illegal, and this prohibition is fairly strictly interpreted. Following a Supreme Court decision of 21 January 2000, company sponsorship of football teams and handball teams by printing the company name of a brewery on their team kits was deemed to constitute the illegal marketing of alcohol. This was the case even though only 40% of the products sold by the breweries involved were alcoholic beverages. Following this decision, the Alcohol Act was amended to include a prohibition against the marketing of non-alcoholic products under a trademark otherwise used for alcoholic beverages. In addition, such products may not feature in ads for other products or services.

The Norwegian Health Directorate is responsible for ensuring compliance with the Alcohol Act. The directorate may order rectifications and impose coercive fines. Its decisions may be appealed to the Market Council.

Infringement of the Alcohol Act can be sanctioned by imprisonment for up to six months and, under certain special circumstances, up to two years.

---

13   Regulation FOR-2010-02-19-184 sets forth a prohibition against money transfers pertaining to bets made and winnings obtained in connection with illegal monetary games. Pursuant to Section 4 of the regulation, the Gaming Authority may impose orders for certain financial institutions to block such payments.

9.3 Pharmaceuticals

Under Section 19 of the Medicines Act of 4 December 1992, all marketing of medicinal products must be true and of a modest standard. The advertisement of a drug that has not obtained a marketing authorisation as a medicinal product is prohibited under Section 20 of that act.

The advertisement of medicinal products is further regulated by Regulation 1839 of 18 December 2009 ('Medicinal Products Regulation'). This encompasses the written and oral presentation of a medicinal product, including pictures, as well as the distribution of samples. The regulation also covers the sponsorship or economic support of activities directed at physicians and other professionals. All presentations must be objective and conform with the approved summary of product characteristics (SPC).

The Medicinal Products Regulation distinguishes between advertising directed at the general public and advertising directed at physicians and other professionals. Only non-prescription drugs may be advertised to the general public, with certain limited exceptions. Such advertising should, among other things:

- not create the impression that it is unnecessary to consult a physician;
- not suggest that effects are guaranteed or that there is no risk of negative side effects;
- not suggest that the marketed medicine is better than other medicines;
- not refer to a recommendation from physicians or other respected persons; and
- not refer to certain specified serious illnesses.

The Medicinal Products Regulation further sets out special requirements on the content of the advertising, such as the inclusion of:

- information about the product's name and active ingredient, and about the use of the product; and
- a request to read the packaging and the enclosed SPC leaflet.

Advertising directed to medical personnel is also subject to special regulation. Certain information must be provided with regard to:

- active ingredients;
- the holder of the marketing authorisation;
- use and dosage;
- indications and contraindications; and
- possible side effects.

Any reference to scientific publications or similar must be accurate and clear, and meet certain qualitative requirements. The distribution of gifts or an offer of entertainment is restricted.

Compliance with the Medicines Act and the Medicinal Products Regulation is overseen by the Norwegian Medicines Agency (NoMA). Infringement of the act and the regulation can be sanctioned by fines and by imprisonment for up to three months (or two years in aggravated circumstances). In certain circumstances NoMA may also ban the further marketing of a medicinal product; and may also order third parties, such as internet providers, to remove content, issue warnings or restrict access to an online interface.

The Association of the Pharmaceutical Industry in Norway has laid down detailed industry guidelines in its Rules for Marketing of Medicinal Products, based on the code of practice adopted by the European Confederation of Pharmaceutical Producers. A voluntary self-regulatory body has been established, through which representatives from the Association of the Pharmaceutical Industry in Norway and the Norwegian Medical Association supervise compliance with the rules.

9.4   Financial products and services

The advertisement of financial products and services is subject to detailed regulations, and the overall principles of good marketing practices and good business practices apply.

Pursuant to Chapter 3 of the Financial Contracts Act of 25 June 1999, certain information must be provided in connection with the advertisement of loans towards consumers, including:

- the total credit being offered;
- the costs;
- the effective interest rate;
- the term of the loan; and
- the required repayment instalments.

There are additional specific requirements on the information that must be provided prior to entering into the loan agreement, combined with a general duty of the lender to provide the consumer with satisfactory information about the characteristics of the contract and how it suits the needs and situation of the individual customer, as well as the consequences of breach of contract.

Non-compliance can result in a fine or imprisonment for up to three months.

The Financial Contracts Mediation Board has the power to issue opinions on complaints regarding compliance with the Financial Contracts Act. Its decisions may be further referred to the ordinary courts.

Chapter 8 of the Securities Funds Act of 25 November 2011 requires financial institutions to provide certain key information about investments, including the costs involved, the historical rate of return and the financial risk. The information must be provided in the Norwegian language, unless specific exemptions apply. Pursuant to Chapter 3 of the Securities Trading Act of 29 June 2007 and the Securities Trading Regulation of the same date, a general prohibition against unfair commercial practices and a general obligation to adhere to good business practices apply. Moreover, any suggestions or recommendations for investments to the public must be followed by correct and detailed information that is reasonable and proper, and that distinguishes facts from predictions. In a 22 March 2013 decision,[14] the Supreme Court overturned a combined investment and loan contract entered into between a bank and a consumer on the grounds that the bank had provided unsatisfactory information about the financial risks involved and the prospects that were foreseen. This decision has been followed by a series of complaints to the Financial Contracts Mediation Board involving allegedly similar cases.

The Financial Supervisory Authority of Norway is responsible for overseeing compliance with the laws and regulations in this field.

9.5   Food

Section 10 of the Act of 19 December 2003 relating to Food Production and Food Safety ('Food Act') sets out the general principle that all food labelling and advertising must be correct and complete, and not misleading. Further detailed provisions are set out in several regulations, including Regulation 187 of 17 February 2010 on Nutrition and Health Claims, which incorporates a reference to EU Regulation 1924/2006 and later amendments. No nutrition claims may be made without being reflected in the authorised list of nutrition claims annexed to EU Regulation 1924/2006; and no health claims may be made without being included in the list of health claims approved by the European Commission in accordance with such regulation and as amended from time to time.

The Norwegian Food Safety Authority is responsible for ensuring compliance with the Food Act and its associated regulations. The authority has the power to order injunctions and coercive fines. Infringements may further be sanctioned by imprisonment for up to two years, depending on the circumstances of the infringement.

The Food and Drink Industry Professional Practices Committee was established in order to issue opinions on compliance with an industry-generated Code for Marketing of Food and Drink to Children. The committee was established in response to a Norwegian government proposal for a total prohibition against any advertising directed at minors (ie, those under the age of 18) with respect to salty products, high-calorie products or products with low nutritional value. Pursuant to the code, the advertisement of such products to children under the age of 13 is prohibited. Furthermore, the code sets forth that the following are not considered to be advertising:

---

14   HR-2013-642-S – Rt-2013-388.

- the actual product, including its packaging;
- an ordinary display of products at the point of sale; and
- sponsorship that includes the use only of the sponsor's name or trademark, including the distribution of samples with the consent of parents and other responsible persons.

Television ads broadcast after 9:00pm will not be regarded as marketing specifically aimed at children.

Chapter 4 of the Marketing Control Act on the protection of children in general applies to all food products.

9.6 Tobacco

The advertisement of tobacco products and tobacco accessories is completely prohibited in Norway (see Chapter 4 of the Act of 9 March 1973 relating to the Prevention of Harmful Effects of Tobacco ('Tobacco Control Act')).[15]

Tobacco products may not be included in ads for other products. Trademarks associated with tobacco products may not be used for other products, and tobacco products may not be launched with the aid of marks used for other products. Tobacco sponsorship is prohibited; as is any kind of free distribution of tobacco products or sale at a discount to consumers. Retail displays of tobacco products are also prohibited and there are special regulations with regard to compulsory health warnings on the packaging.

The Norwegian Directorate of Health is responsible for ensuring compliance with the tobacco legislation. The authority may order rectification or impose fines (coercive or lesser).

9.7 E-cigarettes

The regulations on tobacco in Chapter 4 of the Tobacco Control Act apply to the sale of tobacco surrogates, including e-cigarettes, meaning that e-cigarettes may be sold only to customers aged 18 years or over. The advertisement of e-cigarettes is completely prohibited.[16]

---

15 Implementing EU Directive 2001/37/EC concerning the manufacture, presentation and sale of tobacco products.
16 The EU Directive 2014/40/EU is not yet fully implemented in Norway.

Poland

Jacek Myszko
Ewa Skrzydło-Tefelska
Sołtysiński Kawecki & Szlęzak

1. Overview of the legal and regulatory regime for advertising

1.1 Legal framework

In Poland, advertising is regulated through a number of statutes. Some issues are addressed in a general manner, while others enjoy very specific industry-tailored regulation. As Poland is a member state of the European Union, many areas of advertising follow the common pattern set by EU law. In some cases, however, the EU directives have not been perfectly implemented, leading to non-compliance or, in extreme scenarios, contradictions with the provisions of the EU directives.

In general, advertising is regulated by:

- the Act of 16 April 1993 on Combating Unfair Competition ('Unfair Competition Act');
- the Act of 23 August 2007 on Counteracting Unfair Commercial Practices ('Unfair Commercial Practices Act'); and
- the Act of 16 February 2007 on Competition and Consumer Protection ('Consumer Protection Act').

Radio and television advertising is additionally regulated by the Act of 29 December 1992 on Radio and Television Broadcasting ('Broadcasting Act'); while advertising in the press is regulated under the Act of 26 January 1984 on Press Law. The term 'press' is understood broadly as any periodical publication that is issued at least once a year and has a title, number and date, notwithstanding the manner of dissemination to the public. Therefore, this includes not only the 'regular' press, but also radio and television programmes, internet portals and other means of dissemination.

The advertisement of specific products or services is also regulated by several specific statutes, the most important of which relate to gambling services (including games of chance that are run for promotional purposes) and alcohol, tobacco and medicinal products. In most cases these sector-specific acts comply with EU regulations; indeed, in some cases they introduce a higher level of protection (see section 9).

In Poland, only some acts include a definition of 'advertising' (eg, the Broadcasting Act and the regulations on the advertisement of alcoholic beverages and medicinal products). Consequently, academic legal commentary must be taken into account in many cases. Usually, the notion of 'advertising' is construed broadly, to encompass every avenue of communication aimed at stimulating the market for products or services, irrespective of whether it is addressed to specified or unspecified recipients.

(a)   Unfair Competition Act

Although it is arguably the most important statute that regulates advertising in Poland, the Unfair Competition Act does not include a general definition of 'advertising' (except for 'comparative advertising' – see section 2). Usually, 'advertising' is understood very broadly in relation to the Unfair Competition Act, and refers to all sorts of activities that incentivise the acquisition of products or services. The act sets forth detailed regulations regarding the following aspects of advertising in particular:

- advertising that is contrary to law or good commercial practice, or that offends human dignity;
- misleading advertising, which may affect consumers' decisions to buy a product or service;
- advertising that refers to emotions causing fear;
- the exploitation of superstitions or the trust of children;
- surreptitious advertising, which presents itself as neutral information; and
- intrusive advertising that significantly interferes in the customer's privacy, in particular through burdensome importuning in public places, the sending of unsolicited goods at the customer's expense or the misuse of technical means of communication.

In practice, problems often arise in relation to misleading advertising because it may influence the decisions of consumers regarding the acquisition of products or services. The 'misleading character' of an ad is evaluated in view of all relevant aspects, including information given in the ad with regard to the quantity, quality, components, manufacturing methods, usefulness, possible use or means of repair or maintenance of the product, as well as consumers' behaviour. The advertiser bears the burden of proving the truthfulness of the information included in the ad; but the tort of unfair competition in advertising might also be committed by an advertising agency or another entrepreneur that prepared the ad.

(b)   Unfair Commercial Practices Act

A number of advertising activities are recognised as unfair commercial practices under the Unfair Commercial Practices Act. This act implements EU Directive 2005/29/EC in Poland and deals with, among other things, unfair business-to-consumer (B2C) commercial practices in the internal market. Within this aspect of unfair business conduct, 'misleading' commercial practices include:

- 'bait' advertising, where the entrepreneur is aware that its stock of the product is insufficient when compared with the scale of the advertising and the attractive price offered;
- 'bait-and-switch' advertising, where the advertiser ultimately offers another product instead of the product initially offered;
- hidden advertising, where a paid-for recommendation of goods is not clearly indicated as such or the advertising makes itself out to be objective information (when it is in fact an 'advertorial');
- the advertisement of a product which is similar to a competitor's product in a manner that suggests it is manufactured by that competitor (which probably has a better brand reputation); and
- the inclusion in marketing materials of an image of an invoice or bill in order to suggest to the consumer that he or she has already purchased the product and is obliged to pay for it.

The Unfair Commercial Practices Act also sets forth a list of 'aggressive' commercial practices, which include ads that directly exhort children to buy the advertised products or to persuade their parents or other adults to buy the advertised products for them. In such cases, the advertiser must prove that the relevant practice is not an unfair practice.

(c)   Consumer protection law

Advertising addressed to consumers also falls within the scope of application of consumer protection law. The standard of B2C communication in Poland is high: information directed to consumers must be clear, unequivocal and not misleading (as required, in particular, by the Unfair Competition Act and the Unfair Commercial Practices Act). Special attention is paid to offers advertised as 'free': if any element is in fact supplied against any sort of remuneration (with only very minor exceptions), the practice may be challenged.

1.2   Sanctions

In sensitive industry sectors (eg, alcohol, medicines, gambling), the sanctions for advertising that does not comply with the law may be severe, including criminal sanctions. However, a breach of the general rules may also result in liability under the civil law (ie, that of a non-public nature), and can include liability for committing acts of unfair competition.

Under the Unfair Competition Act, a business whose interests have been threatened or impaired may demand:

- cessation of the prohibited activity;
- elimination of its effects;
- publication of one or several corrective statements;
- payment of damages and account of profits; and
- if the activity was deliberate, payment of a specific amount to a social cause.

The (civil) court may also adjudicate on the products, their packaging, advertising materials and other objects directly connected with the commission of the act(s) of unfair competition. Similar (to some extent) claims may be brought against an advertiser by a consumer under the Unfair Commercial Practices Act. Actions based on the Unfair Competition Act may be taken by the competitors of a given entity; while actions based on the Unfair Commercial Practices Act may be taken by consumers. Furthermore, a national or regional organisation that protects the interests of entrepreneurs (eg, competitors of an entity that is in breach), a local commissioner of consumers or a national or regional organisation that protects the interests of consumers might also instigate proceedings.

Unfair (especially misleading) advertising may be also deemed to infringe collective consumers' interests; such conduct is severely punished in Poland (by fines of up to 10% of the turnover of the perpetrator).

1.3 Self-regulation

In Poland, the system of self-regulation in advertising is relatively well developed. The Advertising Council (together with its adjudication body, the Advertising Ethics Committee) plays the most prominent role among the self-regulatory bodies. The members of the council are trade associations of advertisers, the media and advertising agencies. Its partners are bound by the Code of Ethics in Advertising and are subject to the decisions of the Advertising Ethics Committee, which may order, among other things, the cessation or revision of advertising activities found to be in breach of the code. The code itself sets out rules on:

- general advertising;
- advertising targeted at children and teenagers;
- 'green' advertising;
- sponsorship;
- direct marketing; and
- sales promotions.

Moreover, it contains specific regulations for the advertisement of beer and for food advertising targeted at children.

Other self-regulatory bodies with codes of conduct that regulate advertising activity include the International Advertising Association in Poland and a number of industry-specific associations (including in the pharmaceutical and beer industries).

2. Comparative advertising

Legal restrictions on comparative advertising are set forth in Articles 16(3) and 16(4) of the Unfair Competition Act, which implements the EU Misleading Advertising Directive (2006/114/EC). 'Comparative advertising' is defined in the Unfair Competition Act as "advertising enabling the identification of, directly or indirectly, a competitor or products or services offered by a competitor".

Broadly speaking, comparative advertising is allowed in Poland unless it is contrary to "honest trade practices". A particular ad must meet all of the following criteria in order to be considered compliant with honest trade practices (and thus allowed):

- It is not misleading;
- It compares (objectively and in a verifiable manner) only products and services that fulfil the same needs or are intended for the same purpose;
- It compares one or more material, characteristic, verifiable and typical features, which may include price;
- It does not create confusion on the market (as far as the compared products, entrepreneurs or trademarks are concerned);
- It does not discredit a competitor's products, services, activities, trademarks, designation of an enterprise or other distinguishing designations of or facts concerning a competitor;
- With regard to products bearing a protected geographical indication or protected designation of origin, it relates to products bearing the same designation;
- It does not unfairly exploit the reputation of a trademark, designation of an enterprise or other distinguishing designation of a competitor, or a protected geographical indication or protected designation of origin of competitive products; and
- It does not present a product or service as an imitation or replica of products or services bearing a protected trademark, protected geographical indication or protected designation of origin, or another distinguishing designation.

Moreover, comparative advertising associated with a special offer, depending on the terms of the offer, must:

- specify clearly and explicitly the expiry date of the offer or, alternatively, state that the offer is valid until stock lasts or until the service is discontinued; and
- if the special offer is not yet valid, specify the starting date of the special price or other specific terms of the offer.

Comparative advertising may constitute an unfair commercial practice within the meaning of the Unfair Commercial Practices Act if it is misleading as to the products or their labelling, trademarks, trade names or other distinguishing designations of the entrepreneur or its products.

3. Online behavioural advertising

There are no specific provisions on online behavioural advertising in Poland; the general rules of advertising apply. However, the rules on data protection and telecommunications must also be taken into consideration.

In this regard, the entry into force of the European General Data Protection Regulation (GDPR) had a significant impact on the Polish data protection regime. Following the EU standards and laws on personal data protection, the Act of 29 August 1997 on the Protection of Personal Data was repealed and replaced by new legal framework, implementing and supplementing the GDPR, consisting of:

- the Act of 10 May 2018 on Personal Data Protection; and
- the Act of 21 February 2019 amending certain acts in connection with the implementation of the GDPR ('Amendment Act').

Due to the entry into force of the Amendment Act, some provisions of the Act of 16 July 2004 on Telecommunications Law and the Act of 18 July 2002 on Provision of Electronic Services have been revised.

Depending on whether the personal data of users is processed in the course of online behavioural advertising, restrictions pertaining thereto must be taken into consideration. The key regulatory requirement relates to the use of cookies and similar devices for the purposes of online behavioural advertising. Under Article 173 of the Telecommunications Law, subscribers or end users must be provided with information relating to:

- the purpose for which the information is stored and accessed; and
- the possibility of defining the conditions under which this information is stored and accessed, by adjusting the settings of the software or the configuration of the service.

Cookies can be used if the subscriber or concerned user has given his or her consent thereto, which may be expressed by means of the service configuration or the settings of his or her software or browser. Such consent must meet the data protection requirements – for example, effective consent requires an unambiguous act of confirmation. In this regard, affirming consent on the website by actively clicking a box shall be admissible as consent; whereas a box that is already pre-checked cannot establish effective consent in the sense of the GDPR. Accordingly, cookie banners which seek to establish consent simply by a user continuing to surf a website are not admissible.

Further, the stored information or access to such information must not cause changes to the configuration of the subscriber's or end user's telecommunications terminal equipment or any software installed on that equipment.

These rules do not apply where storage of or access to the information is necessary to perform a transmission through a public telecommunications network, or to provide a telecommunications service or an electronically supplied service requested by the subscriber or end user.

4.   Sales promotions

Under Polish law, the sale to consumers of products or services combined with the award, to some or all of those purchasers, of a free bonus consisting of a product or service dissimilar from the main object of sale is recognised as an act of unfair competition (a so-called 'bonus sale').

The following exemptions apply such that unfairness does not take place:

- the offer of bonuses consisting of products or services that are identical to the main object of sale;
- bonuses of small value or samples; and
- bonuses constituting prizes in lotteries (games of chance) or competitions (games of skill).

There are no clear guidelines as to what is considered a 'small value' bonus. The decisive factor is usually whether the addition of a bonus is likely to influence the customer's decision to acquire the main product rather than products offered by competitors without the bonus.[1]

All forms of promotions in which the winners are selected randomly (by way of a draw, irrespective of whether entry is free or against remuneration) are, in principle, recognised as games of chance in Poland and are thus covered by the broad regulatory category of 'gambling'. Running games of chance is somewhat challenging in Poland; in particular, it requires the issue of a permit by the authorities (the related procedures being rather complicated and time consuming). Moreover, promotions are classified as games of chance in which an element of a skill-based contest is present, but the actual result depends on chance alone. It is therefore recommended to organise promotions based purely on the knowledge or skill of the participants (ie, the best entrant wins).

Such promotions are governed by the general provisions of the Civil Code (according to the principle of the so-called 'public promise'), by various consumer regulations and by other applicable laws (eg, privacy or electronic

---

[1]   There is an argument that these restrictions regarding bonus sales are contrary to EU law as being too restrictive (see in particular Joined Cases C-261/07 and C-299/07). However, at the time of writing, these restrictions remain in force in Poland.

communication). Knowledge/skill-based promotions may be organised without any notification or permit from the authorities – although some obligations may still arise depending on the particularities of each event (eg, where the personal data of entrants is being processed).

It is recommended that the terms and conditions of the contest include at least the following:

- the name and address of the organiser;
- a specification of the type of contest;
- the eligibility criteria;
- the contest period;
- the mode(s) of entry;
- the criteria for and manner of selection of winning entries;
- the promise of a prize, along with a specification of the prize(s) offered;
- privacy-related information (eg, on the handling and storage of personal data);
- the complaints procedure; and
- if the contest is organised via a means of electronic communication, specification of the technical requirements necessary to participate in the contest, along with a prohibition (addressed to entrants) on the supply of illegal content.

Loyalty programmes that allow participants to benefit from discounts or free goods or services in return for regular purchases are considered a form of advertising and are generally allowed in Poland. They may be classified as an abuse of a dominant market position under the Consumer Protection Act if they are carried out by an entity that is dominant in the relevant market (when their scale discourages consumers from purchasing the goods and services of smaller competitors). They may also be considered to hinder access to the market, which constitutes a specific tort of unfair competition.

Specific restrictions apply to sales organised by retail stores with a floor space of more than 400 square metres: these are not permitted to hinder smaller businesses' access to the market by selling products at prices that do not include a profit margin. Exceptions to this restriction include the following:

- end-of-season sales organised no more than twice a year, at the end of summer and winter, for a maximum period of one month;
- discount sales as a result of the imminent expiry of the use-by date or the best-before date of products; or
- sales of goods pending liquidation of a retail store, which must not last for more than three months from public notification of the store's liquidation, or more than one year in the case of liquidation of all stores belonging to an entrepreneur due to the winding-up of its business.

5. Ambush marketing

There are no specific regulations on ambush marketing in Poland; the general regulations on advertising apply. Ambush marketing may constitute a tort of unfair competition – in particular, where it is misleading as to the designation of a product or service or involves the dissemination of misleading information; or it may constitute the tort of passing off.

Moreover, ambush marketing may infringe the IP rights of a given event's organisers in relation to registered trademarks (which, in the case of big sporting events, will often be reputable and therefore more broadly protected). Artwork and logos connected with events may also be protected by copyright, and their imitation may therefore constitute copyright infringement.

In practice, entities tend to extend their monopoly over the organisation of famous events to the point where in fact such monopoly is legally unjustified; this pattern was evident in Poland in the course of FIFA's Euro 2012 football championship. However, it is not possible to ban any reference to the symbols of a sporting event, especially where those symbols are not protected by IP rights. However, the line is very fine and must be evaluated on a case-by-case basis.

6. Direct marketing

In Poland, sending unsolicited commercial information addressed to a specified individual by means of electronic communications (in particular, by email) is prohibited under the Act on Provision of Electronic Services. It is allowed only where a recipient has expressed his or her prior consent to receive such information, in particular by making his or her email address available. The consent must be clear and independent from other declarations made by the recipient (in the sense that it cannot be presumed from other consents given by the recipient), and the consent may be withdrawn by the individual at any time. In any circumstances other than the foregoing, such activity is considered a tort of unfair competition.

The Telecommunications Law bans the use of automated calling systems for direct marketing purposes, unless a subscriber or end user has given his or her prior consent to such use. Under the Telecommunications Law, a marketer cannot obtain consent after making first contact with the end user; the explicit consent regarding the use of automatic calling systems must be granted beforehand (general consent to use personal data for marketing purposes is insufficient).

The general rules of the Unfair Competition Act prohibiting advertising that interferes with privacy or abuses a technical means of communication apply to post and telephone marketing. That apart, there are no specific rules or requirements for post and telephone marketing, provided that such marketing is not coupled with making an offer to conclude a contract (which requires the recipient's prior consent). In practice, it may be difficult to delimit purely advertising content from an actual offer.

There are no legally binding 'opt-out' registers. However, an opt-out database (a so-called 'Robinson list'), based on the Robinson List Rules, is maintained by the Polish Marketing Association (SMB), which is binding on SMB members only. Currently, due to ongoing work to introduce legal changes, the operation of the database has been temporarily suspended.

7. Product placement

Product placement is regulated, directly and indirectly, by various statutes.

Under the Broadcasting Act, 'product placement' is defined as "a commercial communication consisting of the inclusion of or reference to a product, a service or a trademark so that it is featured as an element of a programme, in return for payment or for similar consideration, including gratuitously making a product or service available". In turn, 'theme placement' is "a commercial communication consisting of a reference to a product, a service or the trademark thereof in a script or dialogue of a programme in return for payment or for similar consideration".

Theme placement is generally prohibited in Poland; whereas product placement is generally prohibited, but subject to certain exemptions. Product placement is admissible in cinematographic films, films or series made for 'audio-visual media services', sports programmes and entertainment programmes. Where certain products or services are made available free of charge for the purpose of a programme (particularly as props or prizes), such product placement is also admissible. However, product placement is always prohibited in children's programmes, and the following products must never be used for product placement:

- tobacco;
- alcoholic beverages;
- medicinal products and services;
- some games within the broad category of gambling;
- psychotropic or intoxicating substances; and
- tanning salon services.

Information on product placement must be included at the beginning and the end of every programme that contains it, as well as after each commercial break. The communication should also fulfil specific requirements set forth in the Regulation of 30 June 2011 on the National Broadcasting Council, which defines the graphical sign to be used, its size and the duration of its broadcast. The advertiser must be indicated neutrally along with the placed product or service at the end of the programme; and undue prominence cannot be given to the placed product or service, whose purchase or use cannot be directly encouraged.

Product placement carried out in media other than those included in the Broadcasting Act (eg, in the press) is not prohibited, unless it constitutes an infringement of the general rules of advertising. In particular, hidden or misleading advertising (also encompassing situations in which the advertising nature of the communication is not revealed, such as advertorials) is not allowed because, under the Unfair Competition Act and the Unfair Commercial Practices Act, recipients must be clearly informed of the nature of the communication directed at them.

8. Native advertising and social media influencers

In Poland, social influencer advertising plays an important role in an effective marketing strategy. However, influencers regularly add posts on social media that promote various products and often do not indicate the commercial nature of their involvement. Some of them just add some hashtags with the brand name – for example, #[Brand name]Time, #[Brand name]Day – to their posts. In this respect, the law has failed to keep up with fast-paced developments and influencer marketing is not yet covered by specific legal regulations in Poland.

However, this form of advertising may constitute an unfair market practice and an act of unfair competition, as it is aimed at creating an impression among consumers that the advertising message is neutral information and thus conceals the promotional nature of the activity. Accordingly, it may also be recognised as a practice that infringes collective consumer interests as defined in the Unfair Competition Act.

9. Industry-specific regulation

9.1 Gambling

The Act of 19 November 2009 on Gambling, which governs the advertisement of gambling in Poland, provides for the following main statutory categories of gambling:

- games of chance;
- card games;
- automated machine games; and
- *pari mutuel* bets, also known as 'the tote'.

These categories are defined broadly in the Gambling Act and their definitions overlap to some extent, on occasion creating problems with the qualification of particular games or bets.

'Advertising' covers all instances of the public dissemination of graphic symbols, trademarks, names and other designations relating to games or entities running such games, as well as information about actual places where such games are run. In turn, the promotion covers any form of public incentive to participate in such games (as specifically listed under the Gambling Act).

The advertisement and promotion of cylindrical games (in particular, roulette), card games, dice games, *pari mutuel* bets and games on automated machines (collectively referred to as 'ARGS') are generally prohibited in Poland. It is also illegal to advertise entities whose advertising image exploits a similarity to or is the same as the markings of gambling games or gambling operators. This rule also applies to the names, trademarks, graphical shapes and packaging of any products or services. This prohibition applies to all marketing and promotional activities carried out in Poland, irrespective of whether the advertised services are accessible by (or directed to) Polish customers or whether the gaming operator is licensed by a Polish or another EU authority. The exemptions include the following:

- the dissemination of information on sponsorship by an entity operating *pari mutuel* bets, where such information is limited to the name or other identification of the sponsor, being an entity that exclusively operates *pari mutuel* betting or *pari mutuel* betting along with another activity that is not subject to any advertising restrictions;
- advertising and information placed in game salons and bookmaking points; and
- in relation to online betting, advertising and promotions appearing on websites covered by an advertising permit and used to operate these bets.

The Gambling Act does not prohibit the promotion or advertisement of games other than ARGS, although such activities remain subject to the restrictions applicable under the general rules on advertising.

9.2 Alcohol

In Poland, the advertisement of alcoholic beverages is strictly regulated under the Act of 26 September 1982 on Upbringing in Sobriety and Counteracting Alcoholism ('Anti-Alcoholism Law'). Pursuant to this law, the advertisement and promotion of alcoholic beverages, except beer, are generally prohibited in Poland.

The advertisement of beer is allowed under certain conditions set forth in the Anti-Alcoholism Law. A separate category of advertising relates to information on sponsorship offered by the producers of alcoholic beverages, as defined under Article 2(1) of the Anti-Alcoholism Law.

The Anti-Alcoholism Law allows producers and distributors whose main business activity consists of the manufacture or sale of alcoholic beverages containing between 8% and 18% alcohol by volume (ABV) of alcohol to disseminate information on sponsorship of 'mass events' (eg, sporting events, music concerts) exclusively by placing their name and trademark inside daily newspapers and magazines, or on invitations, tickets, posters, products or information boards tied to a specific event. Information on sponsorship offered by producers or distributors of alcoholic beverages whose business activity consists of the distribution of alcoholic beverages containing more than 18% ABV is prohibited in Poland.

More specific restrictions apply to information on sponsorship on radio and television – for instance, such information must not be presented on television by an individual or in a way that employs the image of an individual.

The restrictions on advertising set forth in the Anti-Alcoholism Law do not apply if the ad, promotion or information on sponsorship is placed:

- inside the premises of a wholesaler trading in alcoholic beverages;
- in separate retail spots trading exclusively in alcoholic beverages; or
- in places where alcoholic beverages are sold for immediate consumption on site (eg, pubs).

Moreover, because of the statutory definitions of 'advertising' and 'the promotion of alcoholic beverages', ads and promotions are also allowed if they are non-public – for example, during closed events (upon invitation only) or in a mailing to named recipients (included in a database).

9.3   Pharmaceuticals

The advertisement of medicinal (pharmaceutical) products is regulated through:

- the Act of 6 September 2001 on Pharmaceutical Law;
- the Regulation of the Minister of Health of 21 November 2008 on the advertisement of pharmaceutical products ('Regulation on Drug Advertising'); and
- the Law of 12 May 2011 on the Reimbursement of Medicines and Foodstuffs Intended for Particular Nutritional and Medical Devices ('Reimbursement Law').

Additional rules and guidelines are provided by soft law, in the form of the following codes of conduct and ethics:

- the Polish Union of Innovative Pharmaceutical Companies (INFARMA) Code of Good Practices in Pharmaceutical Industry;
- the INFARMA Disclosure Code;
- the International Federation of Pharmaceutical Manufacturers and Associations Code of Practice;
- the Polish Chamber of Pharmaceutical Industry and Medical Devices Code of the Pharmaceutical Marketing Ethics of Prescription-Only Medicines; and
- the Physicians' and Pharmacists' Code of Ethics.

The 'advertisement of a medicinal product' is broadly defined in the Pharmaceutical Law as any activity that informs on or encourages the use of a medicinal product, with the aim of increasing the number of prescriptions, delivery, sale or consumption of that product. It does not comprise the following:

- the placement of information on, or the attachment of information to, the packaging of a medicinal product, as long as it complies with the relevant marketing authorisation;
- any communication, along with materials of an informative character, that is necessary to answer questions regarding a specific medicinal product;
- public announcements such as safety warnings, information on a change of packaging and so on, provided that they do not refer to the features of the medicinal product;
- commercial catalogues and price lists containing only the name, dosage, form and price of medicinal products, as long as they do not refer to the features of the medicinal product, including therapeutic indications; or
- the provision of information regarding human and animal health or diseases, as long as it includes no direct or indirect reference to medicinal products.

The advertisement of medicinal products may be conducted only by either the marketing authorisation holder or a parallel importer, or on behalf of the marketing authorisation holder or parallel importer. It must also meet a number of conditions set out in the Pharmaceutical Law and in the Regulation on Drug Advertising – for example, it should present the product objectively and should provide information on its rational use.

An absolute ban on the advertisement of medicinal products applies to:

- medicinal products that are not authorised for use in Poland;
- medicinal products that are authorised for use under statutory exemptions (ie, without the requirement to obtain 'regular' marketing authorisation); and
- advertising that contains information that does not comply with the product's characteristics.

The Pharmaceutical Law prohibits advertising addressed to the general public (and thus does not apply to advertising addressed to professionals) for prescription drugs or other medicinal products dispensed without prescription, if the name of the medicinal product is identical to that of a medicinal product available on prescription only. This also applies to medicinal products containing narcotic or psychotropic substances, and to medicinal products reimbursed through the public health insurance system (or products with an identical name to that of a reimbursed medicinal product).

A variety of restrictions apply with regard to the content and mode of dissemination where medicinal products are advertised to the general public. A warning on the need to verify the content of the leaflet or to consult a doctor or pharmacist must also be included.

The advertisement of medicinal products directed at health professionals should meet specific requirements – for instance, it must contain information that complies with the product characteristics. Very specific regulations apply to the provision of samples of medicinal products. Advertising for items relating to medical practice may not consist of any incentives (eg, gifts, prizes, trips or promotional meetings with excessively generous hospitality), unless the combined value of those incentives does not exceed PLN 100 (about €23).

9.4   Financial products and services

The use of many terms in the banking and financial sector is restricted in Poland, and such terms may be used in advertising only under certain conditions and only by authorised entities. These terms include 'bank', 'savings association', 'payment service', 'investment fund', 'pension programme' and 'pension fund'. The use of such terms by an unauthorised person may result in high fines (eg, PLN 10 million (approximately €2.2 million) with respect to the terms 'bank' and 'savings association').

The advertising carried out by banks is controlled by Poland's Financial Supervision Authority (FSA). The FSA is authorised to issue decisions that are binding on banks regarding advertising in the banking sector. Moreover, the FSA has adopted a set of rules for advertising, which is not binding on banks, but which acts as a form of code of good practice.

Specific requirements regarding the advertisement of consumer credit agreements are set out in the Act on Consumer Credit. Information provided to the consumer about the costs of the loan and the advertiser (creditor or credit intermediary) must include specific details, such as the borrowing rate and the actual annual interest rate, which should be illustrated by means of a representative example (ie, one that the creditor or intermediary would expect to apply to two-thirds of the advertised credit agreements).

The Act of 27 May 2004 on Investment Funds and Management of Alternative Investment Funds ('Act on Investment Funds') restricts the use of the term 'investment funds' to investment funds within the meaning of that act. However, it also introduces an obligation to use the term in advertising for authorised investment funds. Such ads must include certain information as provided in the Act on Investment Funds. These rules also apply to foreign investment funds that conduct promotional activities in Poland. No investment funds other than open investment funds may refer to compliance with the rules on collective investment in securities in their advertising.

Specific regulations on commercial communications made by investment firms are set out in the Regulation of 29 May 2018 on organisational requirements and operating conditions for investment firms and banks, defined in Article 70(2) of the Act of 24 September 2012 on Trading in Securities and Trust Funds.

9.5 Food

EU Regulation 1169/2011 on the provision of food information to consumers is generally applicable in Poland; specific regulations are also set out in the Act of 25 August 2006 on the Safety of Foodstuffs and Nutrition. These statutes constitute the primary source of law regarding food labelling and advertising. Among other things, food advertising cannot:

- mislead the customer;
- ascribe to the food any properties that it does not have;
- suggest that the food has special properties when in fact all similar foods have such properties; or
- in general, attribute to the food any properties relating to the prevention or cure of a disease, or refer to such properties or use health claims or nutritional claims in a manner contrary to EU Regulation 1924/2006.

The Pharmaceutical Law in general prohibits ascribing the characteristics of medicinal products to other products, including dietary supplements and food products, under penalty of a significant fine.

A number of regulations set forth specific restrictions on the advertisement of foodstuffs for particular nutritional uses – for example, infant formula feed. Pursuant to the Act on the Safety of Foodstuffs and Nutrition, infant formula feed may be advertised only in popular science publications specialising in childcare knowledge or in scientific publications, and must be limited to scientifically proven information. Moreover, such advertising may include health claims in accordance with the Regulation of 16 September 2010 of the Minister of Health on Foodstuffs for Particular Nutritional Uses. Also, ads for natural mineral water may include certain health claims under the conditions listed in the Act on the Safety of Foodstuffs and Nutrition and in the Regulation of 31 March 2011 of the Minister of Health on Natural Mineral Water. Some specific requirements for food supplements are included in the Regulation of 9 October 2007 on the Composition and Labelling of Food Supplements. In particular, ads for food supplements must not include the suggestion that a balanced and varied diet cannot in general provide a sufficient dose of nutrients for the human body.

9.6 Tobacco

The advertisement of tobacco products is completely prohibited under the Act of 9 November 1995 on the Protection of Health from the Consequences of Tobacco Use and Tobacco Products ('Anti-Tobacco Act'). The advertisement of tobacco products consists of the dissemination of communications or brand images of tobacco products, e-cigarettes, refill containers, tobacco paraphernalia and symbols connected thereto; as well as the names and graphical representations of producers of tobacco products, e-cigarettes, refill containers or tobacco paraphernalia, where:

- these are identical to the names and graphical representations of tobacco products, e-cigarettes, refill containers, tobacco paraphernalia or symbols connected thereto; and
- the aim is to promote certain brands of tobacco products, e-cigarettes, refill containers or tobacco paraphernalia.

The concept of 'advertising' in relation to tobacco products does not include commercial information used among companies engaged in the manufacture, distribution or trade in tobacco products, e-cigarettes, refill containers or tobacco paraphernalia.

The 'promotion' of tobacco products means:

- the dissemination of tobacco products, e-cigarettes, refill containers or tobacco paraphernalia to the public;
- the provision of samples;
- the bonus sale of tobacco products, e-cigarettes, refill containers or tobacco paraphernalia;
- the offer of tobacco products to consumers at reduced prices (compared with the printed price indicated on the package);
- the organisation of competitions based on the purchase of tobacco products, e-cigarettes, refill containers or tobacco paraphernalia; and
- any other forms of public encouragement to purchase or use such products, irrespective of the form in which they are addressed.

The ban on tobacco advertising covers any advertisement or promotion of tobacco products, e-cigarettes, refill containers, tobacco paraphernalia or imitations thereof, and of symbols relating to the use of tobacco, tobacco products, e-cigarettes or refill containers. Imitations of packages for tobacco products, e-cigarettes and refill containers cannot be displayed in stores. Moreover, manufacturers and importers of tobacco products and related products are prohibited from sponsoring sport, cultural, educational, health and socio-political activities.

9.7   E-cigarettes

The advertisement of e-cigarettes is regulated by the Anti-Tobacco Act, which was amended in 2016 in order to implement the provisions of EU Directive 2014/40/EC. Due to these changes, the ban on the advertisement and promotion of tobacco products also covers e-cigarettes and refill containers (as defined in section 9.6).

Russia

Yulia Yarnykh
Gowling WLG

---

1. Overview of the legal and regulatory regime for advertising

The Russian Constitution guarantees:

- a common economic space;
- protection of competition;
- freedom of thought and speech; and
- the right to freely look for, receive, transmit, produce and distribute information by any legitimate means.

This general rule, established by the primary Russian statute, constitutes the foundation of advertising business regulation in Russia, which is further developed in the Law on Advertising. This is the most important piece of federal legislation governing the advertising industry in Russia.

Article 1 of the Advertising Law defines its main goals as:

- facilitating the development of the market economy based on the principles of fair competition; and
- ensuring the common economic space.

The law prevents false or misleading advertising and sets out industry-specific regulations and requirements on how competitors may deal with each other and how businesses should treat their customers.

The first Advertising Law was adopted in 1995, in the early days of the emerging Russian market economy. As the competitive environment evolved, the need for more sophisticated legislation became apparent. In response, the State *Duma* passed the current federal law on 13 March 2006. Since the date of its enactment, the Advertising Law has undergone 65 amendments, with the latest introduced on 31 July 2020.

Because of the large number of questions relating to the enforcement of the Advertising Law that have been considered by the Russian arbitration courts, on 8 October 2012 the Plenum of the Supreme Arbitration Court of the Russian Federation (SAC) adopted Ruling 58 on Certain Issues of Enforcement of the Federal Law On Advertising by the Arbitration Courts. The SAC ruling clarified important legal issues, with special emphasis on:

- the concept and definition of 'advertising';
- the specifics of certain types of advertising; and
- enforcement of the Advertising Law by the arbitration courts.

The Federal Anti-monopoly Service of the Russian Federation (FAS), which is the state administrative body responsible for enforcing the Advertising Law, also issues explanation letters on the application of the law on a regular basis.

The FAS initiates administrative cases *ex officio*, on a submission of the public prosecutor or at the petition of individuals and legal entities; it also carries out inspections, brings administrative and legal actions against infringers and issues mandatory orders to rectify discovered violations. The FAS's orders or rulings can be challenged in court in the manner prescribed by the Arbitration Procedure Code of the Russian Federation. The limitation period for the institution of administrative cases under the Advertising Law is one year from the date of commission of the violation.

Violation of the Advertising Law results in administrative and civil liability for the advertiser, advertising producer and advertising distributor, as the case may be. The administrative procedure is initiated by the FAS, which determines the case and imposes an administrative fine on the infringer; whereas civil liability is incurred upon judicial consideration of the case initiated by the rights holder. A person whose rights have been infringed by the inappropriate advertising can apply to court and claim compensation for losses (including lost profits), recovery of damages, compensation for moral damages and public refutation of false advertising. In one case, the Russian court held that advertising in which a private security agency, Femida, claimed that it had not made a deal with the National Guard to allow apprehended apartment thieves go free was negative towards the National Guard, which ensures public order, and denigrated the honour, dignity and business reputation of National Guard officers, as well as the business reputation of the Ministry of Internal Affairs. The court obliged Femida to cease the advertising and pay a fine for defamation.[1]

Violations of the Advertising Law are not subject to criminal penalties (eg, imprisonment).

1.1 False and misleading advertising

The general requirements for advertising are set forth in Article 5 of the Advertising Law, which states that the advertising should not be false or misleading.

An ad is considered false if it:

- contains an incorrect comparison of the advertised product with other products in circulation produced by other manufacturers and sold by other sellers;

---

1 Ruling of the Second Arbitration Appellate Court dated 27 February 2017 in Case N 02AP-10936/2016.

- denigrates the honour, dignity and business reputation of other persons;
- advertises products that are prohibited from being advertised if this is done under the guise of the advertisement of other products whose trademark is identical or confusingly similar; or
- constitutes an act of unfair competition.

In 2018 a Russian court found that the dissemination by insurer Rosgosstrakh of leaflets alleging that one of its former agent no longer had an insurance licence constituted false advertising. The leaflets distributed to potential customers implied that Rosgosstrakh's former agent was not entitled to act on behalf of another insurer, but contained no evidence to support these allegations. Therefore, the court found that this constituted false advertising and ordered Rosgosstrakh to cease the infringement.[2]

One of the most common cases of false advertising is the groundless positioning of a brand, product, manufacturer or service provider as 'the best' or 'number one'. Both the FAS and the Russian courts require that an advertiser prove superiority by indicating the criteria on which the comparison is based and, if necessary, providing documentary confirmation of the facts claimed.

The FAS has previously found that an ad which claimed that sports club chain World Class was "number one in Russia" constituted false advertising, as the advertiser was unable to prove that its chain was indeed ranked number one in Russia.[3]

In another case, the court agreed with the FAS and ruled that the actions of communication service provider MTS and its slogan "MTS is the Country Internet Leader" constituted false advertising. The court stated that a formal indication of the comparison criteria included in small font was insufficient.[4]

The Advertising Law contains an extensive list of information on products (services) and their manufacturers (providers) that may be considered misleading advertising, including information on:

- the advantages of the advertised products in comparison with products produced by other manufacturers and sold by other sellers;
- the characteristics of the products, including their nature, composition, method and date of manufacture or qualities;
- the product range, and the period during which and place at which they are sold; and
- the price of the products, payment method, discounts, tariffs and other terms and conditions of purchase.

---

2   Ruling of the First Arbitration Appellate Court dated 9 July 2018 in Case N 01AP-2927/2018.
3   Ruling of the Moscow FAS Arbitration Appellate Court dated 12 April 2016 in Case N 3-16-44/77-16.
4   Ruling of the First Arbitration Appellate Court dated 25 July 2017 in Case N 01AP-4700/17.

The Advertising Law further defines 'misleading advertising' as advertising that contains untrue information about other persons' IP rights and means of individualisation (eg, trademarks, company names or trade names). In a 2018 case, the Russian court found that Visa Center Yaroslavl LLC had violated the Advertising Law and infringed Visa Center LLC's exclusive right to its name, which existed through its use of the designation VISA CENTER in its firm's name and trade name. The court affirmed the claim and stated that by using the claimant's firm's name in its advertising, the defendant had misled potential consumers.[5]

As was clarified by a 2012 SAC ruling, the use of a trademark with respect to products that have been duly introduced into civil circulation is allowed by other parties in order to advertise the fact that they sell those products. The fact that such use has not been authorised by the trademark owner does not automatically imply that such advertising is misleading, as long as customers would recognise it as advertising for an independent seller or service provider. The Russian courts have previously found that a limited liability company did not violate the Advertising Law by using the KAMAZ trademark, which belonged to a well-known truck manufacturer, because it was not presenting itself as an official vehicle service provider, but was rather informing potential customers about the products and services that it provided.[6]

2. Comparative advertising

The Advertising Law does not prohibit comparative advertising as such, unless the ad:

- contains an incorrect comparison of the advertised product with other products produced by other manufacturers and sold by other sellers (Article 5.2.1); or
- makes dubious claims about the advantage of the advertised products over competitor products (Article 5.3.1).

The Advertising Law does not define the criteria for an 'incorrect comparison', leaving this to the discretion of the FAS and the courts, as the case may be. As per the 2012 SAC ruling, a comparison based on a 'disparate' criterion or an incomplete comparison is prohibited. The SAC has also stated that an advertiser should be held liable for the dissemination of false information with respect not only to the advertised products, but also to the products of competitors.

In a 2016 case, the court found that the slogan "No Tandem with Fakes" used by the Rio shopping mall constituted an incorrect comparison and false

---

5   Ruling of the Second Arbitration Appellate Court dated 22 February 2018 in Case N A82-10247/2017.
6   Ruling of the Fourth Arbitration Appellate Court dated 9 February 2017 in Case N A19-14104/2016.

advertising. The court ruled that the ad aimed to promote the Rio shopping mall solely through the advertiser's reference to another shopping mall, Tandem, in the same city, and through a direct indication of the sub-standard quality of products sold at the Tandem mall. The advertiser failed to support its claim and the information contained in the advertising was thus qualified as false.[7]

3. Online behavioural advertising

Online behavioural advertising in Russia is not regulated by the Advertising Law. However, the general principle set forth in Article 23.2 of the Russian Constitution guarantees the privacy of correspondence and other communications. In addition, the federal Law on Personal Data provides for the protection of certain types of information by which an individual can be identified. The unauthorised use of such data, including in online advertising, can result in administrative liability in the form of a fine. The Federal Supervision Agency for Information Technologies and Communications (Roskomnadzor) – the state body responsible for enforcing the Personal Data Law – is entitled to initiate administrative proceedings against and impose an administrative fine on an infringer.

Despite the lack of specific rulings, the FAS is now paying considerable attention to the activities of internet companies.

In a 2017 decision the Moscow Arbitration Court agreed with the trademark owner and awarded compensation for the unauthorised use of its ZANDZ trademark in a competitor's online advertising. The court dismissed the defendant's argument that it did not operate the website www.ezrf.ru, which was shown in the results of a Yandex search for the ZANDZ trademark. The court noted that the websites http://shop.ezrf.ru/ and www.ezrf.ru were connected, and that the www.ezrf.ru site, operated by the defendant, contained a link to http://shop.ezrf.ru/, informing clients of a new store opened by the defendant.[8]

In another case, the FAS held airline Pobeda liable for violation of the Advertising Law as an electronic ticket obtained by a customer of the airline included advertising information. The FAS stated that the customer's permission for the airline to process his personal data did not imply his automatic consent to receive advertising, and that the airline should have obtained two separate consents from the customer. The airline argued that its data protection policy provided that each client who entered into an air carriage agreement or used its services through its website or app was considered to have consented to personal data processing.

However, the court agreed with the FAS that advertising will be considered

---

7   Ruling of the Second Arbitration Appellate Court dated 24 May 2016 in Case N A82-9898/2015.
8   Decision of the Moscow Arbitration Court dated 4 December 2017 in Case N A40-79046/2017.

to have been disseminated without the recipient's prior consent if the advertising distributor does not prove that such consent has been obtained. The airline's argument that its customer had automatically agreed to receive advertising by filling out a ticket purchase form was rejected by the court.[9]

As a result of the amendments to the Personal Data Law, all personal data of Russian citizens must be stored and processed in databases located within the Russian territory. Failure to comply with this obligation may lead to administrative fines and the blocking of access to the website of the personal data operator.

One major case in this space concerning a data operator's refusal to localise the personal data of Russian citizens on servers in Russia involved LinkedIn; in 2016, the court ordered that access to the entire website be blocked. Although the defendant was a foreign entity without a legal presence in Russia, the court agreed with Roskomnadzor that the website was aimed at Russian citizens and the Russian territory – in particular, by having a Russian language website and by advertising in Russian.[10]

4.   Sales promotions

Sales promotions are not specifically regulated by the Advertising Law; therefore, the Russian courts apply general principles on the prohibition of false and inaccurate advertising. For example, the FAS considered the advertising campaign of Siberian Giant LLC misleading because leaflets distributed to store customers did not specify that the discount applied only to purchases of at least three items. The FAS did not agree with the advertiser that the price of one item of the product was determinative to consumers' purchasing decisions, and stated that the ad lacked some of the significant information that should have been included, which thus misled consumers.[11]

In accordance with amendments to Federal Law 138-FZ dated 11 November 2003 on Sweepstakes, promotional sweepstakes can now be conducted only by state bodies authorised by the government. This ended the widespread practice of promotional sweepstakes run by private market participants.

Other promotional events that do not qualify as promotional sweepstakes are not expressly regulated by the Advertising Law. Certain requirements are set forth in Article 9, which provides that advertising for promotional events, including promotional sweepstakes, should contain information on the duration of the promotional event and the source where detailed information on the event can be obtained.

For instance, in *Chuvashia*, the FAS fined a local entrepreneur for failing to

---

9   Ruling of the Seventh Arbitration Appellate Court dated 23 May 2019 in Case N 07AP-3679/19.
10   Ruling of the Moscow City Court dated 10 November 2016 in Case 33-38783/16.
11   Ruling of Novosibirsk FAS dated 12 December 2017 N 06-153/17P.

provide full information on a prize draw. The entrepreneur argued that all required information had been brought to consumers' attention, including the contact information and the source where detailed information on the prize draw could be obtained. The FAS disagreed and stated that the entrepreneur should have indicated not only the source, but also the type of information available to consumers – that is, information on the event organiser, the terms and conditions, the prizes, the timing and the place and procedure for awarding and accepting prizes.[12]

5. Ambush marketing

With regard to the regulation of ambush marketing, attention should be paid to the general prohibition imposed by the Advertising Law on the use of the means of individualisation of third parties or the official symbols of international organisations. In addition, advertisers should observe the prohibition on unfair competition imposed by the Advertising Law and the Competition Law.

Special laws are usually introduced in anticipation of major international sports events in Russia. For example, an express prohibition on the use of the Olympic Games symbols without a licence from the relevant Olympic body was set forth in Article 6.3 of the federal Law on Organising and Conducting the XXII 2014 Winter Olympic Games and XI Winter Para Olympic Games in the City of Sochi. This measure aimed to protect the interests of the Olympic Games sponsors, and provided that advertising containing false information on the advertiser's relationship to the Olympic Games or sponsorship status with respect to the games was deemed unfair advertising.

A similar regulation was implemented prior to the FIFA World Cup in 2018. The federal Law on the Preparation and Holding of the FIFA Football World Championship 2018, FIFA Confederations Cup 2017 in the Russian Federation and Amendments to Certain Legislative Acts of the Russian Federation also prohibited use of the World Cup symbols and the creation of a false impression of a connection between the advertiser and the World Cup organisers and FIFA. The FAS stated that the absence of the World Cup symbols in an ad would not automatically render it compliant with the Advertising Law, as the ad might include other information which could create a false impression about the advertiser's connection to the event organisers.

The FAS also stated that the market participants' use of the World Cup symbols in the advertising had to be qualified as unfair competition.

Thus, the use of the slogan "Charge up for the Mundial!" in a sales promotion run by store Stop Express was considered unfair competition by the FAS.[13]

---

12   FAS Chuvashia Ruling dated 30 August 2018 in Case N 04-08/6044.
13   https://fas.gov.ru/news/25237.

In most such cases, the Russian courts have found against companies that have used the Olympic or FIFA symbols, or identical or similar designations, in their advertising. A rare example of an alternative court practice is the 2011 *Tekhnograd* case, in which the court found for the advertiser. In its ruling, the FAS stated that in the ad in question, the images of the products sold by Tekhnograd were presented in an arrangement that was similar to the official symbol of the 2010 Vancouver Winter Olympic Games. The court disagreed and found that the company had an affiliation to and relations with the games organisers.[14]

By contrast, in a 2012 case, the court decided against General Motors Company and ruled that it had illegally used the Olympic symbol in its trademark OLYMPIC WHITE for the colour of its Chevrolet cars.[15]

In a similar case from 2016, the FAS stated that an advertising banner placed on a river port building with the slogan "Volgograd – the City of Great Victories", the inclusion of the terms 'Volgograd 2018' and 'Football 2018' and the emblem of Volgograd created a false impression that the advertiser was associated with FIFA events which were scheduled to take place in the city during the 2018 World Cup. The FAS held that the advertising banner violated the restrictions on the use of the FIFA symbols, and thus constituted unauthorised (ambush) marketing and an act of unfair competition.[16]

6.   Direct marketing

Similar to other types of advertising that are not expressly covered by the Advertising Law, direct marketing is not specifically regulated as such. Therefore, advertisers must observe the general principles on false and misleading advertising set out in Article 5 of the Advertising Law. That law also states that advertising through telecommunications networks (including telephone, email and SMS) can be distributed only if the recipient's prior consent has been obtained. The burden of proving that such consent has been obtained rests with the advertising distributor.

In addition, the requirements of the federal Law on Personal Data Protection should be taken into consideration by marketers – in particular, the prohibition on using and further processing personal data without the data subject's explicit written consent.

The advertising market has lately seen an increasing number of cases in which companies were fined by the FAS for either:

- failing to obtain consumers' consent to the receipt of advertising; or

---

14   Ruling of the Federal Arbitration Court of the North-West Region dated 23 May 2011 in Case N A56-37558/2010.
15   Ruling of the Federal Arbitration Court of the Moscow Region dated 10 September 2012 in Case N A40-105222/11-144-932.
16   FAS Ruling in *Volgograd* dated 15 November 2016 in Case N 16-03-5-02/538.

- using automatic electronic tools without obtaining call recipients' prior consent in their advertising activities.

For instance, in the 2020 *Rostelecom* case, the company was held liable for sending text messages to a subscriber informing him of a fitness club promotion. Rostelecom was unable to prove in court that the subscriber had consented to the receipt of such advertising text messages; thus, the advertising was considered to be inappropriate and to violate the Advertising Law.[17]

7.   Product placement

The Advertising Law is somewhat ambiguous in its approach to product placement. On one hand, a mere reference to a product, its trademark or its manufacturer will not fall within the scope of the Advertising Law where it is "naturally integrated into a work of science, literature or art and is not aimed at promoting the referenced object". On the other hand, the Advertising Law prohibits hidden advertising used on radio or television, or in video or in the cinema. 'Hidden' advertising is defined as "information affecting an unaware consumer by any means, including video inserts and double sound recording".

The challenge that advertisers face is to safely find a balance between hidden advertising and a naturally integrated reference. The Advertising Law does not define 'natural integration'. In an information letter dated 25 May 2011 (AK/20129) (an official document prepared by the FAS explaining certain issues), the FAS noted that 'natural integration' occurs when the information constitutes an integral element of the plot and is used as an additional characteristic of the character or the situation. In these circumstances:

- the focus is not on the product or the advertiser;
- the product or the advertiser does not replace the main characters and does not disrupt the storyline; and
- it is not possible to remove the product without affecting the general impression created for the audience.

One of the major Russian television channels, VGTRK, was held administratively liable for hidden advertising in its television programme *Risk Zone. Food Products*. The programme showed shelves stacked with fish products and the trademark of a fish-canning factory on the uniforms of its workers. The court agreed with the FAS that the inclusion of the manufacturer's trademark was aimed at attracting attention to the fish-canning factory to promote its products by subconsciously influencing consumers.[18]

---

17   Ruling of the Arbitration Court of Volgo-Vyatsky District dated 14 February 2020 in Case N F01-8441/2019.
18   Decision of the Arbitration Court of Moscow dated 13 October 2016 in Case N A40-172298/2016-145-1522.

8.   Native advertising and social media influencers

Native advertising and social media influencers are not specifically regulated by the Advertising Law. Absent special regulation, the general requirements of Article 5 of the Advertising Law – that advertising should not be false and unfair – must be observed.

Article 5, Section 9 of the Advertising Law prohibits hidden advertising which has a subconscious effect on the consumer. Although initially this requirement applied to advertising involving the use of technical means of influence, the FAS now adopts a wider interpretation of 'hidden advertising', including with regard to information posted by influencers that meets the criteria of advertising, but is not indicated as such.

For a long time, the FAS was unclear as to whether websites located in foreign domains fall under the jurisdiction of Russian law. The regulator's view was that only websites registered in the '.ru', '.su' and '.рф' ('.rf' in Cyrillic) domains should be subject to control by the FAS; advertising on YouTube, Facebook and Instagram was thus beyond the regulator's control.

However, in 2019 the FAS changed its position and held Russian blogger Ilya Varlamov liable for advertising Dewar's whisky on his YouTube channel in violation of the Advertising Law. The FAS found that the information in the podcast met the criteria for advertising, was aimed at Russian consumers and disregarded the prohibition against alcohol advertising on the Internet.[19]

This trend continued in 2020, when the operator of YouTube channel *Bar in a Big City* was held liable on similar grounds for advertising Jim Beam whisky in violation of the Advertising Law and its prohibition against alcohol advertising on the Internet.[20]

9.   Industry-specific regulation

9.1   Gambling

Once a major industry, gambling is now tightly regulated in Russia. Since 1 July 2009, gambling has been allowed only in special gaming areas. The procedure for establishing and closing such areas falls under the jurisdiction of the Russian government.

The legislative changes with respect to the gambling business also affected the advertisement of gambling. Article 27 of the Advertising Law sets out an exhaustive and detailed list of requirements for the advertisement of gambling. Gambling ads should not:

- be aimed at minors;
- create an impression that gambling is a source of income for players;

---

19   Ruling of the Ninth Arbitration Appellate Court dated 19 December 2019 in Case N A40–169842/19.
20   Decision of the FAS Russia dated 28 February 2020 in Case N 08/05/21-4/2020.

- exaggerate the chances of winning or minimise the risk of failure;
- refer to persons who won, but did not actually receive their prizes;
- assert that gambling is important for personal success or similar;
- condemn non-participation in gambling activities;
- convey an impression that victory is guaranteed; or
- use images of human beings or animals.

Gambling advertising is allowed:
- on television and radio from 10:00pm until 7:00am;
- in gambling facilities and buildings, except for public transport infrastructure such as metro stations, airports and railway stations; and
- in specialised print publications.

The exception to this rule is the advertisement of bookmakers' offices during live or recorded transmissions of sports events, provided that the duration of such advertising is less than 20% of the time allocated for advertising during such transmissions.

Gambling ads should always inform potential customers of the duration of any prize draw and the source where relevant information on the prize draw may be located.

In 2018 the FAS found that Sports.ru LLC had violated the law on the advertisement of bookmakers' office Fonbet. The FAS stated that at the time the ad was distributed, the advertiser's website was not registered as a web publishing outlet specialising in sports materials. Therefore, the company had violated the Advertising Law, which prohibits the distribution of ads for gambling organisers.[21]

9.2   Alcohol

The advertisement of alcohol is prohibited in printed materials and on the Internet. In an information letter dated 3 August 2012, the FAS stated that the Advertising Law applies to information placed on websites in the '.ru', '.su' and '.рф?' ('.rf') domains, and on Russian-language websites aimed at Russian consumers, even when these are located in other domains. An exception to this rule applies to information placed on the official websites of alcohol manufacturers or sellers to inform customers about the commercial range of products and the terms of purchase. Information on the manufacturer's or seller's business and related promotional activities is also excluded from the scope of application of the Advertising Law.

In addition, the advertisement of alcohol is not allowed:
- on billboards;

---

21   https://fas.gov.ru/publications/14674.

- in cinema or video facilities;
- on all public transport infrastructure or in public locations; or
- within 100 metres of such places.

The advertisement of alcohol products containing 5% or more of alcohol by volume is allowed only in stores in which alcohol is sold or offered for tasting.

In 2015 the FAS reviewed a complaint over an ad placed outside a café stating, "We have the smallest retail margin on alcohol", with the following information underneath: "Vodka 0.5 L from RUR 220. More details are in the menu." The FAS considered this advertising inappropriate, which was further confirmed by the courts.[22]

Under Article 21.3 of the Advertising Law, alcohol ads must at all times be accompanied by warnings regarding the harm that alcohol causes to health and must not:

- assert that alcohol consumption is important for personal success;
- condemn sobriety;
- assert that alcohol consumption causes no harm to health, or that there are vitamins or biological additives in alcohol products;
- suggest that alcohol quenches thirst;
- be aimed at minors; or
- use images of human beings or animals (including animations).

An exception from the general restriction on alcohol advertising relates to wines produced in Russia. Ads for such wines are allowed in printed media, except for the first and last pages of newspapers and the front and back covers of magazines. However, this exception does not apply to online advertising, including websites which are registered as online media outlets.[23]

Marketing events at which alcohol products are offered to consumers are allowed only in stores where they are sold or offered for tasting, and minors cannot be invited to participate. The advertisement of promotional events in which the purchase of alcohol products is a condition of participation is not allowed, except for special promotional events for alcohol products.

The requirements on alcohol advertising also relate to the advertisement of trademarks registered for alcohol products. The prohibition on the use of images of humans or animals in alcohol advertising also extends to the use of trademarks containing such images. The exception is where the advertising demonstrates product packaging that bears such a trademark, rather than the trademark only. For example, an image of a beer can or bottle branded with a

---

22   Ruling of 12th Arbitration Appellate Court dated 9 September 2015 in Case N 12AP-8311/2015.
23   FAS explanation letter dated 25 September 2019 AK/83509/19 "On Explaining of the Questions of Advertising in the Internet".

trademark containing the image of a human or animal falls outside the statutory prohibition if the packaging is shown in full. Nonetheless, alcohol producers and sellers should still take care when displaying their products with restricted images in their ads.

In 2019, a famous Russian blogger was fined for advertising Dewar's whisky on his YouTube channel in violation of the Advertising Law. The blogger first enthused about his fascination with Amsterdam, which was followed by another person's negative opinion in the next frame. After that, the blogger summarised: "Having two opinions, dear friends, is better than just one, because that gives you an opportunity to see things from different perspectives and get an objective picture. Twice is better. Dewar's is also vatted twice, so that it acquires a better and richer taste. Check it for yourselves and we will continue." The court agreed that the blogger had acted as an advertising distributor and upheld the FAS's decision.[24]

9.3 Pharmaceuticals

The Advertising Law contains detailed regulations on pharmaceutical advertising. The FAS is also very active in supervising compliance with these provisions.

Article 24 of the Advertising Law provides that pharmaceutical advertising must not:

- be addressed to minors;
- refer to specific cases of cures or health improvements as a result of use (unless the ad is aimed at healthcare practitioners at medical forums or in medical printed material);
- express gratitude to persons for using the advertised medicine or equipment (unless the ad is aimed at healthcare practitioners at medical forums or in medical printed material);
- imply any advantages by referring to the studies that are mandatory to obtain marketing authorisation;
- make consumers think that they have medical problems;
- create an impression that healthy persons should use the advertised medicine (unless the ad refers to preventive medicine);
- create an impression that it is not necessary to consult a doctor;
- guarantee a positive effect, safety, effectiveness or lack of side effects;
- present the advertised medicine as a food supplement; or
- assert that safety and effectiveness are guaranteed by the 'natural' origin of the product.

---

24   Decision of the Moscow Arbitration Court dated 12 September 2019 in Case N A40-169842/19-148-1022.

The scope of the information included in pharmaceutical advertising should not go beyond what is written on the label of the product. Another important requirement is that the ad inform on contra-indications as well as the need to read the product label.

The advertisement of medicines that are subject to prescription is allowed only if it is aimed at healthcare practitioners, including at medical forums or in medical printed material. The advertisement of medicines that contain narcotic substances is completely forbidden.

In one significant case, a bank offered credit services to employees of state-funded organisations. The advertising booklets included an image of a person in a white medical gown with a phonendoscope. The court stated that consumers would associate this image with healthcare professionals, which left no doubt about the profession of the person depicted in the ad. The court dismissed the advertiser's argument that phonendoscopes can be used in different fields of work and concluded that the use of the image of a healthcare professional in an ad for financial services fell under the restrictions of the Advertising Law.[25]

In 2018, the Recommendations on Compliance with the Law on Advertising for Over-the-Counter Medicines developed by the Association of International Pharmaceutical Manufacturers, the Association of European Business and other associations were approved by the FAS. The recommendations concern issues such as:

- the information on such medicines that can be included in advertising;
- incorrect comparisons and promises of the medicine's effectiveness; and
- the words and phrases that can be used and those that should be avoided.

9.4   Financial products and services

The advertisement of financial services and securities is regulated by Articles 28 and 29 of the Advertising Law. The relevant provisions apply to the advertisement of:

- bank, insurance and asset management services;
- the solicitation of consumers' money for housing construction; and
- the purchase of securities.

The provisions further require that the ad indicate the name and contact details of the financial organisation or individual entrepreneur rendering such services or products.

Ads for financial services should not guarantee the effectiveness of investments if this cannot be calculated when the contract is made. They

---

25   Ruling of the Fifth Appellate Court dated 21 January 2016 in Case N 05AP-11809/15.

should also include information on the relevant terms and conditions that influence the amount of profits gained and costs incurred in using the advertised services.

Ads for asset management services (eg, securities management, investment reserves of the share investment funds, mutual funds, pension reserves of private pension funds) should specify the source of information that is subject to mandatory disclosure and the contact details of the organisation where consumers can obtain all information relating to the proposed financial services and products. Such ads should not contain unjustified information or assert that it is possible to achieve future results which are similar to those that have previously been achieved.

Securities that cannot be offered to the general public cannot be advertised. Furthermore, ads for securities should:

- not promise dividends unless the payment of dividends is provided for in the issuer's resolution or the issuance rules; and
- always include information on the securities issuer and the source of information that is subject to mandatory disclosure.

The advertisement of tradable bonds is forbidden, unless they are allowed for trade by the Stock Exchange. The Advertising Law does not allow for the advertisement of interests that are not certified by securities.

A common problem that advertisers face in promoting financial services is that the Advertising Law does not expressly specify the manner in which consumers should be informed of the details of the relevant service, including the amount of profit gained and the costs incurred as a result of using the service. As there is much information to be disclosed, it can be a real challenge to incorporate everything into the advertising copy. This gives rise to the problem of 'fine print', where the relevant information is sometimes presented in a manner that makes it very difficult – or even impossible – for consumers to read. The controlling authorities take a case-by-case approach, as there is no regulation on the size of the text and other related requirements.

A 2020 case involved a Gazprombank ad that stated: "GAZPROMBANK – from 10.8% annual rate on credit. CREDIT? EASY! WITH CLOCKWORK PRECISION." The FAS concluded that the essential terms of the credit were included in small font, which could cause confusion among consumers who were unable to read them. The courts agreed with the FAS and stated that the absence from the ad of the essential terms which could influence consumers' decisions to use the bank's services should not distort the meaning of the advertising and create confusion among consumers.[26]

---

26   Ruling of Arbitration Court of Volgo-Vyatsky District dated 25 May 2020 in Case N A79-8624/2019.

9.5 Food

Food advertising is not specifically regulated by the Advertising Law. However, certain regulations on the labelling of food products are set out in the State Standards and Technical Regulations of the Customs Union on Food Products Labelling. Furthermore, Article 25 of the Advertising Law provides for special requirements with regard to biologically active additives and baby food.

In particular, the Advertising Law requires that ads for food additives not:
- create the impression that they have a medical effect;
- refer to specific cases of recovery or health improvements; or
- make consumers ignore healthy nutrition.

Ads for baby food should not:
- create the impression that it fully replaces breast milk; or
- assert any advantages of artificial infant feeding.

Information on age limitations and the need to seek advice from a specialist must be included in ads for products used as breast milk substitutes or for infants during their first year of life.

Biologically active additives are commonly used in Russia. Because uninformed consumers can confuse biologically active additives with medicines, the FAS closely scrutinises ads for such additives, to ensure that the statutory requirements are observed.

In its 2021 ruling, the SAC stated that ads for food additives could be considered as creating the impression that such food additives are medicines with a curative effect if the ad contains the name of the illness or its symptoms and a simultaneous indication of the product as a treatment with health-promoting effect.

An ad including the slogan "AD NORMA – blood pressure is in the norm!" was held to violate the Advertising Law as it contained the following information: "Vegetative complex AD NORMA normalizes blood pressure, builds vessels walls and enhances heart performance. Not a medicine. Inquire in pharmacies." The FAS found that the ad created the impression that the supplement had treatment qualities. The court disagreed with the FAS and noted that the ad did not contain the name of an illness or its symptoms along with an indication of the name of the food supplement. Thus, no violation of the Advertising Law was established.[27]

9.6 Tobacco

On 1 June 2013 the federal Law on Protecting the Health of Citizens from the

---

[27]   Ruling of the Arbitration Court of the East-Siberian District dated August 2 2018 in Case N A19-21340/2016.

Impact of Tobacco Smoke and the Consequences of Tobacco Consumption ('Tobacco Control Law') came into force. Article 16 of that law provides for a complete ban on tobacco advertising, promotion and sponsorship, including:

- the distribution of tobacco and tobacco products to the general public, including as gifts;
- the use of sale discounts, including coupons;
- the use of tobacco trademarks on other products;
- the use and imitation of products that are similar to tobacco and tobacco products;
- the demonstration of tobacco products and the smoking process in media and entertainment;
- promotional events that require the purchase of tobacco as a condition of participation;
- cultural, sporting and other mass events relating to tobacco promotion or for which tobacco products are used as prizes;
- the use of means of tobacco individualisation (eg, tobacco firms' names or trademarks) in charity activities; and
- tobacco product placement in media and entertainment.

If smoking or tobacco products are shown in movies or similar, such movies should be accompanied by social advertising to warn the audience of the harmful consequences of tobacco smoking.

9.7 E-cigarettes

In June 2020, amendments to the Tobacco Control Law were adopted. Among other things, the amendments introduced a new category of 'nicotine-containing products' (NCPs), such as heated tobacco and solutions and liquids containing nicotine.

The main aim of the initiative was to unify the regulation of tobacco and NCPs, which are now subject to the same restrictions and prohibitions as are imposed on traditional cigarettes.

The new law also introduced a definition of 'devices for consumption' of NCPs, which include electronic nicotine delivery systems and heated tobacco devices, except for those registered as medical devices.

Among other things, the following are prohibited:

- the sale of NCPs and devices for the consumption of NCPs to minors;
- the sale of NCPs via vending machines and the Internet, as well as through open displays in stores;
- the consumption of NCPs in restaurants and commercial facilities; and
- the advertisement, promotion, sponsorship and demonstration of NCPs and devices for the consumption of NCPs.

The purchase and use of NCPs is allowed only in locations where the purchase and use of tobacco products are also allowed.

The government plans to amend the existing technical regulations on tobacco products to address the sale and use of NCPs.

The new law came into effect on 31 July 2020, except for certain rules that provide for a transition period, including with regard to:

- the prohibition against the use of NCPs in restaurants and cafes;
- the restrictions on retail sales; and
- the prohibitions regarding the advertisement, promotion and sponsorship of NCPs and devices for the consumption of NCPs.

Spain

Mónica Esteve Sanz

Gómez-Acebo & Pombo Abogados SLP

1. Overview of the legal and regulatory regime for advertising

1.1 Legislation and codes of practice

(a) Legislation

In Spain, there are numerous laws that regulate advertising. This is due, on the one hand, to the existence of three different legislative sources (the European Union, the Spanish state and the autonomous communities of Spain); and on the other hand, to the fact that advertising legislation can be of a civil, administrative or even criminal nature. Some laws regulate advertising in general, while others refer to it in an incidental or accessory way. It is important to take into account autonomic legislation, as each community has exclusive competence over advertising, provided that its laws do not contradict state legislation.

Advertising is mainly regulated by the General Advertising Act (34/1988) and by the Unfair Competition Act (3/1991). These two acts underwent a major reform in 2009 with the approval of Act 29/2009, which amended the legal regime on unfair competition and advertising to strengthen the protection of consumers and users.[1] This act was mainly adopted to implement into Spanish law the Unfair Commercial Practices Directive[2] and the Misleading and Comparative Advertising Directive.[3]

Apart from the General Advertising Act and the Unfair Competition Act, other laws contain provisions that regulate or affect advertising, including the following:

---

1   Act 29/2009 also amends the consolidated version of the General Act for the Defence of Consumers and Users and other complementary acts (approved by Legislative Royal Decree 1/2007 of 16 November 2007 and Act 7/1996 of 15 January 1996 regulating retail commerce).
2   Directive 2005/29/EC of the European Parliament and of the Council of 11 May 2005 concerning unfair business-to-consumer commercial practices in the internal market and amending Council Directive 84/450/EEC, Directives 97/7/EC, 98/27/EC and 2002/65/EC of the European Parliament and of the Council and Regulation (EC) 2006/2004 of the European Parliament and of the Council ('Unfair Commercial Practices Directive').
3   Directive 2006/114/CE, of the European Parliament and of the Council of 12 December 2006 concerning misleading and comparative advertising.

- the Commercial Code;
- Legislative Royal Decree 1/2007, approving the consolidated text for the General Act for the Defence of Consumers and Users and other complementary rules ('Consumer Defence Act');
- Act 7/1996, regulating retail trade;
- Organic Act 1/1982 on the civil protection of the right to honour, personal and familiar intimacy and one's own image;
- Organic Act 1/1996 on the legal protection of minors, as well as modification of the Civil Code and the Civil Procedure Act;
- Organic Act 1/2004 on measures for protection against gender violence;
- Legislative Royal Decree 1/1996 approving the reformulated text of the IP Act in order to regularise, clarify and harmonise certain legal provisions;
- Organic Act 3/2018 on personal data protection and the guarantee of digital rights ('Personal Data Protection Act'), which adapted the General Data Protection Regulation[4] (GDPR) to Spanish law;
- Act 17/2001 on trademarks; and
- the Criminal Code, especially Article 282 on false advertising.

Furthermore, certain sector-specific laws that regulate the advertisement of given products or services must be taken into account (for more details see section 9).

From the above, it can be seen that the legal risks incurred by advertisers will depend on the law on advertising (or law affecting advertising) that has been infringed; and infringement may be of a civil, administrative or even criminal nature. This chapter analyses the advertising industry in Spain from two perspectives:

- the general regime on advertising, regulated in particular by the Unfair Competition Act and the General Advertising Act; and
- certain special provisions aimed at regulating advertising in certain sectors.

(b)   Codes of practice

In Spain, there is also an advertising self-regulatory system, which is administered by the Commercial Communication Self-Regulation Association (Autocontrol), a non-profit organisation created in 1995 whose main objective is to help ensure that advertising is truthful, legal, honest and fair, to the benefit of consumers, competitors and the market. Autocontrol has more than 550

---

4   Regulation (EU) 2016/679 of the European Parliament and of the Council of 27 April 2016 on the protection of natural persons with regard to the processing of personal data and on the free movement of such data, and repealing Directive 95/46/EC.

members, including the most relevant advertisers in Spain (across all sectors of industry and commerce), advertising agencies, media organisations (eg, television, press, outdoor, radio, Internet) and advertising industry associations.

To achieve its main objective, Autocontrol undertakes three kinds of activities:

- the elaboration and application of advertising codes of practice, with either a general or sectoral character. These codes of practice are voluntarily binding on the industries and companies that have committed themselves to them;
- the out-of-court resolution of complaints, which is performed by Autocontrol's Jury and which may be initiated by Autocontrol on its own initiative or by an individual or entity with a legitimate interest. Claims must relate to advertising material that is considered to infringe the Autocontrol codes or the legislation in force at the time. The Jury is composed of independent members who are highly specialised and renowned in different sectors, such as law, economics, advertising and marketing, sociology and consumer affairs. Its decisions are binding on all Autocontrol members and non-members that expressly or implicitly accept the jurisdiction of the Jury to decide the case. The Jury is a highly prestigious body, which – when combined with the speed with which it resolves disputes (proceedings before the Jury might last less than one month from filing of the claim until a decision is rendered; whereas proceedings at first instance before the mercantile courts take between 12 and 18 months on average) and the relatively low costs that these proceedings incur – means that this system of dispute resolution is often preferred over litigation; and
- the provision of pre-launch advice in the form of a non-binding opinion issued by the Technical Department of Autocontrol on the legality or correctness of a given ad at the request of the advertiser, its agency or the channel through which the ad will be launched.

The Spanish self-regulatory system has traditionally benefited from a recognised level of prestige, which has been validated on several occasions by case law and legislation. Furthermore, since 2009, the Unfair Competition Act has contained a chapter dedicated to "Codes of Practice", which aims to encourage their development, recognise them and clarify the conditions with which they must comply. There is also a section that regulates misleading practices regarding codes of practice, such as:

- claiming to observe a code of conduct where this is not the case; or
- claiming that a given code of conduct has been endorsed by a public organisation or any other accreditation when it has not.

1.2 Overview of advertising in Spain

Under Article 2 of the General Advertising Act, 'advertising' means "any form of communication made by a natural or a legal person, public or private, in the exercise of a trade, business, craft or profession in order to promote directly or indirectly the contracting of real or personal property, services, rights and obligations". The 'recipients of advertising' are defined as the people to whom the advertising message is directed or the people reached by it.

Illegal advertising is dealt with in Article 3 of the General Advertising Act, which sets forth the following examples:

- advertising that breaches either a person's dignity or the values and rights recognised under the Spanish Constitution. Article 3 specifically states that this includes showing women in a vexatious or discriminatory way – either by using their body or parts thereof as a mere object disassociated from the promoted product, or by using their image associated with stereotypical behaviours that violate the foundations of the Spanish legal order, contributing towards the type of violence to which Organic Act 1/2004 on integrated protection measures against gender violence refers;

- advertising directed at minors that incites them to purchase products or services by exploiting their inexperience or credulity, or in which children appear persuading parents or guardians to purchase. This includes depicting children, without good reason, in dangerous situations, or misleading consumers as to the characteristics or security of the products, or the required ability or skills for children to use them without injuring themselves or others;

- 'subliminal advertising', which is defined in Article 4 of the General Advertising Act as advertising that could influence the addressee without being consciously perceived as such;

- advertising that violates the provisions of specific laws governing the advertisement of certain products, services or activities (see section 9); and

- misleading advertising – in this regard, the Unfair Competition Act, to which the General Advertising Act refers in relation to misleading advertising, distinguishes between 'misleading acts', 'misleading acts through confusion' and 'misleading acts by omission'. Each of these types of misleading advertising is described further below, as well as four further forms of illegal advertising.

(a) Misleading acts

'Misleading acts' are defined as "any conduct that contains a false statement or a statement that, even though true but because of its content or presentation, misleads or might mislead its addressees, being capable of altering their economic behaviour". In order to be deemed misleading, an act must also relate to a certain aspect of the relevant product or service (eg, its availability, its price or the consumer's rights).[5]

Thus, two essential conditions must be met for an ad to be deemed misleading. First, the ad must be misleading or capable of being misleading. It is therefore irrelevant whether the public has been effectively misled; rather, the ad must merely be capable of misleading. The misleading character of an ad might derive from false information or from information that is accurate but, because of how it is presented or because of its content, is capable of generating a false expectation among its addressees.

With regard to the former hypothesis (false information), an ad's misleading character is automatically presumed from the falsity of the information, and therefore no further analysis need be carried out to determine whether the information is misleading; it is down to the advertiser to prove the accuracy and truthfulness of its claims.[6] With regard to the latter hypothesis (truthful information that could generate a false expectation among its addressees), its misleading character is not presumed; the message must rather be analysed on a case-by-case basis in order to determine whether it is misleading or likely to mislead.

In this respect, the Unfair Competition Act, case law and Autocontrol decisions have established some criteria for this analysis. Broadly speaking, the message must be interpreted from the point of view of the average consumer, who is reasonably attentive and discerning. This implies that:

- the message should not be interpreted in its literal or grammatical terms;
- the message should be analysed in its entirety; and
- the intention of the advertiser is not relevant – the sole relevant element is the meaning that the message has for its addressees or the interpretation that they would make of the message. If this interpretation corresponds to reality, the message will not be considered misleading.[7]

The second condition that must be met for an ad to be misleading is that it must be considered capable of influencing the economic behaviour of its addressees. Article 4 of the Unfair Competition Act defines the 'economic behaviour' of consumers or users as any decision by which they decide to act or not act in relation to:

---

5   A list of the relevant aspects is set out in Article 5 of the Unfair Competition Act.
6   Article 217.4 of the Civil Procedure Act, which establishes a reversal of the burden of proof in cases of misleading advertising.
7   See, for example, the Autocontrol Jury's decision of 7 February 2013, in which the Jury considered that the claim encapsulated in the slogan "If it exists, it is at Toys R Us" was not misleading because the average consumer would not interpret it as meaning that every toy in existence in the world could be found at Toys R Us shops.

- the selection of an offer or of the person that makes the offer;
- the contracting of products or services, as well as, if relevant, the way in which and the conditions under which they are contracted;
- the payment of a price;
- the retention of a product or service; and
- the exercise of contractual rights in relation to products or services.

It is not necessary, in order for this condition to be met, that the practice indeed affects the economic behaviour of consumers; it will suffice merely if it is capable of doing so.

Finally, Article 5 of the Unfair Competition Act contains an exhaustive list of the characteristics of the products or services about which consumers could be misled.

Even if, as stated, the misleading character of an act is analysed case by case in light of the conditions mentioned above, Articles 21 and following of the Unfair Competition Act contain a blacklist of acts that in all cases will be considered as misleading. This list concerns and regulates, among other things:

- misleading practices on the adherence to codes of practice or the holding of other quality distinctions;
- 'lure' practices and promotional misleading practices (see section 4);
- misleading practices on the nature and properties of the products or services, their availability and after-sales services;
- pyramid selling schemes; and
- undercover commercial practices.

(b)   *Misleading practices by confusion*

Article 20 of the Unfair Competition Act prohibits 'misleading practices by confusion', which are defined in Article 20 as commercial practices – including comparative advertising – which, in their factual context and taking into account all of their characteristics and circumstances, create confusion, including a risk of association, with any products or services, registered trademarks, commercial names or other distinctive trademarks of a competitor, provided that they are capable of affecting the economic behaviour of consumers and users.

This definition refers specifically to confusion (including the risk of association) with the distinctive signs (registered trademarks, commercial names and other distinctive trademarks) of a competitor. Traditionally, the Spanish courts have considered that where the same behaviour might qualify as trademark infringement under the Trademarks Act and an act of unfair competition under the Unfair Competition Act, the application of the Trademarks Act shall prevail, as this is the specific law on the matter, leaving the application of the Unfair Competition Act for those cases in which the use of a competitor's distinctive sign cannot be pursued under the Trademarks Act.

Thus, Article 20 of the Unfair Competition Act might be invoked to pursue cases in which the Trademarks Act does not protect against the risk of confusion with a competitor's trademark (eg, a non-registered, not well-known trademark) or by persons that do not have right of standing to claim trademark infringement under the Trademarks Act, but whose interests are exposed to a risk of confusion because of the use of a third party's trademark (eg, consumers).

(c)   *Misleading omissions*

Article 7 of the Unfair Competition Act qualifies as unfair the omission or obscuring of information that is necessary for an addressee to adopt or be able to adopt an informed decision relating to his or her economic behaviour. Unfairness also exists where:

- the information is unclear, unintelligible or ambiguous;
- the information is not offered at the necessary time; or
- the commercial purpose of the practice is not made known when it is not evident from the context.

The key (apart from affecting the economic behaviour of the consumer, as discussed above) to determining whether an omission of information is to be considered as unfair is whether the information omitted was necessary in order for the addressee to adopt or be able to adopt an informed decision. The 'necessary' characteristic of any information is evaluated case by case, considering:

- the information itself;
- the context of the message; and
- the message from the point of view of the average consumer.

In this regard, Article 20.2 of the Consumer Defence Act states that the omission of information imposed by EU law, or of certain information that is judged as substantial and necessary in invitations to buy (eg, the principal characteristics of the product, the identification of the trader, the price and the procedures for payment and delivery), is considered as an unfair misleading practice.

Also, in order to evaluate whether necessary information has been omitted in cases where limitations of time or space are imposed on the advertiser, account must be taken of the totality of the advertising campaign. In this sense, Article 7.2 of the Unfair Competition Act establishes that these limitations and the measures adopted by the advertiser to transmit the necessary information through other means should be taken into account.

(d) Aggressive advertising

'Aggressive advertising' in this context is defined in Article 8 of the Unfair Competition Act as any behaviour that, taking into account its characteristics and circumstances, is capable of reducing in a significant way – through harassment, coercion (including the use of force) or undue influence – the freedom of election or the conduct of an addressee in relation to the product or service being offered, and that consequently affects or could affect his or her economic behaviour.

In order to determine whether any advertising conduct encompasses harassment, coercion or undue influence, account should be taken of the following elements:

- the place in which and time at which it takes place;
- its nature or persistency;
- the use of threatening or insulting language or behaviour;
- the intentional exploitation by the advertiser of any misfortune or specific circumstances that are sufficiently serious to reduce the consumer's capacity of discernment in order to influence his or her purchasing decision with respect to the product or service;
- any non-contractual, onerous or disproportionate obstacles imposed by the advertiser where the consumer wishes to exercise his or her legal or contractual rights, including in order to end the contract, to change the products or services, or to change provider; and
- any communication that a certain action will be taken, when legally it cannot be taken.

Articles 28 to 31 of the Unfair Competition Act set out a catalogue of practices that are automatically considered as aggressive without any need to determine whether they comply with the conditions to be considered as coercion, harassment or undue influence under Article 8. These include:

- practices that make a consumer believe that he or she cannot leave an establishment without buying something (which in some circumstances might be a criminal rather than a civil offence);
- personal visits to a consumer's home, ignoring requests to leave and not return;
- repeated unwanted proposals by phone, fax, email or other communication media (see also section 6);
- advertising that includes any direct exhortation to children to acquire products or use services, or to persuade their parents or other adults to purchase the advertised products or services; and
- the express notification of a consumer that the trader's job or livelihood is at risk if the consumer does not purchase the products or services.

(e) Denigrating advertising

Article 9 of the Unfair Competition Act qualifies as unfair the realisation or dissemination of assertions regarding the activities, services, premises or commercial relations of a third party that are capable of harming its reputation on the market, unless they are accurate, true and pertinent. Allegations regarding the nationality, beliefs or ideology, private life or any other circumstances that are strictly personal to the affected party are not considered as pertinent.

(f) Comparative advertising

Comparative advertising is dealt with fully in section 2.

(g) Parasitic advertising

Article 12 of the Unfair Competition Act qualifies as unfair the taking of undue advantage of the commercial, industrial or professional reputation acquired on the market by a third party. Within the framework of advertising, this provision especially applies where use is made of a third party's trademarks, symbols or initiatives, where there is no risk of confusion but only a taking of advantage of the third party's reputation.

1.3 Injunctions for infringement

Infringement of the provisions of the Unfair Competition Act or the General Advertising Act concerning illicit advertising give rise to the corrective or penalising actions provided for in Article 32 of the Unfair Competition Act, to be exercised before the mercantile courts. These actions include:

- a declaration of the unfairness of the advertising material;
- rectification of misleading, incorrect or false information;
- a requirement that the advertiser cease and/or desist from using the advertising material;
- repair of the effects caused by the advertising material;
- remedies for loss and damage caused by the advertising;
- publication of the adverse decision at the advertiser's expense; and
- potentially, an unlawful enrichment claim.

2. Comparative advertising

Comparative advertising is regulated by Article 10 of the Unfair Competition Act,[8] which includes some kind of implicit or explicit allusion to a competitor.[9]

---

8   Which implements EU Directive 2006/114/EC of 12 December 2006 on misleading advertising and comparative advertising.

9   The fact that in comparative advertising a competitor must be identified (explicitly or implicitly) distinguishes it from other forms of advertising – in particular, 'advertising of an excluding tone', in which the advertiser acclaims its own products as compared to those of competitors, but where it is not possible to identify any specific competitor or competitors.

According to this provision, comparative advertising is lawful in Spain if all of the following conditions are met.

First, the compared products and services must have the same purpose or satisfy the same needs. The Court of Justice of the European Union (CJEU) has established that these shall be understood as products for which there is a real possibility of substitution or products that display a sufficient degree of interchangeability for consumers.

Second, the ad must make an objective comparison between one or more than one essential, relevant, verifiable and representative features – including price – of the compared products or services. It is sufficient if the ad compares just one feature of the products or services; it is not necessary to compare all of the features or even several features selected in an equitable way. However, the advertiser is not totally free while choosing the feature(s) to be compared, as the following rules apply in this regard:

- The selection of the feature must not cause the resulting comparison to be misleading; and where a sole feature is chosen – which is particularly relevant in relation to price comparisons – the general impression must not be misleading;
- The feature or features compared must be material, relevant, verifiable and representative of the products or services. In general, this condition refers to those features that consumers take into account while forming their preferences; and
- The comparison must indeed be made objectively. To be lawful, comparative advertising thus must not include declarations that consist of mere value judgements or refer to subjective elements, such as personal opinions, tastes, impressions or preferences; and assertions must be demonstrable through objective means.

Third, in the case of products covered by a designation of origin or a geographical indication, specific denomination or guaranteed traditional speciality, the comparison must be made only with products of the same designation.

Fourth, products or services cannot be presented as imitations or replicas of others to which a protected trademark or commercial name applies. According to the CJEU,[10] this condition is not fulfilled, and thus the comparative advertising must be qualified as unlawful, if:

- the advertiser states explicitly or implicitly in comparative advertising that the product marketed by it is an imitation of a product bearing a well-known trademark; and
- the advertising is considered to take unfair advantage of the reputation of that mark for the benefit of the advertiser.

---

10   Judgment of 18 June 2009, Case C-487/07, *L'Oreal v Bellure.*

This case referred to the use by the advertiser of perfumes, whereby comparison lists indicated the word mark of the fine fragrance of which the perfume being marketed was an imitation.

Finally, the comparison must not contravene the provisions of the Unfair Competition Act on misleading acts, denigration and exploitation of a third party's reputation, as discussed in section 1.2. In this regard, all comparisons imply, *per se*, a certain degree of denigration of the competitor with which the comparison is made, in order to enhance the superiority of the advertiser's products or services. Thus, this prohibition refers to the unnecessary discrediting of the competitor – which will happen, for example, where there is an allusion to the strictly personal circumstances of the competitor, or where expressions or images that might be considered as excessive, overly aggressive or unnecessarily offensive are used.

3. Online behavioural advertising

On 30 March 2013, Spain implemented the amendments to Article 5 of the e-Privacy Directive (2002/58/EC) into national law through an amendment to Article 22.2 of Act 34/2002 on Information Society Services and Electronic Commerce ('E-commerce Act'). Article 22.2 of that act relates to the use of cookies (eg, for online behavioural advertising). It states that service providers may use storage and retrieval data devices (including cookies) on 'terminal equipment' (ie, computing devices) of recipients, provided that the latter have given their consent after receiving clear and comprehensive information on the use of such devices and, in particular, on the purposes of processing the data, in accordance with the Personal Data Protection Act.

In particular, the Personal Data Protection Act states that users must previously be informed explicitly, precisely and unequivocally about several points. Consent must be collected through any manifestation of the free, specific, informed and unequivocal will of the user, whether by declaration or by clear affirmative action; implied consent is thus acceptable where it consists of an unequivocal action. The Spanish Data Protection Agency (AEPD) has listed in several legal reports cases in which consent is considered to be unequivocal, although implied. In relation to cookies, the relevant points to be informed about are:

- the purpose of collecting the data;
- the recipients of the data;
- the retention period; and
- the identity and address of the data controller or of its representative, if any.

Account should also be taken of the Interactive Advertising Bureau (IAB) Europe's self-regulatory Framework for Online Behavioural Advertising of 14

April 2011. This framework outlines good practice aimed at enhancing transparency and consumer control. It has been signed by the online industry's leading businesses and is binding on those companies and associations. The framework has had a significant influence on Spanish regulation, as the IAB itself participated in the drafting of both the first Spanish Cookie Guide in May 2013 and the new version of the Spanish Cookie Guide issued in November 2019, which aims, among other things, to provide guidance on online behavioural advertising.

The European Advertising Standards Alliance Best Practice Recommendation on Online Behavioural Advertising of 12 April 2011 is another useful reference.

Furthermore, account should be taken of the self-regulatory code approved by the association Confianza Online on 28 November 2002 and last amended in May 2018. Confianza Online is an association which has established a comprehensive self-regulatory system for online commerce with consumers and digital advertising, and which was created by Autocontrol and the Spanish Association for Digital Economy in 2003.

4.   Sales promotions

4.1   Retail Trade Act

Sales promotions are regulated in Title II of Act 7/1996 on the retail trade ('Retail Trade Act'), as last amended by Royal Decree Act 20/2018. Specific legislation may apply in each Spanish autonomous community in which sales take place, which should be taken into account to assess whether a sales promotion is legal. However, this legislation is beyond the scope of this chapter.

The guiding principle of this legislation is that of transparency, as further described below.

According to Article 18.1 of the Retail Trade Act, "sales promotion activities are sales such as promotional sales, sales or promotional offers, sales of [stock] balances, liquidation sales, complimentary gift sales, and direct-to-consumer sales offerings". Those descriptions may be used in marketing materials only where the promotion is consistent with the legal definition – incorrectly describing a promotion can give rise to administrative fines and to a misleading act prohibited by Article 5 of the Unfair Competition Act.

Announcements of sales promotion activities must specify the duration and, if necessary, the special applicable rules, as well as the items concerned. Where a special offer does not include at least half of the articles for sale, the promotion in question may not be advertised as a 'store-wide' sale, but must be referred to only in terms of the articles or sections actually involved.

Offers of reduced-price items must clearly state the previous price along with the reduced price of each item, except for those offered for sale for the first time; where the reduction consists of a percentage of a group of articles, a general reference for that group is sufficient. If items are offered at both a regular price and a reduced price, these must be sufficiently separated in order to avoid any confusion between them; and this price distinction must be made for promotional sales, sell-offs, clearance sales and complimentary gift sales.

(a)   *Promotional sales*

'Promotional sales' (Article 27 of the Retail Trade Act) are sales made at a lower price or under more favourable conditions than usual, in order to promote the sale of certain products or the development of one or more businesses or establishments (and which are not specifically covered by the definitions of other sale promotional activity regulated by the Retail Trade Act). Items traded as promotional sales items must be acquired by the retailer for this exclusive purpose, and must not be damaged or be of lower quality than the same products offered at the regular price in the future.

(b)   *Complimentary gift sales*

'Complimentary gift sales' (Articles 32, 33 and 34 of the Retail Trade Act) are sales involving the offer of a promotional gift of any nature, either straightforwardly or by participation in some sort of contest. Products or services that are offered as promotional gifts or incentives must be delivered to buyers within a maximum timeframe determined by the relevant autonomous community of Spain in which the promotion is taking place; this must never exceed three months from when the buyer met the applicable requirements to receive the gift or prize.

If the offer of the gift or prize is made on the product packaging, the right to obtain the offered benefit may continue to be exercised in the three months following the end of the sales promotion.

If the offered gifts are a part of a group or collection of products, the company responsible for the offer must exchange any of the items forming part of the collection with a different one, unless the public offer of the incentive establishes a different procedure for acquiring any items within the collection.

The offer of a product with a prize or gift is considered a misleading act under the Unfair Competition Act where the consumer does not actually receive what could reasonably be expected according to that offer.

It is prohibited to offer jointly two or more items as a single unit to be purchased, except where:

- the items offered are functionally related (eg, a razor and a razor blade);
- the sale of multiple items is common business practice in relation to the particular item (eg, a pack of four yogurts);
- the consumer can buy the articles separately and at the usual price; or
- multiple items are packaged jointly for aesthetic reasons or for the consumer to offer them as gifts.

(c) Discount sales seasons

Discount sales seasons (see Articles 24, 25 and 26 of the Retail Trade Act) can be established whenever the retailer wishes and for as long as it wishes. Items sold under the qualification of discount sales seasons must have been previously offered for sale under ordinary price conditions. Damaged items must not be offered as discount items.

(d) Sell-offs

Articles 28 and 29 of the Retail Trade Act deal with sell-offs – that is, the promotional sale of products whose market value has decreased due to damage, flaw, disuse or obsolescence. This does not necessarily include products that are a production or seasonal surplus. Sell-off sales must be identified as such or promoted as 'remainder sales'. If items are damaged or defective, this circumstance must be made clear.

(e) Clearance sales

Clearance sales (see Articles 30 and 31 of the Retail Trade Act) are aimed at clearing certain stocks of products, and take place in execution of a judicial or administrative decision, or are carried out in one or more of the following circumstances:

- total or partial cessation of trading activity; if the cessation is partial, the cleared products affected must be clearly indicated;
- a change in trading branch or a substantial change in the orientation of the business;
- a change in premises or the performance of important functions within those premises; or
- any *force majeure* event that causes serious interference with the normal conduct of commercial activity.

Announcements for clearance sales must indicate their cause. Products that are not part of the stock of the establishment or that are acquired by the merchant in order to include them in the clearance sale cannot in fact be subject to this type of sales promotion. The clearance sale must cease if the cause that motivated it disappears or if the products sell out. The maximum duration of a clearance sale is one year.

4.2 Unfair Competition Act

As stated in section 1.2, the Unfair Competition Act contains a blacklist of actions that in all cases will be considered as misleading without any need to analyse whether the conditions for the action to be qualified as misleading are met. Concerning sales promotions, the following acts are considered as misleading practices:

- making a commercial offer of products or services at a given price without revealing the existence of reasonable doubts about the lack of availability of those products or services, or equivalent ones, at the offered price for a sufficiently long period and in a reasonable quantity, taking into account the types of products or services, the scope of the advertising that has been made in relation thereto and the price in question;
- offering products or services at a specified price and then, with the intention of promoting a different product or service:
  - refusing to show the products or services first offered;
  - refusing to accept orders or requests for supplies;
  - failing to supply the products or services within a reasonable timeframe;
  - showing a defective sample of the promoted products or services; or
  - discrediting the products or services;
- offering a prize, either automatically or through a contest or raffle, without then awarding that prize (or another of equivalent quality and value) to winners;
- describing products or services as 'free', 'a gift', 'without charge' or an equivalent, where the user or consumer must pay something in addition to the unavoidable cost of responding to the promotion and collecting the product or paying for its delivery;
- holding a clearance sale where the conditions for holding such a sale are not met, or where the business suggests, without this being true, that it is ceasing its activities or moving; or
- creating a false impression that the user or consumer has already won, will win or will receive a prize or any other equivalent advantage if he or she carries out a specific act, where such prize or any equivalent advantage does not exist, or where the relevant act is subject to an obligation to make a payment or to pay a cost.

5.   Ambush marketing

Ambush marketing is not specifically regulated in Spain. However, certain ambush marketing practices could lead to potential trademark infringement claims where, for example, a third-party trademark is used that identifies the relevant event or its official sponsors.

Furthermore, the following articles of the Unfair Competition Act may be relevant in the context of ambush marketing, provided that the conditions for their application are met (as explained in section 1.2):

- Article 4 (acts contrary to good faith, which include acts that interfere with the competitive position of a third party in the market);
- Article 6 (misleading acts); and
- Article 11 (profiting from a third party's reputation).

These provisions may be invoked, for example, against ambush marketing practices such as:

- organising parallel events close to the place where the major sponsored event is taking place;
- offering or providing assistance to the public to reach the main event;
- creating and distributing promotional products in which the trademark of the ambusher (rather than the contracted sponsor) appears; or
- publishing misleading advertising that gives the impression that the advertiser or ambusher is sponsoring the event.

However, as of the time of writing, no reported cases in this area have yet come to court.

6. Direct marketing

The practices qualified by Articles 28 to 31 of the Unfair Competition Act as automatically considered as aggressive include:

- making personal visits to consumers' homes, ignoring requests to leave and/or not return; and
- making repeated unwanted proposals by telephone, fax, email or other communication media, except insofar as this is legally justifiable in order to comply with a contractual obligation.

Article 28 further states that a business must use, in these kinds of communications, systems that allow consumers to express their opposition to receiving commercial proposals; and where communications are made by telephone, calls must come from an identified telephone number.

Article 21 of the E-commerce Act prohibits unsolicited commercial communications through the means of electronic communications (including both email and text message) or equivalent means of electronic communication. In particular, it is prohibited to send advertising or promotional communications by electronic mail or another equivalent means of electronic communication where they are not solicited or expressly authorised in advance by the recipient. However, there is an exception to this requirement for prior consent where a prior contractual relationship exists and the provider has legally obtained the recipient's contact details as part of a sale or negotiation, and has used them to send commercial communications referring to products or services that are similar to those initially at issue in the contract between the provider and the customer.

In any case, the provider must always offer the recipient the opportunity to object, free of charge and in an easy manner, to the processing of his or her data for promotional purposes, both at the time the data is collected and on the occasion of each commercial message addressed to the recipient. For communications sent by email, this 'easy manner' must necessarily consist of the inclusion of a valid email address through which the right to object can be exercised. The sending of communications that do not include this email address is forbidden.

7. Product placement

Product placement is regulated by the General Audio-visual Communication Act (7/2010). In Article 31 of that act, 'product placement' is defined as "any form of audio-visual commercial communication consisting of, including, displaying or referencing a product, service or trademark appearing on such programme".

Article 17 recognises the right of providers of audio-visual media services to broadcast (subject to the conditions below) feature films, short films, documentaries, movies, television shows, sports programmes and entertainment programmes containing product placement in exchange for compensation. If, instead of payment, the compensation consists of the free supply of products or services (eg, material aids to production or prizes) for the purpose of including them in a programme, the act will qualify as product placement and will be permitted only if the supplied products or services have significant value.

Product placement may take place only under the following conditions:

- If the programme is produced or commissioned by the service provider or one of its subsidiaries, the public should be clearly informed about the existence of product placement at the beginning and end of the programme, and after commercial breaks;
- The product placement must not affect the editorial independence of the programme maker; nor can it directly incite the purchase or leasing of products or services, make specific promotions of products or services or give undue prominence to a product; and
- Product placement is prohibited in children's programming.

8. Native advertising and social media influencers

At the time of writing, native advertising and advertising through social media influencers are not specifically subject to legislation. The general advertising principles and legal limitations established by the general legislation referred to above are applicable, such as the General Advertising Act, the Unfair Competition Act, the E-commerce Act and the Consumer Protection Act. In this sense, like all advertising, native advertising and advertising through social media influencers must comply with the legislation in force (eg, they must not be illegal in the sense of Article 3 of the General Advertising Act (see section 1.2); they must comply with industry-specific regulations (see section 9); and they must not be false, inaccurate, or misleading). The general authenticity principle, according to which advertising must be identifiable as such, is of particular relevance. This principle is embodied, among other things, in the following legislation:

- Article 26 of the Unfair Competition Act, which qualifies surreptitious commercial practices as unfair, due to their being misleading. According to this article, surreptitious commercial practices include the publication in media as information of communications to promote products or services in exchange for payment, without clearly specifying – in the content or through images or sounds that are clearly identifiable by consumers or users – that the content constitutes advertising; and
- Article 20 of the E-commerce Act, which provides that commercial communications must be clearly identifiable as such, and that the legal or physical person on whose behalf they are made must also be clearly identifiable.

From a self-regulatory point of view, Rule 13 of Autocontrol's Code of Conduct establishes that commercial communications must be identifiable as such regardless of their form, format or support. This rule further specifies that where a commercial communication, including native advertising, appears in a medium that contains news or editorial content, it must be presented in such a way that it is easily recognised as advertising and is labelled as such where necessary. Finally, this rule specifically forbids, without limitation, communications that promote the sale of products or services in the guise of, for example, market surveys, consumer studies, user-generated content, private blogs, private publications in social media or independent analysis.

On 13 December 2018, the European Advertising Standards Alliance approved the Best Practice Recommendation on Influencer Marketing. Following this recommendation, Autocontrol and the Spanish Association of Advertisers (*Asociación Española de Anunciantes*) approved a Code of Conduct on the Use of Influencers in Advertising, in agreement with the Ministry of Economic Affairs and Digital Transformation and the Ministry of Consumption Affairs. The code, which entered into force on 1 January 2021, establishes the ethical framework that applies to advertising by influencers and is compulsory for all companies that are members of the Spanish Association of Advertisers or Autocontrol, as well as for all natural and legal persons (advertisers, media, agencies, agents and influencers) that voluntarily adhere to it.

Under the code, advertisers must acknowledge the need to comply with its rules in the agreements that they sign with influencers.

The code applies to all advertising content, defined as all posts and other content (graphics, audio or visual) that:

- are aimed at promoting products or services;
- are disclosed within a framework of reciprocal collaborations or commitments (ie, the disclosure of such content subject to payment or other consideration by the advertiser or its representatives; and

- are subject to editorial control by the advertiser or its agents (ie, by generating some or all of the content and/or validating the content).

According to the code, 'consideration' includes:
- direct payments or indirect payments (ie, through agencies);
- free delivery of a product;
- free tickets to events;
- free provision of a service;
- gift vouchers;
- gift bags; and
- gift trips.

In contrast, content of a purely editorial nature and content that is posted independently by influencers on their own initiative, with no relationship to the company whose products are mentioned or its agents, does not qualify as advertising content and thus is not subject to the code.

The basic principle established by the code is that all posts and content generated by an influencer of an advertising nature must be clearly identifiable as such to his or her followers. To this end, the code includes the following provisions:

- The code recommends the use of clear and generic indications, such as '*Publicidad*' ('Advertisement'), '*Publi*' ('Ad'), '*En colaboración con*' ('In collaboration with') or '*Patrocinado por*' ('Sponsored by'); or alternatively, descriptive mentions based on the specific collaboration in question, such as '*Embajador de*' ('Ambassador of'), '*Gracias a*' ('Thanks to') or '*Regalo de*' ('Gift of').
- The code discourages the use of:
  - generic indications (eg, '*Informacion*' ('Information'), '*Legal*' or similar);
  - indications that require an action (eg, a click) from the user; and
  - unclear indications (eg, '*Colab*', 'Sponso' or 'Sp').
- The indication that the post or content is of an advertising nature should be retained or added when the influencer shares or reposts content in other social networks, platforms or webpages.

Although the code does not require the inclusion of a specific type of advertising label or tag, it does require that this be "explicit, immediate and adequate to the medium and message". Therefore:

- the user should not have to carry out an additional action to learn of the advertising nature of the message in question (eg, by clicking on part of the post or browsing the contents of the post before seeing the tag); and
- the tag cannot be diluted among the rest of the advertising content.

The code contains an exemplary list of where and how the indication of advertising content should be included, taking into account the various format of different social media, as follows:

- Blogs: Include the identifying word or tag in the title of the post.
- Facebook: Include the identifying word or label in the title or entry of the post.
- Instagram: Include the identifying word or label on the title or above the photo, or at the beginning of the text displayed. If only an image is displayed, the image itself must include the identifying word or tag at the beginning of the message. The identifying tag established by the platform ('paid partnership tag') may also be used.
- Pinterest: Include the identifying word or tag at the beginning of the message.
- Twitter and Snapchat: Include the identifying word or tag at the beginning of the message, as a tag.
- Vlogs, YouYube, Twitch and other video platforms: Overlay the identifying word or tag while commenting on the product or service, or indicate it verbally before mentioning the promoted product or service.

The Autocontrol Advertising Jury is responsible for resolving any claims of infringement of the ethical rules contained in the code. Its resolutions are made public.

Finally, IAB Spain (a major association of digital communication, advertising and marketing companies) has issued several guides on this matter, such as *Marketing by Influencers, The Basic Guide to Online Advertising, The Branded Content Guide* and *The Guide to Influencer Kids*.

The first reported case relating to influencer advertising was subject to non-binding advice rendered on 28 November 2019 by the Autocontrol Jury and confirmed by the Plenary Jury on 8 January 2020. It concerned a post made on Instagram by a famous influencer, comprising a picture of her holding the wireless headphones of a Swedish company, and text elaborating on the characteristics and benefits of the product. The Autocontrol Jury considered that this post infringed Rule 13 of Autocontrol's Code of Conduct, because there were insufficient indications that the post served the purpose of advertising and it thus was not sufficiently and expressly identified as advertising, instead appearing as the personal opinion of the influencer. The Plenary Jury further considered that the mention of the word 'ad' in the post was insufficient, because it appeared at the end of the message; and that the lack of economic compensation was irrelevant, as the characteristics and circumstances of the message – which focused exclusively on the positive characteristics of the product – sufficed to conclude that the message had the nature of advertising.

9.   Industry-specific regulation

9.1   Gambling

Gambling is regulated by the Gambling Act (13/2011).

Article 7 of that act prohibits the advertisement, sponsorship or promotion, in any way, of gambling or of gambling operators without due authorisation from the Directorate General for the Regulation of Gambling (DGOJ). Article 7 further provides that the conditions and limits of authorisation to advertise shall be determined through implementing regulations. Accordingly, several royal decrees and ministerial orders that regulate each type of gambling (eg, sports betting, horse betting, contests, roulette, bingo, poker, blackjack) contain additional provisions relating to advertising, which must be observed. Moreover, any regulations on the advertisement of gambling that have been adopted by the legislatures of one or more Autonomous Communities in which the gambling activity is undertaken must also be observed.

Article 7 of the Gambling Act further states that any entity, advertising agency, audio-visual or electronic communication provider, media company or information society service that disseminates ads involving the direct or indirect promotion of gambling or of its operators must confirm that anyone seeking to place such ads:

- holds the necessary authorisation to do so from the DGOJ; and
- has been authorised by the DGOJ to advertise as requested, refraining from any such practice if it does not hold such authorisation.

The DGOJ maintains an updated list of authorised operators. Where an ad infringes the above rules, the DGOJ has the administrative authority to require that it be withdrawn; and the entity, advertising agency, audio-visual or electronic communication provider, media company or information society service that has published or broadcast the ad must comply with this requirement within a two-day period. If the advertiser previously obtained copy advice and approval from a self-regulatory body such as Autocontrol (which has produced the Commercial Communications on Gambling Activities Code), with which the DGOJ has a convention, it is considered to have acted in good faith.

Non-compliance with the provisions of the Gambling Act concerning advertising is qualified as a severe infringement which can incur penalties including a written subpoena and fine of up to €100,000.

Article 8 of the Gambling Act contains provisions on the protection of consumers, together with policies on responsible gambling that, among other things, oblige gambling operators to develop action plans to mitigate the harmful effects of gambling and that include basic rules on responsible gambling policies.

Royal Decree-Law 11/2020, adopting urgent measures in the social and economic field to address COVID-19, prohibits commercial communications that implicitly or explicitly refer to the situation of exceptionality derived from COVID-19 or encourage gambling activity in this context. It also contains some measures that were in force only during the state of emergency.

A self-regulatory code of practice on commercial communications of gambling activities was adopted on 2012 and amended on 2019, in collaboration between the DGOJ and the Audio-visual Authority.

9.2   Alcohol

Article 5.5 of the General Advertising Act prohibits the advertisement of spirits of more than 20% alcohol by volume (ABV) on television and in places where their sale or consumption is not permitted. Article 5.5 further sets out an obligation to limit through regulation the form, content and conditions of ads for alcoholic beverages, taking into account:

- the protection of the health and security of the general public, and of those to whom the advertising is addressed; and
- the requirement not to promote indiscriminate consumption, directly or indirectly, or make any association between alcohol and education, health or sports.

The prohibition on the advertisement on television of alcoholic drinks of more than 20% ABV is also contained in the General Audio-visual Communication Act, which further prohibits the advertisement on television of alcoholic drinks of less than 20% ABV:

- between 6:00am and 8:30pm;
- if it is directed to minors; or
- if it induces immoderate consumption or associates consumption with better physical performance, social success or improved health.

The regulations on labelling foodstuff products (see section 9.5), which include alcoholic drinks, also have implications for the advertisement of alcoholic drinks (in particular Article 9, which relates to the indication of the alcoholic strength of the product).

Account must also be taken of the various laws of the autonomous communities on this matter. Depending on the autonomous community, these extend the prohibitions or limitations on the advertisement of alcoholic drinks set out in state law (eg, completely banning the advertisement of alcoholic drinks of less than 20% ABV on television broadcasts in the relevant autonomous community; or prohibiting the advertisement of alcoholic drinks of more than 20% ABV in any kind of medium, or in certain media or places; or prohibiting or restricting certain types of advertising (eg, product placement, mailings, telephone)).

Various self-regulatory codes of practice have been adopted by alcoholic beverage manufacturers and suppliers – for example, the self-regulatory code of the Spanish Spirits Federation, the self-regulatory code of the association of Spanish brewers and the Code on Commercial Communications of Wine.

9.3 Pharmaceuticals

Advertising in the pharmaceuticals sector is principally regulated by:

- the General Healthcare Act (14/1986);
- Royal Legislative Decree 1/2015, approving the revised text of the Act on Guarantees and the Rational Use of Pharmaceuticals and Healthcare Products ('Pharmaceuticals Act');
- Royal Decree 1416/1994, regulating the advertisement of pharmaceuticals for human use;
- Royal Decree 1591/2009, regulating healthcare products;
- the Ministry Order of 10 December 1985, regulating advertising messages referring to pharmaceuticals and certain healthcare products; and
- laws of the autonomous communities relating to the promotion and advertisement of pharmaceuticals and healthcare products. Among others, the Autonomous Communities of Madrid and Catalonia (where most Spanish pharmaceutical companies are based) have approved guidelines on the application of certain provisions of Royal Decree 1416/1994 in relation to promotional activities.

In general, the legislation on advertising pharmaceutical products distinguishes between advertising targeted at the general public and advertising addressed to healthcare professionals.

Concerning the former, the Pharmaceuticals Act contains the basic rules on the advertisement of pharmaceuticals, which include the following:

- a prohibition on the advertisement of:
  - pharmaceuticals that have not obtained authorisation for commercial use;
  - pharmaceuticals that are financed with public funding;
  - pharmaceuticals that are dispensed on prescription only; and
  - psychotropic or stupefacient substances;
- the subjecting of ads to administrative control – mainly prior authorisation and an obligation to communicate campaigns to the administrative authorities;
- provisions on the minimum content of ads – in particular, they must include:
  - a clear indication that the product is a pharmaceutical;
  - an indication of the name of the pharmaceutical product and its active substance(s);

- identification of the laboratory responsible for its commercial production;
- all information necessary for the normal use of the pharmaceutical;
- an explicit invitation to read attentively the instructions on the packaging and in any enclosed leaflet;
- a recommendation to consult a pharmacist on the correct use of the product, and information on side effects, precautions and important warnings;
- an indication of the principles that ads must respect – including an encouragement to use the product responsibly and an objective (unexaggerated) presentation of the product; and
- the establishment of certain prohibitions – for example, on:
  - ads directed at children or inciting consumption of the product;
  - claims that the effect of the pharmaceutical is assured or that the product has no secondary effects;
  - claims that the effect of the product is superior or equal to another treatment or medicament; and
  - any abusive, alarming or misleading references to testimonies.

With regard to the advertisement of pharmaceuticals to healthcare professionals, Article 10 of Royal Decree 1416/1994 regulates the different types of advertising that are permitted, which include:
- documentary advertising;
- medical visits;
- the supply of free samples;
- the grant of incentives; and
- the sponsorship of scientific meetings.

Moreover, Royal Decree 1907/1996, on the advertisement and commercial promotion of products, activities or services intended for health purposes, regulates the advertisement of products presented as useful for the diagnosis, prevention or treatment of diseases without reporting clearly on their content, composition, nature or effect.

Finally, there are various self-regulatory codes of practice adopted by the pharmaceuticals industry in Spain – for example:
- a good practice code on the relationship between the pharmaceutical industry and patient organisations;
- the good practice code of Farmaindustria, adopted under the umbrella of Autocontrol, last amended in 2016; and
- the good practice code of the Spanish Health Technology Companies Federation.

9.4   Financial products and services

The Spanish legislation on financial products and services is traditionally classified according to the nature of the products or services offered and the organisation that supervises them. In this sense, a distinction may be drawn between:

- the advertisement of banking products and services which are authorised, controlled and supervised by the Bank of Spain;
- the advertisement of investment products and services, which are supervised by the National Securities Market Commission; and
- the advertisement of insurance funds and pension schemes, which are supervised by the General Insurance and Pension Schemes Directorate.

The advertisement of banking products and services and of investment products and services is regulated, respectively, by two orders adopted on 11 June 2010 by the Economy and Tax Ministry:

- Order 1718/2010 for banking products and services, further developed by the Bank of Spain; and
- Order 1717/2010 for investment products and services, further developed by the National Securities Market Commission.

These two orders establish the following principles:

- Ads for such products must provide sufficient information (in particular, to ensure the truthfulness, clarity and objectivity of the message), and meet other criteria determined by the Bank of Spain, to enable consumers to make informed decisions;
- The compulsory and minimum information that must appear in an ad will depend on the products or services offered; and
- Entities must carry out internal controls and establish procedures to protect the legitimate interests of consumers and address the risks to which consumers might be exposed as a result of the advertising activity.

The advertisement of insurance products and services is regulated by:

- Act 30/1995 on the organisation and supervision of private insurance companies;
- Royal Decree-Law 3/2020 on urgent measures implementing several EU directives in the field of public procurement in several sectors of private insurance, social schemes, tax and tax litigation;
- Royal Decree 1060/2015 on the organisation, supervision and solvency of insurance and reinsurance entities; and
- Legislative Royal Decree 1/2002 approving the consolidated text of the act regulating pension schemes and funds.

As far as insurance products and services are concerned, these regulations – apart from regulating the principles that ads must respect and the minimum information that they must contain – establish the possibility for private insurance companies to obtain prior copy advice from the General Insurance Directorate on costly advertising campaigns or campaigns with a broad national scope, in order to ensure before publication that they meet all necessary legal requirements.

9.5   Food

Foodstuffs are mainly regulated by:

- Royal Decree 1334/1999, approving the general law on the labelling, presentation and advertisement of foodstuffs (with the exception of unpackaged foodstuffs, which are regulated by Royal Decree 126/2015); and
- Royal Decree 930/1992, approving the labelling law with regard to the nutritional properties of foodstuffs.

The existing legislation sets out specific categories of foodstuff products, such as:

- dietetic products (regulated by Royal Decree 1412/2018, approving the procedure for the communication of placing on the market of foodstuffs for specific population groups); and
- supplementary products (regulated by Royal Decree 1487/2009 on food supplements).

The labelling, presentation and advertisement of several foodstuff products (eg, water, yogurts, coffee, fruit juice, refreshing drinks, alcoholic drinks, meat) are regulated by specific laws, without prejudice to the application of the general rules on the matter.

Royal Decree 1334/1999 establishes the general principle that the labelling and advertisement of foodstuff products must not be misleading in terms of their characteristics – in particular, their nature, identity, quality, composition, quantity, duration, origin or precedence, and means of production. The royal decree also contains a non-exhaustive list of specific cases in which labelling or advertising is misleading – for example, where it:

- attributes to the product some effects or properties that it does not in fact possess;
- suggests that it has particular characteristics when they are common to all similar products; or
- attributes to a product preventive, therapeutic or curative characteristics for a human illness (without prejudice to provisions regarding natural waters and foodstuffs related to a special diet).

9.6 Tobacco

The advertisement of tobacco products is regulated by Act 28/2005, as last amended in 2017. The general rule is that the advertisement of tobacco products is generally prohibited, except for:

- publications and representations that are addressed exclusively to professionals in the tobacco trade;
- promotions inside tobacconists' stores, as long as they are:
  - not addressed to minors;
  - not part of the window display; and
  - not extended outside the premises or in some other way visible outside;
- publications containing ads for tobacco products that are edited or printed in non-EU countries, as long as those publications are not principally addressed to the EU market and are not principally addressed to minors; and
- the free distribution of tobacco products, or related products or related merchandising, to Spanish tobacconists.

The broadcast, in any medium (including online), of programmes or images in which presenters, collaborators or invited persons appear smoking, or mention or show – directly or indirectly –trademarks, commercial names, logos or other signs identified or associated with tobacco products, is prohibited.

9.7 E-cigarettes

E-cigarettes are also regulated by Act 28/2005, as last amended in 2017. The act includes within its scope any device capable of delivering nicotine, and qualifies as a severe infringement the unauthorised advertisement, promotion or sponsorship of such devices and their refills.

The act prohibits, in relation to these products:

- commercial communications on information society services, in the press and in any other printed publications with the direct or indirect aim of promoting these products, except for:
  - publications addressed exclusively to professionals in this sector; and
  - publications printed and published in third countries, if their principal destination is not the European Union;
- commercial communications whose aim or effect is to promote such products on the radio;
- any public or private contribution to radio programmes whose aim or effect is the promotion of such products;
- any form of public or private contribution to any act, activity or individual whose aim or effect is the promotion of such products in several EU member states or that otherwise has cross-border effects; and
- audio-visual commercial communications that promote such products.

The advertisement of e-cigarettes is further regulated by Title II of Royal Decree 579/2017, regulating certain aspects relating to the manufacture, presentation and commercialisation of tobacco products and related products. This royal decree implements Directive 2014/40/EU into Spanish law.

Finally, several autonomous communities – such as the Basque Country, Asturias and the Valencian Community – have introduced regulations in relation to e-cigarettes.

Sweden

Rebecka Harding
Advokatfirman Delphi

---

1. Overview of the legal and regulatory regime for advertising

The main legislation governing marketing in Sweden is the Marketing Act (SFS 2008:486). The Marketing Act applies to the marketing of all types of 'products', which are defined in the Marketing Act as "goods, services, real property, employment vacancies and other commodities". The Marketing Act implements EU Directive 2005/29/EC on unfair business-to-consumer commercial practices and EU Directive 2006/114/EC on misleading and comparative advertising. Annex 1 of Directive 2005/29/EC (the 'blacklist'), which sets out a list of commercial practices that are always to be considered as unfair marketing, has also been incorporated as an annex to the Marketing Act.

According to the Marketing Act, marketing must comply with good marketing practice, and all marketing claims must be accurate and therefore not misleading. The Marketing Act also regulates matters relating to, for example, comparative advertising and different types of offers. When determining whether advertising is compatible with good marketing practice, consideration shall be given to whether the marketing complies with, among other things:

- authorities' advisory notices (eg, the Swedish Consumer Agency's advisory notices);
- established standards (eg, the International Chamber of Commerce (ICC) Code of Advertising Practices); and
- case law.

Further, in accordance with the so-called 'principle of unlawfulness', marketing that is in breach of other legislation is also *per se* in violation of the Marketing Act's provision on good marketing practice.

For marketing to be in violation of the Marketing Act, the marketing in general must have – or at least be likely to have – caused the recipient of the marketing to make a transactional decision that he or she would not otherwise have made. This economic impact is assessed through a hypothetical test which is called the 'transactional test'. The transactional test must be carried out when assessing whether marketing is in breach of good marketing practice, for example; but not when assessing whether the marketing is in breach of the blacklist or the provisions on comparative advertising and direct marketing.

It is not only marketers that risk being held responsible for marketing in violation of the Marketing Act; anyone that has materially contributed to the marketing (eg, the marketer's employees and other persons acting on behalf of the marketer, advertising agencies, affiliate networks) can be held responsible under the Marketing Act.

The Marketing Act contains several sanctions depending on the nature of the violation, such as prohibitions (which can be subject to a conditional financial penalty), third-party damages and a market disruption charge.

The Swedish Consumer Agency is the supervisory authority that ensures compliance with the Marketing Act (as well as many other marketing rules set out in other laws, such as the Gambling Act (SFS 2018:1138)). The Swedish Consumer Agency is led by a director general, who is also the Consumer Ombudsman. The Consumer Ombudsman represents consumer interests and, among other things, has the authority, in cases of minor importance, to issue injunctions (prohibitions and orders) combined with a conditional financial penalty for breach of the Marketing Act, which the trader (eg, the marketer) can choose to accept to avoid legal proceedings in court. The ombudsman's decisions can be appealed to the Patent and Market Court. Under certain conditions, the ombudsman may also pursue legal action in court within those areas for which the Swedish Consumer Agency is the supervisory authority; the Patent and Market Court and the Patent and Market Court of Appeal are the competent courts for such cases. An action before the competent courts regarding breach of the Marketing Act may also be pursued by other parties, such as a trader affected by the marketing in question or a group of consumers, traders or employees.

In addition to complying with the Marketing Act's general requirements on marketing, marketing must comply with requirements under any applicable specific legislation, such as industry-specific regulations. For example, the Alcohol Act (SFS 2010:1622) sets out further requirements on the marketing of alcoholic beverages. Examples of various industry-specific regulations and their rules on marketing are outlined in section 9.

Marketers should also be wary of the risk of infringing the IP rights of others. For example, if an ad or logo is too similar to that of another business, the marketer may find itself subject to a claim for infringement under the Trademarks Act (SFS 2010:1877) or the Act on Copyright in Literary and Artistic Works (SFS 1960:729), among others. However, details of these aspects are beyond the scope of this chapter.

There are several self-regulatory organisations in Sweden. One such organisation is the Swedish Advertising Ombudsman (RO), which reviews whether advertising complies with the ICC code. Anyone (eg, consumers, companies and organisations) that considers an ad is in breach of the ICC code can file a complaint to the RO about the ad. The RO cannot impose any financial or legal sanctions where the complaint is upheld. However, the RO will post its decision on its website, which can cause PR issues for the marketer. Examples of industry-specific self-regulatory organisations are outlined in the relevant sections below.

2. Comparative advertising

Comparative advertising is regulated by the Marketing Act. Comparative advertising is advertising in which the marketer directly or indirectly refers to another trader or its products. The Marketing Act permits comparative advertising subject to the following conditions:

- It is not misleading;
- It compares products that meet the same needs or are intended for the same purpose;
- It objectively compares one or more material, relevant, verifiable and representative features of the products;
- It does not create confusion between the marketer and another trader, or between their products, trademarks, business names or other distinctive marks;
- It does not discredit or disparage another trader's business, circumstances, products, trademarks, business name or other distinctive marks;
- With regard to goods bearing a designation of origin, it always pertains to goods of the same designation;
- It does not take unfair advantage of the reputation associated with another trader's trademark, business name or other distinctive marks or the designation of origin of the products; and
- It does not present products as imitations or replicas of products that bear a protected trademark or business name.

It is also important to ensure that the comparative advertising does not infringe any third party's IP rights (eg, trademarks or copyrights) by, for example, using a competitor's logos, pictures or similar in an unlawful manner.

3. Online behavioural advertising

Online behavioural advertising is often facilitated through the use of cookies. The most relevant statutes regarding the use of cookies are:

- the Electronic Communications Act (SFS 2003:389), which implements the EU e-Privacy Directive (2002/58/EC); and
- the General Data Protection Regulation (2016/679) (GDPR).

Under Chapter 6, Section 18 of the Electronic Communications Act, it is prohibited to store information on or gain access to information from an internet user's device (eg, through a cookie), unless:

- this is necessary – for example, to provide a service explicitly provided by the user; or
- the user is provided with information about the purposes of the storage of, or access to, the information; and
- the user has given his or her consent.

The Electronic Communications Act applies regardless of whether the use of cookies involves the processing of personal data. The information and consent requirements are often fulfilled through the implementation of a so-called 'cookie policy' and some sort of consent mechanism. The nature of appropriate consent mechanisms has been the subject of debate in Sweden over the years, but was clarified by the October 2019 decision of the Court of Justice of the European Union in Case C-673/17. The court found, among other things, that implied consent and pre-ticked boxes are not acceptable; and that in order to be valid, consent should involve an "active behaviour with a clear view" of consent.

The Swedish Post and Telecom Authority is the supervisory authority that ensures compliance with the Electronic Communications Act. The Electronic Communications Act sets out several sanctions depending on the nature of the violation, such as fines and prohibitions (which may be subject to a conditional financial penalty).

If the use of cookies involves the processing of personal data, account must also be taken of the GDPR. This will be the case only where the cookies collect data which could be used to directly or indirectly identify an individual (eg, IP addresses, which in Sweden are typically considered to be personal data). If personal data is being collected for the purposes of online behavioural advertising, then the 'data controller' (ie, the natural or legal person that determines the purposes and means of the data processing) must comply with the requirements set out in the GDPR. These include obligations to:

- ensure that there is a legal basis for the processing of the personal data (eg, legitimate interest or consent); and
- provide the person whose personal data is being processed with certain information (eg, information on the processing and the rights of the data subject).

The Swedish Data Protection Authority is the supervisory authority that ensures compliance with the GDPR. The GDPR contains several sanctions depending on the nature of the violation, such as administrative fines and third-party damages.

A more detailed analysis of these aspects is beyond the scope of this chapter.

4.   Sales promotions

'Sales promotions' is a collective term for various marketing measures, such as combined offers, promotional lotteries and sales competitions. In Sweden, there is no uniform legislation on sales promotions or special rules on how to combine offers. However, the Marketing Act contains several basic principles that all marketers should bear in mind when arranging sales promotions and some specific requirements regarding the use of certain expressions in marketing.

All sales promotions must comply with the Marketing Act's general requirements, such as that marketing comply with good marketing practice and that all marketing claims be accurate and not misleading. In order to avoid being misleading, a sales promotion should contain clear information on the terms and conditions of the offer, such as:

- the nature and value of the offer;
- the start and closing date of the offer; and
- other restrictions that apply to the offer.

Where there is limited time or space to give details of the promotion (eg, in 'teaser ads', such as in a banner), the full terms and conditions need not be included, but can be limited to 'significant' conditions, such as the value of the offer and the start and closing date. The full terms and conditions can then be made available elsewhere (eg, on a website).

The blacklist also prohibits certain marketing measures, such as:

- short deadlines for participating in the offer; and
- misleading information on the chances of winning that falsely creates the impression of a free offer.

The Marketing Act contains further restrictions on how to use certain terms that are often used in sales promotions. The term 'free' and similar terms may not be used if, in order to obtain the product to which the term refers, the consumer must pay anything other than the unavoidable cost of responding to the offer and collecting or paying for delivery of the product. If the term 'free' is used in conjunction with the purchase of another product, it may be used only if the price of that other product has not been increased to cover all or part of the cost of the 'free' product.

The terms 'realisation', 'discount sale' and similar terms may be used only if:

- the products offered for sale form part of the trader's ordinary range;
- the sale takes place during a limited period; and
- the prices are significantly lower than the trader's normal prices for equivalent products (Section 17 of the Marketing Act).

'Limited period' normally means a maximum of a few consecutive weeks and an aggregate maximum of two months per year. 'Normal price' means the price at which the trader normally sells the product, which generally should have applied for a continuous period of at least four weeks immediately before the promotion. 'Significantly lower' is what is objectively perceived as favourable to consumers of the product in question, which will vary depending on the industry and product type. Similar restrictions apply to the use of the term 'clearance sale' (Section 16 of the Marketing Act).

Specific legislation may also impose requirements on sales promotions. For example, if the sales promotion takes the form of a lottery, the strict rules set out in the Gambling Act must also be taken into consideration. The provision of a lottery or similar typically requires a licence. However, a licence is not required if the participation does not require a payment (eg, social media activities where participation merely requires the 'liking' of a post on social media).

The ICC code also sets out requirements on the arrangement of a sales promotion, which specify, among other things:

- the information that should be provided when organising a sales competition; and
- how the term 'free' and similar terms should be used.

5. Ambush marketing

There is no uniform legislation on ambush marketing in Sweden. Depending on the execution of the ambush marketing, a variety of Swedish laws may apply, including:

- the Marketing Act;
- the Trademarks Act;
- the Act on Copyright in Literary and Artistic Works;
- the Design Protection Act (SFS 1970:485); and
- the Act on Names and Images in Advertising (SFS 1978:800).

Names, logos, products and other distinctive features may be protected by designs, copyright and trademarks, as either unregistered and/or registered rights. Hence, any unauthorised use of these or similar IP rights by an ambusher in the course of trade may constitute design, copyright and/or trademark infringement. The Act on Copyright in Literary and Artistic Works also restricts the ambusher from using the photographs and copyright-protected works of others without the permission of the rights holder. Ambush marketing may also be in breach of the Marketing Act, such as the provisions on comparative advertising, good marketing practice (which includes a prohibition against passing off) and misleading advertising.

Where the ambusher uses a person's name or picture (including lookalikes, famous nicknames and so on), the ambusher must have obtained that person's prior approval in accordance with the Act on Names and Images in Advertising (SFS 1978:800).

6. Direct marketing

In Sweden, all direct marketing must comply with the GDPR and the Marketing Act. In the context of the GDPR and direct marketing, marketers must ensure, among other things, that:

- there is a legal basis for the processing of the personal data for direct marketing, such as legitimate interest or consent;
- the data subjects are informed that their personal data is being collected for marketing purposes;
- the personal data is not processed beyond acceptable retention periods;
- any transfer of the personal data outside the organisation complies with the GDPR; and
- the personal data is not used for a purpose which is incompatible with the purpose notified to the relevant data subject.

The Swedish Data Protection Authority is the supervisory authority that ensures compliance with the GDPR. The GDPR contains several sanctions depending on the nature of the violation, such as administrative fines and third-party damages.

The Marketing Act's rules on direct marketing mainly apply to direct marketing to natural persons (ie, individuals and private companies, as they are not legal entities), and vary depending on the method of direct marketing. Direct marketing without prior consent to natural persons by electronic mail (eg, email, SMS and MMS), fax, automatic calling device or a similar automatic system for individual communication that is not operated by an individual is generally prohibited. However, prior consent for direct marketing via electronic mail is not required if the following conditions are met:

- The marketer obtained the natural person's electronic mail address in the context of the sale of a product to that person;
- The natural person has not objected to the marketer's use of his or her electronic mail address for marketing purposes;
- The marketing pertains to the marketer's own similar products; and
- The natural person is clearly and explicitly given the opportunity to object, simply and without charge, to the use of his or her electronic mail address for marketing purposes, both at the time it is collected and in conjunction with each subsequent marketing communication.

The Marketing Act permits a marketer to use other methods for direct marketing than those described above, provided that the natural person has not clearly objected to the use of such method (eg, by registering with the so-called

'NIX registers' or putting a "No thanks to marketing" sign on his or her post box). Further, the Marketing Act stipulates that marketing via email must always include a valid address to which the recipient may send a request for cessation of the marketing practice. This provision applies with regard to marketing to both natural persons and legal persons. Regardless of the aforementioned, direct marketing targeting children under the age of 16 is generally in breach of the Marketing Act's principle on good marketing practice.

In addition to the statutory rules on direct marketing, the Swedish Data and Marketing Association (SWEDMA) – a national trade association – has adopted several guidelines on the subject. SWEDMA's Ethical Rules on Marketing to Companies via Email are of particular relevance, as (among other things) they clarify that direct marketing can be sent to an employee's work mail in his or her professional role where:

- the marketing is relevant to the employee in his or her professional role; and
- the employee has not objected to the use of this method of direct marketing.

7. Product placement

Product placement in television programmes or via television on demand is regulated by the Radio and Television Act (2010:696), which implemented the EU Audiovisual Media Services Directive (2018/1808) into national law. The Radio and Television Act defines 'product placement' as "the presence in a programme or a user-generated video of a product, a service or a trade mark, if this is done for a marketing purpose and in return for payment or for similar consideration to the media service provider or the video-sharing platform provider, or to the user having created or uploaded a user-generated video on a video-sharing platform, unless the good or service is of little value and has been provided free of charge".

Product placement in television programmes or via television on demand is prohibited in the following programmes:

- news and current affairs programmes;
- consumer affairs programmes;
- religious programmes; and
- programmes aimed primarily at children under 12 years of age.

Product placement in other types of programmes is permitted subject to the following conditions:

- The product placement is not for:
  - infant formula;
  - non-beverage alcoholic preparations according to the Alcohol Act (SFS 2010:1622);

- gambling products where the marketer does not have the necessary licence under the Gambling Act;
- prescription-only pharmaceuticals or medical treatments;
- alcoholic beverages or other products from companies whose principal activity is the manufacture or sale of alcoholic beverages; or
- tobacco products, e-cigarettes or refill containers or other products from companies whose principal activity is the manufacture or sale of such products.
- The product placement does not unduly benefit commercial interests by containing sales promotions (eg, promoting the purchase or rental of products or services), or promote a product or service in an improper manner.
- The product placement does not affect the relevant programme's content, scheduling or structuring in a catalogue in such a way that it affects the editorial independence of the media service provider.
- A neutral indication of the inclusion of product placement and the relevant product or service is given at the beginning and end of the programme, as well as following commercial breaks.

The Broadcasting Commission monitors compliance with the provisions on product placement under the Radio and Television Act. The sanction for violation of the provisions on product placement is a fine, payable to the state, of between SEK 5,000 and SEK 5 million, in accordance with Chapter 17, Sections 5 and 6 of the Radio and Television Act.

8.   Native advertising and social media influencers

There is no uniform legislation on native advertising and influencer marketing, which are regulated and assessed in the same way as all other types of marketing. Native advertising and influencer marketing must thus comply with the Marketing Act, among other statutes. The most relevant provision of the Marketing Act is Section 9, which sets out the requirements on the identification of advertising and sender identification. The former requires that all marketing be formulated and presented in such a way that it is clear that it is marketing. Subliminal advertising is thus prohibited. The latter requires that the identity of the marketer be clearly indicated in all marketing, except in marketing whose sole purpose is to attract attention ahead of follow-up marketing (eg, 'teaser ads', such as in banners). The Marketing Act does not stipulate how an ad should be formulated to fulfil these requirements. However, the ad must be assessed as a whole; and features such as font size and colours can be used to ensure that the disclosure is sufficiently clear. The blacklist also prohibits marketing where it is not clear that the content is marketing and at whom it is targeted (Points 11 and 22).

Traditionally, the marketer has been considered primarily responsible for influencer marketing that does not comply with the Marketing Act, while the influencer has contributory liability.

The Marketing Act applies only to representations with a commercial purpose. Representations with no commercial purpose may instead be covered by freedom of speech or freedom of the press. In practice, this means that if an influencer, on his or her own initiative and outside of any collaboration, mentions a product in his or her channels, this falls outside the scope of the Marketing Act, and requirements such as those on the identification of advertising and sender identification will not apply.

In addition to the statutory rules on native advertising and influencer marketing, the Swedish Consumer Agency has issued Guidelines on Marketing in Social Media, which set out its guidance on how native advertisement and influencer marketing should be formulated to fulfil the requirements of Section 9 of the Marketing Act. Articles 7 and 8 of the ICC code further correspond to Section 9 of the Marketing Act.

9. Industry-specific regulation

9.1 Gambling

Specific rules on the advertisement of gambling are set out in the Gambling Act. The advertisement of gambling to consumers must be moderate, which means, for example, that such ads should be objective, balanced and not misleading. Ads targeted at consumers must also:

- include clear information on the minimum age to gamble (minors under the age of 18 may not engage in gambling that requires a licence); and
- not specifically target minors under the age of 18.

Gambling ads (including in venues where gambling takes place, but excluding marketing via radio) must also include the contact details of an organisation that provides information on and support for problem gambling. The advertisement of gambling products on television or radio where the marketer does not have the necessary licence under the Gambling Act is prohibited. It is also prohibited to send direct marketing on gambling to anyone who has opted for self-exclusion from gambling. Direct marketing to anyone who has closed his or her player account is further permitted only if that person actively approved the marketing in connection with the account closure.

The European Commission has issued its Recommendation on Principles for the Protection of Consumers and Players of Online Gambling Services and for the Prevention of Minors from Gambling Online (2014/478/EU), which provides guidance on how the moderate marketing requirement should be interpreted. The two trade organisations – the Swedish Trade Association for

Online Gambling and the Swedish Gambling Association – have also adopted joint guidelines on ethical and moderate marketing.

The Swedish Consumer Agency is the central supervisory authority that ensures compliance with the provisions on the advertisement of gambling. The sanctions for violation of the rules of on the advertisement of gambling set out in the Gambling Act are regulated through the Marketing Act in accordance with Chapter 15, Section 4 of the Gambling Act.

9.2 Alcohol

Specific rules on the advertisement of alcohol are set out in the Alcohol Act. When advertising alcoholic beverages or non-beverage alcoholic preparations (greater than 2.25% alcohol by volume (ABV)), the following should be considered:

- The advertising must be particularly moderate – for example, it may not be intrusive or insistent, or encourage the use of alcohol.
- The ad may not target or depict people under the age of 25.
- The ad may not contravene good practice in the context in which it appears.
- The ad may not use inappropriate methods for the consumer.
- The ad may not be misleading.
- Images in ads may only show the product or the raw materials included in the product, individual packaging or trademarks and other comparable distinctive marks.
- It is generally prohibited to give such beverages or preparations away as a gift, but it is permitted to give them away as a sample under certain conditions.
- It is generally prohibited to advertise such beverages or preparations in television programmes, via television on demand or on radio.
- A provider of a video-sharing platform may not show ads for such beverages or preparations before, during or after user-generated videos or television programmes on the platform.
- In addition to the general marketing requirements just mentioned, ads in periodicals (eg, newspapers and magazines that are published at least four times a year according to a publishing schedule) and equivalent publications:
    - may not be for alcoholic beverages that exceed 15% ABV (or create confusion with such beverages), unless the publication is provided only at the point of sale;
    - must contain a warning about the harmful effects of alcohol and state the ABV in a clear and neutral way; and
    - may not exceed tabloid format (2,100 column millimetres).

The advertisement of low-alcohol beverages (up to 2.25% ABV) may not create confusion with alcoholic beverages.

In addition to the statutory rules on the advertisement of alcohol, the Swedish Consumer Agency has issued an advisory notice on the marketing of alcoholic beverages to consumers (KOVFS 2016:1), which provides clarification on its interpretation of the statutory rules (eg, how the particularly moderate marketing requirement should be interpreted). The industry has also adopted a recommendation on the advertisement of alcoholic and low-alcohol beverages; and the self-regulatory body – the Swedish Alcohol Suppliers' Scrutineer (AGM) – monitors the marketing of alcoholic beverages in Sweden. Anyone (consumers, companies and organisations) that considers an ad is in breach of the recommendation can file a complaint with the AGM regarding the ad. The AGM cannot impose financial or legal sanctions where it upholds a complaint. However, it does post its decisions on its website, which can lead to PR problems for the marketer.

The Swedish Consumer Agency is the central supervisory authority that ensures compliance with the provisions on alcohol advertising. The sanctions for violation of the rules of on the advertisement of alcohol set out in the Alcohol Act are regulated through the Marketing Act in accordance with Chapter 7, Section 8 of the Alcohol Act.

9.3 Pharmaceuticals

Specific rules on the advertisement of pharmaceuticals for human use are found in the Medicinal Products Act (SFS 2015:315). Clarification on those rules may be found in the Swedish Medicinal Products Agency's Regulation LVFS 2009:6 on the marketing of medicinal products for human use. The Medicinal Products Act and Regulation LVFS 2009:6 are based on Directive 2001/83/EC on the Community code relating to medicinal products for human use. According to the Medicinal Products Act, it is prohibited to advertise:

- prescription-only pharmaceuticals (except for vaccination campaigns for human infectious diseases) to the general public;
- pharmaceuticals targeting children; and
- pharmaceuticals that have not yet been approved for sale in Sweden.

The advertisement of pharmaceuticals for human use must:

- be relevant, objective and balanced;
- accord with good marketing practice;
- include such information that is of particular importance to the recipient; and
- not be misleading.

Ads targeted at the general public must further be formulated in a way that makes clear that they constitute the marketing of a pharmaceutical, and not in a way that could cause the pharmaceutical to be used in a harmful way or that could encourage people not to seek appropriate care. Regulation LVFS 2009:6 sets out further rules on how pharmaceuticals may be marketed, such as:

- how the advertising should be formulated (eg, mandatory information to include in marketing targeting the general public; that all advertising must correspond to the summary of product characteristics in all respects); and
- a prohibition on dispensing free samples of pharmaceuticals.

Specific restrictions on pharmaceutical advertising through product placement and sponsorship on television and radio are set out in the Swedish Radio and Television Act.

Further, the Swedish Association of the Pharmaceutical Industry (LIF) – a national trade association – has adopted its own Ethical Rules for the Pharmaceutical Industry. The rules regulate the advertisement of pharmaceuticals to healthcare professionals and to the general public. The rules also regulate cooperation between pharmaceutical companies and healthcare providers/healthcare professionals, pharmacy employees, politicians and user organisations, interest groups and the general public. The LIF has two regulatory bodies – the Information Examiner Committee (IGN) and the Information Practices Committee (NBL) – which supervise compliance with the rules. The IGN and NBL may, among other things, impose fines on members that violate the rules.

The Swedish Medicinal Products Agency is the supervisory authority that ensures compliance with the provisions on the advertisement of pharmaceuticals under the Medicinal Products Act and LVFS 2009:6. The Medicinal Products Act contains several sanctions depending on the nature of the violation, such as a prohibition (which may be subject to a conditional financial penalty).

9.4 Financial products and services

Swedish law contains specific rules on the marketing of certain types of financial products and services.

Specific rules on the advertisement of consumer credit are set out in the Consumer Credit Act (SFS 2010:1846). The advertisement of credit products must comply with good lending practices – for example, the marketing should not particularly emphasise the ability to obtain a quick loan. The advertisement of credit products must also be moderate – for example, it must:

- be objective, balanced and not intrusive; and
- not give the impression that a loan is a worry-free solution to a consumer's financial problems or entice the consumer to make an unforeseen decision to commit to a loan.

The Consumer Credit Act further requires that certain information be provided in the marketing, including information on the effective interest rate for the credit, with a representative example. In addition to the statutory rules on the advertisement of consumer credit, the Swedish Consumer Agency has issued an advisory notice on the marketing of consumer credit (KOVFS 2020:1) which clarifies how it will interpret the statutory rules, such as the requirement that marketing be correct, objective and neutral.

There are also specific rules on the advertisement of various saving and investment products. For example, the Alternative Investment Fund Managers Act (SFS 2013:561), the Deposit Insurance Act (SFS 1995:1571), the Deposit Business Act (SFS 2004:299), the Investment Savings Account Act (2011:1268) and the Investment Funds Act (SFS 2004:46) set out information requirements regarding the marketing of the different saving and investment products that they regulate. The Swedish Consumer Agency and the Swedish Investment Fund Association have also jointly adopted an agreement on rules for the marketing of funds (BÖ 2015:02), which aims to clarify what constitutes good marketing practice for the marketing of funds. The agreement applies to both members and non-members of the Swedish Investment Fund Association.

The Swedish Consumer Agency is the central supervisory authority that ensures compliance with the provisions on the advertisement of financial products and services. Sanctions for violation of these provisions may include a prohibition (which can be subject to a conditional financial penalty).

9.5   Food

Several statutes regulate the advertisement of food. General principles and requirements on food advertising are set out in regulations such as:

- EU Regulation 178/2002, which sets out the general principles and requirements of food law; and
- EU Regulation 1169/2011 on the provision of food information to consumers.

EU Regulation 178/2002 stipulates that food advertising may not be misleading. EU Regulation 1169/2011 on the provision of food information to consumers also sets out several basic principles that all marketers of food should bear in mind – for example, food advertising must be accurate, clear and easy to understand for the consumer, and must not be misleading. Food advertising is misleading if, for example:

- it attributes to a foodstuff effects or properties which that foodstuff does not possess; or
- it suggests that the food possesses special characteristics when in fact all similar foodstuffs possess such characteristics.

There are also several specific rules on food advertising. For example, EU Regulation 1924/2006 on nutrition and health claims made in relation to foods regulates the use of nutrition claims and health claims. Only nutrition and health claims that meet the requirements set out in the regulation may be included in marketing. The rules are EU-wide and apply to all labelling, presentation and advertisement of foods. To be permitted for use in marketing:

- nutrition claims must:
  - be listed in the annex to the regulation; and
  - meet the requirements set out in the regulation (eg, quantity requirements and other conditions); and
- health claims must be approved by the European Commission.

In general, non-specific benefits of the nutrient or food (eg, through the name of the product) must be accompanied by an approved health claim. The regulation also explicitly prohibits certain health claims, such as health claims which suggest that health may be affected by not consuming the food or refer to the rate or amount of weight loss. EU quality schemes also set out requirements on the use of certain names in marketing (eg, 'prosciutto di Parma' and 'feta').

The Swedish Consumer Agency is the central supervisory authority that ensures compliance with the provisions on food advertising. The sanctions set out in the Marketing Act may be applicable in case of non-compliance with the requirements on food advertising.

9.6 Tobacco

Specific rules on the advertisement of tobacco products and similar products (ie, e-cigarettes and refill containers, herbal products for smoking and enjoyment products which correspond to tobacco in their intended use, but do not contain tobacco) are found in the Act on Tobacco and Similar Products (SFS 2018:2088). The general rule is that the advertisement of tobacco products is prohibited. An exception to the general rule is certain advertising at the point of sale which consists of solely supplying tobacco products for sale or commercial messages that:

- are not intrusive or insistent, and do not encourage the use of tobacco; and
- to the extent possible, are placed so that they are not visible outside of the point of sale.

Marketers should also be aware of the rules on the indirect advertisement of tobacco products, which restrict marketers of non-tobacco products from using signs that are used for tobacco products. There are also rules which restrict the sponsorship of activities that may be assumed to promote the sale of tobacco products. Specific restrictions on the advertisement of tobacco products through product placement and sponsorship on television and radio are set out in the Swedish Radio and Television Act.

In addition to the statutory rules on the advertisement of tobacco, the Swedish Consumer Agency has issued an advisory notice on the marketing of tobacco to consumers (KOVFS 2019:3), which clarifies how it interprets the statutory rules.

The Swedish Consumer Agency is the central supervisory authority that ensures compliance with the provisions on the advertisement of tobacco products. The sanctions for violation of the rules on the advertisement of tobacco products in the Act on Tobacco and Similar Products are regulated through the Marketing Act in accordance with Chapter 7, Section 8 of the Act on Tobacco and Similar Products.

9.7 E-cigarettes

Specific rules on the advertisement of e-cigarettes and refill containers are set out in the Act on Tobacco and Similar Products (SFS 2018:2088). The general rule is that it is prohibited to market e-cigarettes and refill containers:

- online (eg, direct marketing via email);
- in periodicals (eg, newspapers and magazines that are published at least four times a year according to a publishing schedule) or equivalent publications; and
- in television programmes, via television on demand or on radio, which are covered by the Swedish Radio and Television Act.

This means that there is no prohibition on the marketing of e-cigarettes and refill containers, for example, at the point of sale, outdoors or on printed matter such as posters, brochures and leaflets. Advertising online, in television programmes, via television on demand or on radio, which are covered by the Swedish Radio and Television Act, which consists solely of the supply of e-cigarettes and refill containers for sale is also permitted, despite the general rule.

Marketers should also be aware of the rules that restrict sponsorship activities which may be assumed to promote the sale of e-cigarettes or refill containers. Specific restrictions on the advertisement of e-cigarettes and refill containers through product placement and sponsorship on television and radio are set out in the Swedish Radio and Television Act.

In addition to the statutory rules on the advertisement of e-cigarettes and refill containers, the Swedish Consumer Agency has issued an advisory notice on the marketing of e-cigarettes and refill containers to consumers (KOVFS 2019:2), which clarifies how it interprets the statutory rules.

The Swedish Consumer Agency is the central supervisory authority that ensures compliance with the provisions on the advertisement of e-cigarettes and refill containers. The sanctions for violation of the rules on the advertisement of e-cigarettes and refill containers in the Act on Tobacco and Similar Products are regulated through the Marketing Act in accordance with Chapter 7, Section 8 of the Act on Tobacco and Similar Products.

Switzerland

Barbara Abegg
Lenz & Staehelin
Michael Noth
TIMES Attorneys

1. Overview of the legal and regulatory regime for advertising

In Switzerland, anyone in principle has the right to advertise. This right may be covered by different fundamental rights, such as:

- freedom of expression and information;
- freedom of assembly;
- the guarantee of ownership; and
- in particular, economic freedom.[1]

Restrictions on these fundamental rights require that such restrictions be:

- based in law;
- justified in the public interest or for the protection of the fundamental rights of others; and
- proportionate.[2]

In Switzerland, the restrictions and regulations that apply to advertising are scattered across different statutes. The legal nature of these provisions varies. On the one hand, there is state law, which covers civil, criminal and administrative issues. Of great importance in all industries is the Federal Act Against Unfair Competition of 19 December 1986 (SC 241) ('Unfair Competition Act'). This act defines the minimum standards that must be applied in all business sectors. Article 2 of the Unfair Competition Act states that any behaviour or business practice that is deceptive or that in any other way infringes the principle of good faith and that affects the relationship between competitors or between suppliers and customers shall be deemed unfair and unlawful. Non-compliance with the Unfair Competition Act may result in imprisonment of up to three years or in financial penalties.[3] Also, some of the other acts dealing with advertising (eg, the Gambling Act and the Therapeutic Products Act) entail sanctions of a criminal law nature.

---

1   Judgment of the Federal Supreme Court of 18 January 2010, No 2C_407/2009, para 3.2.4.
2   Article 36 of the Federal Constitution of the Swiss Confederation of 18 April 1999, SC 101.
3   Article 23 of the Unfair Competition Act.

On the other hand, some self-regulatory bodies have set out their own rules. In particular, the Swiss Commission of Fair Trading, founded in 1966, has adopted the Principles of Good Faith in Commercial Communication.[4] Since then, the Swiss Commission of Fair Trading has been equally managed by consumers, media professionals and advertisers.[5] It functions as a kind of arbitration board, with the aim of ensuring consistency between concrete advertising measures and both the principles of good faith in commercial communication and the practice of the International Chamber of Commerce. The Swiss Commission of Fair Trading is committed to advertising that is lawful, truthful and non-discriminatory. Anyone that thinks a specific advertising measure has infringed the principles of good faith in commercial communication can notify the Swiss Commission of Fair Trading, at no cost. However, as the Swiss Commission of Fair Trading is a non-governmental organisation, it does not have the decision-making powers of a court and can only make recommendations or requests.

Furthermore, advertisers should be wary of the risk of infringing the IP rights of competitors or other third parties. In particular, advertisers must ensure that they do not use logos, brands, slogans or other signs that are identical or confusingly similar to the trademarks, designs or copyright-protected works of third parties.

2. Comparative advertising

Comparative advertising is primarily regulated by the Unfair Competition Act. The Unfair Competition Act does not define 'comparative advertising'. However, Swiss doctrine and jurisprudence have clarified that 'comparative advertising' refers not only to advertising that compares an advertiser's own products with those of a competitor, but also to any advertising that refers in any way – explicitly or implicitly – to a competitor or its products. Superlative or sole-position advertising is also covered by the notion of comparative advertising.[6]

As comparative advertising promotes transparency in the market, it has always been allowed in Switzerland, subject to certain conditions. According to the Unfair Competition Act, comparative advertising must not be incorrect, misleading, unnecessarily injurious or unnecessarily imitative.[7]

'Incorrect' comparative advertising covers:

- comparisons that are based on incorrect statements;
- comparisons that are based on correct but non-comparable data; and

---

4   At the time of writing, the latest published version of these principles is dated January 2019.
5   See www.faire-werbung.ch/.
6   Judgment of the Federal Supreme Court of 2 May 2003, No 129 III 426, para 3.1.2.
7   Article 3(1)(e) of the Unfair Competition Act and Rule B.3 of the Principles of Good Faith in Commercial Communication.

- comparisons that use unsuitable data (eg, where apples are compared with oranges).[8]

A comparison is also deemed incorrect if the statements are incorrectly presented or wrongly described as complete and comprehensive.[9] The information on both the advertiser's own product and the competing product referred to must be correct. In principle, the burden of proving the correctness of a statement lies with the advertiser.[10]

Advertising is 'misleading' if it:

- conceals or omits important facts (ie, facts which are important according to the expectations of the target audience);
- creates a false impression – even if everything stated may be literally true; or
- does not take into account the average understanding of the target audience.

Comparative advertising will be deemed misleading if:

- it compares single advantages and disadvantages, and other elements are not identical; or
- it creates confusion among the target audience concerning the relationship between the market participants, their brands, other characteristics or their products.[11]

However, if not all possible comparison criteria are considered, a comparison is not necessarily unfair, as long as it does not suggest or imply that all characteristics of the product have been taken into account in the comparison.[12]

A comparison is 'unnecessarily injurious' in particular if:

- it is biased or disproportionate because inappropriate comparison parameters are used; or
- certain competitors are vilified by unnecessarily aggressive or spiteful attacks.[13]

Not all negative statements will be deemed sufficient to qualify as unnecessarily injurious; they must have a certain severity, which is usually the case if they denigrate or decry the competitor or its products – for example, if a third party claims that a product is not worth its price, or is unusable or defective.[14]

---

8   Rule B.3 Fig 3 of the Principles of Good Faith in Commercial Communication.
9   *Ibid*.
10   Article 13a(1) of the Unfair Competition Act and Rule A.5 of the Principles of Good Faith in Commercial Communication.
11   Rule B.3 Fig 4 of the Principles of Good Faith in Commercial Communication.
12   Judgment of the Federal Supreme Court of 28 August 2006, No 4C.170/2006, para 3.2.
13   Judgment of the Federal Supreme Court of 3 June 1999, No 125 III 286, para 6.
14   Judgment of the Federal Supreme Court of 9 February 1996, No 122 IV 33, para 2c.

Comparative advertising is 'unnecessarily imitative' if a third party's products or services are used in the advertiser's own ad in a way that suggests or implies that the third party's image will be transferred to the advertiser's own offers.[15] Thus, advertisers will be deemed to have acted unfairly if they attempt to transfer a positive brand image to their own products by evoking associations with a competitor's products or services. In particular, advertising that conveys the message 'substitute for' or 'equally good as' is unfair under Swiss law.[16]

Further legislation deals with comparative advertising. For instance, the Ordinance on Price Disclosure regulates price comparisons.[17] The Ordinance on Advertising of Medicinal Products stipulates the conditions for comparative advertising of medical products.[18] The Law on Consumer Information includes provisions concerning financial contributions regarding comparative tests conducted by consumer protection organisations.[19] The Federal Act on Alcohol prohibits advertising that contains a price comparison.[20] The Ordinance on Tobacco regulates tobacco advertising, providing that the packaging of a tobacco product must not give the impression that it is less harmful than others.[21]

3. Online behavioural advertising

In Switzerland, there is no specific act that generally regulates advertising on the Internet. However, the use of cookies for the purposes of online behavioural advertising is subject to the general provisions of the Federal Act on Data Protection.

If personal data is collected through the use of cookies, this is permitted only if the user has consented to this voluntarily and after appropriate information has been provided. However, consent may implicitly arise from the user's behaviour. Usually, there is no need for explicit consent to use.[22]

The Federal Act on Data Protection is currently in revision. The draft act stipulates an additional requirement that consent must be given unambiguously.

With regard to the use of cookies, Article 45c of the Telecommunications Act[23] must also be taken into consideration. In particular, it provides that the processing of data on external equipment by means of transmission using

---

15   Judgment of the Federal Supreme Court of 26 May 2009, No 135 III 446, para 7.1; Rule B.3 Fig 6 of the Principles of Good Faith in Commercial Communication.
16   Judgment of the Federal Supreme Court of 26 May 2009, No 135 III 446, para 7.1.
17   Ordinance on Price Disclosure of 11 December 1978, SC 942.211, and in particular Article 16.
18   Ordinance on Advertising of Medicinal Products of 17 October 2001, SC 812.212.5, and in particular Article 7.
19   Federal Act on the Information of Consumers of 5 October 1990, SC 944.0.
20   Article 42b(2) of the Federal Act on Alcohol of 21 June 1932, SC 680.
21   Article 17 of the Ordinance on Tobacco of 27 October 2004, SC 817.06.
22   Article 4(5) of the Federal Act on Data Protection.
23   Telecommunications Act of 30 April 1997, SC 784.10.

telecommunications techniques (eg, a cookie) is permitted only if the user is informed about:

- the processing and its purpose; and
- his or her right to refuse to allow such processing.

The General Data Protection Regulation (2016/679) also affects the use of cookies by Swiss businesses, insofar as they must adhere to the standards set out in the regulation if:

- they are processing the personal data of EU data subjects; and
- the processing activities relate to the offering of products and services or the monitoring of the data subjects' behaviour.[24]

In addition, guidelines on online advertising have been adopted by some organisations (eg, the Swiss Agency for Therapeutic Products (Swissmedic)).[25]

4. Sales promotions

4.1 Sales and clearance sales

Under Swiss law, sales and clearance sales are generally allowed; exceptions apply to a few products, such as spirits.[26] Marketing activities by third parties such as unauthorised dealers with well-known branded products are also allowed, because the mere fact that the advertiser profits from the attraction of branded products does not qualify as a misuse of competition.[27]

The general principles stipulated in the Unfair Competition Act must be observed. Thus, all information with regard to the sale – in particular, the use of terms such as 'sale', 'clearance' or 'liquidation' – must be correct and must not be confusing.[28] Furthermore, it is not allowed to repeatedly offer selected products, works or services below cost price; or to make particular mention of such offers in any ad so that customers are deceived as to the advertiser's capabilities or those of its competitors.[29] Deception will be presumed where:

- customers believe, as a result of the relevant offer, that the loss leader is representative of the entire product range; or
- the sale price is lower than the cost price for comparable purchases of products, work or services of the same type, which constitutes a reversal of the burden of proof for the benefit of the claimant.

---

24 Article 3(2) of Regulation (EU) 2016/679 of the European Parliament and of the Council on the protection of natural persons with regard to the processing of personal data and of the free movement of such data of April 27 2016.
25 www.swissmedic.ch/swissmedic/de/home/humanarzneimittel/marktueberwachung/arzneimittelwerbung/fragen-und-antworten/internetrichtlinie—passwortschutz.html.
26 Articles 41(1)(g) and 41(1)(h) of the Federal Act on Alcohol.
27 Judgment of the Federal Supreme Court of 12 May 1981, No 107 II 277, para 4b.
28 Article 3(1)(b) of the Unfair Competition Act.
29 *Ibid*, Article 3(1)(f).

4.2 Free-of-charge items

Under Swiss law, free-of-charge items are generally allowed, as long as there is no deception regarding the value of a product.[30] Furthermore, the distribution of free-of-charge items is forbidden or strongly restricted for certain products – in particular, for spirits, tobacco products and certain medical products.[31]

4.3 Snowball systems, avalanche systems and pyramid schemes

Under Article 3(1)(r) of the Unfair Competition Act, distribution systems such as snowball systems (also known as 'avalanche systems' or 'pyramid schemes') are illegal in Switzerland.

This kind of distribution system is characterised by the fact that the benefit for participants results mainly from the recruitment of new participants, rather than from the sale of products. The main goal is the aggressive redistribution of money from the people at the base of the pyramid to those at the top of the pyramid, which is often linked to the sale of special products or services that serve to disguise the real nature of the system. Illegal snowball systems are often designed in a way that the number of participants increases very quickly and uncontrollably.

4.4 Competitions and prize draws

Prize draws and competitions are allowed only where:

- they do not meet the characteristics of a lottery or lottery-like undertaking; and
- as part of a competition or draw, a prize is promised whose redemption is not dependent on:
  - calling a premium-rate service number;
  - paying a service charge;
  - buying an item of merchandise or a service; or
  - participating in a sales event, promotional trip or another prize draw (Article 3(1)(t) of the Unfair Competition Act).

Competitions with alcoholic spirits as a prize or as an advertising object, and competitions that require the purchase of some spirits, are forbidden.[32] However, in practice, non-commercial competitions such as tombolas and private lotteries that include minor quantities of spirits as prizes are usually tolerated.

---

30   *Ibid*, Article 3(1)(g).
31   Article 41(1)(k) of the Federal Act on Alcohol; Article 18(f) of the Ordinance on Tobacco; and Articles 10, 19 and 21(1)(e) of the Ordinance on Advertising of Medicinal Products.
32   Article 42b(4) of the Federal Act on Alcohol.

5.   Ambush marketing

There are no specific rules that regulate ambush marketing in Switzerland. In the context of the 2008 UEFA European Football Championship in Austria/Switzerland, the Swiss Federal Council did not deem it necessary to establish specific rules governing ambush marketing. Thus, the legality of ambush marketing must be assessed under Switzerland's general legal principles – in particular, those set out in the legislation on intellectual property, unfair competition (the Unfair Competition Act) and possession. Consequently, there are both legal and illegal forms of ambush marketing. The line between legal and illegal practices is not always clear – particularly in relation to cases in which no obvious IP violation seems to have arisen.

In many cases of ambush marketing, unfair competition law is essential. Article 2 of the Unfair Competition Act forbids, among other things, free riding on reputation. Where a third party systematically attempts to ride on the coat-tails of an event in order to benefit from its power of attraction, reputation and prestige, and to exploit the resulting advantage without paying any financial compensation or making any efforts of its own, such use will be regarded as an unfair advantage within the meaning of Article 2 of the Unfair Competition Act.

6.   Direct marketing

In Switzerland, all direct marketing must comply with both the Unfair Competition Act (in particular, Articles 3(1)(h), (o), (s), (u) and (v)) and the Principles of Good Faith in Commercial Communication (especially Rule C2). In addition, the relevant provisions of the Federal Act on Data Protection should be taken into account.

In principle, direct marketing is permitted only if consumers can identify the marketer and, where there is an offer of products or services, can seriously consider the offer.[33]

It is crucial that the marketer does not impair the customer's freedom of decision by using particularly aggressive sales methods.[34] Practices that significantly impair the consumer's freedom of choice are forbidden. It is not allowed to bypass or blindside consumers through harassment or coercion.

Telephone marketing is allowed only if:

- a business relationship already exists between the caller and the customer; and
- the caller uses and displays an authorised telephone number which is registered in the telephone directory.[35]

---

33   Rule C.2 of the Principles of Good Faith in Commercial Communication; and Article 3(1)(s) of the Unfair Competition Act.

34   Article 3(1)(h) of the Unfair Competition Act; see also Rule C.4 Fig 2 of the Principles of Good Faith in Commercial Communication.

35   Articles 3(1)(u) and 3(1)(v) of the Unfair Competition Act.

A so-called 'Robinson list' exists for mail advertising. This is an opt-out list of private individuals who do not wish to receive mail marketing transmissions. The list is funded by the *Schweizer Dialogmarketing Verband* and is managed within the scope of self-regulation.

With regard to mass direct marketing (ie, so-called 'spam'), Article 3(1)(o) of the Unfair Competition Act must be observed. The automatic mass transmission of marketing by email, text message, fax or telephone is allowed only if:

- recipients have at least implicitly given their consent (eg, in connection with an opt-in system, meaning that the seller may use the information provided by the buyer for its own advertising purposes for similar products under Article 3(1)(o) of the Unfair Competition Act if the seller has informed the buyer of the opt-out possibility and the buyer has not made use of this option);
- the sender is clearly identified; and
- a note clearly points out that there is an easy, free-of-charge option to opt out from receiving such messages (eg, where a link is included in an email which, when clicked, blocks the recipient's address).[36]

Further, in the fight against mass electronic marketing, the Swiss legislative authority has also imposed a series of rules on telecommunications service providers. In particular, telecommunications service providers must protect their customers from receiving unfair mass marketing.[37]

With regard to data protection, the use of postal addresses or telephone numbers for the purposes of direct marketing qualifies as 'data processing' in terms of the Federal Act on Data Protection. Data processing and the establishment of data files are permitted only where the data subject has given his or her consent. Such consent is valid only if given voluntarily on the provision of adequate information.[38]

7. Product placement

Under Swiss law, product placement in audio-visual commercial communications is generally allowed.[39] However, clear reference (eg, "the following programme contains product placements from X and Y") must be made in relation to product placement at the beginning and end of the relevant broadcast, and after each commercial break.[40]

Product placement must be distinguished from 'surreptitious advertising',

---

36   See also Rule C.4 Fig 2 of the Principles of Good Faith in Commercial Communication.
37   Article 45a of the Telecommunications Act and Article 83 of the Ordinance on Telecommunications Services.
38   See Article 4(5) of the Federal Act on Data Protection.
39   Article 21(1) of the Ordinance on Radio and Television of 9 March 9 2007, SC 784.401.
40   *Ibid*, Article 21(3). A single reference suffices for product placements, production aids and prizes of a low value of up to CHF 5,000 (around €4,000).

which is expressly prohibited by law.[41] Product placement cannot represent products or services in the style of advertising.[42] The narrative form of the programme must not be influenced by the product placement itself. The product placement must not directly encourage the purchase or rental of products or services – in particular, by making special promotional references to those products or services – and must not give undue prominence to the product in question.[43] Advertising that has been intentionally inserted in news programmes and where the provider is responsible for its broadcasting is forbidden.[44]

However, not every advertising effect in editorial programmes will fall under the prohibition of surreptitious advertising. Some may be justified by the principles of journalism or public information. Advertising further will not fall under the prohibition of surreptitious advertising if the pictures broadcast depict reality or if the provider cannot influence the pictures – for instance, when perimeter advertising boards in football stadiums appear incidentally in a sports programme.[45]

Whether advertising on television and radio qualifies as permitted product placement or as illegal surreptitious advertising will depend on the overall impression created by such marketing activity.[46]

8. Native advertising and social media influencers

Swiss legislation contains no specific rules on native advertising (ie, the use of paid ads that match the appearance, form and function of the user experience in which they are placed, and thus that do not really look like ads at first glance) and influencer marketing. The legality of these two types of advertising must therefore be assessed under general legal principles, and particularly under the Unfair Competition Act.

Under the Unfair Competition Act, surreptitious advertising is prohibited and the so-called 'transparency requirement' applies. Native advertising and influencer marketing on social media will thus constitute 'unfair commercial practices' if editorial content is used to promote a product without making this clear in the content or through images or sounds.[47] Thus, if an influencer uses a social media platform to advertise for third parties, this fact must be unambiguously recognisable and the 'advertising' must be clearly separated

---

41   Article 10(3) of the Federal Act on Radio and Television of 24 March 2006, SC 784.40.
42   Judgment of the Federal Administrative Court of 24 October 2011, No A-825/2011, para 6.5.1.
43   Federal Office of Communication, Advertising and Sponsoring Directive 2019, p21.
44   News programmes and programmes on political current events, as well as programmes and sequences of programmes which are related to the exercise of political rights, may not contain product placement in general: Federal Office of Communication, Advertising and Sponsoring Directive 2019, p 21.
45   Judgment of the Federal Administrative Court of 24 October 2011, No A-825/2011, para 6.4.
46   Federal Office of Communication, Advertising and Sponsoring Directive 2010, p21.
47   See also Directive 10.1 of the Swiss Press Council's Directives relating to the Declaration of the Duties and Rights of the Journalist of 18 February 2000.

from other content. This means that if the influencer receives sponsored products or similar consideration or benefits in kind, he or she must disclose his or her relationship to the sponsor or other provider.[48]

However, there is no general duty to explicitly mark such posts as advertising. Rather, the commercial character of the communication must be explicitly clear from an overall appraisal of the circumstances.[49]

For example, the Swiss Commission of Fair Trading recently held that the average Swiss Instagram follower would know and clearly recognise that athletes present brand logos on posts for commercial reasons. Thus, a world-renowned tennis athlete did not need to explicitly mark a post that showed him with his sponsor's logo on his headband and jacket, among other things, as advertising.[50]

9.   Industry-specific regulation

9.1   Gambling

Lotteries and gambling are regulated by the Federal Act on Gambling[51] and its ordinances.

Anyone that wants to conduct money games requires a licence or a concession.[52] The following lotteries and games of skill are not subject to the Federal Act of Gambling:

- short-term promotional lotteries and games of skill that do not involve the risk of excessive gambling and where participation is exclusively through the purchase of products or services offered at no more than market prices;[53] and
- lotteries and games of skill carried out by media companies for a short period of time for sales promotion purposes that involve no risk of excessive gambling, and in which it is also possible to participate free of charge under the same access and participation conditions as if a monetary stake had been placed or a legal transaction had been concluded.[54]

Ads for money games:

- must not be obtrusive (ie, pushy, insistent or so intrusive that they cannot be avoided) or misleading; and

---

48   Rule B.15 Figs 1 and 2 of the Principles of Good Faith in Commercial Communication.
49   Decision of the First Chamber of the Swiss Commission of Fair Trading of 11 September 2019, Nos 154/19 and 159/19 para 11.
50   Decision of the Plenum of the Swiss Commission of Fair Trading of 6 May 2020, Nos 154/19 and 159/19, para 14.
51   Federal Act on Gambling of 27 September 2017, SC.935.51
52   *Ibid*, Article 4.
53   *Ibid*, Article 2(2)(d).
54   *Ibid*, Article 2(2)(e).

- must not be directed at minors or at players at risk of gambling addiction whose participation in such activities has been suspended.

Advertising in Switzerland for money games which are not authorised is prohibited.[55]

9.2 Alcohol

Under Swiss law, the promotion of spirits on radio and television is completely prohibited.[56] By contrast, the advertisement of wine, cider and beer on radio and television is allowed;[57] although there are some restrictions regarding the representation of these ads.[58]

The advertisement of spirits in or around public buildings, or parts thereof,[59] in sports grounds and at sporting events,[60] and in pharmacies, drugstores and health food shops is prohibited.[61] Furthermore, the advertisement of spirits on products and their packaging is not allowed if the products have no connection with spirits.[62]

Other kinds of advertising for spirits – especially ads and posters – must be exclusively product related: that is, the content of such ads must be restricted to factual information on the product and its qualities and attributes (including geographical origin).[63] Any information suggesting that spirits are a normal part of social life (eg, drinking and party scenes) is forbidden. Depictions that represent zest for life, light-heartedness, vitality, freshness or similar are all prohibited. By contrast, factual pictures showing fruits and plants from which alcoholic spirits are made are allowed.[64]

Commercial communications aimed specifically at minors are prohibited for all kinds of alcoholic beverages. The following are also prohibited:

- advertising at events that are regularly frequented by minors;
- advertising in publications targeted mainly at youths; and

---

55   Article 74 of the Federal Act on Gambling.
56   Article 10(1)(b) of the Federal Act on Radio and Television, in conjunction with Article 2(1) of the Federal Act on Alcohol and, explicitly, Article 42b(3)(a) of the latter act. This regulation also applies for alcoholic mixed drinks (in particular, so-called 'alcopops').
57   Article 10(1)(b) of the Federal Act on Radio and Television, in conjunction with Article 2(2) of the Federal Act on Alcohol. For the conceptual distinction, it is important for the alcohol content to be over 15% by volume and for the alcoholic beverages to have been obtained exclusively by fermentation (Article 2(2) of the Federal Act on Alcohol).
58   For requirements of the presentation of the advertising, see Article 16(1) of the Ordinance on Radio and Television. The primary aim of the regulations is to protect minors. These provisions are consistent with the food legislation, which applies to all media (see section 9.5).
59   Article 42b(3)(b) of the Federal Act on Alcohol.
60   *Ibid*, Article 42b(3)(d).
61   *Ibid*, Article 42b(3)(f).
62   *Ibid*, Article 42b(3)(g).
63   *Ibid*, Article 42b(1).
64   *Sektion Alkoholmarkt und Werbung der Abteilung Alkohol und Tabak* examines advertising designs for free. www.ezv.admin.ch/ezv/de/home/themen/alcohol/spirituosen_werbung.html. The *Abteilung Alkohol und Tabak* also provides guidelines on the advertisement of spirits. See www.ezv.admin.ch/ezv/de/home/themen/alcohol/spirituosen_werbung/werbeleitfaden.html.

- advertising on products that are mainly used by minors or made available to minors free of charge.[65]

In addition, ads for alcoholic beverages must not contain any information relating to health.[66] Hence, terms such as 'for more power', 'calming' or 'supports your circulation system' are not allowed.

9.3 Pharmaceuticals

Only medicinal products that are permitted and registered in Switzerland may be advertised.[67] The advertisement of medicinal products is unlawful if:

- it is misleading or contrary to public order and morality;[68] or
- it may incite the excessive, abusive or inappropriate use of medicinal products.[69]

The specific requirements for ads for ready-to-use medicinal products for human or veterinary use directed at professionals and the public are set out in the Ordinance on Advertising of Medicinal Products.[70] Advertising directed at the public is permitted only for non-prescription medicines.[71] Advertising directed at the public is unlawful for medicinal products that contain narcotic or psychotropic substances, that are frequently the object of abuse or that lead to addiction or dependence.[72]

All information contained in ads intended for the public must comply with the latest product information approved by Swissmedic.[73] The ad must:

- present the medicine objectively, properly and without exaggeration in terms of wording, images and sound;[74]
- be recognisable as such (clearly separated from editorial text);[75] and
- include some basic information, such as:
    - the product name (brand);
    - the name of the authorisation holder;

---

65 Article 43 of the Foodstuffs and Utility Articles Ordinance of 16 December 2016, SC 817.02.
66 *Ibid*, Article 12(2)(h).
67 Article 32(1)(c) of the Federal Act on Medicinal Products and Medical Devices of 15 December 2000, SC 812.21.
68 *Ibid*, Article 32(1)(a).
69 *Ibid*, Article 32(1)(b).
70 Article 1(1) of the Ordinance on Advertising of Medicinal Products. Swiss pharmaceutical enterprises have also imposed a binding code of conduct that is of particular relevance to the promotion of, and information about, medicinal products (Pharma Code of 4 December 2003, partially revised on 1 October 2006, 12 June 2008, 1 September 2010, 1 November 2011, 1 June 2012, 1 December 2012 and 6 September 2013). The Pharma Code applies to the promotion of, and information about, medicinal products to healthcare professionals.
71 Article 14 of the Ordinance on Advertising of Medicinal Products and Article 32(2)(a) of the Federal Act on Medicinal Products and Medical Devices.
72 Articles 32(2)(b) and (d) of the Federal Act on Medicinal Products and Medical Devices.
73 Article 16(1) of the Ordinance on Advertising of Medicinal Products.
74 *Ibid*, Articles 16(2) and 21(1)(b).
75 *Ibid*, Articles 16(3) and 21(1)(c).

- the indication or application options and
- a note stating "This is a medical product – please read the patient information".[76]

Television and cinema ads must be followed by the text: "This is a medicinal product. Please take advice from a health professional and read the patient information."[77]

All information in ads directed at professionals – that is, all ads that target persons who are allowed to prescribe, dispense or use medicines in a professional capacity and under their own responsibility[78] – must comply with the latest product information approved by Swissmedic. In particular, only those indications and methods of use that have been approved by Swissmedic may be advertised.[79] Statements in ads intended for professionals must be precise, balanced, factually correct, not misleading and provable.[80] Ads must also be recognisable as such.[81] Copy used in ads must comply with the current status of scientific knowledge and reflect this. It may refer only to clinical trials that have been carried out in compliance with the requirements of good clinical trial practice and whose results have been published or accepted for publication.[82] Furthermore, ads directed at professionals must contain some minimum basic information, such as:

- the product name (brand);
- the name and address of the authorisation holder; and
- the indication or application options.[83]

9.4 Financial products and services

Various provisions of banking and capital markets law contain advertising restrictions and mandatory content information requirements. These provisions mainly aim to prevent inexperienced users from being induced to participate in risky transactions through misleading advertising.

The term 'bank' or 'banker', alone or in combination with other words, may be used in a company's name, in the description of its business purpose and in business advertising only if the user has obtained a banking licence from the Swiss Financial Market Supervisory Authority.[84] The term 'saving' may be used in business advertising only by banks that publish annual financial statements.[85]

---

76   *Ibid*, Article 16 Abs 5.
77   *Ibid*, Article 17(1).
78   *Ibid*, Article 2(c).
79   *Ibid*, Article 5(1).
80   *Ibid*, Article 5(3).
81   *Ibid*, Article 5(4).
82   *Ibid*, Article 5(5).
83   *Ibid*, Article 6 of the Ordinance on Advertising of Medicinal Products.
84   Article 1(4) of the Federal Act on Banks and Savings Banks of 8 November 1934 (the Banking Act), SC 952.0.
85   *Ibid*, Article 15(1).

Both in Switzerland and abroad, banks must abstain from misleading or obtrusive publicity within their Swiss domicile or Swiss traditional practices or institutions.[86]

The Financial Institutions Act declares that the terms 'portfolio manager', 'trustee', 'manager of collective assets', 'fund management company' and 'securities firm' may be used, alone or in compound terms, in a company's name, in the description of its business purpose or in commercial documents only if the corresponding authorisation has been obtained.[87]

Various rules apply to the prospectus and further means of advertising in connection with the issuance of securities.[88] For example, Article 71(3) of the Federal Act on Collective Investment Schemes[89] states that in advertising, material reference must be made to the special risks involved in alternative investments.

Advertising for consumer loans must not be aggressive. Commercially active lenders have outlined in a private law agreement the kinds of advertising that will be considered aggressive.[90] According to this agreement, the ad must not create an impression that loans are suitable for the short-term repayment of debts. Furthermore, the advertisement of loans in the vicinity of casinos is prohibited. It is also forbidden to direct such advertising specifically at children and young adults.[91] The Unfair Competition Act also contains specific rules on advertising for providers of consumer loans.[92] Such advertising must contain various items of information, such as:

- the company name of the loan provider;
- the net amount of the loan;
- the real price of the purchase object;
- information on the total cost of the loan; and
- the effective annual interest rate.[93]

Moreover, the information must state the rule that the granting of loans is prohibited if it leaves the consumer over-indebted.[94]

---

86 *Ibid*, Article 4*quater*.
87 Article 13(2) of the Federal Act on Financial Institutions of 15 June 2018, SC 954.1.
88 Articles 68 and 69 of the Federal Act on Financial Services of 15 June 2018, SC 950.1.
89 Collective Investment Schemes Act of 23 June 2006, SC 951.31.
90 Articles 36a (1) and (2) of the Federal Act on Consumer Credit of 23 March 2001, SC 221.214.1
91 Convention on advertising restrictions and prevention in consumer loans and leasing business; https://konsumfinanzierung.ch/files/224/konvention-werbung-u-pr-vention-def-27-11-2015.pdf
92 In Articles 3(1) (k), (l) and (n) of the Unfair Competition Act, the act uses the term 'public advertising'. This covers promotional activities that are not directed against a limited group of persons defined by clear criteria (judgment of the Federal Supreme Court of 18 October 1994, No 120 IV 287, para 2a).
93 Articles 3(1)(k) and (l) of the Unfair Competition Act.
94 *Ibid*, Article 3(1)(n).

9.5 Food

To protect consumers from deception relating to foodstuffs,[95] special provisions on the advertisement of foodstuffs have been adopted. The prohibition against deception is vital in this regard. All information relating to foodstuffs must be true;[96] and ads for foodstuffs, as well as their presentation and packaging, must not mislead consumers.[97] In particular, such information is considered to be misleading if it is likely to deceive the consumer as to the manufacture, composition, qualities, method of production, storage life, origin, particular effects or value of the foodstuff in question.[98]

The Federal Department of Home Affairs prohibits making reference to any illness prevention, illness relief or curative effects of food, as well as to therapeutic or slimming effects. Foodstuff packaging that gives the product the appearance of a medicinal product is also forbidden.[99]

Special provisions apply to the use of the term 'Swiss', the Swiss cross and other terms[100] indicating Swissness for all products, including food (eg, chocolate, cheese). Food can be advertised using the term 'Swiss' if at least 80% of the raw material weight that makes up the foodstuff originates from Switzerland. For milk and dairy products, the weight of milk as the raw material must equal 100%.[101] The details are regulated in the Ordinance on the Use of Swiss Indications of Source for Foodstuffs.[102]

9.6 Tobacco

The advertisement of tobacco products on radio or television is strictly prohibited.[103] Tobacco advertising targeted primarily at minors is also forbidden.[104] Tobacco advertising is illegal:

- in public places frequented especially by youths;
- in young people's magazines and journals;
- on school materials (eg, school folders, cases, pens);
- on promotional gifts (eg, shirts, caps, flags or balls) that are intended to be distributed to youths;
- on toys;

---

95   Article 1(c) of the Federal Act on Foodstuffs and Utility Articles of 20 June 2014, SC 817.0.
96   *Ibid*, Article 18(1).
97   *Ibid*, Article 18(2).
98   *Ibid*, Article 18(3).
99   Article 12(2) of the Foodstuffs and Utility Articles Ordinance. For further information on the advertisement of foodstuffs, see the Ordinance on the Federal Department of Home Affairs on the Information of Foodstuffs of 16 December 2016, SC 817.022.16.
100   Rule B.11 of the Principles of Good Faith in Commercial Communication; see also Articles 47 *et seq* of the Federal Act on the Protection of Trademarks and Indications of Source of 28 August 1992, SC 232.11.
101   Article 48b (2) of the Federal Act on Foodstuffs and Utility Articles.
102   Ordinance on the use of Swiss indications of source for foodstuffs of 2 September 2015, SC 232.112.1
103   Article 10 (1)(a) Federal Act on Radio and Television.
104   Article 18 of the Ordinance on Tobacco.

- through the free distribution of tobacco products and cigarettes to young people; and
- at events organised predominantly for young people.[105]

The Ordinance on Tobacco declares that all descriptions, indications and images that are used on the packaging of tobacco products, or in ads for tobacco products, must be correct and must not mislead the public as to the nature, geographical origin, manufacturer, composition, method of production or effects of such products.[106] The inclusion of references to health in tobacco advertising is prohibited.[107]

This ordinance is subject to change, as the Parliament is currently drafting a Federal Act on Tobacco Products and Electronic Cigarettes.[108] However, the requirements for advertising will not change in terms of content.

Given the major dangers connected with tobacco consumption, the tobacco industry in Switzerland has adopted some self-regulatory restrictions in the field of marketing and communications for tobacco products. It is generally prohibited to place tobacco ads in any printed publications, unless there is a realistic chance that at least 80% of the readers are adults.[109]

9.7 E-cigarettes

According to current law, e-cigarettes qualify as utility articles, and the Federal Act on Foodstuffs and Utility Articles and its provisions on advertising will apply. As mentioned in section 9.6, a new Federal Act on Tobacco Products and Electronic Cigarettes will soon be enacted. According to this new law, e-cigarettes will qualify as tobacco products rather than utility articles, and will thus be subject to the same restrictions as traditional cigarettes. In the meantime, representatives of the Swiss Tobacco Trade Association and independent market participants have issued two codices, under which they undertake not to address e-cigarette advertising primarily at minors. In particular, they will refrain from advertising:

- in places where mainly minors are present:
- in newspapers, magazines or other publications specifically intended for minors;
- on student materials (eg, school folders, cases, fountain pens);
- on promotional items given free of charge to minors, such as T-shirts, caps, flags and bathing balls;

---

105   *Ibid*, Article 18.
106   *Ibid*, Article 17(1).
107   *Ibid*, Article 17(2).
108   The current plan is that the new Federal Act on Tobacco Products and Electronic Cigarettes will enter into force in 2022
109   Agreement dated 27 April 2005 with the Swiss Cigarette and Swiss Commission of Fair Trading on voluntary self-regulation in advertising.

- on toys;
- by supplying free of charge nicotine-containing e-steamers and liquids to minors; and
- at cultural, sporting or other events which are mainly attended by minors.[110]

---

110   See www.swiss-tobacco.ch/wp-content/uploads/2019/01/CODEX-f%C3%BCr-Tabakprodukte-und-elektronische-Zigaretten_def.pdf and www.svta.ch/kodex.

United Kingdom

Andrew Butcher
Paul Jordan
Bristows LLP

---

1.   **Overview of the legal and regulatory regime for advertising**

The UK advertising industry operates a self-regulatory regime. For non-broadcast advertising, the Committee of Advertising Practice (CAP) writes, reviews and enforces a code to which non-broadcast advertising must adhere.[1] CAP is made up of trade and professional bodies of the advertising industry. The Advertising Standards Authority (ASA) is a body, independent of both the UK government and the advertising industry, that adjudicates on complaints about advertisements alleged to breach the CAP Code.

The Broadcast Committee of Advertising Practice (BCAP) regulates broadcast advertising in the United Kingdom. BCAP (in a similar way to CAP) is made up of advertising industry stakeholders that enforce the UK Code of Broadcast Advertising ('BCAP Code'). The role of the ASA also includes adjudicating on complaints about broadcast advertisements alleged to breach the BCAP Code. Therefore, UK consumers can make complaints to the ASA in respect of advertising in any medium.

The overarching principles of the CAP and BCAP codes are that advertisements should:

- be legal, decent, honest and truthful; and
- not mislead or cause serious or widespread offence or harm, especially to children or the vulnerable.

Arguably the most important and fundamental aspect of both codes is the requirement that advertising not mislead consumers.

A prohibition on misleading advertising is also contained within UK legislation: the Consumer Protection from Unfair Trading Regulations 2008 ('Consumer Protection Regulations'). These regulations implement EU Directive 2005/29/EC concerning unfair business-to-consumer commercial practices. They prohibit commercial practices (including advertising) which constitute misleading actions or omissions that are likely to cause a consumer to take a transactional decision that he or she would not otherwise have taken. Although

---

1   The UK Code of Non-broadcast Advertising and Direct and Promotional Marketing.

consumers do now have a private right of action in respect of misleading actions and aggressive practices by traders (which are prohibited by the Consumer Protection Regulations), in most cases enforcement of the regulations is undertaken by either local authority Trading Standards services and/or the Competition and Markets Authority (CMA). Trading Standards and the CMA will generally work with traders who might be breaching the Consumer Protection Regulations to attempt to change their practices and secure undertakings regarding their future conduct. However, in serious cases, both enforcement bodies have the ability to commence criminal court proceedings against traders, with the potential penalties being a fine or, in particularly serious cases, imprisonment. Where offences have been committed by a company, the regulations provide for the prosecution of an officer (eg, a director, manager or secretary) as well as the company itself.

Television and radio broadcasters are responsible for ensuring that the ads they transmit comply with the BCAP Code. Unlike non-broadcast advertising, all broadcast advertising must go through a clearance process before it is aired. Television advertising requires clearance from Clearcast, while radio advertising requires clearance from Radiocentre. However, clearance by Clearcast or Radiocentre provides no guarantee of an ad's compliance with the BCAP Code and the ASA might still rule that the ad breaches the BCAP Code.

If an advertiser fails, when asked, to amend or withdraw an ad that breaches the CAP or BCAP Code, the ASA has a number of sanctions at its disposal to attempt to ensure compliance. One of the most effective of these sanctions, and probably the easiest for the ASA to use, is adverse publicity. When the ASA formally investigates a complaint made about an ad and finds the ad to breach the CAP or BCAP Code, it will publish its decision on the ASA website. In addition, the ASA will provide details of its decision to media outlets (under embargo) the day prior to its publication on the ASA website. Details of a non-compliant advertising campaign can frequently be found in mainstream news outlets, particularly where the campaign involves a well-known brand.

Other sanctions at the ASA's disposal include:

- denial of media space to non-compliant advertisers;
- withdrawal of trading privileges and recognition by trade associations or professional bodies; and
- imposition of a requirement that all marketing communications be approved by CAP and the ASA prior to publication.

In addition, advertisers that persistently breach the CAP or BCAP Code and produce misleading marketing communications, or communications containing unlawful comparisons (see section 2), may be referred to Trading Standards. As indicated above, in the most extreme cases, Trading Standards can bring criminal proceedings against advertisers, with the possibility of fines being imposed or even prison sentences being handed out to company directors.

Advertisers should also be wary of the risk of infringing the IP rights of other businesses. If ads or individual logos are confusingly similar, or even copied, from another business, the advertiser may find itself subject to a claim for copyright infringement under the Copyright, Designs and Patents Act 1988 or for trademark infringement under the Trade Marks Act 1994, or through the tort of passing off.[2] Unscrupulous advertisers that make false claims about competitors could have claims brought against them for trade libel or malicious falsehood.

2. Comparative advertising

In the United Kingdom, comparative advertising is regulated by the Business Protection from Misleading Marketing Regulations 2008 ('Business Protection Regulations'). These regulations implement the EU Comparative Advertising Directive (2006/114/EC).

Under the Business Protection Regulations, 'comparative advertising' is defined as "advertising which in any way, either explicitly or by implication, identifies a competitor or a product offered by a competitor". The regulations permit comparative advertising provided that the following conditions are met:

- It is not misleading;
- It compares products that meet the same needs or are intended for the same purpose (including, where relevant, products with the same designation of origin);
- It objectively compares material, relevant, verifiable and representative features of the products;
- It does not create confusion between the advertiser and a competitor, or between any of their distinguishing products or features, such as trademarks;
- It does not discredit or denigrate a competitor's distinguishing activities, products or features, such as trademarks;
- It does not take unfair advantage of the reputation of a competitor's distinguishing marks, such as trademarks; and
- It does not present products as imitations/replicas of products bearing a protected trademark or name.

There are specific additional rules for ads that contain price comparisons, which have been developed largely on the basis of the judgments of the Court of Justice of the European Union (CJEU). These ads must state the basis of the comparison and be for an identical or substantially equivalent product. Any significant differences between the products must be explained clearly to

---

2   Details of these aspects are beyond the scope of this chapter.

consumers. Ads containing price comparisons which fall foul of this rule are regularly seen in ASA rulings against supermarkets. In particular, the ASA has ruled that where a low-cost supermarket compares the price of its own-brand products with the price of branded products in another supermarket (rather than that supermarket's own-brand alternative), this is an unfair comparison.

If comparative advertising does not comply with the Business Protection Regulations, as well as being vulnerable to a claim for trademark infringement, the advertiser may also be vulnerable to claims of passing off, trade libel, malicious falsehood and/or copyright infringement.

In the United Kingdom, responsibility for ensuring that comparative advertising complies with the applicable regulations falls to Trading Standards and the CMA. Under the Business Protection Regulations, these bodies are given the power to bring proceedings seeking an injunction against non-compliant comparative advertisers, with the breach of such an injunction being punishable by a fine or even imprisonment. Such proceedings cannot be brought by individuals or companies.

The conditions to be fulfilled by lawful comparative advertising as laid down in the Business Protection Regulations are mirrored in the CAP and BCAP Codes. Thus, complaints about comparative advertising can be made to the ASA, as indicated in section 1.

3.   Online behavioural advertising

The two pieces of UK legislation in the areas of privacy and data protection that are most relevant to the tracking of internet users' online activity for the purposes of online behavioural advertising are:

- the Privacy and Electronic Communications (EC Directive) Regulations 2003 ('e-Privacy Regulations'), which implement the EU e-Privacy Directive (2002/58/EC); and
- the UK General Data Protection Regulation (GDPR) – a domestic UK version of the EU's General Data Protection Regulation which took effect following the United Kingdom's departure from the European Union.

The Data Protection Act 2018 also contains some supplementary provisions on data processing which may in some cases be relevant to online behavioural advertising.

Under Regulation 6 of the e-privacy Regulations (following an amendment that took effect on 26 May 2011), it is prohibited to store information – for example, a cookie – on an internet user's device or gain access to information (eg, a cookie) on an internet user's device unless:

- the user is provided with clear and comprehensive information about the purposes of the storage of, or access to, the information; and
- the user has given his or her consent.

Given that online behavioural advertising is often facilitated by the use of cookies and similar tracking technologies which access or store information on a user's device, these provisions have been interpreted to require that information regarding cookies be made available to users (eg, in a cookie policy or notice) and a valid consent mechanism be implemented. While the nature of the appropriate consent mechanism has previously been the subject of much debate in the United Kingdom, following the implementation of the GDPR, the UK data protection regulator – the Information Commissioner's Office (ICO) – has made clear that consent for cookies must meet the GDPR's strict requirements. Among other requirements, this means that consent must be given by:

- a statement or clear affirmative action (ie, 'opt-in') rather than implied from silence or a failure to opt out;
- specific to a purpose for processing (eg, analytics and advertising cookies can be consented to separately); and
- capable of being withdrawn at any time.

However, a detailed discussion of cookie consent requirements is beyond the scope of this chapter.

The provisions of the GDPR apply to data processing (eg, the accessing of cookies on a user's web browser) for the purposes of online behavioural advertising only to the extent that the data collected constitutes 'personal data'. Strictly speaking, this will be the case only where the data collected could be used to identify an individual. However, the GDPR contains a very wide definition of 'personal data', which includes 'online identifiers' that enable indirect identification of an individual. In addition, EU data protection regulators (including the ICO) have indicated that they consider the use of cookies and similar identifiers to take decisions about individuals (eg, to serve them a personalised ad) to constitute personal data processing, even where the underlying identity of the individual is unknown. If personal data is being collected for the purposes of online behavioural advertising, the 'data controller' will need to comply with the requirements of the GDPR, which include obligations regarding data security and to process personal data fairly.

In November 2018 a revised Section 10 of the CAP Code came into effect, covering 'use of data for marketing'. The revised Section 10 replaced both the old Section 10 (which covered only 'database practice') and Appendix 3, which dealt specifically with online behavioural advertising.

The changes in Section 10 of the CAP Code were introduced to ensure that the rules set out in the code:

- cover the data protection issues most relevant to marketing; and
- are aligned with the standards introduced by the GDPR.

A consumer or business that believes an advertiser has breached the rules in Section 10 of the CAP Code can complain to the ASA in the same way as regarding a breach of the rules in any other section of the code.

4. Sales promotions

Section 8 of the CAP Code contains detailed and extensive rules on sales promotions. The code defines a 'sales promotion' as the provision of "an incentive for the consumer to buy by using a range of added direct or indirect benefits, usually on a temporary basis, to make the product more attractive". A non-exhaustive list of offers and mechanisms which fall within this definition is provided, including:

- 'two for the price of one' offers;
- money-off offers;
- text-to-wins;
- instant wins; and
- competitions and prize draws.

The CAP Code also provides that the rules do not apply to the "routine, non-promotional, distribution of products or product extensions, for example one-off editorial supplements (in printed or electronic form) to newspapers or magazines".

While the CAP Code's rules on sales promotions are detailed, there are a number of basic and fundamental principles within them that any advertiser should bear in mind when producing marketing communications about a sales promotion in the United Kingdom. First of all, advertising copy about a sales promotion in which there is limited time or space to give details of the promotion must include as much information as practicable about 'significant' conditions; full terms and conditions can then be made available through an alternative source (eg, a website).[3] Under Rule 8.17 of the CAP Code, before purchase or, if no purchase is required, before or at the time of entry or application, promoters must communicate all applicable 'significant' conditions. 'Significant' conditions include:

- how to participate;
- the start date (if applicable) and closing date;
- any proof of purchase required;
- the nature and number of any prizes; and
- any restrictions or limitations that apply (eg, age restrictions).

Under Rule 8.17.9 of the CAP Code, the promoter's full name and correspondence address must also be stated, unless these are obvious from the

---

3   Rule 8.18 of the CAP Code.

context or unless entry into an advertised promotion is only through a dedicated website containing that information in an easily found format.

Rule 8.2 of the CAP Code contains another fundamental principle for the marketing of sales promotions: promoters must avoid causing unnecessary disappointment to consumers. This rule could be breached in a number of ways – for example, failing to make clear that a particular group of consumers is not eligible for the promotion. Rule 8.2 also states that: "Promoters must conduct their promotions equitably, promptly and efficiently and be seen to deal fairly and honourably with participants and potential participants." This means, for example, that promoters cannot create and enforce terms and conditions retrospectively – a principle emphasised in an ASA adjudication against a UK newspaper which was running a competition to win a 'family holiday'. When the newspaper contacted a potential winner to confirm that she complied with the competition's terms and conditions, the winner asked whether she could take her sister's children with her on the holiday, as she did not have children of her own. The newspaper did not allow this, pointing to the 'family holiday' description of the prize. However, the ASA considered that if the winner was required to have parental responsibility for the children taken on the holiday, the terms and conditions should have made this clear.

One other core principle to bear in mind when producing marketing communications about a UK sales promotion is contained not in Section 8 of the CAP Code, but in Section 3 on misleading advertising. This principle[4] concerns use of the word 'free' and similar: marketing communications must not describe a product as 'free', 'gratis', 'without charge' or similar if the consumer must pay anything other than the unavoidable cost of responding and collecting or paying for delivery of the item.

This principle is particularly relevant in the context of sales promotions – for example, where consumers are encouraged to buy a magazine because a particular item can be obtained 'free with' a particular issue. In such a scenario, the cost of the magazine must not be inflated to cover the cost of the 'free' item; and if the item must be delivered separately to the consumer, then the postage cost must not be inflated. The wording used in the CAP Code is equivalent to a prohibition in Schedule 1 to the Consumer Protection Regulations, which lists various commercial practices that are considered to be unfair in all circumstances.

The rules concerning use of the word 'free' to describe a promotional item should not be confused with the rules applicable to the delivery of prizes to the winners of prize draws or competitions. The October 2012 judgment of the CJEU in the *Purely Creative* case (a reference to the CJEU from an action initially

---

4   See Rules 3.23–3.26 of the CAP Code.

brought in the English High Court by the Office of Fair Trading)[5] made clear that when a consumer is told that he or she has won or may have won a prize, the consumer cannot be required to incur any cost at all in claiming, enquiring about or receiving the prize; he or she cannot even be required to pay for a postage stamp.

The CAP Code definition of a 'sales promotion' expressly includes prize draws and competitions. In certain situations, a prize draw could constitute a lottery under UK legislation, the operation of which requires a licence. In light of this, promoters must take special care to ensure that any prize draw they operate could not be deemed an unlicensed, and therefore unlawful, lottery. Competitions that require entrants to demonstrate a genuine element of skill will not fall within the definition of a 'lottery'. However, a random prize draw in which a premium is charged for entry (eg, a charge in excess of an entrant's standard text message rate) may be considered a lottery.

If a promoter wishes to charge a premium for entry to a prize draw, then it should also offer a free entry route (eg, via mail or online, rather than via a premium-rate text message) that is equally well publicised and that does not place entrants at any disadvantage in comparison with the premium-charging route. The rules in Northern Ireland are even stricter: if a promoter simply wishes to require entrants to make a purchase to enter a prize draw, even if no premium is added to the normal price of the promotional product, then a free entry route must also be provided to prevent the prize draw constituting an unlawful lottery.[6]

A common form of sales promotion in the United Kingdom is the offer of a discount on the trader's own previous price. The Guidance for Traders on Pricing Practices, which is published by the Chartered Trading Standards Institute, suggests that a consumer must be satisfied that the quoted saving is genuine and not unfair. A promotion should therefore be made for a period that is the same or shorter than the period during which the higher price was offered. The guide does not specify how long this period should be, but a previous version of the guidance required the higher price to have been charged for at least 28 consecutive days, so this is likely to be a good baseline. If a quoted comparison price does not fulfil this criterion, the promotion is more likely to constitute a misleading action under the Consumer Protection Regulations, potentially carrying criminal liability.

5.   Ambush marketing

A variety of UK laws, rules and rights may be infringed by ambush marketing activities, depending on the event that is targeted and the execution of the

---

5   *Case C-428/11: Purely Creative v Office of Fair Trading.*
6   Article 130(1)(c) of the Betting, Gaming, Lotteries and Amusements (Northern Ireland) Order 1985.

ambush. Where the name, logos or emblems of the ambushed event have been registered as trademarks, any unauthorised use of such intellectual property by an ambusher in the course of trade may constitute trademark infringement. Where the event organiser has not registered its name or other distinctive features as trademarks, the law of passing off may still enable that organising body to prevent ambushers from using its intellectual property without permission. Sponsorship agreements between brands and event organisers typically contain a trademark licence that expressly permits the official sponsor to use the trademarks, logos and emblems of the event in promotional materials.

In addition to the protection offered by registered and unregistered trademark rights discussed above, copyright enables the creators of original works to prevent those works being copied or adapted by ambush marketers without permission. In the United Kingdom, organisers of the types of events targeted by ambush marketers often spend significant time, effort and money developing characters, logos and other graphic elements to promote their event. Copyright will also protect event organisers' exclusive right to use photographs that they own, taken at past events, in the promotion of current and forthcoming events.

In the United Kingdom, ticket terms and conditions for major events are often extensive and restrictive. Therefore, an ambush marketer that pays or otherwise persuades attendees to take banners or other unofficial marketing materials into a sporting event or festival may find that those attendees are refused entry or ejected from the venue on the grounds of breach of the terms and conditions of ticket purchase. In addition, ticket terms and conditions often prohibit the transfer of tickets and the use of tickets as competition prizes, meaning that only official sponsors can use event tickets as part of their promotional activities.

The International Olympic Committee usually requires the host country of the Olympics to enact bespoke legislation which ensures the protection of Olympic IP assets. During the London 2012 Olympic Games, three bespoke pieces of legislation were in force to deter ambush marketers and protect the investment of official sponsors. These prohibited the unauthorised use of the Olympic symbols, words or mottos, and also any representation which was likely to suggest an association with the London games. In addition, no unauthorised outdoor advertising was allowed during the event period in certain zones around venues, to ensure that the official sponsors' branding was exclusively seen in these areas. A law was passed in Scotland to create similar restrictions for the purposes of the Euro 2020 matches which were due to take place in Glasgow (however, the 2020 tournament was postponed due to the COVID-19 pandemic).

In the United Kingdom, not all forms of ambush marketing are against the law. A form of marketing that is often employed in the United Kingdom to great effect in the lead-up to major sporting events is the sponsorship of individual athletes/players. In the minds of consumers, certain high-profile individuals might be inextricably linked to the forthcoming event because of the expectations surrounding their performance at the event. Thus, advertising featuring these individuals will associate the relevant brand with the forthcoming event without any mention of the event being necessary.

Headphone brand Beats has been known to release ads featuring athletes in the run-up to major events. For example, it released an ad prior to the 2014 World Cup featuring Brazilian footballer Neymar warming up. The ad showed his pre-match routine, which viewers would associate with the upcoming football tournament; but it contained no references to the event or FIFA branding at all.

During the 2018 Football World Cup, mobile network Three rebranded some of its UK storefronts with three lion emojis, in a reference to the English national team's Three Lions emblem. The stores were opened by famous footballers and the brand hosted football competitions for fans to compete in, but made no direct reference to the tournament and used none of its protected intellectual property.

6. Direct marketing

In the United Kingdom, all direct marketing must comply with both the GDPR and the e-Privacy Regulations. In addition, the Direct Marketing Association (DMA) (a national trade association) has its own Code of Practice with which members must comply; and the CAP Code also contains rules that broadly reflect the legislation just referred to.

A key principle of the GDPR is that all processing of personal data must be both fair and lawful. In the context of direct marketing, this means that marketers must ensure, among other things, that:

- individuals understand that their personal data is being collected for marketing purposes;
- individuals are given the opportunity to opt out of receiving direct marketing material;
- personal data is stored in a secure manner; and
- personal data is not used for a purpose beyond that notified to the relevant individuals.

Under the e-Privacy Regulations, direct marketing by electronic means requires opt-in consent. The regulations govern communications made by telephone, fax, email and text message, and possibly also push notifications and other in-app messaging (although this is open to interpretation). They apply to communications sent by not-for-profit organisations, charities and political parties, as well as commercial organisations. For direct marketing sent by email or text message, the regulations allow for limited exceptions to the general requirement for opt-in consent; this is known as 'soft opt-in'. Soft opt-in consent applies where the marketer:

- has obtained the recipient's contact details in the course of the sale of products or services;
- carries out direct marketing in respect of its own similar products and services;
- gives the recipient a simple means, without charge, at the initial point of collection, to opt out of the use of his or her contact details for direct marketing purposes; and
- includes in each subsequent email or text message a means by which the recipient can opt out of future direct marketing.

The Consumer Protection Regulations also address direct marketing. They specifically list the making of persistent and unwanted solicitations by telephone, fax, email or other remote media as a commercial practice that is automatically considered to be unfair and therefore prohibited.[7]

As mentioned above, direct marketing is also subject to self-regulation by the advertising industry, with both CAP and the DMA publishing relevant guidance. The sections of the CAP Code that are of particular relevance are Section 9 (on distance selling) and Section 10 (on use of data for marketing). Both the CAP Code and the DMA's Code of Practice provide clear guidance on the type of consent that must be obtained before particular methods of direct marketing are undertaken.

7. Product placement

The Audiovisual Media Services Regulations 2009 (dealing with on-demand programme services) and the Audiovisual Media Services (Product Placement) Regulations 2010 (dealing with television services) (together, the 'AVMS Regulations') came into force in December 2009 and April 2010 respectively. The AVMS Regulations implement the EU Audiovisual Media Services Directive (2010/13/EU) and made a number of changes to the rules on product placement contained in both the Communications Act 2003 and the Ofcom Broadcasting Code.

Ofcom licenses all commercial television and radio services in the United Kingdom, and the Ofcom Broadcasting Code sets out the rules that television and radio broadcasters must follow in order to retain their licence to broadcast. Section 9 of the Ofcom Broadcasting Code is entitled "Commercial References on TV" and includes a dedicated sub-section on product placement. There are

---

7   Schedule 1, para 26 to the Consumer Protection from Unfair Trading Regulations 2008.

equivalent provisions contained in Ofcom's On Demand Programme Service Rules.

'Product placement' is defined in the AVMS Regulations for both on-demand programme services and television services as "the inclusion in a programme of, or of a reference to, a product, service or trademark where the inclusion is for a commercial purpose and is in return for valuable consideration paid to the broadcaster or the programme's producer (or a person connected to either of those entities), and is not prop placement".[8] 'Prop placement' is:

> *the inclusion of, or of a reference to, a product, service or trademark where:*
> - *that which is provided for inclusion in the programme has no significant value; and*
> - *neither the broadcaster nor the programme's producer (nor a person connected to either of those entities) receives any valuable consideration in exchange for the inclusion (disregarding any costs saved in having the product, service or trademark provided for free).*[9]

Within the Ofcom Broadcasting Code, there is an absolute prohibition on product placement of tobacco products and prescription medicines, along with an absolute ban on product placement within any genre of television programme other than films, series made for television (or other audiovisual media services), sports programmes and light entertainment programmes. The Ofcom code goes on to specifically prohibit product placement within any of these four permitted genres where the programme itself is a news programme or a children's programme. In every case, product placement must not influence the content or scheduling of the programme in which it is found in a way which affects the editorial independence of the broadcaster. To emphasise this restriction, the Ofcom Broadcasting Code also states that references to placed products/services/trademarks must not be promotional or 'unduly prominent'.[10]

Further and more extensive restrictions apply to product placement in programmes 'produced under UK jurisdiction'. Essentially, these programmes are those that are produced or commissioned either by a UK broadcaster or by any person or entity with a view to the first showing being made in the United Kingdom. In respect of UK television programmes, product placement is not permitted in religious, consumer advice or current affairs programmes, and placement of the following products and services is prohibited:
- alcoholic drinks;
- food or drinks that are high in fat, salt or sugar;

---

8   Regulation 9 of the Audiovisual Media Services (Product Placement) Regulations 2010 and Schedule 11A para 1(1) to the Communications Act 2003.
9   Regulation 9 of the Audiovisual Media Services (Product Placement) Regulations 2010 and Schedule 11A para 1(2) to the Communications Act 2003.
10   Rules 9.6–9.11 of the Ofcom Broadcasting Code.

- gambling;
- baby formula;
- medicinal products;
- smoking-related products, including e-cigarettes; and
- any product, service or trademark that cannot otherwise be advertised on television in the United Kingdom.[11]

Where product placement is included in television programmes (and films made for the cinema) that are produced or commissioned by a UK broadcaster, the fact that placement is occurring must be signalled to the audience by the appearance of one of the logos shown in Figure 1 at the beginning and end of the programme, and when the programme recommences after a commercial break.[12] Logo 1 should be used against predominantly dark backgrounds, while Logo 2 should be used against predominantly light backgrounds.

Figure 1. Product placement logos for UK broadcasters

Logo 1   Logo 2

Commercial references and communications in radio programming are subject to different legislative requirements from those in television programming, which are addressed in Section 10 of the Ofcom Broadcasting Code. The first rule of Section 10 requires that radio programming that is subject to or associated with a commercial arrangement (essentially, an arrangement in which some form of consideration is given in exchange for a reference to a brand, product or service) be appropriately signalled to ensure that listeners are aware of the commercial arrangement. Following this principle, the Ofcom Broadcasting Code also requires that commercial breaks on radio be clearly separated from programming.

Section 10 goes on to specifically prohibit the association of commercial references and commercial arrangements with particular types of programming:

- Commercial references must not be included in or around news bulletins;
- Commercial references are not permitted in programming for children; and
- No commercial arrangement is permitted to influence the selection or rotation of music tracks played in radio programming.

---

11   *Ibid*, Rules 9.12–9.13.
12   *Ibid*, Rule 9.14.

In overall terms, the rules in Section 10 of the Ofcom Broadcasting Code are intended to ensure the transparency of commercial communications in radio programming.

The AVMS Directive was amended by Directive 2018/1808, which the United Kingdom has until 19 September 2020 to implement. The key change with respect to product placement is that the revised directive removes the general prohibition on product placement (together with the exceptions to the general prohibition). Instead, the revised directive expressly allows product placement in audiovisual media services, including on video-sharing platforms, except for placement in news and current affairs, consumer affairs, religious and children's programmes. The intention is to give broadcasters and on-demand service providers greater flexibility to use product placement. The UK government has consulted on its proposed approach to implementation and has published its response, along with a stated intention to implement the changes (via changes to the Communications Act 2003 and the Ofcom Broadcasting Code) by 19 September 2020.

8. Native advertising and social media influencers

When people spoke about native advertising in the United Kingdom as recently as 10 years ago, they were probably thinking of so-called 'advertorials' in conventional magazines. For example, an ad for make-up in a women's magazine might reproduce the style, layout and appearance of genuine product reviews carried by the magazine, meaning that readers who missed a small 'advertisement' label somewhere on the page might not realise that they were consuming a message that was conceived and paid for by the relevant make-up brand. However, over the last five years or so, there has been an explosion in a different form of native advertising: individuals (often celebrities) with a large following on social media discussing, reviewing and/or praising products in exchange for payment from the relevant brand owner. In many instances, these influencers do little or nothing to inform their followers that they have been incentivised by a brand to post the relevant message.

In view of the significant impact that social media influencers have on the purchasing decisions of their loyal followers, the UK advertising regulators – the ASA and CMA – believe it is very important that influencers disclose the existence of any commercial relationship which lies behind a specific post, video or message. In respect of the rules and legislation enforced by the ASA and CMA respectively, the provisions relevant to native advertising and the activities of social media influencers are as follows.

In the CAP Code (enforced by the ASA), Rule 2.1 provides that: "Marketing communications must be obviously identifiable as such." The issue of what sort of content the ASA deems to be a 'marketing communication' is considered below. As far as the CMA is concerned, the relevant legislative provisions which it (along with regional Trading Standards bodies) is responsible for enforcing are contained in the Consumer Protection Regulations. The Consumer Protection Regulations prohibit unfair commercial practices and Schedule 1 to the Regulations lists 31 practices which are considered unfair in all circumstances. In the context of native advertising, two of these are particularly relevant:

- "Using editorial content in the media to promote a product where a trader has paid for the promotion without making that clear in the content or by images or sounds clearly identifiable by the consumer (advertorial)"; and
- "Falsely claiming or creating the impression that the trader is not acting for purposes relating to his trade, business, craft or profession, or falsely representing oneself as a consumer."

In order for the ASA to deem a particular social media post from a celebrity to be a marketing communication, two elements are required:

- There must be a payment from the relevant brand to the celebrity; and
- The brand must exert a degree of control over the content posted by the celebrity.

The payment need not be monetary – it could be a gift, an event ticket or some other form of benefit. As for the level of control that the brand must have exerted, the ASA's remit goes beyond situations where the brand has provided a detailed script which the celebrity must follow. The ASA will also examine the labelling of content even if a brand:

- has merely asked for specific phrases, hashtags or affiliate links to be included;
- approves content prior to it being posted (or even just reserves the right to do so); or
- determines when or how many times particular content is posted.

The CMA's remit with regard to native advertising content is even broader than the ASA's. Unlike the ASA, the CMA is not concerned about the degree of control that the brand has over the relevant content. For the CMA, if a social media influencer is receiving payment or any other form of benefit in exchange for talking about a particular brand or product – even if the influencer has total freedom as to what he or she says about the brand or product – the CMA considers that there is a commercial relationship underpinning the post which must be disclosed to the consumer.

If social media content falls either within the ASA's remit in respect of native advertising or within the broader remit of the CMA, the key requirement for compliance with the CAP Code and/or the Consumer Protection Regulations is that the content be easily recognisable as an ad before the consumer engages with it. In other words, it is not acceptable for a consumer to discover that an entire YouTube video is an advertisement only after he or she has been watching for two minutes – the consumer should have been able to see that the video was an ad before he or she clicked through to watch it. Equally, it is not acceptable for the hashtag #ad to be buried within a large number of other hashtags at the end of a lengthy tweet.

In terms of the labels that should be used for content that has been paid for (and potentially also controlled by) a brand, neither the ASA nor the CMA is particularly prescriptive about the specific label that should be used. As mentioned above, the key requirement is that the content be easily recognisable as an ad before the consumer engages with it. That said, the ASA and CMA have expressed a preference for the following labels: 'ad'; 'advert'; 'advertising'; 'advertisement'; and 'advertisement feature'. These labels can be used with or without a hashtag, but on social media it is conventional to add one (eg, #ad), and the ASA and CMA are comfortable with the #ad label. On the other hand, the ASA and CMA have said that (depending on the context) the following labels are less likely to comply with the CAP Code and/or the Consumer Protection Regulations, and should generally be avoided: 'supported by'/'funded by'; 'in association with'; 'thanks to [brand] for making this possible'; '@[brand name]'; 'gifted'; 'sponsorship/sponsored'; and 'affiliate/aff'; 'spon/sp'.

The ASA has no legal powers. As such, the main sanction that it can administer in respect of inadequately labelled social media advertising is to publicly 'name and shame' the responsible brands and social media influencers. In recent years the ASA has published a large number of decisions which call out both brands and specific influencers for failing to clearly label social media content as advertising.

In contrast to the ASA, the CMA (together with regional Trading Standards bodies) can enforce the Consumer Protection Regulations by issuing court proceedings against brands and/or influencers that fail to disclose relevant commercial relationships to consumers (ultimately, only a court can decide whether a particular practice does not comply with the regulations). In practice, however, court proceedings are unlikely in the context of inadequately labelled native advertising. As an alternative, in 2019 the CMA secured undertakings from 16 celebrities, under which they committed to clearly disclose in future social media posts whether they had been paid or received a gift in exchange for endorsing a particular product. The celebrities who provided undertakings to the CMA included Ellie Goulding and Rita Ora, and a number of others were also sent warning letters regarding their conduct online.

9. Industry-specific regulation

9.1 Gambling

The advertisement of gambling is addressed by both the CAP and BCAP Codes, in Sections 16 and 17 respectively. In essence, the two codes aim to ensure that gambling ads are socially responsible and have particular regard to protecting vulnerable groups such as children. For example, both codes prohibit ads that:

- portray, condone or encourage gambling behaviour that is socially irresponsible or could lead to financial, social or emotional harm;
- suggest that gambling can provide an escape from personal, professional or educational problems such as loneliness or depression;
- suggest that gambling can enhance personal qualities;
- link gambling to seduction, sexual success or enhanced attractiveness;
- suggest that gambling is a rite of passage; or
- include anyone who is, or seems to be, under 25 years old, or portray anyone acting in an adolescent, juvenile or loutish way.

The CAP and BCAP Codes specifically state that these rules do not apply to advertising for facilities such as hotels and cinemas that are in the same complex as, but separate from, gambling facilities.

Further guidance is available from the Gambling Commission, an independent regulator established under the Gambling Act 2005.

9.2 Alcohol

Alcohol advertising is addressed by Section 18 of the CAP Code and Section 19 of the BCAP Code. The key principle in both is that the advertisement of alcoholic drinks should not be targeted at people under 18 years of age and should not imply, condone or encourage immoderate, irresponsible or anti-social drinking. For example, the codes prohibit ads that:

- claim or imply that alcohol can enhance confidence or popularity;
- imply that drinking alcohol is a key component of the success of a personal relationship or social event; or
- link alcohol with seduction, sexual activity or sexual success, or imply that alcohol can enhance attractiveness.

Furthermore, an alcohol strength comparison with another product can be made only when the comparison is with a higher-strength product of a similar beverage; and advertising must not imply that a drink may be preferred because of its alcohol content or intoxicating effect.

Section 32 of the BCAP Code contains strict requirements regarding the scheduling of alcohol advertising, to ensure that it is not shown during television programming that is likely to be viewed by significant numbers of children.

Alcohol advertising is also regulated by the Portman Group, an industry-supported body whose Code of Practice applies to the naming, packaging and promotion of alcoholic drinks. Advertising should therefore comply with both the Portman Group's Code of Practice and either the CAP or BCAP Code, as applicable.

Advertisers should also be aware of additional restrictions in Scotland, where the Alcohol etc (Scotland) Act 2010 prevents certain types of alcohol promotions, such as 'buy one get one free' offers. Furthermore, there is a minimum sale price of £0.50 per unit of alcohol in Scotland.

9.3 Pharmaceuticals

Pharmaceuticals advertising is governed by Part 14 of the Human Medicines Regulations 2012, which has replaced the Medicines Act 1968 and the Medicine (Labelling and Advertising to the Public) Regulations 1978. Guidance on the Human Medicines Regulations is provided by the Medicines and Healthcare Products Regulatory Agency, a government agency responsible for the regulation of medicines and medical devices, in its publication known as the Blue Guide.

The Human Medicines Regulations contain separate provisions depending on whether medicines are being advertised to the public or to persons qualified to prescribe medicines. The key principle is that prescription-only medicines must not be advertised to the general public. Furthermore, no pharmaceutical advertising should suggest that one product is better than (or equivalent to) another identifiable treatment or product, or that the effects of taking the medicine are guaranteed. Advertising should not dissuade consumers from seeking medical advice or suggest that health can be enhanced by taking a medicine.

Particular care should be taken so that consumers are not misled as to the benefits of the medicine in comparison to other products in the category. Marketers should be aware that the Human Medicines Regulations make it the responsibility of anyone that promotes a medicine to ensure that it complies with the law – this includes the licence holder, as well as third parties such as journalists, publishers and public relations agencies.

Pharmaceuticals advertising is also addressed by specific sections of the CAP and BCAP Codes. Section 12 of the CAP Code and Section 11 of the BCAP Code state, for example, that:

- prescription-only medicines and treatments may not be advertised to the general public;
- objective claims must be backed by evidence;
- consumers should not be discouraged from seeking essential treatment; and
- claims should not lead consumers into making a mistaken diagnosis.

The Association of the British Pharmaceutical Industry (ABPI) is involved with self-regulation within the industry and pharmaceuticals advertisers should be aware of the ABPI Code of Practice for the Pharmaceutical Industry, which aims to ensure that UK pharmaceutical companies operate in a responsible, ethical and professional manner. This code of practice includes requirements for the provision of information regarding pharmaceutical products to patients and the public.

9.4 Financial products and services

Particular care should be taken when advertising financial products and services in order to ensure compliance with the restrictions found in Section 21 of the Financial Services and Markets Act 2000 and in the Financial Services and Markets Act 2000 (Financial Promotion) Order 2005 (as amended). The regulation of financial promotions is the responsibility of the Financial Conduct Authority (FCA). The key principle of the legislation is that a financial promotion (eg, an invitation to buy or sell shares) can be communicated to the public only by a person authorised to do so by the FCA, or if the contents of the promotion have been approved by such a person. Exemptions are available, but these are less likely to apply to real-time communications such as a personal visit or telephone call, because consumers are deemed to require more protection in these situations.

The Financial Services and Markets Act 2000 (Regulated Activities) (Amendment) (No 2) Order 2013 transferred the responsibility for regulation of ads for consumer credit to the FCA. The law relating to the advertisement of consumer credit is contained in Chapter 3 of the FCA's Consumer Credit Sourcebook (CONC 3). CONC 3's overarching principle is that ads for consumer credit must be clear, fair and not misleading.

Section 14 of the BCAP Code contains additional requirements in relation to financial promotions that are regulated by the FCA. The BCAP Code states, for example, that broadcasters are responsible for ensuring that ads carried by them comply with all relevant legal and regulatory requirements. The CAP Code (in Section 14) has a small number of additional rules that apply to financial marketing communications that are not regulated by the FCA. The CAP Code requires, for example, that offers of financial products be set out in a way that allows them to be easily understood by the audience being addressed, and make clear that the value of investments is variable and, unless guaranteed, can go down as well as up.

9.5 Food

Food advertising is regulated by the Food Safety Act 1990, the Food Information Regulations 2014 and Regulation (EC) 1924/2006 on nutrition and health claims made on foods. A list of authorised and non-authorised nutrition and health claims can be found on the EU Register of Nutrition and Health Claims

Made on Foods, with authorised claims being subject to very specific conditions of use. A key principle of the applicable legislation and guidance is that marketing material that contains a nutritional, health or weight-loss claim must be substantiated by evidence.

Excessive food consumption should not be condoned, and there are further restrictions in relation to the broadcast advertising of food products to children – especially if those foods have been assessed as being high in fat, salt or sugar (HFSS) by the Food Standards Agency.

The legislation referred to above is supplemented by both the CAP and BCAP Codes, each of which has specific sections on food (Sections 15 and 13 respectively), and on weight control and slimming (Sections 13 and 12 respectively). The CAP and BCAP Codes include additional requirements, particularly regarding the advertisement of foods and soft drinks to children. For example, the CAP Code prohibits marketing communications that encourage children to eat or drink a product (other than fresh fruit or vegetables) only to take advantage of a promotional offer; and ads with promotional offers must avoid creating a sense of urgency or encouraging the purchase of an excessive quantity of the product. Particular care should be taken where licensed characters and celebrities are used to appeal to children, as both the CAP and BCAP Codes state that such use must be responsible in nature. HFSS product ads that are targeted directly at pre-school or primary school children through their content are entirely prohibited from using licensed characters or celebrities popular with children.

9.6 Tobacco

The advertisement of tobacco products and associated paraphernalia (eg, rolling papers and filters) is tightly regulated in the United Kingdom. Tobacco products may not be advertised to the public at all.[13] Furthermore, tobacco products must not be displayed to the public in shops and must comply with standardised packaging rules in accordance with the Tobacco and Related Products Regulations 2016 and the Standardised Packaging of Tobacco Products Regulations 2015. Such packaging must not include branding other than the product name in a standard size, colour and font, and must contain prominent health warnings covering the entire area reserved for it by the regulations. Further guidelines can be found in the Tobacco Packaging Guidance published by the UK Department of Health.

Section 21 of the CAP Code sets out requirements for the advertisement of rolling papers and filters, and provides that such ads should not encourage non-smokers to start smoking or encourage smokers to increase their consumption.

---

13   See Rule 10.3 of the BCAP Code and Rule 21.1 of the CAP Code, which reflect the provisions of the Tobacco Directive (98/43/EC).

In addition, ads for rolling papers or filters must not play on the susceptibilities of the young or immature, or suggest that smoking can lead to social, sexual, romantic or business success.

Marketers should also be aware of the restrictions imposed on tobacco producers in relation to the promotion of non-tobacco products. The Tobacco Advertising and Promotion (Brandsharing) Regulations 2004 prevent tobacco producers, when advertising a non-tobacco product, from using any feature that is the same as, or similar to, a feature connected with a tobacco product if the purpose or effect of that use is to promote a tobacco product. The BCAP Code contains a similar provision at Rule 10.4 and thus prohibits the use, in an ad for a non-tobacco product, of any design, colour, imagery, logo or style that might be associated in the audience's mind with a tobacco product.

9.7   E-cigarettes

The use of e-cigarettes has increased significantly in recent years, with many individuals and public health bodies believing that they are a less harmful alternative to smoking. However, alongside the growth in popularity of e-cigarettes is increasing concern that:

- nicotine is a highly addictive substance whose use is not necessarily without its own harmful effects; and
- e-cigarettes have particularly strong appeal for children, who might become addicted to nicotine at an early age (without ever having a harmful smoking habit from which to move to the use of e-cigarettes).

UK regulators are attempting to find a balance between allowing the promotion of e-cigarettes as an alternative to tobacco and preventing non-smokers from being drawn into nicotine addiction via the use of e-cigarettes.

It is possible for e-cigarettes to be licensed as medicines in the United Kingdom by the Medicines and Healthcare Products Regulatory Agency (MHRA). Alternatively, e-cigarettes may be sold without a licence from the MHRA, simply as consumer products (such e-cigarette products are referred to here as 'non-medicinal e-cigarettes'). The vast majority of e-cigarette products available in the United Kingdom are non-medicinal e-cigarettes, and the promotion of these products is subject to two important restrictions which do not apply to the promotion of MHRA-licensed e-cigarettes. First, non-medicinal e-cigarettes cannot be promoted as a smoking cessation device – that is, it is not permissible to suggest that a non-medicinal e-cigarette can help the user to quit smoking. Second, there are significant restrictions on the media in which non-medicinal e-cigarettes may be promoted. Essentially, non-medicinal e-cigarettes cannot be advertised in any medium which might have 'cross-border effects' – that is, which might come to the attention of consumers outside the United Kingdom. This means that the promotion of non-medicinal e-cigarettes in the

United Kingdom is limited to outdoor advertising, UK-based transport media, cinema advertising and hard-copy direct mail.

A strange quirk of e-cigarette advertising regulation in the United Kingdom is that, although non-medicinal e-cigarettes cannot be advertised online, they can be lawfully sold online. The ASA has produced guidance which seeks to create a distinction between 'promotional' and 'factual' claims about non-medicinal e-cigarettes, with only 'factual' claims being permitted online. The ASA's guidance indicates that ingredient lists, instructions for use and price statements are permitted online. However, promotional pricing descriptions such as 'buy one get one free' and significant use of imagery which is unrelated to the product are prohibited online.

Other key restrictions on the promotion of (both non-medicinal and MHRA-licensed) e-cigarettes in the United Kingdom are as follows:

- Ads must make clear that the product does not contain tobacco, but does (if applicable) contain nicotine;
- E-cigarettes may be presented as an alternative to tobacco, but ads must not encourage the use of e-cigarettes alongside tobacco use;
- Non-smokers or non-nicotine-users must not be encouraged to use e-cigarettes;
- Health professionals must not be used to promote e-cigarettes; and
- E-cigarette ads must not be directed at under-18s or be likely to hold particular appeal for under-18s.

The majority of the rules on e-cigarette advertising described above are contained in the CAP Code, enforced by the ASA (within the United Kingdom's self-regulatory system for advertising). However, many of the relevant CAP Code rules implement provisions of the Tobacco and Related Products Regulations 2016, which in turn implement the Tobacco Products Directive (2014/40/EU). The regulations are enforced by regional Trading Standards bodies, with breach of certain rules applicable to e-cigarette advertising constituting a criminal offence (punishable by a fine).

The publisher acknowledges the contribution of Sacha Wilson to this chapter in the previous edition.

United States

Melissa Landau Steinman
Venable LLP

---

1. **Overview of the legal and regulatory regime for advertising**

    In the United States, the federal, state and local consumer protection laws, regulations and ordinances that prohibit false or deceptive marketing acts and practices generally govern the advertising and marketing of products and services. The backbone of federal consumer protection law is Section 5 of the Federal Trade Commission Act, which is enforced by the Federal Trade Commission (FTC) and declares that unfair and/or deceptive acts or practices are unlawful. Most states have statutes modelled on the Federal Trade Commission Act, which are known as 'mini-FTC Acts'. Some of these statutes expressly provide that the relevant mini-FTC Act may be interpreted in accordance with FTC guidance and case law.

    In addition, there are federal, state and local laws, regulations and ordinances that regulate specific types of advertising and marketing activities, including:

    - legal standards for advertising and marketing through particular media (eg, telemarketing and email marketing);
    - the advertisement and marketing of particular products and/or services (eg, warranties, food and dietary supplements); and
    - the promotion of products, services and brands through particular methods (eg, rebates and prize promotions).

    The FTC is the principal federal consumer protection agency and state attorneys general are primarily responsible for enforcing state consumer protection laws. Other federal and state agencies are also tasked with enforcing certain laws regulating advertising and marketing activities, which enforce certain provisions relating to advertising via specific media, such as:

    - broadcasting and telecommunications (the Federal Communications Commission (FCC)) or postal mail (the United States Postal Service); and/or
    - particular types of products and services, such as:
        - food and drugs (the US Food and Drug Administration (FDA) and/or the US Department of Agriculture (USDA));

- bank and financial products (the Consumer Financial Products Board); and
- stocks and other securities products (the Securities Exchange Commission).

Other federal and state advertising and marketing laws, including unfair competition laws (eg, Section 43(a) of the Lanham Act, the federal trademark statute), prohibit false and misleading representations in advertising; and some provide for private rights of action against allegedly offending marketers.

In general, remedies for violations of laws regulating advertising and marketing practices may include:

- monetary civil penalties;
- restitution;
- temporary and permanent injunctions; and
- orders for marketers to issue corrective advertising.

Some federal and state consumer protection laws also provide remedies to consumers and other private parties.

Television and radio broadcast networks have standards that ads must meet in order to air on the networks. Additionally, advertising self-regulatory entities – including the Council of Better Business Bureaus, Inc, the Direct Marketing Association, the National Advertising Division (NAD), the Electronic Retailing Self-Regulation Program (ERSP), the Children's Advertising Review Unit, the Mobile Marketing Association and the Word of Mouth Marketing Association – set standards for and police advertising and marketing practices.

Marketers should also be mindful of laws that prohibit the infringement of IP rights, including trademark rights, copyright and privacy and publicity rights. For example, if a marketer uses a logo or brand that is confusingly similar to an existing trademark, the marketer may infringe the trademark owner's trademark rights under federal and state statutory and common trademark laws, including Section 43(a) of the Lanham Act.

Two particularly hot areas which have recently received special attention and guidance from the FTC concern environmental or 'green' marketing claims and 'Made in USA' claims.

1.1 Environmental marketing claims

As a growing number of US consumers seek to purchase environmentally friendly products, from recycled paper to compostable nappies, companies have responded with 'green' marketing claims, touting the environmental benefits of their products.

The FTC has issued national guidelines to help reduce consumer confusion and prevent the false or misleading use of environmental terms such as 'recyclable', 'degradable' and 'environmentally safe' or 'environmentally friendly' in advertising, labelling and other forms of consumer marketing. These Green Guides, last revised in 2012, explain how consumers are likely to interpret certain environmental claims and educate marketers on substantiating and qualifying such claims to avoid deceiving consumers. The guides are the most frequently cited source of guidance for green marketing in the United States and apply not only to marketers making green claims directly to consumers, but also those making such claims to distributors and retailers, as claims are often 'passed along' to consumers.

The Green Guides caution against making broad, unqualified environmental benefit claims because, according to the FTC, few – if any – products have the specific and far-reaching benefits that consumers appear to perceive, making such claims nearly impossible to substantiate. Any qualifications or disclosures should be sufficiently prominent to prevent deception; and it should be made clear whether the claims apply to the product, the package or a component of either.

In the context of environmental marketing claims, a reasonable basis of support often requires competent and reliable scientific evidence, defined by the FTC to include "tests, analyses, research, or studies that have been conducted and evaluated in an objective manner by qualified persons and are generally accepted in the profession to yield accurate and reliable results".

The Green Guides also advise on more specific claims, such as compostable, ozone, recyclable and recycled content and source reduction claims. For example, marketers are advised not to make an unqualified degradable claim for a solid waste product unless they can prove that the entire product or package will completely break down and return to nature within one year of customary disposal. Recent additions to the guides include new sections on:

- certifications and seals of approval;
- carbon offsets;
- 'free-of' claims;
- 'non-toxic' claims; and
- 'made with renewable energy' and 'made with renewable materials' claims.

Unsubstantiated environmental marketing claims have been, and will continue to be, an enforcement priority for the FTC. In late 2019, for example, one national retailer paid $1.76 million to settle FTC allegations that its bath and beauty products were neither "100% organic" nor "certified organic" by the USDA as advertised. And in 2018, the FTC entered into consent orders with four paint companies that allegedly misled consumers through claims that their products were free of emissions and volatile organic compounds.

Several individual state laws specifically regulate environmental marketing claims, and many states incorporate compliance with the FTC's Green Guides as a safe harbour or defence. Recent state enforcement actions include:

- a 2018 lawsuit alleging that a Florida restaurant made misleading claims that its food products were "farm to table", "locally sourced" and "sustainable"; and
- a $1.5 million settlement involving claims by California district attorneys that a global e-commerce company deceptively advertised plastic products as "biodegradable" and "compostable" without appropriate certification.

1.2   'Made in USA' claims

Many customers prefer to 'buy American' and may even pay more to do so. However, the FTC and many states have created specific statutes and guidance on what it means for a product to be of domestic origin, and federal enforcement in this area has been ramped up.

The FTC's Enforcement Policy Statement on US Origin Claims and its business guide, *Complying with the Made in USA Standard*, provide detailed guidance, with examples of accurate and inappropriate US origin claims. Under FTC guidance, 'Made in USA' – or 'Manufactured in the USA' or 'Crafted in the USA' – means that "all or virtually all" of the product has been made in America. In other words, all significant parts, processing and labour must be of US origin, and the product should contain no – or only negligible – foreign content. Among other factors that the FTC considers in order for a product to be considered "all or virtually all" made in the United States, the final assembly or processing of the product must take place there. The FTC may also consider the portion of the product's total manufacturing costs that is attributable to US parts and processing.

When a product is not "all or virtually all" made in the United States, origin claims should be adequately qualified to avoid consumer deception. Such qualified claims may be:

- general, indicating merely the existence of unspecified foreign content (eg, "Made in USA of U.S. and imported parts"); or
- more specific, indicating, for example, the amount of US content (eg, "60% U.S. content") or the parts or materials that have been imported (eg, "Made in USA from imported leather").

Marketers may also make claims that a particular manufacturing or other process was performed in the United States.

One state departs slightly from the FTC's "all or virtually all" standard, providing that companies may not make 'Made in USA' claims "if the merchandise or any article, unit, or part thereof, has been entirely or substantially made, manufactured, or produced outside of the United States".

California's statute also provides a 5% safe harbour provision, stating that: "This section shall not apply to merchandise made, manufactured, or produced in the United States that has one or more articles, units, or parts from outside of the United States, if all of the articles, units, or parts of the merchandise obtained from outside the United States constitute not more than 5 percent of the final wholesale value of the manufactured product."

In September 2019, the FTC held a public workshop discussing and seeking comments from the public on whether to update its Enforcement Policy Statement on US Origin Claims. Although no updates have yet been implemented, the FTC has continued enforcement actions against these claims. In March 2020, for example, a national housewares and home furnishings company paid $1 million to settle FTC charges that it deceptively claimed in promotional materials that certain of its products were "all or virtually all made in the United States", when in fact they were wholly imported or contained significant imported materials or components. Class action plaintiffs also continue to be active in the 'Made in USA' space.

2.   Comparative advertising

In the United States, comparative advertising is regulated by a number of state and federal laws, including the Lanham Act and the Federal Trade Commission Act. It is also regulated informally by the Better Business Bureau Code of Advertising.

Generally speaking, comparative advertising must be truthful and non-misleading. A comparative claim is false only if:

- an actual substantive claim is made in the ad (as opposed to mere puffery);
- the nature of the advertising claim is material such that it would actually impact on a consumer's decision; and
- the material claim is actually false.

The proof required to show that a material claim is false will depend on whether the claim is a generalised claim, such as a statement that a product is "better" than a competitor's product, or a specific claim, such as a statement that a product is "10 times more effective" than a competitor's product. In the case of a general claim, the advertiser need not prove prior verification or substantiation. In contrast, if an advertiser makes a specific claim, it must be able to substantiate or verify that claim in order to defend against a claim of falsity.

Comparative advertising often arises in the setting of competitor comparison price advertising campaigns, and advertisers should abide by the following requirements when comparing prices to competitors' pricing:

- The price must be current – ideally, the ad should disclose the date on which the price comparison was made;

- The stores must be in the same geographic marketplace in which the seller is offering the sale;
- Unless a specific competitor is identified as the subject of the comparison, the products must be comparable and the prices must be 'regular prices' – that is, those commonly offered by a reasonable number of sellers in the geographic area; and
- The prices must be properly verified and substantiated, with records kept that identify information such as:
  - the date(s) and method of comparison;
  - the name of the party that performed the comparison;
  - the location of the seller and the competitor stores where the prices were compared
  - the products compared; and
  - the prices of the compared products.

In addition to potential sanctions or litigation under state and federal laws, if comparative advertising does not comply with trademark and copyright laws, the advertiser may also be liable for trademark and copyright infringement, as well as for claims such as passing off and trade defamation.

Comparative advertising is regulated at the federal level by the FTC, which acts on behalf of the public, bringing claims under the FTC Act against comparative advertising campaigns that are likely to cause harm to the public due to their false or misleading nature. If the FTC deems a particular ad to be false or misleading, it can impose civil penalties on the advertiser. State attorneys general and other state consumer protection bodies can also bring enforcement actions against advertisers that engage in deceptive or false comparative advertising.

At the private level, competitors can sue each other over false or misleading comparative advertising under the Lanham Act. Alternatively, competitors can file a complaint with the NAD, an informal self-regulatory group that is part of the Better Business Bureau. Whether a party wants to subject an advertising campaign to the evaluation of the NAD is entirely voluntary; but if the NAD rules that an advertising campaign is false or misleading and the offending party does not rectify the situation, the matter may be referred to the FTC for further investigation.

3.   Online behavioural advertising

In the United States, rules and regulations relating to online data privacy come from multiple sources. Federal and state laws, in addition to industry self-regulatory codes of conduct, provide data privacy rules that businesses engaging in a variety of online data collection, use and disclosure practices must follow.

At the federal level, several sectoral laws apply to the use, collection and disclosure of certain types of information. For instance, requirements for operators of websites or online services that are directed to children under the age of 13, or that have actual knowledge that children under age 13 provide personal information to the website or online service, are set forth in the Children's Online Privacy Protection Act (COPPA). Among other rules, COPPA mandates parental notice and consent for the collection, use and disclosure of a wide variety of personal information about children under the age 13, including IP addresses and other persistent identifiers. Federal statutes such as the Health Insurance Portability and Accountability Act, the Gramm-Leach-Bliley Act and others also include directives relating to the collection, use and disclosure of specific types of information. In addition, the FTC may use its authority under Section 5 of the FTC Act to bring enforcement actions for unfair or deceptive acts or practices related to privacy and data protection.

In addition to federal statutes, state laws impose certain requirements that are relevant to data privacy. Laws in California, Nevada and Delaware obligate operators of commercial websites or online services to make disclosures about data use and collection practices. California's Shine the Light Law also sets forth notice requirements for businesses that disclose personal information to third parties for their own direct marketing purposes.

In addition to these more narrowly focused state laws, recently enacted state statutes provide more broadly applicable rules. The California Consumer Privacy Act of 2018 (CCPA), for example, is a state data privacy law that gives California residents the right to access, delete and opt out of "sales" (ie, transfers) of a wide swathe of personal information, including online identifiers. A ballot initiative titled the California Privacy Rights Act of 2020 (CPRA) stands to materially amend the CCPA if it gains enough signatures to qualify for the state's November 2020 ballot and Californians approve of the measure at the polls. Additionally, in 2019, Nevada passed a new law giving residents the right to opt out of certain limited exchanges of covered information, including identifiers that allow a specific person to be contacted online. Maine also passed a law in 2019 requiring broadband internet access service providers to obtain consumers' express consent before using, disclosing, selling or permitting access to web browsing history and other information generated by a consumer's use of the service.

Industry self-regulatory codes of conduct supplement many of these laws. For instance, the Digital Advertising Alliance (DAA) has promulgated Self-Regulatory Principles for Online Behavioural Advertising and a corresponding YourAdChoices programme to provide consumers with transparency and choices regarding the practice. Additionally, while not serving as self-regulatory requirements, the DAA has created CCPA-related tools to assist companies in their efforts to offer consumers the ability to opt out of "sales" of personal information under the law.

## 4.	Sales promotions

### 4.1	Prize promotions

Prize promotions – including sweepstakes and contests – are subject to a wide range of federal, state and local regulation, depending on factors such as the entry and winner selection processes and the medium through which they are advertised. At the federal level, the US Department of Justice, the US Postal Service, the FCC and the FTC each has jurisdiction over sweepstakes, promotions and games of chance (collectively, 'promotions'). State laws and regulations for prize promotions also have their own specific requirements, which are often even more onerous.

A threshold issue in structuring a prize promotion in the United States is whether the promotion would fall foul of applicable lottery laws. Federal and all state laws prohibit lotteries, except for state-run versions. A 'lottery' is generally defined as a promotion in which all three of the following elements are present:

- Element of chance: Winners are selected by a randomising process;
- Prize or award: Something of value is awarded to winners, even if the value is nominal; and
- Consideration: A payment or purchase ('monetary consideration') is required from the entrant – although in a handful of states, a non-monetary expenditure of time or effort by the consumer that benefits the promotion sponsor in some direct way may suffice to render the promotion illegal, and even third-party consideration may present some risk.

Many states also have laws regulating 'games of skill', which are promotions in which winners are determined on the basis of *bona fide* skill (eg, via judging). Some states prohibit games of skill for which consideration is required to participate, even though the element of chance is not present and thus there is arguably no lottery even if consideration is present.

All prize promotions should have a set of official rules. Federal law and some state laws require specific disclosures of certain terms and conditions (generally referred to as 'material terms') in advertising for prize promotions. Some such laws apply to prize promotions advertised and/or conducted through any media, and some apply to particular forms of media. For example, the federal Deceptive Mail Prevention and Enforcement Act regulates direct mail sweepstakes and contests and, among other things, requires that direct mailers advertising prize promotions make specific disclosures and provide a mechanism by which recipients may opt out of receiving future prize promotion solicitations via mail. The Federal Communications Act of 1934 and its regulations require the disclosure of certain material terms in broadcast advertising for sweepstakes.

In some states – such as New York, Florida, Rhode Island and Arizona – certain prize promotions must be registered and/or bonded.

The penalties for violating laws regulating prize and other sales promotions range from civil penalties to restitution, injunctions and remedies for consumers.

4.2 Gift cards, coupons and rebates

The federal Credit Card Accountability Responsibility and Disclosure Act of 2009 ('Credit Card Act') requires certain disclosures and includes strict limitations on when dormancy fees and expiration dates may be imposed on gift cards. Many states have gift-card-specific laws and regulations that restrict the imposition of expiration dates and/or dormancy fees, and require certain disclosures on gift cards. Many states also have escheat or abandoned property laws providing that property such as gift cards must be reported to the state if there is no activity with respect to the property for a specified period (and thus the property may be presumed abandoned).

Coupons and rebates are subject to general federal and state consumer protection statutes, as well as laws and regulations that specifically govern discount promotion items. Many states require certain disclosures on coupons and rebates and in advertising for such items. It is generally unlawful (and in many states, expressly forbidden) to advertise a price that is the net of any manufacturer's rebate and coupon without disclosing that the advertised price was calculated after these deductions. A number of states require that if a net price after coupon or rebate redemption is advertised, the actual price must be disclosed in the ad as well. Connecticut and Rhode Island law wholly prohibits the advertisement of a net price after rebate or coupon unless the seller is prepared to give the coupon or rebate for redemption at the point of purchase.

5. Ambush marketing

The United States has no specific law or statute that explicitly addresses the issue of ambush marketing. Sponsors and sporting event brands generally rely on certain provisions of trademark and unfair competition law, contracts and their rights as lessees or operators of sporting venues to protect the exclusivity of official sponsorship. A sporting event brand in the United States that owns a federal, state or common law trademark may seek an injunction under the Lanham Act, state law or common law against an ambush marketer's unauthorised use of its trademark. To prevail, the trademark owner must demonstrate a likelihood of confusion – this means, for example, that consumers would likely believe that the infringing ambush marketer was somehow affiliated with, or sponsoring, the event.

In practice, however, it is not easy for sporting event brands and sponsors to successfully prosecute ambush marketers for trademark infringement. Many ambush marketers are shrewd enough to avoid infringement and may use marks, signage or other indicia to garner attention without using a sponsor's trademark. Further, many seek to use constitutional defences based on their First Amendment rights. US courts recognise a company's First Amendment right to engage in commercial speech without liability if there is no consumer confusion. Consequently, organisations such as the US Olympic Committee (USOC) and FIFA, along with their official sponsors, have sought other means to protect their relationships and the benefits of corporate sponsorship.

Although there is no general law against ambush marketing in the United States, the US Congress passed the Olympic and Amateur Sports Act in 1978 (and amended it in 1998) to give the USOC the exclusive right to control the use of various Olympic symbols, including the interlocking-ring logo and the word 'Olympic'. As a result, the USOC need not prove that an ambush marketer's use would cause consumer confusion and ambush marketers cannot claim fair use as a defence. Free speech defences are still available, however; and the Olympic and Amateur Sports Act cannot be used to prevent ambush marketing tactics that do not use protected Olympic symbols.

In the United States, the Lanham Act provides a cause of action for false advertising if the sporting event brand can point to a false or misleading statement or implied statement by the ambush marketer, although the sporting event brand must also show that it was damaged by the statement. Courts generally also require a plaintiff to show that:

- consumers are likely to be misled; and
- the false or misleading statement would be material to consumers' purchasing decisions.

Thus, if the nature of an ad would lead a reasonable consumer to believe that an ambush marketer is an event sponsor even though it is not, and sponsorship would matter to the consumer, then the sporting event brand may have an actionable claim. Litigation based on unfair competition claims can be expensive, as such claims can be tough to prove. Moreover, the laws on unfair trade are not uniform, as nearly every state within the United States has its own law governing unfair trade practices.

6. Direct marketing

6.1 Telemarketing
In the United States, federal regulatory agencies such as the FTC, the FCC and the Postal Inspection Service oversee the activities of direct marketers; in addition, the individual states themselves play a role in regulation, as well as national trade associations. Telemarketing is restricted at the federal level by the FCC's Telephone Consumer Protection Act and the FTC's Telemarketing Sales Rule.

The Telephone Consumer Protection Act limits the use of automatic dialling systems, artificial or pre-recorded voice messages, SMS text messages and fax machines. It also specifies several technical requirements for fax machines, auto-diallers and voice messaging systems – principally with provisions requiring identification and contact information of the entity using the device to be contained in the message.

Beginning in October 2013, the Telephone Consumer Protection Act started requiring prior express written consent for all auto-dialled or pre-recorded telemarketing calls (including text messages) to wireless numbers and residential lines. Among its other restrictions, the act:

- prohibits direct marketing agents from calling residences before 8:00am or after 9:00pm (absent proper consent);
- requires direct marketers to keep a company-specific 'do not call' list of consumers; and
- bars solicitations to residences that use an artificial voice or a recording without having a written agreement to do so.

These rules – particularly the express written consent requirement – extend to text messages to mobile numbers in addition to calls. The Telephone Consumer Protection Act imposes damages ranging from $500 to $1,500 for each unsolicited call or text message.

The FTC's Telemarketing Sales Rule similarly prohibits commercial telemarketing calls to consumers – and imposes a penalty of $16,000 per call – made by sellers and telemarketers that transmit pre-recorded messages to consumers who have not agreed in writing to accept such messages. The Telemarketing Sales Rule also establishes a Do Not Call Registry, which makes it illegal for a telemarketer to call consumers who have registered their names and numbers with that national list.

In addition to these federal regulatory regimes, telemarketers calling nationally must adhere to separate state regulations. Most states have adopted 'Do Not Call' lists of their own, only some of which are shared with the FTC's Do Not Call Registry. In addition, each state has its own regulations concerning:

- permission to record calls;
- permission to continue with the call;
- Sunday and national holiday calling restrictions; and
- fines and punishments exacted for telemarketing violations.

6.2   Email marketing

With respect to email marketing, the FTC's Controlling the Assault of Non-Solicited Pornography and Marketing Act of 2003 ('CAN-SPAM Act') establishes the national standards for sending commercial email messages. The CAN-SPAM Act permits email marketers to send unsolicited commercial emails as long as they adhere to three basic forms of compliance, affecting 'unsubscribe' issues, content and transmission behaviour. The CAN-SPAM Act also bans false or misleading header information – that is, the email's 'from', 'to' and routing information must be accurate and identify the person that initiated the email. Finally, the CAN-SPAM Act prohibits address harvesting and other fraudulent ways of sending spam email.

6.3 Direct mailings

A marketer's direct postal mailings in the United States can fall foul of various civil and criminal federal laws relating to the mail service. Under the Postal Service's laws, the agency is authorised to collect payments made as a result of a company's fraudulent representations with respect to its mailings. This provision can extend to advertisers that, for example, avail themselves of discounted postage rates that are available only to non-profit entities.

In addition, states may initiate actions against direct marketers under the respective state's deceptive acts and practices statutes. Common law actions for fraud may also be brought in the context of direct marketing, but the government (or private plaintiff) must meet the same standards of proof applicable to all civil fraud actions. Notably, the mere act of sending direct mail solicitations to a state or of contracting within a state for the provision of direct mail services is a sufficient basis under many state 'long-arm' statutes to establish jurisdiction over the non-resident marketer.

As in other areas of advertising, industry participants in direct marketing generally prefer self-regulatory efforts to governmental enforcement. Some of the largest trade associations in the United States greatly impact on the areas of direct mailing and telemarketing. Most notably, the Direct Marketing Association's general Guidelines for Ethical Practices are broadly applicable to direct marketing activities.

6.4 Negative option marketing

The FTC and state regulators have focused increasing scrutiny on consumer advertising and marketing that utilises a negative option (or 'automatic renewal' or 'continuity') approach. Four types of plans generally fall within the negative option marketing category:

- pre-notification negative option plans, under which consumers receive periodic notices offering products and will receive such products and incur a charge unless they specifically reject the offer;
- continuity plans, under which consumers agree in advance to receive periodic shipments of products or provision of services and receive such products or services and incur related charges until they cancel the arrangement;
- automatic renewals, under which sellers automatically renew contracts,

such as subscriptions, at the end of a fixed period unless consumers instruct otherwise; and

- free-to-pay (or nominal fee-to-pay) conversion plans, under which consumers receive a product or service for free (or at a nominal price) for an introductory period and incur a charge (or pay a greater amount) only if they do not take affirmative action to cancel, reject or return the product or service before the end of the trial period.

At the federal level, the FTC regulates negative option marketing pursuant to the Restore Online Shoppers' Confidence Act (ROSCA). A violation of ROSCA is considered an unfair or deceptive act or practice under the FTC Act, which may subject sellers to civil penalties. In addition to ROSCA, the FTC relies on the Negative Option Rule – which addresses pre-notification plans in particular – and the Telemarketing Sales Rule to combat harmful negative option practices.

Approximately half of US states have implemented some form of automatic renewal statute addressing negative option programmes. Where federal and state regulation overlap, federal standards set the minimum bar for compliance, while states can – and do – impose more stringent and extensive requirements. ROSCA gives state attorneys general a cause of action under the FTC Act, but states may also bring actions under their own automatic renewal and consumer protection laws. In fact, several states consider violations of their automatic renewal laws to be *per se* violations of their unfair and deceptive acts or practices laws.

Companies that engage in negative option marketing must comply with both minimum federal standards and the laws of the states in which they do business. While state laws differ significantly, overarching requirements imposed on advertisers and sellers by both federal and state law include:

- clearly and conspicuously disclosing the material terms of the proposed offer before obtaining the consumer's payment information;
- obtaining affirmative, express informed consent before charging the consumer for a negative option programme;
- providing a post-order confirmation containing all material terms;
- disclosing any modifications to the automatically renewing programme; and
- providing a simple cancellation mechanism for consumers to cease recurring charges.

7.   Product placement

Product placement is primarily regulated by the federal sponsorship identification laws, which generally require broadcasters to disclose to their listeners or viewers if matter has been aired in exchange for money, services or other valuable consideration. In other words, while the integration or display of products in media content is permissible, disclosure is required in certain situations.

The Communications Act of 1934 establishes the general obligation of broadcast stations and cable television operators to air sponsorship identification announcements whenever any "money, service or other valuable consideration" is paid or promised in exchange for the broadcast of programme material. However, whenever a service or property is provided without charge or at a nominal charge to a station in connection with a broadcast, disclosure is not required, unless it is furnished in consideration for identification that is "beyond an identification which is reasonably related to the use of such service or property on the broadcast".

The FCC is responsible for implementing and enforcing the Communications Act, including the sponsorship identification requirements. Its sponsorship identification regulations closely track the language of the statute. The requirements apply to broadcast radio and television and original programming on cable (regardless of whether the programme is primarily commercial or non-commercial, and regardless of the duration of the programming). They do not apply to motion picture films (unless originally made for television) or newer media such as video games and music videos. The rules do not require sponsorship identification where both the identity of the sponsor and the fact of sponsorship of a commercial project or service are obvious.

The FCC enforces the sponsorship identification rules through an administrative process outside the federal court system. Any person or entity that is determined by the FCC to have wilfully or repeatedly failed to comply with the statute or rule issued by the FCC is liable for a monetary penalty. The FCC's Forfeiture Policy Statement sets a base forfeiture amount of $4,000 for sponsorship identification violations.

In 2008, the FCC issued a notice of inquiry and notice of proposed rulemaking (NOI/NPRM) seeking comment on, among other things, whether modifications to the sponsorship identification rules are warranted to address new developments in the use of embedded advertising techniques. It also sought comments on a proposed rule change to make the disclosure requirement more obvious to the consumer. Although the comment and reply comment periods have been closed for some time, the FCC has taken no follow-up action on this NOI/NPRM.

Product placement in children's television programming is more heavily regulated. The FCC has longstanding policies that are designed to protect children from confusion that may result from the blending of programme and commercial material in children's television programming. Specifically, the FCC requires broadcasters to use separations or 'bumpers' between programming and commercials during children's programming. The FCC also considers any children's programming associated with a product in which commercials for that product are aired to be 'programme-length commercials', which likely would violate the FCC's time limits on commercial matter in children's programming (because, under the Children's Television Act, the amount of commercial matter that can be aired during children's programming is statutorily limited to a certain number of minutes per hour of programming).

The FTC has issued guidelines concerning the use of endorsements and testimonials in advertising, which were updated in 2010 to account for new media platforms such as Facebook and Twitter. Under these guidelines, ads that feature a consumer and convey his or her experience with a product or service as typical when that is not the case must clearly disclose the results that consumers can generally expect. The FTC has also restated its longstanding principle that 'material connections' (often payments or free products) between advertisers and endorsers that consumers would not expect must be disclosed.

8.   Native advertising and social media influencers

8.1   Native advertising
Native advertising aims to seamlessly integrate sponsored content and marketing messages with non-advertising content. The FTC defines 'native advertising' as "content that bears a similarity to the news, feature articles, product reviews, entertainment, and other material that surrounds it online". Examples include sponsored tweets, advertorials, search ads and other types of online editorial content, including influencer content.

Because of its potential to blur the line between advertising and content, native advertising can be considered deceptive or unfair if appropriate disclosures are not provided. Therefore, in December 2015 the FTC published long-anticipated guidance in *Native Advertising: A Guide for Businesses* and in its Enforcement Policy Statement on Deceptively Formatted Advertisements, which explain how it applies established truth-in-advertising standards in the native advertising context.

The FTC's guidance identifies disclosure practices that prevent deceptive use of native advertising, with numerous examples, and makes clear that potential liability extends to "[e]veryone who participates directly or indirectly in creating or presenting native ads", including advertising agencies and operators of affiliate advertising networks. In order to ensure that disclosures are clear and prominent on all devices and platforms that consumers may use, the FTC makes recommendations such as:

- placing disclosures in front of or above the headline of the native ad;
- for multimedia ads, delivering disclosures to consumers before they receive the advertising message to which the disclosure relates;
- ensuring that disclosures remain when native ads are republished by others; and

- ensuring that disclosures stand out so that consumers can easily read or hear them, including through the use of visual cues such as contrasting text colour and shading, and that they are understandable, or "in plain language that is as straightforward as possible".

Although the FTC and the NAD are most likely to undertake enforcement actions in the native advertising space, there is limited case law and enforcement precedent. Among recent precedent, in March 2016, a national retailer agreed to settle FTC charges that it deceived consumers by paying for native ads, including a seemingly objective article in an online publication and Instagram post, without disclosing that the article and post were actually paid promotions for the retailer's clothing collection. And in May 2016, as part of its routine monitoring programme, the NAD reviewed an online retailer's ad that appeared in the online version of *People Magazine* and expressed concern that it appeared in a format that blurred the line between editorial content and advertising in a way that would confuse consumers. The NAD determined that express disclosures were required in video links themselves or text surrounding the links, even where other "visual and audio cues" made it clear that consumers were viewing a video ad.

8.2 Influencer marketing

Advertisers increasingly view social media as a valuable opportunity to have influencers – celebrities and other social media personalities with large followings – promote their products and services.

The FTC has made it clear, however, that the rules that generally apply to testimonials and endorsements also apply in the social media context. In November 2019, the FTC released a new publication for online influencers, *Disclosures 101 for Social Media Influencers*, which provides guidance on when and how to disclose relationships or "material connections" between a brand and an influencer, including what wording to use and where to place the disclosure, depending on the platform at issue.

Basic principles require the clear and conspicuous disclosure of any financial, employment, personal or family relationship with a brand. Such relationships include not only paid compensation, but also discounted products, gifts, trips, loyalty points and even sweepstakes entries.

9. Industry-specific regulation

9.1 Gambling

Regulation of advertising of gambling in federal law has been limited since a 1999 Supreme Court case, *Greater New Orleans Broadcasting Association, Inc v United States*, struck down the FCC's restrictions on the radio and television advertisement of casinos on First Amendment grounds. The court considered 18 USC §1304, a federal law that imposed a broadcast ban on ads for 'lotteries', broadly defined as any enterprise that offered prizes based in whole or in part upon chance. The FCC interpreted this provision to prohibit any gambling advertising, regardless of whether the activity was legal in the jurisdiction where the ad was being broadcast. A unanimous court struck down the FCC's interpretation on behalf of a group of Louisiana broadcasters, which sought a declaratory ruling that the ban was unconstitutional when applied to broadcasting ads for legal local casinos. The statute itself remains in effect today and is applied to gambling ads in jurisdictions where the gambling activity being advertised is not lawful. Violation of the statute is a criminal offence and can result in a maximum penalty of a fine or up to one year in prison.

The federal government also regulates use of the mail system for the purposes of gambling advertising. Under federal law 18 USC §1302, it is a criminal offence to use the mail system to deliver a "publication of any kind containing any advertisement of any lottery, gift enterprise, or scheme of any kind offering prizes depending in whole or in part upon lot or chance". Violation of the statute can result in a maximum penalty of a fine or up to two years in prison.

Both statutes 18 USC §1302 and 18 USC §1304 exempt ads for legal state-run lotteries.

Many states also have similar laws regulating the advertisement or promotion of gambling. In some states, gambling 'promotion' could be construed broadly enough to include advertising activity. In states where some forms of gambling are legal, there are often laws that regulate the content of the ad. For example, in New Jersey, casino advertising must contain language providing information about assistance for problem gamblers.

9.2   Alcohol

The Federal Alcohol Administration Act sets forth standards for regulating the labelling and advertisement of wine (containing at least 7% alcohol by volume), distilled spirits and malt beverages. The federal Alcohol and Tobacco Tax and Trade Bureau (TTB) – a bureau under the Department of Treasury – enforces the statute. The Federal Alcohol Administration Act and the TTB's implementing regulations are aimed at prohibiting misleading statements about alcoholic beverage products and providing consumers with adequate information regarding the identity, quality and alcohol content of such products.

States and local governments also have laws that specifically regulate the marketing of alcoholic beverages. In all 50 states, the minimum age for alcohol consumption is 21. Under several federal and state laws, government agencies undertake efforts to curb and prevent underage drinking, including by investigating and issuing reports on relevant industry and state government measures.

The advertisement of alcoholic beverages is also subject to self-regulatory guidelines. The primary self-regulatory organisations that set and impose such guidelines are the Beer Institute, the Distilled Spirits Council of the United States and the Wine Institute.

In addition, television and radio broadcast networks have standards specifically for alcoholic beverage advertising.

9.3 Pharmaceuticals

In the United States, the regulation of advertising for drugs depends on the status of the product, as prescription only or over the counter (OTC).

(a) Prescription drugs

The labelling and advertisement of prescription drugs are generally regulated by the FDA. However, the federal False Claims Act and Anti-Kickback Statute also govern how companies may promote their prescription drug products. State laws also govern the promotion of prescription drugs.

The FDA acts under the authority of the federal Food, Drug and Cosmetic Act to regulate products in significant measure based on their labelling. For drugs that require FDA approval, including all prescription drugs and a few OTC drugs, the labelling must also be reviewed and approved by the FDA. The labelling components that are reviewed and approved by the FDA include:

- container labels;
- package inserts (or professional labelling);
- the patient package insert;
- medication guides;
- instructions for use; and
- risk management materials.

Other 'promotional labelling' need not be approved, but must be accompanied by the approved labelling. The scope of the claims that may be made for the product is limited by the approved labelling.

The FDA also regulates ads for prescription drugs, including oral presentations and "advertisements in published journals, magazines, other periodicals and newspapers, and advertisements broadcast through media such as radio, television and telephone communication systems" (21 CFR § 202.1(l)(1)). Anything else promotional in nature is considered 'promotional labelling'. Ads need not be accompanied by the full prescribing information found in the FDA-approved package insert. They must, however, include a brief summary relating to the side effects, warnings, precautions and contraindications.

The FDA has authority to take both administrative actions and judicial actions to punish persons and companies found to be violating the law and to deter violations. The FDA frequently issues warning letters or untitled letters to companies advising them of alleged violations of the Food, Drug and Cosmetic Act. Judicial actions include seizures of products, injunctions, criminal prosecutions and certain civil monetary penalties.

In addition, the False Claims Act is a federal statute that prohibits inappropriate claims for reimbursement under Medicaid and Medicare. This statute can come into play when a company promotes a drug that is reimbursed under Medicaid or Medicare for an off-label use (ie, a use that goes beyond the intended use of the drug as approved by the FDA). Where a company promotes a prescription drug for an off-label use that is not reimbursable under Medicare or Medicaid, and claims for reimbursement are submitted for that off-label use, the company may be deemed to have caused the submission of false claims if the company knew or should have known that the use was not reimbursable. The US government has brought cases under the False Claims Act based on general allegations that the company was involved in a scheme to promote an off-label use for a drug.

The Anti-Kickback Statute is a federal statute designed to protect the integrity of government payment programmes. The statute prohibits the payment of any form of remuneration in return for, or intended to induce the referral (by a healthcare professional) of, any federal and state healthcare programme business, such as Medicare and Medicaid. The term 'remuneration' covers almost anything of value and includes, among other things, cash equivalents, such as coupons. The government has been aggressive in enforcing the Anti-Kickback Statute against pharmaceutical companies. Many cases have resulted in significant fines and penalties (in the hundreds of millions of dollars).

On the self-regulatory side, the Pharmaceutical Research and Manufacturers of America (PhRMA) is a trade association that represents the country's leading pharmaceutical research and biotechnology companies. PhRMA has developed a voluntary Code on Interactions with Healthcare Professionals, which governs drug companies' interactions with healthcare professionals as they relate to the marketing of drug products.

(b)   *Over-the-counter drugs*

The advertisement and labelling of OTC drugs are regulated by the FTC, the FDA, state law and via voluntary compliance proceedings before the NAD or the ERSP.

The FDA has primary responsibility for regulating the labelling of OTC drugs. For OTC drugs being sold pursuant to the monograph system, the monograph dictates the scope of the claims that may be made for the product. For OTC drugs that are approved by the FDA, the scope of the claims that may be made for the product are limited by the approved labelling. The FDA may indirectly regulate OTC drug advertising based on labelling and approval requirements that may flow from the advertising. As is the case with prescription drugs, the FDA has authority to take both administrative action and judicial action to penalise persons and companies that violate the law, and to deter violations.

The FTC has primary responsibility for regulating the advertisement of OTC drugs, including print, broadcast and internet advertising. The FTC acts pursuant to:

- Section 5 of the Federal Trade Commission Act, which prohibits "unfair or deceptive acts or practices"; and
- Sections 12 and 15 of the same law, which prohibit "any false advertising" that is "misleading in a material respect".

If the FTC has reason to believe that the FTC Act or regulations have been violated, it may seek relief through either administrative proceedings or judicial actions brought in a federal district court. Depending on the forum, the FTC can seek preliminary or permanent injunctive relief, including equitable monetary relief, consumer redress or fines of up to $16,000 for each violation of a consent or final order.

States also have the authority to regulate product advertising through their respective attorney general's office and, in some states, the county district attorney. In addition, lawsuits brought by consumers alleging violations of state unfair competition and/or deceptive advertising laws are commonplace.

Finally, the NAD and the ERSP are arms of the advertising industry's self-regulation programme. On their own initiative or through a competitor challenge, these entities review claims in product advertising to ensure proper substantiation exists. While compliance with NAD and ERSP decisions is voluntary, if a company refuses to make the recommended changes, the NAD or the ERSP will refer the case to the FTC, which can invite additional regulatory scrutiny.

9.4   Financial products and services

Entities that offer financial products to consumers via a commercial medium such as television, radio, print or the Internet must comply with a myriad of state and federal laws. For purposes of this discussion, we identify those laws that apply to consumer lenders generally.

Lenders may also be required to comply with state law and with requirements that are unique to a particular loan product. For example, lenders that offer mortgage loans are subject to additional stringent advertising requirements that are not discussed below.

(a)   Consumer credit legislation

As required by Regulation Z – the implementing regulation for the Truth in Lending Act for any advertisement for consumer credit – the ad must be accurate and offer only credit terms that are actually available. For example, if a lender only makes loans up to a dollar value of $10,000, it cannot advertise loans in dollar values in excess of that threshold. This requirement will apply to lenders as well as to any third party that offers ads on behalf of a lender.

In addition to the requirement to advertise actually available credit, and in order to comply with both the Truth in Lending Act and Regulation Z, lenders and their advertisers must ensure that all ads contain all applicable disclosures. Thus, if an ad for a loan contains a 'trigger term', the ad must also contain certain required disclosures. The trigger terms for closed-ended loans under the Truth in Lending Act are:

- the amount or percentage of any down payment;
- the number of payments or period of repayment;
- the amount of any payment; and
- the amount of any finance charge.

Any ad that includes a trigger term must provide the following disclosures:

- the amount or percentage of the down payment;
- the terms of repayment; and
- the annual percentage rate using that term.

If the rate may be increased after consummation, the fact of that potential increase must be disclosed. For open-ended loans, different trigger terms and disclosures apply.

(b) *Fair lending legislation*

Consistent with the anti-discrimination provisions that arise under the Equal Credit Opportunity Act and its implementing regulation, Regulation B, lenders must make credit available to all qualified applicants and are prohibited from discriminating against any person based on his or her status as a member of a 'protected class'.[1] Lenders are also prohibited from dissuading persons who are members of a protected class from applying for credit. And lenders are prohibited from targeting (or excluding) zip codes for credit offers, which targeting could result in excluding persons of a protected class from accessing credit.

Additionally, if a lender provides an application for credit along with an ad, the lender must ensure that the application conforms with Regulation B. This means, for example, that if the application requests a title (eg, 'Ms', 'Mr', 'Miss'), the applicant must understand that providing such information is optional, and

---

1   See 12 CFR 1002.2(z). A 'protected class' relates to race, skin colour, religion, national origin, sex, marital status or age (provided that the applicant has the capacity to enter into a binding contract); the fact that all or part of the applicant's income derives from any public assistance programme; or the fact that the applicant has in good faith exercised any right under the Consumer Credit Protection Act or any state law upon which an exemption has been granted by the Bureau of Consumer Financial Protection.

that any information requested about an applicant's status as a protected class member is solicited and used only as required by applicable law.

In addition to the more specific advertising requirements that arise under federal consumer protection laws, lenders must ensure that their ads for credit do not violate the requirements set forth in the FTC Act in relation to unfair, deceptive or abusive acts or practice. This is a broad prohibition that prevents creditors from undertaking such activities as making claims without substantiation or advertising credit in a way that could cause the consumer to be confused about the actual cost and terms.

9.5   Food

The advertisement and labelling of food and dietary supplements are regulated by the FTC, the FDA, the USDA, state law and via voluntary compliance proceedings before the NAD or the ERSP.

The FTC has primary responsibility for regulating food and dietary supplement advertising, including print, broadcast and internet advertising. The FTC acts pursuant to:

- Section 5 of the FTC Act, which prohibits "unfair or deceptive acts or practices"; and
- Sections 12 and 15 of the same act, which prohibit "any false advertising" that is "misleading in a material respect".

If the FTC has reason to believe that the FTC Act or related regulations have been violated, it may seek relief through either administrative proceedings or judicial actions brought in a federal district court. Depending on the forum, the FTC can seek preliminary or permanent injunctive relief, including equitable monetary relief, consumer redress or fines of up to $16,000 for each violation of a consent or final order.

The FDA has primary responsibility for regulating the labelling of food. The distinction between 'labelling' and 'advertising' (see previous paragraph) can be somewhat misleading, however, as the FDA takes the position that it may use claims made in advertising as evidence of the intended use of the product, which has a direct effect on the product's regulatory classification. The FDA acts pursuant to Section 403(a) of the Food, Drug and Cosmetic Act, which prohibits "labelling [that] is false or misleading in any particular". In addition, Section 403(r) of the same act limits the types of claims that may be made for food and dietary supplements. The FDA has authority to:

- take both administrative and judicial action to protect the public from dangerous and unlawful products;
- penalise persons and companies found to be violating the law (acting through the Department of Justice); and
- deter violations.

The FDA frequently issues warning letters or untitled letters to companies advising them of alleged violations of the Food, Drug and Cosmetic Act.

Administrative actions include product recalls and withdrawal of facility registration; while judicial actions include seizures of products, injunctions, criminal prosecutions and certain civil monetary penalties.

The USDA has primary responsibility for regulating the labelling of meat, poultry and certain egg products. The USDA acts pursuant to the Federal Meat Inspection Act and the Poultry Products Inspection Act. The USDA's regulations specify the information that must appear on food labels within its jurisdiction; and the USDA pre-approval of labels is required for products that contain poultry, meat and egg products.

States have the authority to regulate product advertising through their respective attorney general's office and, in some states, the county district attorney. In addition, lawsuits brought by consumers alleging violations of state unfair competition and/or deceptive advertising laws are commonplace.

The NAD and the ERSP are arms of the advertising industry's self-regulation programme. On their own initiative or through a competitor challenge, these entities review claims in product advertising to ensure that proper substantiation exists. While compliance with decisions of the NAD and ERSP is voluntary, if a company refuses to make the recommended changes, the NAD or ERSP will refer the case to the FTC, which can invite additional regulatory scrutiny.

In addition to FTC regulatory oversight generally, a number of entities are involved in regulating and overseeing food marketing directed at children. The FCC is charged with enforcing the Children's Television Act of 1990, which restricts the amount of commercial matter that can be aired per hour of children's programming. Television networks may also issue guidelines relating to children's advertising in the networks' Advertising Standards and Guidelines, including guidelines relating to the separation of commercial and non-commercial content and the advertisement of conventional food, sweets, snacks, chewing gum and soft drinks. In addition, several self-regulatory groups – including the Children's Advertising Review Unit of the Council of Better Business Bureaus and the Children's Food and Beverage Advertising Initiative – are involved in evaluating child-directed advertising and/or developing self-regulatory guidelines.

9.6   Tobacco

The advertisement of tobacco products in the United States is closely regulated. In 2009, Congress passed the Family Smoking Prevention and Tobacco Control Act ('Tobacco Control Act'), which gave the FDA broad authority over 'tobacco products', including advertising. The Tobacco Control Act gives the FDA the authority to "restrict tobacco product marketing and advertising, strengthen cigarette and smokeless tobacco warning labels, reduce federal pre-emption of certain state cigarette advertising restrictions, and increase nationwide efforts to block tobacco product sales to youth".

Before the Tobacco Control Act took effect, tobacco products were subject to a long, storied advertising history that resulted in a patchwork of advertising restrictions through legislation and litigation. Cigarette ads were banned from television and radio in 1970 under the Public Health Cigarette Smoking Act. Years later, smokeless tobacco advertising on television and radio was also banned. A master settlement agreement was then reached between major tobacco companies and 46 US states, resulting in further restrictions and warning requirements.

Tobacco products, including e-cigarettes, must include a number of warnings on labelling and in advertising. The Tobacco Control Act also imposes a series of additional restrictions on the advertisement and marketing of tobacco products, which are designed to reduce youth access to tobacco products and tobacco product advertising. For example, the use of descriptors such as 'mild' and 'light' is now regulated. The following restrictions also apply:

- tough limits on sponsorship of events;
- a ban on outdoor advertising; and
- bans on the use of samples and gifts, tobacco product vending machines or self-service displays, and tobacco-branded merchandise.

9.7   E-cigarettes

In 2016, the FDA finalised its much-awaited 'deeming rule', which expanded the definition of 'tobacco products' to include electronic nicotine delivery system (ENDS) products. In the time between the Tobacco Control Act taking effect and the finalisation of the FDA's deeming rule, novel ENDS products proliferated on the market. These novel products were not only beyond the scope of the FDA's jurisdiction before the rulemaking, but also outside the scope of the settlement agreements of the 1990s that restricted the advertisement of other tobacco products – namely, conventional cigarettes. Consequently, vape products became increasingly popular, perplexing public health advocates grappling with the lack of data on health effects – particularly when ENDS products are used as an alternative to traditional, combustible tobacco products. With vaping now characterised as an 'epidemic', both the FTC and FDA are acutely focused on restricting the advertisement of ENDS products, particularly to youth.

Unlike traditional cigarettes, ENDS products – including e-cigarettes and vaping products – may be lawfully advertised on television, radio and the Internet, with limited restrictions. From an FDA perspective, ENDS products must include the following, prominent warning statement on all advertising: "WARNING: This product contains nicotine. Nicotine is an addictive chemical."

Beyond the nicotine warning, e-cigarette advertising must be truthful, non-misleading and not intended for a therapeutic use, including for smoking cessation. The FDA and the FTC work hand in hand to restrict false and misleading advertising of ENDS products and focus primarily on advertising targeting children and adolescents. Despite the lack of sweeping legal restrictions on the advertisement of ENDS products, given the mounting health concerns over increased vaping among teenagers, several television networks have instituted policies prohibiting the advertisement of ENDS products. The FTC has also ordered six major ENDS product manufacturers to provide information and data on sales, advertising and promotional practices in the United States, to better understand the "rapidly growing e-cigarette market". It is yet to be determined what impact, if any, the FTC's review will have.

About the authors

Barbara Abegg

Associate, Lenz & Staehelin

barbara.abegg@lenzstaehelin.com

Barbara Abegg's practice focuses on IP and unfair competition matters. She represents clients in litigation before the Swiss courts, in arbitration proceedings and in administrative matters before governmental authorities. In addition, she regularly advises on a broad range of other issues in the context of IP and unfair competition law. Barbara is a case editor for the Swiss journal for IP, information and competition law, *sic!*.

Daniela Ampollini

Partner, Trevisan & Cuonzo

dampollini@trevisancuonzo.com

With more than 20 years of experience in the IP field, Daniela Ampollini advises both Italian and international clients on the exploitation and protection of innovation, using all tools contemplated by IP law. Her experience covers both contentious work (including multi-jurisdictional litigation) and non-contentious work. Her practice encompasses marketing and advertising law, and she advises clients in various industry sectors – including chemicals, pharmaceuticals and medical devices, electronics, mechanics, household and personal care, cosmetics, fashion and apparel, seeds, food and beverages – on the design and defence of their communications and marketing strategies.

Daniela regularly takes part in national and international conferences in the IP field, including as a speaker, and has contributed to several publications on intellectual property.

Pauls Ančs

Associate, Ellex Klavins

pauls.ancs@ellex.lv

Associate Pauls Ančs specialises in issues relating to the EU market freedoms for goods and services. His main fields of activity are online trading, digital services, unfair commercial practices, advertising, consumer rights and product safety. He represents clients in communications and disputes with business partners and authorities in areas that require product-specific legal knowledge. Pauls is looking forward to 2022, when the Omnibus Directive and other directives relating to the New Deal for Consumers will become effective.

As an expert from Latvia, Pauls has participated in a European Commission project which resulted in the creation of a useful tool for both industry and consumers: an EU-wide, multilingual database of legal acts, case law, legal doctrine and other materials relating to 11 of the most significant EU directives on consumer protection, from each of the EU member states.

George A Ballas

Senior and managing partner, Ballas,
Pelecanos & Associates LPC
george.ballas@balpel.gr

George A Ballas is senior and managing partner
of Ballas, Pelecanos & Associates LPC and head
of the firm's IP, IT and CT practice group. He
read law at the Universities of Athens and Paris
and was admitted to practice by the Athens
Bar Association in 1972. He is a lawyer before
the Greek Supreme Courts, as well as in all
lower courts, and a European patent attorney.

In addition to heading the firm's litigation
practice in complex pharmaceutical patents
and anti-counterfeiting cases, George regularly
advises clients on developing and managing
strategic initiatives for optimising the
protection, exploitation and enforcement of
their intellectual assets. His diverse background
includes the office of secretary general of the
Greek Parliament.

Simen Blaker Strand

Partner, GjessingReimers
sbs@gjessingreimers.no

Simen Blaker Strand is a partner at boutique
law firm GjessingReimers, and specialises in IP
and marketing law. He has nearly 20 years'
experience advising on marketing law and IP
law, as well as a broad range of technology-
related legal issues.

Simen is a member of the Norwegian
Alternative Dispute Resolution Committee for
the country-code top-level domain '.no'.

Andrew Butcher

Senior associate, Bristows LLP
andrew.butcher@bristows.com

Andrew Butcher advises across the full range

of soft IP rights, with advertising and
trademark law being his principal practice
areas. He assists clients with company name
disputes, domain name disputes and IP
litigation in the High Court and below; while
on the non-contentious side, he advises on
trademark filing strategy and compliance of
advertising copy with UK regulations. Andy
has advised major brands on compliance with
ambush marketing legislation for global sports
events and has substantial experience in
ensuring compliance of promotional
mechanics and terms and conditions with UK
advertising rules. He also advises intermediary
service providers such as search engines and
social media sites regarding their liability for
third-party content accessed via their service.

In addition to his experience in private
practice, Andy has completed secondments
with several international clients, where he
advised on online brand protection and filed
and defended UK Advertising Standards
Authority (ASA) complaints.

Alexander Cizek

Founding partner, CIZEK I IP
alexander.cizek@cizek-ip.at

Alexander Cizek studied law in Vienna, Austria
and the United States, and was admitted to the
New York Bar in 1996 and the Austrian Bar in
2000. After 14 years' affiliation with a large
international business law firm, where he
headed the IP and technology practice group
in the Vienna office, he founded his own IP/IT
boutique, CIZEK I IP.

Alexander specialises in all aspects of IP law,
including unfair competition and trade practices
law. He has extensive experience in unfair
competition and IP-related litigation, including
preliminary injunction proceedings, contractual
work and the worldwide filing and prosecution

of trademarks; and provides legal advice to both national and international clients.

Alexander is recognised as a leading practitioner in the IP field and is listed in various professional publications. He has been distinguished by *Chambers & Partners*, *Legal 500* and other legal guides for his brand protection and unfair competition work.

Carlos Dávila-Peniche
Partner, Baker McKenzie Mexico
cdp@bakermckenzie.com

Carlos Dávila-Peniche is a partner at Baker McKenzie in Mexico City. A litigator by trade, he is a well-established and experienced IP attorney, advising on trademark, copyright and entertainment law.

From a trademark law perspective, Carlos regularly handles and coordinates effective, holistic legal strategies in matters involving copyrights, trade secrets and trademarks, as well as expansion based on IP rights, such as licensing and franchising. Likewise, he counsels clients on potential disputes, infringement and enforcement actions in different industries, such as consumer goods and retail, technology, media, hotels, industrials, manufacturing and transportation.

Additionally, Carlos assists entertainment, internet and multimedia companies with their domestic entertainment law needs, including transactional issues such as acquisition of rights, option, talent, producer and synchronisation agreements; mechanical licences; distribution; production and post-production issues; and general compliance issues for film productions in Mexico.

Johanna Flythström
Principal associate, Roschier
johanna.flythstrom@roschier.com

Johanna Flythström is a Helsinki-based principal associate who specialises in marketing and consumer law, as well as IP law. Her experience also includes advising clients on contractual and regulatory matters, in particular in the fields of life sciences, digitalisation and technology, media and telecommunications. Johanna also has considerable experience of acting as a counsel in marketing and consumer law disputes, as well as in IP and technology disputes, including in multi-jurisdictional IP litigation.

Johanna regularly advises major international brand owners and other clients on marketing and consumer law and regulatory matters, such as marketing campaigns, consumer contracts, product information and marketing requirements (including pricing and labelling), as well as sector-specific prerequisites for market entry. She also represents clients regularly in marketing and consumer law disputes, as well as before the supervisory authorities.

Toshiya Furusho
Partner, Oh-Ebashi LPC & Partners
furusho@ohebashi.com

Toshiya Furusho is a partner at Oh-Ebashi LPC & Partners, and is admitted to practise law in Japan and New York State. His practice focuses on counselling, licensing and litigation in the IP field, including patents, trademarks, industrial designs and trade secrets. Toshiya is also experienced in various kinds of commercial dispute resolution, including unfair competition, contract disputes and tort claims. He is a part-time lecturer on patent law at Kwansei Gakuin University Law School.

About the authors

Ida Gjessing
Partner, GjessingReimers
ig@gjessingreimers.no

Ida Gjessing is a partner at boutique law firm GjessingReimers, with expertise in IP and marketing law. She is a highly ranked litigator with a focus on advertising law, as well as patent and trademark cases. On the non-contentious side, she advises on all aspects of IP law and marketing law.

She regularly represents major players within the food and pharmaceutical industries, and has handled a wide range of cases on all aspects of advertising law, including trade dress, nutrition and health claims, misleading advertising and comparative advertising. Her assignments involve both business-to-business and business-to-consumer (B2C) matters.

Ida chairs the Council dealing with Unfair Marketing Practices, an out-of-court dispute resolution body appointed by the industry and advertising community.

Rebecka Harding
Senior associate, Advokatfirman Delphi
rebecka.harding@delphi.se

Rebecka Harding is a senior associate in the tech and IP department of Delphi in Stockholm. She specialises in IP and data protection issues, including marketing law, consumer law and e-commerce questions.

She advises clients on all matters within her specialist areas. Her experience includes advising on IP protection, advertising clearance, branch launches, products and websites, intermediary liability, IP and advertising disputes, data privacy compliance projects and data breach incidents. She regularly speaks on matters within her areas of expertise.

Marina Hurtado-Cruz
Partner, Baker McKenzie Mexico
marina.hurtado@bakermckenzie.com

Marina Hurtado-Cruz is a partner at Baker McKenzie in Mexico City, with expertise in IP advertising and marketing law. She has more than 10 years of experience in the areas of patents, consumer protection and regulatory work. She has a special interest in industries such as food and beverages, consumer goods and retail, cosmetics and pharmaceuticals.

Marina has extensive experience advising companies on advertising campaign and labelling clearances, sweepstakes, contests and promotions, in both a preventive and defensive capacity. She also advises clients on their successful defence against false or misleading advertising by competitors.

Due to her vast experience in IP and advertising law, she is highly proficient in dealing with the Mexican Institute of Industrial Property, the Federal Consumer Protection Agency, the Health Authority and the Interior Ministry of Mexico.

Carina Hyldahl
Attorney, Gorrissen Federspiel
cahy@gorrissenfederspiel.com

Carina Hyldahl is admitted to the Danish Bar and works in the IP and digital business department of Danish law firm Gorrissen Federspiel. She advises Danish and international clients on marketing law and IP law, including in relation to advertising campaigns, advertising clearance and IP contracts.

Carina also has experience with corporate, business and contract law, including national and international mergers and acquisitions.

Emmanuelle Jardin-Lillo

Partner, TGS France Avocats

emmanuelle.jardin-lillo@tgs-avocats.fr

Emmanuelle Jardin-Lillo is a partner in the contract, competition and distribution department at TGS France Avocats. The firm is a member of the TGS France Group and the TGS Global business network, which has expertise in advisory, audit, law and accounting. Emmanuelle recently joined the firm to develop its contract law practice and share her expertise in advertising and marketing law.

With 20 years of experience in business law, Emmanuelle assists French and foreign clients in the negotiation and management of their commercial relationships (contracts, distribution networks, contract management) and the implementation of communications strategies (advertising, marketing, e-commerce, personal data), in order to guarantee them legal security in the development of their activities, both in France and internationally.

In particular, Emmanuelle advises companies on setting up distribution and marketing networks for their products and services, with expertise in product regulation, contract management and sector-specific advertising such as alcohol advertising.

Paul Jordan

Partner, Bristows LLP

paul.jordan@Bristows.com

Paul Jordan is a partner in the IP department and heads the firm's advertising and marketing group. He joined Bristows in 2009.

Although his experience covers the full range of IP issues (both contentious and non-contentious), Paul focuses on advertising regulation, content licensing and trademark and copyright infringement. His experience includes advising on multi-platform advertising clearance projects, social media campaigns, comparative advertising disputes and the preparation and defence of ASA, Phone-paid Services Authority, Trading Standards and Competition and Markets Authority investigations.

Paul regularly speaks on brand protection and advertising law matters, and has been widely published. For almost a decade, all major legal directories have recognised him as a leading expert in the field of advertising law. He continues to represent some of the world's biggest brands and advertising agencies.

Mizuki Kanno

Partner, Oh-Ebashi LPC & Partners

kanno@ohebashi.com

Mizuki Kanno is a partner in the competition/antitrust practice at Oh-Ebashi LPC & Partners. She specialises in competition law, consumer protection, data protection and other compliance matters. She advises both foreign and domestic clients on various matters, including merger filings, cartel investigations, leniency applications, Consumer Affairs Agency investigations and litigation.

Mizuki received her JD from the University of Tokyo and her LLM from the University College London. She is licensed to practise law in Japan.

Anikó Keller

Partner, Szecskay Attorneys at Law

aniko.keller@szecskay.com

Anikó Keller leads the competition and compliance team at Szecskay Attorneys at Law. Anikó and her team work in all areas of business and industry in relation to competition and antitrust law, state aid, unfair competition and unfair commercial practices, and advertising law matters. Anikó has represented multinational companies in both antitrust and unfair commercial practice cases before the Hungarian Competition Authority and courts. She regularly advises clients on antitrust and advertising compliance programmes, carries out competition audits and prepares compliance policies. She is fluent in English and German.

Susan Kempe-Müller

Partner, Latham & Watkins LLP
susan.kempe-mueller@lw.com

Susan Kempe-Müller heads the German IP practice of Latham & Watkins, specialising in advertising, copyright and trademark law. She advises on a broad spectrum of IP matters, including M&A due diligence and transaction agreements on intellectual property and information technology, licensing arrangements, brand development and product branding strategy, outsourcing and cooperation agreements, with experience in both contentious and non-contentious work. Her client base covers a broad range in the technology, consumer products, financial, IT, e-commerce and media sectors.

Susan has a special interest in the healthcare industry and has extensive experience in this area. She represents clients before trademark and patent offices, as well as before all German civil courts. Susan has written a book about pharmaceutical law and is the author of numerous specialist publications on IP topics. She was ranked among the best lawyers for intellectual property and arbitration/litigation/mediation in Germany in 2019 and 2020.

Theodore J Konstantakopoulos

Senior associate, Ballas, Pelecanos & Associates LPC
theodore.konstantakopoulos@balpel.gr

Theodore J Konstantakopoulos is a senior associate with Ballas, Pelecanos & Associates LPC and a member of the IP, IT and CT practice group, the company, tax and employment practice group and the consumer rights practice group. Theodore has been a member of the Athens Bar since 2005. A graduate of Athens University Law School (LLB), Theodore earned a master of laws degree from *Leibniz Universität*, Hannover, Germany, following which he was awarded a second master of laws from Queen Mary College, University of London in computer and communications law.

Theodore is a certified data protection officer (ISO/IEC 17024) and advises Fortune 500 companies on all aspects of electronic communications, information technology, media, telecommunications and e-commerce law, with a particular focus on data protection issues.

Charmaine Koo

Partner, Deacons
charmaine.koo@deacons.com

Charmaine Koo heads the IP commercial and litigation practice group at Deacons. She advises on all aspects of IP work, including commercial exploitation of intellectual property, anti-counterfeiting strategies and enforcement. She has won a number of high-profile court cases resulting in ground-breaking decisions in the Hong Kong IP field. She is one of Hong Kong's leading entertainment lawyers and was previously in-house counsel for one of the world's largest entertainment and media companies. She has extensive experience in copyright, personal data privacy and cutting-edge technology, internet and e-business issues.

Charmaine regularly advises on compliance and regulatory issues relating to marketing and advertising, including copyright and privacy issues, product development, branding and clearance of IP rights, contests, promotions, packaging, design agreements, advertising campaigns and service agreements, co-branding, sponsorship, endorsement, talent and licensing agreements, agreements and disputes with advertising and design agencies.

Charmaine represents many of the world's leading advertising and public relations companies.

Yuki Kuroda

Partner, Oh-Ebashi LPC & Partners

kuroda@ohebashi.com

Yuki Kuroda is a partner at Oh-Ebashi LPC & Partners and is in charge of data protection and data security issues. He has handled a number of law and technology cases throughout his legal career. His practice includes Japanese and international data protection issues such as the General Data Protection Regulation and the Chinese Cybersecurity Law. He regularly assists clients with everything from planning new data-intensive businesses to implementing robust data protection/security compliance programmes.

Yuki received his JD from Osaka University and his master's from the University of California, Berkeley School of Law. He is licensed to practise law in Japan and New York. He is also the specially appointed associate professor (Part-time) at the Artificial Intelligence Centre for Medical Research and Application of Osaka University Hospital.

Kenneth Kvistgaard-Aaholm

Partner, Gorrissen Federspiel

kka@gorrissenfederspiel.com

Kenneth Kvistgaard-Aaholm works in the IP and digital business department of Danish law firm Gorrissen Federspiel. He has extensive experience in advising Danish and international clients on marketing law, inluding in relation to advertising campaigns, online marketing practices and multi-jurisdictional advertising clearances. He also advises clients on all aspects of IP law, including matters relating to the intersection between competition law and IP law.

Kenneth's practice also includes litigation, arbitration and contractual aspects and IP strategies. He is particularly well known for his patent practice and advises technology-heavy clients, spanning areas such as electronics, mechanics and pharmaceuticals.

Kenneth is a trained lecturer and teaches at the University of Aarhus and the Danish Institute for IPR Training, as well as at various seminars. He has also authored various publications within his specialised areas.

Irena Lišková

Partner, Randl Partners, advokátní kancelář, sro

liskova@randls.com

Irena Lišková is an attorney at law and a partner at Randl Partners law office. She leads the data privacy and marketing practice group. Irena specialises in commercial, data privacy, marketing and consumer law and intellectual property, including litigation, and has extensive experience in infringement and unfair competition cases.

Irena works with clients across a variety of industries, and has expertise in advertising and marketing in the gastronomy and hotel, pharmacy and food, HR and real estate and development sectors.

As the Global Advertising Lawyers Alliance (GALA) exclusive member for the Czech Republic, Irena assists in global promotional and advertising campaigns and projects.

Kelley Loo
Partner, Deacons
kelley.loo@deacons.com

Kelley Loo is a partner in the IP commercial and litigation practice group at Deacons. Her practice covers all aspects of IP work, including enforcement of IP rights and IP protection strategy. She has extensive experience advising on contentious and non-contentious IP issues; she handles IP litigation matters at the Hong Kong courts, arbitrations and proceedings at the Hong Kong Trade Marks Registry, and has won a number of cases for her clients.

Kelley also advises in the area of product and advertising clearance, including regulatory compliance. Her clients include players in the luxury goods, sports, social media, biotechnology, film distribution, financial and co-working industries.

Ladislav Mádl
Associate, Randl Partners, advokátní kancelář, sro
madl@randls.com

Ladislav Mádl is an attorney at law at Randl Partners law office, who specialises in commercial and marketing law. He is experienced in advising both Czech and international clients on the marketing and advertising of food and pharmaceuticals, including Czech and EU regulatory and compliance issues and litigation.

Ladislav regularly assists in global advertising campaigns and projects, and currently focuses on issues relating to the COVID-19 pandemic in the area of marketing and advertising.

Patricia McGovern
Partner, DFMG Solicitors LLP
pmcgovern@dfmg.ie

Patricia McGovern is head of the IP department at DFMG Solicitors LLP in Dublin. She is a solicitor, an Irish trademark agent and a European trademark and design attorney.

She has practised in almost all areas of IP law, both contentious and non-contentious. She also advises on data protection; the competition aspects of intellectual property; issues affecting e-commerce and the Internet; all aspects of technology agreements; all types of media contracts; the IP aspects of employment; advertising and sales promotions; and defamation.

Patricia is a current member and former chairman of the IP & Data Protection Committee of the Law Society of Ireland.

Patricia is active in many IP organisations, both in Ireland and abroad. She has written and lectured extensively both in Ireland and internationally on general business law and IP topics. Under her leadership, the firm has been the recipient of many awards.

Jennifer McKenzie
Partner, Bereskin & Parr LLP
jmckenzie@bereskinparr.com

Jennifer McKenzie is a partner with Bereskin & Parr LLP. She is the leader of the regulatory, advertising and marketing practice group and a co-leader of the cannabis and COVID-19 practice groups.

Jennifer has extensive experience with

regulatory, advertising and marketing law. She reviews advertising for clients in a wide range of industry sectors, from pre-packaged consumer goods to regulated products such as food and drugs. Jennifer has represented clients in competitive trade disputes before Ad Standards and advises clients on privacy legislation. She also helps clients in relation to promotion and contest design.

Jennifer additionally has extensive experience in trademark prosecution and enforcement.

She is recognised as a leader in both advertising and IP law, and has been ranked in a number of directories, including the *Chambers Canada Guide*, *Best Lawyers in Canada*, *Canadian Legal Lexpert Directory* and *Who's Who Legal: Trademarks*.

Paula Bezerra de Menezes
Partner, Soerensen Garcia Advogados Associados
pmenezes@soerensengarcia.com.br

Paula Bezerra de Menezes' practice encompasses domestic and international prosecution of patents, industrial designs and trademarks; disputes; and client counselling. She specialises in the development and management of trademark enforcement and anti-counterfeiting programmes. She has extensive experience in infringement and unfair competition cases and domain name and other internet-related disputes. She advises clients on cross-border issues, including how import and export control requirements affect IP rights.

Paula also counsels clients on enforcing their rights in coordination with Customs and regularly represents them in customs proceedings. She also assists clients with the development and implementation of sweepstakes and commercial promotions, and advises them on compliance with the relevant regulations and on tax consequences.

Paula has a master's in legal procedure with a focus on evidence law and is currently pursuing a PhD exploring the impact of implicit biases on judicial decision making at the University of Birmingham, United Kingdom.

George Ch Moukas
Senior associate, Ballas, Pelecanos & Associates LPC
george.moukas@balpel.gr

George Ch Moukas is a senior associate with Ballas, Pelecanos & Associates LPC. He obtained his law degree from the University of Athens in 1989 and was admitted to the Athens Bar Association in 1992. He is a lawyer before the Greek Supreme Courts and the litigation coordinator at Ballas, Pelecanos & Associates. He has extensive experience in the litigation of IP rights, the implementation of the anti-counterfeiting customs intervention legislation and liaison with Customs and the police.

George has advised many multinational brand owners on the implementation of the customs intervention legislation and since 2003 has been co-author of the Greece report for Borderwatch (LawInContext – Interactive Knowledge from Baker McKenzie), a global online information product for IP owners on the protection of IP rights through customs controls. He also participated as a lecturer in the training programme for police and customs officials in Estonia, sponsored by the European Union.

Jacek Myszko

Partner, Sołtysiński Kawecki & Szlęzak

jacek.myszko@skslegal.pl

Jacek Myszko manages the life sciences practice at Sołtysiński Kawecki & Szlęzak. He focuses on regulatory issues relating to pharmaceuticals, medical devices and foodstuffs, as well as on IP and advertising law.

Jacek graduated with a law degree from the Nicolaus Copernicus University in Torun, Poland, and with a diploma in EU studies from the J Monnet European Studies Centre. He also completed an IP law programme at the Jagiellonian University in Krakow, Poland, and various international courses organised by the University of Cambridge (English and EU law), the Catholic University of America and the Columbus School of Law (business and trade law).

Jacek advises Polish and foreign clients on all aspects of advertising issues, including unfair advertising, the unauthorised use of health claims and advertising in regulated sectors, such as alcohol, medicinal products and foodstuffs. Jacek has successfully litigated various trademark and patent disputes, including before the Polish Supreme Court.

Michael Noth

Partner, TIMES Attorneys

noth@timesattorneys.ch

Michael Noth has more than 20 years' experience in the field of intellectual property and advertising regulation. He is one of the founders of TIMES Attorneys, a leading boutique law firm in Switzerland.

Michael focuses on trademark law, copyright law, unfair competition law and advertising law. He has vast experience in IP-related litigation and arbitration, IP-related contractual work and regulatory and compliance issues in advertising and marketing in a broad range of industries, including entertainment, sports, life sciences, IT and luxury goods. *Chambers Europe* has described Michael as "one of the key IP lawyers in Switzerland".

Michael is recognised as a leading practitioner in the IP field and is listed in various professional publications. He is a partner of the Competence Center for Luxury Management of the University of St Gallen and a member of numerous professional associations. He regularly speaks and publishes articles on IP, life sciences and sports law.

Juan Carlos Ojám

Managing partner, Ojam Bullrich Flanzbaum

jcojam@ojambf.com

Juan Carlos Ojám has more than 30 years' experience in the IP field. Through his practice in IP boutiques and leading teams in commercial firms, he has gained expertise in all IP issues, including in relation to corporate and financial matters, and law in general.

His specialist knowledge encompasses advertising law, consumer law, unfair competition, false advertising, comparative advertising, antitrust and marketing compliance issues. He regularly represents clients both in court and before specialist self-regulatory bodies.

Clients reported in *Chambers and Partners* that "Juan Carlos works with us for our most serious cases"; and that "He is a great lawyer and strategic thinker who takes the time to really get to know our business".

Juan Carlos is a professor at several universities, both in Argentina and abroad, where he enjoys creating an environment in which students can constantly improve and objectively judge how they are developing.

Manon Rieger-Jansen

Partner, Bird & Bird

manon.rieger.jansen@twobirds.com

Manon Rieger-Jansen is a partner in Bird & Bird's IP practice and heads the brand management team in The Hague, the Netherlands. She has over 20 years of experience and has a particular focus on both contentious and non-contentious trademark, design, copyright, domain name and advertising law matters.

Manon's practice includes global strategic advice on IP rights and the protection and registration of IP portfolios. She is a seasoned litigator and handles high-profile IP disputes, including multi-jurisdictional litigation, as well as trademark office proceedings. She regularly advises and litigates on matters involving comparative and misleading advertising, with a focus on IP-related advertising, such as the use of competitors' trademarks and copyright, keyword advertising and social media-related matters.

Manon contributes regularly to publications on IP-related topics and is a teacher in the vocational education for Benelux trademark and design attorneys.

Mónica Esteve Sanz

Of counsel, Gómez-Acebo & Pombo Abogados SLP

mesteve@ga–p.com

Mónica Esteve Sanz has a degree in law from *Université Libre de Bruxelles* (1993) and a master's in European and international law from *Université Catholique de Louvain* (1994). In 1993, she was a *stagiaire* at the European Commission (IP and Unfair Competition Law Unit). She started working as an associate at the Brussels office of Gómez-Acebo & Pombo in 1994. Since 1998, she has been working in the IP and technology practice area at the firm's Madrid office, where she is of counsel. Her areas of specialisation are trademarks, franchising, distribution, unfair competition and advertising law. She provides contractual assessments and handles litigation before the national and EU courts, as well as within Autocontrol. Mónica has published several works on IP, franchising, advertising and unfair competition law. She has also lectured on several master's courses and is a frequent speaker at conferences. She speaks Spanish, French, English and Italian.

Stephanie Scott

Senior solicitor, von Muenster Legal

stephanie.s@vonmlegal.com

Stephanie Scott joined von Muenster Legal in 2017, where she works as a senior solicitor practising in contentious and non-contentious commercial matters. She specialises in intellectual property (including all aspects of trademark law and copyright), and has expertise in consumer law in the advertising and marketing sector. Stephanie is a founding member of the Australian Influencer Marketing Council, having advised on its Code of Practice.

Stephanie completed her JD at the University of Technology, Sydney in 2016. She also holds a bachelor of business communication majoring in advertising and a bachelor of arts majoring in film and television and cultural studies from the University of Queensland.

Her background and experience working in film and television production and arts funding provide a wealth of industry-specific knowledge to draw on in her legal work.

Mikael Segercrantz

Partner, Roschier

mikael.segercrantz@roschier.com

Mikael Segercrantz is a Helsinki-based partner and head of Roschier's marketing and consumer practice. His practice focuses on marketing and consumer law, intellectual property and regulatory matters, including litigation. Mikael regularly advises clients – including multinational brand owners – on various types of regulatory and marketing law issues, such as marketing campaigns, product classification, pricing and labelling issues, with a particular focus on the pharmaceutical, medical device, food and cosmetics industries. He has also handled and coordinated a number of product recall campaigns in Finland and the Baltic States.

Mikael also has extensive experience in IP litigation in Finland and before the Court of Justice of the European Union (CJEU), as both first and second chair, in disputes relating to patents, trademarks, copyright and designs, as well as other IP rights, and involving matters such as preliminary injunctions, infringing acts and invalidity claims.

Takamitsu Shigetomi

Partner, Oh-Ebashi LPC & Partners

shigetomi@ohebashi.com

Takamitsu Shigetomi heads the IP practice department at Oh-Ebashi LPC & Partners. He is admitted to practise law in Japan and New York, and specialises in IP licensing and litigation of all types, including unfair competition and advertising-related issues. Takamitsu is a frequent author and lecturer on IP topics, and teaches as an adjunct professor at the Graduate School of Science, Technology and Innovation of Kobe University.

Ewa Skrzydło-Tefelska

Partner, Sołtysiński Kawecki & Szlęzak

ewa.skrzydlo-tefelska@skslegal.pl

Ewa Skrzydło-Tefelska joined Sołtysiński Kawecki & Szlęzak in 1999 and became a partner in 2006. She coordinates the firm's intellectual and industrial property law practice and its advertising, life sciences and EU law practice. She advises clients on the protection of their IP rights, including unfair competition disputes. She represents clients in litigation regarding industrial property rights before the Polish common and administrative courts, including the Supreme Court; and in numerous disputes before the EU IP Office and the CJEU. In the area of advertising, in addition to day-to-day advice and litigation, she assists with the organisation of games and promotions.

As GALA's exclusive member for Poland, Ewa advises on global promotional and advertising campaigns. She assists clients with matters relating to the global management of large trademark portfolios, and has significant experience in providing legal advice and assistance in disputes regarding nutrition and health claims for food.

Sarmis Spilbergs

Associate partner, Ellex Klavins

sarmis.spilbergs@ellex.lv

An associate partner and head of the technology, media and communications practice, Sarmis Spilbergs specialises in various regulatory fields, such as data protection, life sciences, IT, e-commerce and communications, licensing and general corporate law. Since joining Ellex in 2005, he has gained extensive experience advising numerous large corporations on implementing their IT projects, organising internal data flows and ensuring compliance with local legislation in dealings with customers, employees and other third parties. He also provides legal advice on the import, sale and licensing of different types of goods (eg, electronic equipment, medicines, tobacco, e-commerce), permits and other issues.

Sarmis has extensive experience in the automotive sector; he also advises pharmaceutical companies on various legal issues relating to their activities in Latvia and retail sector companies on General Data Protection Regulation compliance matters.

Melissa Landau Steinman
Partner, Venable LLP
mlsteinman@venable.com

Melissa Steinman focuses on advertising and marketing, including litigation, antitrust, trade regulation and consumer protection. Melissa is particularly knowledgeable about the technology, retail, media, gaming and hospitality industries. She also actively represents clients in government investigations and defends clients in class action cases. Melissa also assists non-profit organisations and others with charitable promotions and commercial co-ventures. She represents celebrities, producers and notable businesses, and trade associations involved in consumer products and services, media, internet gaming, gambling, software, technology and telecommunications.

Verna Syrjänen
Associate, Roschier
verna.syrjanen@roschier.com

Verna Syrjänen is a Helsinki-based associate working in Roschier's marketing and consumer and IP practices. Since joining the firm in

2018, Verna has been involved in assignments relating to marketing and consumer law and regulatory matters, as well as IP litigation and IP and technology transactions.

Roelien van Neck
Partner, Bird & Bird
roelien.van.neck@twobirds.com

Roelien van Neck is a specialist in digital business and technology-related matters. She has specific expertise in the field of (digital) B2C matters, and advises clients on all aspects of trading practices, marketing and advertising. She also advises on commercial contracts covering distribution, sales, agency, cooperation and procurement arrangements.

Roelien is chair of the Netherlands Association of Computer Lawyers, and regularly speaks at seminars and courses. She is a co-editor of legal journal *Juridisch up to Date* and a frequent contributor to other leading legal journals.

Roelien was admitted to the Bar in 2000. She graduated from Leiden University and subsequently completed an LLM at University College London. She also holds a postgraduate *cum laude* degree in IT law.

Otávio Saraiva Padilha Velasco
Partner, Soerensen Garcia Advogados Associados
opadilha@soerensengarcia.com.br

Otávio Saraiva Padilha Velasco is a lawyer with further specialisation in commercial agreements, marketing and intellectual property. His practice focuses on domestic and international contract negotiations, strategic alliances and other commercial dealings involving clients' IP assets. He regularly drafts and negotiates technology transfer agreements, licence agreements and distribution and agency agreements, and litigates disputes arising from such arrangements. He manages IP due diligence efforts in connection with clients' mergers, acquisitions and divestitures.

Otávio specialises in the establishment and management of trademark enforcement and anti-counterfeiting programmes. He also represents clients on matters of unfair competition, franchising, consumer rights and corporate law before the Brazilian courts.

Stephen von Muenster

Partner, von Muenster Legal
stephen.vm@vonmlegal.com

Stephen von Muenster is a practising solicitor and partner at von Muenster Legal. He has specialised in advertising, communications, marketing and media law since 1995. He has a keen interest in emerging technologies, media and the interactive and digital mediascape, and advises extensively on disruptor technology platforms, social media, online reputation management and artificial intelligence technologies. He is presently assessing the Australian Competition and Consumer Commission response to the Digital Platforms Inquiry and the related Ad Tech Inquiry. In the COVID-19 world, Stephen is assisting agencies with stakeholder transformation.

Stephen also specialises in agency mergers and acquisitions, and was legal counsel on a number of recent high-profile independent agency and media acquisitions across the communications spectrum. He is the legal adviser to numerous industry bodies and regularly presents to them on matters of legal and regulatory compliance. He is also a guest lecturer at the University of Sydney and the University of Technology Sydney.

Vasileios A Xynogalas

Trainee lawyer, Ballas, Pelecanos & Associates LPC
vasileios.xynogalas@balpel.gr

Vasileios A Xynogalas is a trainee lawyer with Ballas, Pelecanos & Associates LPC and participates in most practice groups of the law firm, including the IP, IT and CT group, the company, tax and employment group and the consumer rights groups. Vasileios has been a member of the Athens Bar since 2019 and received an LLB from the University of Athens.

Yulia Yarnykh

Partner, Gowling WLG
yulia.yarnykh@gowlingwlg.com

Yulia Yarnykh is a partner in the Moscow office of Gowling WLG. Her practice focuses on IP, corporate and commercial law matters. She advises Russian and foreign clients on a wide range of IP issues, including enforcement of IP rights, unfair competition, regulatory and commercial intellectual property.

Yulia has broad experience in advertising and marketing, media, e-commerce and data protection matters. She assists major international companies in conducting anti-piracy campaigns against counterfeiters and parallel importers, and in structuring their franchise and distribution networks in Russia. She is actively engaged in various IP transactional work.

Yulia is also dedicated to assisting others in need in the not-for-profit sector.

Edvijs Zandars
Senior associate, Ellex Klavins
edvijs.zandars@ellex.lv

Senior associate Edvijs Zandars specialises in IP, IT and competition law. He regularly advises international and local clients on the protection and enforcement of IP rights and licensing. He has significant experience in protecting the IP portfolios of major international clients. He also regularly represents clients before the Latvian courts and IP enforcement institutions, and assists in various opposition proceedings at the Latvian Patent Office, the World Intellectual Property Organization and the EU IP Office. He is also a registered patent attorney for trademark matters in Latvia.

Edvijs is also experienced at providing regulatory guidance to multinational technology companies, providers of electronic communications services and content, and e-commerce companies. He also assists international telecommunications companies with setting up and managing their business in Latvia. He is a key point of contact with the Latvian regulatory authorities on innovative technologies and solutions, helping clients to successfully establish their services in Latvia.

About Globe Law and Business

Globe Law and Business was established in 2005. From the very beginning, we set out to create law books which are sufficiently high level to be of real use to the experienced professional, yet still accessible and easy to navigate. Most of our authors are drawn from Magic Circle and other top commercial firms, both in the UK and internationally.

Our titles are carefully produced, with the utmost attention paid to editorial, design and production processes. We hope this results in high-quality publications that are easy to read, and a pleasure to own. Our titles are also available as ebooks, which are compatible with most desktop, laptop and tablet devices. In 2018 we expanded our portfolio to include journals and Special Reports, available both digitally and in hard copy format, and produced to the same high standards as our books.

We'd very much like to hear from you with your thoughts and ideas for improving what we offer. Please do feel free to email me at sian@globelawandbusiness.com with your views.

Sian O'Neill
Managing director
Globe Law and Business

www.globelawandbusiness.com